Contents

Preface *xv*

Chapter 1
The Middle School Student *1*

Early Adolescence: The Great Transition   2
Knowledge about the Age Group   2
    Three Phases of Adolescence   3
    Common Attributes   5
Early Adolescent Development   6
    Developmental Tasks   6
    Physical and Sexual Development   7
    Implications for Middle Schools   9
Cognitive Development   10
    Constructivism   11
    Conceptions of Intelligence   11
Moral Development   16
    Moral Development among Middle Schoolers   17
    Identity Formation   19
The At-Risk Middle School Student   23
    The New Significance of Poverty, Race, and Ethnicity   25
    Programs for At-Risk Youth   27
    Components of Effective Programs for At-Risk Students   28
    Seven Cardinal Principles   29
Focus on the Middle School Student: Summary   30

Chapter 2
The Middle School Movement and Concept *38*

The Middle School Concept Emerges   39
Early Efforts to Educate the Young Adolescent   39
The Junior High School   40

Toward a Different School in the Middle 41
Expediency Leads to Many More Middle Schools 43
Definition and Description of the Middle School 45
Desirable Characteristics of Exemplary Middle Schools 48
    Three Goals of Middle School Education 51
    The Educational Zip Code 52
The Middle School Concept: Unique and Transitional 54
Schools in the Middle—21st Century Trends and Issues 58
    Interdisciplinary Team Organization 59
    Curriculum 60
    Scheduling 61
    Technology 62
    Instruction 63
    Grouping for Instruction 64
    The Corporate Presence 64
    School Leadership 65
Conclusion 67

Chapter 3
Middle School Curriculum 73

Standards-Based Reform versus Learner-Centered Curriculum 74
    The Rationale for Standards-Based Education 74
An Example of a Curriculum Based on State Standards 78
    Standards-Based Reform in a Typical State 79
    Standards within Each Strand of the Middle School Curriculum 81
    Benchmarks within Each Middle School Standard 83
    Standards in Other States 86
Criticism of Standards-Based Reform 87
Standards-Based Reform and the Middle School Curriculum 92
Working to Combine Standards and Integrated Curriculum in the Classroom:
    A Classroom Model 95
Integrated Curriculum: An Ideal for Middle Level Classrooms 99
    The Rationale for the Integrated Curriculum 100
    Interdisciplinary Approaches 102
    Brown Barge Middle School 105
    Problems or Concerns with Moving to an Integrated Curriculum 109
    The Curriculum Wars 111
Exploration in the Curriculum 112
    Exploratory Courses 113
    Examples of Exploratory Programs 114
Clubs and Special Interest Activities 118
Health and Physical Education 121
    Health Education 122
    Physical Education 123

Intramurals, Interscholastic Sports, Other Extracurricular Programs, and the
Role of Competition   124
Technology and the Curriculum   131

Chapter 4

Instruction   151

Characteristics of Effective Instruction in the Middle School   152
Traditional Whole Class Instruction   158
  Classroom Management and Whole Class Instruction   159
  Whole Class Instruction: Steps in the Process   161
  Important Modifications of Whole Class Instruction   163
Differentiating Instruction   166
  The Problem with Lecture   166
  Defining "Differentiation of Instruction"   167
  Differentiating Instruction in the Regular Classroom   168
  Initial Steps in Differentiating Instruction   170
  Supplementing the Traditional Classroom   176
  Small Group Activities   184
  Cooperative Learning   192
  Other Major Methods for Differentiating Instruction   198
  Technology and the Differentiation of Instruction   202
Consultation and Co-Teaching   205
  Cooperative Consultation   206
  Co-Teaching   207
  Implementation of the Consultation and Co-teaching Models   209
  Recommendations   210
  Precautions and Promises   211
  Concluding Comments   213

Chapter 5

Managing and Mentoring Middle Schoolers   225

Developing Relationships with Middle School Students   226
  Student Development and Behavior Management   227
  Middle School Organization and Student Behavior Management   235
  Problems with the Traditional Junior High School Organization   235
  Behavior Management and the Middle School Concept   238
  Using the Interdisciplinary Team to Improve School and Classroom
    Discipline   243
Mentoring Middle Schoolers: The Teacher as Advisor   252
  Alternative Designs for Teacher-Based Guidance or Advisory Programs   255
  Daily Large Group Programs   255
  One-on-One Programs   258
  Requirements for Successful Schoolwide Advisor-Advisee Programs   260
  Purposes of the Advisor-Advisee Program   272

Goals of the Advisory Program   275
Teacher Roles   277
Conducting an Advisor-Advisee Group   278
Successful Activities for Daily Advisory Programs   281
Occasional Activities   283
Research on the Advisory Program   284
Guidance and Counseling in the Middle School   289

Chapter 6
Interdisciplinary Team Organization   301

Interdisciplinary Team Organization: Operational Core of the Middle School
        Concept   302
Sharing: The Basis for Organizing the Middle School Faculty   302
The Nature of the Interdisciplinary Team Organization   304
Four Phases of Interdisciplinary Team Life   305
Phase One: Organization   306
Phase Two: Community Building   308
Phase Three: Teamed Instruction   310
Phase Four: Governance   311
Characteristics of Highly Effective Teams   312
Alternative Types of Interdisciplinary Team Organization   313
Roles and Responsibilities of Teams and Their Members   323
Teaching Responsibilities   324
Arranging the Physical Environment   324
Structuring Academic Class Time   325
Grouping Students   325
Scheduling Students   325
Selecting and Distributing Texts and Other Materials   327
Teamed Instruction   327
Other Student Matters   331
Relating to Other Staff Members   331
Team Planning   332
The Team Leader   341
Purposes and Possibilities of the Interdisciplinary Team Organization   344
Advantages: Instructional   344
Advantages: Affective and Behavioral   346
Precautions   352
Balanced Teams   352
Ten Commandments of Teaming   355
Teams and Team Meetings: Problems to Avoid   357
Planning for an Interdisciplinary Team Organization in the New Middle
        School   359

Chapter 7
Grouping Students in the Middle School 365

Organizing Students for Instruction 366
  Organization in Elementary and High School 366
  Organizing Students at the Middle Level 368
Student Development and School Organization 369
  A Model of Student Development and School Organization 370
  Departmentalization 372
  Gradewide Interdisciplinary Teams 374
  Core-Style Grouping 375
  Grade Level Interdisciplinary Teams 378
  Long-Term Teams 379
  Developmental-Age Grouping 390
  Parker Intensive Core Program 392
Advantages and Disadvantages of Alternatives to Age-Grade Grouping 395
  Advantages 395
  Disadvantages 400
  Requirements for Success 400
Inclusion: Grouping Students with Learning Problems in the Middle School 401
  Schoolwide Arrangements 402
  Resource Rooms 404
  Inclusion and the Interdisciplinary Team 408
  Inclusion and the Regular Teacher 413
Tracking and Ability Grouping: Which Way for the Middle School? 414
  Synthesis of Research on Ability Grouping 415
  Why Tracking and Ability Grouping Fail 415
  Which Way for the Middle School? 416
  Strategies for "De-Tracking" 417
  Getting Off the Track: Options and Alternatives 422

Chapter 8
Organizing Time and Space in the Middle School 435

Organizing Time in the Middle School 436
The Flexible Block 436
  Implementation of the Middle School Concept 437
  The Flexible Block Responds to Clearly Established Priorities 441
  The Flexible Block Schedule Yields Instructional Responsiveness 444
The New Long Block Schedule 445
  Varieties of Long Block Schedules 446
  Reasons for Adopting a Long Block Schedule 454
  Reported Outcomes of the New Long Block Schedules 455
  Problems and Concerns Surrounding Block Schedules 457

Ten Steps to Designing an Effective Middle School Schedule 459
    Master or Servant? 459
    Steps in Designing the Master Schedule 460
    No Single Right Way to Schedule a Middle School 465
    Scheduling in Perspective 466
Organizing Space in the Middle School 466
    The Middle School Building 466
    Adapting Older Buildings 470
An Emerging Consensus on the Nature of Facilities for the Exemplary Middle
    School 477
    Pods, Team Areas, and Houses 479
    General Considerations for Specifications for New Buildings 493
Concluding Comments 494

Chapter 9

Planning and Evaluating the Exemplary Middle School 500

Exemplary Middle Schools Follow Similar Planning Pathways 501
    Six-Step Middle School Implementation Plan 501
    Strategic Planning for Middle School Implementation 502
Revitalizing Existing Middle Schools 513
    Revitalizing Middle Schools: A Case Study 515
Staff Development for Middle Schools: Guidelines and Roles 524
    Successful Staff Development Strategies: Eight Recommendations 526
    The Focus of Middle School Staff Development: Skills 532
    Special Planning Concerns for Exploratory Teachers and Their
        Programs 534
Evaluation of the Middle School 537
    Formative Evaluation of a Middle School 538
    Self-Study Programs: School Improvement and Accreditation 543
    Summative Evaluation and the Middle School 544
Evaluating the Middle School Movement 548

Chapter 10

Middle School Leadership 555

Core Components of Middle School Leadership 556
Middle School Leadership and Vision 556
Maintaining the Middle School: Shared Decision-Making 557
    The Program Improvement Council or Building Leadership Team 558
Raising Academic Achievement: The Middle School Leader's Challenge 562
    Strategy #1: Utilizing a Breakthrough Planning Process 563
    Strategy #2: Improving School Climate, Faculty Cohesiveness, and Student
        Behavior Management 563
    Strategy #3: Strategic Use of School Achievement Data 564
    Strategy #4: Enhancing Professional Development 566

Strategy #5: Curriculum Alignment 566
Strategy #6: Finding Additional Time for Learning 567
Strategy #7: Implementing Special Standards-Based Curriculum Programs and Instructional Strategies 568
Strategy #8: Components of the Middle School Concept 569
Strategy #9: Promoting the Test 570
Strategy #10: Changing School Leadership Style 571
Concerns about Standards-Based Reforms in Middle Schools 572
Other Challenges for Leaders of the Middle School Movement 573
What the Middle School Movement Has Accomplished 573
What More Must Be Done? 575
The Generative School 584

References *591*
Roster of Middle Schools *605*
Author Index *611*
Subject Index *615*

Preface

The Exemplary Middle School is a basic textbook for students in the field of middle school education. It is comprehensive in scope beginning with a discussion of the characteristics and needs of the students, describing in detail exemplary middle school programs that best meet those needs, and proceeding to a discussion of leadership and the implementation of these programs. We have prepared the book to be of substantial and specific help both to the advanced beginner in middle school education and to the practitioner seeking continued improvement in already exemplary schools.

BACKGROUND

Educators have long been deeply involved in the search for better education for children in the middle school years. This search lasted throughout the 20th century, with the junior high school becoming the dominant school between elementary and high school during the 1920 to 1960 period. Dissatisfaction with the junior high school and with the still common K8–4 plan of organization (without a school in the middle) led William M. Alexander and other educators to propose early in the 1960s the alternative organization now commonly called the middle school. The middle school concept has caught on widely since 1960, with some 15,000 schools now using this organization (usually, but not always, three or more years including grades 6 and 7). As researchers, consultants to school districts and faculties, and trainers of middle school personnel, we have been actively involved in the search for effective middle schools that would help achieve the long sought goal of education continuity from early childhood through adolescence, linking elementary and secondary with a dynamic program for children in the middle.

Despite the thousands of middle schools in existence, they have only begun to develop a uniformity of the characteristics educators have agreed are essential for effective education in the middle of a child's school career. Perhaps the early years of the middle school movement exhibited too much of a bandwagon effect, with many middle schools being established for social, budgetary, or political reasons only indirectly associated with the needs of the students. We examine the movement in detail and call attention to the remaining gap between the consensus-based characteristics of middle school and actual practices—although much has been accomplished in narrowing this gap since the first edition of this textbook appeared 20 years ago. This third edition bridges the gap between theory and practice, aiming toward a significant increase in the number of exemplary schools and in exemplary practices in schools.

We believe that most books on the middle school published since *The Emergent Middle School* by William Alexander and his colleagues (Holt, Rinehart, and Winston, 1968) have lacked an adequate balance among theory, research, and illustrative practices. To help readers relate theory and research to practice, we have been eager to include many illustrations of exemplary practices and schools. Using our experience and knowledge, the recommendations of other middle school educators, and the literature on middle school education, we identified more than 1,100 middle schools throughout the United States, Canada, and beyond as being representative of exemplary practices. In all three editions of this book, we have asked the leaders of these schools to share materials explaining their schools, and exemplary practices therein, and have been pleased with the wealth of materials provided. We have visited and studied closely many of the schools referred to in this book. We include a roster, which, while incomplete, is a useful directory of exemplary middle schools. We regret the impossibility of including all good middle schools, as well as our failure to hear from a few schools in time to include them.

ORGANIZATION AND CONTENT

The organization and content of the text are based on the characteristics of middle school students described in Chapter 1 and the definition of the middle school and its essential characteristics presented in Chapter 2. Chapter 1 summarizes the information available on this age group, and it looks closely at a new group of students—those identified as "at risk." Chapter 2 offers a history of the middle school movement and a concise explanation of the middle school concept as it has emerged. Chapter 3 is devoted to the middle school curriculum, the recent standards-based reform movement, and other trends in the process of curriculum development that promise to be significant in the next decade. Our concern for providing readers with specific examples, sometimes with a how-to quality, is evident in Chapter 4, on instruction. Chapter 5 examines the nature of the student-teacher relationship at the middle level and the teacher's role in managing and mentoring young adolescents. Chapter

6 illustrates another unique feature of exemplary middle schools, the interdisciplinary team, which bridges the gap between the self-contained classroom of the elementary school and the departments of the high school. Illustrations are drawn from many new schools, and major new descriptions of exemplary teams are offered in this third edition. Chapter 7 focuses on alternative methods of grouping middle school students, with sections concentrating on the important trends of ability grouping and inclusion. In Chapter 8, we attend to the problems of time and space (schedule and building), which are critical because so many middle schools have inherited the buildings of predecessor organizations and sometimes maintain their schedules. We illustrate new building conceptualizations that we believe will more nearly match the middle school concept in the 21st century. Chapter 9 studies the processes of planning and evaluating middle schools, with step-by-step instructions born out of our involvement in such activities over the past decade. Chapter 10 turns to the critical matter of leadership roles in the middle school, with special attention to the challenges of standards-based reform.

FEATURES OF THIS REVISION

We consider the extensive use of up-to-date illustrative materials a unique feature of this book, and we are indebted to the educators who provided these examples. Readers may also find the roster of exemplary schools and the index references useful in identifying schools and practices of special interest to them. We've also added the following new chapter-ending features to promote student mastery:

- Content Summary provides an overview of core chapter concepts.
- Connections to Other Chapters covers how the chapter relates to other chapters.
- Action Steps provides suggested activities for individual and group work.
- Questions for Discussion facilitates critical thinking and reinforces knowledge of chapter content.
- Suggestions for Further Study provides useful references in the areas of theory and research. These lists include bibliographic information on ERIC documents and doctoral dissertations dealing with middle school education. These studies provide significant resources for further implementation and support for middle school theory and desired practices.

ACKNOWLEDGMENTS

We are grateful to all the personnel of the middle and other schools in which we have worked as teachers and consultants for the stimulus given to our thinking and writing about middle school education. We are also influenced by and are grateful for the challenges from and other contributions of the hundreds of students in our middle school education courses at the University of Florida. Especially, we wish to thank again the principals and other personnel of the exemplary middle schools cited in this text for their valuable assistance.

We wish to thank the following reviewers for their insightful comments: Jo Alexander, Auburn University–Montgomery; Laura Allen, Trinity University; Thomas S. Dickinson, Indiana State University; Antonio M. Eppolito, LeMoyne College; Tom Erb, University of Kansas; Scott Page, Minnesota State University–Mankato; Stephen E. Phillips, Brooklyn College; Rosalie Romano, Ohio University–Athens; Sandee L. Schamber, Black Hills State University; Sheila Wright, Minnesota State University–Mankato.

We want to provide special acknowledgment for the assistance of Molly McGill and Xenia Hadjioannou in updating the references and compiling the roster of middle schools. Finally, we wish to gratefully acknowledge the cheerful and determined support that Reisa George devoted to the development of this manuscript throughout all three editions.

About the Authors

Paul S. George is professor of education in the School of Teaching and Learning, College of Education, at the University of Florida, in Gainesville, Florida. Dr. George has been involved in the study of middle school education since he became a ninth grade teacher in 1964. He has written 11 books and produced approximately 150 monographs, articles, and videos on the topic of middle school education. Dr. George has served as a consultant to educational groups of all kinds in nearly all 50 states and nine foreign countries. In the past 30 years, he has addressed a total audience numbering nearly 100,000 at state, national, and international meetings, conferences, and workshops, including guest lectures at more than 25 universities in the United States, Canada, France, and Japan. Dr. George has also spent considerable time in the study of Japanese education and in the investigation of organization and leadership in the corporate world, seeking insight into what those areas might offer to American education. The American Association of School Administrators has referred to Professor George as "the foremost expert on middle schools in the country." He is married and the father of three children.

William M. Alexander (deceased) was professor of education at the University of Florida, in Gainesville, Florida, for several decades. Often called the "Father of the Middle School," Dr. Alexander was involved in middle level education for half a century. He was a man of "firsts" in that regard. He was the senior author of the first textbook on the subject of middle school education (*The Emergent Middle School,* published by Holt, Rinehart, and Winston in 1968). He initiated the first league of middle schools, the still successful Florida League of Middle Schools, in 1972. He established the first program in middle school teacher education in the nation, at the University of Florida. He presented one of the first keynote addresses to the National Middle School Association (NMSA) and was one of the first recipients of the prestigious Lounsbury Award, given by the NMSA. And Dr. Alexander was an early president of the Association for Supervision and Curriculum Development.

*The Exemplary
Middle School*

THE MIDDLE SCHOOL STUDENT

8-YEAR-OLD WOMEN

The American Academy of Pediatrics, collaborating with Marcia Herman-Giddens on a study of 17,000 girls across the country, concluded that the onset of puberty (measured by the appearance of breast buds) was 9.96 years for all girls and 8.87 years for African American girls. Even more surprising, close to a third of the African American girls had started puberty between their 7th and 8th birthdays, and half of that group had entered puberty before their 9th birthday. Otherwise healthy girls are entering puberty at least a full year earlier, on average, than was previously thought. These are first- and second-grade girls.

In their struggle to explain this striking phenomenon, developmental psychologists have identified a number of possible contributing factors. Girls who are obese seem to enter puberty earlier. Certain foods, especially milk and other dairy products, may contribute to girls' earlier entry into puberty; food additives may play a role, too. Girls who live in families in which the biological father is absent are likely to mature, physically, more quickly. This may happen even faster when a nonrelated male is present in the home. Even the media, with the ubiquitous presence of what must be identified as soft porn, may contribute. Herman-Giddens responds, "Is it going to keep getting lower? And is this supposed to be happening? I don't think so. I don't think this is what nature intended."

Based on "The Making of an 8-Year-Old Woman," by L. Belkin, in the New York Times Magazine, *Dec. 24, 2000, pp. 38–43.)*

WHAT YOU WILL LEARN IN CHAPTER 1

This is the most important chapter in the book. All of the rest of the book matters little if study proceeds without amplification, in the reader, of a compassionate understanding of the characteristics and needs of the young adolescent. So, in this chapter, we examine the nature of early adolescence as a period of life as well as the risks and opportunities that characterize what others have described as the great transition. We look at physical, cognitive, moral, and other aspects of development. We describe the importance of the search for identity. We recognize how many of today's young adolescents can be identified as at-risk. We conclude with the seven cardinal principles of developmentally responsive middle schools.

EARLY ADOLESCENCE: THE GREAT TRANSITION

Research and experience in the last several decades (George & Anderson, 1989) indicated that a close correlation has existed between the longevity of quality middle school programs and the degree to which the members of the school staff possess what might be described as a compassionate understanding of the characteristics and needs of the learners in the school. Educators who are able to organize and open an exemplary middle school, and then maintain the school program at a high level of quality for a decade or more, point to such an understanding as one of the most important enabling factors associated with their success. Over the last three decades, we have visited hundreds of middle schools. Every outstanding school we have ever visited has had, among the staff, a clear understanding of the nature and needs of the students and an irrevocable commitment to meeting those needs in the school setting. Educators in such schools are willing to do whatever is necessary, and in their power, to create schools that fit the needs of their students. Evidently, such a sufficiently direct connection is found between exemplary middle school programs and a committed understanding of the characteristics of the students that proceeding with any endeavor related to middle school education is folly without first focusing firmly on the nature and needs of the developing adolescent. Hence, we begin this textbook with a closer examination of the student in the middle level school.

KNOWLEDGE ABOUT THE AGE GROUP

Early adolescence is a unique and significant period in human development. It marks the end of an individual's childhood years and the beginning of youth or young adulthood. It is a time of great transition. For a period of two to four years, during which this transition occurs, early adolescents are in a state of metamorphosis. No longer children, but not yet adults, they are in a world of their own somewhere in between. (Caissy, 1994, p. 2)

Prior to the 1980s, little attention was paid to the characteristics of students between the ages of 10 and 15, except by harried parents and educators. Both of these groups seem to have sensed that special differences separated this age group from younger children and older adolescents. But little confirmation of this intuitive understanding was available from professionals in research on human development, medicine, the criminal justice system, the church, or other areas. A quarter-century ago, Lipsitz (1980) asserted that "we are less informed about this stage of development than about any other among minors in America."

At that point, professionals found it difficult to agree even on the proper terminology to describe the age group. For some, the term *transescence* coined by Donald Eichhorn (1966) had a great deal of appeal, because of their personal acquaintance with and fondness for Eichhorn, one of middle school education's most important pioneers. Others used the term *developing adolescent;* still others chose more informal terms such as *in-between-ager.* Each of the terms *later childhood, preadolescence,* and *emerging adolescence* describes definite and large groups of the middle school population, but each fails to be inclusive of the total range of ages and development that fall into the middle school years. To use all of these terms in a single reference is tedious. So we ourselves are inclined to use these terms somewhat interchangeably, especially the terms *early adolescent* and *young adolescent.* In this text, we will talk about young adolescents, boys and girls, learners, or students in the middle school or of middle school age, and sometimes we just abbreviate the reference to *middle schoolers.* In the same sense that we have difficulty defining and using concepts such as fun and obscenity in wholly satisfactory ways, we have difficulty coming to agreement, yet, about the dimensions of this age group, let alone the proper descriptive terms. Similarly, however, most would agree that "they know early adolescence when they see it."

Three Phases of Adolescence

Generally, scholars and researchers have come to agree that the now long period of adolescence, which lasts from about age 10 until age 20 or ever later, has three distinct phases. Early adolescence encompasses the period from ages 10 to 14, virtually beginning and ending with the middle school years. Middle adolescence, from ages 14 to 18, is congruent with the high school years. Late adolescence is thought to encompass the years from 18 until the person establishes authentic independence, which, in today's society, could last, for some youth, well into their third decade of life. Middle schoolers, then, are involved in a stage of development that begins just prior to puberty and extends through the early stages of adolescence. It involves many changes in physical, sexual, social, emotional, moral, psychological, and intellectual dimensions.

Regardless of the term used to identify these learners, or the exact dimensions of the developmental phase, unanimity about the significance of this period of growing up is being reached. A variety of professional organizations has devoted substantial time and resources to the nature of these students and to the importance of improving schooling during these years: National Middle School Association, American Association of School Administrators, Association for Supervision and Curriculum Development, National Association for Secondary School Principals, the Carnegie Foundation, National Science Foundation, and others. These organizations offer workshops, give journal space, and highlight many conference sessions on the young adolescent student and the implications for schooling that flow from a knowledge of those students. The National Middle School Association membership has grown from about 1,000 to over 30,000 during the time between the first and third editions of this text (from 1983 to 2003), an indication of growing interest in and concern about the age group and its education. No less prestigious a group than the Carnegie Foundation has devoted impressive resources to the age group and its education. In *Turning Points 2000* (Jackson & Davis, 2000, p. x), an influential publication of the Carnegie Task Force on Education of Young Adolescents, the authors underlined their convictions about the importance of this developmental period by writing that

> adolescents make choices that have fateful consequences both in the short term and for the rest of their lives—choices affecting their health, their education, and the people they will become.

Human development research and scholarship has increasingly identified the importance of early adolescence as a unique phase of growing up. Since psychologists Shave and Shave wrote in 1989 about early adolescence "as a distinct developmental phase that is quantitatively different" from both earlier and later periods, a professional consensus has affirmed this position. Today's researchers agree with Shave and Shave that the changes experienced during early adolescence are "developmentally unique in both the intensity and the reactivity of early adolescents to self-experiences and life situations." Human development specialists Feldman and Eliott (1990) articulated the now-prevailing view that early adolescence is a pivotal stage of life when the person is defined, by society, as being neither adult nor child. Adolescents are, wrote Feldman and Eliott, "changing physically, maturing sexually, becoming increasingly able to engage in complex reasoning, and markedly expanding their knowledge of themselves and the world about them. These and many other factors foster an urge in them to gain more control over how and with whom they spend their time" (p. 4). According to the Carnegie Council on Adolescent Development, "This is a time of immense importance in the development of the young person" (1989, p. 21).

In recent years, knowledge of this phase of human development has evolved to the point that its importance has definitely been determined and a realization exists that the experience can be vastly different from one individual to another (Roeser et al., 2000). For girls, the tremendous changes usually happen earlier than for boys. For some youngsters of both sexes, it may be "an exceptionally stressful time in the life course"; for others, possibly the majority, the supposed tumult of the period in and of itself—the "storm and stress"—may be much less significant; and for some, it may be virtually nonexistent (Simmons & Blyth, 1987). Early adolescents show as much variability in their backgrounds, life experiences, values, and aspirations as do adults. Regardless of the nature of the experience itself, however, a majority of American youth have managed, somehow, to come through the critical years of this period relatively unscathed.

With good schools, supportive families, and caring community institutions, a slim majority of young adolescents grow to adulthood meeting the requirement of the workplace, the commitments to families and friends, and the responsibilities of citizenship. Even under less than optimal conditions for healthy growth, many youngsters manage to become contributing members of society. Some achieve this feat despite threats to their well-being that were almost unknown to their parents and grandparents. Resilience is one attribute of successful young adolescents (Roeser et al., 2000).

Common Attributes

Even though variability may be the most outstanding characteristic of the entire population of the age group, this should not imply that early adolescents as an age group exhibit no important commonalities of experience. All middle school students experience many similar changes; physically, intellectually, and emotionally they are in a period of extraordinary transition. Even though the transition from child to adult is no longer viewed as a predictable and immutable sequence of stages, most members of the age group are influenced and react to similar stimuli, both internal and external, some endocrinological, but mostly social and psychological. Striving for independence and a sense of identity, most middle schoolers undergo the common difficult task of balancing the pressures of family, friends, church, community, and school, with the desire to define a value system that fits their own needs, while experiencing phenomenal changes intellectually, physically, and otherwise.

Lists of the characteristics of this age group abound. One such list (Knowles & Brown, 2000, p. 2), perhaps more amusing than others, would, nonetheless, likely find much affirmation from teachers and parents—and scholars, too.

- They eat all the time.
- Their music is too loud.
- They take social issues very seriously.
- They frequently exclaim, "You don't understand."
- They cry a lot.
- They laugh a lot.
- They are sure that nobody has ever felt what they are feeling.
- They like hanging out at home and being with their parents.
- They hate hanging out at home and being with their parents.
- They have difficulty attending to something for more than a minute at a time.
- They are plagued with acne.
- They are seldom satisfied with the way they look.
- They are loyal to their friends.
- They talk behind their friends' backs.
- They outgrow their clothes every few months.
- Their voices crack when they sing in mixed chorus.
- They want to be independent.
- They do not want to let go of their childhood.

EARLY ADOLESCENT DEVELOPMENT

Much of the research and theory focused on adolescence and early adolescence during the last century has been conducted in a paradigm that assumed the existence of discrete stages or periods, arranged hierarchically, through which youth passed on their way from childhood to young adulthood. These stage theorists include some of the most well known names in the study of human development. In recent years, writers have placed less emphasis on these discrete stages and more emphasis on the plasticity of human development and the fact that change and development happen at all ages and are continuous throughout human life. Here, we acknowledge the value of both perspectives.

Developmental Tasks

For much of the history of research on adolescence, writers such as Robert J. Havighurst (1972) have portrayed human life as a series of discrete stages of development, with each stage involving unique challenges, or tasks, that must be mastered for successful progress to the next stage to occur. For Havighurst, a developmental task was "a task which arises at or about a certain period in the life of an individual, successful achievement of which leads to his happiness and to success with later tasks, while failure leads to unhappiness in the individual, disapproval by the society, and difficulty with later tasks" (1972, p. 2). Developmental-stage theorists such as Sigmund Freud, Jean Piaget, Erik Erikson, and Lawrence Kohlberg have contributed greatly to the understanding of the important transition from childhood to adulthood known as adolescence.

Levinson's highly regarded research (1978) supported the belief that these transitions are critical to smooth and successful development from one stage to another and that the problems of later life can often be traced to inadequate completion of the developmental tasks that were required for an earlier transition from one stage to another. So, stage theorists suggest that adolescents are persons negotiating their way simultaneously through several important areas of development, each of which is likely to have specific stages, with unique tasks that must be mastered for the adolescent to move successfully toward young adulthood.

Havighurst saw individuals striving to learn the developmental tasks of life to become and to feel like healthy members of society. He delineated critical times when certain tasks are most easily learned, and he outlined eight tasks central to successful development that begin in early adolescence (Cobb, 2001).

1. Achieving mature relations with age mates of both sexes
2. Achieving a masculine or feminine social role (which today involves choosing from a variety of possibilities)
3. Learning about one's body and using it in healthy ways
4. Gaining emotional independence from parents and other adults
5. Preparing for marriage and family life
6. Preparing for a career
7. Developing a set of values and an ethical framework or ideology or both as a guide
8. Striving for and achieving socially responsible behavior

If these eight tasks are successfully managed at various times during the adolescent period, success throughout adulthood is far more likely, according to Havighurst. After 30 years since Havighurst proposed these tasks, they still have relevance.

Physical and Sexual Development

"Puberty and entrance into middle school typically define the beginning of adolescence," write Roth and Brooks-Gunn (1999, p. 63). So many changes are connected to the onset of puberty that this one particular biological transition has a direct effect on other aspects of physical growth, cognitive functioning, and social development. Few developmental features throughout the span of human life have so much impact on so many other parts of life.

Ample evidence shows that physical growth and development surrounding puberty, during early adolescence (ages 10–14), is unparalleled in other periods of life, with the possible exception of the first year following birth (Steinberg & Levine, 1997). Puberty is the time of the legendary growth spurt (accelerated rate increase in height and weight) and sexual maturation, when young adolescents undergo rapid physical changes in what seem to parents and teachers as impossibly brief periods of time. What are, at least in some young adolescents, dramatic changes in body size and symmetry, and in the primary and secondary sex characteristics, emphatically mark this transitional time.

Physical maturation has been occurring earlier and earlier in successive generations due to several factors, including nutrition, social circumstances, and quality of medical care (Belkin, 2000). The average age of entrance into puberty has dropped from 16 to 12 years of age over the last 150 years (Urdan & Klein, 1999). With these trends combining with other social and psychological factors, sexual activity is beginning earlier and teenage pregnancy rates have increased. The incidence of adolescent AIDS and ARC (AIDS-related complex) is also on the rise. AIDS is now the sixth leading cause of death among 15- to 24-year-olds (The Adolescent Years, n.d.). As a result of earlier maturation, sexual relations, pregnancy, and sexually transmitted diseases are now issues of heightened concern at the middle school. This trend and its ramifications make understanding this period critical for the middle school educator.

Further complicating the matter, girls generally experience the growth spurt and reach sexual maturity earlier than boys. Female maturity is most frequently defined as the age of menarche, about 12 years of age (Urdan & Klein, 1999), although reproductive capability may not be reached until several months or even a year or more later. For boys, maturity is often measured as the peak of the growth spurt, at about 14 years of age (Simmons & Blyth, 1987). Girls reach maturity then, on the average, two years before boys. At a time when students are learning to relate to one another in social situations, the developmental lag between boys and girls can be awkward and embarrassing for those involved.

Boys of the same age are usually not of interest to girls unless the boys are early maturers. Instead, mature girls will often be attracted to older boys, who may have sexual knowledge and drive that can be confusing or overwhelming to a young girl. Early maturing girls may have particular difficulties in social adjustment (Lenssen, Doreleijers, Van Dijk, & Hartman, 2000). Late maturing females are sometimes tall and thin, with no evident sexual development. Being different can lead to extreme self-consciousness and withdrawal. Consequently, self-esteem and self-concept are closely related to physical development. Adolescent females report significantly lower self-esteem, sense of self-stability, and self-image and higher self-consciousness than do males (Simmons & Blyth, 1987).

The overall health of young adolescents has been declining over the past few decades. For many, young adolescence is the time for the beginning of engagement in high-risk behaviors that can lead to serious injury or death. Each day, some 3,000 young adolescents smoke their first cigarette. Some groups of young adolescents are already acquiring risk factors for heart disease, high blood pressure, and diabetes. More than half of American middle schoolers are overweight, while many young adolescent girls have a punishing obsession with thinness (California Middle Grades Task Force, 2001).

This transitional period involves not only visible external physical changes, but also internal ones. Hormonal fluctuations may cause mood swings. Rapid physical development brings increased nutritional demands. Middle schoolers in the throes of such development may become alternately excitable and lethargic. In the past, many people have attributed what has been deemed the erratic behavior of middle schoolers to such hormonal changes. However, recent research has shown that the physiological changes are only a portion of what contributes to the well-known emotional states and behaviors of middle school students (Urdan & Klein, 1999).

Physical development and appearance can be related to self-esteem. The girl who is not yet menstruating and has no breast development may invent excuses to avoid physical exercise that requires undressing in front of other girls. Late maturing males may also suffer from feelings of inadequacy, particularly at a time when athletic prowess begins to take on added importance and early maturing boys, with more developed muscles, are at a definite advantage in most sports. Late maturing girls and boys may assiduously avoid the gang shower.

Physical development, in which diversity is the rule rather than the exception, is of great concern to middle schoolers. Any development perceived by the student to be abnormal can cause great anxiety and influence social and emotional development. Early maturing boys may excel in physical activities and, as a consequence, develop increased self-confidence and feelings of competence. Conversely, late maturing boys and girls may become insecure and withdrawn, feeling unable to compete with larger, more mature children. The question "Am I normal?" is never far away from the minds of middle school learners, and physical development is a very important part of the answer. When an average middle school classroom presents a six- to eight-year physical age span, it may be difficult for any one in the room to decide what is normal.

Implications for Middle Schools

In many ways, these dramatic physical changes can be seen positively, as an "enabling mechanism" that propels students toward exciting growth and development (Urdan & Klein, 1999). Physical development can also be a stress factor of major proportions. To make the most of this development, middle school students need frequent opportunities for physical movement as well as for rest and change of activity. They also need help in diet, nutrition, personal hygiene, and coping with such physical factors as menstruation, growing beards, changing voices, and outgrowing clothes. The opportunity for positive intervention from educators on such matters is unparalleled.

We believe that middle school educators should vigorously oppose attempts to eliminate physical education as a frequent, if not daily, experience. Financial exigencies or the pressures of standards-based reform should not allow this fundamental need to be given less than the full priority it deserves in the education of young adolescents.

COGNITIVE DEVELOPMENT

Until relatively recently, middle school educators had accepted the theories and concepts of famous Swiss psychologist and biologist Jean Piaget without question or modification. Piaget (1977) described four stages in the development of cognitive thought: sensori-motor (0–2 years old), preoperational thought (2–7 years old), concrete operations (7–11 years old), and formal operations (11–12 years old into adulthood). The Piagetian theory, especially as it applies to students from ages 11 to 15, has frequently been used as the justification for widely differing middle school program changes. At times, educators have argued that schools should place more emphasis on complex intellectual tasks, because Piaget held that formal operations began at age 11. At other times, educators have asserted that complex subjects such as algebra should be delayed until high school, because concrete thinking dominated the middle school years.

Educators have known for some time, as a result of other research studies (e.g., Miller, 1980; Eson & Walmsley, 1980) that great numbers of students do remain in the stage of concrete operations throughout their tenure in the middle school. Children in the concrete operations phase are often unable to generalize to broad contexts—that is, to hypothesize from existing facts. They may have great difficulty dealing effectively with the past, in a realistically chronological way. They may be unable to reverse mental operations or consider situations that appear to be contrary to their personal observations. Teaching a class with students operating at concrete levels can be difficult, to say the least, given that most middle school curriculum has been designed to involve substantial amounts of hypothesizing, conceptualizing, and symbolizing. Providing diverse learning experiences, with varied instructional delivery, can help communicate the subject matter to students in either stage.

Several decades ago, some suggested that because many early adolescents are not ready to move into complex operations at the age that Piaget suggests, pushing them too hard to make the transition might be harmful (see Toepfer,

1980). Children, it was argued, are in a plateau period of brain growth from 12 to 14 years. Researchers suggested that pushing adolescents to attain higher levels of thinking skills based on Piaget's theories might cause frustration and lower self-esteem. Our experience is that most middle school educators believe that their students are, in fact, far less mature in the stage of intellectual development that they have reached than was previously believed to be the case. If the observations of many classroom teachers are accurate, many students remain in the concrete stage throughout the middle school years, and far fewer have advanced to formal operations by their arrival at the middle school door than was once believed to be normal. None of this should be taken, however, as our endorsement of the idea that middle schools should be less intellectually rigorous than they now are. On the contrary, we believe that all middle school students deserve and require a rich, meaningful, and challenging educational experience.

Constructivism

Research and theory in the area of cognitive development suggest that young adolescents are far from being merely passive vessels awaiting the arrival of a biologically delivered capacity for complex thinking (Urdan & Klein, 1999). Middle school students are much more accurately described as students capable of playing a major role in their own cognitive development. Constructivist perspectives on teaching and learning (Brooks & Brooks, 1993), which evolved in the 1990s, asserted that individuals are much more in charge of their intellectual development than once thought and that teachers have a far greater role to play in the cognitive development of their students. Knowledge and cognitive development are both the products of interaction with information, materials, instruction, and other students.

Early adolescence is rightly conceived as a period usually marked by improvements in students' capacities to think abstractly and hypothetically. These changes are brought about by a combination of biological maturation, experiences, interaction, socialization, and good teaching. Early adolescent students can envision what they want to be like in the future, and, most importantly, they can design and choose to follow pathways that help them become this kind of person. Or not. Much depends upon the actions of educators in the face of students with such characteristics and needs (Urdan & Klein, 1999).

Conceptions of Intelligence

A great deal of research and writing has occurred in the area of the meaning and measurement of the still elusive concept of intelligence. Always a controversial topic because of the many potentially significant possible implications for race, ethnicity, socioeconomic status, and other factors, current discussions about intelligence are no different. Because this work is germane to middle school education reform, but not exclusively tied to the middle school, we briefly summarize the significant work of several writers and suggest that interested readers consult the reference list for sources of more detailed information.

Nature versus Nurture   Questions and issues surrounding the source and mutability of intelligence seem to return to the headlines in the United States on a regular basis. In the early 1970s, for example, debate burst on the scene following the publication of Arthur Jensen's widely read monograph in the *Harvard Education Review* (1969). Jensen strongly suggested that human intelligence was immutable and that this fact of fixed intelligence limited the worth of the expensive and widely implemented educational enrichment programs that had been established during President Lyndon B. Johnson's Great Society. In a book published shortly thereafter, Harvard University professor Richard Herrnstein (1973) claimed that these immutable differences in intelligence were largely attributable to genetics. Counterarguments followed, and the debate has continued.

Richard Herrnstein and Charles Murray (1995) added fierce new energy to debates about intelligence with the publication of *The Bell Curve*. Most of the controversy generated by the book focused on the authors' claim that racial differences in intelligence quotient (IQ) are largely genetic. Herrnstein and Murray also suggested that the United States was rapidly becoming a caste society rigidly stratified by IQ, with an underclass stuck at the bottom and an intellectual elite in charge of every aspect of American life. Echoing Herrnstein's argument in the early 1970s, the authors charged that, because of the genetic components of IQ, government or the education system could do little to change the structure of the society. Herrnstein and Murray went so far as to assert that no racial or ethnic discrimination was evident in the American workplace and that such discrimination that did exist was reverse discrimination aimed at whites and Asians. All such efforts at government intervention, said the authors, should be immediately halted.

A fusillade of criticism of *The Bell Curve* quickly followed its publication. Charging that publication of the book damaged race relations in a country already deeply divided over the issue, critics also suggested that the timing of the publication contributed to the efforts of conservative politicians to cut welfare payments (Dickens, Kane, & Schultze, 1995). Dickens and his colleagues stated that a large and widely accepted body of research contradicts the theory that IQ is the dominant factor determining economic and social position. If IQ were all that mattered, they pointed out, the American society would be a great deal more egalitarian than it is now. The famous bell curve, or normal distribution, reveals that most people are similar in intelligence and grouped around the middle of the curve.

Other critics reacted to different weaknesses they perceived in the Herrnstein and Murray work. Feuerstein and Kozulin (1995) pointed to the great danger that could follow reducing human worth to a single number, especially when that number (IQ score) comes from a testing process that so many psychometricians believe to be severely limited. Fraser edited a book (1995) in which many of the most highly regarded names in American social science took aim at *The Bell Curve*. In *The Bell Curve Wars: Race, Intelligence, and the Future,* Howard Gardner, Stephen Jay Gould, Thomas Sowell, Henry Louis Gates Jr., and Nathan Glazer all inveighed against the various theses promulgated by Herrnstein and Murray.

These authors pointed to the evidence that suggests that IQ differences between African American and majority culture children, for example, can be almost completely eliminated by adjusting for differences in neighborhood, economic conditions, family poverty, maternal education, and learning experiences. They asserted that poverty and home environment explain the gap in IQ, not the reverse. Herrnstein and Murray's statistical methods, their depiction of American class structure, and their ultraconservative policy recommendations are all condemned as faulty and too likely to lead to destructive outcomes were the conclusions of *The Bell Curve* to influence practice in American schools. Unfortunately, we predict, the argument about nature versus nurture is not over, nor are the influences of such struggles on the organization and operation of middle schools.

Multiple Intelligences Harvard University professor Howard Gardner was among those most strongly objecting to Herrnstein and Murray's theses. Gardner had been involved in developing new theories about intelligence since shortly after the first set of charges and countercharges about intelligence were generated in the 1970s. At the beginning of the 21st century, no theoretician since Piaget had been more widely read, with greater effect on classroom practice, than had Gardner. His theory of multiple intelligences (Gardner, 1983, 1991, 1993) runs against the traditional American educational practice of giving value to and assessing only linguistic and logical-mathematical abilities. Instead of arguing about the origin of IQ, Gardner identified seven areas or intelligences, six of which had little to do with the arguments connected to *The Bell Curve*.

1. Spatial (think of artists)
2. Musical ("I think in sounds," said Maurice Ravel)
3. Bodily Kinesthetic (think of dancers, athletes, mimes)
4. Interpersonal (the ability to understand people's moods, feelings, motives)
5. Intrapersonal (the ability to know one's self, to read the internal landscape)
6. Linguistic (language and symbol systems; think of authors, journalists, poets)
7. Logical Mathematical (symbol systems of math and science; think of science, medicine, and technology)

Middle school educators who support Howard Gardner's work find limiting the concept of intelligence to the IQ and its analytical functions far too restrictive for effective educational practice. Gardner and others view intelligence as far more complex than earlier IQ-oriented intelligence theorists had. Gardner has developed a theory of multiple intelligences that many middle school educators consider critical in tapping into young adolescents' multifarious talents and varying ways of learning. Middle school students, from this perspective, have a variety of ways of being intelligent, and individuals have legitimate learning strengths that may not necessarily lie in the cognitive realm. Responding to multiple intelligences in the classroom means that successful teachers vary instructional strategies and types of activities to tap into students' intellectual strengths and support their weaknesses.

Gardner claims that these intelligences exist independently in individuals' neural systems. Thus, he stated, the traditional understanding of intelligence as a single entity should be reconsidered and reconceptualized. Thinking of intelligence in this way helps educators and others realize that value and worth are not, or should not be, determined by a single number (IQ) and that schools and society can and should develop ways of recognizing the value of different intelligences and working to enhance them.

How might this influence classroom practice at the middle school level? While Gardner has expressed some reservations about misapplication of his theories, middle school educators clearly can make use of these ideas, and middle school educators have embraced Gardner's theories with unbridled enthusiasm. Bringing music into the classroom, so that students might tap into this aspect of their intelligence by creating raps, songs, and jingles that accompany other subjects, appeals to educators of young adolescents. Using visual images and graphic organizers such as webs, Venn diagrams, and the creative use of color and other concrete visual tactics ought to enhance learning in virtually every classroom. Evidence has accumulated to show clearly that these practices are directly connected to increased academic achievement (Marzano, Pickering, & Pollock, 2001). Having students use mental rehearsal, a technique borrowed from top athletes, might improve science lab work, speeches, or other projects that could be visualized before the task was performed. Complex concepts can be summarized effectively in cartoons, paintings, and symbols; words are not the only way. Thousands of middle school teachers are using manipulatives to teach and reinforce sophisticated mathematics concepts. Alternative assessment strategies that use one or more of the intelligences would certainly enhance the ability of students to express what they know (Daniels & Bizar, 1998).

Honoring those who excel in areas of intelligence other than the traditional IQ may be the most important implication of Gardner's work for middle school educators, considering the central commitment of the middle school concept to the success of all students. Middle school educators can work harder to reinforce the value and worth of music programs, art experiences, and dance performances. Interpersonal and intrapersonal intelligence can be explored more openly and with more enthusiasm, without sacrificing the school's traditional commitment to linguistic and logico-mathematical intelligence.

Emotional Intelligence   An important extension of the concept of multiple intelligences came with the publication of Daniel Goleman's *Emotional Intelligence* (1995). Continuing Gardner's argument that traditional conceptions of intelligence are far too narrow, Goleman stated that conceptions such as those advanced by Herrnstein and Murray ignored a crucial range of human abilities (intelligences) that matter immensely in terms of how well a person does in life. Goleman drew on brain research and behavioral evidence to highlight the factors at work when people with high IQs fail and when those with modest IQs do very well. He stated that, even when people with high IQs do well, the real reasons for their success may have more to do with their "EQ" (emotional quotient) than their IQ.

Emotional intelligence is, according to Goleman, probably a broad range of abilities, seeming to combine much of the interpersonal and intrapersonal intelligences identified by Gardner. A person with emotional intelligence is skilled at self-awareness, reins in emotional impulses, can read another's feelings, experiences empathy, keeps relationships on track, displays social deftness, and possesses the sort of self-motivation that helps one persevere despite setbacks. The lack of emotional intelligence can often create havoc in one's life. Low EQ can destroy one's rational mind, ruin otherwise promising careers, cause problems in important relationships such as marriage and family, and lead to poor physical health. Good mental health is closely tied to emotional intelligence.

Young adolescents, says Goleman, may suffer most from low emotional intelligence. Depression, eating disorders, unwanted pregnancies, low motivation, aggressiveness, and violence in adolescence are all tied to low EQ. Young adolescents need to bring intelligence to their emotions to protect against such tragedy. They need to realize that they have two distinct brains (i.e., one brain with two important parts), two different kinds of intelligence, to harmonize. Goleman wrote that instead of interfering with rational minds, emotional intelligence is an integral part of thought processes.

Fortunately, Goleman stated, like Gardner and others, that emotional intelligence is not fixed at birth anymore than rational intelligence. It can be nurtured and strengthened in all people all their lives, but like other intelligences, raising the EQ when the person is young is far more effective. Before their emotional intelligence is hard-wired, by adulthood, children and youth are taught emotional lessons and coached in emotional habits that, for better or worse, last throughout their lives. Goleman believes so strongly in the capacity of schools to educate and strengthen emotional intelligence, he stated that such emotional education may be the most important way for America to find its way out of the cultural difficulties that surround it. Some middle schools around the country are beginning to integrate emotional literacy into the curriculum. We believe this trend cannot be anything but a positive step in the education of young adolescents in the 21st century.

MORAL DEVELOPMENT

Piaget (1977) contributed to the early work in one of the most well known theories of moral development. Piaget assumed that cognitive and moral development progress together, that moral development is the development of the thought process. Distinguishing between right and wrong, he theorized, is moral, but it is primarily an intellectual task. Piaget held that both intellectual and moral development proceed through a series of discrete stages or phases. The stages of moral judgment, as elaborated by Piaget, are seen as sequential and universal. That is, children and youth always develop through the same stages, in the same order, wherever they are in the world. They may not all reach all of the stages, he believed, but development occurred in an orderly manner.

The first stage, as Piaget conceived of moral development, is moral realism, in which children judge objectively. For example, greater damage done to another person is worse than less damage, no matter what the cause. The second stage, morality of cooperation, applies to middle schoolers. In this stage, judgments about morality are made subjectively, usually according to the perceived intent. Piaget offers the example that a child operating in the morality of cooperation stage would consider a boy to be naughtier who breaks 1 cup while trying to sneak some jam out of the cupboard than the child who breaks 15 cups by opening a door and accidentally knocking over the cups.

Lawrence Kohlberg (1981), building on Piaget's classifications, proposed that individuals develop moral judgment by moving through a series of six stages contained within three levels. Continuing research in this area confirms much of Kohlberg's original ideas. They are as follows.

LEVEL ONE: PRECONVENTIONAL

> Stage One—Punishment and Obedience: literal obedience to avoid punishment
>
> Stage Two—Individual Instrumental Purpose and Exchange: serving one's own or others' needs for personal benefit

LEVEL TWO: CONVENTIONAL

> Stage Three—Mutual Interpersonal Expectations, Relationships, and Conformity: the desire to please others and conform to perceived norms of right and wrong

Stage Four—Social System and Conscience Maintenance: doing one's duty to preserve the social order

LEVEL THREE: POST-CONVENTIONAL AND PRINCIPLED

Stage Five—Prior Rights and Social Contract: commitment to relative social order; rules may be changed if needed

Stage Six—Universal Ethical Principles: action determined by conscience, based on self-chosen ethical principles

Moral Development among Middle Schoolers

Middle level educators are most likely to see students who are thinking and acting, in terms of moral development, in stages one to four. Some middle school students will continue to demonstrate the predominance of stage one, where "what they can get away with" determines what is right to them. Near age 10, some children will begin to enter stage two, where what is right and wrong depends on who is involved and their relationship. In stage two, relationships and their outcomes are important in moral reasoning. However, relationships are often limited to one-on-one situations in which what is right depends on the nature of the relationship. Groups are not yet important. If the other person is important to the decision-maker or actor, then one is bound to consider him or her when making decisions or acting in one way or another. If the other person is not a central character in the constellation of the person's relationships, then one is not bound to act with the other person's interests in mind. In other words, right is what produces pleasure for me in our relationship; wrong is whatever does not produce pleasure.

Middle school students are, typically, thought to be involved in stage three, and many are. During early adolescence, many students progress from egocentric behavior in stage two to the desire to please others and win acceptance in stage three. Stage three is where approval from groups is important. This includes not only peers but also adult role models and perceived community norms. In stage three, the student becomes sensitive to the opinions and values of groups of people that they know, care about, and interact with on a regular basis: their peers, their family, their church group, and other reference groups. Agreeing with what these groups define as good and rejecting what they define as bad becomes central.

Perhaps only a minority of students move into stage four during their middle school years. Moving into stage four requires an understanding of the need for social order beyond individual benefit and beyond the approval of groups that are made up of people who are known and cared for. Stage four is very advanced, in terms of moral development, insofar as it involves a willingness to do what is right because one knows that institutions (such as schools) will cease to function effectively unless most group members voluntarily act in moral ways, following the rules and behaving for the good of the institution.

Several years ago, Paul S. George (1980) spent a brief period of time at the Center for the Study of Moral Education, at the Harvard University School of Education, in extended conversations with Lawrence Kohlberg on the significance of these concepts of moral development for middle school educators. Among the areas of agreement was that there is one very crucial point in moral development, a sort of "go–no go" spot, and it has to do with the years students spend in middle level schools. Kohlberg asserted that if students have not fully mastered stage three before they move on to high school, they probably never will. That is, students who have not matured to the point where they identify with groups they care about by the time they leave middle school may never understand, for example, the ideas that support the rule of law and the importance of maintaining the social order, let alone understand the Constitution or universal principles of justice and morality that characterize the highest stages of moral development.

The special readiness of early adolescents for learning about group citizenship, in the sense of moral identification with groups that is the heart of stage three, holds special meaning for middle school educators. Middle school educators may be able to make important contributions to the continued moral development of early adolescents by organizing and operating middle schools so that positive group involvement, loyalty, duty, responsibility, ownership, and citizenship are emphasized. This makes advisory groups, interdisciplinary teams, long-term relationships, and other aspects of middle schools even more important.

Research in comparative education (George, with Evan George, 1995; Duke, 1986) confirms our belief that early adolescents in both Japan and America move through a period of distinctive, virtually unparalleled, readiness to learn about group citizenship. The Japanese believe that, prior to the middle grades, children are too young to learn the important lessons of group involvement and that, if the lessons have not been internalized by the time the students move on to high school, it may be too late to do so. Consequently, Japanese educators organize and operate their middle level schools to capitalize on what they believe is the prime time in life to learn concepts such as duty, responsibility, loyalty, involvement, and commitment. In what may be the most academic schools in the world, Japanese junior high schools, almost 10 hours a week are devoted to learning to be an important member of an important group. Homerooms, clubs, school duties, and other components of the school experience are designed to teach the concepts of group citizenship that are related to the third stage of moral development. We believe that American middle school educators must move in similar directions.

Identity Formation

For more than four decades, educators and psychologists have shared a growing certainty that the formation of a positive sense of identity may be the most challenging and critical task faced by young adolescents. General understanding of the complexities of identity development has also grown over these years.

Erik Erikson While indebted to Sigmund Freud's ideas in many ways, Erik Erickson's socio-psychoanalytic theory focused on identity formation in a way that went far beyond Freud's attention to psychosexual development. Erikson (1963, 1968) placed much less emphasis on early childhood than Freud, believing that each stage has its own importance to human development. Erikson stated that family and society could have deeply positive effects on individual development. Further differences with Freud centered on Erikson's belief that conscious reason (the ego) had a much greater capacity to resolve crises in human development. Erikson's emphasis on life-long development was unusual for the time in which he was writing and is responsible for the value placed on his interpretations of human development by current scholars engaged in the study of early adolescence (e.g., Roeser et al., 2000), somewhat in contrast to Freud's work.

Erikson contended that an individual strives, throughout life, to maintain a positive ego identity as he or she passes through what Erikson delineated as eight key stages of human development. Identity development depended on the successful negotiation of a series of turning points, each with a unique set of challenges (what Havighurst called "developmental tasks"). Infants, in the first year of their lives, must, for example, resolve a dilemma between the issues of basic trust in or mistrust of other persons. Young children, ages 2 and 3, must wrestle with shame and doubt as they build a sense of autonomy; children ages 4 and 5 must develop a sense of initiative (Erikson, 1963, p. 249). Older children must establish a sense of industry, as opposed to a feeling of inferiority (Erikson, 1963, p. 258).

Erikson's conception of the major task of adolescence as a struggle of identity formation versus identity (or role) diffusion still holds sway in current discussions about adolescence (Erikson, 1963, p. 261). Erikson believed that if an individual adolescent is unable to develop an identity that the person feels is valuable, the failure to do so may lead to an inability to forge a clear sense of identity (identity diffusion) or even an identity grounded solely in opposition to others (negative identity) (Goodenow & Espin, 1993).

Erikson viewed adolescence as a time characterized by the dichotomy of identity versus isolation. For Erikson, the task of adolescence—what all adolescents must do—is the establishment of one's unique identity. Erikson described adolescence as a necessary turning point, a time for "marshaling resources for growth, recovery and further differentiation" (Peshkin & White, 1990, p. 11). An individual moved into young adulthood when able to merge his or her identity with another's without a loss of personal identity in the process, developing a capacity for intimacy. Adulthood emerges through the formulation and reformulation of personal values and key identifications and fantasies with plans, opportunities, and realistic expectations.

Youths' ego identities sometimes involve the maintenance of folk heroes as substitute identities, according to Erikson. While basketball star Charles Barkley made headlines with his controversial claim, "I am not a role model," the record-breaking sales of Michael Jordan basketball jerseys offered strong evidence of the power of Erikson's idea. Minority students' love for heroes of their own ethnic background (e.g., Gloria Estefan) is one way for youths today to negotiate the complex terrain of identity formation.

Contemporary scholars in the area of human development do insist, however, that thinking about identity formation and other areas of development must consider important factors such as gender, factors that received little if any consideration in the male-dominated paradigms of earlier decades. Carol Gilligan (1982), for example, has critiqued Erikson's work in the area of identity formation, charging that "identity comes to be identified with separation, and attachments appear to be developmental impediments, as is repeatedly the case in the assessment of women" (pp. 12–13).

In her book *In a Different Voice*, Gilligan stated that, while Erikson did note that for men identity precedes intimacy, the two fuse together for women. While Erikson acknowledged that women come to understand themselves through intimate relationships with others, his overarching theory did not acknowledge this conception. He maintained that identity precedes intimacy (Garrod, Smulyan, Powers, & Kilkenny, 1992). In such models, Gilligan and others assert, women, who prize intimacy and attachment, are inaccurately portrayed as developmentally impaired. And theories of human development that do not include important aspects of life, such as gender, fail to fully understand the enormous complexity of human development and are, therefore, incomplete.

Still, contemporary educational psychologists affirm the clarity of Erikson's insights into the importance of the stage of identity formation, limited though it might have been by the restrictions of the time in which Erikson worked. Bengston (1996, p. 1), for example, described adolescence, particularly early adolescence, as a period when individuals begin to identify their "abiding, personal interests." This identification is personal, as compared with that of children, who often act on their parents' suggestion. When things go well, the emerging adolescent develops a set of interests in a variety of areas (intellectual, vocational, artistic, recreational) that begins to describe what they are about—who they are. One's interests define one's identity; a young person is, in a very real sense, what the person is interested in. The development of identity through the identification of abiding personal interests does not necessarily imply parent-child stress, nor does it have purely masculine connotations.

In the case of either boys or girls, according to Bengston (1996, p. 3),

> persons without interests become a burden to themselves and others. Their condition can be variously characterized, in its least to most virulent forms, as mechanical conformity, apathy, learned helplessness, the possession of or by a negative identity, clinical depression, autism, and psycho- or sociopathology.

Bengston agrees that young adolescents without interests also "lack what Erikson terms a temporal perspective" (1996, p. 3). Adolescents who do not develop this basic sense of identity do not have a sense of where they have been or where they are going. This temporal perspective is critical to the capacity for persistence and the ability to engage, with absorption, in work and study—characteristics critical to the successful negotiation of the other tasks of adolescence. The implications for middle school programs are enormous.

William Glasser (1965, 1972, 1985, 1990) has, for many years, written with clarity and a sense of urgency about the importance of identity formation and education in the American school. In *The Identity Society* (1972), Glasser illustrated how life in contemporary America no longer focused, at least for the relatively affluent majority, on survival. Instead, adolescents and others saw their major developmental task as the development of a "success identity." Identity factors such as personal power and control over one's own life, meaningful relationships, and a sense of success are far more important to young adolescents than ever before, and many young adolescent students are failing to develop such positive identities (Roeser et al., 2000). Identity formation is the central task of adolescent development and will rarely succeed without a firmly constructive beginning in the middle school.

Self-Esteem   One's sense of identity and a sense of self-esteem are clearly related. Cotton's (1985) comprehensive review of the literature points out the importance of the transition into early adolescence for both identity and self-esteem. Early adolescence is a sensitive and vulnerable time for self-esteem. The transition into this stage of life almost always brings lower self-esteem as the person grapples with the turbulence and confusion of major growth experiences. But, when these experiences are completed successfully, self-esteem is likely to return to a more positive position.

Because of the emergent nature of identity development and the parallel formation of moral reasoning, middle school students are known for their vacillating self-esteem. Middle school teachers know the unpredictable nature of students, in this regard, often from one day to the next. The desire to fit in, please peers as well as parents, while attempting to incorporate the values of the community, local church, family, and friends can be exhausting and confusing for the middle schooler. Television serves as a conveyor of values and beliefs as well as images of success and beauty, and it can have both positive and negative influences on adolescent viewers and their self-esteem (Greeson & Williams, 1986; Luker & Johnston, 1988). Not looking, sounding, or acting in a certain way can have negative effects on adolescent self-esteem.

Self-consciousness is at its peak in early adolescence and decreases thereafter (de Rosenroll, 1987), but the student with poor self-esteem may not see self-consciousness as a stage. The lonely adolescent, seeking ways either to become part of the group or to dull rejection, may turn to alcohol or other drugs (Roeser et al., 2000). Much of the research on dropouts and at-risk youth shows that these students feel alienated in the school environment and report negative perceptions of themselves in relation to the school (Roeser et al., 2000).

Low self-esteem has far-reaching implications. Affective education—teaching about emotions, feelings, and relationships—is critical in the middle school. Students at the middle level are in need of learning experiences that recognize and accommodate the changing nature of the young adolescent's psychological and social development. That is, middle schoolers need guidance in developing social skills and learning how to interact appropriately with other children and adults. Oliner (1986, p. 390) said, "In order to restore personal and social balance, appropriate self-interest needs to be augmented by a sense of community responsibility. The schools also have a legitimate role to play in cultivating a sense of community."

Peer Pressure

> Young people can also be remarkably clannish. . . . It is important to understand . . . such intolerance as a defense against a sense of identity confusion. For adolescents . . . help one another temporarily through much discomfort by forming cliques and by stereotyping themselves, their ideals, and their enemies. (Erikson, 1963, p. 262)

In the past, many theorists asserted that peer pressure was responsible for adolescent deviance. Drug and alcohol abuse, sexual experimentation, and other undesirable behaviors have been blamed on the influence of peer pressure. Recently, however, educators and adolescent psychologists have begun to hypothesize that peer influence is only one part of what makes adolescents behave the way they do. Peer pressure is a reality, but it is not the ultimate controller of an adolescent's actions. "Adolescents do generate their own norms and rules, but this process does not and cannot develop in isolation from the institutional context of the communities in which they live and learn" (Ianni, 1989, p. 679). Scheidlinger (1984, p. 393) suggested that the adolescent peer group is "better characterized by notions of growth and adaptation than those of turmoil and conflict." The peer group can be responsible for negative behavior, but it more often acts as a sounding board and a reference for more positive, adaptive behavior.

Peer pressure implies a passive acceptance of a barely resistible power. From the dynamic viewpoint of peer clusters, every member of a peer cluster is seen as an active, participating agent in shaping the norms and behaviors of that cluster. From the outside, it may look like peer pressure is leading to conformance, particularly if a parent or counselor wants to believe in the innocence of a particular child. What is actually occurring is a considerable amount of behavior norming, with each youth moving toward a commonly defined set of behaviors.

Peer relations allow the early adolescent to redefine a sense of self in terms of what is normal in everyday life. Relationships with peers and then adults begin to be reciprocal instead of "unilaterally controlled" by adults (Schwartz, Merten, & Bursik, 1987). Early adolescents look to peers for reinforcement and comfort; adults need to allow room for individual growth and diversity of relationships. Learning to relate to others is one of the primary lessons a school can teach. "Excessive attention to individual achievement and success has obscured one of the fundamental missions of schools, which is to produce people capable of living with some degree of responsibility and care for one another" (Oliner, 1986, p. 404).

THE AT-RISK MIDDLE SCHOOL STUDENT

Research on the growth and development of the young adolescent indicates that educators interested in making the most of their opportunities to "cultivate positive youth development" must undertake a dual endeavor. The first strategy is to design and implement schoolwide reform efforts that "benefit all young adolescents during this critical developmental period." The second strategy is to implement targeted intervention and prevention programs that focus on "subgroups of adolescents with specific vulnerabilities and needs" (Roeser et al., 2000). In this textbook, we attend to both of these important directions. In this section, however, we look specifically, albeit briefly, at the second—assisting at-risk middle school youth.

Unfortunately for everyone, a significant trend to emerge with substantial clarity since the first edition of this textbook was published in 1981 is that ever-growing numbers of middle school learners, across all social groups, are not successfully negotiating the twists and turns in the course of human developmental challenges and are emerging increasingly unlikely to ever reach their full potential (Jackson & Davis, 2000). All Americans struggle with the high rate of divorce, economies regularly disrupted by distant wars, the declining influence of organized religion, radically increased personal freedom, what President Jimmy Carter once called a "cultural malaise," and now the events of September 11, 2001. But only early adolescents must develop their sense of self and their personal momentum for their future in such a milieu. The good news may be that not even more youth are placed at risk by the challenge of development during such trying times.

The bad news is that millions of today's early adolescents personally endure increasing poverty, continuing racial prejudice, parental unemployment, family disruption, and community disintegration (Kozol, 1991). They are regularly exposed to life-limiting opportunities (e.g., easy availability of drugs and alcohol, social glorification of sexual promiscuity), the consequences of which may forever limit their options. For early adolescents, simultaneously denied the guidance and support they require, such obstacles can permanently hamper physical and emotional health, destroy motivation and ability to succeed in school and jobs, and damage personal relationships and the chance to become an effective parent.

As the Carnegie Council on Adolescent Development (1989, p. 8) pointed out:

> Unfortunately, by age 15, substantial numbers of American youth are at risk of reaching adulthood unable to meet adequately the requirements of the work place, the commitments of relationships in families and with friends, and the responsibilities of participation in a democratic society. These youth are among the estimated 7 million young people—one in four adolescents—who are extremely vulnerable to multiple high-risk behaviors and school failure. Another 7 million may be at moderate risk, but remain a cause for serious concern.

A teacher in South Florida said of her students at the end of the 20th century, "The students may not realize it, but they have a lot more things to worry about than we ever did." An Alabama teen put it this way (Public Agenda, 1997, p. 29):

> I think it's harder today because there's more stuff to do wrong. They didn't have as many people killing each other, and people fighting as much, at least I don't think so from what I've heard. There's just more stuff to get into. There wasn't as much damage to be done.

While they may have little with which to compare their experiences, middle school students in the 21st century clearly face a set of challenges that no other group of young adolescents in the United States has been asked to negotiate. Whether students consciously realize how much more challenging it is to grow up now, today's youth exhibit behaviors that indicate that growing up is, in many ways, far more difficult for them than it was for previous generations (Hechinger, 1992).

Yet researchers and writers who focus on early adolescence insist that it remains a time not only of challenge, and therefore of great risks, but also of great opportunities, even for the at-risk student. The period of early adolescence, from 10 to 14, is no longer viewed solely as a time of danger and risk. It is also a time of exciting possibility and opportunity, and of seeing older children and youth as societal assets instead of societal liabilities. Early adolescence is a time of tension between "multiple stressors and new possibilities for growth" (Urdan & Klein, 1999). When schools respond effectively, the results can be positive.

Thorough research (e.g., Roeser et al., 2000; Roth & Brooks-Gunn, 1999) indicates that educators must be careful about generalizations regarding the nature of this great transition. Stark, bimodal differences describe the success of this generation of American youth as its members attempt to negotiate this crucial passage in human life.

More than half of all young adolescents are able to successfully manage the stress without experiencing major problems. This slight majority of young adolescents is able to avoid what one researcher (Dryfoos, 1990) referred to as the "new morbidities" of early adolescence: poor motivation to learn, poor grades, school failure and truancy, depressed mood, misconduct, and negative peer affiliations. This group of approximately 51% of young adolescents achieves academic success, continues positive relationships with teachers and parents, maintains good mental health, and avoids affiliating with bad crowds. This successful half experiences early adolescence as a time of exciting explorations of their identity, their relationships, their bodies, and their success in school.

However, many young adolescents are far from successful. Roeser, Eccles, and Sameroff (2000, p. 444) report that

> somewhere between 25% and 50% of all young people in the United States between the ages of 10 and 17 are at-risk for curtailed educational, economic, and social opportunities due to their engagement in high-risk behaviors and activities that include violence and vandalism, unprotected sex, abuse of alcohol and drugs, skipping and failing school, and so on. And 60% to 80% of the youth most at risk dwell in disadvantaged inner-city environments. Currently the challenges to successful adolescent development are serious, and millions of U.S. young people are at serious risk for unsatisfying and unproductive lives.

The New Significance of Poverty, Race, and Ethnicity

At the beginning of the 21st century, young adolescents, ages 10–14, in the United States number approximately 20 million. Approximately 20% of them live below the poverty line and nearly 30% are members of minority groups (Carnegie Council on Adolescent Development, 1996). Thirty years ago only 1 in every 100 children born in the United States was of mixed race. Today that number is 1 in 19, and in states such as California it is closer to 1 in 10 (Clemetson, 2000). Added to the challenges of moving into adolescence in a time of great cultural stress, therefore, are the increasing numbers of poor children, minority children, and recent arrivals to the United States, creating new and more formidable tasks for themselves, the nation, and its educators.

Harold Hodgkinson (2001), a respected demographer with a special interest in education, asserts that educators should recognize that the students in the

21st century middle school will increasingly come from economically stressed homes. By the year 2020, because of higher birth rates among minority populations and patterns of immigration, nearly half of all school-age children will be non-Caucasian. Continuing to allow minority youth to face extraordinary risks of failure is a direct threat to the U.S. national standard of living and democratic foundations (Carnegie Council on Adolescent Development, 1989, p. 27).

These middle school students will represent racial and ethnic groups in a multicultural mix that is very different from what the typical teacher faced throughout the last two centuries. Because poverty is the best predictor of school failure, and more and more students placed at risk by poverty are coming to American secondary schools, Hodgkinson says that the task is clear. He believes that the new American middle school should unabashedly focus its efforts more on the poorest, and most at-risk, 40% of middle school students.

> The specter of a divided society—one affluent the other poor—looms ever more ominously on the American horizon. Inherent in this scenario is the potential for serious conflict between generations, among races and ethnic groups, and between the economically disenfranchised and middle and upper-income groups. It is a disturbing scenario, which must not occur. (Carnegie Council on Adolescent Development, 1989, p. 32)

The decade of the 1990s witnessed the fulfillment, across the nation, of what Sharon Fritz, principal of the Taylor Middle School in Millbrae, California, had experienced much earlier. In speaking of the transition that had occurred at her school during the previous decade, she said in March 1991:

> Ten years ago this school population of 550 was predominantly Caucasian, college bound, and conservative. Twenty teachers primarily lectured to seventh and eighth grade students almost every period. Discipline problems consisted of students being sent to the office for not having a pencil, forgetting a book, or talking without raising their hands. One out of ten were ESL [English as a second language], primarily native speakers of Chinese or Japanese.
>
> Today the school population consists of 650 students who speak 22 different languages. One out of four is enrolled in our ESL program. . . . Last week we identified close to 100 students who we feel are academically in need of support. We allocate a large portion of our money to provide a homework center for our kids after school. If someone had told us ten years ago that this is the way it would be, we would have laughed.
>
> We are very proud of our kids and each other. But we are also grappling with the following realities which did not exist ten years ago:
>
> Multiple languages in each classroom
> More and more single family homes (many of our kids live with their grandparents or various other relatives)
> More disparity between the haves and the have nots . . . [with] more have nots

Greater numbers of parents who have no parenting skills

Latch key children

The staff at Taylor Middle, and thousands of other middle level schools, has every right to be proud of its students and of its professional efforts to serve those students. At Taylor Middle, for example, the commitment to the students' welfare had, if anything, become more positive and constant during this period of time. Staff development has been continuous, state department reviews have resulted in numerous commendations including a designation as a "California Distinguished School," and interdisciplinary units were taught frequently. Many middle school educators there, and elsewhere, seemed to feel, however, that events may be outpacing their efforts to keep up, especially with the demographic changes that the student population continued to present.

Feldman and Eliott (1990) argued that, among other initiatives, a dramatically expanded research effort is needed to learn more about minority youth, especially African American and Hispanic early adolescents. Precious little is known about the normal development of minority adolescents, especially those who come from socioeconomically advantaged settings. Why so little is known and how this paucity of knowledge can be corrected are important issues to be confronted by human development scholars, educators, and the society as a whole. Recent research studies, however, do support the contention that at-risk students profit from direct training interventions designed to increase their academic achievement motivation, self-efficacy, persistence, confidence, responsibility, and citizenship (Felner et al., 1997; Roeser et al., 2000).

Programs for At-Risk Youth

A few such programs based on the characteristics of at-risk young adolescents have demonstrated admirable early progress. The Accelerated Schools Project, at Stanford University, in Stanford, California, has caught national attention. Accelerated schools focus on high expectations on the part of parents, teachers, and students; specific deadlines when students are to meet certain requirements; stimulating and relevant instructional programs; and a fundamental shared decision-making process. Perhaps the most common feature of accelerated schools, all of which may be different in some ways, is the insistence that all children in the schools should be brought to a certain level of competence by specific deadlines and should adhere to a core of curriculum, instructional, and organizational practices (Slavin, 2001; Goldberg, 2001).

The Program for Disadvantaged Youth, of the Edna McConnell Clark Foundation (Mizell & Gonzalez, 1991) began as an initiative focused on five urban school systems (Baltimore; Louisville, Kentucky; Milwaukee, Wisconsin; Oakland, California; and San Diego, California) and the reform of their middle level schools. The objectives of the program included completion of the middle grades curriculum, by all students, on time; exhibition of mastery of higher order thinking, reasoning, and comprehension skills; more positive attitudes toward self and school; and increased clarity about options for high school and beyond. A total of 12 middle schools attempted to implement new programs bent upon these outcomes. After a decade of effort, aimed mostly at establishing a rigorous curriculum congruent with standards-based reform, the foundation related its surprise at how difficult reform can be in urban middle grades schools (Lewis, 1999).

In a somewhat similar framework, the College Board developed a number of initiatives throughout the 1990s aimed at fostering improved articulation between middle and high schools so that "greater numbers of diverse students . . . pursue a more challenging curriculum in high school." The new programs hope to induce more poor and minority group students, who make up large proportions of at-risk students, to enroll in Advanced Placement courses and to engage middle and high school educators in exploring new methods for preparing these students for doing so. The initiatives propose that curriculum plans focus on the development of a rigorous curriculum for all students, with new diagnostic assessment procedures, groups of mentors, familiarity with college entrance tests such as the Scholastic Assessment Test, "SAT," and other components aimed at the goals of the initiatives. One example of these initiatives is a partnership between the College Board and the Florida Department of Education (College Board, 2001).

Most recently, the Center for the Social Organization of Schools, at Johns Hopkins University, in Baltimore, has developed a whole school reform model called the Talent Development Middle School (Talent Development Middle Schools, 2000). The model, based on what we consider to be carefully chosen components consistent with the middle school concept, is aimed at reforming serving "high-poverty populations." Among the components of the talent development model are cooperative learning, organizational strategies familiar to middle school educators, rigorous curriculum in mathematics and science, multicultural approaches to the social studies, high-quality staff development, and vigorous attempts to connect schools and communities. Because the components of the model are congruent with the middle school concept, and because the center has a record of success, we expect that the talent development model will provide educators with important new insights in the education of urban middle school students.

Components of Effective Programs for At-Risk Students

Educators in thousands of middle schools are employing special efforts to respond more effectively to the education of at-risk young adolescents. These might be labeled as "drop-out prevention" programs or have some other, less pejorative, title. All such programs, most importantly, recognize that a direct connection exists among three factors: the demographic characteristics of the students, their success in school, and the way in which the staff of the school works to make certain that an appropriate fit is made between the needs of the students and the components of the school they attend (Roeser et al., 2000). That is, the success of students in a school depends, overall, on the extent to which educators organize and operate the school with the particular needs of their students in mind. Do the educators in a school make the commitment to the success of their particular students, and the related programmatic changes, or cling to the traditional program that may or may not have worked decades earlier? Two roads diverge, to paraphrase poet Robert Frost, and the road less taken, until recently, can make all the difference.

Seven Cardinal Principles

What are the components of successful programs for the education of young adolescents, especially those at risk, in the 21st century? Upon what principles are effective schools for young adolescents based? We are persuaded that a synthesis of contemporary research (Felner et al., 1997; Lee & Smith, 1999; Osterman, 2000; Roeser et al., 2000; Urdan & Klein, 1999; and many others) specifies school programs that establish an effective match, a fit, between the needs of young adolescent students and the school program and environment, based on the following seven principles:

1. Emotional support and encouragement during the learning process, especially when difficulties are encountered, so that students feel known and cared for
2. Opportunities for young adolescents to exercise appropriately autonomous control over aspects of their own learning
3. Support for the development of competence in noncompetitive, nonjudgmental, and noncomparative ways
4. Meaningful, rigorous, unfragmented, and socially approved curriculum, connected to the lives of students, with high expectations for the success of all students
5. Organizational and operational strategies that yield a sense of personal identity, a feeling of smallness even in large schools
6. Particular support for the sizable and growing cohort of students who need more than the basic services to continue to be academically successful
7. Constructivist-style, active, social, experiential classroom learning experiences

We recognize that these are only general principles, with little descriptive detail accompanying them. That is what the remainder of this book is about. For now, suffice it to say that schools that establish an effective fit based on these principles are able to avoid being too large and too departmentalized.

They are able to avoid being highly competitive, academically and socially. They refuse to focus on the success of only the more able students, within the boundaries of a traditional curriculum. They avoid the narrowing of opportunities for student decision-making and self-management. The environment of schools that fit their students is more personal, less restrictive, and more cooperative, for students and for staff members (Roth & Brooks-Gunn, 1999).

In this textbook, we will focus on how educators in exemplary middle schools can build developmentally responsive schools, based on the knowledge educators currently possess about the nature and needs of this age group and the characteristics of schools that respond appropriately and effectively. We do this tentatively, however, in the knowledge that developmental psychologists and others continue to press forward to learn more about all aspects of this phenomenally important period of growth and development.

The challenges students face each day require ingenious responses from teachers and other school personnel. Fractured family lives, both parents working, the potential for encountering violence, alcohol and drug abuse, and a dozen other factors complicate the lives of today's middle school students. Nonetheless, this textbook echoes recent researchers' positive perspectives and the belief that organizing and operating the exemplary middle school in substantially different and more effective ways is possible. We offer many vivid examples of schools forging new strategies, new curricula, and new alliances to address the educational and social needs of young adolescents and to encourage their success.

FOCUS ON THE MIDDLE SCHOOL STUDENT: SUMMARY

The foregoing section has only briefly identified some of the most salient characteristics of middle school learners, and it is hoped that interested readers will use additional sources (such as those suggested at the end of the chapter) for further information. The point of greatest significance is that the middle school must be uniquely planned, staffed, and operated to provide a program that is truly focused on the rapidly moving and changing learners in the great transition from childhood to adolescence. In truth, this entire book is devoted to implications of the focus on the learner, for we see the exemplary middle school as one with a facility, organization, curriculum plan, student services, instruction—indeed, every aspect—developed and utilized to serve the needs and characteristics of this unique student population (see Box 1.1). The chief implication of our knowledge about middle school age learners is that they need a school focused sharply on their needs, the exemplary middle school, and that educators, with the help of researchers in related fields, must keep searching out these needs and the best means for their satisfaction.

**BOX
1.1**

A Summary of the Chapters in This Textbook

1. The primary focus of the middle school should be on the learners in these schools, usually about ages 10–14 and having the many unique needs and interests of early adolescents. Chapter 1 is devoted to these learners and their characteristics, needs, and interests.

2. Middle school planning should recognize as fully as possible historical factors in the development of the middle school and its rationale and desired characteristics (the middle school concept). Chapter 2 deals with these matters.

3. The middle school curriculum should include provision for its three basic domains or areas: personal development, continued learning skills, and basic knowledge. This chapter discusses what seems like a curriculum war that is currently ongoing. Chapter 3 presents examples of exemplary middle school curriculum opportunities as well as middle school curriculum planning.

4. Although no single chapter can adequately deal with how to teach, current information from theory, practice, and research as to instructional methodology should be utilized fully in every middle school and classroom. Relevant information is summarized in Chapter 4.

5. The middle school should provide an adequate guidance program, with special attention to types and plans for teacher-based guidance. Besides covering that topic, Chapter 5 deals with the new role of the teacher as advocate for the student in and beyond the school building.

6. An interdisciplinary team organization, characteristic of an effective middle school, is the focus of Chapter 6.

7. Exemplary middle schools can and should utilize appropriate means of grouping students. Alternative methods are described in Chapter 7.

8. Flexible scheduling and various types of space utilization should be planned for each middle school for its maximum effectiveness. These are discussed in Chapter 8.

9. Exemplary middle schools depend upon effective planning and implementation. Furthermore, middle schools, new and established, should be evaluated on the extent to which they attain goals related to the needs of the students who are their clients. Chapter 9 deals with these concerns.

10. Sooner or later every middle school takes on the characteristics of its leadership. Chapter 10 considers this most important concept and recent changes in the roles played by middle school leaders.

CONTENT SUMMARY

Early adolescence is usually defined to include the years between 10 and 14 or 15, surrounding the onset of puberty and related developmental changes. Scholars now recognize that this period of life is far more important than they formerly realized. Many crucial changes happen in this great transition: physical, sexual, cognitive, moral, and social. The development of a sense of identity may be the central task of early adolescence. Many millions of young adolescents are at risk of failing to craft such an identity and, consequently, failing in school. Middle schools can make a big difference in the degree of success such students experience.

CONNECTIONS TO OTHER CHAPTERS

The contents of this chapter are important to all the other chapters in the book. Becoming an effective middle school teacher and implementing programs for an exemplary middle school are both dependent on the development of a compassionate understanding of the characteristics and needs of young adolescents.

QUESTIONS FOR DISCUSSION

1. How well do the portrayals of early adolescence (e.g., intellectual, moral, identity development) fit with your own personal knowledge of today's young adolescents?
2. Does your own conception of human development seem more like those of stage theorists such as Jean Piaget and Lawrence Kohlberg, or do you believe that culture and environment play a more important role?
3. How well do contemporary middle schools provide for the development of abiding, personal interests in today's young adolescents? How could it be improved?
4. What are the implications from the recent emergence of conceptions of multiple intelligences for middle school curriculum and teaching?
5. Can you make some guesses about the specific programs or organizational strategies that exemplary middle schools use to create the best match or fit between the school and its students?

ACTION STEPS

1. This might be a good time to use the shadow study technique to learn more about today's middle school students. In a shadow study, you

make advance arrangements with a nearby middle school to spend the day there observing one student as he or she moves through the school day. It works best if the student is unaware that he or she has been selected for the study and you make your observations surreptitiously. Study a copy of the student's schedule, ahead of time if you can, and make every attempt to be in proximity to that student throughout the whole day—before school, at lunch time, and until the student leaves campus at the end of the day. Take careful and voluminous notes of what you observe, then review this chapter to help organize your findings.

2. The members of a class or a staff development training program using this textbook might want to employ a cooperative learning technique called curriculum jigsaw to become more familiar with the recent research on early adolescence published after this book was printed. In a curriculum jigsaw, students in a class, or workshop participants, are members of two groups: a home-base group or study group, and an expert group. The jigsaw begins when the class is organized into study groups of about five persons each. Each person in the study group agrees to become an expert on some aspect of research on adolescence (e.g., gender, minorities, sexual development, etc.). The next step is for these experts to get together in groups, divide up the labor, and work together to learn what is most important in each area. For example, members of the expert group on gender would compile a list of the most recent references, read those they take responsibility for, and get back with the other members of the expert group to synthesize their information and organize a presentation. Then, study groups or home teams re-form; each member of the home team is now an expert on a different area of early adolescence. The last part of the curriculum jigsaw is formed when members of the home team teach each other what they have learned about various aspects of contemporary early adolescence.

3. So much research on the characteristics of early adolescence has been conducted that research journals reporting these new insights have proliferated. It will be enlightening to become familiar, in a beginning way, with some of those journals. As an individual, or as part of a group, identify the ones that seem to fit your interests.

Adolescence
Child Development
Childhood Education
Family Relations
Gender and Education
Journal of Black Studies
Journal of Black Psychology
Multicultural Review
Journal of School Health
Urban Review
Journal of Child and Adolescent Substance Abuse
Journal of Adolescent and Adult Literacy
Psychology of Women Quarterly
Journal of Career Development

SUGGESTIONS FOR FURTHER STUDY

Books

Balk, D. (1995). *Adolescent development: Early through late adolescence.* Pacific Grove, CA: Brooks/Cole Publishing Co.

Caissy, G. (1994). *Early adolescence: Understanding the 10 to 15 year old.* New York: Insight Books.

Carnegie Council on Adolescent Development (1996). *Great transitions: Preparing adolescents for a new century.* New York: Carnegie Corporation of New York, 1996.

Cowen, E., Hightower, A., Pedro-Carroll, J., Work, W., & Wyman, C., with Haffey, W. (1996). *School-based prevention for children at risk: The Primary Mental Health Project.* Washington, DC: American Psychological Association.

Finn, J. (1998). *Class size and students at risk: What is known? what is next?* Washington, DC: National Institute on the Education of At-Risk Students.

Gil, N., & Thomas, E. (1993). *The moral self.* Cambridge, MA: MIT Press.

Johnson, N., Roberts, M., & Worell, J. (1999). *Beyond appearance: A new look at adolescent girls.* Washington, DC: American Psychological Association.

Jordan, W., & Murrey Nettles, S. (1999). *How students invest their time out of school: Effects on school engagement, perceptions of life chances, and achievement.* Baltimore: Center for Research on the Education of Students Placed at Risk.

Lipka, R., & Brinthaupt, T. (1992). *Self-perspectives across the life span.* Albany, NY: State University of New York Press.

Santrock, J. (1996). *Adolescence: An introduction.* Madison, WI: Brown & Benchmark.

Santrock, J. (1997). *Life-span development.* Madison, WI: WCB Brown & Benchmark Publishers.

Wavering, M. (1995). *Educating young adolescents: Life in the middle.* New York: Garland Publishers.

Periodicals

Buysse, W. (1997). Behaviour problems and relationships with family and peers during adolescence. *Journal of Adolescence, 20*(6), 645–659.

Damon, W., & Gregory, A. (1997). The youth charter: Towards the formation of adolescent moral identity. *Journal of Moral Education, 26*(2), 117–130.

DuBois, D., Felner, R., & Lease, A. (1996). Early adolescent self-esteem: A developmental-ecological framework and assessment strategy. *Journal of Research on Adolescence, 6*(4), 543–579.

Drummond, W. (1997). Adolescents at risk: Causes of youth suicide in New Zealand. *Adolescence, 32*(128), 925–934.

Flieller, A. (1999). Comparison of the development of formal thought in adolescent cohorts aged 10 to 15 years (1967–1996 and 1972–1993). *Developmental Psychology, 35*(4), 1048–1058.

Hacker, D. (1994). An existential view of adolescence. *Journal of Early Adolescence, 14*(3), 300–327.

Helwig, C. (1995). Adolescents' and young adults' conceptions of civil liberties: Freedom of speech and religion. *Child Development, 66*(1), 152–166.

Lewis, S., Mirowsky, J., & Ross, C. (1999). Establishing a sense of personal control in the transition to adulthood. *Social Forces, 77*(4), 1573–1599.

Perry, C., & McIntire, W. (1995). Modes of moral judgment among early adolescents. *Adolescence, 30*(119), 707–715.

Royse, D. (1998). Mentoring high-risk minority youth: Evaluation of the brothers. *Adolescence,* 33(129), 145–158.

Sinkkonen, J., Anttila, R., & Siimes, M. (1998). Pubertal maturation and changes in self-image in early adolescent Finnish boys. *Journal of Youth and Adolescence, 27*(2), 209–218.

Stringer, S. (1994). The psychological changes of adolescence: A test of character. *ALAN Review, 22*(1), 27–29.

Wigfield, A., & Eccles, J. (1994). Children's competence beliefs, achievement values, and general self-esteem: Change across elementary and middle school. *Journal of Early Adolescence, 14*(2), 107–138.

ERIC

De Haan, L., & Gunvalson, D. (1997). *Factors associated with early risk for school-aged children living in rural poverty* (ERIC microfiche ED408131).

Dryfoos, J. (1998). *Safe passage: Making it through adolescence in a risky society* (ERIC microfiche ED425225).

Gardner, H. (1991). *The unschooled mind: How children think and how schools should teach* (ERIC microfiche ED368451).

Harter, S. (1999). *The construction of the self: A developmental perspective* (ERIC microfiche ED429699).

Rothenberg, D. (1997). *Supporting girls in early adolescence* (ERIC microfiche ED407185).

Sizer, T., & Sizer, N. (1999). *The students are watching: Schools and the moral contract* (ERIC microfiche ED433342).

Sugar, M. (1993). *Female adolescent development* (ERIC microfiche ED357890).

Web Sites

Multiple Intelligences Developmental Assessment Scales (MIDAS)

http://www.angelfire.com/oh/themidas/index.html

Provides an efficient method of obtaining a descriptive assessment of a student's multiple intelligences profile. The site also provides a concise presentation of Howard Gardner's theory of multiple intelligences.

Center for Adolescent Studies

http://education.indiana.edu/cas/

The mission of the Center for Adolescent Studies is to advance the understanding of the psychological, biological, and social features of normal adolescence. Important site components include the following.

- Developmental Tasks of Normal Adolescence
- Teacher Talk—practical advice, strategies, and lesson plans for secondary teachers who want to enhance the social and emotional growth of their students.
- Teacher Talk Forum—a teacher's guide to the Web. Sets of links to lesson plans, educational resources, field trips, and more.

National Institute on the Education of At-Risk Students (U.S. Department of Education, Office of Educational Research and Improvement)

http://www.ed.gov/offices/OERI/At-Risk/

The institute supports a range of research and development activities designed to improve the education of students at risk of educational failure because of limited English proficiency, poverty, race, geographic location, or economic disadvantage.

The Pulsar Program

http://www.pulsarprogram.org

PULSAR Inc. is a nonprofit organization that brings together police officers, educators, and youth by utilizing the leadership of at-risk youth. The group focuses on reducing the damage of stereotypes held by members of various groups.

Studies in Moral Development and Education

http://www.uic.edu/~lnucci/MoralEd/

This Web page links together educators, scholars, and citizens who want to share their work and learn more about research, practices, and activities in the area of moral development and education. Important site components include the following.

- Featured articles on issues of moral development and character education

- Classroom applications and policies in classroom practices for moral development and character
- Examples from classroom practice
- Information about professional literature related to moral development and character formation
- Overview of moral development and education theory and approaches

THE MIDDLE SCHOOL MOVEMENT AND CONCEPT

WAKULLA MIDDLE SCHOOL

Wakulla Middle School (WMS), in Crawfordville, Florida, has been offering a high-quality, developmentally appropriate education to approximately 750 young adolescents, annually, for about a quarter-century—quite a feat of distinction in today's educational climate. WMS is, furthermore, an example of the complete middle school concept in action. The school's philosophy is grounded in a thorough commitment to the characteristics and needs of its students. Since the school's founding, the faculty has continuously embraced teacher-based guidance programs. WMS educators have been committed to small interdisciplinary teams (two to three teachers) nestled in a school-within-a-school organization for 25 years. The school maintains and uses a team-based flexible schedule. An emphasis on student-centered curriculum results in frequent interdisciplinary offerings, a robust special interest activity program, and rich exploratory and unified arts offerings. Differentiating instruction is important to the teachers there. Academic achievement is among the highest levels in the state, demonstrating the efficacy of the middle school concept concerning academic outcomes. Parent support is, consequently, extremely high, so much so that, recently, the district opened a new middle school designed like WMS. We predict that a visit to Wakulla County a decade from now will demonstrate that educators there are continuing to offer the best education programs for the young adolescent. This book is about what it takes to offer such programs in districts in every state.

WHAT YOU WILL LEARN IN CHAPTER 2

In this chapter, we trace the beginnings of the middle school concept and the educational movement surrounding that concept. The first real middle level school was the junior high school. Although this model was largely unsuccessful in implementing developmentally appropriate program components, it did pioneer the ideas that are at the center of today's middle school concept. In this chapter, we define and illustrate this concept in depth and bring our awareness to 21st century trends and issues.

THE MIDDLE SCHOOL CONCEPT EMERGES

The 21st century middle school usually covers grades 6–8, 5–8, or just 7–8, and it is intended to help young adolescents make a smooth transition from elementary to high school, from older childhood to adolescence. At the opening of the first decade of the new century, approximately 15,000 such schools dotted the educational landscape. This chapter aims to sketch the evolution of American education at the middle level and to highlight the critical steps and issues necessary for its further development. We describe the current meaning of the middle school concept, as it appears in the literature and in the experiences of middle school educators and students. We also identify contemporary research about the effectiveness of the middle school concept in action and current disquiet among critics of middle level education.

EARLY EFFORTS TO EDUCATE THE YOUNG ADOLESCENT

In the thinly populated agrarian society of early America, schools were small, almost family affairs, requiring little internal grouping of students in grades or otherwise. The legendary one-room schoolhouse attempted to meet the needs of students of all ages and may have done well with the resources at its disposal. As the population increased and larger communities developed, however, two levels of education appeared. Grammar, or elementary, schools constituted the first phase of schooling for American students. Those who succeeded in this school, and whose parents could afford their continuation in school, could seek admission to the prep school, academy, or finishing school for girls, which, in time, became the high school. In some communities, one school might embrace both elementary and high school years, or in others the upper schools might be completely independent of any elementary schools, relying on home, church, or other agency for their students' preparation in the three R's. Gradually, however, with ever-increasing population and school enrollments, two distinct levels of education below college became the common pattern. Eventually, elementary and secondary education became crystallized as the two levels of American public school education (Pulliam & Van Patten, 1995). Unfortunately, in a sense, many American educators and citizens still think of education that way.

THE JUNIOR HIGH SCHOOL

The junior high school (grades 7–8 or 7–9), a school that older members of your family may have attended, was America's first middle level school. Beginning after World War I and becoming common across the country following World War II for the next quarter-century, the junior high school became popular as a result of dissatisfactions with the two-level, 8–4 elementary-high organization (eight years of elementary school, four years of high school). Ironically, the middle school most common today probably received its initial form as a consequence of dissatisfactions with the junior high school and the 6–3–3 plan that it engendered (six years of elementary school, three years of junior high school, three years of high school). A troublesome question for many middle school proponents is whether today's middle school will meet the same fate as its predecessor.

The philosophy of the early junior high schools was similar to today's middle school concept. A century ago, advocates and theoreticians argued for a school based on the needs of the young adolescent and suggested program components such as integrated (core) curriculum, team teaching, and flexible schedules. The advocates of the junior high concept and those who support today's middle school concept would probably find themselves comfortable with each other.

The real reasons the junior high school spread nationally, however, had little to do with the recognition that the age group deserved a unique educational experience. The reasons for the widespread implementation of the junior high school may have actually been in conflict with the needs of the young adolescent. Van Til, Vars, and Lounsbury (1961), in their popular text of the 1960s junior high school, indicated that creation of the junior high school had more to do with the concern of college educators for getting better-prepared students and the related belief that earlier (than grade 9) introduction of college preparatory subjects, especially mathematics and foreign languages, was highly desirable. College level educators believed that extending the period of secondary education into what had been elementary grades, and bringing a more rigorous academic focus to those years (grades 7 and 8), would be good. Advocates for the junior high school believed that they could also improve the drop-out problem if the 9th grade was moved out of the high school. Students would be likely, educators believed, to stay through the end of the junior high school (9th grade) and not drop out at the end of the traditional elementary school (8th grade), thereby keeping a whole nation of students in school for another year of secondary education.

The junior high school movement spread rapidly after 1920. The increased birthrate after World War I, and other factors boosting the U.S. population, meant mounting school enrollments and bulging schools. One answer to crowded elementary and high schools was to move grades 7–9 into a new building (or into the old high school) and just build one new building instead of a new elementary school and a new high school. Also, genuine improvements in education were made in many junior high schools. Whatever the reason, instead of the situation in 1920, when four of every five high school graduates had attended an 8–4 organization, 40 years later, in 1960, four of every five high school graduates had attended a 6–3–3 one. The junior high school had become common, but it was already coming under criticism and another school in the middle was in the offing (Van Til, Vars, & Lounsbury, 1961).

TOWARD A DIFFERENT SCHOOL IN THE MIDDLE

By the early 1950s, about the time the junior high school had become the common experience for America's young adolescents, dissatisfaction with both the junior high school and the earlier, still continuing 8–4 elementary-high school organization began to gain momentum. Dissatisfaction with the education of young adolescents, however it is conducted, seems to be perennial.

The 8–4 and the 6–3–3 plans were both considered, by many, as unsuitable to the needs and interests of young adolescents. The first publication with which we are familiar that voiced these dissatisfactions was a monograph published by the Association for Supervision and Curriculum Development (1954, p. 47). In its concluding chapter, "Toward Better Programs for Young Adolescents," the authors identified several serious problems with the junior high school, problems that will sound familiar to educators reading about them now, more than a half-century later.

The junior high school was seen, ironically, as being too secondary, as having been too successful in bringing the high school program down into what had been elementary school grades. Critics charged that the departmentalized, high school- or university-style organization of teachers caused more problems than it solved. Students had adjustment problems moving into the subject-centered junior high school. Organizing teachers by the subject they shared was, critics asserted, too abrupt a change from the predominantly self-contained classroom of the elementary school. This departmentalization produced little relationship between the subjects and the needs of young adolescents, causing students to disengage from school. Departmentalization was also faulted for preventing cooperation among teachers who shared the same students and making it difficult, therefore, for teachers to work together to provide the kind of active educational experiences (e.g., field trips) needed by young adolescents. Sadly, the evidence is still strong that such problems continue to plague students moving out of the elementary school into the middle level (Eccles & Midgley, 1989).

The educators who promulgated the Association for Supervision and Curriculum Development document did not suggest creating a completely new grade organization. However, they did propose changes from departmentalization to what they called flexible, block scheduling and "little school" arrangements (a type of teacher team organization) and to broader choices of exploratory subjects and activities as well as other special interest activities. These would all be characteristic of the middle schools to be planned later. Some type of such reorganized junior high schools was either already existing or soon to come. In Upper St. Clair, Pennsylvania, a study had been conducted of the schools needed by young adolescents, and the plan was for a new middle school. Donald Eichhorn, one of the founders of today's middle schools, then assistant supervising principal of the Upper St. Clair Township School District, related in his pioneer work (1966, p. 2) his district's efforts to persuade the state department of education to permit the establishment of a new school in the middle.

> We are requesting that the school be composed of grades 6–7–8. The reasons why we believe that this program is desirable and educationally sound are as follows:
> 1. From the physical and psychological point of view it is a more natural grouping. There appears to be less of a differential in maturity between the sixth and eighth grade than between the seventh and the ninth grade.
> 2. The social patterns are more nearly the same in grades 6, 7, and 8 than in the conventional pattern of grades 7, 8, and 9. The social maturity of the ninth grade student more nearly parallels that of the older students. A better social program could be carried on without the ninth grade student.
> 3. The transition from the self-contained classroom to a departmentalized program may be more gradual.

This school, the Fort Couch Middle School (still an exemplary middle school), and the district became early models in the middle school movement.

Grades 6–8 schools, variously called junior high, intermediate, and senior or upper elementary schools, were located elsewhere even before the term *middle school* became the common one. Thus, the exemplary Skokie Junior High School, in the Winnetka, Illinois, Elementary School District, as early as the 1940s, had modular scheduling, interdisciplinary organization and teaching, teacher advisory groups, special interest activities (called "enterprises" at Skokie), and other characteristic features of many middle schools today. The Saginaw, Michigan, Township Community School District developed the 4–4–4 plan of organization (four years of elementary school, four years of junior high school, four years of high school) that has been used many places in later decades. An article by George Mills (1961, p. 6) justified the plan then in operation in the Saginaw Township Community School District, adjacent to Saginaw, as follows:

> For some time the junior high school concept has been under scrutiny. . . .
> In practice it has resulted in junior high schools becoming miniature senior
> high schools, with the social activities, the athletic program, and the instructional programs of the senior high school moving into the lower educational
> levels. . . . As we studied the 320 physical, mental, emotional and social
> growth characteristics and teaching implications for boys and girls, from
> kindergarten through the 12th grade, we concluded that there were centers
> of similarity in this 13 year span that merited close study. . . . These conclusions led us to establish the primary school, which includes kindergarten
> through grade 4, the middle school with grades 5 through 8, and the four-year
> high school with grades 9 through 12.

Although new middle level schools had various grade structures and names, among the first newly constructed middle schools in America were Amory, Mississippi, Middle School (1963); Barrington, Illinois, Middle School (1965); Bedford Middle School, Mt. Kisko, New York (1966); Matlin Junior High School, Plainview, Long Island, New York (1963); McIntosh Middle School, Sarasota, Florida (1962); Pleasant Hills Middle School, West Jefferson Hills School District, Pleasant Hill, Pennsylvania (1965); Henderson Junior High School, Little Rock, Arkansas (1965); Kennedy Junior High, Natick, Massachusetts (1965); Ardis C. Egan School, Los Altos, California (1963); Giana School, Rawlon School District, Rowland Heights, California (1964); and Del Mar Community Intermediate School, Reed Union School District, Tiburon, California. And so, by 1965, the middle school movement seemed firmly launched across the United States (Murphy, 1965).

For the next 35 years, the middle school movement experienced dramatically rapid growth. Middle schools numbered nearly 500 in 1967 (Cuff, 1967). Scarcely a year later, the number had doubled to 1,101 (Alexander, 1968). Alexander and McEwin (1989b) identified 5,466 after another 20 years. Recent estimates indicate that the number of schools in the middle continued to grow into the 2000s, numbering near 15,000 in the early years of that decade. The middle school is clearly the dominant form of education for the young adolescent in America. Why did this happen?

EXPEDIENCY LEADS TO MANY MORE MIDDLE SCHOOLS

The reasons that the number of new middle schools was growing rapidly then, and now, appear (just as in the case of the earlier junior high school) to have had little to do with an authentic attempt to meet the needs of young adolescent learners. More often, school district decision-makers were motivated to consider a new grade configuration for important reasons that were far from focused on the early adolescent as a person and a learner.

In the South, and elsewhere as well, one of the important factors in producing hundreds of new middle schools during the 1960s and 1970s was the pressure to accommodate school district racial desegregation. In dozens of districts of all shapes and sizes, school planners and policy-makers made an important discovery. One could redesign a district to facilitate racial desegregation by closing the junior high school(s) and moving the 9th grade to the newly desegregated high school. Fifth grade or 6th grade or both then could be moved out of the segregated elementary schools to create new and desegregated middle schools. The result was a plan for a dramatically more desegregated school district that would be likely to receive court approval. Hundreds of middle schools opened in the late 1960s and 1970s were products of this effort.

A few years later, in the 1970s and 1980s, the changing demographic patterns in the Northeast and Midwest brought new challenges to managing school enrollments for planners in those districts. Buildings in some districts were far below capacity in the upper grades, to the point that high schools might have to be closed, a hitherto unheard of and undesirable option. High schools tend to be the subject of great loyalty and nostalgia. In other districts, new growth brought a surge of new enrollment in the early grades of the elementary school, leaving crowded classrooms in those buildings. In still other districts, both things happened at once, causing simultaneous crowding in some of a district's schools and underutilization in others.

A school planner or policy-maker in a district with both overcrowded and underutilized schools likely first had an insight that became serendipitously beneficial to the middle school movement. Why not close the junior high school, move the 9th grade into the high school(s) and increase enrollment there by 25%; and then move the 6th grade out of the elementary school(s) and create a new middle school program for the district? Thus, one could be conservative in terms of school district capital outlay and innovative (via the new middle school program) at the same time. This was, as time proved, an almost irresistibly attractive motive for those involved. Hundreds of middle schools were, and still are, being organized to accommodate the need to more fully and equitably utilize the school facilities in the district(s) involved.

Another wave of new middle schools emerged as a result of the educational tumult following the publication of *A Nation at Risk* (National Commission on Excellence in Education, 1983). Virtually every state in the nation implemented laws intended to infuse high school programs with new rigor. In many states, the 9th grade continued to be counted as a high school year. Consequently, the 9th grade program became more intensely dominated by graduation requirements and other contingencies that made its presence in a middle school increasingly anomalous.

More and more, district decision-makers seemed to find it difficult to defend the presence of the 9th grade in a junior high school organization. This was especially true if there were other pressing reasons for those students to be relocated to the high school, such as enrollment or school desegregation concerns. At this time, momentum for districts to reorganize into a middle school configuration took on increasing power and speed. One crucial additional factor came into play: The middle school concept was proving to be very popular in districts that had adopted it over the preceding two decades (George & Oldaker, 1985).

A middle school program that was effectively implemented (emphasizing "effectively" here) appeared to produce the sorts of outcomes that pleased parents, policy-makers, and practitioners alike. Student behavior and attitudes improved, home-school relationships became closer, interethnic interaction became more positive, students enjoyed school more, teachers grew increasingly more appreciative of the opportunity to work together, and in many situations academic achievement held steady or improved slightly while these other more positive outcomes became pleasantly obvious. Presented with this sort of evidence, anecdotal though it was, the active resistance of traditional junior high school educators abated. Consequently, in the 1980s and 1990s, the middle school concept became a more popular alternative, one that educators sought to implement for its own sake. By 2001, when school districts needed to construct new buildings, middle schools were the choice.

DEFINITION AND DESCRIPTION OF THE MIDDLE SCHOOL

Now, for the more important question: What is a middle school? We will start with a definition and follow with a description of what has come to be known as the middle school concept. In this book, when we group all structures between elementary and secondary as middle ones, we usually use the term *middle level schools* or *schools in the middle,* leaving the term *middle school* to designate grades 5–8, 6–8, and others that call themselves this. We see the term *middle school* as most appropriate for *a school planned and operated as a separate school to provide a developmentally appropriate educational experience for students usually enrolled in grades 6–8 or 5–8 and 10–14 years of age, building on the elementary and leading toward the high school,*

We believe that the reason the middle school concept has appealed to educators for so many years, over and above the expedient reasons that prompted the appearance of thousands of new middle schools from 1965 to 2000, has been and remains its focus on developmental appropriateness for the education of young adolescent students. Is it developmentally appropriate? Is it based on the characteristics and needs of the students? These are the twin questions that have guided middle level educators for many decades, and they are the questions that bring educators continuously back to the middle school concept. An exemplary middle school provides a developmentally appropriate education for its students.

In 1977 the newly organized National Middle School Association (NMSA) appointed a Committee on Future Goals and Directions to set out goals for the middle school (and the association). The committee took the following position, specifying developmentally appropriate opportunities for young adolescents, later adopted by the association (National Middle School Association, 1977, p.16).

> We recognize the absence of any universal definition of the middle school and of middle school goals, and intend to reject any set of standards that prescribed specific goals. At the same time we feel that the NMSA should stand for certain priority goals, and hoped this would influence members to incorporate these goals into their own school statements:
> 1. Every student should be well known as a person by at least one adult in the school who accepts responsibility for his/her guidance.
> 2. Every student should be helped to achieve optimum mastery of the skills of continued learning together with a commitment to their use and improvement.
> 3. Every student should acquire a functional body of fundamental knowledge.
> 4. Every student should have opportunities to explore and develop interests in aesthetic, leisure, career, and other aspects of life.

We wholeheartedly accept this concept of developmental appropriateness and the goals for middle school education that can be derived from it. We only wish they had been fully implemented and achieved for all the millions of adults who have been through the middle level schools during the last 50 years.

As middle schools have been created out of former elementary and junior high schools and often have inherited their faculties and students from the former organizations, their basic rationales were sometimes overlooked or overruled, to not rock the boat or for lack of essential personnel, facilities, or funds. But many schools were more successful, and the basic aim of providing a developmentally appropriate education continues to predominate in the planning and maintenance of middle schools. A significant 1987 report of the Superintendent's Middle Grade Task Force, *Caught in the Middle: Educational Reform for Young Adolescents in California Public Schools,* included a foreword from State Superintendent Bill Honig, who emphasized the basic function of schools in the middle in such statements as these:

> For too long, the middle grades have been treated as a wild card for solving facilities and enrollment problems. Now it is time to face the critical educational issues at stake in these "neglected grades."

The success of the educational reform movement depends on meeting the needs of middle grade students—both academically and socially. Failing to address these needs jeopardizes efforts for educational excellence and, more importantly, for these students' future success. (Honig, 1987, p. v)

In Florida, three years earlier, the Speaker's (of the state House of Representatives) Task Force on Middle Childhood Education had found

that between the entry into the 4th grade and exit from the 8th grade, students must accomplish a number of developmental tasks, and middle childhood programs must recognize the developmental diversity and needs of students. Careful attention, therefore, should be given to program structure, curriculum, student services and personnel. Students should master these developmental tasks during grades 4–8, if they are to enter high school at a readiness level in order to complete their high school education, and successfully enter adult society. (Speaker's Task Force, 1984, p. v2)

Other states and many school districts have conducted similar reviews of their programs as to their developmental appropriateness for young adolescents, with a considerable impetus from a significant and much publicized report by the Carnegie Council on Adolescent Development, *Turning Points: Preparing American Youth for the 21st Century*. Although certainly not approving the current status of education at the middle level, the report emphasizes the basic rationale of middle level schools.

Middle grade schools—junior high, intermediate, and middle schools—are potentially society's most powerful force to recapture millions of youth adrift, and help every young person thrive during early adolescence. Yet all too often these schools exacerbate the problems of young adolescents.

A volatile mismatch exists between the organization and curriculum of middle grade schools and the intellectual and emotional needs of young adolescents. Caught in a vortex of changing demands, the engagement of many youth in learning diminishes, and their rates of alienation, substance abuse, absenteeism, and dropping out of school begin to rise. (Carnegie Council on Adolescent Development, 1989, pp. 8–10)

And Carnegie's "A Plan for Action" emphasizes the urgency of the need for improvements of middle grade schools, based on developmental appropriateness, in such statements as these:

The early adolescent years are crucial in determining the future success or failure of millions of American youth. All sectors of the society must be mobilized to build a national consensus to make transformation of middle grade schools a reality. The Task Force calls upon all sectors that care about youth to form partnerships that will create for young adolescents a time of purposeful exploration and preparation for young adulthood.

The Task Force calls upon the education sector to start changing middle grade schools now. Teachers and principals are at the center of this process. We urge superintendents and boards of education to give teachers and principals the authority to make essential changes, and work collaboratively to evaluate student outcomes effectively. (Carnegie Council on Adolescent Development, 1989, p. 10)

In 2000 the Carnegie group released a new publication, *Turning Points 2000: Educating Adolescents in the 21st Century* (Jackson & Davis, 2000). In this widely anticipated book, the authors asserted that in the intervening decade there had been a meteoric rise in the number of middle schools. Furthermore, the report made clear two very important conclusions: (1) developmentally appropriate educational experiences were being implemented effectively in thousands of middle schools across the nation, and (2) the evidence indicated that such programs, implemented effectively, produced the positive outcomes educators and parents desired. The middle school concept works well when it is effectively implemented.

DESIRABLE CHARACTERISTICS OF EXEMPLARY MIDDLE SCHOOLS

The year 1965 seems to have been the first in which advocates of new schools in the middle tried to summarize what it meant, specifically, to provide a developmentally appropriate education. In December 1965, on the basis of their study of the scant relevant professional literature and of the discussion in a faculty-student seminar at the University of Florida, plus school visitations and discussions there, Alexander and Williams (1965, p. 219) proposed the following "Guidelines" for "A Model Middle School":

A real middle school should be designed to serve the needs of older children, preadolescents, and early adolescents.

A middle school organization should make a reality of the long-held ideal of individualized instruction.

A middle school program should give high priority to the intellectual components of the curriculum.

A middle school program should place primary emphasis on skills of continued learning.

A middle school should provide a rich program of exploratory experiences.

A program of health and physical education should be designed especially for boys and girls of the middle school years.

An emphasis on values should underline all aspects of a middle school program.

The organization of the middle school would facilitate the most effective use of the special competencies and interests of the teaching staffs.

Two decades later, George and Oldaker (1985, p. 19) took a different approach to the basic characteristics and effectiveness issues. They identified some 160 middle schools across the nation that had been recommended by others as exemplary middle schools because of the schools' major features and effectiveness. The big surprise of this study was that the schools reputedly providing a developmentally appropriate education were incredibly alike in their organization and program. George and Oldaker reported that the schools' common features included interdisciplinary team organization, a flexibly scheduled day, home base or advisor-advisee (AA) teacher guidance program, curriculum provisions for student personal development, a favorable school learning climate, and other such critical elements.

The Association for Supervision and Curriculum Development used a much larger sample of schools for its survey, yielding very similar results. Cawelti (1989, p. 9) reported this study's findings and conclusions as follows:

> Regardless of their organization, most U.S. schools enrolling 10- to 14-year-olds do not address all the program characteristics recommended for this age group.
>
> The middle school form of organization is far more likely to provide these program characteristics needed by the early adolescent. (This key finding might seem self-evident, but it is important to document that many school leaders have, in fact, responded to the essential features advocated for such an institution.)
>
> Despite the superiority of the middle school program, simply placing grades 6–8 or 5–8 in a single building does not assure that the program characteristics suggested for youth of this age will be present. Many schools with grades 6–8 continue to be more similar to than differing from junior high schools.

Also in 1989, the influential Carnegie Task Force on Education of Young Adolescents made broad, forceful recommendations that encompassed the basic characteristics of middle schools and added other critical ones involving families and communities (Carnegie Council on Adolescent Development, 1989, p. 9):

> Create small communities for learning. . . . The key elements of these communities are schools-within-schools or houses, students grouped together as teams and small group advisories that ensure that every student is known well by at least one adult.
>
> Teach a core academic program. . . .
>
> Ensure success for all students through elimination of tracking by achievement level, flexibility in arranging instructional time, and adequate resources (time, space, equipment, and materials) for teachers.

> Empower teachers and administrators to make decisions about the experiences of middle grade students. . . .
>
> Staff middle grade schools with teachers who are expert at teaching young adolescents who have been specially prepared for assignment to the middle grades.
>
> Improve academic performance through fostering the health and fitness of young adolescents. . . .
>
> Reengage families in the education of young adolescents. . . .
>
> Connect schools with communities, which together share responsibility for each middle grades student's success.

Studies by Epstein (1990) and MacIver (1990) of the Johns Hopkins University Center for Research on Elementary and Middle Schools, based on a large sample of all types of schools, identified the following as key practices in the middle grades that are more likely to be adopted in more schools than other practices:

> Interdisciplinary teams of teachers
>
> Common planning time for teams of teachers
>
> Flexible scheduling
>
> Students assigned to the same homeroom or advisory teacher for all years spent in the middle grades
>
> Cooperative learning as an instructional approach
>
> Exploratory courses and mini-courses
>
> Parental involvement in workshops on early adolescence; and parents as volunteers in the middle grades

As to practices, grade spans, and effectiveness, these conclusions were drawn:

1. Most schools that contain grade 7 have not yet developed educational programs based on recommended practices for the middle grades. . . .
2. Some practices are more prominent in certain types of middle-grade schools than in others. . . . Overall, middle schools (6–9) and 7–8 schools use more of the practices that are recommended for middle-grade education than do other schools. . . .
3. Regardless of grade span, good practices make stronger programs. . . .
4. There is much more to be learned.

One of the most remarkable aspects of the middle school concept is how stable and consistent the basic tenets have remained across the nearly 50 years it has been evolving. Examining statements from 1965 to 2000 reveals an amazing congruence and continuity around what it means to design and implement a developmentally appropriate education for young adolescents. Virtually every list seems to include:

- Smaller communities for learning (teaching teams, house organizations)
- Grades 6–8 plans (also 5–8, 7–8)

- Exploratory opportunities in the curriculum
- Instruction that would lead to success for all students
- Teachers expert on the young adolescent
- Flexible schedules and space
- A core curriculum for all students
- An emphasis on guidance and health
- Reconnecting schools with homes and communities

Three Goals of Middle School Education

In the early years of the 21st century, a national consensus emerged on the nature of the middle school concept (Jackson & Davis, 2000). We believe that this national consensus reflects an equally solid agreement among educators and citizens on the goals to which such school characteristics should contribute. All exemplary middle level schools seek to accomplish three central essential goals for their students: academic learning, personal development, and group citizenship.

Academic Learning   Every institution in American society has a primary mission. The military, for example, has a primary mission it seeks to perform for society. The corporate world, the family, and the church—each has a special mission to perform. So, too, the school has a primary mission: learning. In the new century, most educators and parents agree that the primary goal of the middle level school, like those at other levels, is to provide a rich and rigorous academic experience for its students. Schools at the middle level must be academically challenging for all students. Middle school must not be a "muddle school." Each middle school, despite the specific characteristics of the students in that particular population, should reach the learning goals embedded in the academic curriculum for the age group, including appropriate knowledge, skills (e.g., critical thinking), and attitudes. No middle level school staff should shrink from analyzing its success or failure in achieving this primary goal, and standardized tests of academic achievement often are an important criterion of such success or failure. Middle schools must have academic achievement as their primary goal.

Personal Development   Institutions in America often endorse secondary purposes or goals that are important to them. Physicians, for example, take an oath to a secondary goal while they pursue their primary goal—healing. Physicians swear to "First, do no harm." They affirm that, while they vigorously pursue the healing process, their patients will not leave worse than they were when they came to see the doctor. In a sense, educators at the middle level take a similar oath, to do no harm to their students, while teachers vigorously pursue the goal of increased learning, of higher levels of challenge and academic achievement. We believe that, because of the unique nature of early adolescence, middle level educators must pay special attention to the personal development of their students. Each school staff should go further in this area than educators at other levels might believe necessary, attempting to provide a school that enhances the personal development of each middle school learner, by enriching the curriculum with expanded age-appropriate curriculum choices and activities. All middle schools should attempt to provide regular success experiences for students, resulting in a school program that, as a minimum, does no harm to the personal development of the students therein. Ideally, middle school students should leave the middle school feeling better about themselves, more motivated for school success at the next level, and able to interact successfully with others like and unlike them.

Group Citizenship Japanese educators are correct when they argue that young adolescents everywhere are moving through a unique phase of development connected to the acquisition of important concepts such as loyalty, duty, involvement, harmony, commitment, and, in Japan, sacrifice for the good of the group (George, 1995). The Japanese believe, and we concur, that young adolescents are at a unique time of readiness for learning these things, that elementary school children are too young and high school students are too old. Japanese educators work extremely hard to inculcate these concepts through their middle level school programs, maybe more diligently than they pursue academic achievement, because they are persuaded that success in the first two goals will be limited by the degree to which middle level educators are successful in this important third area. Each and every middle school should, then, attempt to inculcate an appropriate degree of group citizenship, group loyalty, and the perception in each student that he or she is an important part of groups to which he or she owes loyalty, duty, and involvement.

How each school organizes and operates to move toward the three overall goals of middle school education—academic learning, personal development, and group citizenship— should depend primarily upon the characteristics of the particular group of students in each school.

The Educational Zip Code

The United States Postal Service made history when it developed the concept of the zip code to help deal with the complexities of accurately delivering the mail. Virtually every American now knows that a zip code indicates a general area within which are often as many as several hundred individual addresses, each one signifying a unique home designed, ideally, to meet the special needs of the group that lives within. Having the mail go astray as a consequence of having been sent to the wrong zip code can be frustrating. Probably every reader has memorized his or her zip code, including the newer nine-digit one.

Not nearly so many Americans know that there are "educational zip codes" every bit as important.

We believe that American education has evolved, in the last half-century, to the point where the developmental characteristics and needs of students at the three levels have produced three distinct educational zip codes, each with common characteristics that distinguish it from the other two. There are now three such widely acknowledged zip codes: elementary, middle, and high school. As with one's knowledge of one's own personal postal zip codes, most professionals know the characteristics of their own educational zip codes, and at least the characteristics of an adjoining zip code. The three educational zip codes, as we think they have evolved, are depicted in Table 2.1.

One can argue that, particularly over the last forty years, the nature of the middle school zip code has become increasingly clear and, simultaneously, more broadly accepted and affirmed by scholars, practitioners, and laypersons. The middle school concept itself has changed very little, from its beginnings in the literature of the junior high school on into the first decade of the 21st century. The basic components of the concept today are, however, far more broadly recognized, understood, accepted, and utilized than ever before. A seemingly infinite number of activities and publications regarding the middle school concept has been offered by professional associations, foundations, state departments of education, universities, and school districts around the nation and the world.

TABLE 2.1   **THE MIDDLE SCHOOL: UNIQUE AND TRANSITIONAL**

Program	Elementary school	Middle school	High school
Student-teacher relationship	Parental	Advisor	Choice
Teacher organization	Self-contained	Interdisciplinary team	Department
Curriculum	Skills	Exploratory	Depth
Schedule	Self-contained	Block	Periods
Instruction	Teacher-directed	Diverse	Student-directed
Student grouping	Chronological	Supportive	Subject
Building organization	Single classroom	Team or house	Department
Co-curriculum	All participate	Broad choice	By ability
Governance	Principal and teachers	Principal and council	Principal and department heads
Teacher preparation	Child-oriented generalist	Flexible resource	Academic specialist

The Middle School Concept: Unique and Transitional

The components of the zip code described in these documents and practices can be characterized by two important terms: *unique* and *transitional*. All of the program components of the exemplary middle school should be unique: that is, different from what students receive in either the elementary school or the high school, but not so severely different that such experiences make the transition from elementary to high school more difficult than it would be without the presence of a middle level of education. Each aspect of the middle school concept is specially tailored to the needs of the students at the middle level, not merely a thoughtless and unplanned downward extension of the high school program or an upward thrust of the elementary school. Yet, each component links the elementary and the high school together so that the process of education from kindergarten to high school is a smoother passage, a more seamless transition, than what students might have otherwise experienced. The middle school concept unifies the whole K–12 educational experience while providing a special learning opportunity for early adolescents that is uniquely tailored to their characteristics and needs. *Unique* and *transitional*— these are the key words that should be used to underline an understanding of which addresses are appropriate for the middle school zip code and which are not. The middle school concept or zip code, then, denotes a number of specific programs for virtually all schools at that level.

Advisors   Educators in all middle schools should be expected to recognize the students' need for teacher guidance and provide some structured opportunity for that experience. Teachers would neither act as quasi-parents (*in loco parentis*), as they would in the elementary school, nor leave the students on their own to seek out relationships with adults on the basis of common interests or personal preferences, much as might legitimately happen in high school. Middle school educators recognize the responsibility to act as advisors to their students. Just as every postal zip code pertains to many addresses, a teacher-based advisory program can be implemented in many different ways. But, fundamentally, young adolescents need at least one teacher who knows and cares about them in a comprehensive way, acting as their ombudsman, the school expert on them.

Teams   Similarly, the middle school concept is centered on a special way in which teachers and students are organized to provide and receive instruction and learning: the interdisciplinary team organization. In an interdisciplinary team organization, teachers share the same students, the same schedule, and the same part of the building. They also share in the responsibility for planning the major academic subjects that students encounter during the school day. Many experienced educators say that the interdisciplinary team is the heart of an exemplary middle school. While an interdisciplinary team can organize and operate in at least a dozen different ways, there is no substitute for the interdisciplinary team organization in a good middle school. Self-contained classrooms belong in the elementary school, and subject-centered, university-style academic departments belong no lower than the high school level. Many school districts are organizing and operating an interdisciplinary team organization in the 9th or 10th grade of the high school (George, McEwin, & Jenkins, 2000), so rigid dividing lines may be inappropriate.

Exploration　The curriculum of the middle school, too, has its own unique but transitional flavor. The middle school curriculum builds on and extends the skills imparted by the elementary school, introduces the world of knowledge students will encounter in depth in high school, and bathes it all in an exploratory, interdisciplinary light. Or, it should. Curriculum is likely the least changed aspect of the middle school concept, in terms of altered practices in real schools in the 20th century. Much of what is being taught in the first decade of the 21st century was designed during the first decade of the previous century.

Flexible Scheduling　In the elementary school, a single teacher is usually in charge of the whole day's schedule, except for recess and for short periods of time when special teachers take the students. At the high school level, the bell controls just about everything. Middle school educators seek to place control of time for learning in the hands of teams of teachers, instead of leaving the bell in charge. Consequently, in many exemplary middle schools bells no longer signal, perhaps every 50 minutes, the time to change classes. More often, teams of teachers have charge of their common students' day, arranging it as they see fit, except for lunch and exploratory classes. Recently, the new long block schedule has become an attractive option in hundreds of middle schools (George, 1999).

Differentiated Instruction　Instruction, at the middle level, needs to be a deft balance of teacher and student initiative. Very young children need a great deal of teacher direction to be successful in formal education. By the time students are 16 years old, no law compels them to learn anything from anyone ever again. Middle school students should become more independent and in charge of their own learning as each day passes. Consequently, middle school teachers may have the most difficult professional responsibilities in the world of education, while working with education's most challenging student group. Differentiating instruction fits students best as they move through a period of great personal diversity.

Supportive Grouping　Grouping students for instruction in the middle school is a complex process and much has been learned, in the last two decades, about how to do so more effectively. Chronological age, perceived ability or prior achievement, and the number of years a student has been in school are no longer adequate bases for grouping when students reach the middle level. They are not entirely ready to group themselves via the subject matter choices they make. Many middle schoolers need a great deal more supportive inter-personal structure in their school environment than they often receive. A great deal of excitement is being generated among middle school educators by new and more effective ways to group early adolescent learners.

Feeling of Smallness   Elementary schools are often organized by grade level, and high schools are almost always laid out according to subject specialization requirements. Exemplary middle schools are organized so that there is a "smallness within bigness," which usually focuses on the interdisciplinary team area. Teachers share the same middle school students and the same part of the building. Often the teams are organized with further "smallness within big-ness" through a "house" or school-within-school organization. Looping (stay-ing with the same students over a period of years) is currently popular. Here, too, much has been learned in the past decade.

Broad Choice   One of the more controversial areas of the middle school pro-gram focuses on the nature of appropriate extracurricular activities for the age group. Essentially, the belief of many middle school educators, growing firmer over the years, is that middle school programs should serve the needs of mid-dle school learners. Extracurricular activities should not be offered primarily as entertainment for the public or merely as support for high school sports programs or exclusively as the province of those students who happen to ma-ture early. Nor should such activities be watered-down versions of high school activities for which young adolescents are too young (e.g., formal nighttime dances, sophisticated newspapers or yearbooks) or that will be repeated again in high school.

High school activities, most middle school educators believe, should be saved for high school. Elementary school activities are almost always open to participation by all children. Many high school activities, particularly in large high schools, are often restricted to those who have the particular talent or ability called for. At the middle level, participation should be open to all who choose to become involved. The middle school is not the place to begin divid-ing students into those who can be successful in an activity and those who can-not. The middle school program is an exploratory opportunity with few options closed to anyone who wishes to participate.

Shared Decision-Making   Middle level schools also manifest a unique and tran-sitional method of decision-making, problem solving, and policy development. Elementary schools are often small enough to involve everyone in the formal decision-making process. High schools are so large that academic divisions take far more responsibility, much in the way of colleges and universities. Governance in exemplary middle schools is a careful balance between spirited leadership and broad empowerment of all the stakeholders. Most often, a governing council of some sort, in which teams have representatives who work with the school administration, is the vehicle. Shared decision-making has been occurring in exemplary middle schools for decades.

Specially Trained Teachers Elementary school teachers are prepared to teach basic skills to young children; high school teachers are prepared for in-depth work in their subjects. Middle school teacher education must include a focus on the characteristics and needs of the learner, and it must prepare teachers who can function as effective learning resources in one or more subject areas. Middle school teachers must be able to teach knowledgeably and enthusiastically, but they must not care more about their subjects than they do about the welfare of the students they teach. Once again, the middle level must perform a double duty.

Most supporters of the middle school concept, then, subscribe to certain unique but transitional common elements believed to be congruent with the goals of educating students in virtually all middle level schools. This is the middle school zip code. Advisory programs, interdisciplinary team organization, an exploratory emphasis on the curriculum combined with a core of common knowledge, flexible scheduling, active instruction, specially trained teachers, shared decision-making among the professionals in the school, success experiences for all students, improved health and physical education, and reconnecting the home and community with the education of early adolescent learners—this is the canon of contemporary middle school education. National, state, and local organizations and associations affirm it (Jackson & Davis, 2000).

Typically, middle school educators attempt to embody these principles in a school philosophy that makes their commitments clear. The school philosophy of Wakulla Middle School, Crawfordville, Florida, for example, has guided program development there for nearly a quarter of a century, from the opening of the school in 1980 to the recognition of the school as a model of exemplary programs in the 1990s, to its continued status as exemplary middle school in 2002. The 1989–1990 version of the school's philosophy states:

> The middle school is an idea designed to meet the needs of children in grades six through eight. These needs stem from the characteristics of the development of the middle school child. We believe strongly that all the programs and practices of the Wakulla County Middle School should be based on a thorough knowledge of the development of middle school children and should be focused on meeting their needs.
>
> While congruent with the educational philosophy of all the Wakulla County Schools, K–12, this school is unique in that it should provide a learning environment for middle school students. The school should not be

either an elementary school or a mini-high school, but possess unique components that will provide a smooth transition from the elementary to the high school.

The environment should be student-centered rather than subject-centered and should provide a structured, orderly environment for learning. At the same time, we recognize the critical role of a middle school in the development of the self-concept and urge the establishment of a supportive, positive emotional climate.

Curriculum and instruction should appeal to the exploratory nature of middle school students, and yet provide challenge and a foundation for future studies. We believe that mastery of the basic communication and mathematics skills is of primary importance in the middle school so that students may possess the skills they need for learning in the depth required of high school students.

Believing that successful educational endeavors must include the home as an integral part, we encourage the community to be involved in all aspects of the school program in an advisory, as well as an operational role.

SCHOOLS IN THE MIDDLE—21ST CENTURY TRENDS AND ISSUES

The national debate about the common characteristics of exemplary middle level schools is over, at least among active participants in the middle school movement. But, just because educators have arrived at a relatively solid national consensus on the attributes of an exemplary middle school does not mean that the middle school concept has become stagnant or that debates over the effectiveness of middle school programs have ended. In the 21st century, the middle school movement continues to evolve, middle school concepts continue to take on new meaning, and critics of middle level programs continue their century-long dissatisfaction with the status quo. At the dawn of the new century, the status of middle school education includes a number of important trends.

Size and Complexity   In the early years of the 21st century, the context for middle level education is visibly and dramatically different, in several important ways, from its origins a half-century ago. New middle schools are large and are becoming larger. They may hold between 900 and 1,400 students, and too many have more than 2,000 students in one facility. Middle schools are more racially desegregated at the school level, but not necessarily at the classroom level. Safety and security are a great concern, and school administrators carry two-way radios at all times. Some schools have more security staff members than they do counselors, and many schools have a police resource officer on campus daily. Other middle schools have abandoned the use of hallway lockers. Uniforms for students are increasingly in evidence, and full-service school models provide more of the health services that were, 50 years ago, at least supposed to be the responsibility of each student's family.

Transition to High School   Transition into and out of middle school remains a problem, especially the transition from middle school to high school. Some districts have created separate 9th grade centers as educational way stations between middle and high school. These centers are frequently additions to the high school site, but they are off to the side and autonomous to the degree possible. To date, and to the surprise of many, the experience of educators with such centers has been positive. When centers are not created physically, districts still attend to transition difficulties, often by organizing the high school's 9th grade teachers into academic teams that resemble the interdisciplinary team organization of the middle school (George et al., 2000). Clearly, high school educators have not been involved in the middle school restructuring process as frequently or as thoroughly as might be best.

Interdisciplinary Team Organization

Academic teaming has triumphed in middle schools, and school leaders are keenly aware of the centrality of interdisciplinary team organization to an exemplary middle school and to the process of raising academic achievement. Of all of the components of the middle school concept, teaming seems to be the place where school leaders have drawn their line in the sand. It is the one thing they have refused to give up.

There are some common aspects to teaming. Most middle schools have team leaders who receive reasonable stipends that often match or exceed those paid to department chairs ($2,000 per year in Dade County, Florida), and most middle schools have teams in which four teachers teach up to 110 or more students. Teams often have names, colors, and mottos—much like athletic teams or military outfits. A great deal of effort is often devoted to group cohesiveness as a part of teaming.

Teaming is not, however, a monolithic thing; the shape of teaming varies from school to school. Not a few schools arrange teachers and students so that they remain together for more than one year. Multiage grouping and looping have become much more popular. Inclusion teams are becoming common, where an Exceptional Student Education (ESE) teacher and a group of students are an integral part of the team, not just a part of a particular class. And, there is a strong trend in the direction of smaller, two- and three-teacher teams in many schools. One large Florida district has two-teacher teams in all 34 of its middle schools. Teaming, of one variety or another, seems here to stay.

Curriculum

In the first decade of the 21st century, two contradictory curriculum paradigms are at war in the nation's middle schools. Many middle school educators remain committed to what they see as a developmentally appropriate curriculum, one springing from the needs of young adolescents as those educators and their students perceive them. The popularity of the integrated curriculum movement is the most evident manifestation of the belief that curriculum should be truly student-centered. Advocates of an integrated, student-centered curriculum are convinced that such plans are in the best interests of today's students and tomorrow's nation.

The competing curriculum paradigm grows from the standards movement and the high-stakes assessment and accountability processes that are so closely linked to it. The pressure of these standards, testing, and accountability programs has led to a comprehensive process of curriculum alignment and pacing to an extent never before witnessed in most states. Once fiercely proud of local curriculum autonomy, many educators have yielded to the pressure to make certain that what is tested is what is taught or that at least a congruence exists among standards, assessments, and the classroom curriculum that students experience.

The arguments from each paradigm's advocates are clear, rational, and strong. Advocates for the integrated curriculum point to the tremendous appeal their approach has for students, how it enlivens the classroom for everyone, and the connection to the best thinking in education from John Dewey to Carl Rogers and on to Jim Beane. Advocates for the standards-based curriculum process point to the popularity of such measures with the public at large. They assert that new testing procedures focusing on real-life application and critical thinking have begun to lift the curriculum to new levels of the well-known Bloom's taxonomy that the middle school philosophy has never achieved. One thing seems certain: The traditional curriculum, based on the century-old pronouncements of the influential Committee of Ten, is on its way out. We explore this situation in depth in Chapter 3.

A potential casualty of the curriculum war is the central concept of teacher-based advisory programs, or advisor-advisee programs. Always enthusiastically advocated but never firmly in place, AA programs have mostly fallen by the wayside in too many middle schools. Weakened by poor implementation, inadequate training, little faculty or leadership support, and parental misunderstanding, AA programs are too often not surviving the onslaught of the now national accountability process. School leaders and teachers feel compelled to devote every available school minute to academic purposes, and in many schools where the time for AA programs is still in the schedule, the curriculum and activities during that period tend to focus on standards and assessment. We address this problem more fully in Chapter 5.

One survivor of the curriculum wars has been the exploratory portion of the day. An important part of the curriculum since the early days of the junior high school, exploratory or elective programs are present in virtually every middle school in the nation. Usually organized on what has come to be called a "wheel," students take one such course daily along with physical education, plus the four or five main academic courses. Typically, 6th graders take all of the courses in the wheel, for about six weeks each, truly exploring art, music, technology, foreign language, family and consumer science, and other subjects. Also typically, the choices narrow the next year and the last. Students who wish, and whose parents insist, can be placed in instrumental music all the way through, eliminating the opportunity for exploration but enhancing the band option.

Technology is a much greater part of the exploratory curriculum than in prior decades. Industrial arts and home economics have given way almost completely to technology. Usually, a 6th grade student will be in a beginning technology course emphasizing keyboarding and this will be followed by more sophisticated options, including the most advanced software application programs in graphics and data management. More and more, middle schools are committing to a substantial monetary investment in technology-based laboratories for business education, home economics, and advanced technology courses. These labs usually feature a centers approach, in which students encounter units in many different areas: robotics, graphic design, Web site construction, flight simulation, rocketry, and so on.

Scheduling

The way in which time is organized for teaching and learning is, itself, a matter of some controversy in 21st century middle schools. For many years, the middle school concept has advocated flexible block scheduling. Usually, this has meant a schedule that placed most of the academic day in the hands of an individual interdisciplinary team, permitting the team to divide up the day into discrete periods or use one big block of time, as the team members saw fit. Once adjusting for physical education, exploratory courses, and lunch, the remainder of the day was at the disposal of the team of teachers. In many middle schools where a team-controlled schedule has been implemented, the sound of bells ringing to announce separate periods has disappeared. Unfortunately, this freedom to be flexible has been present often in possibility but not actuality. In the great majority of American middle schools, standard six- or seven-period days remain the norm.

In the last five years, however, the long block schedule popular in many high schools has found its way to the middle school. In Florida, for example, approximately one-third of middle schools have implemented, or are planning to implement, a block schedule such as the 4 × 4 or A/B plan, which we explore in Chapter 8. These longer periods, ranging from 85 to 120 or more minutes, are quickly gaining popularity. It seems likely that as many as half of Florida's 500 middle schools will be using a block schedule in the next five years, and the trend should be a national one, if Florida is truly a bell-wether state.

Technology

At a new middle school of 1,200 students in one large school district, each classroom has 6 computers, each science classroom has 10 computers, and three computer labs have 30 computers in each—for a total of 700 networked, Internet-connected computers in the school. In this school, the debate about whether to place scarce computer resources in teachers' classrooms or in centralized computer labs had been bypassed—by eliminating the scarcity.

What many middle school teachers and their students are doing, with the aid of technology, is dazzling. Email, for example, has become ubiquitous. Teachers and administrators now communicate by email, not by memo or loudspeaker; even parents now conference with their children's teachers by email. New Web-based school computer search engines permit students to gain access from their homes. Teachers no longer spend hours figuring out grade averages, because computer programs do it for them easily. Live TV crews from studios that would, 30 years ago, have made network news crews proud now conduct the daily announcements, in virtually every middle school. Wireless computer and Internet labs, with 20 I-Books, are present, wheeled from room to room on large carts by the technology specialist much like the librarian used to move library materials to classrooms where teachers had requested them. And the librarian who had become the media specialist is now being transformed into the technology specialist in many schools.

More important, perhaps, is the freshness and vitality that the Internet has added to school curriculum resources. In a social studies class one of us observed, the library's 30-year-old books on Latin America were quickly dispensed with by students using newer compact discs (CDs) and having immediate access to each country's own Web pages. Students who would have been condemned to reading materials outdated by decades now had online access to the most current information available. In another classroom in that same school, students were engrossed in studying the campaign literature available on Al Gore's and George W. Bush's separate 2000 presidential campaign Web pages. In yet another, students were collecting data on birds outside their classroom and comparing it with patterns of data on the same birds in 10 other states as reported that day on various Web pages. In hundreds of other elective and exploratory classrooms in many middle schools, 6th grade students are learning to use computer applications that most current adults will never learn: presentation, database, and video software that is close to the cutting edge of availability.

Educators in middle schools have begun to envision schooling dramatically transformed by technological resources. One leader, for example, forecast middle schools where personalized learning would allow each student to learn exactly what that student needed, exactly when that student needed to learn it. New data warehouses will collect all data on individual student performance in one place, for teacher, parent, and other uses.

In such schools, every student would have an Individual Education Plan (IEP), which could be continuously updated, along with suggested instructional strategies. Electronic textbooks will be coming soon, these leaders believe, and every student will have a laptop or palm-held Internet connection device that companies such as Apple predict will be available at a reasonable cost within the next five years.

Other leaders speak of the potential elimination of barriers between public schools and home schooling. Students will be able to move back and forth between the two sites with ease and impunity. Differentiated staffing will, some predict, be back with new possibilities for creating levels of professionalism in teaching. And this is just the beginning. We deal with these issues further in Chapters 3 and 4.

Instruction

While much has changed in middle schools in the last three decades, some things have remained largely the same. The way teaching is conducted has, for example, only begun to be altered by the advance of technology. In many classrooms, teachers seem caught in what their students might call a time warp, continuing to rely almost exclusively on traditional teacher-directed, whole class instruction. Presentation, question and answer, practice, and reteaching are components of the most common instructional sequence in too many middle school classrooms; but even this has begun to give way to change.

Teachers and school leaders have recognized the need to differentiate instruction even if they have not been able to accomplish it widely. Cooperative learning has, consequently, become a permanent part of hundreds of middle school classrooms, in every subject, at every level. Few question its utility, especially with group-oriented middle school students. Other methods of differentiation (case studies, Socratic seminars, simulations, independent study) have come only slowly, usually in schools attempting to challenge gifted students in the regular, heterogeneous classroom. One instructional strategy may hold particular promise for the middle grades. The workshop classroom popularized by language arts educators seems ideal for young adolescents and has found adherents and advocates in increasing numbers. In Chapter 4, we attend to instruction in detail.

Grouping for Instruction

The way in which students are grouped for instruction is a special source of concern to many middle school educators. The concern rises from educators' decades-long advocacy of educational equity for all groups of students and of opportunity for individual students to achieve whatever level of excellence their talent permits. Two particular groups of students are being singled out for attention: special education students and gifted students.

Inclusion   Special education students are, in many, if not most, middle schools, increasingly joining the mainstream in inclusive classrooms. In some large districts, at almost every school, every team is an inclusion team, and the schools have a support specialist at each grade level to help teachers make inclusion work. Such circumstances more often involve inclusive teams, in which one team on each grade level contains a substantial number of that grade's special education students. Special education teachers become members of the team, as do their students, in every way. This sort of co-teaching and collaboration is leading to daily benefits for every student on the team, not just those with special needs or disabilities. Most teachers readily embrace inclusion, when the process entails teacher empowerment and the opportunity for regular training and frequent common planning time for educators involved in inclusion.

Ability Grouping and Education of the Gifted   Middle school educators have been unable to close the debates on tracking and the education of the gifted. As schools become more demographically diverse, parents of highly able, majority culture, middle- and upper-middle-class students have effectively increased the pressure to group their students in separate classrooms for large portions, if not all, of the school day. While many middle schools remain completely heterogeneous in their instructional grouping, the great majority provides at least advanced and standard sections for math and language arts courses, if not social studies and science. Some middle schools have four or five levels of classes in subjects such as mathematics. A few schools organize wholly separate teams for gifted students, who have little or no opportunity to interact with other students in the school. In not a few schools, isolated islands of educational plenty are surrounded by a sea of discouragement and disappointment, which only further increases the fevered advocacy for special separate programs for gifted, mostly white, upper-middle-class students. Chapter 7 is the location of further discussion on these controversial topics.

The Corporate Presence

Practices and paradigms from the corporate world increasingly influence middle school leadership. Many school district central offices have initiated centralized planning processes (e.g., strategic planning, Total Quality Management) that remove much of the traditional autonomy-building leaders enjoyed during the years of school-based management. District leaders envision and work to ensure a system in which every school day, in every school, reflects the state and district goals toward which the district hopes to move. State standards and district goals are a part of every school's annual School Improvement Plan. Classroom plans are expected to be congruent with school and district goals as well as state standards.

The distance between classrooms of middle school students and the corporate world has also narrowed dramatically in the last three decades, apart from the substantial influence on their daily lives exerted by the corporate-style planning in which adults engage. Large numbers of students watch brief news shows every morning, which include two minutes of commercials for products such as Snickers, Juicy Fruit, Pepsi, and Pop Tarts. Companies offer free computers to schools, in exchange for monitoring the students' Web-surfing habits, broken down by sex, age, and zip code, and potentially linked to the parents' credit card numbers. Other middle schools, weakened by diminished resources in a time of great corporate profits, compete to sign up as many corporate partners as possible. Banners announcing the presence of such partnerships hang in hallways and auditoriums of many schools, with some school lobbies festooned with more corporate symbols than a NASCAR race track.

What will the next decade bring? Will the testing companies that already publish textbooks "created by the same company that created your state assessment program" find more ways of penetrating the school "market"? Will textbooks have as many ads as *People* magazine? Certainly the advertising on the Internet that students now encounter daily suggests that such things are possible, perhaps probable. Will Nike sponsor school lunches? More than a few school lunchrooms are already dominated by Subway, Pizza Hut, and fast-food fare that does, at least, replace the once ubiquitous "mystery meat."

The corporate paradigm appears to have an ever-increasing influence on education in general and middle school programs in particular. Centralization threatens local autonomy and school-based planning. Standardization may completely replace curriculum planning based on students' perceived needs and interests. Competition between and among students, teachers, school leaders, and schools replaces trust, cooperation, and collaboration. Assessment and accountability managed from a distance supplant local decisions about effectiveness, worthiness, and the assignment of resources. Chapter 10 touches on these issues.

School Leadership

The person inside the middle school principal's office today is much more likely to be female, and she is not the secretary. And it is no longer a rarity for African American or Hispanic or Latino educators to be leading middle schools, especially in larger, more urban districts. Often, these leaders move into their positions as a result of having done well on new, much more complex and objective administrative selection assessments. Shared decision-making, real faculty involvement in the decisions that are made at the school level, is often found in the settings to which these new leaders are assigned.

Instructional Leadership   Today's middle school principals now see themselves as instructional leaders. Everything else is viewed as an irritating distraction from their responsibility for instruction. While the best leaders have always cared deeply about instruction, recent programs initiated by the state government have mandated this change: Instructional leadership is now a professional survival strategy as well as the desirably central aspect of middle school leadership. Athletic programs are scarcely noticeable if not totally absent in the language of middle school leaders who now speak with great familiarity of what each teacher in the building is teaching and how well he or she is performing.

However, the accountability movement in many states appears to have driven some middle school principals beyond instructional leadership to an all-consuming preoccupation with academic achievement as measured by statewide assessment tests. Scores on these tests determine a school's status in the community, may dictate bonuses for the staff, bring public praise or disapprobation, and may result in termination or promotion for school leaders and teachers. In many schools today, nothing else matters as much as test scores. We take a long look at accountability in Chapter 10.

Middle School versus "Muddle School"   Does an inherent conflict exist between the middle school concept and rigorous academic classrooms leading to higher academic achievement? Does the middle school concept place an inordinate amount of attention on the social, emotional, and physical needs of the young adolescent? Forty years after the middle school movement began to replace the junior high school, advocates for the education of this age group find themselves on the defensive again. Critics charge that middle school educators accept low expectations for their students' achievement, leading to a muddle at the middle level where students who do well in elementary school slip behind badly, when compared with students in other nations. We examine this continuing controversy in some depth in Chapter 10.

We will assert now, and argue later in the book, that the middle school movement of the last 35 years has been one of the most dynamic and successful educational innovations in the history of American education. The remainder of this textbook deals with the specifics of how you, as an educator, can help to extend the success and deepen the stability of the middle school movement during the early years of the 21st century.

CONCLUSION

So much has changed in America's middle schools during the last quarter-century, and, yet, the challenges remain relatively constant. Can educators find a balance between elementary and secondary education in the middle school? Can educators build and operate schools that feel small regardless of their size? Can educators find opportunities to create curriculum experiences based on the true needs of young adolescents? Can educators satisfy their patrons, especially those who are affluent and influential, without sacrificing the children of the poor? Can educators find a new generation of effective leaders for the nation's middle schools? We hope that you, the reader, will join the new generation of middle level educators working to find answers to these important questions.

CONTENT SUMMARY

Educators have been focusing on schooling for the young adolescent for more than a century. The earlier strategies (K–8 elementary school and the grades 7–9 junior high school) seemed inadequate. Today's middle school, a composite of many important concepts, emphasizes developmental appropriateness. There are now about 15,000 middle schools, most often in a building housing grades 6–8. As the 21st century dawns, dissatisfaction with middle level education continues, and many trends and issues occupy the minds of middle school educators.

CONNECTIONS TO OTHER CHAPTERS

What you have learned in Chapter 2 is connected to all the other chapters in the book. Most important, perhaps, is the connection with Chapter 10. In Chapter 10, we return to the important trends and issues, because leaders are usually the ones most closely involved with making decisions and solving difficult problems.

QUESTIONS FOR DISCUSSION

1. What is it about the nature of middle level education that, compared with the other two levels, inspires such dissatisfaction from the public?
2. Where, in your opinion, should be the balance between developing a sense of community in which students feel known and cared about and

emphasizing a rich and rigorous curriculum in which all students are effectively challenged?

3. Do the three goals for middle schools seem complete to you? Should there be others?

4. What do you see as the most important trends and most critical issues challenging the effectiveness of contemporary middle level education?

5. Have significant issues or trends in middle level education emerged since the publication of this book in 2002?

ACTION STEPS

1. Arrange for a visit to, and brief tour of, a nearby middle level school. Collect enough data to permit you to make judgments about the degree to which the school offers a developmentally appropriate education for young adolescents, the concerns educators have about contemporary middle level education, and whether you see evidence that the school attempts to meet all three goals of the middle school concept.

2. Attempt an oral history. Identify people who had their middle level education in each of these three situations: K–8 school, junior high school, and middle school. Develop questions to ask them about their experience and their satisfaction or dissatisfaction with it. Conduct interviews and prepare a short paper describing the results.

3. Conduct your own public opinion poll, in which you identify adults in the community from two different groups. First, identify those who do not have children in the school system. Ask them a series of questions about their beliefs about the efficacy of today's middle level schools. Then find a group of equal size, comprised of those who have children in a middle level school, and ask the same questions. Compare and contrast the answers.

4. Seek out your state middle level education association. Find out when the annual conference is being held and attend it.

SUGGESTIONS FOR FURTHER STUDY

Books

Borman, K., & Nancy, P. (1994). *Changing American education: Recapturing the past or inventing the future?* Albany, NY: State University of New York Press.

Clark, S., & Clark, D. (1994). *Restructuring the middle level school: Implications for school leaders.* Albany, NY: State University of New York Press.

David, R. (1998). *Moving forward from the past: Early writings and current reflections of middle school founders.* Columbus, OH: National Middle School Association.

Dickinson, T. (Ed.) (2001). *Reinventing the middle school.* New York: Routledge/Farmer.

Jackson, A., & Davis, G. (2000). *Turning points 2000: Educating adolescents in the 21st century.* New York: Teachers College Press.

Lieberman, A. (1995). *The work of restructuring schools: Building from the ground up.* New York: Teachers College Press.

Lipka, R., Lounsbury, J., Toepfer, C., Vars, G., Alessi, S., & Kridel, C. (1998). *The eight-year study revisited: Lessons from the past for the present.* Columbus, OH: National Middle School Association.

Pace, G. (1995). *Whole learning in the middle school: Evolution and transition.* Norwood, MA: Christopher-Gordon Publishers.

Raebeck, B. (1998). *Transforming middle schools: A guide to whole-school change.* Lancaster, PA: Technomic Publishing Co.

Wheelock, A. (1998). *Safe to be smart: Building a culture for standards-based reform in the middle grades.* Columbus, OH: National Middle School Association.

Periodicals

Backes, J., Ralston, A., & Ingwalson, G. (1999). Middle level reform: The impact on student achievement. *Research in Middle Level Education, 22*(3), 43–57.

Felner, R., Jackson, A., Kasak, D., Mulhall, P., Brand, S., & Flowers, N. (1997). The impact of school reform for the middle years. *Phi Delta Kappan, 78*(7), 528–532, 541–550.

Fry, D., & Jobe, M. (1996). Importance and implementation of middle school concepts: A study of East Texas Middle School principals. *ERS Spectrum, 14*(1), 31–36.

Lipsitz, J., Mizell, H., Jackson, A., & Austin, L. (1997). Speaking with one voice: A manifesto for middle-grades reform. *Phi Delta Kappan, 78*(7), 533–540.

Muth, D., Hart, L., Letendre, G., Ference, R., & Naumowicz, D. (1998). Middle grades education in the 21st century: The role of cross-disciplinary research in practice and policy. *Research in Middle Level Education Quarterly, 21*(4), 1–13.

Osuch, J. (1997). Beyond early childhood: Restructuring efforts at the middle level. *Childhood Education, 73*(5), 282–285.

Seghers, M., Meza, J., & Kirby, P. (1997). More evidence for the implementation of middle level practices. *NASSP Bulletin, 81*(591), 98–107.

Williamson, R., et al. (1995). Agenda: The achievement agenda for middle level schools. *Schools in the Middle, 5*(2), 6–9.

ERIC

Berkowitz, J., & Uline, C. (1999). *A changing school culture: The case study of Galion Middle School: Transforming learning communities* (ERIC document ED436847).

Boniface, R. (1998). *Collected papers from the OERI conference on adolescence: Designing developmentally appropriate middle schools, Washington, DC, May 7–8, 1998* (ERIC document ED433926).

Brooks, D. (1999). *Teacher-leaders, trust, and technology: The case study of Talawanda Middle School: Transforming learning communities* (ERIC document ED436843).

DeFord, M. (1996). *A comprehensive literature review in valuing the concept of caring in middle and secondary level schools* (ERIC document ED404041).

Dougherty, J. (1997). *Four philosophies that shape the middle school* (ERIC document ED408082).

Gullatt, D. (1995). *Effective leadership in the middle school classroom* (ERIC document ED388454).

Kahle, J., Tobin, K. G., & Rogg, S. R. (1997). *Impressions of reform in Ohio schools* (ERIC document ED425544).

Kellough, R., & Kellough, N. (1999). *Middle school teaching: A guide to methods and resources* (ERIC document ED423985).

Lounsbury, J. (1996). *Key characteristics of middle level schools* (ERIC document ED401050).

McEwin, K., Dickinson, T., & Jenkins, D. (1996). *America's middle schools: Practices and progress: A 25-year perspective* (ERIC document ED396842).

McLeod, B. (1996). *School reform and student diversity: Exemplary schooling for language minority students.* Washington, DC: National Clearinghouse for Bilingual Education, George Washington University, Institute for the Study of Language and Education (ERIC document ED392268).

Morrow, L., Martin, K., & Glascock, C. (1999). *An evolutionary journey: The case study of East Muskingum Middle School: Transforming learning communities* (ERIC document ED436850).

Romano, L., & Georgiady, N. (1997). *The middle school distinction* (ERIC document ED415016).

Scales, P. (1996). *Boxed in and bored: How middle schools continue to fail young adolescents—And what good middle schools do right* (ERIC document ED406506).

Siu-Runyan, Y., & Faircloth, V. (1995). *Beyond separate subjects: Integrative learning at the middle level* (ERIC document ED404036).

Takanishi, R., & Hamburg, D. (1997). *Preparing adolescents for the twenty-first century: Challenges facing Europe and the United States.* Johann Jacobs Foundation Conference Series, 4 (ERIC document ED419153).

Thompson, S., & Wallace, M. (1999). *Reform issues: A review of methodology and results* (ERIC document ED438369).

Trubowitz, S., & Longo, P. (1997). *How it works—Inside a school-college collaboration* (ERIC document ED404431).

Wavering, M. (1995). *Educating young adolescents: Life in the middle* (ERIC document ED388447).

Wheelock, A. (1998). *Safe to be smart: Building a culture for standards-based reform in the middle grades* (ERIC document ED435773).

Wolfe, E., & Gregoire, M. (1999). *Using the Rasch model to assess the implementation of exemplary middle school practices: A pilot study of Florida's middle schools* (ERIC document ED431017).

Videotapes

George, P. (1996). *The case for the middle school: Rationale and research.* Gainesville, FL: Teacher Education Resources.

Web Sites

The National Forum to Accelerate Middle-Grades Reform

http://www.mgforum.org

The National Forum to Accelerate Middle-Grades Reform is included in the home page of the National Middle School Association. Made up of a distinguished group of individuals committed to promoting the academic performance and healthy development of young adolescents, the forum is enhancing the middle level school movement by developing common goals and understandings, strengthening individual efforts to improve middle grades schools, collaborating across institutional and other boundaries, and working together to mobilize others in the larger middle grades community. Important site components include the following.

- Information about the forum
- Information about the Southern Forum
- Tools and resources
- Updates on relevant research and policy
- Criteria for exceptional schools and relevant research

Midlink Magazine

http://www.ncsu.edu/midlink/middle level.eds.2000.bio.htm

Presents original classroom work that reflects creative learning processes.

The mission is to highlight exemplary work from the most creative classrooms around the globe. This nonprofit organization is supported by North Carolina State University and the University of Central Florida. Any school, teacher, or student is invited to participate.

Middle Web: Exploring Middle School Reform
http://www.middleweb.com
A large and helpful site sponsored by the Edna McConnell Clark Foundation, which is dedicated to school-based reform that results in increased academic achievement for all students, particularly those in urban, integrated middle schools. The site features hundreds of articles, dozens of links, and opportunities to chat with teachers and leaders in the middle school reform movement.

MIDDLE SCHOOL CURRICULUM

BROWN BARGE MIDDLE SCHOOL

Brown Barge Middle School (BBMS), a school for able learners in Pensacola, Florida, features a comprehensively integrated curriculum virtually unduplicated anywhere in the nation. All 450+ students and teachers at BBMS teach and learn together in fully integrated curriculum streams, multiage-grouped interdisciplinary teams focused on a particular curriculum theme. Each stream lasts for 12 weeks, with all students and teachers choosing, during the previous spring, which three 12-week streams they want to teach and learn in for the coming year. A group of four teachers and 120 students may, for example, be formed around the theme of bridges, while others might group around arts motifs, flight, the environment, or a dozen other possibilities. The stream is the total educational experience of both teachers and students for the 12 weeks, all day every day, except for unified arts and physical education programs during one two-period block of the day. With the exception of the last 12 weeks of the 8th grade year, students have no separate classes in mathematics, language arts, or other traditional subjects. Yet virtually every student tests out of 9th grade mathematics during his or her first few days of high school. Seven hundred students are on the waiting list to gain admission via lottery to this incredibly innovative, amazingly popular, urban, diverse, public middle school.

WHAT YOU WILL LEARN IN CHAPTER 3

In this chapter, we illustrate the curriculum mandated by standards-based reform, and we profile the rationale and process supporting the integrated curriculum movement. In addition, we highlight that important, but oft-ignored, area of the middle school curriculum—the exploratory, unified arts program. We also profile special efforts to enrich middle school curricula through special interest programs, magnet programs, technology, and others.

STANDARDS-BASED REFORM VERSUS LEARNER-CENTERED CURRICULUM

Two contradictory curriculum paradigms battle for primacy in America's middle schools. Two movements pull educators, parents, and students in opposite directions. Many middle school educators remain committed to a developmentally appropriate curriculum, one in which lessons spring from the needs and interests of young adolescents as those educators and their students perceive them (Beane, 1997). The popularity of the decades-long integrated curriculum movement is the most evident manifestation of the widespread belief among educators that curriculum, at its best, is truly student-centered. The competing curriculum paradigm grows from another movement, the newer standards-based reform movement and the high-stakes assessment and accountability processes that have become so much a part of it. Many politicians, and conservatives in general, are persuaded that improvement is desperately needed at every school level, and especially at the middle level, given that the clearest opposition to standards-based reform is under way at the middle level.

The Rationale for Standards-Based Education

Content or curriculum standards are public, written statements of educational expectations. They describe the knowledge and skills Americans want students to attain. Standards focus on measured student outcomes, stressing implied learning outcomes, instead of curriculum covered, credits earned, or time in school. Standards are for all students, not just a few. Standards, then, are intended to guide what is taught in the middle school classroom, especially in the core subjects of language arts, mathematics, science, and social studies. But standards have also been developed for the arts, health education, physical education, and foreign languages. In standards-based education, curriculum standards are matched with instructional activities, assessment, and measures of school accountability in achieving those standards.

The current phase of the standards-based education movement may have begun with a political event—President George Bush's 1989 "education summit" with the nation's governors—and continued political interest seems to have taken it to where it is today (Bush, 2001). The movement for standards-based reform was bolstered by the U.S. Department of Labor's 1991 publication of the Secretary's Commission on Achieving Necessary Skills (SCANS) report, *What Work Requires of Schools.* The SCANS report produced some of the first examples of standards, of what students should know and be able to do to be successful in adult work life. The New Standards Project began, in 1993, to collect and analyze tests and documents from other countries where students were perceived to be doing well on international tests and holding jobs that required a high level of skills and also paid well. A major outcome of this work was the conclusion that schools were successful when they set clear, consistent, demanding standards and used performance assessments that determined the academic proficiency of their students.

By 2000, 49 states were involved, with 27 going so far as to require students to pass the state assessment to graduate from high school (Hardy, 2000). Once fiercely proud of local curriculum autonomy, many educators, parents, and politicians have embraced the idea that there should be, as a minimum, a congruence among public standards established at the state or national levels, accompanying assessments, and the classroom curriculum.

A joint public statement by the California State Board of Education and the state school superintendent laid out the case for standards-based education in that state and elsewhere (Middle Grades Task Force, 2001, p. 1).

> A shortcoming of [school reform] up to this point has been the lack of focus on rigorous academic standards. The desire to improve student achievement . . . lacked a comprehensive, specific vision of what students actually needed to know and be able to do. . . . For the first time we are stating explicitly the content that students need to acquire at each grade level. . . . These standards are rigorous. With student mastery of this content, California schools will be on a par with those in the best educational systems in other states and nations. . . . Fifteen years from now, we are convinced, the adoption of standards will be viewed as the signal event that began "a rising tide of excellence" in our schools. No more will the critical question "What should my child be learning?" be met with uncertainty of knowledge, purpose, and resolve. These standards answer the question. They are comprehensive and specific. They represent our commitment to excellence.

Mediocre Performance Modern standards-based reform probably began in 1983, with the vitriolic attack on public education contained in the well-known *A Nation at Risk* report, which indicted American schools as having experienced a "rising tide of mediocrity." That report, and years of succeeding reports and legislation, charged that American schools had fallen drastically short of the best hopes for them and behind the best systems of schooling in Asia and Europe. The most recent major education report (U.S. Department of Education, 1999), on the Third International Mathematics and Science Study (TIMMS), continued to assail American schools for their mediocre performance in these key areas. So, for the greater part of the last two decades, the national press has presented the arguments of advocates for standards-based reform that American schools have failed and that drastic measures were necessary.

Standards-based reform, it is asserted, will focus educators' attention on, and force them to respond to, the gaps in their knowledge of their subjects and the deficiencies in their teaching practices. Reformers believe that truly talented teaching has never been widely available and that only a fortunate few students have, in the past, been part of exciting and effective learning experiences. Much more frequently, contend the advocates of standards-based reform, students have been confined to a classroom where fragmented curriculum is dominated by textbooks; where immense amounts of time are wasted in unproductive activities that go unmonitored; and where curriculum, instruction, and assessment have no connection to each other. The community has had no real knowledge of what was occurring, advocates alleged, until the standards-based reform got under way and assessment results became public knowledge. When the knowledge of what appeared to be shockingly poor performance became widely recognized, the public was furious and demanded drastic reform measures.

Focused, Public Design   Drastic measures included a dramatic shift away from local control of education, to the idea that standards should be publicly derived and available. After 1983, state legislatures and departments of education initiated new curriculum and testing requirements that effectively removed local school-based educators from any important formal role in the curriculum planning process. Whatever one's opinion of the outcomes of these movements in education nationally, for the last two decades local educators have had increasingly less influence in the design and development of middle school curriculum.

This was necessary, advocates said, because educators needed to move away from "naïve, comforting assumptions about what is happening in the classroom, toward a more honest and productive reckoning with what and how well children are actually learning" (Schmoker, 2000). Advocates asserted that standards need to be publicly derived, because curriculum decisions made by individual teachers were likely to be arbitrary and idiosyncratic, based on what the teacher felt confident in teaching. Supporters of standards charged that too many classrooms have, for far too long, been characterized by a curriculum composed of the content from the teacher's favorite college courses, whether or not it fit the needs of the students. In the schools of a democracy, it was argued, curriculum decisions ought not be made behind the closed doors of individual classrooms. In a hundred thousand such classrooms, a hundred thousand different curriculum plans would be implemented.

The challenges of contemporary schooling and life in 21st century society, say advocates of standards-based reform, require that educators be much more deliberate, and much more clear, about what should and is being taught. What constitutes successful achievement, in today's diverse society, needs to be much more publicly available, because the consensus on the nature of schooling from the "good old days" has dissolved.

Success for All Students Standards-based reform is intended, its supporters state, to focus on raising expectations for all students, especially for those who have experienced the least effective education—urban, minority, and poor students. Instead of the silent acceptance of failure of millions of such students, a common set of high expectations for all students will elevate the performance of more than the talented and fortunate few. True equity will result when all students have access to consistently high expectations provided by teachers using a rich, public, assessed, standards-driven curriculum.

Standards-based education, with its emphasis on monitoring student progress, will also encourage a more equitable distribution of resources than has existed to date. When it becomes clear that some students need more assistance to reach the expectations that have been set for all, targeted assistance and additional resources can be made available. Systemic progress, instead of scattered and isolated improvements, can be the result. The complacent acceptance of widespread failure can no longer be tolerated and, advocates allege, the results of standards-based reform, so far, indicate that poor and minority students are receiving more resources and doing much better.

Curriculum Alignment Supporters of standards-based education stress that the alignment of curriculum, teaching, and assessment will deliver many benefits to a system beleaguered by fragmentation, inconsistency, and unaccountability. When they become familiar with the standards for their curriculum, for example, teachers are often amazed at how familiar they are with the standards and how much of what they already teach is built into the standards. Teachers in possession of standards no longer feel pressured to cover all the possible content in their subject or pushed to make crucial decisions about what to include or exclude from their classroom curriculum. Teachers feel more effective, advocates say, responding to the targeted needs of their students and more successful when they can move students forward.

In these circumstances, teachers can make more reasonable judgments about all aspects of their curriculum and teaching. They can, for example, examine textbooks more judiciously, and they can make informed decisions about professional development opportunities. They can think more clearly about questions relating to the use of time or particular schedules. Standards become the referent for all such decision-making. They make curriculum alignment possible.

Teacher, Student, and Parent Support   Advocates for standards-based education contend that there is no backlash against the use of standards in today's classrooms. One poll, for example, indicated that 87% of teachers agreed that standards-based reform was a "step in the right direction." Teachers in high-poverty areas agreed, at about the same level, that expectations have risen, the curriculum has become more demanding, and students were working harder. Even students agree that they would work harder if pressed to do so (Doherty, 2001).

Some advocates for the standards movement insist that if standards-based reform is not successful, the American common school experience is in jeopardy. If standards-based reform collapses, they assert, what will ensue will be a "Darwinian world of education" in which public education becomes pauper schooling. "This is the last best chance to save American education as we know it, and we've got to make it work," says Harvard professor S. Paul Reville (Lindsay, 2000, p. 37).

Success in standards-based education, then, promises a number of improvements for middle schools.

- Higher expectations, with a rigorous and world class education for all young adolescents
- Focused instruction, on a common curriculum, without dictating teaching methods
- Aligned curriculum, with appropriate testing and monitoring
- Extra help for low-performing students
- Meaningful professional development, along with evaluation of teacher performance
- Improved parent involvement
- Restoration of public confidence in the schools

AN EXAMPLE OF A CURRICULUM BASED ON STATE STANDARDS

In previous editions of this text, we described the content of the middle school curriculum in painstaking detail. Readers who require such detailed descriptions are referred to the previous edition (George & Alexander, 1993) or to the groups developing comprehensive lists of standards that we identify here. In this edition, we attempt to satisfy, simultaneously, the need to provide descriptive details of the middle school curriculum and illustrate the process being taken by the standards movement. To do so, we examine the middle school curriculum as laid out by standards-based reform in the state of Florida.

Standards-Based Reform in a Typical State

Florida's standards-based reform movement is based on the Sunshine State Standards, which purportedly identify what students should know and be able to do after they complete grades PreK–2, 3–5, 6–8, and 9–12 (Florida Department of Education, n.d.). Unless Florida is unique, the same general standards are likely to be found in the lists of the other 48 states that have developed standards documents. The Florida standards are organized in four ways.

1. General academic subject areas (e.g., language arts)
2. Strands—subdivisions of those general areas (e.g., writing)
3. Standards—descriptions of general expectations of knowledge or skills within a strand
4. Benchmarks—the most specific and precise statements about student knowledge and skill at one of the four developmental levels (e.g., middle school)

The organization of the curriculum in Florida middle schools resembles an inverted pyramid (see Figure 3.1), with general subject areas at the most universal level and benchmarks at the most specific level.

Middle School General Subject Areas   For middle schools, most state and national organizations have specified strands, standards, and benchmarks, in the traditional areas most educators expect. Florida does the same. The world of the

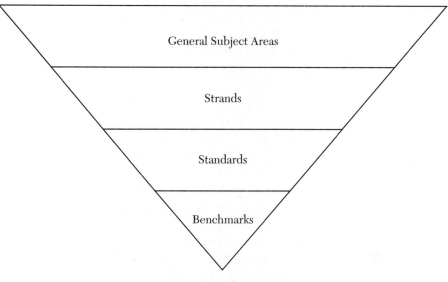

FIGURE 3.1

FLORIDA CURRICULUM: SUNSHINE STATE STANDARDS

middle school curriculum is divided much as it always has been and in new standards documents as

- Language arts
- Mathematics
- Science
- Social studies
- Foreign languages
- The arts
- Health and physical education

Strands within Middle School Subject Areas   Within each general subject area, specific stands are identified, also like descriptions of the middle school curriculum across the last several decades. Nothing is radically new here.

In language arts:
  Reading
  Writing
  Listening, viewing, and speaking
  Language
  Literature
In mathematics:
  Number sense, concepts, and operations
  Measurement
  Geometry and spatial sense
  Algebraic thinking
  Data analysis and probability
In science:
  The nature of matter
  Energy
  Force and motion
  Processes that shape the Earth
  Earth and space
  Processes of life
  How living things interact with their environment
  The nature of science
In social studies:
  Time, continuity, and change (history)
  People, places, and environments (geography)
  Government and the citizen (civics and government)
  Economics
In foreign languages:
  Communication
  Culture

Connections
Comparisons
Experiences
In the arts:
Dance
Music
Theatre
Visual arts
In health and physical education:
Health education
Physical education

Standards within Each Strand of the Middle School Curriculum

Florida identifies 109 specific standards across these subject areas and strands of the middle school curriculum. Because similar documents are readily available in virtually every state, we will not fully list all 109 here, choosing instead to give you the flavor of each area.

Language Arts   Language arts has 11 standards, among which are the following.

- The student uses the reading process effectively.
- The student constructs meaning from a wide range of texts.
- The student writes to communicate ideas and information effectively.
- The student uses viewing strategies effectively.
- The student responds critically to fiction, nonfiction, poetry, and drama.

Mathematics   Mathematics has 17 standards, such as the following.

- The student understands the different ways numbers are represented and used in the real world.
- The student understands the effects of operations on numbers and the relationships among these operations, selects appropriate operations, and computes for problem solving.
- The student uses estimation in problem solving and computation.
- The student uses expressions, equations, inequalities, graphs, and formulas to represent and interpret situations.
- The student uses statistical methods to make inferences and valid arguments about real-world situations.

Science   Science has 17 standards, including the following.

- The student understands that all matter has observable, measurable properties.
- The student understands that types of motion may be described, measured, and predicted.

- The student recognizes that processes in the lithosphere, atmosphere, hydrosphere, and biosphere interact to shape the Earth.
- The student recognizes the vastness of the universe and the Earth's place in it.
- The student understands the competitive, interdependent, and cyclic nature of living things in the environment.

Social Studies   Florida identifies 12 standards in social studies, such as the following.

- The student understands the world from its beginnings to the time of the Renaissance.
- The student understands Western and Eastern civilization since the Renaissance.
- The student understands U.S. history to 1880.
- The student understands U.S. history from 1880 to the present day.
- The student understands the world in spatial terms.
- The student understands the structure, functions, and purposes of government and how the principles and values of American democracy are reflected in American constitutional government.
- The student understands the characteristics of different economic systems and institutions.

Foreign Languages   Nine standards are proposed for foreign languages, including the following.

- The student engages in conversation, expresses feelings and emotions, and exchanges opinions.
- The student understands and interprets written and spoken language on a variety of topics.
- The student demonstrates an understanding of the relationship between the perspectives and products of the culture studied and uses this knowledge to recognize cultural practices.
- The student uses the language within and beyond the school setting.

The Arts   Twenty-nine standards cover the arts, including these representative ones.

- The student identifies and demonstrates movement elements in performing dance.
- The student performs on instruments, alone and with others, a varied repertoire of music.
- The student reads and notates music.
- The student acts by developing, communicating, and sustaining characters in improvisation and formal or informal productions.

- The student creates and communicates a range of subject matter, symbols, and ideas using knowledge of structures and functions of visual arts.
- The student assesses, evaluates, and responds to the characteristics of works of art.

Health and Physical Education   Fourteen standards are established for health and physical education, such as the following.

- The student knows health-enhancing behaviors and how to reduce health risks.
- The student analyzes the influence of culture, media, technology, and other factors on health.
- The student demonstrates competency in many movement forms and proficiency in a few forms of physical activity.
- The student achieves and maintains a health-enhancing level of physical fitness.
- The student understands how participating in physical activity promotes inclusion and an understanding of the abilities and cultural diversity of people.

Benchmarks within Each Middle School Standard

Continuing with the inverted pyramid-like organization, within each subject area, then within each strand, and then within each standard, specific benchmarks are identified. The process goes from subject area to strand, to standard, and finally, to benchmarks. Across all middle school subjects, strands, and standards, Florida identifies a total of 418 benchmarks for the middle school level, constituting the portion of the middle school curriculum mandated by the state. Here, we identify only a few of this large number, several in each major subject area. The reader should understand that benchmarks constitute the body of each standard.

Language Arts   In the subject area of middle school language arts, one of the five strands is reading. Within the reading strand, there are only two standards, reflecting the fact that most of the work in reading is to be done in prior years at the elementary school level. Standard 1 says: "The student uses the reading process effectively." Contained within this standard are four benchmarks.

1. Uses background knowledge of the subject and text structure knowledge to make complex predictions of content, purpose, and organization of the reading selection.
2. Uses a variety of strategies to analyze words and text, draw conclusions, use context and word structure clues, and recognize organizational patterns.

3. Demonstrates consistent and effective use of interpersonal and academic vocabularies in reading, writing, listening, and speaking.
4. Uses strategies to clarify meaning, such as rereading, note taking, summarizing, outlining, and writing a grade level appropriate report.

Mathematics In the subject area of mathematics, one of the five strands is algebraic thinking, which includes two standards, one of which is: "The student describes, analyzes, and generalizes a wide variety of patterns, relations, and functions." Contained within this strand are only two benchmarks.

1. Describes a wide variety of patterns, relationships, and functions, through models, such as manipulatives, tables, graphs, expressions, equations, and inequalities.
2. Creates and interprets tables, graphs, equations, and verbal descriptions to explain cause-and-effect relationships.

Science Within the subject area of science and its seven strands, there are 17 standards, one of which is: "The student understands the interaction and organization in the Solar System and the universe and how this affects life on Earth." Four benchmarks comprise the specific expectations for this standard.

1. Understands the vast size of the solar system and the relationship of the planets and their satellites.
2. Knows that available data from various satellite probes show the similarities and differences among planets and their moons in the solar system.
3. Understands that the sun is one of many stars in the galaxy.
4. Knows that stars appear to be made of similar chemical elements, although they differ in age, size, temperature, and distance.

Social Studies Within the subject area of social studies, and its four strands, there are 12 standards, one of which says: "The student understands the structure, functions, and purposes of government and how the principles and values of American democracy are reflected in American constitutional government." Six separate benchmarks identify the specific content of this area.

1. Knows the essential ideas of American constitutional government that are expressed in the Declaration of Independence, the Constitution, the *Federalist Papers,* and other writings.
2. Understands major ideas about why government is necessary and the purposes government should serve.
3. Understands how the legislative, executive, and judicial branches share power and responsibilities.

4. Knows the major parts of the federal system including the national government, state governments, and other governmental units.
5. Knows the major responsibilities of his or her state and local governments and understands the organization of his or her state and local governments.
6. Understands the importance of the rule of law in establishing limits on both those who govern and the governed, protecting individual rights, and promoting the common good.

Foreign Languages   In the subject area of foreign languages, and its five strands, there are nine standards, one of which says: "The student acquires information and perspectives that are available only through the foreign language and within the target culture." Three benchmarks comprise this standard.

1. Uses the target language to establish contact with members of the target culture.
2. Uses the target language to gain access to information and perspectives that are only available through the target language or with the target culture.
3. Uses films or texts produced in the target language to gain knowledge and understanding of various aspects of the arts, music, literature, history, or economics of the target culture.

The Arts   The four strands of the arts contain 29 standards, one of which reads: "The student improvises melodies, variations, and accompaniments." This standard has two benchmarks.

1. Improvises simple harmonic accompaniments for a given melody.
2. Improvises short melodies over given rhythmic accompaniment.

Health and Physical Education   This subject area contains two strands and 14 standards, one of which is: "The student knows health-enhancing behaviors and how to reduce health risks." This standard has six benchmarks that identify it.

1. Knows the importance of assuming responsibility for personal health behaviors.
2. Understands the short-term and long-term consequences of safe, risky, and harmful behaviors.
3. Knows strategies for managing stress.
4. Knows strategies for improving and maintaining personal and family health.
5. Knows techniques for avoiding threatening situations.
6. Knows injury-prevention and injury-management strategies for personal and family health.

Standards in Other States

What we have reproduced is only a part of the total package of subject areas, strands, standards, and benchmarks for the middle school curriculum as defined and described in what we believe is a typical state. The comprehensive nature of such efforts prevents us from complete replication here. Complete sets of curriculum standards for your own state, which we suspect will be similar to the result in Florida, can be easily found. Look in the literature and Web sites of state departments of education and check national curriculum groups such as the National Council for Teachers of Mathematics. Also consult the collections published by groups such as the Mid-Continental Regional Educational Laboratory (McREL), the Council for Basic Education, and the National Center on Education and the Economy. The Consortium of National Arts Education Associations has produced a set of curriculum standards for dance, music, theatre, and visual arts for grades 5–8, containing standards and benchmarks in all areas.

An annual survey on standards and on the ways they are being used is issued each winter by *Education Week* and another is put out each spring by the American Federations of Teachers. Foundations, such as the Edna McConnell Clark Foundation, have committed sizable resources to the elaboration of standards in all areas of the middle school curriculum. Standards have been developed for language arts, mathematics, science, social studies, the arts, health and physical education, and foreign languages. Dozens of such standards have been established for every subject area, far too many to be listed here.

We recommend, therefore, that readers in need of lists of specific standards refer directly to their individual state department of education. Readers who are interested in social studies standards, in Texas, for example, will be referred to the *Texas Social Studies Framework, Kindergarten–Grade 12: Research and Resources for Designing a Social Studies Curriculum* (Texas Education Agency, 1999). The Florida State Department of Education publishes lists of standards (*Sunshine State Standards, Grades 6–8*) and offers helpful resources for test preparation and so on. Readers seeking information about standards in California will find that the California State Department of Education has produced a substantial amount of resources in addition to specifying standards. *Taking Center Stage: A Commitment to Standards-Based Education for California's Middle Grades Students* (Middle Grades Task Force, 2001) not only lays out information on specific standards in the California middle grades curriculum, but it also provides readers with in-depth resources for understanding standards-based education in California and for making standards work in authentic middle schools. The report argues, at length, that no conflict exists between "a sound middle school philosophy and the goals of standards-based education" (p. 1).

Educators who support standards-based reform, in these and other states across the nation, assert that rigorous and consistent standards can be implemented while maintaining a dynamic student-centered school culture. They believe that a commitment to the essentials of an exemplary middle school can be demonstrated while simultaneously aligning curriculum, instruction, and assessment practices with the state-mandated content. They are convinced that the contributions of diverse, multicultural populations can be identified and injected at the same time that standards are implemented. And they argue that specificity finally brings clarity and wholeness to a curriculum long in desperate need of such improvement. None of these claims is without challenge and outright censure from a host of critics of standards-based reform.

CRITICISM OF STANDARDS-BASED REFORM

Critics of standards-based education are primarily educators and others who believe that the best teaching and the most relevant learning happen when decisions about curriculum, about what is to be learned, occur as close to the learner as possible. Ideally, these educators believe, formative decisions about curriculum ought to arise out of the interests of the students as expressed in questions they have about themselves and the world (Beane, 1997). Curriculum should be based on the concerns of those who study it. Many middle school educators subscribe to these beliefs about curriculum, and the 30,000-member National Middle School Association (NMSA) puts it this way:

> Relevant curriculum involves students in activities that help them understand themselves and the world around them. It is rich in personal meaning. Teachers address students' own questions and concerns, which are then examined in a wider context. Making curriculum relevant thus does not mean limiting content solely to students' preexisting interests. Challenging curriculum creates new interests; it opens doors to new knowledge and opportunities; it "stretches" students. (National Middle School Association, 1995, p. 21)

Critics raise a number of serious objections to standards-based reform. The most serious reservations come from the way in which high-stakes testing and harsh accountability programs have become so much a part of the standards movement. Even though critics are not thrilled with the standards movement itself, when combined with testing and grading of schools and teachers, they are often horrified at the consequences for middle school education.

Irrelevance   Critics of standards-based reform argue that, if Rip Van Winkle awoke today, he would recognize few things in contemporary America. One of the familiar items, however, would be the school curriculum that advocates for standards-based reform seek to install in every middle school. The critics of standards-based reform argue that the secondary curriculum established by the Committee of Ten, in 1893, remains largely unchanged more than a century later. So, the primary argument of these critics is that students do not recognize any relevance to their lives of the curriculum brought to the classroom by an emphasis on sets of standards established by state departments of education. "The kids are bored to death" is not an uncommon lament. At the very least, an overemphasis on standards leaves too little time for curriculum decisions based on teacher expertise or student interest, leading to a lifeless curriculum and poor teaching.

Inaccurate Charges of Mediocrity   Advocates for a learner-based curriculum assert that the current standards campaign is an extension of a centuries-old tendency for people to blame their schools for almost anything that seems to go wrong in the society around them. In modern America, they charge, school bashing has been elevated to an art form, one of the media's favorite sports, and politicians of all stripes eagerly take advantage of every opportunity to criticize and blame the schools for every manner of fault. The schools, however, are never credited with positive contributions, such as having anything to do with the great economic boom of the 1990s. Schools are always at fault when things go wrong, but they are never responsible for things that work well.

Advocates for learner-based curriculum point out that schools are better, astonishingly better, than they were in the "good old days." In 1940, for example, American schools had a 50% drop-out rate, pregnant girls were expelled, and the handicapped and learning disabled were warehoused out of sight. In 1940, 75% of all poor and minority students were isolated in segregated schools. Illiteracy was four times higher than today, and the life expectancy for a 16-year-old was six years shorter. Critics of standards-based reform assert that to argue 1940 was great is to argue that a segregated, stratified school system serving only a minority of its students was superior to schools of today. Unfortunately, and inaccurately, Americans always seem ready to believe that today's youth represent the worst in history and that schools are cauldrons of ignorance, crime, and failure (Carson, Huelskamp, & Woodall, 1992).

Advocates for a learner-based curriculum point out that charges of mediocre performance are often inaccurate or plainly false. No evidence exists, for example, of declining test scores; if anything, test scores have been going up for the last 30 years, without any public celebration. Scores on tests such as the Scholastic Aptitude Test, "SAT," the National Assessment of Educational Progress (NAEP), and Advanced Placement (AP) tests are all positive, compared with any year in the past. U.S. economic competitiveness has not suffered, and American schools do not compare unfavorably with those of other nations (Berliner & Biddle, 1995).

Accountability and Standards-Based Reform   Many critics argue that standards-based reform, while well intentioned, has been pushed roughly aside in favor of politically motivated massive testing and harsh accountability measures that have a series of negative consequences. In states such as California, Florida, North Carolina, South Carolina, and many others, schools now receive publicly announced grades on the basis of how well their students do on tests, and they receive punishment or reward based on how well or poorly they score. In such circumstances, critics avow, fear replaces joy as the central emotion of learning. Teachers and school leaders fear the loss of their jobs, and students and parents fear the possibility of failing to graduate unless the final, big test is passed. Differentiating instruction is discouraged, in favor of large group teaching. A "drill and practice" mentality abounds, and the curriculum is "a mile wide and an inch deep" (U.S. Department of Education, 1999).

Harsh accountability measures, critics of standards-based education allege, drive out much of what is positive and exciting about quality curriculum. Students who will do very well or very poorly on tests (gifted and very low performing students) may be ignored, in favor of groups of students whose test scores can be influenced by short-term intensive cramming efforts. Programs such as recess, electives, class meetings, health, discussions of current events, the arts, and even science and social studies are eliminated or pushed into the background. Tracking and ability grouping, practices with very negative outcomes, flourish in high-stakes testing and accountability atmospheres.

Unwieldy, Poorly Planned, Knee-Jerk Efforts Those who abhor standards-based reform charge that it has been implemented in a careless, hurried, "ready, fire, aim" approach. Warren Simmons, of the prestigious Annenberg Institute for School Reform, for example, argues that too many states have test-driven reform masquerading as standards-based reform. Sets of standards can be too lengthy, too cumbersome, too prescriptive, too fact-based. The result is a curriculum that forces both teachers and students to race through the year without any time to reflect and without opportunity for deep inquiry. And, virtually everyone admits, the best educational experiences are those in which students and teachers arrange the curriculum to delve deeply into topics of great interest. Standards-based education endangers such pursuits, critics declare.

Tests and accountability measures have been implemented while they were being planned, leaving many educators and students confused about both procedures and outcomes. A school's grade can change dramatically from year to year—one year a "D," the next an "A," and the third year a "C." Such volatility cannot possibly reflect real changes in learning or school quality. Often, standards documents are burdensomely large, because the consensus process results in the inclusion of every committee member's pet interest. In addition, reliance on such tests ignores other measures of success, such as the number of students in a district who are admitted into top colleges and universities.

Punishing the Victim   Critics state that, instead of supporting the improvement of education among minorities and the poor, standards-based reform has further stigmatized and punished those students and the schools where they learn. Cynical educators charge that the square footage of homes in a school's area, or the number of students in the school wearing braces, is more closely correlated with a school's scores on state tests than the type of curriculum taught. One study of the accountability process in Florida, for example, showed that a school's scores could be very accurately predicted on the basis of four factors closely related to socioeconomic status: the number of students on free and reduced-price lunch, the number of gifted students in the school, the attrition rates during the year, and the size of the school (Hunter, 2000).

Alfie Kohn (2000) charges that the whole process works like a gigantic, social-class-based sorting device, defeating efforts at educational equity. Because the bar for success in meeting the standards is continuously raised, increasing numbers of schools serving minorities and poor, and the students in those schools, will be labeled as failures. When accountability measures are not paired with serious attempts to improve the schools, the result is frustration, anger, and failure. The real problem, critics such as Jonathan Kozol argue, is not the absence of standards, it is the presence of poverty.

Antidemocratic Nature   Carl Glickman (2001) warned that standards-based reform may be much more fundamentally antidemocratic than educators and parents realize. He states that narrow standards, which dictate single-format tests based on one group's idea of what students should learn, may be dangerously antidemocratic. If standards-based reform leads to the establishment of a single, mainstream idea of education, with little or no allowance for dissent, democracy will inevitably suffer. When standards lead to standardization, diversity takes a back seat. Unilateral state control over anything as important as the curriculum invites dogmatism, intolerance, and other challenges to democratic procedures.

Deborah Meier (2000) insisted that when decisions about curriculum are removed from the hands of teachers and school leaders (the adults students know), the natural authority of the local community is undermined and an unnatural and unhealthy regard for remote officialdom is fostered, which places democracy at risk. In standards-based reform, school boards become largely irrelevant, and the future of students is increasingly placed in the hands of remote state or federal officials, once again a challenge to community-based democracy.

These procedures, critics argue, lead to the installation of a common, highly specific, back-to-the-basics style core of knowledge that much resembles the curriculum of E. D. Hirsch's best-selling 1987 book, *Cultural Literacy.* Such compendiums of prescriptions are ridiculed by critics such as Alfie Kohn as nothing more than a long list of names, dates, and isolated facts, "from

Plato to NATO." This sort of conservative curriculum, the result of greater increments of state and federal control, does not represent the diversity, or the learning needs, of an evolving America.

Arthur Costa (1995, p. 23) argued that curriculum derived from such conservative sources is drawn from discrete academic disciplines that emerged from "largely male-and-western-oriented ways of thinking." As American culture evolves, incorporating more female and non-western voices, Costa stresses that the school curriculum must reflect richer, more diverse views of how humans construct meaning. In fact, Costa points out, the old disciplines, upon which the curriculum has been traditionally based, are themselves being supplemented, if not replaced, by more generalized, transdisciplinary, problem-focused bodies of knowledge. Insisting on rooting the curriculum of the future in the disciplines of the past may be foolish as well as antidemocratic.

Best Practices in Teaching Are Discouraged Standards-based education, critics claim, punishes constructivist, problem-based teaching styles, because it implies that there is nothing for learners to construct, only memorize. Arthur Costa, a long-established writer about curriculum, declares that "learners need to discover that they can be self-referencing, self-initiating, self-evaluating—that comprehension comes from within." He asserts that quality learning suffers when students learn only discrete parts of content, losing sight of "the beauty, interconnectedness and spirituality in the world" (Costa, 1995, p. 23). Standards-based education, Costa says, leads to a view of learning as passing a test, not constructing meaning and developing wisdom. At the least, good teaching and learning are too complex to be judged by any single measure such as a standardized test, which leaves out creativity, ingenuity, effort, and other important intangibles. America, Costa continues, may be great because of such intangibles, because it values and teaches creativity, problem solving, teamwork, and life-long learning instead of the right answers that are connected to standards.

Other critics of standards-based reform believe that, at its worst, the emphasis on standards, testing, and accountability squeezes out the energy, enthusiasm, and the legitimacy of efforts to build curriculum experiences around the real needs and interests of the students. A long series of highly respected educators, from John Dewey and Carl Rogers to contemporary advocates such as James Beane and Gordon Vars, has firmly established the principle that student motivation, engagement, and authentic learning are highest when teachers are able to construct their curriculum in harmony with their students' own interests. They assert that if teachers are pressured to adhere to a single, state-mandated and tested monolithic curriculum, it will be the opposite of what decades of research and experience have led educators to accept as best practice.

Jay McTighe, co-creator of the Understanding by Design program, likens the approach of teaching to the test to "trying to cover a mattress with a bedspread: the content is stretched out to encompass all of the test material, but the result is a thin level of understanding rather than a deeper and more meaningful one" (Education Update, 2001, p. 4). This kind of knowledge is seldom retained or applied because it "simply does not 'sink in.'" "Most people," says McTighe, "remember cramming to study for a quiz or a test in high school, but soon after the test, they forgot the material because it was never presented to them in a meaningful way." Constructivist teaching, the kind of instruction that focuses on the creation of meaning and leads to frequent application and long-term retention of the material, may suffer badly under standards-based reform.

The middle school movement has flourished, many say, because of its almost single-minded devotion to the characteristics and needs of the young adolescent. This being the case, middle school educators might be expected to be present in large numbers among those who criticize the process of making curriculum decisions on the basis of state standards identified by bureaucrats working at a great distance from the middle school classroom. And this is the case. In June 1991, the Board of Trustees of the National Middle School Association was considering for adoption 10 statements to express the strong beliefs of the group. The first one dealt with curriculum. It stated:

> Just as a middle level school is organized to meet the needs of young adolescents, NMSA believes that middle school curriculum, instruction, and assessment should
> * Relate to the lives of students
> * Integrate knowledge
> * Focus on the process of learning and
> * Be delivered in an environment in which exploration is pervasive and which is activity-based and students can learn from failure.
> The NMSA Board of Trustees stated its belief that each of these characteristics is a necessary facet of the middle school curriculum and contributes to learning that is dynamic and meaningful. (NMSA, 1991, 1)

STANDARDS-BASED REFORM AND THE MIDDLE SCHOOL CURRICULUM

Are middle level educators required, because of their commitment to the young adolescent, to reject the totality of the standards-based education process? Or must educators committed to the middle school movement deferentially succumb to the demands of standards-based reform? Is there a balance point between political and pedagogical emphases in educational reform? Can conscientious middle school educators respond to the demands of standards-based reform while remaining loyal to their commitments to the young adolescent and the middle school concept? Where does this leave middle school educators concerned about making the right curriculum decisions? We believe, with a strong note of caution about the tentativeness of such possibilities, that such a rapprochement may be possible.

The National Forum to Accelerate Middle-Grades Reform   The work of the National Forum to Accelerate Middle-Grades Reform may be one pathway to this end.[1] The forum, working during the 1990s with a number of national charitable foundations, commissioned the Education Development Center (EDC) to draw up a set of comprehensive guidelines for making middle school curriculum decisions.[2] *Aiming for Excellence* was the result of their attempts to craft curriculum guidelines that fit the forum's three basic requirements for middle school curriculum: academic rigor, equity, and developmental appropriateness. *Aiming for Excellence* is a comprehensive set of guidelines for making curriculum decisions based on a standards approach. The entire set of comprehensive guidelines can be downloaded from EDC's Web site.

While many of the most vigorous defenders of learner-based middle school curriculum (e.g., James Beane, Gordon Vars) were not invited to be members of the forum, many of the participating professionals have given years of time and effort to the middle school movement. The forum attempted to commit, simultaneously, to both standards-based reform and to improving the quality of education for the young adolescent. The members of the forum asserted their belief that a rigorous standards-based curriculum can be offered that is also fundamentally equitable and developmentally appropriate. Vigorous critics of standards-based reform would hasten to point out, however, that the guidelines of the forum do not support learner-based curriculum as firmly as they would wish.

Combining Standards and Integrative Curriculum   Even vigorous, decades-long defenders of learner-based, integrated curriculum, however, seem to have come to grips with the power of the standards-based reform movement. In a series of position papers, Vars and Beane assert that middle school educators can "reap both the benefits of genuine student-centered, integrative curriculum and instruction and also develop student competencies in state-mandated standards so that students can make acceptable scores of typical standards-based tests" (Vars & Beane, 2000, p. 1).

The process begins with the identification of generic competencies that cut across the barriers of subject matter lines. Because virtually all of the state

---

[1]For more information about the aims of the National Forum to Accelerate Middle-Grades Reform, see Lipsitz, Mizell, Jackson, & Austin, 1997.

[2]Education Development Center Inc., 55 Chapel Street, Newton, MA 02458-1060. Phone: 614-969-7100. Online at www.edc.org.

standards (and the tests that accompany them), and those of groups such as the National Forum to Accelerate Middle-Grades Reform, are set up in terms of conventional subject matter areas, this barrier of separateness must be overcome for integrated curriculum to thrive. Common learnings must be a high priority in classroom curriculum planning.

Vars and Beane (2000) cite several organizations that have produced sets of standards that cut across subject areas, focusing on common learnings, but do so in a way that manages to capture the essence of the separate subject standards. The venerable National Study of School Evaluation (NSSE) and the Alliance for School Reform have collaborated to examine the standards established by other national organizations and develop "Schoolwide Goals for Student Learning" in six categories.

1. Learning to Learn Skills
2. Expanding and Integrating Knowledge
3. Communication Skills
4. Thinking and Reasoning Skills
5. Interpersonal Skills
6. Personal and Social Responsibility

The Center for Occupational Research and Development (CORD), in Waco, Texas, has also identified common learnings drawn from the standards developed by national organizations. The group has, according to Vars and Beane, generated a database of 38 sets of standards and 53 core standards that are suitable for integrated curriculum planning. McREL developed a set of standards that cut across subject areas at the same time that it was developing a comprehensive set of subject standards. Even some commercial publishing companies have begun to develop sets of standards that can be used to plan integrated curriculum programs.

Vars and Beane assert that teachers who are eager to engage their students in integrated curriculum studies could use any, or a combination, of those sets of common learning standards. In doing so, the teacher could be confident that his or her students would also be engaged in content that was essential to the standards developed at the state department of education. A teacher might be planning a unit that would focus on communication skills, for example, but could be confident that he or she would, at the same time, be teaching essential language arts standards.

Vars and Beane suggest that teachers who want to plan an integrated curriculum can refer to state standards before, during, and after they have generated their unit plans with their students. As they plan units with their students, teachers can identify standards that have been included. During a unit, perhaps as a part of a transition to a new topic, teachers can highlight subject standards that are embedded in what the students are learning. Teachers can even use a technique Vars and Beane call "back mapping." Here, teachers conclude their teaching unit by "identifying and labeling the standards and competencies included in a unit" that had just been completed (Vars & Beane, 2000, p. 3).

Vars and Beane recommend that using common learning standards is one way to teach in more exciting, learner-based ways and still satisfy administrators and parents that essential state standards have been effectively incorporated. They suggest that involving students in the process of selecting standards provides excellent opportunity for the development of critical thinking skill, collaborative skill, and other outcomes that are part of many state standards.

Vars and Beane also cite a number of research reviews (e.g., National Association for Core Curriculum, 2000) that conclude that students working in "any type of interdisciplinary or integrated curriculum do as well as, and often better than, students in a conventional departmentalized program" (2000, p. 2). The positive outcomes for integrated curriculum programs are found in self-contained classes, block time programs, or as a part of the more commonly found middle school interdisciplinary team. Furthermore, these results were found in studies for which subject-centered standardized tests were the determining variable.

WORKING TO COMBINE STANDARDS AND INTEGRATED CURRICULUM IN THE CLASSROOM: A CLASSROOM MODEL

Mary Jo Ziegler and Barbara Brodhagen were partner teachers at Sherman Middle School, in Madison, Wisconsin. Their approach to combining integrated curriculum with state standards is described in a series of articles published in the *Core Teacher*, a newsletter of the National Association for Core Curriculum.[3] Those who are familiar with their teaching say that this partner team represented a high level of skill and enthusiasm for combining both learner-based curriculum and state standards into an exciting program of studies for their classrooms. Their two-person team provided science, social studies, math, and language arts to a group of about 50 6th graders, diverse in terms of their ethnic and socioeconomic backgrounds.

Curriculum Development Aiming to develop a democratic classroom, which they viewed as essential to a learner-based curriculum, Ziegler and Brodhagen provided a great deal of opportunity for their students to shape the studies in which they will engage. So, the annual curriculum development process began with students identifying the big questions they have about themselves and the world around them. First as individuals, later in small

---

[3]National Association for Core Curriculum, 1100 East Summit Street, Suite #5, Kent, OH 44240-4094. GVarsNACC@aol.com.

groups, and finally as a class, students brainstormed and developed common questions that then became common themes. Themes were given titles, and the content involved became units that structured the learning and teaching for the year. One year, the small team of partners Ziegler and Brodhagen and their students planned, taught, and learned in a series of units with intriguing titles such as Water World, Circle of Life, The Young and the Restless, People and Money, How Things Work, Space and Beyond, Weird and Weirder, and Where Is Peace?

At this point in the planning process talented teaching is required. When themes had been chosen, the class voted on which unit would be the first one for the year. All of the questions connected to that unit were collected, students suggested activities that might be productive, and the teachers pulled it all together in a design that they believed would engage the students, answer their initiating questions, and cover the required state standards. The teachers "work to keep learning interesting by incorporating many group projects and hands-on activities. We use performance, portfolio, and traditional assessments to collect data on our students' learning" (Ziegler, 2000a, p. 2).

Eventually, the teachers felt pressured to assure parents and others that students were not just having fun but were also mastering the standards that the state had intended for that grade level and its curriculum. So, Ziegler and Brodhagen identified the Wisconsin standards and the corresponding benchmarks and organized them into a document that parents and other teachers could understand. A few colleagues worried that the team had capitulated to standards-based education and the teachers had to respond frequently to the question "You aren't planning to teach to the standards, are you?" (Ziegler, 2000b, p. 5). The teachers' response was along the lines of "No, we're teaching the way we always have; we just make sure that standards are included."

When asked about whether the attention to standards made a positive contribution to her students' learning, Ziegler (2000b, pp. 5–6) put it this way:

> At the time this question was asked, I had no good answer because I was just beginning the project. And the standards did seem like a lot of documentation for the administration to play politics with. But after sitting down and looking through the standards and actually documenting what we had taught, our work really will, in the end, benefit my students. Why? Because it caused me to be a more reflective teacher. The students leaving my classroom might have had a less outstanding mathematics experience during their sixth and possibly their seventh-grade years. Our mathematics program will be strengthened dramatically because we looked through the standards and made some improvements.
>
> I am not naïve enough to think that there are no dangers involved in setting standards for education. I am not a proponent of the standards being used to evaluate teacher performance. . . . I feel standards and benchmarks,

along with action research, can be used as a wonderful tool for reflective teaching, as a mid-year analysis in order to make adjustments, or as an end of the year check to make those few tweaks in programming that could really bring it all together for the students who enter my classroom the following year. These are steps that can make a strong teacher's curriculum even stronger.

Most important of all, we as teachers are set free by the standards and benchmarks. "How?" you ask. Well, they are very general, concept-and-skill-driven documents. Therefore, as long as we cover those concepts during the school year, we are doing our jobs. This means that we can choose the teaching style we feel most comfortable with. We can develop our curriculum in the way we feel most appropriate to our students. We can use the materials and activities we feel work best with our class and style to bring these standards and benchmarks to life in our classrooms.

It would be very beneficial if students and parents could see the documentation of the standards and benchmarks they have met and have yet to meet at conference times and before heading to high school. I feel that it would give them more confidence and motivation in their learning.

Gordon Vars, longtime advocate for integrated curriculum, reflected on Ziegler's story and argued that

it is not the standards, themselves, that pose a threat to curriculum integration. As Mary Jo says, the public that supports schools has a right to state their expectations. If they are reasonable in number, developmentally appropriate, and stated in language understandable by teachers, parents, *and students*, they provide useful guidelines for teacher-student planning of the curriculum and instruction.

The damage comes when expectations are converted into absolute mandates, imposed uniformly on all students, regardless of their individual differences, and then enforced with high-stakes tests that cannot possibly assess the subtle nuances of person-centered, democratic education. (2000, p. 7)

Watershed Teacher and author Mark Springer, of Radnor Middle School (RMS), in Wayne, Pennsylvania, has been identified with another example of the best that integrated curriculum can offer, as an acceptable alternative to standards-based reform. On a 7th grade team at RMS, an integrated curriculum program that has come to be known as Watershed replaces the entire curriculum for that grade. Watershed covers essential skills and concepts "through an integrative, thematically oriented combination of classroom and on-site learning experiences. Skills and concepts taught in traditional disciplines are integrated and focused on the comprehensive examination of a specific watershed (in the Brandywine River Valley). Elements and processes from English, mathematics, science, social studies/history, reading, art, music,

BOX
3.1

King Middle School Curriculum

At King Middle School (KMS), in Portland, Maine, longtime school leader Mike McCarthy has helped the staff move to a vision of curriculum that provides an exciting melding of standards and integrated curriculum. At King, an exemplary middle school in many respects, the faculty has fully adopted the Expeditionary Learning model, an integrated curriculum design promoted by the New American Schools, based on Outward Bound programs.

At King, all teachers and students are assigned to interdisciplinary, heterogeneous, looping teams that are organized in two grades 6–8 houses, Windsor and York. Within these teams, the organizing principle for much of the curriculum is what is called an "expedition." Expeditions are interdisciplinary units organized around a set of state standards, but with a radically unusual focus. Each unit, after being grounded in state standards, is built around a provocative theme that is connected to both school and community concerns. Connection to the community and service are required components of every expedition. Two such 9–12-week units from the 2000–2001 school year were "A Park Grows in Portland" and "Dream On."

Each unit always begins with a guiding question that provides a continuing focus for the unit. In the case of "A Park Grows in Portland," the guiding question was "What does a park mean to a city?" At the beginning, and throughout the unit, this question keeps calling teachers, students, and community members back to the heart of the unit. Each unit also always ends with individual and group presentations.

In the case of the unit "Dream On," a mathematics-centered unit, students were involved in an expedition that challenged their team to work with the city committee in charge of designing a new aquarium. Students on the team designed their own aquarium and presented their design to the city committee. So impressed with the work of the middle school students, the members of the city committee decided to move their meetings to the school.

The fact that 28 languages are spoken by the 700 students in the school, and a quarter of the student body is classified as LEP (limited English proficiency), makes what happens at KMS even more significant. The faculty at King would assert that all students can learn in a model such as theirs. Other schools—for example, Crabapple Middle School, near Atlanta, Georgia, a great middle school in its own right—have been persuaded to adopt the model as a consequence of the success at King.

industrial arts, and physical education are included" (Arnold, Silcox, & Springer, 1998, p. 2).

Among the many active learning experiences connected to the year-long project, students are involved in conducting laboratory tests, examining geological history, analyzing and constructing maps, learning the skills required for safe stream exploration, and researching the history of the stream and its role in the region's agriculture, industry, and culture. Guest speakers abound. Field trips are frequent and focused. The result, observers and participants report, is an opportunity for students to see the interrelated nature of learning, to see their own connection to that learning, and to develop personal meaning as a consequence of their experience in the year-long unit (Arnold et al., 1998, p. 3). (For another example of combining standards and integrated curriculum, see Box 3.1.)

INTEGRATED CURRICULUM: AN IDEAL FOR MIDDLE LEVEL CLASSROOMS

Curriculum can be developed and introduced into middle school classrooms in many ways, and, for decades, if not centuries, much discussion and even heated debate has taken place about definitions and interpretations of various curriculum designs and their value for learners. The current debate seems to have devolved to a match between advocates of standards-based reform and those who hold high the banner for student-centered, integrated curriculum. Having already considered that debate here, the reader should easily grasp the meaning of the term *integrated curriculum* and understand why so many middle school educators support the idea of integrated curriculum. Far from being a revolutionary proposal, however, an integrated curriculum turns out to be fairly conventional when examined closely. In an integrated curriculum, teachers, such as Ziegler and Brodhagen, draw the content of the unit from a combination of three important and less than controversial areas: student needs and interests, adult concerns, and curriculum standards.

Student Needs and Interests First, and most significantly, supporters of integrated curriculum tap into their knowledge of the characteristics and needs of early adolescents to be sure that planning learning experiences centers on important aspects of those attributes. Ideally, the students themselves are drawn into the planning process, to suggest the needs that they feel most strongly. Teachers plumb student interests and needs for problems and concepts that can be turned into themes for the curriculum. Given that the middle school movement is based on a dedication to the characteristics and needs of the young adolescent learner, why these educators find the idea of integrated curriculum so appealing should be obvious.

Adult Concerns   Second, the teachers recognize that early adolescents share many profound human concerns with adults and others. These concerns of the larger world, which early adolescents share, become the second well from which curriculum content is drawn. Early adolescents are, for example, fiercely interested in the issues of fairness and justice, on a number of levels. The United States, for more than 200 years, has been struggling to fairly balance freedom and justice in the lives of many different Americans. Two important strands thus intersect: the personal concerns of early adolescents and the social concerns of all Americans. Out of the fusion of these two perennial concerns might come a unit titled "The Struggle for Freedom in the United States." The objectives of such a unit would not simply be American history in disguise but would involve early adolescents in an examination of the meaning of concepts such as responsibility, community, liberty, and so on, in their own daily lives as they "struggle for freedom" on their own. Such a unit, comprehensively planned, might involve a team and its students for two to three or more periods of the school day and might last for several weeks.

Curriculum Standards   Because even teachers of integrated curriculum work in the real world of public schools, planning does acknowledge and include the subject matter from state and national standards and other sources. It may be more realistic to envision the integrated curriculum as the intersection of three sets: student needs, adult concerns, and curriculum standards set by the state or national organizations or both. Such a curriculum would draw, perhaps equally, from the concerns students have about their own lives, the social problems of the larger world, and the subject matter that has been designed and mandated for the curriculum from more remote sources.

The Rationale for the Integrated Curriculum

While few middle school educators have argued that the entire curriculum design should be drawn from this framework, James Beane and Gordon Vars (Beane, 1993, 1996; Vars & Beane, 2000; Vars, 1997, 2001b) have, however, continued to present a forceful case for this very concept. A number of theses presented by Beane, Vars, and others regarding the desirability of the integration of the middle school curriculum are summarized as follows:

- The curriculum should be based on the living concerns of those who study it. Real problems or puzzling situations are much more likely to provoke strong motivation and persistent efforts. An integrated curriculum is based on this assumption.
- The curriculum should be presented in a way that provokes what John Dewey called a "reconstruction of experience." Dewey, a great American philosopher and psychologist, argued that learning is what happens after experience, that reflecting and integrating experiences into prior learn-

ings is what leads to new and significant learning. An integrated curriculum is much more likely to lead to this reconstructive experience.

- Grouping for instruction should always be flexible and based on the interests of the learners. An integrated curriculum makes this much more possible.
- Young adolescents should be encouraged to become increasingly independent, as they strongly wish to be. The choices and options embedded in an integrated curriculum facilitate this increasing independence.
- Significant learning always involves interaction with the environment and with other learners. An integrated curriculum builds in such opportunities as the heart of the instructional process.
- Integration is a psychological activity that persons must do for themselves. An integrated curriculum cannot be presented as the traditional curriculum almost always is. Integration comes from the encounter with exciting but disparate concepts that invite the learner to act on them in an integrative way.
- Middle school education ought to be general education. Only an integrated curriculum permits a focus on the combined general interests of learners and society instead of the increasingly specialized and segmented curriculum of the traditional program.
- Middle school learners have serious questions about themselves and their world that can serve as a legitimate base for a curriculum plan. An integrated curriculum has a natural integrity.
- Middle school youth should have a significant role in the development of the curriculum they study. An integrated curriculum promotes involvement and ownership of the course of study that results.
- Middle school students should have the opportunity to select at least part of what they want to learn, share new learning, hear peer opinions, challenge what they encounter, engage in cooperative effort, and sometimes be taught by other students. Instructional strategies that accompany an integrated curriculum (e.g., cooperative learning) are much more likely to provide these opportunities.
- Teachers who act as facilitators of learning, instead of as the "sage on the stage," are more likely to promote long-term, high-quality educational outcomes. An integrated curriculum makes this possible.
- The most productive classrooms are those in which students learn more, remember more, and apply more of what they learn to their own lives. An integrated curriculum is dedicated to these sorts of outcomes.
- A curriculum that covers fewer topics, but in much greater depth, is more likely to lead to a level of mastery that facilitates future learning and increases retention and transfer. The unit approach of the integrated curriculum makes this happen.
- Students can capitalize on prior knowledge when they approach problems and ideas from a variety of perspectives. This is inherent in the integrated curriculum.

- Students can surprise teachers with what they know and can do when the topic is not limited to a particular subject area. The integrated curriculum makes it much more likely that teachers will discover more about the capabilities of even their least successful students.
- Knowing is reinforced by application. Application is a natural part of the integrated curriculum.
- Many early adolescents, slower to develop intellectually than some of their classmates, require learning experiences that are concrete. The hands-on approach characteristic of the integrated curriculum works for both the advanced and the slower developing student.
- The traditional curriculum often ignores process and assumes skills have already been acquired. The integrated curriculum includes these areas as content as often as concepts and more traditional knowledge.
- Concrete experiences in one area of knowledge improve learning in other areas, providing for deeper understanding. The integrated curriculum brings this about naturally.
- Career teachers are renewed and invigorated as a result of planning and teaching concepts, skills, and processes that are fresh and new. The integrated curriculum forces this to happen.

Interdisciplinary Approaches

Finding teams of teachers working to implement occasional interdisciplinary units is much more common than encountering what Beane might identify as fully integrated curriculum. At Sebastian Middle School, in St. Augustine, Florida, the faculty has been working for several years to produce schoolwide interdisciplinary units like the one on the Olympics. Profoundly concerned about linking curriculum to student interests, faculty at Sebastian refer to this curriculum effort as Real Life Scenario Thematics. Richmond Heights Middle School (RHMS), east of Cleveland, Ohio, is a good example of the thousands of middle schools where an effort to infuse the curriculum with interdisciplinary flavor has paid great dividends in student interest and engagement. An 8th grade team at RHMS, led by teacher Andrea Dulik-Manes, featured, during one recent year, the following interdisciplinary units, all including the five basics (reading, language arts, mathematics, science, and social studies).

September:	Bubble Gum (history, chemistry, marketing)
October:	The Truth about Pumpkins (measurement, agriculture, holidays)
November:	Elections
December:	Gingerbread Men (anatomy, biography, novels, cooking)
January:	Careers
February:	Coins (history, mathematics, coinage and numismatics)
March:	Rockets

April: Birds and Worms (simulation on coloration, poetry)
May: Baseball (history, mathematics, and physics of the game)

In most middle schools where the creation of interdisciplinary units is a common experience, teams of teachers usually produce one such unit per semester, with a maximum of two per year. Monthly unit teaching, such as that at RHMS, is far less common.

Interdisciplinary approaches are not limited to thematic units produced by middle school teams. Much work is being done within traditional subject areas to broaden them in interdisciplinary, thematic ways. At Lewis and Clark Middle School (LCMS), in Jefferson City, Missouri, for example, the school's mathematics curriculum is organized in "thematic modules that connect big mathematical ideas to real-world applications." This curriculum is, furthermore, congruent with the standards of the National Council of Teachers of Mathematics. Language arts classes at LCMS utilize the workshop approach, and science uses the Foundational Approaches to Science Teaching (FAST) program, which is a series of interdisciplinary courses relating the traditional sciences to human use of the environment.

Pioneers of the Fully Integrated Curriculum   At Shelburne Middle School, in Shelburne, Vermont, teachers and students in grades 5–8 have long been persuaded of these advantages and have been involved in integrating the curriculum for many years. A long-standing organizational strategy there involves every teacher and student in one of three truly integrated, interdisciplinary teams: technology, humanities, and communications. Each student spends 12 weeks on each team. Each team involves a third of the faculty in the development of a yearly theme. Students and teachers meet in these team arrangements two afternoons a week, for two periods each session, all year long.

At Homer Junior High School (HJH), in Homer, Alaska, teachers created what amounts to a combination of exploration and integrated curriculum in what they call their "Cross-Curricular Program." For the last 12 days of school each year, students and teachers engage in what they describe as a "wholistic/thematic educational approach." Aimed to engage students with high-interest active learning, teachers extend the traditional curriculum into life-related application minicourses. Students not only earn course credit, but they also find school more meaningful and motivating. During one year, the following short, but intensive, 12-day courses were offered during this "fifth quarter."

Sew What (quilting, batik, silk-screen, etc.)
Marine Mysteries (exploring the Kachemak Bay)
Discover Homer (camping, beach walks, and canoe trips)
Touch and Goes (aviation and aerospace)
911 (careers and service in emergency and disaster relief)
Birds of a Feather (all about Alaskan birds)

Sports Literature

No Business Like Show Business (performing a musical review)

For Land's Sake (exploring the land bordering the local bay)

Caves to Castles (frame house building)

A.W.E.S.O.M.E. Experience (that is, art while enjoying some of our majestic environment)

Trails and More Tales (outdoor education)

At the Middle School of the Duke School for Children (DMS), a quasi-private university-affiliated school in Durham, North Carolina, the integrated curriculum is in full implementation. Small teams of two teachers and 48 students, similar to that of Ziegler and Brodhagen, pursue a fully integrated curriculum based on themes or questions that are the "connective tissues which tie together the work of a year in the classroom." In 2000–2001, students investigated the following large questions.

5th grade

What is human about being human?

What is my place in the world?

What changes and transitions will I experience?

How am I the same as and/or different from others?

In the 5th grade, these questions were addressed in a series of interdisciplinary units, such as Exploring New Worlds, Ships and Explorers, Human Body, 20th Century, and Inventions.

6th grade

What is civilization?

How are all things connected?

Does cooperation lead to survival?

What is technology and how does it affect human society?

How do we learn from the past?

In the 6th grade, students were involved in units with these topics: Survival, Community Building, Early Civilizations, Astronomy, Habitats, Patterns in Nature, and World of the Invisible.

7th grade

What is community?

What is community good for?

What does community do for me?

Where has it been and where is it going?

Seventh graders at DMS studied North Carolina, Community—Terra Nova, Progress and Change, Family Study, and Durham Study.

8th grade

How can change be described and predicted?

How is the world changing and how can I ensure a secure future?
What are rights and where do they come from?
What are my rights as a citizen and a global citizen?
How can I make a difference right now?

Eighth graders were involved in units that included Diversity/Study of America, Law and Justice, The Future, and Asia.

Educators at DMS are persuaded that centering the curriculum around these large, meaningful questions, and constructing units from them, helps students master important skills and content knowledge at the same time they come to realize that school can be a place that "helps them discover themselves and the world." We imagine that this is true. We speculate that the last three weeks of school at HJH are likely to feature a great deal more student time-on-task than might be likely if the Cross-Curricular Program were not in place. For years, efforts like those at Shelburne and Homer were exceedingly rare. In recent years, however, dozens of other exemplary middle schools have established similar programs, and information about such programs is widely available in dozens of books, conference programs, journals, and on the Web.[4] The Duke Middle School is one example of high level implementation in a small and private school setting.

Brown Barge Middle School

Brown Barge Middle School (BBMS), a school for able learners in Pensacola, Florida, offers an example of integrated curriculum at its intended best, in a public school setting. BBMS was created a decade ago, in an old, dilapidated, inner-city elementary school building, as a part of the school district's effort toward racial desegregation. To make certain that the school served its purposes well, a visionary principal, Camille Barr, was appointed early, to plan the program and hire the staff, far in advance of the usual time provided for such tasks. Barr was fascinated by the rationale for the integrated curriculum proposed by Beane and others. This fascination, and the vision of how it might be brought into daily practice, was to have profound consequences for the new school plan. Barr, and the other members of the school planning team, created a design for a school that was unique, especially in the way it combined three or four important aspects of the program.

Curriculum Streams Barr and her team were committed to the ideal of a fully integrated curriculum, seeking to go far beyond the more typical situation in which students might encounter an interdisciplinary unit once or twice a year,

---

[4]See, for example, Apple and Beane, 1995; Arnold, 1990; Forte and Schurr, 1994; Roberts and Kellough, 2000; and Stevenson, 1992.

if they were lucky to be on a good team. Using the funds from several planning grants, Barr and her colleagues created a vision and a plan for the school that remains, we believe, unmatched. The planning team created what came to be called "curriculum streams," groups of teachers and students who would teach and learn together for an entire 12-week period within the context of a particular thematic integrated curriculum.

The members of the planning team, acquainted with the challenges to effective integrated curriculum, believed that it would be virtually impossible to plan such complex and comprehensive curriculum units on the sort of spontaneous basis usually implied by advocates of integrated curriculum. So, while other plans for the new school in the old building were under way, curriculum planning teams began developing streams, learning units that were based on the needs and interests of young adolescents but offered on a regular basis without the need to reinvent the wheel every 12 weeks. New units, or streams, continue to be created today, just as many old favorites stay in place.

Student Choice   One way in which the faculty planned to maximize the engagement of students in the curriculum plans, and to offset the problem created by the fact that students would not be directly involved in the planning of each unit, was to radically increase the choices and options available to students and teachers regarding what they would learn and teach. Consequently, from the beginning at BBMS, every teacher and each student had the opportunity to choose which units he or she wished to be a part of in each year. In the late spring of each year, therefore, students and teachers have an opportunity to view the units, or streams, that will be part of the school plan for the coming year. Each teacher and every student then chooses in which units they wish to participate, with teacher-advisors assisting students with their choices. These advisors, or "teachers of record" as they are called, keep careful account of the choices made by their advisees, so students are not making choices on the basis of their friendships or swimming in the same stream year after year. Advisors also help students plan alternatives when their favorite is unavailable to them.

Figure 3.2 presents the schedule for three trimesters during a typical year at BBMS. During the fall (first) trimester, 7th and 8th grade students were enrolled in one of three multiage-grouped streams: Bridges, Environment, or Flight. Sixth graders, and others new to the school, were enrolled in the Orientation stream. In the second trimester, through February, all students could choose from four different streams: Today's Technology, Conflict/Compromise, Environment, or Art Motifs. The spring offerings for this particular year were Futures, Global Awareness, a repeat of the Flight unit, and the Exit stream.

Multiage Grouping   Being able to choose the stream in which one wished to learn means, also, that at BBMS students were grouped in multiage fashion,

First trimester				
Bridges	Stream 9:05 a.m.–10:18 a.m. 73 minutes	Encore/plan 10:20 a.m.–11:23 a.m. 63 minutes	A lunch 11:25 a.m.–11:50 a.m. 25 minutes Encore lunch	Stream 11:52 a.m.–3:30 p.m. 218 minutes
Environment	Stream 9:05 a.m.–11:48 a.m. 163 minutes	Encore/plan 11:50 a.m.–12:53 p.m. 63 minutes	D lunch 12:55 p.m.–1:20 p.m. 25 minutes	Stream 1:23 p.m.–3:30 p.m. 127 minutes
Orientation	Stream 9:05 a.m.–12:18 p.m. 193 minutes	C lunch 12:21 p.m.–12:52 p.m. 31 minutes	Encore/plan 12:55 p.m.–1:58 p.m. 63 minutes	Stream 2:00 p.m.–3:30 p.m. 90 minutes
Flight	Stream 9:05 a.m.–11:50 a.m. 165 minutes	B lunch 11:53 a.m.–12:18 p.m. 25 minutes	Stream 12:20 p.m.–2:25 p.m. 125 minutes	Encore/plan 2:27 p.m.–3:30 p.m. 63 minutes

Second trimester					
Today's Technology	Teacher of record 9:00 a.m.–9:15 a.m. 15 minutes	Stream 9:15 a.m.–10:13 a.m. 58 minutes	Encore/plan 10:15 a.m.–11:18 a.m. 63 minutes	A lunch 11:20 a.m.–11:45 a.m. 25 minutes	Stream 11:47 a.m.–3:30 p.m. 223 minutes
Conflict/ Compromise	Teacher of record 9:00 a.m.–9:15 a.m. 15 minutes	Stream 9:15 a.m.–11:45 a.m. 150 minutes	B lunch 11:47 a.m.–12:12 p.m. 25 minutes	Stream 12:14 p.m.–1:20 p.m. 64 minutes	Encore/plan 1:22 p.m.–2:25 p.m. 63 minutes / Stream 2:27 p.m.–3:30 p.m. 63 minutes
Environment	Teacher of record 9:00 a.m.–9:15 a.m. 15 minutes	Stream 9:15 a.m.–12:13 p.m. 178 minutes	C lunch 12:15 p.m.–12:40 p.m. 25 minutes	Stream 1:42 p.m.–2:25 p.m. 103 minutes	Encore/plan 2:27 p.m.–3:30 p.m. 63 minutes
Art Motifs	Teacher of record 9:00 a.m.–9:15 a.m. 15 minutes	Stream 9:15 a.m.–11:38 a.m. 143 minutes	Encore/plan 11:40 a.m.–12:43 p.m. 63 minutes	D lunch 12:45 p.m.–1:10 p.m. 25 minutes	Stream 1:12 p.m.–3:30 p.m. 138 minutes

Third trimester					
Futures	Homeroom 9:00 a.m.–9:15 a.m. 15 minutes	Encore/plan 9:20 a.m.–10:23 a.m. 63 minutes	Stream 10:25 a.m.–12:55 p.m. 150 minutes	D lunch 11:55 a.m.–1:20 p.m. 25 minutes	Stream 1:20 p.m.–3:30 p.m. 130 minutes
Flight	Homeroom 9:00 a.m.–9:15 a.m. 15 minutes	Stream 9:20 a.m.–11:20 a.m. 120 minutes	Encore/plan 11:22 a.m.–12:25 p.m. 63 minutes	C lunch 12:27 p.m.–12:52 p.m. 25 minutes	Stream 12:54 p.m.–3:30 p.m. 156 minutes
Exit	Homeroom 9:00 a.m.–9:15 a.m. 15 minutes	Stream 9:20 a.m.–11:18 a.m. 118 minutes	A lunch 11:20 a.m.–11:50 a.m. 30 minutes	Stream 11:52 a.m.–2:25 p.m. 153 minutes	Encore/plan 2:27 p.m.–3:30 p.m. 63 minutes
Global Awareness	Homeroom 9:00 a.m.–9:15 a.m. 15 minutes	Stream 9:20 a.m.–11:53 a.m. 153 minutes	B lunch 11:55 a.m.–12:25 p.m. 30 minutes	Stream 12:27 p.m.–1:02 p.m. 35 minutes	Encore/plan 1:05 p.m.–2:08 p.m. 63 minutes / Stream 2:10 p.m.–3:30 p.m. 80 minutes

FIGURE **3.2**

MASTER SCHEDULE AT BROWN BARGE MIDDLE SCHOOL

Reprinted with permission from Brown Barge Middle School.

where what a student seeks to learn took precedence over the number of years a student has been in school. (In Chapter 7, we explore the practice of multi-age grouping in some depth.) Flexible grouping seems to be an integral part of flexible curriculum and teaching.

Student as Worker   Theodore Sizer, creator of the Coalition of Essential Schools, is credited with a story about a Martian spy who comes to Earth to learn about education here. At the end of the story, the spy tells the Martian superiors that education, on Earth, is largely a process of having "the old people in the school work very hard while the youngest sit and watch." Sizer argued that it ought to be the students who are the workers in school. From the beginning, school leaders and teachers at BBMS took that admonition seriously, believing that students should shoulder the responsibility for their own learning. This meant something beyond making responsible choices about what one wished to learn. At BBMS, it also meant that the student was in charge of conducting the learning experience, of doing the work of learning as much as the teachers.

Consequently, as Figure 3.2 indicates, 6th graders and other newcomers were enrolled in the Orientation stream for the first 12 weeks of the school year. During this orientation, students learned how to swim in a curriculum stream, in a school that had abandoned traditional, familiar subject area lines. They also had to learn how to learn, because the faculty was dedicated to the concept of student as worker. During each 12-week stream, students had to pursue their own learning goals, collaborating with others as they did so. They had to demonstrate what they had learned and how their learning applied to their own lives and the life of the community. And they had to learn how to use the tools of learning responsibly.

Unification of Curriculum and Technology   The faculty at BBMS believed that the knowledge explosion and the revolution in technology that had occurred in the waning years of the 20th century had profound implications for teaching and learning in their school. They believed that not only should students be in charge of, and responsible for, their own learning, but they also believed that easy access to knowledge and the assistance of technology liberated both teachers and students from always following traditional ways of teaching and learning. So, every classroom at BBMS is inundated with the materials that are required by students engaged in their own learning: books, calculators, computers, the Internet, and everything else teachers could make available to students. Funds from a continuing series of grants have been dedicated to the wedding of curriculum and technology in a way that would facilitate the integrated curriculum at BBMS.

The results of all these efforts appear to have been impressively positive. Student success at BBMS, and in the high schools that they attend in their later years, is remarkably high. A waiting list of 700 students testifies to the satisfaction of parents and their children. The fact that the new principal was chosen from one of the staff members of the school, with the mandate to continue the mission of the school, indicates that central office leaders in the district are convinced of the value of the program there.

There seems to be little question that BBMS is a big success. But, does this indicate an unqualified endorsement of integrated curriculum as implemented at the school? Would all leaders have an equally compelling vision and the capacity to persuade so many others to join in the pursuit of that mission? Would all students be capable of success in such settings? Would the teachers in every building be able to do what the teachers at BBMS have accomplished? Would all parents be happy for their students to be enrolled in such a school? Is BBMS simply an anomaly?

Problems or Concerns with Moving to an Integrated Curriculum

Readers might reasonably ask why (if the rationale for the integrated curriculum is so strong, and the example of schools such as BBMS so inspiring) have only a few schools, or a few classrooms in many schools, moved to fully implement this strategy for planning and teaching? As with many ideal or model programs or processes, full and effective implementation is difficult to accomplish quickly or easily, or without opposition. Here are some of the possible reasons that the integrated curriculum plan is not fully present in school after school.

- Teachers may feel threatened by a curriculum with which they have no familiarity and uncomfortable when they are asked to teach what they themselves do not already know. The integrated curriculum may force teachers to abandon what they know for what they do not know.
- Most secondary teachers have studied a single subject, often for many years, to become proficient. The integrated curriculum may give little attention to this preparation.
- Effective classrooms are based on the concept of momentum. The best teachers can keep things moving. Doing so requires a familiarity with the curriculum that is difficult with the constant changes required by the integrated curriculum.
- Teachers improve what they teach from year to year as they accumulate more resources and refine their lessons. The integrated curriculum requires teachers to forgo improving upon what they have done well and to constantly improvise and fashion new lessons and units based on the needs of their current students.
- The integrated curriculum abandons special subject areas with which teachers have come to identify. Many teachers think of themselves as teachers of a specific subject. "I'm an English teacher. I even have a coffee cup that proclaims how important English teachers are." In an integrated curriculum, teachers sometimes are led to believe that their

subject areas are perceived as less important, secondary, and underval-
ued. This can be threatening, if not insulting, to experienced teachers.

- Teachers at the middle level have precious little planning time as it is.
The integrated curriculum requires considerable planning time, so that
teachers would have less time for the myriad tasks that teaming and
teaching will require of them every day, such as parent conferences, discussions of students, and so on.
- Standards-based reform focuses on specific subjects. In an integrated
curriculum, what is taught is not what is tested. As a result, test scores
may go down, the students will be at a disadvantage compared with others, and parents will complain.[5]
- What is taught in an integrated curriculum at the middle level is not
likely to be taught, at least in the same way, at the high school or recognized as having value by high school or college instructors. High school
teachers will be critical of the program, and students may suffer by comparison to those who have learned the traditional curriculum.
- The outcomes of the integrated curriculum may have little congruence
with the knowledge and skills that are required for admission to Advanced Placement courses in high school. Students may not be able to
enter such courses, and their college admission plans may suffer.
- Teacher certification is one of the few instruments that helps determine
whether teachers are minimally qualified. The integrated curriculum ignores teacher certification. There may be no way to supervise teachers
or to determine whether they have the necessary knowledge to teach the
curriculum in an integrated program.[6]
- Parents are already concerned about the academic soundness of the middle school concept. Many do not understand or accept the goals of an integrated curriculum. Dismantling the traditional curriculum may further
undermine parental confidence in and support for the middle school.
- Parents are suspicious of a whole host of strategies that accompany the
integrated curriculum: cooperative learning, the teacher as facilitator,
heterogeneous grouping, and the values that may emerge from such a
so-called new age curriculum. Even being successful with the integrated
curriculum may lead to failure as far as parent support is concerned.
- The human mind integrates what it learns under any circumstances. It is a
natural process of the mind. Mentally integrating and reconstructing one's
experience does not require a pre-integration of the curriculum. An integrated curriculum may even prevent the natural processes from working
well.

---

[5]However, the evidence from research seems to suggest that students in an integrated curriculum
setting do as well as or better than those who are not taught in this way.

[6]However, several states offer certification to teachers in broad fields or integrated curriculum in a
way that would make these concerns moot.

- Many subjects do not require integration of the sort required in a formally integrated curriculum. Understanding history, for example, does not require connections to science or math. Nor does understanding mathematics require a study of history.
- Some subjects, such as history, may not fare well or may even suffer when used as the focus of an integrated curriculum. Too many activities, for example, alphabetizing the capitals of the states, are not good ideas to begin with. Such activities find their way into an integrated curriculum far more frequently when teachers struggle to find ways of integrating subjects that do not naturally fit together.
- For 2,000 years, education has emphasized the individual nature of teaching and learning. The integrated curriculum does not recognize the value of that tradition and has an uphill battle even if the integrated approach was a better way.
- Learning for application, touted by the integrated curriculum, takes much more time to achieve. A great portion of the curriculum now covered in public schools would be ignored with an integrated curriculum. This would have both political and pedagogical consequences.
- Teachers may not have the skill to effectively plan an integrated curriculum. Collaborative planning and unit development are not part of the average teacher's repertoire, and the integrated curriculum demands more than teachers have to give.
- The integrated curriculum implies that teachers will set aside the traditional direct instruction style that they have always used. Simply put, some teachers do not have the skill to change their teaching in such major ways. Advocates of standards-based reform argue that the majority of teachers do not possess the skills required to effectively implement integrated curriculum. Only a relatively few lucky students have such teachers on a regular basis.
- The integrated curriculum may be a good theory, opponents assert, but, they say, it may be far less effective placed in widespread practice. A few excited and expert teachers will do a great job. Many teachers will do it reasonably well, and many others will refuse or do it poorly. This is just the way it is now, say those who caution others about implementation of new and complex efforts such as the integrated curriculum. Putting tremendous effort and hope into the integrated curriculum may be going on a fool's errand, they say, especially in light of the tremendous pressure to go in other directions being exerted by advocates of standards-based reform.

The Curriculum Wars

We are not sufficiently prescient to be able to predict the outcomes of the current struggle for control of the middle school curriculum. We are unwilling to predict the shape that will be taken by the curriculum in the next decades. We do earnestly hope, however, that the struggle over the curriculum is resolved and that the students to which the middle school concept is devoted are the ultimate beneficiaries.

EXPLORATION IN THE CURRICULUM

As one of the 10 fundamental tenets proposed for the junior high school, more than half a century ago, authors Gruhn and Douglas (1947) asserted that middle level schools should "provide opportunities for pupils to explore present interests and talents and to encourage them to identify new interests and talents which may lead to further education, vocational careers, and cultural, intellectual, and avocational pursuits" (p. 65). Educators in junior high schools saw themselves as being involved in providing exploration in the academic program and beyond.

Nearly a half-century later, most states continued to endorse the importance of exploration in the middle school curriculum. The Maryland Task Force on the Middle Learning Years wrote that

> an essential part of the curriculum for the middle grades is academic and non-academic exploration. Early adolescents are curious and inquisitive. They need to explore a variety of topics in many subjects to identify their own interests and talents, appreciate the abilities of others, and understand the contributions of many diverse individuals to society. In addition to academic exploration, a wide range of school-sponsored activities encourages students to investigate various areas of potential interests and talents. (1989, p. 46)

In 1995 the members of the National Middle School Association emphasized the importance of exploration in the manifesto of the organization, *This We Believe*.

> The entire curriculum, not just certain courses or activities, should be exploratory. There are three earmarks of an exploratory curriculum. First, it enables students to discover their particular abilities, talents, interests, values, and preferences. This self-knowledge helps students to prepare for adult life, not only in terms of vocation, but also as family members and citizens. Second, all courses and activities are taught so as to reveal opportunities for making contributions to society. Finally, exploratory experiences acquaint students with enriching, healthy leisure-time pursuits, such as lifetime physical activities, involvement in the arts, and social service. Such a curriculum helps to develop young adolescents who will become well-rounded adults. (pp. 23–24)

Middle level schools, regardless of name or time frame, have always and everywhere attempted to honor the exploratory nature of the young adolescent by providing equivalent curriculum experiences. The last two decades of the 20th century, however, have been unkind to an exploratory emphasis in the curriculum, including the integrated curriculum. Nonetheless, leaders in many exemplary middle schools are continuing and expanding the exploratory program regarded by many educators as the most significant contribution of the precursor to the middle school, the junior high school. Middle school educators hold staunchly to the belief that young adolescents have not lost their inherent curiosity or inquisitiveness and that the need to explore their talents and interests has not faded. Consequently, in spite of what others may demand of the schools in the middle, educators there insist on maintaining that exploratory emphasis. In spite of the pressure, in the early years of the 21st century, to attend primarily, if not exclusively, to narrow academic goals, middle school educators continue to inject exploration into the curriculum.

Some middle schools call all of these experiences "exploratories," while other schools refer to them all as "electives." Other schools differentiate the more formal ones as courses in an area often called Unified Arts, or Encore, and others as "activities." Some schools make some experiences, usually the more formal ones, required and the others elective.

Exploratory Courses

The characteristic credit-earning, graded, exploratory courses of the junior high were art, music, home economics, and industrial arts, and these four in some form remain prominent in middle school offerings a century later. However, now, along with typing (now word processing) and more computer science, a broader business course, drama and speech, health and physical education, and other courses, these exploratory courses may be termed Electives, Related Arts, Exploratories, Encore, or Unified Arts. In the 1990s, instruction in the area of computer science became a common part of many exploratory programs; the state of Florida has, for example, declared this area the "fifth basic." The original intent of the exploratory program was to have relatively brief, introductory courses for beginners, with longer, more intensive courses available another year for those interested. Curriculum developers in California expressed their continuing commitment to this exploratory emphasis, in a publication focused, ironically, on standards-based reform.

> Exploratory programs capitalize on the innate curiosity of young adolescents, exposing them to a range of academic, vocational, and recreational subjects for career options, community service, enrichment, and enjoyment. Exploratory topics include foreign languages, intramural sports, health, clubs, student government, home economics, technological arts, independent study projects, music, art, speech, drama, careers, consumer education, and creative writing. (Middle Grades Task Force, 1991, pp. 100–101)

Examples of Exploratory Programs

Because it is a very large school (3,200 students in 2001), Creekland Middle School (CMS), near Atlanta, Georgia, can offer a wealth of opportunity for exploration. At CMS, students in grades 6–8 are involved in two such courses every day, on a random, rotational basis, with most courses lasting for nine weeks. Here is what their size enables them to offer daily: art, band, chorus, computer science, family and consumer science, foreign languages (nine-week surveys and year-long), general music, health, physical education, strings, technology education, and theater arts.

At another large middle school, Mandarin Middle School (MMS) in Jacksonville, Florida, size enables the following daily exploratory offerings.

2D art (drawing, painting, printing)
3D art (ceramics, sculpture, fiber, fabrics)
Home economics
Technical education
Exploring manufacturing
Power and transportation
Business
Computer science
TV production
Drama
Graphics
Band
Chorus
Foreign language (Spanish, German)

At Sequoia Middle School, in Redding, California, during the 2000–2001 school year, the following electives were in place: band and advanced band, music appreciation, chorus, orchestra, art/crafts, art, drama, technology exploration, vocational education, social skills, and foreign language (Spanish and French). The course in technology exploration is typical of the sophisticated courses being offered in this area now. It included content in graphic projects (including Photoshop), editing projects (AVID Media Suite Pro), HyperStudio projects (including animation for the morning bulletin at school), video (including 19 different programs, projects, and formats), TV studio, teacher assistance in technology, home design, Web page design, and student-generated projects.

In the Silicon Valley area of California, the Union School District permitted the offering of the following separate exploratory or elective options in middle school: art, astronomy, careers, ceramics, current events, drama, exploring cultures, environmental design, flight technology, foods, foreign language, Good News, home economics, journalism, life skills, Quest, art technology, technology/computers, technology/keyboarding, and woodshop.

Another approach, illustrated by the Ballston Spa, New York, Middle School Humanities Program, utilizes the time traditionally allotted to music, art, industrial arts, home economics, and study hall and provides in this block a wider range of activities as follows: block printing, children's TV, clothing, colonial Ballston, copper foil, craft design, creative painting, crocheting and knitting, drama, food exploration, graphics, guitar, home decoration, lamp or pet cage construction, musicals, power mechanics, TV news, tutoring, tutoring projects, and tie-dyeing/macramé.

The Exploratory "Wheel" An example of a typical "wheel" sequencing of exploratory courses is the one followed by students at the two middle schools on the post at Fort Campbell, Kentucky. Sixth graders take six weeks of six of these: art, German, home economics, technology education, communications enrichment, music and drama, Spanish, and instrumental music. The same components are available to 7th graders for nine weeks and to 8th graders for 18 weeks. Beginning and intermediate band are offered at both the 7th and 8th grade levels.

At Lewis and Clark Middle School, in Jefferson City, Missouri, the wheel offers these six-week experiences to 6th graders: health, art, keyboarding, foreign language exploration, and Quest. In the 7th grade at LCMS, students take six weeks of foreign language exploration, MathWorks, art, technology education, family and consumer science survey, and research 1. In the 8th grade, students have a one-semester six-week wheel of creative and critical thinking, research 2, and analytical reading. Eighth graders also are offered semester and full-year elective courses in art, vocal music, orchestra, family and consumer science, technology education, Web publishing, speech and drama, instrumental music, and foreign languages. Hundreds of American middle schools follow similar rotating wheel-like procedures in their exploratory offerings.

At Chain of Lakes Middle School, in Orange County, Florida, the technology component of the exploratory program illustrates the sophistication in this area. At CLMS, students enter a technology exploratory class where they encounter all of these components: packaging, digital design, computer graphics, lights and lasers, broadcasting, flight technology, rocketry, robotics, electronics, plastics, mechanics, engineering, weather, and video production. This lab approach to technology, becoming more common in exemplary middle schools, is a far cry from older industrial arts programs experienced by previous generations.

At Kinawa Middle School, in Okemos, Michigan, one of the earliest exemplary middle schools in America, educators cling to a robust and varied exploratory emphasis that enriches the curriculum for every student. In a seven-period day, most students at all three grade levels can take two exploratory or elective classes. The program is carefully designed to ease the transition from elementary school to 6th grade at the middle level. Students in 6th grade choose from a long list of high-interest exploratory classes that change every six weeks throughout the first year in a wheel-like format. Here are just a few of the nearly 50 exploratory minicourses that were offered to 6th graders in the 2000–2001 school year.

ABC's of Kinawa	Babysitter Training
Art around the World	Bugs, Frogs, and Copepods
Castles, Codes, and Calligraphy	Classroom City (simulation)
Computer Graphics	Harry, Bilbo, Meg, and Dorothy
Medieval Banquet	Puppets and Plays
Serving Our Community	Singing for Fun
Two Amigos (foreign language exploration)	Kinawa Kares for Kritters

In the 7th and 8th grades, students choose their own year-long or trimester elective classes from a much more conventional list. When Kinawa students reach the 7th grade, they must make choices from a list of electives that includes, among many, a full year of band, choir, or orchestra; trimesters of art lab; ceramics; drawing; mixed media; several life skills courses (fabrics, food, consumer technology, or sewing); integrated technology; school newspaper; sports and games; drama; debate; and student assistant seminar. In the 8th grade, a full year of French, Spanish, or German becomes available along with the electives from the 7th grade.

The Special Situation of Band At many exemplary middle schools, the decision about how to place band in the exploratory offerings is an important one, and sometimes a difficult one to resolve satisfactorily. Middle school educators are often firmly committed to having students examine a broad range of interests and opportunities prior to making life-shaping decisions. This commitment rises naturally from an understanding of the characteristics and needs of young adolescents. At the same time, some students reach middle school having already discovered an interest, and perhaps a talent, in instrumental music. They may also be accompanied to school by influential parents who are committed to having their child continue to progress in music and to having the students ready to participate in the high school marching band when the time comes. This is particularly the case in areas where the marching band has long been a staple of the community experience and when expectations for contest-winning high school marching bands are extremely high. Under such circumstances, high school band directors, under pressure to produce to the level of community expectations, may, in turn, exert pressure on middle school instrumental music teachers to conform to their wishes for longer, more intense, and more exclusive instrumental music programs. When these pressures are combined, many middle school leaders find themselves under fire when they attempt to offer a curriculum that provides an exposure to instrumental music to all students and a program that also expects students who are talented musically to explore art, technology, home economics, and foreign language. What may be best for the middle school student may not always fit with what the community desires. Educational statesmanship, public relations skills, and the art of compromise thus may all need to come into play.

Typically, all 6th grade students are expected to participate in the school's 6th grade exploratory program. Then, in many schools, after having given one year to exploration, students who are irrevocably committed to instrumental music are permitted to opt out of additional exploratory participation and move to continuous involvement in instrumental music. In Orlando, Florida, for many years, all 6th grade students participated in a semester introduction to the exploratory curriculum, in units lasting only four and a half weeks each. All students took exploratory music during this period. Then, after the first semester, students interested only in band could remove themselves from further exploratory experiences.

In the new century, few seem satisfied by such compromises. All too often, instrumental music teachers complain that they are unable to offer the specialized training that they were prepared to provide and their talented music students are ready to receive. Scheduling that permits academic teams of teachers to plan together may force music teachers into grade level band arrangements, instead of woodwinds one period and brass another, or beginning band one period and concert band another. However, middle school curriculum leaders point out that the typical 6–8 grade middle school is "one third younger" than the former 7–9 grade junior high school and that "business as usual" is not developmentally appropriate and will not work. Further, others argue that the traditional approach to instrumental music in the middle grades (an intensive focus on the few and the talented), when judged by the criterion of continued participation in high school, college, and adult bands, is a staggering failure. It may well be that parents of instrumental music students understand, instead, that participation in band requires the development of a considerable amount of self-discipline in the student and that this is sufficient, in and of itself, to make the middle level band experience desirable. When association with many of the brightest, most talented, and affluent students in the school is offered as an added inducement, few parents may be able to resist.

Experience in Orlando's (Orange County) middle schools and many others, thus far, indicates that interest in instrumental music is increased, considerably, by the exploratory music program. But more data must be collected, from more programs, to be able to make a persuasive case to anxious parents and to those whose careers in instrumental music may seem to be at stake.

CLUBS AND SPECIAL INTEREST ACTIVITIES

As standards-based reform influences more middle schools to tailor their curricula to the requirements of state and national objectives, the curriculum consequently becomes more standardized. As a result, students may find much of their experience less interesting, certainly less personally meaningful, or just plain dull. For many years, educators in exemplary middle schools have been attempting to inject more interest and vitality into the curriculum. Special interest opportunities give young adolescent students the chance to explore without long-term commitment or concerns about their grade point average (GPA). They can investigate a new hobby or career possibility. They might find a way to be involved in leadership at some level or provide service to the school or community. Variously called "classes," "activities," "minicourses," and other terms, the short-term, noncredit, learning opportunities, which we are classifying as "special interest activities," have the following distinguishing characteristics.

- Student participation in organizing, selecting, planning, and conducting is encouraged.
- The activity meets much less frequently and for a shorter term than the traditional exploratory courses.
- Teacher responsibility for an activity is a part of the teacher's assignment, but teachers have much freedom in proposing and planning the particular activities they guide.
- The students' participation is voluntary and teachers give no grades. However, the teacher-advisor does help students make choices of appropriate activities.
- Students throughout a middle school may choose activities so that grades or ability levels or other factors toward homogeneity do not organize these activities. In some schools the activities are organized within teams. If the teams are heterogeneous, the activity groups are likely to be also.

Examination of the descriptions of special interest activity programs indicates various titles and examples. The Rupert A. Nock Middle School in Newburyport, Massachusetts, has the SPARK program: "The program is based on Service, Participation, Activity, Recreation and Knowledge, and in keeping with its purpose, it will be referred to as the SPARK program." The basic principles of the program, as stated in a bulletin for parents and others, further explained and illustrated the goals and nature of this special interest activity program.

- The SPARK program offerings are student-initiated.
- The SPARK program is established to develop a student's role as a cooperative, successful, and well-adjusted group member.

- The SPARK program offers a natural outlet for the curiosity, interest, and talents of the students.
- The SPARK program is to help students to develop positive interests and activities for leisure time.
- The SPARK program is a necessary creativity outlet for students to meet the adjustment needs for the transitional period between childhood and adolescence.

Separate lists of activities available for one quarter for students in grades 5–6 and grades 7–8 in each of the three houses of the school showed that each student has more than 40 activities from which to choose.

As principal of the Louisville Middle School, in Louisville, Colorado, and later at Broomfield Heights Middle School, in Broomfield, Colorado, Walt Grebing provided a SEARCH program (Students Educational Activities in Research and Creative Hobbies) and used PALS (Persons Assisting Louisville Middle School) in operating the program. During one quarter, 24 activities were offered on Mondays, 28 on Tuesdays, and 23 on Wednesdays. Activities open to all students in grades 5 through 8 included Silent Study, A Bank, School Services, New Games, Liquid Embroidery, Country Carvings, Ping Pong, Crewel, Minute Mysteries, String Program, All about Horses, Indoor Games, Outdoor Games, Puppetry, Soccer, Sign Language, Creative Writing, and Guitar, with many other activities restricted to one, two, or three grades. One list of activities for a recent year's programs had 44 separate possibilities, listed alphabetically from Adopt a Grandparent and Fun Fitness with the Principal on to Public Domain and Strategy Software for the Apple and finishing up with Writing Music: A Beginner's Guide. Accompanying descriptions made the options all seem attractive.

At the American School of Paris, France, an exemplary middle school has been in place for many years. The middle school offers a relatively large exploratory program for such a small school. Courses meet once weekly for a trimester, thus three possibilities are offered during the year. In the winter 2001 trimester, the offerings included minicourses in airplane design, photography, "movie madness," word processing, nutrition for girls, video production, the Web, chess, Knowledge Bowl, ping-pong, band, and Czech civilization (not a typical exploratory class). Students get "S" (satisfactory) or "U" (unsatisfactory) grades for these experiences.

At Marie Drake Middle School, in Juneau, Alaska, special activities were arranged for every Friday afternoon during the winter months, January to March. In one year, 29 activities were available in a school housing only 470 students, a wide range. Choices included BB guns, cartography, chess, computer adventure, Mathcounts, swing band, and a Tlingit language group. Similarly, at Thurgood Marshall Middle School, in Olympia, Washington, every Friday has been Exploratory Day, when students have four 90-minute periods of electives. Every teacher at Marshall offers an exploratory class, producing a wide range of options to tweak student interest. For example, 68 different minicourses were offered in a recent quarter.

Thunder Ridge Middle School (TRMS), in Aurora, Colorado, may win the prize for the most fervent commitment to special interest activities. According to enrichment program coordinator Ned Gilardino (2000), TRMS has offered more than 400 different minicourses during a 10-year period. Courses meet four days a week and last about four weeks each. The school organizes eight "MiniCourse" sessions in each school year. Each last-period-of-the-day enrichment class is open to students from any grade. All classes are created by faculty members, but a governing board consisting of teacher volunteers approves all of the classes on the basis of several criteria: sample lesson plans, incorporation of district academic priorities, and the use of the basic learning skills. All students receive grades for their work in the courses. Gilardino declares that registration of 1,250 students for the MiniCourses, eight times a year, has been the most daunting part, but a new computer program has allowed the registration process to be completed in one day. Ending every school day with a period devoted to courses teachers are eager to teach, and students have chosen to be a part of, has to be a good experience for everyone.

Clubs   Clubs often disappeared with the change from junior high to middle school, on the assumption that younger students had fewer sustaining interests that would lead to productive club membership. This may have been a mistake, and in the 21st century, many schools offer an enriching club program. Centennial Middle School, in Lino Lakes, Minnesota, has an activities program that combines intramurals and clubs into an exciting after-school program. The purpose is to "create fun and educational activities that meet the desires of the student body. It is our belief that activities make students feel better about school, themselves, and their future." We agree.

All clubs at Centennial meet from 2:30 p.m. to 3:45 p.m. once weekly. Activity busses are provided. During the winter of the 2000–2001 school year, clubs were active in the areas of art, chess, drama, Future Problem Solvers, Future Cities Competition, strategy games, guitar, holiday baking, Knowledge Masters, mathematics team, newspaper, science, scrapbook, speech team, stamps, and weight training.

Wakulla Middle School, in Crawfordville, Florida, is one of the highest scoring schools in the state, a pillar of academic achievement. Every Thursday the faculty offers a special interest schedule that makes room for an extra period. At Wakulla Middle School, exploratory clubs meet on a special schedule every two weeks for one semester, with membership and topics changing at the semester break. Among the clubs offered at Wakulla in recent years were 4–H, aerobics, checkers, cheerleading, chorus, comic books, crafts, crocheting, current events, Florida Future Educators, girls basketball, girls softball,

Junior Optimist Club, Just Say No, library aides, model making, movies, National Junior Honor Society, National Junior Art Honor Society, National Geographic Club, newspaper, running club (open to staff and students), science Olympics, small wood projects, stock market game club, student council, No Club (card games), yearbook, and Young Authors.

At Mt. Slesse Middle School, in Chilliwack, British Columbia, 24 clubs invited student membership during the 1999–2000 school year. In addition to those traditional clubs that might be expected were school beautification, electric car, floor hockey, ski and snowboarding, weight lifting, Web page, jazz, homework, and curling (a special sport in Canada). As long as they are not forced on students or teachers, and students can change clubs when their interests change, club programs make useful contributions to students' curriculum experiences. This is especially so, we think, in light of the severe curriculum alignment efforts pressuring many middle schools to eliminate courses, programs, or activities that do not match the state or national tests.

HEALTH AND PHYSICAL EDUCATION

The dominance of physical growth and development and related characteristics in the life of the middle school child demands that the program of health and physical education—health education, including sex education; physical education; and intramurals—be carefully planned and implemented. Concern about health and physical education continues to grow among many groups that examine the education of young adolescents. The Carnegie Council on Adolescent Development (1989) recommendations in this area were particularly well stated. Of the eight recommendations the council submitted, the one dealing with health and fitness was the only area of the curriculum singled out for special attention. The Carnegie Council urged educators to consider better health and fitness as the path to improving academic performance.

> Because of the direct link between the health of young adolescents and their success in school, the Task Force on Young Adolescents concludes that middle grade schools must accept a significant responsibility, and be provided sufficient resources, to ensure that needed health services are accessible to young adolescents and that schools become health-promoting environments. Schools need not deliver the services directly, but should make sure they are provided. Moreover, the school's role will vary with the availability of family and community resources and with community values. It is essential, however, that every middle grade school have a coordinated system to identify health problems and provide treatment or referral to outside health agencies and individuals.

The transformed middle grade school can meet these objectives by:

1. Ensuring student access to health service; and
2. Establishing the school as a health-promoting environment.
    (Carnegie Council on Adolescent Development, 1989, p. 61)

Echoing the concerns of the Carnegie Council, the National Middle School Association issued, as its first resolution of the 1989–1990 school year, the following statement.

> WHEREAS, young adolescents experience enormous physical growth and change, and WHEREAS, research suggests that for youngsters 10–15, health and fitness are not abundant, be it RESOLVED that all involved in the education and welfare of our young adolescents promote programs and practices which sustain integrated and activity-centered programs of health and physical education, ensuring the improvement of the nourishment, hygiene, safety, and health of our emerging young teens. (National Middle School Association, 1990, p. 56)

In 2000 the Carnegie Foundation renewed its commitment to healthy schools for young adolescents (Jackson & Davis, 2000), calling for program components that go far beyond traditional services in these areas. The Carnegie Council adamantly affirmed that "for middle grades students, health and learning are inextricably linked" (1989, p. 170). A healthy environment for learning would, it argues, include positive interethnic and interracial relationships, peer mediation and conflict resolution programs, peer support groups, and school-based clinics, as well as a modern health and physical education curriculum.

Health Education

Although aspects of health education may be treated in physical education, science, homemaking, and other classes, the great need for instruction in this area suggests separate classes with qualified instructors and adequate instructional materials. A school health coordinator, as envisioned by the Carnegie Council, with planning and advisory groups representing various related school areas and the parents and community, should help to develop and maintain an effective program. Typical content for the health program includes hygiene and personal care; nutrition; drugs, alcohol, and tobacco; communicable diseases, which includes AIDs education in many schools; mental health; community health services; consumer health; chronic diseases; and first aid and safety education.

Few middle schools deal with health education more thoroughly than do educators at Talent Middle School (TMS), in Talent, Oregon. A school of fewer than 700 students, TMS maintains a comprehensive health education program. Like most middle schools, TMS teachers work diligently in drug awareness activities, parent education, and cooperating with other agencies to provide special services for high-risk students. Beyond that, however, every student takes health for a semester, for each of the three years they attend TMS. In the other semester they take science. Three health teachers form an extended team with the school's mathematics and science teachers. Students are part of a multiage class, within a science, mathematics, and health team, with rotating content that is not dependent on the grade of the student. So, students at TMS experience health as one of the regularly scheduled classes they take as part of that team, not as an occasional topic on rainy days in their physical education class. The three semesters of health education at TMS is far beyond the typical health education young adolescents get. It is a goal for all middle schools to emulate.

Programs like those at Talent, built on an understanding of the characteristics and needs of early adolescence, might also include education and screening for maladies that typically make their appearance during this time of life, including epilepsy and scoliosis. Sex education can be provided in various ways. Although its provision has been and may remain controversial in some communities, the need for emerging adolescents to understand their changing bodies and the specifics of human sexuality is critical. In the new century, fewer communities find such programs objectionable. Teenage pregnancies and sexual diseases have become national problems and local emergencies, and the related problem of changing life styles and mores as to marriage and the family also need to be considered. For certain, any specific course, unit, assembly, or other approach to sex education must be carefully planned with, and sponsored by, parent representatives along with representatives of the health professions and the church. Concentrated programs involving medical and other community representatives, along with a definite unit in the health program and related instruction as appropriate in science, physical education, and other subjects, seem a good combination.

Physical Education

Frequent physical movement is characteristic of the middle school student. One comical definition of the typical 6th grade boy, frequently heard in workshops and conferences, is "someone who runs everywhere he goes and when he gets there, he hits something or someone." Attempts to keep these students sitting still for the greater part of the day are, one might guess, doomed to failure. Unfortunately, although daily vigorous exercise is "critical to adolescents' immediate and future physical and mental health" (Jackson & Davis, 2000), nearly half of America's young adolescents are not physically active in any meaningful way, and as they get older they exercise even less. "Physical education," says the Carnegie Council, "should be provided regularly to all middle grades students as a matter of course within the curriculum" (Jackson & Davis, 2000). Sadly, daily physical education seems to be even less a part of the curriculum than it was decades ago, at the very time that adolescent and adult obesity is reaching record levels. It may be that the provision of regular, daily physical education is suffering as a consequence of the harsh accountability measures that threaten to eliminate everything in the curriculum that is not directly and immediately relevant to the next state examination. Conscientious middle school educators cannot ignore the important role physical education should play in the daily life of the school.

The exemplary physical education program characteristically includes a program of daily physical movement and exercise, lifetime recreational activities, and sports activities. The instructional program aims at a balance among these aspects of physical fitness. For example, a physical education curriculum guide for the middle schools of Fort Campbell, Kentucky, stated that

> physical education teachers recognize the uniqueness of the age group we teach. We feel it is important to help each child develop and maintain a suitable level of physical fitness through large group games, team sports, and movement activities. The curriculum emphasizes lead-up skills, individual sports, and intramural activities. Each child should be stimulated to participate and derive enjoyment from recreation.

The list of activities at Fort Campbell middle schools is extensive, although not atypical.

Physical fitness conditioning—two weeks
Softball skills and games—two to three weeks
Falcon football—two to three weeks
Soccer—three weeks
Strength training—two weeks
Wrestling—two weeks
Aerobics—two weeks
Volleyball—three to four weeks
Rhythmic activities—two weeks
Basketball—three weeks
Tumbling and gymnastics—two weeks
Cheerleading—one week
Archery—two to three weeks
Recreation games—two weeks
Physical fitness testing—two weeks
Track and field—one week

Intramurals, Interscholastic Sports, Other Extracurricular Programs, and the Role of Competition

Middle school educators, perhaps more than any others, seem to struggle with the place of competition as a component of the middle school curriculum. These professionals are caught between an awareness of the characteristics of early adolescence that make competition a hazardous activity and the existence of tremendous stress in American society on the importance of such rivalry. The accumulated research on competition in education (Kohn, 1986) speaks loud warnings against permitting too much such activity into the school lives of young adolescents. One experienced educator, John Winton, then principal of Shelburne Middle School, in Shelburne, Vermont, put it exceptionally well.

An interesting and humbling aspect of teaching young adolescents over a period of years is that one becomes aware that making predictions about the future achievement of students is hazardous. Often we are both surprised and delighted with some of the students who had exhibited modest talents . . . [and] make significant achievements in high school or later in life. Because we are often surprised we learn to be especially thoughtful about labeling boys and girls at a time in their lives when change and dis-equilibrium are so prominent. We would like our students to keep an open mind about their own potentials and to give themselves a chance to grow and mature before making a firm decision about their strengths and weaknesses. An important implication of this has to do with competition.

Competition is a part of our lives. No matter what we do, individuals will find ways to be competitive. That is neither a good thing nor a bad thing so long as we are not dealing with extremes. What is commonly overlooked is that while our society seems to foster competition, it may be the most cooperative society in history. Think of how many people share our roads in automobiles, for instance. The real work of our society is done through cooperation. Competition has its place, but it should not be the dominant factor, especially in the lives of boys and girls who have yet to realize their full growth and whose assessment of their own potentials is at best incomplete. We want adolescents to try. We wish to encourage them. . . .

Creating curriculum strategies and activities that permit all students to find some success is not soft pedagogy. It is just good sense. Those who speak in terms of letting down standards are willing to sacrifice some boys and girls in order to motivate others. That can't be part of a public school philosophy. If we train children to feel success only when they can see that others have failed, we have done them all a great disservice. Our standard should be that of the greatest possible growth for each student within the limits of his or her own abilities. All middle school students must be winners.

Middle schools reduce the competitive aspects of education for students by avoiding selective activities, by stressing participation, and through individualization. At the Shelburne Middle School we have not put a heavy emphasis on grading, our classes are almost all grouped heterogeneously, and we stress participation by making it possible for all to take part at some level in school activities. As do most middle schools, we give priority to our intramural programs although we still maintain interscholastic teams for seventh and eighth graders.

We recognize participation in activities and students receive many awards and certificates. Helping in the library, taking part in a play, being on a basketball team, or tutoring a younger student are all valued and recognized equally. (Winton, 1989, pp. 3–4)

Although many middle schools provide interscholastic athletics, as did their junior high predecessors, this practice remains decidedly controversial, and many educators and parents vigorously oppose its excesses and abuse. The major basis for continuing opposition is the conviction that most children of middle school age are not yet ready to profit from participation in intensely competitive and highly selective sports activities. Most middle school educators, we believe, seek to avoid the traditional secondary school model of some athletics-dominated high schools and junior high schools. Relevant, too, is the widespread desire for the middle school to be a unique institution focused on the needs of its own population instead of modeling itself after a higher level with too little thought to the special needs of a younger group. But to us, the most significant argument is that all the students in the middle school need to have experience in sports, experience that is appropriate for their physical status and that can yield feelings of satisfaction to many children who would never make the varsity team. The possible physical damage of inappropriate activities, such as occurs too frequently in tackle football for early adolescents, must also be avoided.

The evidence against the traditional interscholastic athletics and in favor of intramurals in the middle school is impressive. Excellent reviews of the issue have been available for 15 years. One early review concluded with this comment:

Middle school people who really are concerned for what is best for their students increasingly are looking for a quiet burial for interscholastic athletic programs with their over-competitiveness and over-organization of these youngsters. They are trying in their middle schools to offer a program of intramural sports and strong physical education programs for both boys and girls, with teachers who understand and are dedicated to the best interests of these transescents. (Romano & Timmers, 1978)

Intramurals are organized in various ways in middle schools—by grades, teams, periods, and advisory groups. At Marie Drake Middle School, in Juneau, Alaska, students who participate in the interscholastic program must first have participated in an intramural program, a unique requirement insofar as we know. Where there is an interdisciplinary team organization, it is a natural outgrowth of the team life to have various types of sports contests within and between teams. The intramurals may be organized by the physical education teachers and certainly should operate under their supervision, but with much interest and support from all members of the staff.

As with the marching band, however, what may be developmentally appropriate and desirable for the curriculum may be difficult to implement successfully. Intramural programs appear to be much easier to talk about than to implement and maintain. Interscholastic athletic programs have many advocates whose salary supplements and hopes for career advancement may depend upon continuing interscholastics at the middle level and on organizing and operating those experiences as if they were farm clubs for the high school varsity sports program. Interscholastic programs also have a momentum from their traditional value as entertainment for the community and the symbols of group pride they represent.

At Centennial Middle School, in Lino Lakes, Minnesota, the 2000–2001 school year had a full intramural schedule, an example of how well such programs can operate. During four different seasons, the school provided boys and girls intramural teams in soccer, basketball, tennis, cross-country running, and volleyball. Coed teams were featured in table tennis, floor hockey, karate, and flag football. Boys wrestling was also on the schedule. Combined with its club program, Centennial offers a great after-school program at a time when young adolescents, nationwide, are in real need of structured, monitored, and high-interest after-school activity.

The school district of Volusia County, Florida, has been particularly successful in developing a viable intramural program at the middle level. At each of the 12 middle schools in the district, intramurals work through the interdisciplinary team organization, at each grade level. Traditionally, three activities are scheduled for each grading period: two outdoor activities and one indoor (e.g., flag football, kickball, and war ball). Each Friday, intramurals are scheduled for two periods for each grade level, instead of the regular physical education period and an exploratory class. The teachers of these classes act as referees and supervisors. At the end of each grading period, the teams with the most wins meet in a "House Championship" in front of their peers. Playoffs are scheduled only at the same grade level, to avoid older students running away with all the competitions. The program is so meticulously designed that the activities for each grade level are based on appropriate themes (e.g., 6th grade, locomotion; 7th grade, body management; 8th grade, fitness). One of us witnessed such a playoff day at DeLand Middle and can testify to the tremendous spirit and pride that interdisciplinary teams generated at this event. Sadly, recent budget cuts in the district have forced educators there to put this fine program on hold.

At Nautilus Middle School, in Dade County, Florida, a carefully planned program also worked exceptionally well. Advisory groups and physical education classes were the twin hearts of the program, which featured almost a dozen different activities throughout the year. Field days and "Funtastic Fridays" for playoffs were held. In Fulton County, Georgia, each of the 11 middle schools offered an intramural program four days a week, after school for 90 minutes each day. Special activity busses provide transportation for the participants. Tennis, volleyball, basketball, gymnastics, track and field, aerobics, badminton, bowling, fitness training, golf, and jogging are available. Extramural culminating events occur in tennis, basketball, track and field, and gymnastics. Each school sends representatives, chosen through school level intramural programs, to the countywide extramural event. The purpose of the extramural event is to "promote good will, sportsmanship, and positive interschool relationships between the students of the eleven middle schools in Fulton County."

Interscholastic Sports   Interscholastic sports programs are not inherently undesirable; it is the abuses to which these programs have been subject that have too often rendered them counterproductive at the middle level. We believe that interscholastic programs can be developed that are effective for this age group, although maintaining their developmental purity is extremely difficult. In the Orange County, Florida, school district, for example, the transition from junior high school to middle school was accompanied by a retention of interscholastic athletics, but in significantly modified and developmentally appropriate form.

When the transition occurred, the interscholastic program was retained but reduced from 12 junior high sports to four in the new middle schools, one for each of the nine-week quarters of the year. The sports that were retained in Orange County were deemed fit for young adolescent needs for physical, social, and affective development: soccer, volleyball, basketball, and track. All four sports where available in boy and girl versions. The season for each sport was tailored to the length of the nine-week grading period, with the number of competitions reduced from more than a dozen to six or eight. Schools competed against five other schools in their cluster, as the district has 18 middle schools. This reduced travel time, distance, and late-night games during the week. Competitive standings and end-of-season tournaments were eliminated. No "most valuable players" are selected. Everyone who wishes to play is a member of the team, and every team member plays in every game. It seems to us that this is what interscholastic athletics was intended to be at the middle level, and we endorse such practices.

The staff of Burlingame Intermediate School (BIS), in Burlingame, California, was out in front of the development of healthy interscholastic programs for its students. During one school year, for example, instead of doing away with interscholastic basketball, the school fielded 18 varsity basketball teams, and although it may have been a scheduling nightmare, we would guess that it was a wonderful experience for players and parents who would not otherwise have had it. We would also guess that the local high school basketball program would benefit substantially from the way it is operated at the middle level. The philosophy of the Burlingame Middle School regarding extra and co-curricular programs was expressed by its developer, principal Bob Welch (personal communication, March 6, 1991).

> At no point in a youngster's formal academic years is there such a burst of energy from every direction, as that which occurs in the life of an emerging adolescent. This energy needs to be directed into a wide variety of activities. These activities should be positive and inclusive.
>
> At BIS we believe that every student should be in more than one activity. There is no elitism at the school. If you go out for an activity or a team, you are automatically a member of the group or team. As an example, this year we have 18 basketball teams that play interscholastic competition. For a school of 640 students, that is a very high level of participation!

At East Grand Rapids Middle School, in Michigan, in 2001, interscholastic sports were offered in what we believe to be a developmentally appropriate program acceptable to both educators and community. Sports programs are offered at four different times of the year, from late August until late May: girls basketball and volleyball, boys basketball and wrestling, and coed cross-country running, tennis doubles, swimming and diving, and track and field. The school takes the firm position that all students who want to play will be placed on a team. There are no cuts. Multiple teams in every sport accommodate students with different levels of skills. Acknowledging that the school exists in a highly athletically conscious area of the country, the most skilled players in each sport are placed on one team and the other students are divided up into additional teams. If, for example, 40 boys want to play basketball, the most skilled players are put on one team and the rest of the players make up three other teams.

Cheerleaders   Whether or not to have cheerleaders is also a controversial issue at the middle level. There seems to us that little fault can be found with cheering enthusiastically for the team of one's choice. School spirit and pride are extraordinarily desirable in these times. Once again, it is with the abuse of these programs that trouble enters the school door. When school leaders permit cheerleading programs to degenerate into popularity contests in which only popular, upper-middle-class, fair-haired, and well-formed young girls ever qualify, the goals of such activities are subverted in unacceptable ways. One exemplary middle school may have found a solution that worked, at least for it. At McCulloch Middle School, in Highland Park, Texas, cheerleaders were not eliminated, but the popularity contest changed. At McCulloch, if a student wanted to be a cheerleader, all that was needed was a white shirt, blue shorts, and school spirit. Consequently, in one year, the school had 140 cheerleaders. At Cope Junior High School, in Bossier City, Louisiana, a similar philosophy worked well. As principal Tim Gilbert explained (personal communication, January 1991):

> Basically, what we did was to devise an alternative plan to popular election of cheerleaders. Each year we had ten or twelve students that felt really great about being elected and about twenty that had every insecurity they ever had reconfirmed because they hadn't been elected. We now allow any students, (not just girls), who are in the eighth grade and academically eligible, to be a cheerleader.
>
> We achieve this by having rotating squads. After initial opposition by a few parents, we have gained very strong parental support. The program was so successful at raising self-esteem and increasing school spirit, that it has been used as a model for all the middle schools in our system.

Educators at Broomfield Heights Middle School, in Broomfield, Colorado, have worked long and hard to maintain a quality intramural program. In announcing its intramural athletics program to its parents, through the first of many newsletters for the year, school leaders made their policy clear.

> Boulder Valley Public Schools has a middle level athletic program that takes into account the nature of the physiological and psychological needs of middle level students. All students are welcome and encouraged to participate in these activities regardless of their skills. Emphasis is on game play and participation for all.

At Broomfield Heights Middle School, a gradually shifting emphasis based on the development of the students moves from complete emphasis on intramurals in the 6th grade to intramurals with more coaching in the 7th grade. In the 7th grade program, some of the intramural sports include a culminating activity such as extramural playoffs. Eighth graders participate in intramurals, but they also have an opportunity for a limited interscholastic program of boys football, wrestling, basketball, and track and girls softball, basketball, volleyball, and track. Even so, parents were informed that "any eighth grader may participate in the fall sports program. Students do not need previous experience. Emphasis is on skill building, participation, and enjoyment of sports." We find such programs refreshing and realistic.

At Talent Middle School, lunchtime intramural programs are supplemented by club sports. As they would in a university setting, club sports programs are available to students who chose not to play on interscholastic teams or who are not chosen to play on those teams. Intramural in nature, these club teams play during the same season as the interscholastic teams, but with a shorter schedule and no traveling to other schools. The TMS interscholastic program begins with 7th grade and includes a number of coed and/or boys and girls sports: track, cross-country running, volleyball, football, basketball, and wrestling.

Other so-called extracurricular issues relate to the transitions in middle level programs. The desirability of having a school newspaper, a sophisticated yearbook, dances, and even proms is hotly debated from school to school, district to district, and within the home between parent and the young adolescent. Many middle school educators maintain that high-school-style programs, of all sorts, should be saved for the high school. Students who experience intensely competitive athletics, sophisticated proms, and lengthy yearbooks in junior high school frequently show less interest in those programs at the high school, when such activities are most developmentally appropriate. Matching middle school curriculum and the resulting activities to the characteristics and needs of the students is the most logical way to proceed. Save high school programs for the high school—a maxim worth repeating.

We recommend the work, and endorse the conclusions, of respected developmental scholars such as David Elkind, author of *The Hurried Child* (1981) and *All Grown Up and No Place to Go* (1984). Elkind argued that students, at this age, need time to grow up, and tremendous pressure from anxious adults to hurry the process is clearly counterproductive. Programs for older teens should not be simply placed earlier and watered-down for younger students. Alternatives must be found. Simply eliminating those extracurricular activities that are inappropriate is not sufficient; it is only half of the process. Many middle school educators in the 1970s and 1980s, in their rush to eliminate inappropriate programs, did so without replacing them with effective ones. School spirit, pride, and group citizenship suffered as a result. Too many middle schools became bland, lifeless places where no robust occasions caught students' attention or commitment. Suitable programs that foster the healthy development of individual students and stimulate school spirit, unity, pride, and citizenship are needed. Much development remains to be done in this area.

TECHNOLOGY AND THE CURRICULUM

In 1991, as the second edition of this text was being prepared, we made a bold prediction regarding technology. We stated that we believed that "before the end of the decade of the '90's, video discs, minicomputers, and other, perhaps even newer technology, will be within the common experience of most middle school learners." We were right. In the last decade, few things have changed so much as the way in which technology has become a part of the school experience of young adolescents. By the year 2001, video had revitalized the use of aging and otherwise rarely used television monitors in classrooms all across America. Modern school television studios have become common as the source of appealingly sophisticated student-generated morning news and announcement programs. Such productions not only rival the quality of local television news shows, but they also are rapidly replacing the already fading memory of the school principal making long and mostly boring pronouncements over the antiquated PA (public address) system. The Internet and the World Wide Web have forever transformed access to and use of information in the classroom. That place in the school once called the library, which became the media center in the 1980s, has become something totally different, now sometimes called the Information Center in many schools.

Middle school teachers are now engaged in educating the "Net Generation" (Tapscott, 1995). The first generation of American youth born and raised in a dot.com world has already passed through the middle school classroom. Don Tapscott, president of New Paradigm Learning Corporation, asserts that the current generation of young adolescents is "bathed in bits" and thriving on it. More important, Tapscott believes that advances in technology have the capacity to transform learning and teaching, from a teacher-centered to a learner-centered process. Classrooms, Tapscott and others illustrate, are already in the process of moving from a book-focused linear learning process to a milieu that is interactive, where knowledge arrives in nonsequential packages. The inquiry-based nature of digital learning is speeding up the process of moving away from teacher-centered direct instruction to learner-centered inquiry and constructivist activity. Memorization is rapidly being replaced by learning how to learn and where to acquire necessary information on a need-to-know timeline. The process of replacing the model of the teacher as "sage on the stage" with the "guide on the side" is being rapidly enhanced by digital opportunities available to both teacher and learner.

Perhaps the best-known example of the application of advanced technology to the operation of the middle school concept, available at the time of publication of the second edition of this book, in 1993, was in the program for the Saturn School of Tomorrow, in St. Paul, Minnesota (Bennett & King, 1991). Saturn was a middle level school, housing about 250 students (with 80 on a waiting list) in grades 4–8, in a renovated YMCA in downtown St. Paul. Students came to Saturn from all over the city as part of the city's magnet desegregation program.

The mission statement for the Saturn School was: "The Saturn School Community is an interpersonal, individualized environment in which students become empowered life-long learners prepared for the 21st century." Core concepts of the program included the following.

- A Personalized Learning Program is devised for each student.
- Learning takes place in mixed age and ability groups.
- Saturn is a textbook-free school.
- Technology is used as a tool to support learning.

- Course offerings are based on student interest and needs.
- Grades are not given; progress is measured by attainment of personal growth goals.
- A primary goal is: Students are responsible for their own learning.
- Instruction is focused on developing learning processes.

Among the exciting programs evolving at the Saturn School was the use, by students and teachers, of what were state-of-the-art learning technologies, primarily videodisc and other systems that brought huge content blocks to the fingertips of young adolescents. Macintosh labs enabled what became known as desktop publishing. Voice mail was new.

It is possible to appreciate the extent of technological advancement at the turn of the century by the fact that dozens, if not hundreds or thousands, of American middle schools are rapidly moving in the direction pioneered by schools such as the Saturn School of Tomorrow. Part of the explanation for this forward movement lies in the natural receptivity of middle school educators to innovation that they perceive to be connected to improving their capacity to educate their students. In the 1990s, advocates for the integration of technology recognized this readiness on the part of middle school educators and responded. Today's middle schools, consequently, exhibit an exciting array of technological capabilities.

For example, Towns Middle School, in Hiawasee, Georgia, was identified by *Time* magazine in May of 2001 as the runner-up for Middle School of the Year. *Time* asserted that Towns, located in one of Georgia's poorest and most isolated areas, was one of the "best-wired middle schools in the U.S." Funded for "e-learning" by the Appalachian Regional Commission, every student is provided with a NetSchools laptop computer that "can be dropped from 5 ft. without breaking." Infrared sensors in classroom ceilings connect the students' laptops to the school's server and to the Internet. Students can take the computers home and tap into the Internet for additional class work, or they can email their teachers or other students with whom they might be working. They can even check the menu in the cafeteria, although laptops may not make young adolescents more positive about their lunches. According to Anne Berryman at Towns Middle School, results in other areas have, however, been positive; attendance and standardized test scores are up, and discipline referrals are down (Roche, 2001).

At Marshall Simonds Middle School, in Burlington, Massachusetts, technology has been a focal point for years. As a result of a grant from Sun MicroSystems, the school is fully networked, and every classroom is connected to the Internet. Two full-time technology specialists work with teams. Each classroom has three computers, and every team has a large screen monitor, scanner, and laser printer. The school houses the district's training center for staff development, with 13 computer stations, zip drives, and CD (compact disc) burners. At Simonds, leaders have developed a careful teacher-training program that has led to greater use of technology in the classroom.

At East Jessamine Middle School, in Kentucky, a student leadership program in technology gets students engaged. Six student teams provide technology leadership throughout the school. The Video Production Team does the morning announcements on video, with news, feature stories, announcements, and training. The Web Team is in charge of all Web-based activities, such as monitoring the school's Web site and encouraging teacher use of the Web in their classes. The school's morning announcements, for example, are automatically put on the school's Web page every day. Teachers' calendars are woven into the Web page. The Maintenance Team keeps the school's labs up and running, cleaning the inside and outside of all computers. Members of this team communicate with each other through email during the four periods of the day. A Service Call Team provides troubleshooters for aging machines, taking calls from teachers and responding quickly. The Programming Team develops and delivers training in the use of a wide variety of program applications, and they train students who wish to join other technology teams. Finally, the Virtual Classroom Team works with teachers to assist students who have been absent. They post information on the Web from each teacher's class, scan handouts, and collect video clips and other things students may have missed during their absence. Students on the technology teams at East Jessamine also work to help teachers and students in a nearby elementary school. At this school, in 2001, half of the parents have submitted their home email addresses, furthering instant communication between home and school.

East Grand Rapids Middle School (EGRMS), in Michigan, seems to typify the directions taken by middle level schools in regard to technology. At EGRMS, educators "infuse technology in all that we do." This effort is supported by a state-of-the-art media center, a distance learning laboratory, three multimedia labs, unlimited access to the Internet, their own TV production facilities, maximum email communication options, a school Web site, and other options as well.

Students at Timothy Edwards Middle School (TEMS) are also moving ahead technologically. TEMS, in South Windsor, was named Connecticut's Middle School of the Year for 2001. Among other fine program components, a modern Computer Education Program is in place. Each academic team works closely with the staff member in the school who provides leadership in computer education. For the nearly 1,200 students at TEMS, there are over 425 networked computers in both classrooms and labs. In 6th grade, students learn word-processing skills sufficiently to produce a short term paper, magazine, or booklet. Sixth graders also learn to use ClarisWorks, Clip Art, The Factory (IBM), and AutoSketch (IBM). Seventh graders progress to using the TEMS home page to conduct research on the Internet, via Netscape and helper applications. In the 8th grade, students at TEMS develop a multimedia presentation of concepts developed in their academic classes, with other documents containing both text and graphics, through HyperStudio and Claris-Works.

The Technology Plan of the East Lyme Middle School (ELMS), in Connecticut, illustrates how far and fast middle school educators are moving in this area. The "Vision of Technology Use at ELMS" mirrors directions identified by Tapscott and others.

> East Lyme Middle School educators must take advantage of computer and communications technology to enhance learning for young adolescents and to prepare students for their lives in a world filled with technological advances and challenges.
>
> When computer and communications technology is accessible, change occurs. Electronic formats enable access to worldwide information crossing the boundaries of age and culture. Students have equal access to information as needed, regardless of grade, course selection, classroom space, or teacher. Networks foster interaction among teachers and students by creating experiences and environments that stimulate the learning process. Students move about in the world, skilled in gathering, managing, and assimilating vast resources of information, building relationships and a sense of community worldwide.
>
> The inclusion of computer and communications technology in our middle school changes teacher-student relationships. Teachers and students are co-learners in this dynamic, problem-solving, integrated learning environment. Teachers are the facilitators of learning; technology becomes the means. Students move from being dependent learners to interdependent thinkers.
>
> Technology at ELMS becomes increasingly accessible to students and educators. As technology becomes more universal, powerful, and flexible, educators and students will design programs that utilize these new opportunities to enhance learning. Computer and communications technology are tools that ensure student success.

Educators at ELMS made one of the first attempts at sketching out a scope and sequence for a technology curriculum at the middle level. See Box 3.2 for their early attempt, in 1999.

At Kinawa Middle School, in Okemos, Michigan, a more typical technological scenario is in place. Sixth graders at Kinawa begin their technological education within an exploratory program. Those students may, and usually do, choose courses in computer graphics or computer keyboarding. In the 7th grade, trimester-length technology electives are available in Integrated Technology, a lab-based course now common in middle schools across the country. In these labs, sometimes known as Technology Labs, students are involved in a stations approach to a wide variety of educational activities: rocketry, airfoil

BOX
3.2

Technology Curriculum at East Lyme Middle School

Computer Graphics

Grade 6: Students will become familiar with the graphics environment and incorporate clip art, CD-ROM, Internet graphics, and data into desktop publishing projects. (exposure/experience)

Grade 7: Students will incorporate graphics from CD-ROMS, the Internet, and scanned images into desktop publishing projects. (experience)

Grade 8: Students will incorporate graphics from CD-ROMS, the Internet, and scanned images into desktop publishing projects. (mastery)

Databases

Grade 6: Students will input and extract information from an existing database through guided class projects. (exposure/experience)

Grade 7: Students will design a database. (experience)

Grade 8: Students will create, edit, and use databases to support a curriculum project. (experience/mastery)

Data Collection/Information Retrieval

Grade 6: Students will use an online catalog to locate materials; use Request to locate materials in other libraries; mark, save, print from CD-ROMS (electronic encyclopedias, atlas, etc.); Internet exposure. Students will use the Internet to conduct a simple search to access information. (exposure/experience)

Grade 7: Students will use more advanced research techniques (Boolean search, keyword) and CD-ROM sources (Newsbank, Current Biography, InfoTank, Time, Almanac). Students will use CD-ROM searches for magazine research and guided Internet searches. (experience)

Grade 8: Students will independently evaluate and choose the best electronic source and independently use all online and CD-ROM sources and incorporate research into a finished product. (experience/mastery) Students will frequently use the Internet for class projects.

Spreadsheets and Graphs

Grade 6: Students will experience the use of electronic spreadsheets and graphs in multiple subject areas via technology. (exposure) Students will read and interpret spreadsheets and graphs. (experience) Students will create simple spreadsheets to generate a graph and use formulas to perform simple calculations. (exposure)

Grade 7: Students will use electronic spreadsheets and graphs in the context of a subject area task/product and use formulas to perform calculations. (experience)

Grade 8: Students will independently gather data and create a spreadsheet/graph. (mastery) Students will use graphing calculators. (exposure) Students will analyze the data in a spreadsheet and reach conclusions. (experience/mastery)

Desktop Publishing

Grade 6: Students will create a one- to two-page, two-column newsletter with simple computer generated graphics. (experience)

Grade 7: Students will create a multipage, multicolumn product with sophisticated graphics (digital camera, CD-ROM, Internet, scanned, student-created). (experience/mastery)

Grade 8: Students will independently apply grade 6 and grade 7 skills to curriculum projects. (experience, mastery)

Digital Multimedia

Grade 6: Students will create a simple electronic presentation. (experience)

Grade 7: Students will create a simple electronic presentation incorporating digital shots, video skills, photos, images, and so on. (experience)

Grade 8: Students will create an electronic presentation incorporating digital shots, video skills, photos, images, and so on. (mastery)

Video Production

Grade 6: Students will experience the basic elements of camera features and creating videos. (exposure)

Grade 7: Students will experience the basic elements of camera features and creating videos. (experience) Students will experience the basic elements of video editing. (exposure)

Grade 8: Students will experience the basic elements of camera features and creating videos. (experience) Students will experience the basic elements of video editing. (experience)

Telecommunications

Grade 6: Students will send and receive email. (exposure, experience)

Grade 7: Students will send and receive email. (exposure, experience)

Grade 8: Students will independently send and receive email. (mastery) Students will share data through an interactive project. (experience) design, land and watercraft design, and a host of computer applications such as Web site construction, flight simulation, and so on. Seventh graders at Kinawa also have a two-trimester technology course in design and problem solving. This course focuses on four modes of transportation: "aero-space, atmospheric, marine, and terrestrial." In 8th grade, the 7th grade offerings are repeated, with individualized options built in for students who take them again.

Farnsworth Middle School (FMS), in Guilderland, New York, has been in a leadership position in middle school education for decades. Its leadership in technology is, consequently, not surprising. "The Technology Plan, 1999–2002" for FMS specifies the following expectations for middle school students.

By 1999–2000:

- All classrooms will be connected to the information superhighway.
- All middle school students have at least one major assignment requiring the use of multimedia or the Internet.
- All 7th and 8th graders will work in cooperative groups using a presentation software package to prepare and present at least one major assignment.
- Students use technology to expand their learning environments by accessing information from community and world organizations via links to World Wide Web pages.
- All middle school teams will review the district's Acceptable Use Policy.

By 2000–2001:

- All middle school students will, in addition to the expectations for the previous year, have at least one major assignment requiring a cooperative learning experience, collecting data in a database, and sharing the results with other students.
- All middle school students participate in a collaborative learning activity by communicating with other students via a specialized Multimedia/Research lab.

By 2001–2002:

- Products of presentations by middle school students using presentation software will be of professional quality ready to be published on the Internet.
- All middle school students participate in a collaborative learning activity by communicating with other students via Internet access from the middle school Web server.

The commitment to this ambitious set of objectives at FMS has several important implications for the school. It means comprehensive planning for training teachers for integrating technology into their classrooms. It means a realignment of the curriculum with the objectives of the Technology Plan. It means hiring technology support personnel, and it means the presence of many more computers in the school than otherwise.

Technology Magnet Schools   Another feature of the rapid infusion of technology into middle school education is the appearance of magnet schools with a technological focus or special houses within middle schools that have a special technology program. Challenger Middle School, in Colorado Springs, Colorado, has a long tradition of being on the cutting edge of "preparing students for tomorrow." In 1966, for example, the school opened as Air Academy Junior High School, building on its location near the United States Air Force Academy. In recent years, the school has become the "technology school of choice" for the district. Using a "distributed technology model," the school has achieved a ratio of one computer for every five students, and three computer labs for whole class use, special instruction, and technology classes.

At the Mount Hebron Middle School of Science and Technology (MHMS), in Upper Montclair, New Jersey, many aspects of curriculum and technology come together. A whole school theme, the environment, is infused in every course students take. The school is equipped with five state-of-the-art Technology Labs as well as computers in every classroom. A "fiber optic backbone" supports the technology infrastructure and allows students and teachers virtually immediate access to the Internet and its global information. All students at MHMS receive 200 minutes of technology training per week, which assists them in many phases of the use of technology: using effective research techniques, employing sophisticated presentation software, working on the school's Web page, creating the school's Intranet, expanding uses of the school email capabilities, and further integrating the curriculum. As MHMS describes it, the "expansion of technology throughout the science program and the visual and performing arts has been realized. The educational community of Mt. Hebron connects school, homes, and the entire community in a global learning environment."

At Vista Middle School, in Las Cruces, New Mexico, a similar transition moved the school to a Technology/Science Magnet program for the district. Every student receives three full semesters of technology training. Applied Technology offers students training in word processing, desktop publishing, graphic design, and Internet research. Music Technology permits students to compose, arrange, record, and edit their own music, as well as learn beginning piano skills. A Technology Lab 2000 provides learning experiences in the use of digital photography, animations, robotics, rocketry, the creation of electronic portfolios, and the exploration of careers in the world of technology. An Enriched Sciences program builds on the training students receive in technology, leading to science research and projects that extend far beyond the old norms for those activities.

Technology in the Years to Come   In 2000, in St. Johns County, Florida, school superintendent Hugh Balbonie (personal communication, February 2000) envisioned a school system in which middle school learners would soon be involved in what he described as a seamless system of "personalized learning." In such a system, not too many years away according to Balbonie, young adolescents and other students, K–12, would "learn the next thing they need to know, when they need to know it," as a result of rapid progress in educational technology. Data warehouses would capture all data on student performance in one place, along with the curriculum, and all of this would be continuously available to teachers, students, and parents. Teachers would, thus, have instant access to student data, allowing for a seamless, continuous diagnosis and prescription cycle leading to the most efficient pathway for student academic growth. Personal Individual Education Plans (IEPs) would be prepared for every student, and such plans would be continuously updated with the help of new technology.

Superintendent Balbonie predicted that Apple and other computer companies would soon be developing Internet connection devices that would eventually be provided to every student, devices that would resemble a laptop but will be wireless. Electronic textbooks would someday soon replace printed ones. Handheld computers would soon be inexpensive enough to permit school districts to distribute them to every student. Technology would permit such dramatically increased communication between home and school that the boundaries between home schooling and public schools would be erased, leading to a blended "public home schooling."

In the spring of 2000, at Haile Middle School, in Manatee County, Florida, 150 Emates, Apple's new small word processor for schools, were already in use, along with four to five regular computers in every classroom. A year later, in the fall of 2001, University of Michigan researchers announced that they were close to unveiling a "suite of educational tools" for such handheld computers, software that will be available for downloading at no charge (Branigan, 2001a). This new software would be created to make the use of handheld computers more practical and financially feasible for school settings. New software programs for handheld devices developed by Palm Inc. would, the company predicted in 2001, soon allow students to do many essential tasks (e.g., word processing, graphing equations, manipulating images, and printing) directly from these personal digital assistants, or PDAs. Such devices, available soon for as little as $150 per student, will function as computer, calculator, emailer, textbook, notebook, and pencil. At the same time, five states have received the green light to start connecting their schools to Abilene, the ultra-high-speed Internet2 that has been developing among government, university, and private sector users (Branigan, 2001b). This new Internet2 is expected to be 100 times faster than current connections to the Internet.

Will middle school teachers be ready to be a part of this rapid development in the use of technology in their classrooms? Unfortunately, some evidence has shown that teacher and student use of technology is not keeping pace with the extent to which hardware and software are available. Most teachers, to date, are either not using technology or only occasionally bringing it into their lessons. And, also unfortunately, when teachers do use technology, the usage does not tend to substantially alter the instructional strategies (Cuban, Kirkpatrick, & Peck, 2001). We are confident, however, that the majority of colleges and universities in America have begun to prepare their future teachers for this role. In the state of Florida, for example, the Florida Education Standards Commission has added the "use of appropriate technology in teaching and learning processes" as the last of 12 "Accomplished Practices" that all teacher education students must master prior to certification. Among the 10 key indicators in the technology area are these:

- "Utilizes appropriate learning media, computer applications, and other technology to address student needs and learning objectives."
- "Utilizes a wide range of instructional technologies such as CD-ROM, interactive video, videotaping, and electronic libraries to enhance the subject matter and ensure it is comprehensible to all students."

We leave our discussion of the subject of technology and the curriculum without making any predictions similar to the one we made in the second edition of this text. We fear that our predictions may be out of date before this text reaches your hands.

CONTENT SUMMARY

We examined the conflict between standards-based reform and the middle school concept, arguing that student-focused education is essential even when standards are present. Second, we presented the rationale for integrated curriculum and described several schools where the integrated curriculum has been fully implemented. Exploration in the curriculum was examined, highlighting the importance of efforts to enhance the basic curriculum with exploratory courses, special interest activities, and clubs. We paid special attention to the area of health and physical education and the issues surrounding intramurals and interscholastic sports. We assert that every aspect of the curriculum in middle schools must be developmentally appropriate. Finally, we described the ways in which technology is having an impact on the curriculum and implied what might be directions for the future.

CONNECTIONS TO OTHER CHAPTERS

What you have learned in Chapter 3 has direct implications for several other chapters. Curriculum does affect everything else in the school and is directly affected by other aspects of the school. Most notably, the curriculum is directly involved with the school schedule, so it will be important to keep this in mind as you read Chapter 8. The same is true for Chapters 6 and 7, where we consider how curriculum affects how students are organized for learning in an exemplary middle school.

QUESTIONS FOR DISCUSSION

1. What is your position regarding the clash between supporters of standards-based reform and advocates for student-focused education?
2. What do you believe to be the three strongest points in favor of integrated curriculum? The three most important concerns?
3. What is a developmentally appropriate program for young adolescents in the area of sports and other extracurricular activities? What should occur in middle school and what should be left for high school?
4. What advances in the use of technology in middle schools have occurred since the publication of this textbook in 2002?
5. What do you believe to be the proper role of technology in teaching and learning?

ACTION STEPS

1. Visit a team of middle school teachers while they are engaged in implementing an integrated curriculum project with their students. Conduct a mini-research study of the process.
2. Conduct a telephone survey of five middle schools to determine the types of exploratory programs that are generally available in those buildings.
3. Arrange a teacher workday devoted to investigating ways in which a school might make progress in merging standards-based reform and student-focused education.
4. Attend a state conference on technology to ascertain the new directions that may be on their way to general availability.
5. Search the Web for examples of school curriculum programs that match the descriptions of programs in this chapter.
6. Talk with a group of parents to determine the extent to which they are pleased with the offerings and organization of the curriculum in the middle school their children attend.

SUGGESTIONS FOR FURTHER STUDY

Books

Abbeduto, L. (2000). *Taking sides: Clashing views on controversial issues in educational psychology.* Guilford, CT: Dushkin/McGraw-Hill.

Airasian, P. (2000). *Assessment in the classroom: A concise approach.* Boston, MA: McGraw-Hill.

Allen, D. (1998). *Assessing student learning: From grading to understanding.* New York: Teachers College Press.

Allen, H., & Splittgerber, F. (1993). *Teaching and learning in the middle level school.* New York: Maxwell Macmillan International.

Chatton, B. (1999). *Blurring the edges: Integrated curriculum through writing and children's literature.* Portsmouth, NH: Heinemann.

Drake, S. (1998). *Creating integrated curriculum: Proven ways to increase student learning.* Thousand Oaks, CA: Corwin Press.

Ellis, A., & Stuen, C. (1998). *The interdisciplinary curriculum.* Larchmont, NY: Eye on Education.

Five, D. (1996). *Bridging the gap: Integrating curriculum in upper elementary and middle schools.* Portsmouth, NH: Heinemann.

Florida Department of Education (2000). *Florida School Recognition Program 1999–2000: Best practices for higher student achievement.* Tallahassee, FL: Florida Department of Education.

Florida Department of State (1990). *Best practices for career development infused into the middle school exploratory vocational wheel.* Tallahassee, FL: Florida Department of State.

Germain-McCarthy, Y. (1999). *Bringing the NCTM standards to life: Exemplary practices from high school.* Larchmont, NY: Eye on Education.

Heller, N. (1994). *Projects for new technologies in education: Grades 6–9.* Englewood, CO: Teacher Ideas Press.

Himley, M., & Carini, P. (2000). *From another angle: Children's strengths and school standards: The Prospect Center's descriptive review of the child.* New York: Teachers College Press.

Jarrett, D. (1998). *Integrating technology into middle school mathematics: It's just good teaching.* Portland, OR: Northwest Regional Educational Laboratory.

Kearns, D., & Harvey, J. (2000). *A legacy of learning: Your stake in standards and new kinds of public schools.* Washington, DC: Brookings Institution Press.

Kendall, J. S., & Marzano, R. J. (2000). *Content knowledge: A compendium of standards and benchmarks.* Aurora, CO: Mid-Continent Regional Educational Lab.

Kordalewski, J. (2000). *Standards in the classroom: How teachers and students negotiate learning.* New York: Teachers College Press.

Mallery, A. (2000). *Creating a catalyst for thinking: The integrated curriculum.* Boston, MA: Allyn and Bacon.

Manning, M., Manning, G., & Long, R. (1994). *Theme immersion: Inquiry-based curriculum in elementary and middle schools.* Portsmouth, NH: Heinemann.

Muth, D., & Alvermann, D. (1999). *Teaching and learning in the middle grades.* Boston, MA: Allyn and Bacon.

Pate, E., Homestead, E., & McGinnis, K. (1997). *Making integrated curriculum work: Teachers, students, and the quest for coherent curriculum.* New York: Teachers College Press.

Sergiovanni, T. (2000). *The lifeworld of leadership: Creating culture, community, and personal meaning in our schools.* San Francisco, CA: Jossey-Bass Publishers.

Speck, B. (2000). *Grading students' classroom writing: Issues and strategies.* Washington, DC: George Washington University, Graduate School of Education and Human Development.

Stein, M., et al. (2000). *Implementing standards-based mathematics instruction: A casebook for professional development.* New York: Teachers College Press.

Stevenson, C., & Carr, J. (1993). *Integrated studies in the middle grades: Dancing through walls.* New York: Teachers College Press.

Underwood, T. (1999). *The portfolio project: A study of assessment, instruction, and middle school reform.* Urbana, IL: National Council of Teachers of English.

Vars, G. (1993). *Interdisciplinary teaching: Why & how.* Columbus, OH: National Middle School Association.

Walvoord, B., Johnson, & Anderson, V. (1998). *Effective grading: A tool for learning and assessment.* San Francisco, CA: Jossey-Bass Publishers.

Wheelock, A. (1998). *Safe to be smart: Building a culture for standards-based reform in the middle grades.* Columbus, OH: National Middle School Association.

Wood, K. (1997). *Interdisciplinary instruction: A practical guide for elementary and middle school teachers.* Upper Saddle River, NJ: Merrill.

Periodicals

Azzara, J. (2000). Training teachers for technology. *Principal, 79*(3), 22–25.

Bergen, D. (2000). Technology in the classroom. *Childhood Education, 76*(2), 116–118.

Bradford, D. (1999). Exemplary urban middle school teachers' use of the five standards of effective teaching. *Teaching and Change, 7*(1), 53–78.

Bragaw, D., Bragaw, K., & Smith, E. (1995). Back to the future: Toward curriculum integration. *Middle School Journal, 27*(2), 39–46.

Bybee, R., & Loucks-Horsley, S. (2000). Standards as a catalyst for change in technology education. *Technology Teacher, 59*(5), 14–16.

Clark, J. (1996). Bells and whistles . . . But where are the references? Setting standards for hypermedia. *Learning and Leading with Technology, 23*(5), 22–24.

Clark, S. (1998). Authentic assessment—Key issues, concerns, guidelines. *Schools in the Middle, 7*(3), 50–51.

Cooke, G. (1992). Encouraging adolescents to prepare for college: Following a dream. *Schools in the Middle, 1*(3), 17–19.

Collison, M. (2000). School of the future? *NEA Today, 18*(4), 8–9.

Cross, L., & Frary, R. (1999). Hodgepodge grading: Endorsed by students and teachers alike. *Applied Measurement in Education, 12*(1), 53–72.

Coutler, B. (2000). Making good: Technology choices. *Principal, 79*(3), 18–21.

Desmond, C., Kerlavage, M., & Seda, E. (1998). An integrated approach to using national and state standards in a school-university. *Journal of Teacher Education, 49*(1), 5–12.

Doggett, K. (1997). CityYouth: A middle school core curriculum model. *Social Studies Review, 36*(2), 28–29.

Doig, L., & Sargent, J. (1996). Lights, camera, action. *Social Studies Review, 34*(3), 6–11.

Enomoto, E., Nolet, V., & Marchionini, G. (1999). The Baltimore Learning Community Project: Creating a networked community across middle schools. *Journal of Educational Multimedia and Hypermedia, 8*(1), 99–115.

Farnan, N., & Dodge, B. (1995). Creating a teaching, technology and restructuring partnership with young adolescents in mind. *Middle School Journal, 26*(5), 17–25.

Gilstrap, R. (1997). The electrified classroom: Using technology in the middle grades. *Childhood Education, 73*(5), 297–300.

Hall, P. (1993). Focus on Meyer Middle School. *Schools in the Middle, 3*(2), 49–51.

Hargreaves, A., & Moore, S. (2000). Curriculum integration and classroom relevance: A study of teachers' practice. *Journal of Curriculum and Supervision, 15*(2), 89–112.

Haviland, V., & McCall, M. (1999). Transformation through technology: How HyperStudio updated middle school research. *English Journal, 89*(1), 63–68.

Hinebauch, S. (1999). Coming of age: Making connections. *Voices from the Middle, 7*(1), 17–23.

Hope, W. (1999). Service learning: A reform initiative for middle level curriculum. *Clearing House, 72*(4), 236–238.

Howe, A., & Bell, J. (1998). Factors associated with successful implementation of interdisciplinary curriculum units. *Research in Middle Level Education Quarterly, 21*(2), 39–52.

Kesson, K., & Oyler, C. (1999). Integrated curriculum and service learning: Linking school-based knowledge and social action. *English Education, 31*(2), 135–149.

Kirkwood, T. (1999). Integrating an interdisciplinary unit in middle school: A school-university partnership. *Clearing House, 72*(3), 160–163.

Lee, J. (1998). The impact of content-driven state education reform on instruction. *Research in Middle Level Education Quarterly, 21*(4), 15–26.

Little, C. (1999). Geometry projects linking mathematics, literacy, art, and technology. *Mathematics Teaching in the Middle School, 4*(5), 332–335.

Manouchehri, A. (1998). Mathematics curriculum reform and teachers: What are the dilemmas? *Journal of Teacher Education, 49*(4), 276–286.

McCade, J., & Boynton, J. (1997). Engineering and the middle school link. *Technology Teacher, 56*(5), 10–14.

Mergendoller, J. (2000). Technology and learning: A critical assessment. *Principal, 79*(3), 5–9.

Otis-Wilborn, A., Terrell, D., Hnat, C., Lemmen, L., & Jefferson, M. (1999). A multicultural curriculum for middle schoolers: The perspective of the Harlem renaissance. *MultiCultural Review, 8*(4), 32–38.

Pena, R., Brown-Adams, C., & Decker, S. (1999). Rethinking curriculum integration by expanding the debate. *Research in Middle Level Education Quarterly, 22*(4), 25–40.

Pottle, J. (1998). Project Flight: Integrating language arts, science, and math. *Clearing House, 71*(5), 312–313.

Powell, B. (1999). Dilemmas of curriculum in the classroom: Ms. Martin's struggle to teach for understanding. *Peabody Journal of Education, 74*(1), 111–145.

Schurr, S. (1998). Teaching, Enlightening: A Guide to Student Assessment. *Schools in the Middle, 7*(3), 22–27, 30–31.

Silverman, S., & Pritchard, A. (1996). Building their future: Girls and technology education in Connecticut. *Journal of Technology Education, 7*(2), 41–54.

Tell, C. (2000). Generation what? Connecting with today's youth. *Educational Leadership, 57*(4), 8–13.

Van Horn, R. (2000). Resolutions for the new millennium. *Phi Delta Kappan, 81*(5), 414–415.

Walker, D. (2000). Process over product: A critique of the present state of problem solving in technology education. *Technology Teacher, 59*(4), 10–14.

ERIC

Alagbe, A., & Lemlech, J. (1998). *Middle school teachers' use of on-line communications* (ERIC document ED419514).

Allen, M., & Alley, D. *Foreign language study in Georgia middle schools* (ERIC document ED365115).

Andrews, K. (1998). *The effect of test-taking strategies on the test scores of middle school level students* (ERIC document ED424285).

Andris, J., Crooks, S., & Hawkins, G. (1999). *Disseminating engaged learning strategies in the middle school through technology* (ERIC document ED432276).

Branderhorst, M., Huizenga, T., & Kruzich, K. (1997). *Developing transfer in middle school student learning* (ERIC document ED412275).

Brazee, E., & Capelluti, J. (1995). *Dissolving boundaries: Toward an integrative curriculum* (ERIC document ED397982).

Carper, L. (1996). *Effectively using technology to develop independent research topics by middle school language arts students* (ERIC document ED401888).

Cole, D., Ryan, C., Kick, F., & Mathies, B. (2000). *Portfolios across the curriculum and beyond* (ERIC document ED438301).

Cunningham, V., & Karr-Kidwell, P. (1999). *Conventional school and curriculum is not for everyone: Guidelines for middle school administrators and teachers* (ERIC document ED427409).

Hecht, D., & Fusco, D. (1997). *Research informed by practice: Lessons learned from a study of service learning* (ERIC document ED415358).

Holland, H. (1998). *Middle start technology facts* (ERIC document ED423318).

Howley, A., Kusimo, P., & Parrott, L. (1999). *Grading and the ethos of effort* (ERIC document ED435728).

Irvin, J. (1997). *What current research says to the middle level practitioner* (ERIC document ED427847).

Kindberg, C. (1999). *Matching actions to words: Espoused curriculum theories* (ERIC document ED436576).

Langer, J. (1999). *Beating the odds: Teaching middle and high school students to read and write well* (ERIC document ED435993).

Lustig, K. (1996). *Portfolio assessment: A handbook for middle level teachers* (ERIC document ED404326).

Mayer, D. (1997). *New teaching standards and old tests: Dangerous mismatch?* (ERIC document ED413348).

Neapolitan, J. (1999). *Teachers' beliefs about redesigning instruction to meet new standards through action* (ERIC document ED430975).

Raebeck, B. (1993). *Exploding myths, exploring truths: Humane, productive grading and grouping in the quality middle school* (ERIC document ED366462).

Raebeck, B. (1998). *Transforming middle schools: A guide to whole-school change* (ERIC document ED422658).

Silverman, S., & Pritchard, A. (1993). *Guidance, gender equity and technology education* (ERIC document ED362651).

Siu-Runyan, Y., & Faircloth, V. (1995). *Beyond separate subjects: Integrative learning at the middle level* (ERIC document ED404036).

Southern Regional Education Board (1998). *Education's weak link: Student performance in the middle grades* (ERIC document ED419278).

Southern Regional Education Board (1999). *Leading the way: State actions to improve student achievement in the middle grades* (ERIC document ED432819).

Strickland, K., & Strickland, J. *Reflections on assessment: Its purposes, methods and effects on learning* (ERIC document ED422342).

Teberg, A. (1999). *Identified professional development needs of teachers in curriculum reform* (ERIC document ED430976).

Warren, L., Allen, M., & McKenna, B. (1998*). South Carolina middle schools' exploratory programs: A research report* (ERIC document ED436310).

Wasley, P. (1998). *Rigor and innovation: Getting both* (ERIC document ED429058).

Web Sites

Middle Web Curriculum and Instruction

http://www.middleweb.com/contntcurr.html

This is part of the large Middle Web site sponsored by the Edna McConnell Clark Foundation. It focuses on middle school reform efforts, especially raising academic achievement among at-risk youth. At this part of the site, teachers can access all kinds of information on middle school curriculum. It is an invaluable resource.

North Central Regional Educational Laboratory

http://www.ncrel.org/

The North Central Regional Educational Laboratory (NCREL) is a not-for-profit organization dedicated to helping schools—and the students they serve—reach their full potential. They specialize in the educational applications of technology. Important site components include the following.

- State profiles
- Curriculum, instruction, and assessment issues
- School and community
- Policy evaluation and research

U.S. Department of Education, Office of Educational Technology

http://www.ed.gov/technology/

The U.S. Department of Education Office of Educational Technology develops national educational technology policy and implements this policy through departmentwide educational technology programs. The site includes information and national reports on budget and legislation, evaluation and assessment, distance learning, Internet safety, and so on.

Northwest Educational Technology Consortium

http://www.netc.org/

The mission of the Northwest Educational Technology Consortium (NETC) is to provide professional development opportunities, access to technical assistance, and support for collegial interaction that allow and encourage educators throughout the Northwest, and especially in K–12 schools, to become informed and fearless users of technology. The site includes information about NETC products, publications, and conference presentations.

North Central Regional Technology in Education Consortium

http://www.ncrel.org/

The North Central Regional Technology in Education Consortium helps schools to integrate technology into their classrooms. Their products and services include the following.

- Tools for Teaching and Learning—Products and services for using technology in the classroom
- Training and Professional Development—Learning how and why to use technology to improve education
- Increasing Technology Capacity—Hardware, software, and infrastructure information and implementation plans

Northwest Regional Educational Laboratory

http://www.nwrel.org/national/

The Regional Educational Laboratories are educational research and development organizations supported by contracts with the U.S. Department of Education Office of Educational Research and Improvement. Important site components include the following.

- Assessment and Evaluation Program—Improving ways to assess educational results
- Child and Family Program—Helping to attain quality education and care for young children
- Comprehensive Center, Region X—Helping all students to meet challenging academic standards

- Education, Career, and Community Program—Helping educators, business, and community leaders prepare youth and adults for a quality work life, active citizenship, and a lifetime of learning
- Equity Center—Promoting equity in the workplace and classroom
- Mathematics and Science Education Center—Supporting effective mathematics and science teaching and learning
- National Mentoring Center—Providing training and technical assistance to mentoring programs through a variety of services and conferences
- National Resource Center for Safe Schools—Providing training and technical assistance that will enable schools and communities to create safe school environments
- Rural Education Program—Assisting small, rural schools
- School Improvement Program—Building capacity for efforts improving education performance
- Technology in Education Center—Assisting with educational applications of technology

INSTRUCTION

A MIDDLE SCHOOL TEACHER FOR ALL SEASONS

Kathy Shewey began teaching young adolescents in 1969. She was still at it when the 21st century dawned. When the school district in which she was teaching reorganized to include middle schools, Kathy moved from the high school to the middle school, became a part of a new thing called an interdisciplinary team, and never left. In a career that has spanned 30 years so far, she has taught in three middle schools in the same district, serving as team leader in all three places. Over the years, she has moved in and out of the classroom, serving several years as the district's middle school coordinator and, most recently, in charge of staff development for the district, including the training of new middle school teachers. Kathy Shewey has been an important part of the Florida League of Middle Schools and the National Middle School Association. Most of her career, however, has been spent in the classroom with hundreds, now many thousands, of young adolescents. When we first observed her teaching, in 1972, it was in an open-space team area with learning centers that covered the walls. She and her teammates were engaged in differentiating instruction and integrated curriculum before many educators had heard of them. When we last observed her, in the fall of 2000, she was teaching a thematic unit on the Vietnam War to a team of 8th grade students in her third middle school. All good middle school teachers, we think, have a little bit of Kathy Shewey in them.

WHAT YOU WILL LEARN IN CHAPTER 4

In Chapter 4, we divide our attention between traditional whole class instruction consistent with standards-based reform and the strategy now known as differentiating instruction. We examine teacher-directed whole class instruction in some depth because it is the method of choice in most middle school classrooms, most of the time. It is also regaining its popularity as a consequence of the new importance of standardized tests of academic achievement. In examining differentiating instruction, we argue that this approach is much more consistent with what we know about the characteristics and needs of the young adolescent. We look closely at methods for modifying and supplementing the traditional approach and at the use of small group activities and cooperative learning as major ways of moving toward differentiating instruction. We also illustrate consultation and co-teaching strategies as extensions of the concept of differentiating instruction.

CHARACTERISTICS OF EFFECTIVE INSTRUCTION IN THE MIDDLE SCHOOL

Middle school educators frequently find themselves torn between two different types of instructional pathways—traditional and familiar teaching strategies that have dominated classrooms for two centuries and alternative instructional strategies that may often be far more satisfying for both teacher and students. Middle school teachers are struggling to respond to two goals that seem, at least on the surface, to be very different, contradictory, and even mutually exclusive. On the one hand, middle school teachers are facing greater pressure than ever to choose instructional strategies that are congruent with the targets set by standards-based reform: teaching methods that yield higher scores on standardized tests of academic achievement. On the other hand, many middle school teachers remain loyal to the fundamental goal of the middle school concept—to guide their practice with a clear understanding of, and commitment to, the characteristics and needs of young adolescent students. This dedication to the young adolescent sometimes brings with it a conviction that the teacher ought to be differentiating instruction, instead of treating the class of students as if they were all alike with whole class instruction.

The choice of teaching methodology for today's middle school teacher is further complicated by factors such as teacher style and tradition and the comfort levels of parents and administrators with alternatives to whole class instruction. Furthermore, the choice is influenced by the fact that differentiating instruction is much easier to talk about than it is to accomplish. Consequently, whole class, teacher-directed instruction is most often what observers of middle school classrooms are likely to encounter. We are persuaded that an important goal of middle school educators, in the 21st century, must be to assist teachers in moving from traditional classrooms to classrooms where differentiation of instruction is more common. This goal is not an easy one to accomplish, because changing one's teaching style may be the most daunting task in the professional lives of teachers at all levels.

In exemplary middle schools, whatever strategy is chosen, effective instruction is the primary goal. The design of the building, the shape of the master schedule, the organization of teachers, and the schoolwide decisions about the grouping of students are prerequisites for the delivery of effective instruction. Even instruction's pedagogical partner, curriculum, is, in a sense, dependent upon instruction for its effective implementation. All of this heightens the significance that should be attached to the design and conduct of instruction in middle schools. The behavior of teachers, as they plan and implement their instruction, is at once both the most obvious and the most difficult aspect of middle school education.

Teaching as Decision-Making   Teaching, at any level, can be thought of as a chain of decision-making. A host of decisions are involved: decisions about who will be taught, about the curriculum to be implemented, about the instructional style to be employed. At the middle school level, educators have felt a commitment to several principles guiding the decisions about teaching. Instruction in the middle school, most educators agree, focuses on helping pupils understand themselves as unique individuals with special needs and important responsibilities. Instruction attempts to guarantee every pupil some degree of success in understanding the underlying principles and the ways of knowing in the academic disciplines. Certainly, instruction aims to promote maximum individual growth in the basic learning skills, while at the same time it permits the widest possible exploration of the world of knowledge and of the personal interests of each student. Finally, effective instruction fosters the ability to work and learn independently and cooperatively on the part of every pupil. Decisions about instruction in the exemplary middle school are strongly influenced by these commitments.

In addition to the principles that form the basis for decision-making about instruction in the middle, a number of other factors affect teaching. Research on teacher behavior and student learning styles should affect instruction. Many states implementing standards-based reform have special learning objectives that elicit particular emphases in teaching. The federal government has a steadily increasing number of guidelines and restrictions that require certain practices, and legislation passed by Congress in early 2002 ("Leave No

Child Behind Act") may eventually intrude even further into the choices teachers make. The state of the art in educational technology both extends and limits what teachers may attempt. The structure of knowledge imposes its own demands, as does teachers' understanding of the process of learning and their preferences for one or another of the current explanations of the process. Long before teachers begin to instruct their pupils, many influences have been felt in the design of that instruction.

No influence is likely to be more significant than the middle school teachers themselves. The literature of middle school education is replete with references to the special characteristics desirable in persons electing to teach middle school youngsters. List after list of special talents has been drawn up, with more recent versions the result of several decades of accumulating insight (e.g., Knowles & Brown, 2000). Yet we believe that the qualities that distinguish a good middle school teacher from a good elementary teacher or high school teacher are probably limited, albeit critically important. We believe that teachers who have the flexibility of the generalist, the expertise of the specialist, and the enthusiasm of one who understands and enjoys the special nature of the middle school student implement effective middle school instruction.

Unique and Transitional   Perhaps the most important characteristic of effective instruction at the middle school level is that it, too, carries the obligation to be different from instruction at the elementary and high school levels and to bridge the gap between the two. In the elementary school, effective instructional practices are often much more likely to be teacher-directed, whereas the high school has the burden of assisting students to become self-directed and responsible for their own learning to a far greater extent than students are capable of in the elementary school. Not that student-directed instruction is impossible or unadvisable in the elementary school, but most young children are in need of a tremendous amount of teacher direction in their learning in school. It would also be foolish to claim that the average high school student is capable of sustained and satisfactory patterns of totally independent learning for prolonged periods of time. Certainly older students need guidance and direction of varying amounts throughout their latter school years, but the amount of student responsibility for their own learning should increase as each year in the public school passes.

The emphasis of instruction in the elementary school is on a teacher-directed introduction to the world of the school and to the process of learning, and the stress at the high school level focuses on developing increasing increments of student responsibility. The middle school's obligation is to weave together these two divergent threads so that students may move from following one to pursuing the other without loss of educational momentum. Middle school teachers strive to accept students who are comfortable with almost total dependence upon the teacher for every learning experience. They act to help these students move to the place where they can survive in an academic environment much less tolerant of the personal idiosyncrasies of each learner. At the same time, the pattern of instruction in the middle school aspires to be sufficient to help students reach success in mastering the learning tasks that the curriculum of the middle grades imposes upon the learner.

The instructional strategies of the middle school are, therefore, a combination of structure, balance, and flexibility—structure, to provide the teacher-directed efforts without which the basic skills of the middle school student would remain largely unextended; balance, to offer the opportunities that will teach students the skills necessary for learning on their own and the attitudes that support such learning; and flexibility, to permit teachers to know when a particular instructional strategy is appropriate and when it is not and to have the disposition to make the changes in style when it is necessary for the students' benefit to do so. Instruction in the middle school emanates from the purposes of the school.

Teaching methods mirror the functions of the total institution, with care needed to relate to knowledge of the characteristics of the students served. Teachers must be prepared to teach a variety of different kinds of students with a wide range of learning skills and styles. The faculty must accept the challenge to become proficient with an array of methods and techniques, choosing one or another in relation to the purposes that motivate their actions.

Flexibility   Middle school educators must never be committed to any one particular instructional strategy to the exclusion of any other. The literature of middle school education from the 1970s seemed to argue that individualized instruction was the only approved method. The same literature, from the 1980s, argued in favor of teacher-directed, large group instruction, and individualized instruction fell from its favored position. Some might argue that cooperative learning assumed the favored spot for the 1990s. In the early years of the 21st century, so much stress has been placed on succeeding on standardized tests that traditional forms of instruction have experienced a resurgence in popularity, at the same time that the constructivist paradigm has achieved prominence (Perkins, 1999). We, however, are convinced that the elevation of one strategy over all others is dangerous and unproductive.

Because middle school educators believe strongly in the special nature of the students they serve, the enthusiasm resulting from this commitment may have caused an overemphasis on the use of individualized instruction in middle schools in the 1970s. While individualized instruction is certainly one of the most important instructional strategies to be employed in middle schools, it is just as certainly not the only such strategy to be used. Middle school and individualized instruction are not irrevocably connected. The same thing can and must be said for direct instruction, or cooperative learning, or any other special methodology and the middle school. Certainly middle schools and standards-based reform are not synonymous. The tremendous effect of the research on teacher effectiveness felt in all public schools during the 1980s probably brought a predictable overreliance on teacher-directed large group instruction. Perhaps cooperative learning will experience the same fate, and we are uncertain of the path down which standards-based reform will lead.

The question is not "What is the best way to teach middle school students?" The evidence of both research and practice clearly shows that there is no one right way to teach all middle school students all the time, just as there is no one right way to organize students and teachers on interdisciplinary teams. The instructional methods chosen depend upon the objectives of instruction, the nature of the particular group of students being taught, and the grade level involved. The right question to ask about instruction in the middle school is likely to be "What is the right method to use for these objectives with this particular group of students?"

Criteria for Selecting Teaching Methods Whatever the method may be, a number of perennially important factors can be considered in the selection of an instructional approach. Most important is the assurance that the method chosen does not conflict with knowledge of the characteristics and needs of the students in the middle school and of the particular needs of students in any one school and classroom. Equally significant, however, is the requirement that the blend of instructional strategies finally designed be consistent with the obligation of the middle school to strike a balance, pedagogically, between the elementary school and the high school. In addition, the selection of teaching methods involves criteria such as clarity of the learning task in the eyes of the learner when using a particular method, motivational power of the method, provision of immediate feedback of a method, opportunities for continuous progress provided, avoidance of excessive frustration and failure, likelihood of transfer of learning to other situations outside the classroom, and the ability to develop and preserve positive attitudes toward self, teacher, subject matter, and school in general.

A consideration of teaching methodology appropriate for middle schools might also include several other factors. First, the particular teaching method must match the instructional skill of the teacher intending to use it. Some methods are considerably more difficult to conduct effectively than others, and the expectation that all teachers will be able to use a method with equal effectiveness is bound to meet with disappointment. Second, the method chosen must not demand more of a teacher's energy than is reasonable. The phenomenon of teacher stress and burnout is too well known to ignore. Teachers in the middle school often seem, by the very nature of their tasks, to be frequently subject to considerably more stress and exhaustion than are teachers at other levels. Methods that demand even more energy and time are likely to be successfully implemented in a few situations and for brief periods of time. Third, methods that require a great deal of staff development time to learn will have a low priority, simply because there is so much competition for in-service education funds and, unfortunately, staff development is rarely as successful as educators would prefer. Finally, methods that, while they may be effective in producing achievement gains, conflict with the basic values and philosophy of the school and community must be examined closely prior to extensive implementation.

In Orange County, Florida, where many exemplary practices in middle school education have been implemented, educators attempted to break new ground in specifying the sort of instruction they wished to encourage in the middle school classrooms. A Middle School Instructional Practices Scale was developed and piloted by several members of the supervisory staff (Thomas, Pickler, & Sevick, 1990). The scale had 14 conceptual areas based on research on teacher effectiveness over the two prior decades. In each of the 14 areas, a "From" statement represents a less desirable practice and a "To" statement describes the ideal level of practice in that area. Then, again in each of the 14 conceptual areas, the developers of the instrument supplied concrete descriptors (not included in our description below) that enabled observers to determine the level on which the concept was practiced in a particular teacher's class or on a particular interdisciplinary team of teachers. Here are several examples of the conceptual areas.

INTRODUCTION OF FORMAL ACADEMIC DISCIPLINES AT THE APPROPRIATE LEVEL
FROM: Subject content is taught without regard to the developmental level of middle school students.
TO: Subject content is presented at a pace and degree of complexity that reflects an awareness of middle school students' developmental characteristics and needs.

PRACTICAL APPLICATION/CURRICULUM RELEVANCE
FROM: Limited opportunities are provided for students to apply skills or concepts learned in a lesson.
TO: Frequent opportunities are provided for students to apply skills and concepts to real-world situations and individual or class interests.

CONTEMPORARY INSTRUCTIONAL PRACTICES
FROM: Instructional planning and delivery consistently reflect the use of methods that are associated with the learning model of the past (single approach, passive learning, overuse of lecture, textbook driven, etc.).
TO: Instructional planning and delivery reflect the utilization of methods that are consistent with recent research on effective instruction and current district staff development efforts.

GROUPING PRACTICES (WITHIN THE TEAM)

FROM: Within the team, students are grouped according to similar ability levels at the beginning of the year, and the groups remain the same.

TO: Within the team, students are grouped and regrouped, for a variety of reasons, for varying lengths of time, and in both homogeneous and heterogeneous patterns depending on student needs and instructional goals.

Selecting instructional strategies for use in middle schools is, regardless of progress in districts such as Orange County, not a simple or easy process. Many factors must be considered, because research and experience recommend a number of methods for use with the students served by the middle school.

TRADITIONAL WHOLE CLASS INSTRUCTION

The Teacher Makes the Difference   In the past 30 years, research on teacher behavior has contributed mightily to the understanding of the relationship between how teachers act and the academic achievement of their students. While for years it was not, now it is very clear that teachers do make a difference in the academic achievement of their students. What students do in the classroom makes a difference in their learning, and what teachers do makes a difference in what learners do. Research has helped show that it is not only the socioeconomic characteristics of the students in a school that determine the achievement within the building. The most recent research (Sanders, 2000) indicates that teacher behavior is a more important variable in academic achievement than grouping strategies, ethnic makeup of a class, per pupil expenditures, class size, or other variables previously thought to be more important than how teachers teach. In any given school, academic achievement will vary from one class to another, based, in large part, on the teaching behavior exhibited in those classes. This behavior could be described as teacher-directed whole class instruction (Sanders, 1998).

Teacher behavior does make a difference, but not so much through single, discrete, separate teaching acts. What do seem to make a difference in student achievement are the teacher behaviors that tend to group together into patterns or clusters. These clusters of teacher behavior appear to be responsible for differences in learning among students exposed to different patterns. Several clusters seem consistently related to increased achievement on standardized tests: patterns of teacher expectations and role definitions, classroom management, and what might be called the direct instruction process.

Total class instruction has always been, and may always be, a mainstay of middle school teaching. It remains particularly appropriate when the focus is academic achievement in the basic skills with less than completely successful students and when standardized tests are the primary measure of success. It is the methodology of choice, we think, when teachers have few opportunities for effective staff development that will prepare them for more complex forms of differentiating instruction on a continuing basis.

For teachers and administrators interested in raising standardized test scores in basic skills, teacher-directed total class instruction of a fairly traditional nature is often superior to discovery approaches, or traditional small group teaching, or individualized instruction as it has often been practiced in middle schools. In 1979 Jere Brophy summarized the effective process of total class, teacher-directed instruction; research in the last three decades adds little to his conclusions.

> The instruction that seems most efficient involves the teacher working with the whole class (or small groups in the early grades), presenting information in lectures/demonstrations and then following up with recitations or practice exercises in which the students get opportunities to make responses and get corrective feedback. The teacher maintains an academic focus, keeping the students involved in a lesson or engaged in seatwork, monitoring their performance, and providing individualized feedback. The pace is rapid in the sense that the class moves efficiently through the curriculum as a whole (and through the successive objectives of any given lesson), but progress from one objective to the next involves very small, easy steps. Success rates in answering teacher questions during lessons are high (about 75 percent), and success rates on assignments designed to be done independently are very high (approaching 100 percent). (Brophy, 1979, p. 34)

Classroom Management and Whole Class Instruction

Time on Task Teachers who are able to produce increased amounts of on-task behavior without increasing the amount of time devoted to discipline or the level of negative teacher affect are teachers who help students score higher on tests of basic skills than the students would be likely to do with some other type of teacher behavior. Apparently this objective is easier to achieve with large group instruction than with most other forms of instruction. Task-oriented but relaxed classrooms (and both aspects are equally important) are places where increased achievement is found. Large group instruction is more likely to display this binary characteristic.

Time spent on task is of the essence in increasing academic achievement, and classroom discipline efforts detract from this time. Teachers who must focus their attention on dealing with deviant and disruptive behavior are likely to have less time to devote to the skills to be tested. Classrooms where a great deal of pupil freedom of movement exists are classrooms where learning of basic skills may be less. Socialization of pupils with each other, and of the teacher with the pupils, is also negatively correlated with pupil growth in the basic skills. Within reasonable limits, the less physical movement and off-task talk the better (Good & Brophy, 2000).

Low Negative Affect   Tight control of the classroom and of negative affect are not the same thing. In fact, positive affect and negative affect are not opposite ends of the same continuum. That is, the elimination of negative teacher affect from the classroom does not always, or even often, mean that the more positive a teacher is, the more learning that will occur. Positive affect on the part of the teacher is on many occasions either unrelated to increased achievement or negatively correlated such that the presence of positive affect produces less achievement. The use of praise is not uniformly helpful, so it must be used specifically and with individuals. According to the research, classrooms with a neutral atmosphere, where neither positive or negative affect abound, are likely to be classrooms where students spend more uninterrupted time at the tasks of learning set before them (R. Soar & D. Medley, personal communication, May 1979).

Establishing a classroom where tasks are taken seriously by both the teacher and the students, and where time is a precious commodity, is important to achievement in the basic skills. How the teacher manages the time of pupils over which he or she has control is as important as establishing a classroom where negative affect is at a minimum. Because learning is a process that takes place in time, and what students do is essential to their learning, influencing how pupils use their time becomes a critical variable. Research has indicated a number of factors associated with uses of time in the classroom and the connection with achievement in the basic skills.

Teachers concerned with managing their classrooms to maximize the effective use of time need to know several things. A number of studies, for example, indicate that what students learn is directly related to the uses to which they put their time. That is, simply, the more time devoted to the study of a subject, the better the subject is learned. If basic skills have a priority, then more time in the school day needs to be devoted to those topics. Research does not seem to indicate a point of diminishing returns; no apparent limit exists to increasing the time devoted to learning tasks. When breaks and wasted time are decreased, learning goes up. Increasing breaks will not raise productive behavior or achievement (Wittrock, 1986).

Although balance with other activities is important, strong research supports spending substantial amounts of student learning time in large groups in face-to-face contact with the teacher (Heistad, 1999). When using a large group instructional strategy, devoting up to two-thirds of the hour to large group teacher-directed instruction might be effective. The remaining one-third of the time could then be spent in closely supervised and monitored seatwork that is directly related to the preceding large group instruction. Seatwork that is not closely monitored by the teacher actively moving around the room is negatively correlated to achievement. Students spend more time on task when working directly with the teacher (84%) than when working alone in seatwork (70%) (Rosenshine & Stevens, 1986).

Whole Class Instruction: Steps in the Process

Assuming that large group teacher-directed instruction does often generate greater degrees of student on-task behavior with less need for negative teacher affect, the question remains as to what specific form this large group instruction should take. Here again, research has some important statements to make. Teaching the basic skills takes definite steps. Rosenshine, referring to the recommended process, called it "direct instruction" (Rosenshine & Stevens, 1986).

Step One Direct instruction, by whatever name, may be thought of as containing a series of specific steps, beginning with the assumption of personal responsibility for student learning by the teacher. Teachers who feel personally responsible for whether or not their students achieve the objectives set for them are, not surprisingly, more effective in producing higher levels of student achievement. Teachers who believe that it is up to the students to learn and that the teacher has no role or duty to motivate, inspire, or promote students' learning are less likely to act in ways that produce it. The power of teacher expectations is manifested clearly in teaching through the direct instruction process.

Step Two The second step in effective large group instruction involves a series of decisions, all made primarily by the teacher. The teacher decides what curriculum goals and objectives should be pursued, not the students. The teacher also decides the materials to be used, the settings in which instruction occurs, and the time to be devoted to the process. The teacher assumes the primary role in planning instruction, and students do little or no such planning.

The teacher makes a considerable effort to focus the time of both teacher and students on academic goals. Distractions, pleasant or otherwise, that draw the class away from the academic objectives at hand are discouraged. Socializing is diminished. All persons involved realize that their job is to pursue the academic objectives that have been set for them. There is no other choice.

Step Three With this mindset, the teacher then sets about to promote, through whole class, direct instruction, extensive coverage of the objectives that have been selected. When the teacher has arranged the class effectively, students will often be sitting with their backs to the rest of the class, while the teacher is facing the class. The teacher begins with an overview of the lesson that ties it to previous work and that prepares the students for the skills work to come. In doing so, the teacher concentrates on the whole class, not a small group.

Some researchers go so far as to specify that this review and orientation should last about eight minutes. Following the introduction, the teacher should collect and check the homework, if there has been some assigned (Good & Brophy, 2000).

Step Four   After the review and the checking of homework in large groups, the teacher continues the total class instruction with about a 20-minute presentation that develops the new concepts or skills. Again, this process is highly teacher-directed, with a minimum of opportunities for student input or questions. As a part of this lesson, however, the teacher should eventually begin to ask questions and solicit student responses on the concepts or skills that have been introduced. Such questions should be of a low cognitive level, simple enough to result in a very high success rate.

Step Five   The question-and-answer session toward the end of the lesson is important, and the research speaks clearly about it. The teacher should do most of the questioning, and the students should do most of the answering. Avoiding extensive student questions and extended answers and amplifications of student questions by the teacher seem to be practices well supported by the research data.

Teachers who have been told that teacher-directed instruction is evil face other surprises, including support for using a predictable pattern when calling on students during the recitation portion of the lesson. Random and unpredictable questioning may be counterproductive, while the structure and stability of the pattern process appears to support the anxious student. When questioning, teachers should wait at least three seconds for the student to answer (the average teacher waits one second), before interrupting with a new question or calling on a new student. Furthermore, teachers should see to it that other students wait to be called upon, and when they do not, to remind them that everyone will get a turn and that they must wait for theirs. Focus on one student at a time, but set up the questioning session so that everyone in the class has had a chance to answer a question. Praise correct answers only, but accept questions in the form that they are asked.

Step Six   The lesson, and question-and-answer session included, should be followed by a shorter period (for example, 15 minutes) of closely monitored seatwork. Such seatwork should be highly correlated to the lesson and should, ideally, lead to uninterrupted successful practice. Effective total class instruction requires that the teacher set the pace at which students work, both during the lesson and while at work at their seats. A teacher who spends the time during seatwork walking from student to student, checking work, and delivering brief praise quietly to specific individuals should hold students accountable for their seatwork. Under appropriate circumstances, and with great care, homework should be assigned. The homework should take little more than 15 minutes but should be collected and checked regularly.

Step Seven   The final step is to conduct weekly and monthly reviews of the concepts and skills that are being taught.

Important Modifications of Whole Class Instruction

The same type of instruction, no matter what style or for what purposes, cannot be applied equally to all types of students. Whole class instruction must also be modified and adapted to the types of students being taught. A directive total class instructional process seems especially appropriate when teaching the basic skills and when teaching students who might be described as less successful, those who are less academically motivated, are more dependent, and are anxious. Some researchers point out that these characteristics often appear with greater frequency in populations of school children from lower socioeconomic groups. Students with what has been called an external locus of control also seem to profit from the direct total class instruction (Brophy & Good, 1986). Teacher-directed whole class instruction might also often be the method of choice when standardized testing is at the forefront of a school's concerns.

With Less Successful Students   When using total class instruction with less successful students and under the circumstances surrounding standards-based reform, the general recommendation seems to be to follow the direct instruction model to the letter, but with some important emphases. Students who are less successful need a slower pace, with more drill and repetition as well as more overlearning in small pieces. More individual monitoring is important, as is more teacher warmth, encouragement, and personalized teaching in general. Students who are anxious and dependent need less challenge, but not less than they are able to handle. They do require lower levels of criticism and of demands, and they need to know that help is always available.

Less successful students need to be gently prodded into making responses each time they are asked a question, but with less rigorous probing and a greater stress on facts and on thinking operations at the lower end of the taxonomy. The oft-repeated statement that factual questions are bad and higher level questions are good is not borne out by the research on academic achievement, as far as these students are concerned. More success with lower level questions, more repetition, and more structured help of all kinds are called for (Rosenshine & Stevens, 1986).

When working with less successful students, teachers need to be aware of expectations that subtly lead to teacher behaviors associated with lower achievement in students. Teachers who expect lower ability students to learn give adequate amounts of feedback, provide equal amounts of individual attention, and are as patient with the slower students as with the higher ability pupils. Negative expectations are not consciously formed in teachers, and when notified of such behaviors, they change immediately (Ysseldyke, 2001).

With Able Students   Using total class instruction with students at the other end of the continuum, those with high ability and a high record of achievement, with an internal locus of control and so forth, requires a different emphasis. Such students should be asked more difficult questions, with more rigorous probing and redirection. Incorrect answers from these pupils should be corrected. More homework should be assigned to these students, or homework of a more detailed and demanding nature. Teachers also can admit more student initiation of teacher-student interaction and be more flexible in response to student input generally. Less structure imposed by the teacher, and more student-designed activity, is desirable with higher ability, less dependent, children (Walberg, 1986).

Teachers using the total class instruction model must also be prepared to further modify the process, depending upon the age or grade level of the students they teach. Generally, middle school teachers can rely on the use of more large group and whole class instruction, and less small group work, than teachers in the primary grades. Older middle school students should be able to handle more extended discussion, with slightly less drill and repetition. More cognitive challenge and higher level cognitive level activity should be encouraged, along with more sustained concentration on academic activities. A more rapid pace than would be comfortable for younger students and less individual feedback are both possible at the middle school level. Less positive affect and praise are necessary, but not to the point of having a higher level of negative affect and criticism.

In the primary grades, and in most of the middle school grades, when basic skills are the focus, and especially where the students are less successful or less academically motivated, total class instruction works well. As students mature and become more successful and the curriculum includes more objectives that are beyond the basic skills, the emphasis on the use of total class instruction should lessen and the search for alternatives that permit more flexibility and more student direction of the learning process should be increased.

With Basic Skills   Brophy points out that the findings concerning the process of direct instruction do generalize to students at the middle school level, but that the most important qualification is that basic skills must be the primary goal. The instructional objective pursued seems to be the guiding factor when deciding what instructional strategy to pursue. When the focus is on basic skills in reading and math, in particular, teachers should consider the total class model. When creativity, problem solving, complex thinking, appreciation, and social and emotional education are the goals, the total class instruction process may not be the best method. The direct instruction process may be inimical to student growth in some areas other than basic skills, especially if students are older or more academically successful. Total class instruction may be inconsistent with the goals of social studies, humanities, the arts, and other essentially less cognitive and less factual areas. It may be less effective than alternatives when heterogeneous grouping is important.

Why Does It Work? Why does total class instruction work better than individualized instruction or discovery modes when teaching basic skills, especially to less successful students? Because using this method, under these circumstances, often makes it possible to encourage higher levels of student on-task behavior with lower levels of negative teacher affect. The traditional whole class method seems easier for many teachers to plan and easier to manage, leaving more time and energy for the teacher to focus on the tasks and objectives at hand. The structure provided by total class instruction apparently helps the anxious, dependent, distractible students to stay on task, and it is easier to establish standards and hold students accountable for the accomplishment of those standards. Whole class instruction provides large helpings of teacher contact, and middle school students, who often measure the significance of tasks they are asked to complete by the amount of attention the teacher pays to them as they work on it, place greater significance on teacher-directed learning tasks than on those that primarily involve materials without teacher intervention. Whole class instruction takes less time in changing activities, requires the training and use of fewer additional adults in the classroom, and, consequently, provides more time for instruction and less time for directions and transitions. There is more modeling and less of the elitism and labeling that sometimes occurs in rigid ability grouping within a class.

Whole class instruction permits teachers to take an active role, one that allows them to, as one teacher told us, "really teach." The goals of instruction seem reachable with this process, as it does not require magical talents or hidden energy reserves to implement and continue. It is realistic and practical, and it inspires confidence in teachers that they pass on to their students. It develops a sense of community. It works.

Alternatives to Teacher-Directed Instruction Teacher-directed instruction clearly is not the method of choice for all objectives, with all students, at all grade levels, or, perhaps, in all centuries. When the objectives go beyond the basic skills, or when teachers are dealing with students who possess a great deal of self-discipline and personal responsibility, other instructional strategies may be preferable. Some of these strategies are effective because they build upon the characteristics of the students with whom middle school teachers work, and these same methods may be preferred because they provide a setting in which social and emotional education may occur along with the academic objectives. Under these circumstances, methods that forsake the large group teacher-directed process become more desirable.

DIFFERENTIATING INSTRUCTION

We believe that a style of teaching that has, at its center, an emphasis on differentiating instruction is to be preferred whenever circumstances warrant. That is, differentiating instruction is to be preferred when teachers are competent and comfortable with its use. It is to be preferred because American middle school classrooms are rocketing toward ever-greater student diversity, accommodated in heterogeneous classrooms that reflect the diversity of the student body as a whole. Differentiating instruction is preferred when school leaders believe that teachers ought to be implementing instruction that is congruent with the characteristics and needs of their students, and these leaders have the courage to "let the test score chips fall as they may," as one brave school leader recently told us. Traditional instructional strategies are, we believe, inadequate to the task of educating the next generation of early adolescents.

The Problem with Lecture

> The increasing reliance on whole-class, lecture-style delivery in middle schools, relative to elementary schools, paired with early adolescents' desire and capacity for inquiry and control, make middle school a boring place for many students. (Urdan & Klein, 1999)

Skillful middle school teachers have long known, in their hearts, that, regardless of what the research has said about the effectiveness of teacher-directed whole class instruction, there was a better way to reach and teach young adolescents. We have heard countless stories and anecdotes told by teachers faced with class after class of students who just cannot sit still and listen to endless presentations by the teacher. The new long block schedule being implemented in hundreds, perhaps thousands, of middle schools also makes it inappropriate, if not impossible, for teachers to lecture for 85, 90, or 100 or more minutes and for students to sit still and learn for that period of time. And, perhaps, lecturing never did work all that well at achieving high levels of time on task with young adolescents. Maybe it just looked that way.

A study that went beyond the way a classroom appears was conducted by Yair and reported in the October 2000 issue of *Sociology of Education*. Yair gave 865 American secondary students digital watches and asked them to record what they were doing when the watch beeped, eight times per day for a week. Overall, students were engaged with their classroom lessons approximately 54% of the time. Students were least engaged when being lectured to by the teacher (54.4%). Students were substantially more engaged during active learning experiences such as laboratory activities, group work, and discussions and in individualized instruction. Yair labeled classroom lecture "low-quality instruction" because of the results he discovered.

A particularly disturbing finding was that from the beginning of middle school (6th grade) until the 12th grade, the percentage of time that students were engaged with classroom learning activities registered a steady decline. This is, most likely, also accompanied by a steady increase in the amount of time teachers spend "giving notes" in the low-quality instructional style excoriated by Yair. He concluded that American secondary schools "provide instruction that encourages mediocre engagement rates and almost equal rates of alienation from instruction" (Yair, 2000, p. 268). We think that pioneering middle school teachers, exploring alternative instructional strategies, have intuitively understood what Yair discovered. Alternatives must be found to traditional whole class, teacher-directed instruction, alternatives that generate high academic achievement and that are within the skill level of the average middle school teacher.

Defining "Differentiation of Instruction"

> Walking into Ms Gage's sixth grade English class, a visitor sees six students seated around a listening center playing a tape of The Outsiders while they complete a graphic organizer comparing Ponyboy's experiences to their own. Another group of six students is seated in a literature circle discussing the themes of the different novels they have read independently. The teacher is in the front of the room with six students conducting a mini-lesson on narrator's point of view using the overhead projector. The remaining four students work independently on self-selected anchor activities related to figurative language. (Brimfield, Masci, & DeFiore, 2002, p. 14)

What is differentiated instruction? The term *differentiated instruction* is used in two different ways. First, educators use it to mean the "adaptation of classroom strategies to students' different learning needs, so that all students experience challenge and success." Second, educators use the term when describing "instructional strategies that move away, dramatically, from traditional forms of teaching, toward more active and interactive learning experiences." Differentiated instruction, as the example of Gage's classroom illustrates, leads to the development of classrooms in which students sometimes work at different paces, on varied tasks, and are assessed with a variety of indicators appropriate to their interests and needs. The process also leads to classrooms where students are working together more frequently, in ways that differ from sitting and taking notes. Differentiated instruction, then, can involve the alteration of what is taught (content), how it is taught (process), and how it is assessed (products).

Differentiating Instruction in the Regular Classroom

Good middle school teachers have always recognized that every student is unique and, to a degree, deserves and requires special attention and adaptation of the learning experience to fit those unique needs, interests, abilities, and attitudes. At the beginning of the 21st century, however, teachers are being asked to work with more broadly diverse groups of learners. The public middle school is bursting with diversity. Providing differentiated classroom instruction, teaching that responds effectively to this diversity, is absolutely essential.

For Gifted Students   Many educators argue that differentiating instruction is especially important in the heterogeneous classroom, where gifted students are to be placed in the regular classroom. Without differentiating instruction, gifted students may otherwise be overlooked in teacher planning because they are perceived to do well in class, frequently make good grades, and cause few discipline problems. In classrooms where a single curriculum is covered by all learners, however, many of these students may find school restrictive, frustrating, and uninspiring. Some of them receive good grades with minimal effort and can come to see themselves as impostors who are not as capable as people believe them to be. Some able learners become addicted to high grades, instead of focusing on learning itself. Many fail to develop study and production skills appropriate for their learning capacities. Many decide that school is a place to be tolerated and that real learning takes place elsewhere. Some lose interest in developing their abilities altogether. Some become discipline problems—and as a result, school staff is less likely to perceive these students as highly able.

In classrooms where instruction is appropriately differentiated for learners, gifted students are more likely to feel challenged, to encounter both struggle and success, to be called on to develop advanced study and production skills, and to be able to develop their particular interests in the context of the classroom. Differentiating instruction, then, is a key to creating learning environments that effectively accommodate the diversity typical of today's classroom, especially where the needs of able learners must be accommodated (Tomlinson, 2000).

For Less Able Students and the Learning Disabled   The mainstreaming and inclusion movements have placed at-risk students in many middle school classrooms, challenging the effectiveness of whole class instruction. Methods that worked in a homogenous, tracked, classroom often are no longer effective. Good teachers, committed to educating all students in a personalized and motivational way, reject the existence or use of one best or single way to teach and, instead, aim to accumulate an "arsenal of approaches appropriate in different circumstances" (Kilgore, Griffin, Sindelar, & Webb, 2002, p. 8). In particular, in classes with large percentages of less successful students, the traditional "tell 'em and test 'em" methods are clearly inadequate. Differentiating instruction, difficult as it may be, is the choice for teachers who will not accept a classroom where growing numbers of students are increasingly less successful.

For the New Citizen   A second, and equally compelling, reason exists for using differentiating instruction in today's classrooms. Many educators are increasingly uncomfortable with what they perceive to be the lack of fit between the traditional classroom experience and the needs of tomorrow's citizens, especially those who ought reasonably be expected to assume positions of leadership. The traditional, authoritarian, classroom may create a culture in which students depend on the teacher for everything, do nothing on their own initiative, and strive to "keep up (or back) with the rest of the class." This can happen, unfortunately, even in many advanced, honors, and gifted classes, where the objectives of learning more, faster, are still out of synch with the needs of students who will be tomorrow's leaders, independent thinkers, researchers, professionals, and artists. Such classrooms can reward conformity when nonconformity may be a more critical outcome. They may reinforce other-directedness when self-direction is the key to increased motivation and a broadened sense of personal and social responsibility.

The Knowledge Explosion   The third reason in support of differentiating instruction has to do with the knowledge explosion and the information revolution that has accompanied it. Both of these have had a tremendous impact on the lives of young adolescents in almost every facet of life except the classroom. Rip Van Winkle would recognize the type of teaching going on in today's schools. Middle school classrooms remain, in the face of an incredible information overload, places where teachers continue to think of their duty as primarily the provision of information by talking and providing students with the opportunity to take notes.

Very little reason exists to support the traditional conception of teaching as primarily the provision of information. Teachers can and should assume important new roles of classroom manager and facilitator of learning. Differentiation of instruction becomes an important strategy for achieving new roles and relationships in the classroom.

But, changing one's instructional style is much easier to talk about than it is to do. Many teachers, we think, are comfortable with the traditional teacher-directed, whole class instructional model. Few teachers have the time, energy, or support for making revolutionary changes in how they teach. This is a real professional dilemma. On the one hand, educators know that diverse classrooms are best, but that they work well only when all students, including the most able learners, experience challenge and success. On the other hand, teachers know how hard it is to change the way they teach, how challenging it is to do a better job of differentiating instruction.

We think that realistic strategies are available that can help teachers create classrooms where all students are successfully challenged, without asking teachers to make radical changes in their instructional style. The first strategy is for teachers to continue with the traditional teacher-directed, whole class instructional model that so many teachers know so well, but modifying that process so that appropriate degrees of challenge and support are more likely to be present. The second strategy is to supplement the traditional teacher-directed classroom with instructional strategies that allow substantial differentiation in what is learned and how it is learned.

Initial Steps in Differentiating Instruction

Confronted with increasingly diverse groups of students in their classrooms, with a correspondingly widening range of achievement, many effective middle school teachers begin the process of adapting their instruction while they remain within the conventional whole class model that they have been comfortable with. Their first steps toward differentiating instruction, abandoning total reliance on whole class teacher-directed instruction, begin within that traditional pathway. These teachers strive to maintain classroom rigor through high content, high expectations, high challenge, and high support. Dumbing-down the classroom experience is the last thing on their minds. They are comfortable with traditional teacher-directed instruction and see no reason, or perhaps little opportunity, to develop totally new techniques or methods.

These teachers still approach their teaching by thinking of the class as a unit. But they wish to challenge the most able learners and support the less successful students so that the class as a unit moves forward, together, as fast as is appropriate for the group and the curriculum. Some teachers may compare their roles with those of the loving shepherd, in classical literature and some contemporary cultures, whose job has been to move a herd of sheep forward at an appropriately rapid pace, while he encourages stragglers to keep up, searches for those who stray, and keeps a lookout for dangers to the progress and safety of all.

What do teachers do to keep the class learning rapidly, while recognizing the diversity in their rooms, challenging all learners, and providing support for all to be successful? Most of the techniques that effective teachers use in such circumstances are tried and true methods familiar to many experienced teachers. Among the most commonly used are the following.

Seating Arrangements   Effective teachers know that "proximity is accountability" and take great care in planning which students sit where. They understand that sometimes able learners, in their zeal to be noticed and approved by the teacher, try to sit as close as possible, while sometimes at-risk students try to avoid uncomfortable involvement in class activities by sitting as far away from the action as possible. Permitting students to select their own seats will, therefore, sometimes lead to the students who most need to be accountable for classroom involvement being seated farthest from the teacher. Effective teachers arrange student seating to maximize involvement.

They also organize desks in the room to allow the teachers as much immediate access to students as possible. Desks are arranged so that students focus attention on the teacher's area. Seating that allows students to turn their backs on the teacher is not permitted.

Progress-Based Grading   Effective teachers press all students for growth, insisting that each student learn knowledge and skills that are important and new. Grades are assigned on the basis of how much progress a student makes, not solely on the level the student attains. How much a student has grown is important to the grading process. Teachers know that effort, persistence, and motivation are the ultimate keys to life-long learning, and these qualities are strengthened and rewarded in the grading process. These teachers demand that every student learn something new, every day.

Tiered Assignments   Effective teachers modify homework and other major and minor assignments to account for the individual skills and abilities of the students involved. Choice is an essential part of assignments that work well in their classes. Different problems may be assigned for homework. Different levels of sophistication or completion may be expected in written work (e.g., essays, reports). Students in the same class may read different versions of the same story. Different experiments may be conducted on the same scientific principle.

Challenge Activities   The teachers should arrange for students to work on extra credit problems or other optional assignments designed to challenge all students near their correct level. One math teacher, for example, offers two "Problems of the Week" as a challenge activity on two different levels. She offers a 100-point bonus problem that requires even the most able learners to sweat in the process of solving it. She also offers a 90-point bonus problem that most of the students in the class can solve with the application of some effort. While students can choose either problem, this teacher's experience is that able learners will almost always choose the 100-point problem, especially with encouragement from the teacher. Less able students can experience success with the 90-point problem, and they enjoy earning almost the same points as other students in the class.

Graphic Organizers   Graphic organizers are supportive tools teachers use to help students organize their thinking, writing, and reporting. Such tools are especially useful for students who are not yet capable of fully abstract, conceptual thinking. Graphic organizers can often help these students keep up with the fast pace of the class as a whole. Teachers provide visual outlines, diagrams, grids, webs, ladders, or charts when they present a complex topic to the class as a whole. The graphic organizer is on the overhead or duplicated for every student. One of the most popular is the fishbone diagram, but there are dozens of other appealing images for graphic organizers.

Grading Rubrics   In the same vein as graphic organizers, a grading rubric brings concreteness to the expectations teachers have for student course outcomes or products. A rubric is a detailed description of what the teacher expects for an assignment, a test, an essay, or a product or outcome in the class. A rubric is a clear target for the student to aim at when doing work for the course or class. The teacher will describe, in writing or some other definite way, the component parts of an assignment that will get an "A," what will bring a "B," and so on. Students who, for example, earn a "D" on a report can look to the scoring rubric for an explanation of what was missing from their report, instead of claiming they did not understand or that the teacher was not fair.

Enrichment Opportunities   For students who already know the content of a lesson, or who finish learning it faster than others, effective teachers plan enrichment activities that are extensions of the basic content of the lesson, but in more depth, complexity, creativity, and sophistication. Such activities are not extra work, which is punishment, but opportunities to earn time away from restudying what students already know, to something that fits their level of achievement and interest. Such activities may not even be graded, unless they are used as a substitute for content students already know, content that other students are required to learn while faster students move to enrichment in the classroom or elsewhere in the school. There are hundreds of possibilities in every subject taught in school.

Collaborative Pairs   Many teachers regularly organize group and independent practice, as well as other classroom activity, so that it occurs with students working in pairs. Collaborative pairs is a simple combination of cooperative learning and peer tutoring, both of which are clearly related to increased achievement in the heterogeneous classroom (Marzano, Pickering, & Pollock, 2001). The documented advantages of the collaborative pair strategy include the following.

- Teaching another promotes greater self-learning.
- Self-concepts of students are improved when they teach others.
- Students who are taught by other students have an opportunity to develop a sense of warmth and recognition as a result of the attention and identification with the other student.
- A more efficient use of human resources results when students are used to help each other.

- Individualized instruction is more nearly possible when students are involved in teaching one another.
- Students are more highly motivated to achieve when involved in tutoring relationships, because students simply like working together.
- Because it depends on a new kind of interaction, collaborative pairs can be a focal point for eliminating some forms of discrimination.
- Students become more active participants in their own learning.
- Academic achievement is higher than in some other forms of instruction.
- It is a relatively easy strategy for teachers to employ.

Often, teachers choose to have students work in pairs, instead of larger groups, finding the smaller partner group easier to implement than more complex cooperative learning strategies. Typically, a teacher will introduce a new concept or skill, followed by whole class work or practice with that concept or skill. Then the teacher will arrange for collaborative pairs to engage in what would otherwise be independent seatwork or practice with the same content.

Collaborative pairs works best, teachers say, when students are paired carefully, according to their achievement or other important criteria. Most often, teachers match a high-achieving student with one who might be moving at an average pace, or a low-achieving student might be paired with a middle level student. Matching high-achieving students with each other is also an occasional way to challenge able learners. Putting two slower students together is often less successful, teachers report.

When students are prompted to engage in "elaborated helping" (Webb & Farivar, 1994) in collaborative pairs, achievement of all students in the class is likely to be higher. Elaborated helping occurs when students are involved in more than just giving the answer to another student. When students explain, persuade, refute, clarify, justify, or otherwise wrestle with a subject together, academic achievement of both members of the pair will often be higher than other situations would provide.

Many different techniques make collaborative pairing easy for teachers and students. One teacher provides a clock to each student at the beginning of the year—a big, simple clock face on a sheet of paper. Students are asked to make appointments with 12 other students in the class—at one o'clock, two o'clock, and so on—and to keep this record in their class notebook. When it is time to work in or to change collaborative pairs, the teacher makes a comment such as "Please work with your six o'clock appointment on this assignment."

Flexible Grouping and Regrouping   While rigid tracking between classes rarely works for all students, flexible grouping and regrouping within one classroom or among the members of an interdisciplinary team can be an effective way to modify large group instruction (George, Renzulli, & Reis, 1997). Students might be temporarily grouped within the class or team, based on interests, achievement, skill deficiency, or other criteria. A two-teacher team of middle school teachers, for example, completed a learning unit in which all of the 60 students on the team were grouped heterogeneously and taught with traditional methods. At the conclusion of the two-week unit, students were presented with four week-long seminar choices. Two seminars were designed to challenge the most able learners, and two were open to all. At the conclusion of this week of seminar work, students returned to the heterogeneous classroom grouping design.

Short-term groups of one kind or another work well on many occasions. Even in cooperative learning, where heterogeneous groups work extremely well, the most able learners in the class should be permitted to work in their own cooperative group, allowing other students to assume leadership in the cooperative groups that are formed by the rest of the class.

Study Guides   Many teachers find that providing written guides for major upcoming tests and assignments helps many students to focus their efforts in productive ways. A one-page study guide provided at the beginning of a curriculum unit, for example, might alert students to the key concepts that will be the focus of the teacher's efforts and later student assessment. A study guide provided during a review for an important test will help raise the achievement of many students.

Questioning Techniques   Effective teachers often adjust the questions they ask, and the way they ask them, on the basis of the different achievement levels of students in the class (Black, 2001). With a less successful student, teachers improve achievement during question-and-answer sessions by

> Asking easier questions with a high success rate
> Working to get some response from the student
> Providing clues, rephrasing, or asking a new question when the student has difficulty
> Allowing the student to finish a partially correct answer begun by another
> Asking low cognitive level, short, simple questions
> Waiting for an answer
> Letting the student volunteer the answer
> Getting around to everyone, quickly
> Naming the student before asking the question
> Asking for the student's opinion on another's answer

With a high-achieving student, teachers can increase achievement during question-and-answer sessions by

> Asking more difficult questions
> Providing positive criticism

Probing the answers for the student's reasoning

Accepting only the precisely correct answer

Asking for elaboration and justification

Concentrating on higher order thinking skills: analysis, synthesis, and evaluation

Asking "why" and continuing with "what if . . ."

Prohibiting the student from calling out the answer

Asking the question before naming the student

Concreteness   Recognizing that a heterogeneous classroom will contain many students who have not yet moved to a formal thinking level, effective teachers attempt to make their instruction more concrete for learners still in this stage. Using graphic organizers and rubrics are examples of this effort. Other techniques used to make lessons more concrete, enabling less mature learners to keep up with others, include using manipulative materials; bringing up real-world problems; providing frequent demonstrations; using media and props; displaying key points and terms; offering many, varied, specific, and redundant explanations; using marker words (e.g., "Now look carefully at this next word") and techniques (underlining, highlighting); drawing up frequent summaries; and making comprehension checks. The use of highlighters is becoming more common in middle schools.

Assessment, Test Preparation, and Administration   Lower achieving students are often intimidated and discouraged by traditional testing; the most able learners are frequently unchallenged by such tests. Understanding that, effective teachers develop alternative assessments for students to demonstrate what they have learned. In many classrooms, for example, students now assemble portfolios, collecting a meaningful set of their work, which demonstrates their overall effort, progress, and achievement in an area or during a grading period. Other teachers rely much more, than in prior years, on alternatives to testing that build on more than one intelligence: artwork, notebooks, study cards, exhibits, videotapes, dances, plays, scrapbooks, journals, collections, interviews, artifacts, mobiles, essays, self-assessments, take-home exams, collaborative tests that require both individual and paired answers, experiments, speeches, models, audio tapes, stories, and many others. All of these items can be contained in portfolios, too.

When teachers are faced with the high-stakes testing that accompanies standards-based reform, several techniques lead to greater student success, especially in the heterogeneous classroom. Here are some testing "Do's" for teachers.

- Teach test-taking skills to the class.
- Tell the students the purpose of the test, its relevance, and how the results will be used to plan further learning experiences.

- Tell the students that the test will be difficult, but express confidence in their readiness for it.
- Cite study references or provide a study guide.
- Tell students what kind of test items will be included.
- Provide opportunities for practice with similar items.
- Set up the classroom ahead of time.
- Be verbally warm when students arrive for the test.
- Monitor the testing carefully.
- Return the test results as soon as possible, provide students with feedback about the test, listen to their comments, and use this information in planning future tests.

Here are several testing "Don'ts" that need careful attention.

- Don't threaten reprisals if the students do poorly on the test.
- Don't make negative predictions about their performance.
- Don't mention report cards.
- Don't post the grades or otherwise publicize who got what grades.
- Don't express your disappointment with their performance or lecture them about the dire consequences of failure.

Supplementing the Traditional Classroom

A number of methods for supplementing the traditional whole class strategy, providing for even more differentiation, are available. Because describing these strategies, and the techniques that are a part of each, in sufficient detail would require at least one textbook alone, we have chosen to identify each strategy, summarize the essential elements, and provide references that contain more information.

Curriculum Compacting   Curriculum compacting is a process of pretesting students on new units of instruction to determine if they already know substantial portions of that material. If they do, the student can be released from the obligation of reviewing what they already know, and they can use that time for enrichment or acceleration. Permitting students who already know the curriculum to move to alternative activities has been a strategy practiced by good teachers for many decades. Teachers in the one-room schoolhouses of the 19th and 20th centuries probably practiced it daily. The process has been refined, tested, and incorporated into more broadly based programs (Renzulli, 2001).

At the beginning of a unit, the teacher uses a pretest (perhaps a version of the end of unit test that will be given later) to determine what the students know. Students who demonstrate that they have mastered more than, say, 85% of the content to be covered are released to alternative activities. These alternatives build on and enrich what students already know, and being forced to work only on their weaknesses does not punish students.

When a student demonstrates that he or she knows the material of a current topic or unit, the student has, in a sense, bought back time to be used for appropriate alternative learning experiences.

Joseph Renzulli and others recommend the use of a three-column form called a compactor or some other clear method of documenting what the student knows, how that was assessed, and what alternate activities the student will pursue with the time purchased. Students who test out are, furthermore, given the "A" they earned on the unit test. They are not punished by being given more work and then graded on that work in a way that might end up being punitive. If a student tests out of the regular unit of work at the level of "A," assigning more work and then giving a grade of less than "A" on that work would lead any clear-thinking student to question the value of passing the pretest in the first place.

The steps taken by the teacher in curriculum compacting include the following.

1. Identify the basic objectives and content for a new unit of instruction.
2. Identify the students who may already know this material.
3. Pretest the students.
4. Eliminate the portions of the curriculum that have been already mastered for the students who have demonstrated that mastery.
5. Provide individual options for students who do not qualify for complete compacting of the unit because they have not yet mastered all of the objectives but who demonstrate that they will be able to do so much more quickly than the rest of the class.
6. Develop enrichment or acceleration options for eligible students.
7. Maintain formal or informal records of this process for accountability purposes.

One practical variation of the curriculum compacting process was developed by Winebrenner (1992). She called it "Most Difficult First (MDF)." This technique offers a way of compacting homework and related assignments. Assume, for example, that a class of students is assigned 15 mathematics problems for skill practice. The teacher identifies which of the problems are the five most difficult. Students who are able to do these problems correctly, with only one error, can skip the rest of the (less difficult) problems.

In MDF, the teacher corrects papers until one student turns in a paper that is perfect. This student then becomes the checker for all other students. Papers that are 80–100% correct on the most difficult problems are given to the teacher, and the others must be worked on to completion of the whole assignment, with no appeal to the teacher. All students who complete the most difficult problems correctly get an "A" on the whole assignment, as do students who complete the entire 15 and get enough correct to earn an "A." Students who are successful with the most difficult problems can use the remaining time in appropriate activities of their own choosing, so long as they stay on task and do not bother anyone else, including the teacher.

Learning Contracts   Learning contracts are agreements between one or more young adolescent students and the teacher regarding specific learning objectives, activities, or assessment procedures. While contracts can be valuable for every student, or for an entire class, in many situations they are an especially effective way of differentiating instruction to challenge gifted and other able learners in the regular classroom. Contracts are particularly useful as a follow-up to the curriculum compacting process. When one or more learners have demonstrated that they have mastered at least a substantial portion of an upcoming learning unit, they can be engaged in enrichment activities through the use of the learning contract. The contract usually lasts for the duration of the learning unit, from several days to several weeks. The contract is typically used, for this purpose, to engage the student in enrichment activities related to the learning unit in which other students are involved.

The components of the learning contract include

- The objectives the student will pursue—learners know exactly what they have to accomplish.
- The particular resources to be used in the learning process—books, media, computers, or human resources.
- The learning activities in which students will engage—reading, writing, viewing, creating, researching, interviewing, experimenting, and other activities the student will pursue to fulfill the terms of the contract.
- How the learning experience will be assessed, how the student will demonstrate what he or she has learned, and to what degree of quality— tests, conferences, papers, portfolios, worksheets, demonstrations, models, and other conventional and innovative assessment strategies might be involved.

Winebrenner (1992) and others suggest the following steps in the contracting process.

1. Preplan the enrichment activities and assemble materials that students will need ahead of time. Check the library, consult teacher's manuals, talk with potential resource people, and so forth.
2. Design a master contract form. It might include activities or assignments that are non-negotiable and those that involve a student choice among options. Non-negotiable items could include components of the learning unit that were not completely mastered, new content that can be quickly mastered by the student, and so on. Negotiable items would include activities that were more complex, more challenging, and thus, more interesting to the student.

3. Pretest the students who seek to move to learning contracts and, while these students are taking the pretest, provide enrichment activities for the students who opt to work through the unit as a group with the teacher.
4. Confer with those students who are able to move to learning contracts for this unit, while other students continue to engage in enrichment activities. At this meeting, explain the expectations, describe the options available, and make certain the students understand the special rules that apply to them during this process.
5. Have the students sign the contracts and take them home for parent scrutiny. After the parents sign the contract, the teacher also signs.
6. Provide a space in the classroom or some other place where supervision and materials can be located, where the students pursuing learning contracts can work without interrupting the teacher and the remainder of the class.
7. Meet regularly with contract students to check on their progress and provide them with the teacher contact, feedback, and guidance that all students require.
8. Evaluate the student work at the end of the learning unit.

Winebrenner recommends that all enrichment work be self-correcting and ungraded. When it is self-correcting, the teacher is not submerged in even more paperwork. When it is ungraded, students need not fear that independent work will cause them to work harder for what might end up being a lower grade than they would have earned if they had simply moved at a slower pace with the rest of the class. They get the grade ("A") that they earned by testing out of the regular curriculum.

This does not mean that the teacher ignores the products that students generate. The students may be asked to make presentations to the rest of the class, meet together in a small group to share with each other, or deposit their work in a continuously developing portfolio. These students require the same praise and recognition for this work as for anything else they do.

Grading Contracts   Grading contracts can also be used to differentiate instruction by presenting a whole middle school class with grading options related to a learning unit that is taught using other methods. The contract, in this case, presents students with a choice of grades ("A," "B," "C," "D," etc.) based on the amount and quality of the work that each student completes during the unit, grading period, semester, term, or course. The most able students, along with others who seek to attain a favorable grade, are encouraged to choose "A" level contracts.

Students in a 7th grade geography classroom, for example, might become involved in contracts during a two-week unit on, say, China. The contract for the unit might present all students with certain options.

The "D" contract: Students attend class regularly, punctually, behave correctly, listen carefully, and give evidence of having read the textbook, by answering a question correctly when called on by the teacher.

The "C" contract: Students complete the terms of the "D" contract and summarize in writing ideas from four written sources about life in China, only one of which can be an encyclopedia.

The "B" contract: Students complete the terms of the "C" contract and receive at least an 80% on the unit test.

The "A" contract: Students complete the terms of the "B" contract and complete an independent project dealing with life in China, choosing from the possibilities assembled by the teacher or a student idea approved by the teacher.

Students also could be offered a contract that would give them the following choices.

The "D" contract: Successfully completes one of four options (unit test, independent project, etc.).

The "C" contract: Successfully completes two of four options.

The "B" contract: Successfully completes three of four options.

The "A" contract: Successfully completes all four options.

In the contracts, the teacher retains the right to exercise judgment regarding the quality of student work. If a student completes all four options, for example, but does so with less than "A" quality work, the teacher can move the grade down to a "B+" or "B." By the same token, if a student chooses a "B" option and does it exceptionally well, a "B+" would be in order.

Using grading contracts gives the teacher the opportunity to guide able learners into more challenging and complex learning experiences while keeping the class together as a group in the study of a particular unit. Individual teachers should adapt grading contracts to their own uses and preferences (Tomlinson, 2001).

Independent Study Independent study (IS) is a strategy in which able learners assume greater responsibility in

- Selecting topics to investigate on their own
- Designing procedures for learning about the topic(s)
- Conducting the inquiry
- Sharing the findings
- Evaluating the process and products of IS

Tomlinson (1993) argues that IS is especially valuable for middle school learners. It builds on a recognition of student differences. It allows the teacher to expand the dimensions of learning units beyond what the whole group will study. It encourages active learning and flexible grouping, two goals of middle school education. Tomlinson reports that IS leads to a more student-centered classroom—an important part of the rationale for challenging gifted students in the middle school and for differentiating instruction for all students.

Topics are usually those that would be unsuitable or unlikely for the class as a whole. IS topics would be related to the main theme of the learning unit, but they might be much more complex or explore a tangent that not all students would find interesting or for whom such an emphasis would not be appropriate. Winebrenner (1992) suggests that IS can be used to help selected students to become "resident experts" on a topic that is a part of the learning unit, one that the student can eventually help the teacher present to the rest of the class.

To be eligible for IS, students must agree to master the regular basic content of the unit on their own. For many able learners, their ability to learn school subjects more quickly than other students makes this a likely prospect. Students thus satisfy the teacher's need to be sure that they know the basics, and they satisfy their own need to avoid the boredom of trudging slowly through material they could learn in a flash. Once they have agreed to do so, students are freed from regular class time to pursue an IS project that they will eventually share with the rest of the class.

Winebrenner says that, ideally, the IS project should not be a written report, and it must be done during school time. This helps to guarantee that the students have something interesting to do during class time, when they might otherwise be bored. It also provides the students with the opportunity to contribute to the class in meaningful ways. Work has to be done in the classroom or at an alternative site in the school, and it cannot be taken home until it is shared with the class.

The 10 steps in the IS process are as follows:

1. Provide an overview of the unit to all students, so that the domain of IS options is clearer.
2. For students without much prior experience with the IS process, provide them with a list of starter suggestions for IS projects. For example, in a recent two-week unit on Japan, when one of us was acting as a substitute teacher, he gave students a list of 25 possible IS projects, including some of the following.
    *   Make a timeline on butcher paper of important events in the history of Japan.
    *   Illustrate a trip to Japan by constructing a map and describing the parts you would like to visit, the preparations you should make, the modes of transportation you would take, and the stops you would make along the way.
    *   Put up a bulletin board display entitled "Japanese Products in America."
    *   Conduct a survey of 10 adults, asking them how they interpret famous Japanese sayings, such as "Words are silver; silence is golden" and

"The nail that sticks out shall be hammered in." Present the results to the class in graphic form.

- Draw up 10 true-false questions about important aspects of Japanese culture and give the quiz to 10 students who are not a part of your grade. Report to the class about your findings.
- Pretend that you are a Japanese radio broadcaster following World War II. Prepare and broadcast (to the class) a story based on fictitious interviews with five Japanese citizens about their lives and how they feel about the United States.
- Draw a series of at least five cartoons depicting important events in the history of Japan or five pictures portraying important aspects of Japanese culture today.
- Develop a photographic essay about life in Japan. Find 7–10 pictures about Japan and describe what they communicate about life there.
- Construct a detailed model of a traditional Japanese home. Label important parts inside and outside the home. Take class members on a tour, explaining the meaning and importance of various areas.
- Imagine yourself a 7th grader in Japan during WWII. Write several poems expressing your (a) admiration for the emperor or (b) your bitterness toward the enemy.

3. Selection of topics, by young adolescents, should follow several guidelines. Topics should, for example, be designed so that the students go beyond just collecting information and reporting it. Answering intriguing questions, solving challenging puzzles, confronting difficult issues, or requiring the creative use of findings—all these will help move the student to a different level of challenge and satisfaction. To keep overeager or inexperienced middle school students from leaping into a topic prematurely, they should explore the content area broadly before making selections. Students choose a topic, preferably one they care about, instead of having the teacher make an assignment. Topics must be ones that have plenty of available resources and references to use in the study process.

4. Communicate with parents about the goals of the independent study, the procedures to be followed, and what parents should and should not do to help their child.

5. The teacher often meets with the independent study students as a group and uses this time to communicate all the rules, guidelines, and conditions attached to the independent study privilege. The teacher presents the students with an independent study contract that requires three signatures: the teacher's, the student's, and a parent's.

6. Teacher and student develop criteria for evaluating the independent study project. This should result in the creation of a rubric that provides a clear description of what an "A" quality project would look like. This

might include options for the final product, when the project itself does not require a specific outcome.

Students who do a project that is mainly research-oriented might be able to choose to bring it all together in a computer program, a video, an art display, an oral presentation, or other means.

7. The teacher helps the students investigate a variety of resources, including the Internet, avoiding the encyclopedia whenever possible.
8. The student develops a schedule for initiating and completing the independent study project, and keeps a journal of their effort. Students, no matter how capable they may be, are sometimes unable to manage time as maturely as adults would like. Helping them make a choice in a timely fashion will be an important start. Supporting the student by requiring a regular check-in with the teacher will help overcome a tendency toward procrastination.
9. Tomlinson suggests that students be required to keep a "process log" of their thoughts and actions as they work through the project. The students record new ideas, difficulties they encounter, and how they felt at different points of the IS project.
10. Winebrenner recommends that the student shares the final product with the class, as the "resident expert" on that topic, co-teaching it with me for that day. Or the students might make a presentation to another audience—their peers, another class, the school administration, or a group of parents.

Students who are able to fulfill the expectations associated with the IS project during one learning unit may qualify to participate in a later project. In addition to successfully completing the IS, the student must have

- Learned the basic content of the unit independently to at least the level of "B."
- Consistently remained on task, without disturbing the teacher when the teacher is teaching and without disturbing the rest of the class in any way.
- Followed all classroom rules and acted appropriately when working in other locations, such as the library or another classroom.
- Refrained from bragging or otherwise demeaning the work of the remainder of the class.

Winebrenner asserted that IS projects should not be graded. The reward for the work should come from the satisfaction of delving into topics of interest, relief from boredom, and the opportunity to share with others.

Curriculum compacting, learning contracts, grading contracts, and independent study represent four strategies for supplementing the traditional classroom, moving toward differentiating instruction without abandoning what teachers are familiar with.

Small Group Activities

Many middle school teachers, seeking to move away from traditional teaching but apprehensive about trying complex cooperative learning strategies, find that small group activities can help them with the task of differentiating instruction. The best teacher-tested activities described here can be used at virtually every grade level with almost every subject, without a great deal of extra preparation. We particularly recommend the work of Spencer Kagan (1994) in the area of small group activities.

Numbered Heads Together   Traditional review sessions are usually little more than a question asked by the teacher answered by one of the cheery hand-waving volunteers who always knows the answer. Other students may or may not even pay attention. No one learns much during such sessions. The Numbered Heads Together technique is especially effective for use in reviewing or checking comprehension (Kagan, 1994). It works well in mathematics classes, where other techniques for differentiating instruction are sometimes less effective. In Numbered Heads Together, the teacher organizes the class into small groups, and each student in each group is given a number. If there were four members in a group, for example, then numbers one through four would be assigned within each group. If there are more than four members in a group, doubling up on the numbers (e.g., two students with the number one in each group) works well.

The teacher then asks a question or poses a problem to the whole class. It can be either a low level recall, right-or-wrong-answer question or a high level analysis and evaluation question or problem, as the teacher chooses. The question is asked in a way that makes it clear that every student in the group must know the answer. The teacher might say, for example, "Make sure that everyone on the team can identify at least one cause of World War II correctly. Now get your heads together and work out the answer." Students then consult with each other until everyone in the group knows the answer to the question. They may have a specific period of time to work this out.

The teacher then randomly calls a number. All students with that number raise their hands or stand up. The teacher then calls on one student who must answer the question. If there is more than one answer to a question, such as the question on causes of World War II, the teacher can turn to the other students with that same number who are still standing and ask if they can supply an additional answer.

The activity can be repeated until the review or comprehension check is completed. Often, a quiz or test immediately follows the review. Appropriate points, rewards, or bonuses can be distributed to the groups whose members all do well. This technique can also be used with chalkboard problems, computer work, or short-answer questions.

Middle School Roulette   Middle School Roulette can be used for a variety of purposes in the long block schedule: review, testing, selection of assignments, independent practice, and other activities. The teacher divides the class into small groups of three or four students. Then, a representative of each group is called to the teacher's desk or some other table or surface. The teacher places a large number of index cards facedown on the desk or table, more cards than there are groups of students. Each card has a question, a problem, a situation, a short reading, or something similar. Each group's representative draws one of the cards and may or may not be permitted to take it back to the group to examine. If the representative, or group, decides to accept this particular card challenge, the group goes to work on it immediately. If not, the group's representative goes back to the table, replaces the first card facedown, and chooses a second card. This card cannot be exchanged, so the group must work on that question or problem. When the groups have completed work, or when time is elapsed, the teacher can choose to collect and check their work. Or the teacher might send a representative from each group to another group, much like the Group Reporter strategy, where the student shares the problem and his or her group's solution and receives feedback from the second group as to the correctness or suitability of the solution.

Stand and Share   In Stand and Share, another excellent Kagan (1994) technique, students form small groups or teams and discuss an issue or problem that has been posed by the teacher, one with numerous possible responses. The discussion continues in each group until every student on the team feels confident that he or she has an idea or a solution to share with the whole class. When every member of the group is ready, the members stand up. When the whole class is standing, the teacher asks one student to share his or her idea. When that student is finished sharing, he or she sits down and, simultaneously, so do other students in the room who had the same idea, concept, answer, or reaction to share. A second student is then called upon to share, and the process repeats itself with the other students who had the same idea in mind taking their seats when the second student does. The process continues until all students are seated. Kagan says that the strength of this structure is that all students see that their ideas have been shared, but nothing gets repeated, so the process moves swiftly. Stand and Share is a great way to bring closure to a topic, to solicit student reactions, and to address questions that have been unresolved. It can be used for review, independent practice, or other purposes.

Spontaneous Lectures   In this strategy, small groups of students deliver 90-second lectures on a topic, after having been given a period of time (maybe 20 minutes or so) to prepare them as a group. The teacher begins the lesson by stating that the students will be in charge of the lesson or review. The teacher introduces a topic that has a number of separate components to it, a topic that is familiar to the class members. The topic may be a series of math problems, reactions to characters from a series of short stories, countries from Latin America, simple science experiments on a theme, and so forth. After the topic is introduced, students are divided randomly into small groups and each group is assigned one aspect of the total topic. The small groups meet together for about 20 minutes to plan the lecture they will present. Provided chart paper and markers, the students write out their group's lecture notes in letters that are large and legible enough to be seen by all the members of the class when the charts are held up. Every group member must take a role in the design and delivery of the Spontaneous Lecture. Some are lecturers, some print the notes, some are timekeepers, some hold up the lecture notes, some post the notes on the wall after the lecture has been completed. When all lectures on the topic have been delivered, the teacher has the option of testing all students individually or having lecture groups become study groups that help each of the members learn the important topics delivered by all groups. Each teacher finds ways of adapting this technique to his or her own needs.

Inside-Outside Circles   As with many small group activities, at least part of the reason for their use is to avoid situations in which one student or a small group of students has the floor of the class, while the others sit passively and listen endlessly. Sometimes, oral reports can seem to go on forever. Inside-Outside Circles is a way of preventing this. There are several ways to do it. In one variation, the teacher divides the class into two large groups. One group forms an inner circle, seated with their backs to the inside, facing outward; the other forms an outer circle facing in, with each student seated facing a member of the inner circle. The teacher then poses a problem, asks a question, or invites an opinion. Each pair then discusses the question, helps each other solve the problem, or listens as the members of each pair make brief presentations on a topic they have prepared or thought up on the spot. Instead of endless individual oral presentations to the whole class, there may be 15 presentations going on at once.

The teacher monitors each round carefully and, in a few minutes, when discussion slows, directs the students in the outer circle to move one seat in a clockwise direction so that they are seated across from a new partner. The new pair can solve a new problem, share an opinion, or give the same presentation that they provided to their last partner. The process continues until the teacher decides to end it.

This activity can also work with pairs, trios, or small groups forming inner and outer circles facing each other. The members of one pair, small group, and so on make a presentation or report to the members of a similar-size group in the other circle. The members of the listening group then respond, saying what they liked about the presentation, agreeing or disagreeing with an answer to a problem, and so forth. Then the other small group takes its turn and gets feedback from the group sitting opposite. Kagan suggests that, at this point, it is possible to pull the groups out of the circle and give them time to improve their presentation.

Following this improvement session, the groups move back into the circles, meeting a new group. Each group repeats the process and moves on to a new group, for as long as the teacher wishes to continue the activity. Using the Inside-Outside Circles activity is a great way to cut down on long and repetitive oral reports to the whole class.

Group Reporters   Group Reporters will work with virtually any subject and for many purposes. First, the teacher divides the class up into a number of small groups. A class of 25 middle schoolers, for example, might be divided up into five groups of five students each. Prior to the class session, the teacher prepares a number of math problems, discussion questions, review items, poems, and so on. Each item or set of items is given to one student who agrees to be the reporter for that question or item. For the first round, each reporter begins with the group in which he or she is assigned. For some reasonable period of time, considering the task, the students in each group discuss the question, try to solve the problem, interpret the poem, and so on. At the end of that time, say five to six minutes, the reporter from each group moves in a clockwise direction to the next group. The reporter introduces the task to the new group but most often does not share a previous group's responses with the new group. Each group now has a new task, problem, or question. The process continues until all of the small groups in the class have dealt with all of the tasks the teacher designed; all reporters have visited every group.

At this point, the teacher can call for a short break or pull the class back together while the group reporters have a minute or two to synthesize the reactions of the groups to the task for which they were responsible. Then, the teacher invites each group reporter to share the results of the group work. Finally, the teacher may synthesize, debrief, or move on to another activity.

Having a pair of group reporters work together in each group may be desirable at times. For example, the teacher may want an able student to support the efforts of a less able student. Other reasons for pairs to work together include synthesizing and presenting the results of the groups' work.

Jigsaw   Originally developed by Elliot Aronson, this small group activity is a way of bringing students into the role of active worker, as Sizer suggests. Jigsaw is a complex process and may take more time than many of the other small group activities, but it almost always works so well that the time and effort are easily justified. First, the teacher identifies an area of study that students can learn and teach to others. The content may be as simple as a chapter from the textbook, or it might be a series of challenging problems or questions, or several poems. It could be the nations of Asia.

The teacher pulls together the content in a set of materials ahead of time or identifies where students can learn what they need to know from, for example, the textbook or the Internet. The teacher places the class into heterogeneous study groups, or home teams, of four or five students. These students examine what it is that they all have to learn (for example, the chapter on Japan), and each student decides which part of the overall task he or she wants to learn and teach to the others in the small group. One student, for example, might want to learn about the geography of Japan; another might want to learn about the major aspects of the culture; a third might investigate school or family life in Japan; a fourth might learn about important events in Japanese history; a fifth might agree to study the materials about the economy in contemporary Japan. Each of these students has agreed to become an expert on that one area.

Expert groups then form. One student from each home team joins with the others in the class, from other home teams, who have agreed to become experts on that same area. All of the students who selected the geography of Japan, for example, work together. These four or five students help each other to master the subject in question, to become so expert that they can go back and teach it to the others in their home team. In an extended Jigsaw, the students may have to do research in the library, on the Internet, or elsewhere. They bring this research to their expert group and teach each other about it. The final part of this step is for the expert groups to plan how they will teach what they have learned to members of their home team, avoiding just telling whenever possible. They might design a game, a series of questions, or some other way of making what they are teaching interesting to their teammates.

When there is a wide range of achievement in a class, it is sometimes wise to pair a gifted student and less successful student to become experts on the same topic, to ensure that the rest of the group will not suffer. The teacher can ensure that the two operate so that each has a meaningful contribution to make, permitting able learners and those less so to work together effectively, without having the gifted student do all the work.

Each expert or pair of experts returns to the home team and teaches the members of that team what they have learned about the subject or content. Everyone in the small home team is also taught what the other experts have learned, so that at the end of the process all students have learned all areas of the topic. If an expert is absent on the day he or she is to teach, two groups can be combined for that part. Evaluation comes next. Each student is assessed, individually, on all areas of the curriculum studied through the Jigsaw process. Then groups that have high average scores, or who have made real progress, may receive a group prize or recognition.

Spencer Kagan (1994) describes a modification of Jigsaw that he calls "Co-Op Jigsaw." In this version, experts come back and teach their home team. Then, each team integrates all the information from the experts and presents a report to the whole class on the topic that the group has been studying. In math, for example, experts may have been learning, separately, about formulas for determining height, weight, volume, and shape of various objects. After each expert teaches these formulas to his or her home team, each home team puts the information all together and teaches the whole class a lesson on how it applies to its object (i.e., a golf ball, baseball, brick, balloon, or eraser). In a geography class, Co-Op Jigsaw might have home teams studying various countries in a region of the world (e.g., different countries in Asia). Experts would, however, work together to learn about aspects of climate, natural resources, history, population, and physical features. Home teams would integrate all of the information about their assigned country and then teach it to the rest of the class.

KWL Charts   Activating prior knowledge is an important part of successfully learning new material. A technique called KWL assists this process. Virtually all uses of KWL techniques are based on three important questions for students.

What do I already *k*now about this subject?
What do I *w*ant to know about this subject?
What have I *l*earned about this subject?

KWL Charts are useful for having individuals and small groups of students assess what they know about a subject, virtually any subject, both before and after a learning experience.

The teacher can design such a chart in about five minutes, one that looks something like Figure 4.1. Students are invited to begin individually, and then they may talk together in small groups about what they already know about the subject or topic and make a list of those items—the K. Then students are asked to identify what they believe to be the important aspects of the topic that they need or want to know, or they may list what they believe to be important questions about the topic to which they need answers.

The teacher may ask individuals or small groups to share, in summary form, what they already know and what they want to learn about the topic—the W. The teacher may synthesize this information on the board or on an overhead transparency. Individual and small group charts are then collected, and the teacher keeps them until the completion of the lesson or the unit. One of the last steps in the instructional sequence for the lesson or the unit will then focus on students completing the remainder of the chart—the L. Once again, the teacher can summarize and record the outcomes of instruction for the class as a whole.

K	W	L
What do I know about this subject?	What do I want to know about this subject?	What have I learned about this subject?

FIGURE **4.1**

A KWL CHART

KWL Charts are effective for helping both the teacher and the students see clearly three important aspects of learning. The first question helps students see that they are not ignorant on most topics, and it helps teachers recognize what students already know so that instruction can be streamlined. The second question helps both teacher and students agree on the focus for the upcoming lesson or unit. The third question is especially useful for helping students (and parents) see that important insights or outcomes have transpired as a consequence of instruction.

Brevino, Snodgrass, Adams, and Dengel (1999) describe a strategy similar to KWL Charts, one they call "Focus Friends." In this adaptation, the teacher places students into trios, prior to an instructional activity of any sort. Each group is given one 5" × 8" index card. On one side of the card, the trios summarize what they already know about this topic or unit, and on the other side they are to list at least three important questions about the topic, one from each student. The lesson is then presented. After the lesson, the trios reconvene to answer the questions they had written beforehand. The teacher then brings the class back as a whole to discuss the learning experience, clarify questions that remain unanswered, and provide a summary and debriefing.

With Two-Minute Interviews, Brevino and colleagues suggest yet another variation of the KWL strategy using pairs of students, but a teacher could also use trios or even quartets. The teacher groups the students and gives each student a piece of paper to take notes from a two-minute interview on what his or her partner remembers from a lesson or perhaps from a reading just completed. The teacher then calls on several students to report on their partner's information (or lack thereof), as a way of assessing what students have learned from a lesson or a unit, as a review or as preparation for a lesson or a test that follows. This strategy can also be used to get students involved in reviewing homework, comparing answers, and correcting work when needed.

Solution Sort Solution Sort is another small group activity aimed at injecting some freshness into the review process. The teacher makes certain that all the students in the class have two pieces of paper and a pencil, then the class is divided into smaller groups of from five to nine students. In the small group, each student is asked to write out a problem on one sheet of paper and a correct answer to that problem or question on another sheet. Alternatively, the teacher may distribute a problem or a question to each student and require the student to write his or her best answer to the problem or question on the second sheet.

Problems or questions will vary with the subject. In subjects such as math or science, the teacher might assign questions from the end of the chapter or section in the textbook, being certain to assign questions carefully, considering the difficulty of the question and the ability of the student. In social studies, when the class is studying an area of the world in geography, the teacher distributes a different question to each student along the lines of "How can India solve its problem of poverty?" In language arts, the students could be asked to interpret a different paragraph or statement from a book. In well-managed classes, students can be trained and invited to write the questions or problems, too.

Students are then asked to fold their solution papers so that no one can read them and to place their solution sheets in a box held by the teacher. Or students can simply exchange solutions around the group. The students keep the papers on which their question or problem is written. The students then select a solution from the box. They do not look at the solution until directed to do so by the teacher. When all students have a new solution, the teacher calls on a student to read his or her question out loud. All the other students in the group then examine the answer they have, to determine whether it fits the question. The activity continues until all students have shared their problem or question and had the solution matched to them.

The activity can also be done in reverse. The teacher can direct students to place their problem or question in the box and keep their solution. Each student would then read the solution out loud, and other students would try to match the solution with the appropriate question or problem.

Three-Step Interview   Three-Step Interview, also popularized by Spencer Kagan (1994), is frequently used to promote divergent thinking, to share individual reactions to learning experiences, or to provide an anticipatory mindset for an upcoming lesson. It also works for reviews. Three-Step Interview is good for sharing information, impressions, reactions, or conclusions. The method also helps build listening skills and other group skills.

The middle school teacher divides the class into groups of four or six students, and each small group is again divided into two or three pairs of students. The members of each pair interview each other.

The teachers must emphasize that it is an interview, not a back and forth discussion. One person asks questions and listens silently but attentively while the other responds. Note taking is permitted. The middle school teacher will have to stress the differences between interview and discussion, and he or she perhaps will have to teach students how to conduct a good interview. Following this interaction, the pairs of students share their thoughts within their small group and then perhaps with the class as a whole. The process might end with one or more of the small groups sharing especially interesting ideas or problem solutions with the whole class.

Kagan suggests that three-step interviews can be used to introduce a topic, using questions such as "What experience have you had with . . . ?" "What do you already know about . . . ?" "What do you most want to learn about . . . ?" This strategy can also be used for closure on a topic or lesson, with questions such as "What did you learn from this lesson?" "How will you use what you have learned today?" "What would you like to know more about . . . ?" It can also be used to review homework or to prepare for a test, with questions such as "What did you find most interesting?" "What did you have the most difficulty with?" "What do you think is going to be most important to know for the test?"

Cooperative Learning

Cooperative learning, during the last two decades, took the middle school by storm and appears, in the new century, to be firmly fixed in the repertoire of desirable techniques for the successful middle school teacher. Perhaps because of the social nature of middle school students, perhaps because of the fascination of middle school educators for effective innovation, perhaps because of the demands of increasingly heterogeneous classrooms, middle school educators seem to feel compelled to involve their students in cooperative learning experiences. Middle school educators may also respect the solid research base that accompanies the claims of cooperative learning proponents.

Research comparing middle level education in the United States with that in Japan may shed light on the popularity of cooperative learning strategies among middle school educators (George with Evan George, 1995). Many Japanese educators believe that young adolescents are at a unique point of readiness for learning about cooperation and positive group involvement. These educators seem convinced that, to use a popular phrase, a "window of opportunity" exists for learning group citizenship, loyalty, duty, cooperation, and so on, which opens during early adolescence and closes shortly thereafter. We tend to agree, and we suspect that the popularity of cooperative learning in middle level schools indicates that many American educators intuitively support these same assumptions about the readiness of young adolescents to learn about group life.

The attempt to develop small group learning strategies that combine both academic inquiry and learning about the democratic process has led to a number of related but somewhat different methods for use in the middle school classroom. Individual teachers have, for the last two centuries, used group projects and other team learning situations to achieve a variety of objectives. Recently, however, several more clearly defined and researched models of group and team learning have made their appearance in the classroom.

These models of teaching have been most carefully cataloged and described by Joyce, Weil, and Calhoun (2000). These authors categorize several types of teaching methods into families of models, which, in the case of cooperative learning, emphasize the social dimension of learning and teaching. Middle school and junior high school teachers have been using these methods, or portions of the methods, for many years without labeling or describing their uses for others. According to Joyce and his colleagues, the origins of these methods can be traced to the theories of John Dewey who, as long ago as 1916, advocated the use of teaching methods that would combine both academic inquiry and democratic learning.

Organizing the students in a class into small groups whose task is to work cooperatively while reacting to, inquiring into the nature of, and attempting to solve social problems that the teacher helps them to select is a method that teachers of older children and early adolescents have used effectively for many years. Herbert Thelen developed one of the earliest versions of cooperative learning. Joyce, Weil, and Calhoun (2000) list six steps in the application of what Thelen called the "group investigation" process.

1. The students in the group are confronted with a stimulating problem that arises naturally or is supplied by the teacher.
2. The students react to the problem, and the teacher draws their attention to the diversity of their responses and reactions to the problem.
3. As the students become interested in the differences in their responses to the problem, the teacher helps them formulate a problem statement.
4. Following the formulation of a problem statement, the students organize themselves to attack and resolve the problem.

5. The students pursue the study of the problem and, at the conclusion of their study, report their results to the teacher and the rest of the class.
6. With the assistance of the teacher and the rest of the class, the investigating group evaluates the solution to the problem.

One can see, immediately, that even in this early version of cooperative learning the teacher plays a much different, decidedly more indirect, role than in the large group, total class instruction process. In all successful versions of cooperative learning, the teacher is careful to ensure that the students examine the process in which they are involved, that they are conscious of the methods they are using, that they are learning interpersonal and social skills involved in effective group work, and that they are involved in the examination of personal meaning in the group context.

The basic conclusion of the research on cooperative learning methods (Marzano, Pickering, & Pollock, 2001) is that all such methodologies require, for success in enhancing academic learning, two basic conditions. First, there must be a common group goal that requires collaboration to be achieved; this is often called positive interdependence. Second, individuals in the group must be held accountable for their own particular contributions to the group's effort and their own achievement; the teams' success depends on the individual learning of each member. This second component is usually termed individual accountability. Both components are essential. In a review of research on cooperative learning, Slavin observed that, when these two essentials were effectively present in the method used, results were consistently positive, not only in academic achievement, but also in such diverse but desirable outcomes as "self-esteem, inter-group relations, acceptance of academically handicapped students, attitudes toward school, and ability to work cooperatively" (1991, p. 71). Little wonder, then, that such methods are popular with middle school educators.

The most extensively researched cooperative learning method appears to be the Student Team Learning (STL) process developed at Johns Hopkins University. STL seems to be taking on the characteristics of a family of methods, given that four or five major versions have been developed and studied. Two STL methods are general strategies adaptable to most subjects and grades: Student Teams–Achievement Divisions (STAD) and Teams–Games–Tournaments (TGT). Elliot Aronson developed a third general method adapted to the STL format, Jigsaw. The other methods are specifically designed for reading and mathematics programs in the intermediate grades. Slavin observes that STL programs require, in addition to positive interdependence and individual accountability, a sort of "equal opportunity for success." The evaluation of individual learning is based on improvement over prior achievement, so that all group members experience an appropriate degree of challenge and are valued for their contribution by other members of the group. In STL, as in most cooperative learning methods, students work together in groups of three, four, or five. Sometimes the students respond to a lesson presented by the teacher by making certain that all group members have mastered the lesson prior to a quiz during which group members may not help each other.

In other methods, somewhat complicated tournaments replace the quizzes. In TGT, students are assigned to learning teams of four or five members. After the teacher presents the lesson, the teams study together, trying to make sure that every team member understands the lesson, because the success of the team depends upon each member functioning effectively in the slot he or she is assigned. At the end of a period of time (for example, a week), the teams engage in a tournament with other teams in the class. Each team member competes with students from other teams on a more or less ability-grouped basis. At the end of the tournament, winners from each competition level move up to the next highest position, competing there with those whose scores on the last set of games classifies them as on the same level. The spirit of competition changes rote memorization from a dead and deadly affair into one of challenge and enthusiasm. Under these circumstances, competition also begets, ironically, higher levels of cooperation.

According to one teacher we know, the equal competition made it possible for every student to have a good chance of contributing equally to the success of the team—an example of Slavin's "equal opportunity for success." A weekly class newsletter prepared by the teacher recognized successful teams and students who contributed effectively to their team's success. The dynamics of the process combined to produce a classroom where the objectives of small group instructional processes were effectively realized. For example, Geoffrey Pyne, former mathematics teacher at Mebane Middle School, in Alachua, Florida, said, "The students love to play the tournaments, and I believe I can honestly say that this was true for all my students. When presented as an alternative to the customary classroom methodologies in mathematics, it is accepted in a very positive manner by the students." The TGT process also allows the teacher in a school where racial issues are unusually sensitive to promote regular interaction without resorting to an unpopular seating chart, because all teams must be balanced—racially, sexually, and academically. As Pyne pointed out, the TGT process does not affect the teacher's own individual style of teaching, because it structures the way in which students work together on any objective or content presented to the class through any chosen style or method of presentation.

The basic idea of this sort of cooperative learning is that when students learn in small, carefully structured learning groups (with group goals, equal opportunity for success, and individual accountability), they help one another learn; gain in self-esteem and feelings of individual responsibility for their learning; and increase in respect and liking for their classmates, which is increasingly important in light of the changing demographics of American middle schools (Marzano, Pickering, & Pollock, 2001). STL and other methods draw upon the group spirit that emerges from common effort, hearkening back to the experiences of each person growing up and participating in team sports, music groups, and other such efforts. The exciting experience of working toward a cooperative goal, either in competition with other groups or in comparison to some ideal goal, provides a strong motivational force that, the originators of the STL process argue, teachers can use to infuse classroom learning with a sense of urgency. Students in an STL-style classroom are involved in a learning process that provides the same kind of peer support, excitement, and camaraderie that are characteristic of team efforts elsewhere.

Research and development efforts at Johns Hopkins extended the cooperative learning model into the area of reading and writing in a whole language workshop-style of instruction. Student Team Reading and Student Team Writing seem to be promising combinations of whole language strategies and team learning. Johnson, Johnson, and Holubec (1998) maintain that learning to be cooperative is as important as being cooperative to learn. They argue, as do others (Kohn, 1991), the critical importance of developing a generation of learners who possess the social skills and propensities that will enable Americans to work together as adults with less interpersonal friction and more intergroup harmony. Like any other skill or attitude, they write, children and youth are not born with the social skills and attitudes they will need to be successful adults; these must be learned.

Effective interpersonal skills and attitudes must, consequently, be intentionally introduced into the school lives of early adolescents. Such skills and attitudes must be taught. Cooperative learning, from this perspective, will not be fully effective unless teachers introduce these skills and attitudes prior to and throughout the whole learning cycle.

Johnson, Johnson, and Holubec propose five essential conditions for fully developed cooperative learning situations. There must be (1) positive interdependence and (2) individual accountability, as with Slavin's versions. The Johnson and others model cites (3) the importance of "face-to-face interaction" as the medium in which motivation, feedback, and social influence grow. They emphasize (4) the direct instruction, modeling, coaching, and practice of interpersonal and group skills. And they see (5) group processing as the way in which group members provide and receive feedback on how well they are achieving their goals and maintaining effective working relationships (Johnson, Johnson, & Halubec, 1998).

As an illustration of the essential components of cooperative learning in action, Johnson and others described an assignment from an English class in a middle level school. The students in the class were involved in writing essays on a story, about the experiences of a time traveler, they had been asked to read. The class was divided into groups of four students, each balanced by gender, race, achievement, and other factors, which made them representative of the class. A series of instructional tasks was assigned over a period of about a week in the class.

1. A pre-reading discussion takes place on what time travel would be like.
2. Each student writes a letter or proposal requesting funds for time travel into the future.
3. Group members read and edit each other's letters, give suggestions for improvement, and mark errors that need correcting.
4. Each student submits revised and corrected letters to the teacher, handed in with the signatures of the group members who edited them.
5. Each member reads the story and responds tentatively to questions from the teacher.
6. Group members discuss the story and reach consensus about answers to the teacher's questions.
7. Each student writes a composition about the meaning of the story and argues in support of his or her conclusions about its meaning.
8. Group members edit each other's compositions, perhaps having each member read those of two others.
9. All final compositions are submitted, along with the signatures of student editors.

The teacher uses a point system for grading the compositions that arrives at both a group grade and individual grades for each participant. As a part of the process, the teacher instructs the students in the important cooperative skills of providing feedback on a person's work without criticizing the person. This is a skill everyone can always develop more fully. At the conclusion of the week, groups spend time processing how well they worked together and how they could improve their working relationships in the future (Johnson et al., 1998, pp. 1:8–9).

Cooperative learning is an important tool for middle school educators interested in moving toward differentiating instruction for the students they teach. Cooperative learning is built, intentionally or not, on a solid grounding in the characteristics of the young adolescent student. It accomplishes the objectives for which middle schools are accountable, academically (Marzano, Pickering, & Pollock, 2001). And it serves effectively in the attempt to pass on to students the social and human relations skills and attitudes that students require for effective citizenship. Middle school teachers who attempt to fashion their instructional styles without any effort to include cooperative learning will, in our opinion, serve their students less effectively than they might.

Other Major Methods for Differentiating Instruction

Differentiating instruction has emerged as a high priority for middle level education. Consequently, a variety of strategies for accomplishing differentiation have become popular.

Learning Centers   Learning centers are one of those old favorites that is experiencing new popularity with the more recent efforts toward differentiating instruction. The learning center seems to provide a popular balance between teacher control of the curriculum and the goals of increasing student self-direction, independence, and responsibility, as well as opportunities of heterogeneous classroom life. Learning centers, or stations, as they are sometimes called, usually refer to "an area for study and activity, in or near the classroom, that has been provided for the structured exploration of a particular subject, topic, skill, or interest. It is a place for using and storing materials that relate to a special interest or curriculum area. It may be on a wall, in a corner, next to a bookcase, or on a table; but it exists somewhere in the physical space of the classroom or school" (Schurr, Lewis, LaMorte, & Shewey, 1996). It is not, however, the library or media center of the school.

Learning centers frequently exhibit the following characteristics.

- Learning centers are auto-instructional. When properly designed they do not require the constant and continuous intervention of the teacher. Students, after consulting with the teacher, may go directly to a learning center and begin work. Consequently, a well-designed learning center will contain clear, easily discovered objectives and plainly written directions for beginning, continuing, and completing work.
- A learning center invites each student to achieve specific objectives that are clearly communicated. The directions must specify the nature of the task and the required exit behavior.
- Each learning center includes a method of recording the student's participation. The teacher may provide individual folders for each student, stored with others in an area removed from the center but convenient to both students and teacher. Students make additions to their folders whenever necessary.
- A learning center offers opportunities for assessment of pupil learning. Ideally, a center contains both pre-assessment and post-assessment, which students can administer to themselves or to each other without constant supervision by the teacher.
- Each learning center provides the opportunity for student decision-making and steps toward the assumption of increased degrees of independent learning. Students should be making decisions about the management of time, use of resources, goals, evaluation of products, and other concerns.

Learning centers in middle school classrooms can be used on a part-time basis to accomplish a wide variety of purposes. Enrichment centers, where students may go for additional work, in greater depth, on a particular topic, are effective, too, especially in heterogeneous classrooms where faster learners must be challenged. For students on the less successful end of the continuum, learning centers can be used for remediation or reinforcement opportunities. Centers can be particularly useful as motivational previews of coming units or themes. And learning centers are a place to bring closure to a unit that used total class instruction or small group learning as the primary instructional strategies.

For several years at Spring Hill Middle School, in High Springs, Florida, a team of teachers led by Kathy Shewey used learning centers as a regular part of each day's instruction. The daily master schedule provided the teachers with a 30-minute unit of time following lunch that seemed too short to do anything difficult or complex. The team decided to encourage students to use the time for independent study. Student interests were surveyed and a dozen or so brightly colored, well-designed learning centers appeared on the walls of the team area. Following a conference with their advisor, each student contracted for an amount of learning centers activity, small group discussions with the counselor, or other independent learning that could be supervised by the teachers on the team. Students who initially had difficulties in taking hold and making the most of the opportunity met with one of the teachers and worked on the skills and attitudes necessary for effective independent study. The program, with learning centers at the heart, lasted for three years and became the favorite time of the day for both students and teachers.

Another effective way to introduce learning centers into the classroom is in the form of a short course within another, larger, unit. In the average six-week unit, for example, usually many different activities are planned, one or more of which can be learning centers involving a self-contained short course. A unit on comparative government might include a short course on dictatorship offered as a learning center, with its own objectives, directions, assessments, and learning activities, all relating to the subtheme of dictatorial government. Another appropriate short course for the same unit might focus on the process of comparing. Such centers can be a part of the unit, but separately so.

Once students have been introduced to using learning centers, know what is expected of them when using a center, and have used them on a part-time basis, additional learning centers can be introduced. They can easily become the major instructional strategy for a short unit or for a particular subject. Centers can be used, in this way, one day a week, one week during a unit, or on any other schedule that a teacher finds effective.

A unit on the Civil War, in an 8th grade American history class, for example, could be taught using learning centers as the primary instructional strategy. Such a unit might have centers on some or all of these topics: the South before the war, the North before the war, the causes of the Civil War, significant battles of the Civil War, music and art of the Civil War period, civilians and the war, the end of the war, the results of the war, and why the North won the war. Individual teachers could manage a unit in their own special ways, using the centers as the focus. Learning centers, thus, can be a supplementary strategy or the major pedagogical tool, depending upon the goals and preferences of teachers.

The process of developing good learning centers follows the same steps involved in designing any good instruction, with a few modifications. Teachers must first decide what role the learning centers will have in their instructional program: enrichment, remediation, motivation, short course, or major method. Will the learning centers be used during the whole period, the entire week, or some other schedule? Will they be required or optional? Will they be used in one classroom or for an interdisciplinary team unit? Many teachers recommend that the teacher new to the use of learning centers begin with one subject or dedicate a few hours out of the day or week. Teachers and students can, in this way, learn how to use centers effectively, with the least amount of disruption or confusion in their classes. Once the teacher has determined the extent to which centers will be used, other steps toward implementation may be taken. Teachers and students may plan the identity of the centers. Learning activities can be designed. Assessment and evaluation plans can be drawn.

In a recent return to the middle school classroom, one of the authors was engaged in teaching a three-week unit on Japan in 6th grade World Cultures, using learning centers as the major instructional strategy. Six centers were designed, dealing with Japanese culture, geography, history, school life, origami, and an independent study center. During the three weeks, students were expected to complete all six centers, as well as a number of other tasks that were presented through teacher-directed whole class instruction. Students spent at least half of their classroom time during the unit actively engaged in the learning centers. The third week was primarily devoted to student presentations on their independent study projects. It all worked beautifully.

The Classroom Workshop   We believe that the classroom workshop model, popularized at the middle level by Nancie Atwell (1987), has become an important addition to the repertoire of many middle school teachers. At first it was limited to reading and language arts areas, but in the last few years attempts have been made to adapt it to instruction in other areas of the curriculum (Daniels & Bizar, 1998).

The reading and writing classroom workshop is based on several important assumptions. First, young adolescents need time to read and write in school. Regular and frequent time, as much as half a period every school day, is critical. This school time is crucial, among other reasons, for establishing the momentum that will permit students to overcome distractions out of school that usually block their attempts to read and write in other settings. Second, young adolescents learn to enjoy reading and writing, and to improve their efforts in both areas, when they take ownership of their reading and writing. This means that students must be given extraordinary freedom in the choice of what they read. Classrooms and media centers must be equipped with high-interest reading, including dozens, if not hundreds, of paperbacks. Ownership also means that choice extends to the selection of writing topics as well. A common assignment that all students would pursue simultaneously might be valuable, but it must be balanced by sufficient opportunities for individuals to choose their own vehicles for expression—short stories, personal narratives, editorials, or whatever. Finally, the workshop model requires that students receive responses to what they read and write, from teachers and classmates.

The workshop approach at Fort Clarke Middle School, in Gainesville, Florida, appeared to have a distinct and coherent structure. Total class instruction, in many of the traditional language arts topics, came in the form of so-called mini-lessons. Students received direct instruction in punctuation, vocabulary, technique and style, and so on. The workshop time, in both reading and writing, was frequent and lengthy. In reading workshops, students entered the classrooms of the language arts teachers, sat down, and immediately began to read. This was the procedure in every period in every language arts class in the 6th grade. Even in math class, when students were finished with a test or an assignment, they immediately took out a novel and began to read. The same thing happened during the period devoted to the writing workshop. At Fort Clarke, as of the beginning of 2002, the workshop classroom had been popularly in place in the language arts curriculum in all three grades for more than a decade.

The workshop approach relies on a great deal of teacher-student and student-student interaction focusing on students' writing and reading. Teachers hold brief conferences with as many as a dozen students during a block of time. Students help each other edit their work. Group-share sessions, at the end of the workshop period, are settings for many listeners to respond to a writer's work. This is what "response" means in a classroom workshop of this sort.

The teacher's role, in the workshop approach, constantly shifts from direct instruction, to one-on-one conferences with students, to facilitating group discussions. Teachers are active, but not in the sense of making endless presentations to students. Students work a great deal on their own, but not passively filling in work sheets or other common assignments made by the teacher. Time on task, as we have witnessed it in workshop classes, tends to be extraordinarily high.

A number of unique experiences confronted one of the authors during a week of observing the workshop approach at Fort Clarke. Students, later identified as learning disabled, eagerly shared their excitement about reading with him. Many wrote to him about their reading and their writing (writing to an adult is a regular feature of this methodology), and this author was required to respond in writing to them. This letter writing immediately established a powerful personal relationship between student and observer. We can only guess at the bond it creates between the regular teacher and the students. Most unusual, however, was a brief discussion with the author in which two 6th grade boys, after hearing about his current writing project, proudly proclaimed that, when they grew up, they, too, were "going to be writers." Never, in 30 years of observing middle school classes had 6th graders volunteered such a desire to him. When this conversation was reported to the teacher, he spontaneously turned to three girls sitting at the nearest table and asked them to tell him what they were going to do over the summer. The three girls, from different ethnic and academic backgrounds, had already made concrete plans to "get together over the summer and write."

Questions may arise about the applicability of the classroom workshop model to a variety of subjects and to special populations of students. Concerns also may surface about the adequacy of instruction in specific reading skills and about reading comprehension. Undoubtedly, however, students in the reading and writing classroom workshop eagerly accomplish a mountain of reading and writing. If a forced choice must be made between preparing students who can read and write well but who hate to do either and taking a chance on missing a few skills but developing early adolescents who eagerly read and write, the choice is clear, we think.

Technology and the Differentiation of Instruction

Many educators hope that the processes involved in middle school instruction will soon be even more drastically modified by the utilization of advances in the design of personal computers, the Internet, and the explosion of software witnessed in the last decade. Since the first edition of this text was published in 1981, great advances have been made toward the development of school and classroom learning systems based on the use of technology. Computers, videodiscs, CD-ROMS, videotapes, laser discs, and films have been introduced and targeted toward the conduct and management of instruction in the middle school classroom. One estimate is that, in 2002, there were about 6 million computers in American schools, about one for every nine students, with about half of public schools linked to the Internet (Jacobsen, Eggen, & Kauchak, 2002). We suspect that the current figures are even higher.

Our observation is, however, that the promise of technology-assisted learning has not yet been kept. In 1981, we wrote:

The present authors, however, believe that those who predict revolutionary growth in individualized instruction via the minicomputer are likely to fall short of their hoped-for quantum leap toward a completely technologically based instructional program for the middle school. (Alexander & George, 1981, p. 247)

Sadly, we remain skeptical about the degree of power that technology has brought to the typical middle school teacher's attempts at differentiating instruction. In the several hundred middle schools we have visited in the last two decades, all too often we have seen computers go unused, sometimes even unpacked, in the majority of classrooms. In the fall of 2001, one of the authors and a companion visited 160 classrooms in nine middle schools in a medium-size urban school district. The computers were turned on in only one of those classrooms. We believe that one of the main reasons for this situation is the predominance of teacher-directed whole class instruction in most middle school classrooms. When teachers are unable to get beyond seeing and treating their classes as a single unit, differentiating instruction with computers becomes difficult, if not impossible.

In an effort to deal with the difficulties of getting teachers to utilize computers in their classrooms, yet despairing of providing effective training in differentiating instruction, many districts have adopted a policy of removing computers from classrooms and installing them in centralized computer labs in different areas of the school. Sometimes fully outfitted computer labs are set up at each grade level. In some schools, often the newest, classrooms have computers and computer labs are also present. These labs are open to teachers to bring their classes, and every student can be on his or her own computer and the teacher can continue to treat the class as a unit, in whole class teacher-directed instruction. Unfortunately, even in these circumstances, we have not witnessed widespread use of the computer labs in ways that move far beyond treating the computers as dramatically more colorful encyclopedias.

In one recent week-long immersion in a 7th grade classroom, for example, we observed a talented teacher take his classes to the grade level computer lab for what he described as a "Web Quest" on the subject of recent Chinese history. After spending his planning time getting the computer lab up and running, the students spent their entire social studies period copying information about China from several colorful Web sites. On the positive side, the students were able to access information about recent Chinese history that allowed them to leapfrog the outdated and miserly references on the subject in the school library. On the negative side, they did little more with that information than they would have with a traditional encyclopedia—filling in the answers to a teacher-developed work sheet.

The lesson could have been designed differently, and in hundreds of classrooms, happily, this is now the case. Bernie Dodge (1995), one of the developers of the idea of the WebQuest, suggests (among other strategies) the use of a Jigsaw-style process, with individual research, group consensus, reporting out of findings to the whole class, and a debriefing process that we believe to be effective. And, in barrier-breaking middle schools such as Rachel Carson Middle School (RCMS), in Alexandria, Virginia, and Brown Barge Middle School, in Pensacola, Florida, technology has found uses that are truly and dramatically leading toward greater differentiation of instruction.

Rachel Carson Middle School exemplifies the cutting edge in middle schools in its use of technology for instruction. At RCMS, students are expected to become "capable of using technology in their pursuit of learning and self development, as productive members and leaders, ready to face the challenges of a global society." The school is equipped with 10 labs devoted to a variety of uses: keyboard instruction, multimedia, iMac, a mobile wireless lab, a dedicated science technology lab, and so on. Parent volunteers supervise labs. All classrooms have an Instructional Management System workstation, multimedia presentation stations, and 10 laptop "loaners." A special elective course is used to maintain a cadre of 36 student Webmasters, presenters, filmmakers, and technicians available to assist teachers and students in any class.

In schools such as RCMS, technology can be used to enhance instruction in many ways. We observed one such method, tele-collaboration, in a recent visit to Chain of Lakes Middle School (CLMS), in Orlando, Florida. CLMS is a new middle school, with more than 500 computers throughout the school. In one class, we observed science students gathering data about the migratory behavior of birds in a specially constructed project outside their classroom. Once the data were collected and collated, the data were shared, via the Internet, with peers in a middle school in California who were partners in the study.

In another classroom at CLMS, we observed students use the Web for examining the political platforms of the two major party candidates for U.S. president in the fall of 2000. Students ultimately used the data they retrieved from these sites to engage in discussions about the election with other students in a distant middle school. These sorts of learning activities, we think, are impressive. Students in both CLMS classrooms were involved in information collection and analysis, problem solving, and interpersonal exchanges regarding their projects. Tele-collaboration can also allow students to communicate with experts in the studied fields through activities such as tele-mentoring, electronic appearances, and impersonations.

We suspect that, like for all aspects of education, a number of pros and cons can be identified with the use of technology, particularly the Internet, in the middle school classroom. Among those most relevant to our discussion of the Internet are the following.[1]

Pro	Con
Is a rich resource	Is an often unreliable resource

---

[1] We are indebted to Cheryl Wickham and Cindy Johnson for the first draft of this list.

Is fun for students	Video games and TV are fun, too
Students need to be familiar with it	Most students already are familiar with it, often too much so
Frees teachers from the traditional	Many teachers do not want to be free from the traditional
Allows for synthesis of masses of information	Synthesis of masses of information is far from automatic
Assists teacher collaboration	Teacher collaboration is minimal and contrived
Is racially and culturally blind	Invites hate groups, porn, and incompetents to full membership
Provides incredible quantities of information	American society seems obsessed with quantity
Promotes critical thinking	Students think that anything that has been published is true
Promotes differentiating instruction	Differentiating instruction is far from guaranteed
Offers a whole new world of curriculum	No evidence exists of achievement increase
Provides access to real-world experiences	Is a gigantically expensive experiment

We discuss additional aspects of the uses of technology in Chapter 3.

CONSULTATION AND CO-TEACHING

Two major movements are responsible for the emergence of promising practices in the education of young adolescents with specific learning disabilities. First, the continuing national emphasis on inclusion attempts to find the most appropriate and most effective, as well as least restrictive, learning environment for the learning disabled student. Exceptional education teachers at the middle level, pursuing the inclusion goal, continue to explore viable alternatives better suited to their students' best interests. This advocacy frequently brings them to the classroom doors of their regular education colleagues.

Second, the evolution of the middle school interdisciplinary team organization has brought together groups of regular classroom teachers who share a common group of students, instead of a single subject or discipline. In such teams, teachers often find themselves in meaningful discussions of their students. More often than not, these discussions focus on students who have special needs. In such discussions, teachers often learn a great deal about the students they teach. Commonly, this increased knowledge of students leads to a more positive feeling toward the students, more empathy with them, and an increased disposition to act on their behalf.

The team organization often brings the regular classroom teacher to a point of far greater readiness to respond positively to the ideas and interests of exceptional education teachers who also teach some of the same students. So, two groups of teachers, in many middle schools, now have a more positive view of the potential of students with specific learning disabilities. These two groups of teachers are willing to make adjustments in the plans they make and the methods they utilize, for the sake of learning disabled students. Such a critical mass of professional concern for specific students is bound to lead to attempts to change the way exceptional students are educated at the middle level. We describe two efforts under way in school districts where exceptional education teachers and regular teachers on interdisciplinary teams are working together to develop new models of cooperative and collaborative effort.

Cooperative Consultation

When general education teachers on interdisciplinary teams work closely together with the exceptional education teachers, inclusion of students with disabilities can be far more effective (Mercer & Mercer, 2001). Instead of scheduling such students, usually with reading or writing difficulties, directly into self-contained exceptional education classes, they are included in as many of the classes on the interdisciplinary team as possible. The exceptional education teacher and the team of general education teachers consult cooperatively with each other in a problem-solving process to define a student's problems and compare the student's abilities with the demands of the educational setting. The teachers brainstorm modifications that will help the student become more successful in the regular classroom.

Usually, the teachers who are working most closely together (e.g., the exceptional education teacher and a reading teacher) commit themselves to a meeting, once a week or so, to monitor the effectiveness of their cooperative plan. Common planning times for interdisciplinary team members also makes it easier for exceptional education teachers to meet with all of a student's general education teachers at once. Some students involved in this sort of program are scheduled into a Learning Strategies class taught by the exceptional education teacher.

A Cooperative Consultation instructional model provides a number of benefits for middle school classrooms. Educators of different perspectives learn from each other, and the general education teacher can receive support in the use of more effective instruction for the Specific Learning Disabilities students on the team. Modifications in teaching methods that result from such consultation spill over and help other students in the class, students who may not be identified as learning disabled but who may be potential dropouts, high-risk, or other less successful students. The Learning Strategies class helps the students to become more effective independent learners in the regular classroom. Generally, many teachers involved in such a cooperative attempt to improve the education of exceptional students believe that their collaborative efforts are effective.

Co-Teaching

The Co-Teaching instructional model is a step toward even further cooperation and collaboration between the exceptional education teacher and the members of the general education interdisciplinary team (Gately & Gately, 2001). Co-teaching involves an exceptional education teacher and at least one general education teacher, from the team, planning and teaching together in the same classroom. Co-teaching is team teaching as it was intended to be. Typically, the general education teacher presents content material to the entire group and the exceptional education teacher works with any students needing more help. The exceptional education teacher also teaches the entire student group, emphasizing strategies for organizing and learning the material of the class, techniques that all middle school students can profitably use.

The special education teacher is not labeled as an exceptional education teacher. He or she is known, in the class, as the co-teacher of the class. Likewise, the students with disabilities are not singled out. They are part of the total class, and they use grade-appropriate textbooks and other materials, right along with their classmates. Accommodations are made in the curriculum and the materials whenever it is necessary to do so. Oral tests, extended time, and differentiated assignments and homework opportunities are among the most common modifications made for students in this direct approach to inclusion.

Requirements for Success   There are several requirements for the success of the co-teaching model at the middle school level. First, the concept and the rationale must be presented in a clear and straightforward manner to teams of general education teachers. Ideally, these teachers help to create the design of the program and have the opportunity to volunteer for the assignment. Classes must, necessarily, be heterogeneous (comprised of about one-third students with disabilities from the team), and they should be slightly smaller than regular general education classes on the team. Most funding formulas permit such arrangements. Finally, and perhaps most important, the exceptional education teacher and the general education teacher involved in such an effort must have some common planning time on an almost daily basis. Programs with these components will be much more likely to be effectively implemented.

Co-teaching does not, however, spring forth fully formed like Athena from the forehead of Zeus. Teachers, especially those with long histories of working alone in a subject-centered classroom, must be trained in knowing how to give assistance and support and how to receive them. Often, secondary school-trained and experienced teachers have few ideas about how to work with another adult in the classroom, in anything other than an aide's role. They may even be extremely uncomfortable, or anxious, with another teacher in the same classroom. They need help making this adjustment (Rice & Zigmond, 2000).

While teams of teachers (exceptional and general education teachers) will do many things differently, early innovators in the practice of co-teaching have emerged with a number of guidelines, which can help the exceptional education teachers demonstrate their value in the partnership. At College Place Middle School, in Lynwood, Washington, the exceptional education teacher works in the regular classroom.

- Serving as a resource to the regular teachers in planning lessons or units that reach all learners in concrete ways, adapting curriculum and instructional strategies
- Providing all students with helpful hints for remembering facts and clarifying concepts
- Helping all students with improving their strategies for learning: using textbooks effectively, using proper form, staying well organized, having assignment calendars
- Employing modeling strategies and techniques for students
- Assisting the general education teacher during class by monitoring class for on-task behavior, providing guided notes for students during lectures, working with small groups of all kinds, helping individual students read particularly difficult passages, giving oral tests
- Being a liaison with counselors, psychologists, and special services personnel
- Serving as a coordinator of parent contacts for exceptional students on the team
- Being a peer coach for general education teachers
- Working in coordinating Individual Education Plan information
- Being a testing specialist
- Serving as an unofficial counselor and advisor for students on the team

At Scott Highlands Middle School, in Apple Valley, Minnesota, general education teachers are assisted by licensed teachers or paraprofessionals who

- Read to or with students
- Assist students in note taking
- Re-teach concepts from a different point of view or different mode of instruction
- Guide students on specific problems or assignments
- Read and interpret test questions
- Interpret assignment instructions

- Assist the classroom teacher with modification of materials and tests to help ensure success
- Provide oral review for tests when necessary
- Monitor progress on assignments and answer questions during student seatwork

Implementation of the Consultation and Co-teaching Models

More than a decade ago, the 18 middle level public schools of Orange County (Orlando), Florida, were reorganized, from junior high schools to the middle school concept. As a result of the lengthy and careful planning that preceded this move, district decision-makers authorized the simultaneous implementation of consultation and co-teaching practices. To assist exceptional students in fully participating in the exciting new middle schools, policy-makers concluded that a different instructional model was necessary, one that departed significantly from what was used in the junior high school programs.

School district planners, and especially the supervisors and teachers involved in the exceptional student education program, were excited about the possibilities of the move to middle school and what that move offered to advance the inclusion mandate. It was a perfect opportunity. Unfortunately, as is too often the case, so many changes accompanied the move to middle school in such a large district that the implementation of the consultation and co-teaching models may not have received the attention that was needed for fully effective implementation.

This is not to say that preparations were not made. Recommendations and guidelines were shared with school administrators throughout the year before implementation. A range of acceptable scheduling options was available, from the most traditional junior high model in which little co-teaching or even consultation would occur to the most advanced interdisciplinary team approach in which co-teaching was a daily event. Staff development was held for many teachers. Eventually, three schools became modified pilot sites for implementing the models.

Inevitably, however, the best-laid plans are rarely implemented perfectly. Such was the case in this instance. Many general education teachers were not involved with the staff development efforts prior to implementation of the models. Staff development opportunities may have been insufficient to the task of preparing those who were involved. Some school principals had their attention drawn away to other seemingly more urgent priorities. The district was involved in a tumultuous reorganization affecting every school, student, and teacher in the district: new high school, new middle schools, as well as new models for instruction. It was an exciting but challenging time in Orange County.

Consequently, the district experienced a wide range of effectiveness in the implementation of consulting and co-teaching models. Terminology was different from school to school. Scheduling options ran the gamut of approved possibilities. Administrative support and understanding were firm in some schools and virtually nonexistent in others. Some general education teachers were openly enthusiastic about the possibilities; others were openly hostile to the presence of another teacher in their private classroom preserve. The results of the first year's experience (e.g., in suspension rates for exceptional education students) indicated the same variations—positive results in the schools where educators were prepared for and enthusiastic about the models, much less success in those schools where preparation and enthusiasm were absent.

In recent years, our experience is that, in middle schools across the nation, results have been all too similar to the experience in Orange County. While many districts have moved beyond consultation and co-teaching to full inclusion models, many schools and districts have yet to move boldly beyond the sort of segregated education that exceptional education students have received in their districts for decades. Many forward-moving districts have incorporated inclusion teams as the model for every school in the district. In other districts, such as one we visited in the fall of 2001, none of the nine middle schools could point to any major steps toward inclusion; consultation and co-teaching were absent and inclusion teams were unknown.

Recommendations

Regular interdisciplinary team teachers and exceptional education teachers, working together, can provide instruction that helps all students to experience more successful learning. This is the goal of differentiating instruction. Teacher collaboration of this sort has enhanced the generalization of effective instructional strategies from exceptional education to the regular classroom, in Orange County and elsewhere. Success depends upon the expertise of the exceptional education teacher, the understanding and enthusiasm of the regular classroom teacher, and administrative support. It appears, from the experience of the last several decades, that several recommendations are important.

1. Consultation and co-teaching models are best suited to situations in which all teachers are comfortable with the middle school concept and volunteer to work together.
2. Some schools may need to offer a transition classroom for 6th grade students coming from full-time exceptional education class settings in their elementary schools.
3. Staff development is critical and must precede implementation.
4. Middle school students with disabilities should be assigned to all teams, perhaps with the more severely disabled students on the same team. This will permit their teachers to provide more concentrated support to subject area teachers and students.

5. Exceptional education teachers, when co-teaching, should stay with the class for the entire period for five days a week.
6. Teachers of students with disabilities need the same amount of planning time as their regular classroom colleagues, and whenever possible common planning time should be available for those who are co-teaching. Duty time and consultation time, for exceptional education teachers, need to be synonymous.
7. Coordinators or other district level support persons must also collaborate (e.g., the exceptional education and the middle school program supervisors).
8. Administrators need as much staff development as teachers. They need to be able to articulate the program clearly to general education teachers and parents.
9. Co-teaching should be restricted to situations in which the exceptional education teacher is experienced and certified in the fields to be taught.
10. Co-teaching should be used in areas identified by individual schools, not on a districtwide basis. One school, for example, might implement the program in 6th grade reading, another in 7th grade mathematics.

Precautions and Promises

Cooperative consultation and co-teaching are wonderful ideas for instruction. Unfortunately, as school budgets continue to decline, effective implementation is problematic.

Precautions Interventions and alterations of teaching practices that have existed unchanged for decades, if not centuries, will not proceed without difficulty. Co-teaching, in particular, is a practice that cannot be easily or effectively forced on a faculty. Teachers who are successful are likely to be more flexible than most and to see their students as their clients. Effective co-teachers will be likely to view adjustments in their teaching mode as an opportunity to deliver services more effectively, rather than as an impertinent imposition upon the way things are supposed to be.

Students must be grouped carefully and correctly for the practices to work smoothly. A careful balance of students with disabilities and regular students is required. Attempting these practices with classes composed of primarily low-track students will not meet with success. It may also prove difficult to schedule the common planning times that co-teaching peers require, but the temptation to go forward without that planning time should be strenuously resisted.

Promises We, the practitioners with whom we have worked, and the evidence from research (e.g., Rice & Zigmond, 2000) affirm that these practices are valuable, when implemented effectively. Most important, to be sure, is the assistance they may provide to the education of individual early adolescents identified as having specific learning disabilities. With inclusion and differentiating instruction, these students have access to the same curriculum, instruction, materials, and equipment as their peers. The strategies used in such co-taught classes usually prove to be effective in assisting the learning of all students, exceptional and otherwise. Teachers of the general education subjects receive direct assistance and support in dealing with the students in their classes who need the most help in coping with the demands of the classroom. Finally, students with disabilities are often thrilled with the fact that they are just "one of the gang" and not sent to special education classrooms for their courses. We believe that, consequently, their motivation to succeed is likely to be increased and their self-esteem is most probably enhanced.

Many middle school educators, for some reason, seem to think that the number of students with special needs is, proportionately, on the rise. Simultaneously, in many states, the funding for such programs becomes more thinly spread with each passing year. Increased inclusion of students with disabilities, if only for financial reasons, is inevitable; perhaps it is overdue. Learning disabled students in a general education class, such as science, will have the opportunity to learn more than they would if they were placed in a resource science class, when accommodations are made for their specific disability. Such students will learn more, in most cases, because many middle school special education teachers are currently asked to teach in so many subject areas and grade levels that their preparations cannot possibly be as thorough or their lessons as enriched as those of the general education teacher specializing in one or two subjects. Subject matter expertise may come at the price of exhaustion for the exceptional education teacher. Consultation and co-teaching models may help change this undesirable situation.

Even though students with disabilities may be a part of inclusion classes for longer periods of time in the consultation and co-teaching instructional models, this does not mean the exceptional education teacher is in danger of extinction. Other teachers become more aware of teaching not only to those who are strong auditorially, but also to those who are visual and kinesthetic learners as well. Regular teachers on teams will utilize the exceptional education teacher more frequently for ideas and methods to meet their students' particular needs. This is why instruction via consultation and co-teaching are such valuable processes.

Consultation and co-teaching offer further important support to the middle school concept as a whole. These practices permit teachers to create the "smallness within bigness" for which the middle school concept is justifiably well known (George & Lounsbury, 2000). They permit educators to prize the diversity of each young adolescent without destroying the unity of the team and school. Each process strengthens the relationships between exceptional education teachers and the members of interdisciplinary teams. As middle level educators struggle for alternatives to the rigid tracking and between-class ability grouping, the co-teaching model offers an especially attractive option to consider. We believe that this model holds equally great promise not only for students with disabilities but also for reintegrating the gifted student into the regular general education classroom. No more important agendas await (George et al., 1997).

Concluding Comments

Much more can be written about effective instruction in the middle school than can be included in a single chapter. We have not presented information about a number of important instructional strategies: problem-based teaching, simulation, and case studies, for example. Little reference was made to the characteristics of effective middle school teachers, to middle school teacher education, or to certification. Nor have teacher burnout and the effects of the school organization as an instructional phenomenon been considered. Further, we have assumed that readers will not look to this volume for beginning instruction in the basics of lesson planning and the other characteristics of effective instruction at any level of schooling. This chapter has, instead, focused on major instructional strategies that have significance for all middle school teachers: whole class instruction and differentiating instruction.

How are teachers to acquire such instructional competencies? Continuous staff development is critical, because until recently, middle school teacher preservice preparation at the college and university level was virtually nonexistent. We believe, however, that the challenges of effective implementation of almost all aspects of the complete middle school program (advisories, the interdisciplinary team organization, an integrated curriculum, as well as new and more appropriate instructional strategies) ultimately depend, for their longevity, on the spread of authentic middle school teacher education.

Until recently universities and colleges seemed unable or uninterested in developing teacher education programs that had as their goal the preparation of teachers specially trained to teach at the middle level (Allen & McEwin, 2001). Where such programs did begin, efforts were often frustrated by the lack of supportive certification regulations. University educators discovered that prospective teachers would not enroll in large numbers for teacher education programs that offered either sharply restricted or nonexistent certification, and therefore severely limited employment opportunities. Pioneering efforts at the University of Florida, Appalachian State University, and the University of Georgia have, however, given way to fine programs at dozens of other colleges and universities in as many states. Nearly 35 states, we estimate, now have middle level certification requirements, which support new and vigorous efforts for preservice teacher education. The National Middle School Association and the National Council for the Accreditation of Teacher Education have collaborated on guidelines for such preparation programs.

Realizing that the majority of teachers who will be practicing in the middle schools of the year 2020 are already teaching, however, makes the hope for a trained cadre of committed teachers emerging from American universities to infuse schools with new vigor and expertise a still doubtful prospect. The training necessary to produce effective middle school teachers may, we lament, continue to occur primarily as a process of in-service education and staff development. Public school educators seem destined to be left with the task of identifying and training the staff of their programs, in addition to designing and implementing those programs.

Like the curriculum of the middle school, the topic of effective instruction for the middle school is complex, and in spite of much progress, it is as yet poorly researched and inadequately understood. Understanding of this topic likely will grow more than, perhaps, any other aspect of the exemplary middle school. The more clearly educators perceive the characteristics of their students, agree upon their purposes and research the effects of their behavior, the more they will experience progress in the area of instructional strategies.

CONTENT SUMMARY

Standards-based reform has reinforced the popularity of traditional whole class, teacher-directed instruction. A great deal of evidence also suggests that this strategy is consistent with gains in scores on standardized tests. We argue, however, for a process of differentiating instruction, in which the teacher ceases to view the class as a unit in which all students have identical learning needs and, instead, searches for ways to disaggregate the classroom. We identify relatively simple ways to move away from traditional approaches, and we discuss the inclusion of students with disabilities as another important reason to move away from traditional models. We also discuss the pros and cons of the Internet as a tool for differentiating instruction.

CONNECTIONS TO OTHER CHAPTERS

Considering methods of instruction is impossible without thinking about curriculum, so referring back to Chapter 3 will be important. Teaching and organization are also inextricably interrelated, so you will want to look at Chapter 6 for information on how teaching and teamwork go together. You will also notice references to issues that relate to grouping, which is dealt with in Chapter 7. As with many topics, there is a considerable overlap. We hope you see this as encouraging, not frustrating.

QUESTIONS FOR DISCUSSION

1. Why is it so difficult for teachers to move away from traditional whole class, teacher-directed instruction? How many important reasons can you identify? What priorities would you assign to these factors?
2. Have you had occasion to be involved with, or to observe, an inclusive classroom where exceptional education teachers and teachers on interdisciplinary teams worked together to meet the needs of students with disabilities? If not, why was this the case? If so, what stands out from the experience?
3. Do you believe standards-based reform can be harmonized with the differentiation of instruction? Have you seen it done?
4. What has been your experience with the use of the Internet in the middle school classroom? Was it positive, negative, or nonexistent? What role do you believe technology will play in the middle school classroom of the future?
5. What is your preferred style of teaching? Has anything in this chapter caused you to think differently about teaching middle school students?

ACTION STEPS

1. Interview a group of five teachers about their use of small group activities in their classrooms. Determine which activities they use most frequently and why they choose to use these.
2. Visit a middle school and assess the extent to which inclusion and the strategies of consultation and co-teaching are in use there. Write a brief analysis of your findings or share it, in some other way, with your peers.
3. Investigate the work of Spencer Kagan as the source of expertise on differentiating instruction. Look at his work in the areas of cooperative learning, multiple intelligences, brain-based teaching, and so on. Identify a minimum of five activities from his work that you would find useful in a middle school classroom.
4. With a group of peers, conduct a debate on this topic: "Resolved—The Use of the Internet Should Be a Part of Every Middle School Classroom."
5. Write a brief essay on this topic: "Traditional Whole Class, Teacher-Directed Instruction—Burden and Blessing for Middle School Classrooms."

SUGGESTIONS FOR FURTHER STUDY

Books

Albers, P., & Murphy, S. (2000). *Telling pieces: Art as literacy in middle school classes.* Mahwah, NJ: Lawrence Erlbaum Associates.

Allen, J. (1999). *Class actions: Teaching for social justice in elementary and middle school.* New York: Teachers College Press.

Allen, J., & Gonzalez, K. (1998). *There's room for me here: Literacy workshop in the middle school.* York, ME: Stenhouse Publishers.

Alvermann, D. (Ed.) (1998). *Reconceptualizing the literacies in adolescents' lives.* Mahwah, NJ: Lawrence Erlbaum Associates.

Aronson, E., & Patnoe, S. (1997). *The jigsaw classroom: Building cooperation in the classroom.* New York: Longman.

Baloche, L. (1998). *The cooperative classroom: Empowering learning.* Upper Saddle River, NJ: Prentice-Hall.

Bruffee, K. (1999). *Collaborative learning: Higher education, interdependence, and the authority of knowledge.* Baltimore, MD: Johns Hopkins University Press.

Callahan, J., Leonard, C., & Kellough, R. (1998). *Teaching in the middle and secondary schools.* Upper Saddle River, NJ: Merrill.

Charles, C. (1999) *Building classroom discipline.* New York: Longman.

Cohen, E., & Lotan, R. (1997). *Working for equity in heterogeneous classrooms: Sociological theory in practice.* New York: Teachers College Press.

Deshler, D. (1999). *Teaching every adolescent every day: Learning in diverse middle and high school classrooms.* Cambridge, MA: Brookline Books.

Edelsky, C. (1996). *With literacy and justice for all: Rethinking the social in language and education.* Bristol, PA: Taylor and Francis.

English, F. W. (2000). *Deciding what to teach and test: Developing, aligning, and auditing the curriculum.* Thousand Oaks, CA: Corwin Press.

Fearn, L., & Farnan, N. (1998). *Writing effectively: Helping children master the conventions of writing.* Boston, MA: Allyn and Bacon.

Freiberg, J. (1999). *Beyond behaviorism: Changing the classroom management paradigm.* Boston, MA: Allyn and Bacon.

Gallegos, A. (1998). *School expulsions, suspensions, and dropouts: Understanding the issues.* Bloomington, IN: Phi Delta Kappa International.

George, P., Lawrence, G., & Bushel, D. (1997). *Handbook for middle school teaching.* New York: Longman.

Gersten, R., & Jimenez, R. (1998). *Promoting learning for culturally and linguistically diverse students: Classroom applications from contemporary research.* Belmont, CA: Wadsworth Publishing Co.

Griffin, G. (1999). *The education of teachers.* Chicago, IL: University of Chicago Press.

Harris, K., Graham, S., & Deshler, D. (1998). *Teaching every child every day: Learning in diverse schools and classrooms.* Cambridge, MA: Brookline Books.

Henson, K. (1996). *Methods and strategies for teaching in secondary and middle schools.* White Plains, NY: Longman Publishers.

Holcomb, E. (1996). *Asking the right questions: Tools and techniques for teamwork.* Thousand Oaks, CA: Corwin Press.

Hurd, P. (2000). *Transforming middle school science education.* New York: Teachers College Press.

Kellough, R., & Kellough, N. (1999). *Middle school teaching: A guide to methods and resources.* Upper Saddle River, NJ: Merrill.

Kingen, S. (2000). *Teaching language arts in middle schools: Connecting and communicating.* Mahwah, NJ: Lawrence Erlbaum Associates.

Lemlech, J. (1998). *Curriculum and instructional methods for the elementary and middle school.* Upper Saddle River, NJ: Merrill.

Linn, M., & Hsi, S. (1999). *Computers, teachers, peers: Science learning partners.* Mahwah, NJ: Lawrence Erlbaum Associates.

Lindquist, T., & Selwyn, D (2000). *Social studies at the center: Integrating kids, content, and literacy.* Portsmouth, NH: Heinemann.

Loehrer, M. (1998). *How to change a rotten attitude: A manual for building virtue and character in middle and high school students.* Thousand Oaks, CA: Corwin Press.

Logan, J. (1997). *Teaching stories.* New York: Kodansha International.

Mehan, H., Villanueva, I., Hubbard, L., & Lintz, A. (1996). *Constructing school success: The consequences of untracking low-achieving students.* New York: Cambridge University Press.

Muspratt, S., Luke, A., & Freebody, P. (1997). *Constructing critical literacies: Teaching and learning textual practice.* Cresskill, NJ: Hampton Press.

Newby, T. (2000). *Instructional technology for teaching and learning: Designing instruction, integrating computers, and using media.* Upper Saddle River, NJ: Merrill.

Peters, K., & March, J. (1999). *Collaborative observation: Putting classroom instruction at the center of school reform.* Thousand Oaks, CA: Corwin Press.

Powell, R. (1999). *Literacy as a moral imperative: Facing the challenges of a pluralistic Society.* Lanham, MD: Rowman and Littlefield Publishers.

Raebeck, B. (1998). *Transforming middle schools: A guide to whole-school change.* Lancaster, PA: Technomic Publishing Co.

Redman, G. (1999). *Teaching in today's classrooms: Cases from middle and secondary school.* Upper Saddle River, NJ: Merrill.

Reksten, L. (2000). *Using technology to increase student learning.* Thousand Oaks, CA: Corwin Press.

Roberts, P. (2000). *Education, literacy, and humanization: Exploring the work of Paulo Freire.* Westport, CT: Bergin and Garvey.

Schumaker, J., & Lenz, K. (1999). *Adapting language arts, social studies, and science materials for the inclusive classroom.* Reston, VA: Council for Exceptional Children.

Shapiro, N., & Levine, J. (1999). *Creating learning communities: A practical guide to winning support, organizing for change, and implementing programs.* San Francisco, CA: Jossey-Bass.

Shulman, J., Lotan, R., & Whitcomb, J. (1998). *Groupwork in diverse classrooms: A casebook for educators.* New York: Teachers College Press.

Snodgrass, D., & Bevevino, M. (2000). *Collaborative learning in middle and secondary schools: Applications and assessments.* Larchmont, NY: Eye on Education.

Solley, B. (2000). *Writer's workshop: Reflections of elementary and middle school teachers.* Boston, MA: Allyn and Bacon.

Soter, A. (1999). *Young adult literature and the new literary theories: Developing critical readers in middle school.* New York: Teachers College Press.

Soven, M. (1999). *Teaching writing in middle and secondary schools: Theory, research, and practice.* Boston: Allyn and Bacon.

Sowder, J., et al. (1998). *Middle-grade teachers' mathematical knowledge and its relationship to instruction: A research monograph.* Albany, NY: State University of New York Press.

Stevenson, C. (1998). *Teaching ten to fourteen year olds.* White Plains, NY: Longman.

Takenishi, H., & Takenishi, M. (1999). *Writing pictures K-12: A bridge to writing workshop.* Norwood, MA: Christopher-Gordon Publishers.

Tharon, H., & Benson, C. (1999). *Electronic networks: Crossing boundaries/creating communities.* Portsmouth, NH: Boynton/Cook Publishers.

Tomlinson, C. (1999). *The differentiated classroom: Responding to the needs of all learners.* Alexandria, VA: Association for Supervision and Curriculum Development.

Vermette, P. (1998). *Making cooperative learning work: Student teams in K–12 classrooms.* Upper Saddle River, NJ: Merrill.

Watson, D., & Downes, T. (2000). *Communications and networking in education: Learning in a networked society,* IFIP TC3 WG3.1/3.5. Open Conference on Communications and Networking in Education, June 13–18, 1999. Boston, MA: Kluwer Academic Publishers.

Weil, D. (1998). *Towards a critical multicultural literacy: Theory and practice for education for liberation.* New York: Peter Lang.

Wolfgang, C., Bennett, B., & Irvin, J. (1999). *Strategies for teaching self-discipline in the middle grades.* Boston, MA: Allyn and Bacon.

Periodicals

Atwell, N. (1996). Cultivating our garden. *Voices from the Middle, 3*(4), 47–51.

deBettencourt, L. (1999). General educators' attitudes toward students with mild disabilities and their use of instructional strategies: Implications for training. *Remedial and Special Education, 20*(1), 27–35.

Bell, K. (1998). In the big inning: Teacher created a positive learning environment. *Teaching Elementary Physical Education, 9*(4), 12–14.

Bevilacqua, M. (2000). Collaborative learning in the secondary English class. *Clearing House, 73*(3), 132–133.

Black, D., Tobler, N., & Sciacca, J. (1998). Peer helping/involvement: An efficacious way to meet the challenge of reducing alcohol, tobacco, and other drug use among youth? *Journal of School Health, 68*(3), 87–93.

Bruce, B. (2000). Searching the Web: New domains for inquiry. *Journal of Adolescent and Adult Literacy, 43*(4), 348–354.

Callison, D. (1999). Inquiry. *School Library Media Activities Monthly, 15*(6), 38–42.

Cesarone, B. (1994). Conflict resolution in the middle grades. *Childhood Education, 71*(1), 55–56.

Chase, K. (1999). Beyond this point. *Educational Leadership, 56*(8), 70–71.

Ciaccio, J. (1998). Teaching techniques for the underachieving middle level student: In the classroom. *Schools in the Middle, 7*(4), 18–20, 45.

Corson, D. (1999). Critical literacy: Another linguistic orthodoxy for the lucky country? *English in Australia* (124), 108–113.

Cruickshank, D. (2000). What makes teachers good? *Mid-Western Educational Researcher, 13*(1), 2–6.

Edmondson, J. (1999). Staying the course. *Voices from the Middle, 6*(3), 15–17.

Elliott, D., & McKenney, M. (1998). Four inclusion models that work. *Teaching Exceptional Children, 30*(4), 54–58.

Firestone, W., Mayrowetz, D., & Fairman, J. (1998). Performance-based assessment and instructional change: The effects of testing in Maine and Maryland. *Educational Evaluation and Policy Analysis, 20*(2), 95–113.

Fu, D. (1998). Unlock their lonely hearts. *Voices from the Middle, 6*(1), 3–10.

Gorman, M., Plucker, J., & Callahan, C. (1998). Turning students into inventors: Active learning modules for secondary students. *Phi Delta Kappan, 79*(7), 530–532.

Haworth, A. (1999). Bakhtin in the classroom: What constitutes a dialogic text? Some lessons from small group interaction. *Language and Education, 13*(2), 99–117.

Hendershott, T. (1997). Under observation: Critical areas of school effectiveness. *Schools in the Middle, 6*(4), 34–36.

Hinebauch, S. (1999). Coming of age: Making connections. *Voices from the Middle, 7*(1), 17–23.

Horner, R., Sugai, G., & Horner, H. (2000). A schoolwide approach to student discipline. *School Administrator, 57*(2), 20–23.

Lee, J. (1998). The impact of content-driven state education reform on instruction. *Research in Middle Level Education Quarterly, 21*(4), 15–26.

Lee, L., & Debevec, S. (1999). Partners in pedagogy: Collaborative teaching for beginning foreign language classes. *Foreign Language Annals, 32*(1), 125–138.

Leland, C., Harste, J., Ocrepka, A., Lewison, M., & Vasquez, V. (1999). Exploring critical literacy: You can hear a pin drop. *Language Arts, 77*(1), 70–77.

Leu, D., & Kinzer, C. (2000). The convergence of literacy instruction with networked technologies for information and communication. *Reading Research Quarterly, 35*(1), 108–127.

Luke, A. (2000). Critical literacy in Australia: A matter of context and standpoint. *Journal of Adolescent and Adult Literacy, 43*(5), 448–461.

Manning, L. (2000). Understanding diversity, accepting others: Realities and directions. *Educational Horizons, 78*(2), 77–79.

Martino-Brewster, G. (1999). Reversing the negative. *Voices from the Middle, 6*(3), 11–14.

McKay, M. (1998). Technology and language arts: Great support for every classroom! *Book Report, 17*(3), 33, 36–37.

Moje, E., Young, J., Readence, J., & Moore, D. (2000). Reinventing adolescent literacy for new times: Perennial and millennial issues. *Journal of Adolescent and Adult Literacy, 43*(5), 400–410.

Murphy, C. (1995). Managing students: Building positive attitudes in the classroom. *Schools in the Middle, 4*(4), 31–33.

Newman, W., & Newman, J. (1996). Teacher education and classroom discipline: A candid conversation between a teacher and a professor. *Thresholds in Education, 22*(4), 2–6.

Obaya, A. (1999). Getting cooperative learning. *Science Education, 10*(2), 25–27.

Ozvold, L. (1996). Does teacher demeanor affect the behavior of students? *Teaching and Change, 3*(2), 159–172.

Pajares, F., & Graham, L. (1998). Formalist thinking and language arts instruction: Teachers' and students' beliefs about truth and caring in the teaching conversation. *Teaching and Teacher Education, 14*(8), 855–870.

Polite, V., & Adams, A. (1997). Critical thinking and values clarification through Socratic seminars. *Urban Education, 32*(2), 256–278.

Prom, M. (1999). Measuring perceptions about inclusion. *Teaching Exceptional Children, 31*(5), 38–42.

Quezada, M., Wiley, T., & Ramirez, D. (2000). How the reform agenda shortchanges English learners. *Educational Leadership, 57*(4), 57–61.

Reid, L. (1998). Teaching reading in middle and secondary schools (professional links). *English Journal, 88*(1), 114–117.

Richardson, D. (1998). Eric's journey: A restructured school's inclusion program and a student with disabilities. *NASSP Bulletin, 82*(594), 74–80.

Rochester, M. (1998). What's it all about, Alfie? A parent/educator's response to Alfie Kohn. *Phi Delta Kappan, 80*(2), 165–169.

Shneiderman, B., Borkowski, E., Alavi, M., & Norman, K. (1998). Emergent patterns of teaching/learning in electronic classrooms. *Educational Technology Research and Development, 46*(4), 23–42.

Sprague, M., & Pennell, D. (2000). The power of partners: Preparing preservice teachers for inclusion. *Clearing House, 73*(3), 168–170.

Stanovich, P. (1999). Conversations about inclusion. *Teaching Exceptional Children, 31*(6), 54–58.

Strike, K. (1999). Can schools be communities? The tension between shared values and inclusion. *Educational Administration Quarterly, 35*(1), 46–70.

Swafford, J., Jones, G., Thornton, C., Stump, S., & Miller, D. (1999). The impact on instructional practice of a teacher change model. *Journal of Research and Development in Education, 32*(2), 69–82.

Townsend, J., & Fu, D. (1998). Quiet students across cultures and contexts. *English Education, 31*(1), 4–25.

Welker, W. (1999). The CRITICS Procedure. *Journal of Adolescent and Adult Literacy, 43*(2), 188–189.

White, B., & Frederiksen, J. (1998). Inquiry, modeling, and metacognition: Making science accessible to all students. *Cognition and Instruction, 16*(1), 3–118.

ERIC

Alvermann, D., Moon, J., & Hagood, M. (1999). *Popular culture in the classroom: Teaching and researching critical media literacy* (ERIC document ED427365).

Andrews, K. (1998). *The effect of test-taking strategies on the test scores of middle school level students* (ERIC document ED424285).

Atwell, N. (1998). *In the middle: New understandings about writing, reading, and learning* (ERIC document ED422343).

Baker, T. (2000). *When school accountability and preservice teachers' needs conflict: Effects of public school testing on teacher education field experiences* (ERIC document ED439093).

Beers, K., & Samuels, B. (1998). *Into focus: Understanding and creating middle school readers* (ERIC document ED412499).

Berghoff, B., Egawa, K., Hartse, J., & Hoonan, B. (2000). *Beyond reading and writing: Inquiry, curriculum, and multiple ways of knowing* (ERIC document ED438508).

Brandt, R. (2000). *Education in a new era: 2000 ASCD yearbook.* (ERIC document ED438621).

Caton, E., Brown, F., & Brewer, C. (1999). *Facilitating teacher-scientist collaborations: Teaching about energy through inquiry* (ERIC document ED434803).

Coleman, P., & Deutsch, M. (2000). *Cooperation, conflict resolution, and school violence: A systems approach* (ERIC document ED439198).

Deering, P. (1994). *Is "cooperative learning" either, both, or neither? Tales from three middle school classrooms* (ERIC document ED371899).

Demchak, M. (1999). *Facilitating effective inclusion through staff development* (ERIC document ED429769).

DiGiulio, R. (2000). *Positive classroom management: A step-by-step guide to successfully running the show without destroying student dignity* (ERIC document ED433334).

Fahy, P. (2000). *Achieving quality with online teaching technologies* (ERIC document ED439234).

Freeman, M. (1999). *Building a writing community: A practical guide. Lessons, models, reproducibles* (ERIC document ED430252).

Gilberts, G. (2000). *The effects of peer-delivered self-monitoring strategies on the participation of students with disabilities in general education classrooms* (ERIC document ED439871).

Gregoire, M. (1999). *Paradoxes and paradigms in an eighth grade pre-algebra class: A case study of a "good" math teacher* (ERIC document ED431600).

Gruber, S. (2000). *Weaving a virtual Web: Practical approaches to new information technologies* (ERIC document ED436787).

Hinson, B. (2000). *New directions in reading instruction* (ERIC document ED437628).

Hunt, G., Wiseman, D., & Bowden, S. (1998). *The middle level teachers' handbook: Becoming a reflective practitioner* (ERIC document ED422283).

Kahre, S., McWethy, C., Robertson, J., & Waters, S. (1999). *Improving reading comprehension through the use of reciprocal teaching* (ERIC document ED435974).

Khalsa, S. (1999). *The inclusive classroom: A practical guide for educators* (ERIC document ED425577).

Kreidler, W. (1994). *Conflict resolution in the middle school: A curriculum and teaching guide* (ERIC document ED377968).

Lane, S., Parke, C., & Stone, C. (1999). *Consequences of the Maryland school performance assessment program* (ERIC document ED434927).

Langer, J. (1999). *Beating the odds: Teaching middle and high school students to read and write well* (ERIC document ED435993).

Langer, J. (1999). *Excellence in English in middle and high school: How teachers' professional lives support student achievement* (ERIC document ED429295).

Lee, F. (2000). *Construct-a-greenhouse: Science by design series* (ERIC document ED439964).

Luft, J. (1997). *Border crossings: The student teaching experience of a multicultural science education enthusiast* (ERIC document ED417144).

Mann, M. (1998). *Technology in education* (ERIC document ED415853).

May, S. (1999). *Critical multiculturalism: Rethinking multicultural and antiracist education* (ERIC document ED433406).

McFarland, K. (2000). *Specific classroom management strategies for the middle/secondary education classroom* (ERIC document ED437340).

Means, B., & Lindner, L. (1998). *Teaching writing in middle school: Tips, tricks, and techniques* (ERIC document ED418412).

Mills, M., & Stevens, P. (1998). *Improving writing and problem solving skills of middle school students* (ERIC document ED420876).

Mills, R. (1998). *Grouping students for instruction in middle schools* (ERIC document ED419631).

Mitchem, K., & Benyo, J. (2000). *A classwide peer-assisted self-management program all teachers can use: Adaptations and implications for rural educators* (ERIC document ED439868).

Moore, J. (1996). *Empowering student teachers to teach from a multicultural perspective* (ERIC document ED394979).

O'Donnell, A., & King, A. (1999). *Cognitive perspectives on peer learning* (ERIC document ED438098).

Parke, C., Cerrillo, T., Levenson, J., O'Mara, J., Hansen, M., & Lane, S. (1999). *Impact of the Maryland School Performance Assessment Program (MSPAP): Evidence from classroom instruction and assessment activities (reading, writing)* (ERIC document ED434939).

Passman, R. (2000). *Pressure cooker: Experiences with student-centered teaching and learning in high-stakes assessment environments* (ERIC document ED440146).

Peters, D. (2000). *Taking cues from kids: How they think; What to do about it* (ERIC document ED439127).

Powell, T., & Taylor, S. (1994). *Taking care of risky business* (ERIC document ED372865).

Rankin, V. (1999). *The thoughtful researcher: Teaching the research process to middle school students* (ERIC document ED431722).

Reames, E., & Spencer, W. (1998). *The relationship between middle school culture and teacher efficacy and commitment* (ERIC document ED428441).

Rougle, E. (1999). *A lifelong middle school teacher never stops learning: The case of Cathy Starr* (ERIC document ED430245).

Seamon, M. (1999). *Connecting learning & technology for effective lesson plan design* (ERIC document ED432982).

Taylor, B., Graves, M., & van den Broek, P. (2000). *Reading for meaning: Fostering comprehension in the middle grades* (ERIC document ED435980).

Van Vliet, L. (1999). *Media skills for middle schools: Strategies for library media specialists and teachers* (ERIC document ED426705).

Whitworth, J. (1999). *Seven steps to successful inclusion* (ERIC document ED436040).

Zorfass, J. (1998). *Teaching middle school students to be active researchers* (ERIC document ED426050).

Videotapes

George, P. (1994). *Middle school discipline.* Gainesville, FL: Teacher Education Resources.

Web Sites

Office of Educational Research and Improvement, Education Consumer Guides

http://www.ed.gov/pubs/OR/ConsumerGuides/

The Education Consumer Guides series is produced by the U.S. Department of Education, Office of Educational Research and Improvement (OERI). It is published for teachers, parents, and others interested in current education themes. Created and edited by OERI's Office of Research, it includes documents on issues such as collaborative learning, performance assessment, and student portfolios.

NASA Quest

http://quest.arc.nasa.gov/home/index.html

NASA Quest is dedicated to bringing National Aeronautics and Space Administration (NASA) people and space science to classrooms through the Internet. The NASA Quest projects allow students to share in the excitement of NASA's authentic scientific and engineering pursuits such as flying the shuttle and International Space Station, exploring distant planets with amazing spacecraft, and aeronautics and airplane research.

Learning Network

http://www.learningnetwork.com

This large and complex site is funded by both commercial and noncommercial sponsors. It has subsites for parents, teachers, students, and school leaders. Several sites for students offer games and other fun activities; others provide research and homework assistance for students. TeacherVision.com should be of particular interest to many middle school teachers. FunBrain.com and Factmonster.com will appeal to middle school students.

MANAGING AND MENTORING MIDDLE SCHOOLERS

SPRING HILL MIDDLE SCHOOL

Spring Hill Middle School (SHMS), in High Springs, Florida, has been serious about the affective components of the education of young adolescents for a long time. In 1969, when the school was opened, it inaugurated what might have been the first advisor-advisee (AA) program in the modern history of middle level education. While homeroom had been an important idea for the early generation of middle level schools (the junior high school), it quickly became a time for taking attendance and collecting milk money instead of a time and place devoted to teacher-student relationships.

Educators at SHMS, a new middle school before most Americans were aware of the middle school concept, designed and implemented a number of programs that were destined to become central parts of the emerging middle school concept. The school held grades 5–8, but teachers and students were organized into three smaller multiage houses. Teachers and students were also organized into one of the first versions of a heterogeneous interdisciplinary team, in which teachers had large blocks of time and offered a team-planned curriculum in every subject. In addition, SHMS was an open-space school, where the space was utilized as designers intended.

Among the central components of the then new middle school that is still in place is the advisor-advisee program. At SHMS, every morning begins, as it has for the last 30 years, with advisory time—20 minutes in which teachers and advisees meet for a variety of important purposes. Never abandoned at SHMS, the advisory program has undergone important changes in response to the changes in local, state, and national priorities. But educators there understand and appreciate the importance of what was created decades ago and what their students need in the 21st century.

WHAT YOU WILL LEARN IN CHAPTER 5

This chapter is about relationships between teachers and students and, to some degree, among students in middle schools. Middle school educators believe that the teacher-student relationship is the fulcrum upon which all other aspects of life in those schools are leveraged. In this chapter, we will examine the characteristics of young adolescents that make teacher-student relationships so important. We will look at how teachers, on teams, can gang up on the students in positive ways. We will examine the most attractive, and most controversial, component of the middle school concept, the advisor-advisee program.

DEVELOPING RELATIONSHIPS WITH MIDDLE SCHOOL STUDENTS

Middle school educators often identify the teacher-student relationship in the middle school as the starting point of the entire program, proclaiming the middle school to be specially suited to the characteristics of this age learner. Among the list of characteristics, which determine the uniqueness of the young adolescent, the need for a particular kind of teacher-student relationship is almost always placed at the top. Written philosophies from individual middle schools consistently strive to highlight the student-centered nature of the program, implying a concern for each student and a commitment to firm teacher-student bonds. Managing and mentoring middle schoolers requires a unique relationship between teacher and student, which is different from relationships between teacher and student in elementary school or high school.

Teacher-Student Relationships in Elementary School   In the early years of the elementary school, the teacher-student affiliation has, perhaps, more significance than at any other time in the educational program. Young children, moving for the first time from the home to the public institution of the school, require a relationship with the adult teacher that closely parallels the association experienced between parent and child. This relationship, in the past, took on the exclusive character of the parent-child affiliation and was formalized by the legal system as in the Latin phrase *in loco parentis.*

Elementary teachers were expected to assume the care of young children, in at least a quasi-parental way, when the child came to school. Many of the activities of teachers in kindergarten and the primary school years today can scarcely be distinguished from those of parents. Young pupils, many educators believe, need an exclusive connection with one adult as they complete the move from the home to school, today as in years past. Following a decade or two of practices which weakened this association between the elementary school teacher and pupils, many teachers and parents seem ready for a return to the conditions that permitted the strong relationship to develop. Even if such a reestablishment of the exclusive relationship experiences between teacher and student in the elementary school did not transpire, many would agree that this is the way it has always been, and still is, in the majority of elementary schools in the United States. Some would argue that the practices that weakened the teacher-student relationship existed in only a few schools in only a few states and never affected the majority of elementary schools.

Teacher-Student Relationships in High School   Six-year-old children need a great deal more guidance and supervision, educators would hope, than do high school students. The American high school has never acknowledged an obligation to establish formal teacher-student relationships. Not that high school educators were or are unconcerned about the nature of the relationships between teachers and students; they are. Such relationships have, however, usually arisen from common subject matter interests, extracurricular pursuits, similar personality or style, and so on, rather than from an attempt on the part of the school to mandate such affiliations. Students who are close to the legal age of adulthood have been presumed to have the maturity to choose their own friends from among the professional adults in the school.

Teacher-Student Relationships in Middle School   The middle school must find a way to weave together these two disparate patterns of teacher-student relationship, to assist students in moving from the exclusive association with one adult to the situation in which the student is equally responsible for establishing and maintaining the rapport. Most middle school students are beyond the need for the self-contained classroom and the relationships it provided, but they are not ready to be completely on their own in a large school. The middle school attempts to help students move from one type of relationship to the other, while providing its own special brand of teacher-student affiliation along the way. Managing and mentoring middle school students depends on teachers who understand and respond positively to the unique characteristics of the young adolescent.

Student Development and Behavior Management

Educators who accurately and emphatically understand the characteristics and needs of young adolescents relate better and connect to them more positively. This positive connection then leads to improved behavior management.

Younger Children and Older Adolescents   Most educators would agree, we think, that young children, in the elementary school, are much easier to deal with, in terms of behavior management, than young adolescents. Young children often love their teachers unconditionally and are eager to do what the teacher requests, once they are taught the correct ways to behave. In the elementary school, behavior management is not the biggest problem.

At the high school, as students move to the higher grades, often the most difficult and unmotivated students have left the school as dropouts or have moved into alternative programs that take them out of the mainstream classroom. Academic tracking frequently segregates the most difficult students into sections with others like themselves, leaving many advanced classes with virtually no discipline problems. And many high school students have matured to the point where they are much more settled and more highly motivated to be successful academically or in the vocational programs they have enrolled in. They have passed through the most rebellious stages of their adolescence and have become intellectually developed enough that they show more interest in the subject. Others may have become so resigned to the system that the major problem they present to the teacher is motivation, and not discipline. They do not challenge the teacher's right to control the classroom; they simply do not participate.

Most educators, we think, would concur with the statement that, as students move up from the 1st grade, closer to, say, the 7th grade, fewer students can be accurately described as loving their teachers and eager to do what the teacher asks. Observing student behavior in the secondary school range, from the 12th grade, the closer one gets to the 7th grade, the more motivation and classroom discipline appear to become more serious challenges. This chapter identifies the attributes of young adolescents that educators must keep in mind when considering classroom management.

Young Adolescents and Behavior Management   What do middle school educators need to know about early adolescents to exert control of the classroom in ways that achieve their goals? Ironically, what makes young adolescents challenging is also what makes them captivating and fun to teach and be with. So, although educators talk about classes of early adolescents as sometimes difficult to manage, the middle school movement is based on a thorough and compassionate caring about the students in the schools. (For more detail about the characteristics and needs of young adolescents, see Chapter 1.)

Physical Development.   Middle school educators know that early adolescence is a tumultuous time in terms of the amount of change that occurs in the bodies, minds, and lives of their students. More change is likely going on than at any other time of life. Certainly, this is true of physical development. It almost makes sense to think of a storm raging in their bodies. Human beings often grow more during early adolescence than at any other time. For many, this means an awkwardness and self-consciousness that may contribute to classroom discipline problems. Arms and elbows elongate; legs, feet, knees, and ankles often seem to be everywhere—in the aisles, on neighbors' desks. Certainly, the expectation that teachers once had for their students to sit up straight, with hands folded and feet on the floor under their desks, seems unrealistic for many contemporary middle school classrooms. Common acne, and more serious problems such as scoliosis and epilepsy, often make their first appearance during early adolescence. Changes associated with sexual development also may contribute to a classroom climate that is more difficult to control.

Mental Development and Hypercriticality. Mentally, middle school students are often changing in ways that also contribute to difficulties with classroom control. Research reports that sometime during ages 10–15, many students begin to acquire new mental abilities. Among the attributes acquired by many middle school students is the ability to think more abstractly, symbolically, hypothetically, and critically. While many of these new intellectual skills allow students to be more successful academically, the changes are not all positive. As middle school students acquire the ability to think critically, for example, they often seem to feel compelled to use this new critical power in their interactions with other students and with adults. Middle school students can often be observed being very critical of their peers. Interpersonal interactions sometimes seem to verge on outright cruelty to one another.

The early adolescent also discovers that parents, teachers, principals, pastors, and even presidents are less than perfect. Their reaction is, sometimes, to be critical of everything adults say and do. Teachers catch a great deal of this student criticism. "This class is boring." "The teacher is dumb." "The activities are babyish." "Nothing about school is cool." This tendency of young adolescent students to be hypercritical can make controlling the middle school classroom anything but easy.

Emerging Sexuality. Another attribute of early adolescent development that contributes to difficulty in middle level classroom management is the emerging sexuality that characterizes the lives of these students. The Carnegie Council on Adolescent Development report *Turning Points* (1989) described the disjunction between the students' biological and social development. Students are able to engage in behavior, biologically, far before they are mature enough, socially, to undertake the responsibility associated with that behavior. Early adolescents certainly seem to spend a great deal more time thinking about sexual development than academic issues. Absorption in that development, attraction to the opposite sex, and the almost overpowering urges that appear constantly regardless of the situation often produce a group of students who seem highly distractible and uninterested in the curriculum the teacher has been mandated to teach. This presents great challenges to the teacher concerned about on-task behavior and engaged learning time.

Social Interaction.   Many young adolescents are, by nature, caught up in a web of social needs from which it seems impossible to extricate them. In fact, middle schoolers are social beings who want to belong. Often, students misbehave at the middle school level because they believe that it will get them the recognition they seek.

Middle school students are often much more concerned about their place in the social constellation than about their academic rank in class. This may cause them to resist adult attempts to make them do almost anything. Acquisition and retention of friends is a much more critical concern of many early adolescents than the acquisition and retention of subject matter.

The evidence says that many early adolescents are willing to sacrifice academic progress for social success. Bright girls, for example, sometimes downplay their abilities in exchange for popularity. African American boys, given the choice between the development of their minds and the maintenance of friendships, may find it hard to focus on school success. This is especially the case if the norms of their group label school success as "acting white."

Everything went smoothly in the author's home when his three teenagers had good friends at school. When they did not, the children's grades would go down, their school behavior became less positive, and teachers found themselves more in need of parental help. Imagine, then, a classroom of 30 or 35 students engaged in a constant struggle for social success and status. Could this situation, common to every middle school classroom, present a problem for classroom management?

Emotional Development.   Emotionally, young adolescents are in transition as well. Young children may have the same emotions as older students, but they seem unable to experience them fully or articulate them clearly. By high school, students have begun to get control over their emotions and the expression of those feelings.

At least some middle schoolers seem to have a rich new sense of their emotions, to experience them fully, and to be, yet, unskilled in managing the expression of those emotions. That, said simply, means that young adolescents are sometimes very emotional beings. Their emotions are very close to the surface and easily tapped. A student can be calm and quiet one minute and a raging storm a little later. Exhilaration seems, sometimes, to turn to depression more quickly for early adolescents than for others.

When all the changes that are happening in other areas of their lives are factored in, they have much to be emotional about. And these emotions spill into the classroom right along with the students.

Self-Esteem.   Another area of development that offers a challenge to the middle school teacher has to do with the students' self-esteem, their concept of self as either positive or negative. Although a great deal more research needs to be done in this area, many middle school educators believe that their students often seem to have considerably more negative self-concepts than the same students had in elementary school. Students who feel badly about themselves tend to project that feeling outwardly toward others, and middle school classrooms can be places where blame and disapproval are common. The same attitude of negativity and blaming can often occur at home as well as school. Parents and their middle school children can often experience long periods of tension in their relationships. Home can be a place where tension leads to one argument after another as students also struggle with their emerging need for autonomy and independence. The arguments and anger that begin at home can carry over to the school, where students can be like simmering pots ready to boil over.

Moral Development. Psychologist Lawrence Kohlberg has helped explain another important area of early adolescent development—moral development and how human beings make distinctions between what is right and wrong, moral and immoral. In a nutshell, many middle school students come to their classrooms with less than mature ways of thinking about right and wrong. Often, right seems to them to be what they can get away with and wrong is only what they are punished for. Or, right can be determined by whether the people involved are friends or not. Middle school classrooms are frequently full of students who think that right and wrong are determined only by consequences or relationships and who seem to be completely unaware of rules, principles, moral precepts, or of the effects of their actions on their classroom and school.

Many middle school students are developmentally immature when it comes to moral thinking. To some high school teachers who come to the middle school to teach, it seems like a sort of moral jungle. Secondary teachers often do not understand why appeals to "do the right thing" seem to fall on deaf ears. They are surprised to learn that many middle schoolers do not understand concepts such as group loyalty, duty, involvement, commitment, belonging, or compromise. Teachers are often also surprised with how important the concept of fairness is for their young adolescent charges.

Spiritual Development. Some middle school theorists have concluded that another area that causes problems for the classroom has to do with spirituality. Discussions of spirituality can be difficult for educators, but this is an area too important to ignore, with implications for behavior management and relationships with young adolescents. Many middle schoolers do not seem to believe that life has a purpose, that it has meaning, or that it makes sense. Many students do not seem to believe that their lives have much direction or promise. They seem to believe that the future, at least for them, holds little to be excited about, little to work hard for, and little to sacrifice for. The Carnegie Council on Adolescent Development describes this state as growing confusion about roles and the years ahead. Consequently, teachers who must ask students to work hard, defer gratification, and put responsibility before pleasure find doing so increasingly more difficult.

Cultural Differences.   Educators have to add the challenges that come with the increased cultural pluralism that characterizes the typical middle school classroom. While diversity adds rich, robust, and wonderful variety to people's lives, some would argue that such diversity does not come without cost. Different communication styles, different values, different goals, and different beliefs about the worth of education—all this makes the middle school classroom a much more complex place than perhaps it used to be. Complex classrooms are more difficult to manage. It is not just that new groups of students from different ethnic, religious, racial, and cultural backgrounds are present in the middle school classrooms. Many teachers would assert that all the students seem different from "the way they used to be."

Researchers Charles Wolfgang and Karla Kelsey (1991) argue that today's middle school students are different from earlier generations because their childhoods are different. Earlier generations came to the middle level classroom having been taught, at home, important lessons about appropriate behavior that today's students have not learned. Earlier generations knew, assert Wolfgang and Kelsey, and today's successful students know that classrooms are places where time must be organized and used effectively. Successful students, then and now, know how to stay engaged and on task for extensive periods of time. Successful students know that they must produce work and finish assignments under the demand of time requirements. They learned this at home, from practicing set times to go to bed, to get up, for eating meals, and for doing one's chores.

Often, in today's homes, argue Wolfgang and Kelsey, time is viewed differently. Parents under stress may forgo trying to implement and enforce the lessons about time in the lives of their children. There may be no set time for meals, perhaps few occasions when the whole family sits down together for any purpose. There may be no set time for going to bed or for getting up. Many students, consequently, arrive at the middle school with a pronounced "here and now" orientation, without a concern for punctuality or orderliness and without any understanding about "what the fuss is all about." This is a perfect setup for conflict with teachers who believe that learning occurs best in incremental, sequential, time-oriented fashion.

Today's middle school students also sometimes fail to understand and appreciate what Wolfgang and Kelsey call "motor and spatial rules." Knowing that when they leave the table in the cafeteria they should pick up their trash, push in their chair, and move away without bumping into anyone is something that should have been learned at home and be performed automatically at school. Students whom educators consider to be well socialized (educators used to say "well-mannered," which is now probably considered out-of-date) understand when and where certain behaviors are appropriate and when they are not.

In earlier years, children were taught that playing ball in the dining room is not appropriate. Every room in the house had a clearly defined use. The children knew that what was okay in one room was not in others. Having toys all over the floor in their bedroom might be fine, but toys scattered throughout the living room would not be acceptable. Children, Wolfgang and Kelsey state, knew how to behave in other spaces, such as someone else's home, a church, or a restaurant. They also knew what behavior was appropriate in the playground, the cafeteria, the classroom, and the gym.

Some of today's students may be growing up in homes where both parents return exhausted from a long and arduous day in the workplace. Parents may have little energy left for teaching their children that their rooms should be neat, that toys do not belong in the kitchen, or that meals are not supposed to be eaten in front of the television in the living room. This lack of structure may leave students with little understanding of what behavior is appropriate in specific contexts. Middle schoolers may, then, tumble into classrooms with behavior more appropriate to the gym. Teachers, who feel strongly about what behavior is acceptable in different places, find themselves exasperated and asking, "Didn't their parents teach them anything?"

The concept of property rights, say Wolfgang and Kelsey, is also something that used to be learned in well-ordered homes, where everything had its place and its owner. Students who do not learn the concept of property rights may seem to operate on the assumption that "I needed it. I found it. I get to use it." They may also believe that they have the right to use force to get what they want. All of this means that many middle school classrooms will contain more than a few students who have not learned important lessons about being members of groups, about the meaning of community. Combine this with students whose normal development leads them to be critical, clumsy, emotional, highly social, sexual, and immature morally and to be without the perspective supplied by a well-developed and positive outlook on life.

Then add the Carnegie Council's cautions about early adolescence at the end of the 20th century. Evidence shows that the period of adolescence is, in many ways, getting longer. Students can be dependent, which is one defining characteristic of immaturity, into their 20s and 30s. This is the case, even in the face of the erosion of family structure and social support for adolescents. Easy access to life-limiting opportunities makes adolescence a much scarier time than it was for many in the past. Increasing poverty and continuing racial discrimination and class division make life difficult for everyone, but especially for those who must try to grow up in the midst of it.

The middle school classroom is a challenging place and among the hardest to manage when filled with 25–35 early adolescent students. Forming and maintaining positive relationships with young adolescents is difficult and time consuming. In face of all of this, the temptation for some might be to choose to teach at the elementary or high school. In truth, this has often been the case. Until recently, many teachers who could find a place at another level have avoided the middle level. Others may succumb to the temptation to view student behavior as willful disobedience and to heap on more and harsher punishments for misbehavior and rule breaking.

However, the middle school movement has helped thousands of educators recognize that this catalog of challenges is not the fault of the students. Aliens have not occupied their bodies. Young adolescents are not just "hormones with feet." Middle school educators understand that blaming early adolescents for important and necessary changes that, successfully negotiated, will move them to become productive, healthy young adults makes no sense. Middle schoolers are what they are because of the important and necessary stage of development through which they are passing and because of experiences they have had and values they have developed long before they ever arrive in middle level classrooms and schools. Educators recognize that what educators face in classrooms are often just younger versions of themselves—tender, vulnerable human beings who need attention, energy, caring, and teaching, perhaps even more than they did earlier or will need in later years.

An affirmative, effective response to the challenge of middle school discipline requires that educators recognize and accept early adolescent students for what they naturally and wholesomely are. Educators must recognize how differently today's children and youth are being raised and that in too many cases they are not being raised, but merely housed. An effective, affirmative response does not, however, require middle school teachers to stand quietly and tolerate behavior that leads to lower academic achievement, less positive personal development, and the destruction of group citizenship.

What can educators do? Educators must recognize and accept that there is nothing inherently wrong with their students or with themselves as teachers. One is not a bad teacher just because of a desire for students to pay attention and observe the rules. But, instead of blaming students or themselves, educators must examine how they can use the middle school concept to help connect to their students and exert control of their schools and classrooms in more effective ways. Educators can use teaming and advisory programs to assist them in developing better relationships with their students and the families of their students. Educators can establish more effective control of middle school classrooms through the use of a proactive structure that encourages appropriate student behavior. Educators can use instructional strategies that maintain classroom momentum and time on task with a minimum of negative teacher affect. And, educators can, when misbehavior does occur, respond in effective ways that avoid being overly harsh, punitive, and coercive.

Educators know that this is a tall order, but the middle school movement has not become the most successful innovation in the history of modern education by avoiding a challenge.

Middle School Organization and Student Behavior Management

The middle school concept is the only innovation in the history of American education based on a compassionate understanding of and dedication to students with their particular characteristics and needs. However, middle school educators are naive about the difficulties associated with organizing and operating middle level schools and classrooms. They want their students to learn as much as possible, feel positive about themselves, and develop a commitment to and skills associated with group citizenship. That can be a difficult undertaking, given the nature of young adolescent students and the conditions in contemporary society. The good news is that educators have discovered some effective ways of responding to the characteristics and needs of middle school students.

This concept, called the middle school, is based on a unique school program that leads students from the elementary school on to the high school in a smooth and effective transition. It begins with the recognition that the students are not just taller elementary students or shorter high school students. They are, for the most part, too old to be treated like children but too young to be treated like young adults. Many of today's early adolescent students are not mature enough, self-disciplined enough, grown-up enough, or capable enough of resisting temptation to be successful in the traditional secondary school. Perhaps 50 years ago, when life in the home and society was much more highly structured, early adolescent students could be successful in a very unstructured school.

Problems with the Traditional Junior High School Organization

The traditional junior high school, operated like a high school or a university, was simply too loosely organized to be effective with today's young adolescent students. The experience of the last 40 years teaches middle school educators that many students need a great deal more positive structure to be successful in their school lives. The middle school concept inserts positive structure into the lives of students in two important ways—in the organization of the school and in the structure of the relationships between teachers and students within the school.

The structure of the middle school needs to match the levels of maturity of the early adolescent student in a much more effective way than the traditional junior high school. The junior high school was organized very much like the traditional high school as well as the university—according to the subject area specializations of the instructors. Teachers in the university, the high school, and the junior high school were organized according to the thing they cared most about, that is, their subject area. The history teachers and professors were together in the history department. The science teachers were placed with each other, and their labs, in the science department. It was the same with English, mathematics, and other subject areas. In college and on today's high school campuses, students move back and forth across the campus according to the subjects in their schedule.

When this concept eventually trickled down to the junior high school, schools for young adolescents were organized the same way as schools for older adolescents and young adults in college. This, it turned out, was developmentally inappropriate in major ways. If the outline of the floor plan in Figure 5.1 was that of a traditional junior high school, the math department would be in one part of the building, the science department in another, the history department in its own part of the building, and English teachers would have their own wing. When the bell rang in this kind of junior high school, students, who had recently been in much smaller elementary schools, sprang from their seats in classrooms in one department area and raced across the school to their next class, unless teachers were standing guard outside their classrooms. Even then, time between classes could be a perilous period of time for younger and more vulnerable students.

Hall duty was one of the more unpleasant tasks assigned to junior high teachers when they were not teaching. At the end of a class, students would come out of their classrooms and race in entirely different directions. Usually this movement between classes, known as passing time, lasted for five or six minutes, officially until the tardy bell rang. Then, dozens of students who were still in the hallways charged past teachers who did not know their names, ran into their classrooms, and raced to their seats, just in time, or later. Classes then lasted for another 50 minutes, or so, and then the bell rang to begin the process all over again.

Counting the bells for the beginning of school and for dismissal, this process could occur eight or nine times in a typical school day. Changing classes thus consumed about 30–45 minutes each day and happened in ways that inevitably filled both the hallways and the dean's office with students who had acted like lemmings heading for a distant cliff. Many junior high teachers and administrators spent their careers observing this maddening daily ritual, trying to maintain decorum as best they could. Estimating eight class changes a day, 180 days a year, for 30 years, that is 43,200 passing times to be supervised over the span of a teaching career.

Sometimes, junior high schools were organized according to the quarter system. This meant that students changed their class assignments and teachers every 12 weeks. A teacher might have as many as 450 different students in a year. And students might have as many as 25 teachers during a year in a tra-

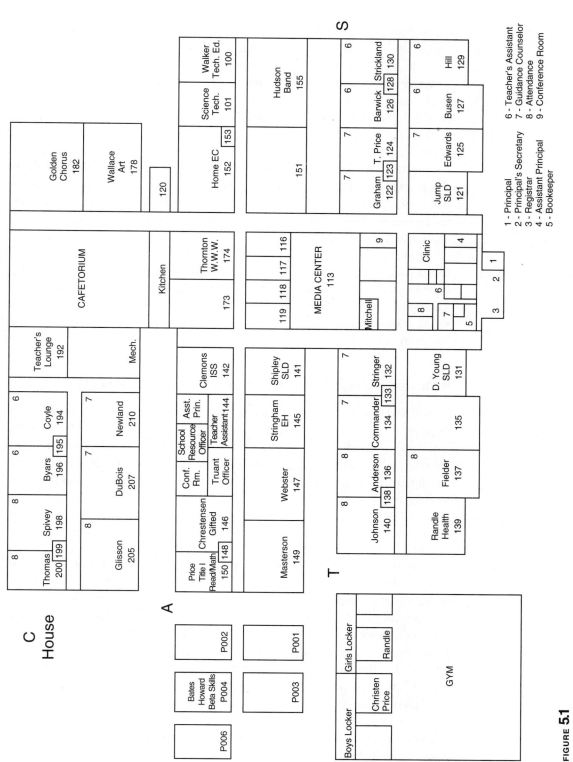

FIGURE **5.1**

WAKULLA MIDDLE SCHOOL IN CRAWFORDVILLE, FLORIDA, 2000–2001

ditional junior high school. Little wonder that few students or teachers were able to develop any sort of meaningful relationship with each other.

Junior high school teachers were often pedagogical lone rangers. Although they were organized in subject area departments, they taught different parts of the curriculum than other members of their department. They always taught different students, often in different grades. And they rarely had the same planning period as their department members, so that when they relaxed in the teachers lounge during a well-deserved break, no one there taught the same subject or the same students. They had very little in common with the other teachers, except their frustrations and disappointment, which may be one reason teachers lounges in traditional junior high schools developed reputations as unsavory and unprofessional places, haunted by people who were known as "lounge lizards."

Junior high teachers were on their own. No wonder they often preferred the calmer, quieter high school, with their names on the transfer list year after year. Teachers who are still teaching in a middle level school organized like a traditional junior high school may be experiencing a great deal more professional pain than necessary. Little wonder that, these days, few educators can be heard calling for a return of the junior high school concept.

Behavior Management and the Middle School Concept

How does the middle school do things differently? The middle school concept requires that educators place their highest priority on the characteristics and needs of young adolescent students, not on the subject matter in which teachers majored. This fundamental reordering of priorities leads to an equally fundamental reordering of virtually everything in the school, including teacher-student relationships and how they are formed. In exemplary middle schools, this reorganization is the result of the implementation of a special brand of positive structure that changes the nature of teacher-student interactions.

Younger Students Advocates of the middle school concept reject the idea of business as usual when students' characteristics and needs are dramatically different from an older group's. This is particularly important when students who attend middle schools are, on the whole, about one-third younger than the students who attended schools with grades 7–9. Middle school educators have discovered that organizing a school for students who are between 10 and 15 years old the same way that universities organize to serve students who are from 18 to 30 years old makes no sense.

When school districts changed from a junior high organization to a middle school organization, they may not have realized that this action created schools that may be 50% younger than what existed before. This is a most important point. When a school for students in grades 7–9 is replaced with a school housing students in grades 5–8, for example, the student body is dramatically younger. In fact, when a district moved to middle school, usually every school in the district housed a younger clientele. Elementary students lost their most mature students—usually the 6th grade and sometimes the 5th. Ninth graders moved to the high school, making the middle level school and the high school both full of younger students. One of the often unanticipated outcomes of the districtwide implementation of middle schools was that all schools in the district had a younger clientele.

In many ways, this was good news, unless the teachers and administrators in those schools thought that what was developmentally appropriate for a much more mature student group was good enough for the much younger students in their buildings. Middle school educators know not to organize and operate schools for students ages 10–14 in the same way as schools for 15- to 19-year-olds, and there is substantial research to affirm this intuitive understanding (Rutter et al., 1979; Felner et al., 1997).

Middle schools are, in this way, a much more conservative school organization than first glimpses would suggest. They are based on the idea that immature students will fail in schools organized for much older and more mature students. Middle schools, properly understood and organized, are the implementation of a process of tightening down on the students in the most positive way possible. The middle school concept requires that teachers and students be organized, always, according to the needs of the students and not according to the subject matter in which the teachers majored in college. Teacher subject specialization, so popular in colleges and universities, is not the only, or the most important, factor in considering how to organize middle school teachers. Positive, supportive structure is often more characteristic of the exemplary middle school.

Positive, Supportive Structure The layout of the conventional middle school, as well as the passing time routine, is different from a traditional junior high school. When and if a bell rings (bells are often unnecessary in exemplary middle schools), the students move out of one class, for example, and in the next door to their next class or just across the hall to another one. Organized into teams or houses according to the students they share, and not the subjects they teach, middle school teachers have their classrooms as close as possible to the classrooms of the teachers on their team who have the same students. Teams of from two to five teachers, who know the names and faces of virtually every student, supervise the changing of classes in two minutes or less. Hallway problems, while not gone completely, can be reduced to an occasional nuisance. (For more information about teams and houses, see Chapter 7.)

In hundreds of middle schools across the country, another level of positive structure helps with the discipline problems. Wakulla Middle School (WMS), in Crawfordville, Florida, for example, is not organized into grade level wings like a conventional middle school (see Figure 5.1), even though educators there use an interdisciplinary team structure that is much more effective with discipline than a departmentalized structure. WMS is organized into houses, based upon a school-within-school design, each covering grades 6–8. Given that the school's sport teams are the Wildcats, the four houses are labeled "C," "A," "T," and "S." "S" House has a small 6th grade team, an equally small 7th grade team, and an 8th grade team. This is also true in "C," "A," and "T" houses. Not only do students stay in the same part of the building during the day, for all of their academic classes, but they also stay in that part of the building for the entire time they are students at Wakulla Middle School.

This structure affects the management of young adolescents in positive ways because it is another level of positive structure built into the school. How does it happen? Look closely at "S" House and think about the following questions, based on your knowledge of young adolescents and their school lives.

- Do the 6th graders coming into "S" House care what the 6th grade teachers say about the rules? Yes, they do, because 6th graders still care deeply about their teachers and what those teachers think and feel.
- Do the new 6th graders care what the 7th and 8th grade teachers say? Yes, they do. Why? They care because they will have those teachers next year and the year after. From the first day of school for 6th graders, and the teachers they will have for the next three years, a new level of accountability is built into the school structure.
- Do the 7th and 8th graders in "S" House pay attention to what the 6th grade teachers say? Yes. Those teachers were their teachers last year and the year before, and a bond virtually always remains.
- Do the 8th grade teachers care how the 6th grade students act? Yes. How about the 7th grade teachers? Yes. Do you see why?
- Are you beginning to see the level of positive structure, of accountability, that may be absent in a building without this type of organization?

At WMS, and dozens of schools like it, a type of three-year informal and, perhaps, unconscious contract binds the teachers and students in each house together in a new kind of positive structure. Even more encouraging, this sort of positive school structure enlists far greater parent support in developing better student behavior management. In fact, at Wakulla and schools like it, parent involvement is often much higher than in schools without the house plan. At WMS, parents know where their children will be and who their children's teachers will be for the entire time they will be at the middle school. This can be a much more positive, inviting structure, especially for the parents of the children with greatest needs. Research and experience speak clearly to the strongly positive effects on classroom discipline that result from increased parent involvement, and close ties with parents are proven to keep parental dissent at a minimum, which can have its own positive effects on classroom discipline.

At Mandarin Middle School, in Jacksonville, Florida, the economics of school construction convinced the school board to open a middle school housing 2,400 6th, 7th, and 8th grade students. Even the most uninformed persons would be likely to agree that 2,400 students is too many and that the problems that come with that number will be likely to far outweigh the benefits of the rich curriculum that might be possible from the economy of scale. If Mandarin were organized into academic departments like a traditional junior high school, the situation would be a management and disciplinary nightmare. At Mandarin, however, the school is organized to build in a new level of positive structure, and it has a salutary effect on school and classroom discipline there. At other large schools, or where students are unusually challenging in terms of school discipline, the same results can be expected.

Educators at Mandarin wisely rejected the departmentalized organization in favor of the interdisciplinary team organization. Mandarin also adopted the house or school-within-school organization that works so well at Wakulla and elsewhere. At Mandarin, however, educators took a big step toward even greater positive structure. At Mandarin and, we estimate, at more than 100 other pioneering middle schools around the country (George & Lounsbury, 2000), the team organization and school-within-school structure are complemented by looping. For example, teachers on the Cosmic Hawks team at Mandarin begin with their 6th grade students and stay with them for three years. At Mandarin, this practice is called student teacher progression (STP).

When thinking about the potential benefits of looping in the area of student behavior management, keep in mind that the two- or three-year connection between teachers and students is not restricted to just the one or two students who might drive a teacher or team of teachers to distraction in a particular year. Looping means that teachers are able to stay connected to all the great kids who they would love to have another year. Four teachers and approximately 130 students stay together through 6th, 7th, and 8th grades. What does this do to discipline? We believe that the evidence available, anecdotal though it may be, suggests that substantial benefits are realized from the practice of team looping.

Consider the following possibilities.

- Imagine the level of intensity that the 6th grade teachers attach to getting their students off on the right foot early in that first year.
- Think about how differently students behave when they know they will have the same teachers for three years.
- Visualize how much more eager parents might be to get involved with teachers on the team that will teach their child for three years.

- Think about how much easier it is to end the 6th grade year, in terms of discipline, when the students, and their parents, realize that the teachers on the current team will be their teachers again next year and the next.
- Consider how much more effective it might be to begin the year when the teachers know all the students and their parents. Students and parents know the team's rules, the team's expectations. Teachers on the team know the students' strengths and their weaknesses. We think that everyone involved likely gets down to work faster and more efficiently.
- Imagine never hearing a student say, ever again, "We didn't have that last year," because the teacher could say, "Oh, yes, you did and I taught it to you."

One of the most difficult times in the lives of middle school teachers happens at the end of the year, usually during the last two weeks. At Mandarin, even the 8th graders stay on task longer, because they have been with these teachers for three years, and, believe it or not, they care about each other. Many times in June, teachers at Mandarin and other schools with the same positive structure have been observed standing in the hallway crying because 8th graders are leaving. In places such as these, discipline cannot be a big problem.

The research evidence supports having teams of the same students staying together even when they cannot have the same teachers for year to year (Rutter et al., 1979; George & Lounsbury, 2000). We assert that expecting these positive outcomes associated with increased positive structure is, in a way, common sense. Consistency and continuity in human relationships is almost always a good thing, cutting down on instability in human relationships and building up the positive structure in people's lives. It works with middle school students, too. Short-term, topsy-turvy, human relationships are unlikely to produce positive outcomes in any sphere of human activity. The most productive corporations, athletic teams, military units, and families are all based on long-term relationships (Kanter, 1983). Educators should not be surprised to learn that practices that lead to such relationships also work well with middle school students.

The middle school concept adds much more positive structure to the school experience for early adolescents. Beginning with advisory groups at the heart of the programs, middle schools add an important layer of positive structure with the introduction of interdisciplinary teams. The house plan, or school-within-school, adds a powerful new level of that same kind of positive interpersonal structure. Looping, and multiage grouping, contributes even more positive structure to the school. Closer and more personal teacher-student relationships lead to fewer challenging and confrontational discipline situations.

Using the Interdisciplinary Team to Improve School and Classroom Discipline

Several years ago, one of the authors spent time in a middle school in Orlando, Florida, where teachers had just changed the way they were organized, from academic subject departments to interdisciplinary teams. Interdisciplinary team organization is a way of organizing the faculty and students of a school so that a group of two to five teachers share

- The same group of students
- The same part of the school building
- The same schedule and planning time
- The responsibility for planning, teaching, and evaluating curriculum and instruction for more than one academic subject area

For more information about interdisciplinary team organizations, see Chapter 6.

As the author explored the effects of this organization on the teachers and students at the Orlando school, he spent some time observing student behavior and interviewing them about this new organization. He will never forget the response of one 8th grade boy who, when asked what this "team thing" was, replied, "The teachers are ganging up on us!" Another student said, "The teachers have unionized against us!"

Both students made these comments with big smiles on their faces, perhaps acknowledging the wisdom of their teachers. They clearly liked it when teachers worked together to improve the effectiveness of the school experience. Even tough 8th grade boys in challenging school situations, which this certainly was, recognized the benefits of having teachers gang up on them in positive ways. He knew then that middle school teachers had a new tool to be used in classroom relationships and behavior management.

Experience indicates that the mutual support that teachers on teams can offer each other is a crucial factor in mitigating the unusual stress of teaching at the middle level. Peer support, via the team, decreases feelings of isolation and stress, and it increases the levels of professionalism of the team members. Teachers who have spent even a short period of time working with early adolescents know, for example, that in disciplining students, consistency is probably more important than almost anything else. Middle school educators also know, as a result of the last 30 years' experience, that when teachers gang up on the kids things almost always go better for everyone.

One of the first ways teachers on teams can use their combined power is in the area of managing student behavior more consistently and effectively than they could acting alone. The goal of ganging up on the kids is to use consistent techniques that are effective with most of the students on the team, most of the time, in most situations. There is no silver bullet for discipline;

nothing works with all students, all of the time. The fundamental effort in this phase of team life is to make the team work for the teachers, to utilize each other's support and strengths to make the school day more pleasant and productive. Teachers on teams can use the team to develop a new sense of consistency in the area of classroom discipline.

A Team Discipline Plan   One way to gang up on the kids, positively, is for teachers to work together on the team to develop and implement a team discipline plan that has the approval and support of the school administration. Teachers will still have a school discipline plan, and their own classroom discipline plans, even if they and their teammates develop one for the team.

The first step in the development of any good team discipline plan is a lengthy and spirited exploration of and eventual consensus on the most important student behaviors that the teachers' collaboration could influence in helpful ways. What specific student behaviors do teachers want to encourage? What precise behavior do teachers on the team want to discourage?

A team discipline plan might or might not include these positively stated rules.

- Students must come to class prepared and on time.
- Gum, candy, and food can be consumed only during snack time.
- Students must raise their hand and wait to be called on before speaking out.
- Students must stay in their seats unless they have permission to leave.
- The teacher dismisses class.

One team had no rules, but they agreed to "HARP" on student behavior. HARP stood for Honor, Ambition, Respect, and Pride, the four most important virtues that teachers on the team worked to instill in their students' behavior. Inappropriate behavior was consistently met with teacher questions such as "Are you showing respect for our class when you act like that?" "Are you demonstrating pride in yourself when you turn in work like this?" "Are you honoring our team when you say things like that?" The plan, and the vigorous efforts teachers made to implement it, had the desired effect.

The second step is to come to agreement on the specific consequences that will result from the group's consistent attention to misbehavior, and the procedure that will be followed, in every classroom on the team, in the application of those consequences. Consequences usually begin with a verbal warning and other classroom actions. They quickly move on to team interventions of all kinds.

The third step in developing a good team discipline plan is to agree on the positive ways in which the team will consistently encourage correct behavior. Rules and consequences, behavior management specialists agree (e.g., Canter & Canter, 1976; Jones, 1987), must be balanced by factors that make life on the team, and staying on task and in line, at least positive, if not fun, for the students. Typically, teams offer special weekly activities, "no homework" passes, computer time, library passes, movie and popcorn parties, treats, tangible rewards such as pencils and tablets, special awards, and field trips. Once these steps have been taken, the team must arrange the components of the discipline plan into a clear, positive, and attractive format for distribution to students, parents, and administrators.

A perusal of good team discipline plans will demonstrate several important factors.

1. The most effective plans are as positive as possible.
2. The plans all spell out specific behaviors.
3. The behaviors in the plan vary somewhat based on the desires and preferences of the teachers on each team. A team discipline plan should reflect what teachers on that team care most about. If teachers do not feel the same way about certain rules, these do not become part of the team discipline plan. They can remain part of an individual teacher's plan.
4. The consequences are arranged in a series of hierarchical steps in which the severity of the response increases as student behavior becomes more serious or when the same misbehavior is repeated.
5. The consequences almost always begin in an individual teacher's classroom but eventually involve serious support from teammates in several ways: team detention, team conferences with a student, team contact and conferences with parents, use of a teammate's classroom for time-out purposes, team demerits, and so on.
6. Referral to the counselor or the house administrator is virtually the last step in the discipline plan, not the first. Sending students out of class to the school office is almost always thought of as one of the team's biggest guns. If the team shoots its biggest discipline guns too soon, on what might be considered trivial infractions, too little may be left for the serious and repetitive student misbehavior. In a school where team discipline plans are well installed, the administration knows that when a student comes to the office the situation is serious, at least one teacher has first tried to correct the behavior, and the entire team has also been unsuccessful.

Teams must remember that, once the team discipline plan has been developed, they must not make the mistake of thinking that because the students are now at the middle school level they will simply read the discipline plan and follow the team's directions. A team will need to bring the students together for an orientation to the plan. At that time, teachers and the students they trust can describe the desired behaviors, demonstrate them, get other students involved in rehearsing them, and solicit feedback from the students about the fairness of the discipline plan and the rules, consequences, and positive factors involved.

One team, the Bears at Southeast Middle School, in Guilford County, North Carolina, implemented its discipline plan and several weeks later identified the students who were having more trouble coping with rules than others on the team. Teachers met as a team with each of the 12 students, stressing their positive concern for the students and emphasizing the expectation that the students would follow the rules more consistently. A team might also consider inviting the dean or school administrator to the team orientation session, to add their support to the plan the team is implementing together.

Team Procedures   A team discipline plan is helpful, but it is not the only way teams of teachers can gang up on the kids in positive ways. Teams can work together to implement consistent team procedures for a range of different student behaviors that consistent collaboration will make work better in each classroom on the team. Many teams develop a team handbook that contains not only the discipline plan, but also team procedures for as many of these areas that were important to the members of the team.

Use of lockers
Late homework
Make-up tests
Headings for papers, tests, and assignments
Test rules
Time between classes
Notebooks
Extra credit
Special help sessions
Grading policies
Entering the team area
Bathroom times
Standards for neatness
Procedures for absentees
Cooperative learning
Hallways
Beginning and ending the day on the team
Announcements

This may seem to cover considerable ground, but veterans can probably add many more items to the list of things that have to work smoothly for student behavior to be at its best in individual classrooms and across the team as a whole.

Team Behavior Contracts   Many teams also find the use of student behavior contracts to be an effective way of ganging up on the kids. A contract is the result of a mutual agreement between the student and the team regarding specific desirable student behavior and how it can be achieved. The contract can be oral or written, depending on the severity or persistence of the misbehavior.

The contract can have either short- or long-term goals, but teams usually find that the shorter the goals the better the change in behavior, because the long term for many early adolescents is an hour from the present moment. This is also why the contract ought to be signed by the student.

Such contracts usually emerge from a team-student conference, perhaps even including parents, in which the following questions might have been asked of the student.

What should you be doing?
What can you do to change?
How can the team help you change your behavior?
What can you do that is different?
Which of these things do you choose?
Can you make a plan?
When will you start?

An Example of a Team Plan   At Southeast Middle School (SMS), in Greensboro, North Carolina, all teams are expected to develop team discipline plans that are congruent with the schoolwide plan. During an advisory group meeting early in the year, students on each team have input into making the rules for their team. Teachers at SMS are convinced that this experience allows students to "feel they have ownership of the procedures because they were instrumental in developing them." In a team planning period that follows, teachers on each team discuss the rules that students have brainstormed, add those they believe should be considered, and suggest modifications. Consequences for breaking rules are decided by the team, and at SMS this always includes positive consequences that will balance the negative ones.

A team meeting including all teachers and students on a team is then held to examine the tentative rules, consequences, and rewards. Students ask questions, and the plan is discussed until everyone is clear about the process and a consensus develops. A vote is taken, and the discipline plan for the team is formally adopted. Copies are made for each student and taken home for parents to examine and sign.

In one recent year at SMS, one team had the following rules.

1. Be prompt.
2. Be prepared.
3. Raise your hand when you wish to speak.
4. Follow directions.
5. Treat others with respect.

The consequences that were attached to this particular plan included the following.

- First offense: Student name is recorded in the classroom discipline log.
- Second offense: Student misses the team "commons break" that day.

- Third offense: Student writes a 250-word essay on how to improve behavior, and parents sign the essay.
- Fourth offense: Student attends a team conference where the team of teachers will decide the consequences, which might be silent lunch, team isolation, or after-school team detention.
- Fifth offense: Office referral.

Positive consequences associated with such a team plan can include rewards for individual students (stickers, positive phone call home, special seat in the class, homework pass, media center pass, etc.), the class (movie, homework pass, popcorn party), and the entire team (recess, field trip, intramurals, ice cream party, dance).

An Example of a Schoolwide Plan   Team discipline plans can connect to schoolwide discipline plans. At another Southeast Middle School, this one located in Columbia, South Carolina, a schoolwide discipline plan that involved every teacher and team made recent school years go much more smoothly and positively. The plan contained schoolwide rules that all team plans had to include.

- Respect: We will respect ourselves and the rights of others.
- Order: We will conduct ourselves in an orderly manner at all times.
- On Task: We will remain on task at all times.
- Safety: We will conduct ourselves in such a way that everyone is safe.
- Property: We will protect school and personal property.

Teachers and administrators at the Southeast Middle School in Columbia took steps to ensure that the students understood the rules. These rules were spelled out clearly in a handbook for students, including specific lists of infractions and the levels of severity that they represented, from those that were typical of daily distractions encountered in middle school to those that required immediate emergency procedures. In addition, carefully designed lesson plans for each rule were designed and taught at the beginning of the year in every homeroom so that no doubt remained about student understanding.

Then, just like the team plan, a series of consequences were laid out. First offenses were met with a series of warnings, verbal or written. Second offenses merited a reflection that included a short conference with the teacher and the completion of a reflection form. Third offenses were met with the loss of a privilege, such as recess, open lunch, canteen, or free time. A team of teachers would decide these situations for the students on their team. Fourth offenses involved a parent conference with the team and a counselor. Referral to an administrator came after this, or when an emergency required it. Teachers and administrators were pleased with the results of this plan on student behavior at the school.

At Fort Clarke Middle School, in Gainesville, Florida, team and school-wide discipline plans are combined.

- Step One: The teacher follows a classroom discipline plan approved by the dean.
- Step Two: A behavior slip is sent from the teacher to the student's advisor and to the parent.
- Step Three: Time out is held in the classroom of the student's advisor.
- Step Four: A team review committee meets with the student and parent to design a behavior improvement plan and the consequences that go with it.
- Step Five: Referral is made to the dean.

"Kid Meetings" When teachers share the same students and a common planning time, they talk a great deal about the early adolescents on their team. As team members talk about their students, they learn more about them. They find out about learning styles, about disabilities, about special gifts, about difficult home situations, among many other things. In some schools, teacher teams take one planning period a week for what they call a "Kid Meeting." At this meeting, the school counselor who works with the team identifies students who deserve the special attention of the teachers as a team. The teachers and the counselor, and sometimes the school principal or another specialist, spend the next 45 minutes discussing these students, increasing their common knowledge about them, and identifying tactics they might use to assist these students in whatever way seems appropriate.

A team might want to use planning time to develop more productive relationships with a number of other staff members: counselors, deans, administrators, unified arts teachers, special education teachers, media specialists, police liaison officers, or others. If team members have no regular contact with these professionals, it will be useful to work out ways to do so.

The more teachers know about their students, the more they can plan effectively to influence student behavior in positive ways. Knowing why a student may be misbehaving helps teachers to have empathy for the student and not to take his or her behavior personally. It also helps teachers find ways of responding that might be more effective if they are matched with the causes of the misbehavior. Experience with middle school teachers on teams also indicates that the more teachers know about the students, the more these teachers become willing to plan curriculum and instruction that will ultimately improve the behavior of the students.

When teachers become well acquainted with their students, the teachers are more eager to adapt their lessons for specific learning styles, to account for disabilities, to be alert to abusive home situations. This process seems to work in somewhat of a positive cycle. Teachers discover important information about their students from their teammates. They develop more positive feelings toward these students whom they come to know so much about, even the most difficult ones. Teachers are then willing to work harder and more creatively to meet the needs of students they care more about. The more they put into their lessons, the more they come to know about their students—and so on. This is, in the very best sense of the phrase, ganging up on the kids.

Parent Conferences   Teams can work together in ways that make parent conferences more productive and pleasant for everyone involved. Because good team-parent conferences almost always lead to improvements in student behavior, teachers usually notice that the number of parent conferences usually increases dramatically when teams are in place. Teachers on a team might choose to contact parents of students who need the assistance that increased teacher-parent contact will bring. The team might also choose to have an occasional conference with a parent whose child deserves special praise and recognition.

Sense of Community   Once organized and operating collaboratively, with discipline plans, consistent procedures, and parent conferences working to improve student discipline, teachers and students usually begin to feel more positively about each other and the new team arrangement. An authentic sense of community may begin to grow. The experience of teachers on the very best teams is that both teachers and students yearn for this group identity and that classroom discipline almost always improves when that sense of community grows. For teachers, the sense of community can be the redeeming virtue of the interdisciplinary team organization. Veteran educators frequently speak of the team arrangement as the factor that enabled them to continue teaching with a sense of joy and commitment that difficult student situations had threatened or damaged. So, the sense of community that can come from teaming is not just for students.

Students require this sense of community even more than the faculty. Older children and young adolescents are at a special time of readiness—to experience and learn the concepts of inclusion, group citizenship, responsibility, and duty. The team offers a turf to belong to and a positive group to join. Teamwork can make a major difference in the level of group feeling that exists on the team and the more positive behavior that can result from that feeling. Proactive strategies that increase the feeling of community, and consequently improve student behavior, include developing team names, colors, mottoes, songs, T-shirts, and other visible common possessions; staging contests, special meals, meetings, field trips, intramurals, and a host of other group activities; and planning interdisciplinary curriculum units involving the whole team.

At Broomfield Heights Middle School (BHMS), in Broomfield, Colorado, staff members welcomed parents and students to one new school year as the "Year of Team Spirit" and invited them to become team parent representatives. The school's Citizen Advisory Council had even established the position of team parent representative coordinator. Schools that involve parents in team life in this manner find parental support of the school to be substantially greater than it otherwise might be. This, then, leads to improved behavior management and more productive relationships with students, because they quickly become aware of increasingly more collaborative relationships between their parents and their teachers.

When teachers are enthusiastic about this aspect of teaming, improved relationships with students and consequently more productive behavior management are almost always the result. For teachers without experience in this area, but with the opportunity to experiment, a "don't knock it if you haven't tried it" position is best. With a team of colleagues, and perhaps with students, teachers who are ready can develop as many of the following as they deem feasible for the team.

Name	Mascot	Colors
Logo	Symbols	Song
Cheer	Slogan	T-shirt
Banner	Signs	Signals

Esprit de corps, of this sort, develops from identity, but it must be nurtured. Teams of teachers and students who feel a real sense of identity will also wish to enjoy that unity—in activities. Adults make friends by doing things together. It also works for teams. Among the dozens of ways that team spirit can be nurtured and enjoyed are the following.

Spirit days
Dress-up days
Talent shows
Field trips
Cleanup days
Brain bowls
Birthdays
Holiday parties
Field days

Often teachers on teams reach a point where they agree that classroom discipline in each of their individual classrooms can be bolstered by working together to provide consistent recognition and reward for positive student behavior. When teams of teachers and students come to know and regard each other positively, opportunities to recognize and celebrate achievements of all sorts come to mean much more. Many teams, for example, operate a "Student of the Week" program in which each of the teachers on the team selects one student from their classes each week to receive this designation, purely for reasons having to do with appropriate student behavior. Students' names and photos are then placed on a bulletin board in the hallway nearest the team, and these students then become the teacher's pets for that week.

At the end of the year, if a team conducts this activity in 30 of the 36 weeks of the year, how many students will be recognized in this way? All of the students on the team would be recognized. If every team in the school were to do it, by the end of the year, all of the students in the school would be identified as Student of the Week, a highly desirable circumstance. This is, still, a manner of ganging up on the kids.

Students who are successful academically are much more likely to behave appropriately. So, every effort teams make to improve academic achievement also contributes to improved student behavior. Teams can, for example, identify their own criteria for such recognition activities as a team honor roll. A schoolwide honor roll usually recognizes only the brightest, most successful students in the school, often those with consistent "A" and "B" grades. The team, however, can decide to honor students for academic improvement, which, in one way of thinking, is as important as consistently high grades. A team could, for example, decide to honor all students who improved their grade point averages (GPAs) by 0.25 in one grading period. One of the authors witnessed a team assembly at Lincoln Middle School, in Gainesville, Florida, in which all of the team's students who had improved their GPAs were recognized with a round of applause from their peers, a certificate, a pat on the back from the team leader, and a handshake from the school principal. Many of the students, perhaps the majority, had never been recognized for academic achievement in their school careers. And six parents called the team to say so.

Another team holds what they called an "I Try" assembly in the spring of the year, for students who always tried their best, no matter the result. The assembly was a marvelous thing for students, with parents in attendance, who had rarely, if ever, received public recognition. The process of using team organization to gang up on the kids by developing recognition activities that reach deeper into the team is one that can, and probably should, be a regular part of life on every team.

MENTORING MIDDLE SCHOOLERS: THE TEACHER AS ADVISOR

The teacher-student relationship in the middle school is often associated with the term *advisor* or, more recently, *advocate* or *mentor*. Each middle school student is seen as needing to reach out and explore the world of adults, while maintaining a type of interpersonal haven until a new level of maturity permits him or her to function as a high school student. Middle school students are encouraged to leave the sheltered atmosphere of an exclusive relationship with one adult behind, but they are guarded from the impersonal anonymity that might characterize a large high school. Exemplary middle schools attempt to see to it that every middle school student interacts with more than one adult, and perhaps as many as a half dozen adults, during a day or week, while maintaining a special connection with one. Each student has a teacher in the school who will know him or her better and care about him or her more than most other adults in the school. Every student will have a teacher who considers himself or herself to be the school expert on that particular child, his or her mentor. In this way the middle school continues to supply a unique educational experience while providing for a smooth transition from the elementary to the high school.

In a survey of hundreds of parents of middle schoolers in the New England area, James Garvin (1987) learned that once a parent knew that their child was safe at school, the concern shifted toward the availability of teacher guidance. Garvin found that parents were extremely eager for the presence in the middle school of a supportive adult who would be a sort of ombudsman for their child. In most districts, contacts from the elementary school to the home are frequent and supportive. This changes dramatically in many districts, when the children move to a middle or secondary level. The once frequent communications often shrink to being virtually nonexistent, which makes many parents uncomfortable and anxious about their child's programs and progress. Parents want their children to move beyond the dependence of childhood, but not more quickly than would be appropriate.

Much has happened in the last half-century to create a milieu in which schools and teachers were expected to shoulder part, sometimes a large part, of what had previously been regarded as the province and responsibility of the home—child rearing (Johnston, 2001). In more households both adults went to work outside the home. Extended family support systems (e.g., grandparents, aunts, and uncles) collapsed under the strain of distance and mobility required to match the new economy. More older adults retreated into age-segregated communities without contact with their children's children. Johnston also adds that, in recent years, an "aura of fearfulness" has come to surround the relationships between children and adults, and "adults distrust the motives of other adults when it comes to their interactions with children" (2001, p. 1). In many areas, then, schools and teachers were expected to become more important affectively, as mentors to young adolescents in their care.

Many lists of objectives for education written to guide program development have, somewhere close to the top, an enthusiastic commitment to objectives, which can best be summarized as affective. The middle school program for older children and early adolescents takes this commitment seriously, as every school philosophy proudly proclaims. While there is a great deal more to affective education than the teacher-student guidance program, we believe that such a program is the hub of affective education in the middle school (Jackson & Davis, 2000).

As defined here, the focal point of the teacher-student guidance program is the advisor-advisee (AA) program. Although known by different names in different places (home base, small group, fourth R, homeroom), the faculty of almost every school that takes this commitment seriously is familiar with this term or recognizes its meaning immediately. Hence, the teacher-student guidance program, mentoring, and the advisor-advisee program will be considered here as one and the same, and the terms will be used interchangeably.

Early surveys of middle school practices failed to inquire about the existence of advisory programs, because such programs were so infrequently encountered. In the 1980s and 1990s, the number of middle level schools implementing a formal teacher-based guidance or advisory program rose dramatically. A national survey indicated that 39% of the responding schools had instituted regularly scheduled advisory programs (Alexander & McEwin, 1989). While popular with middle school theorists, experienced practitioners report much less success with the implementation of such programs than would have once been predicted (Johnston, 2001).

Sadly, the advisory function of the middle school teacher, vested in the advisor-advisee program, has failed to achieve its purposes in many schools where it has been implemented. There are several reasons for this. The typical AA program was often implemented as a part of wholesale conversion of schools in a district from junior high school to a middle school format. The vision and commitment to ensure such a program's success were too rarely present. Those who attempted to implement the program had no experience and often called for help from consultants who also had no direct experience. Often, no curriculum was present; in other cases, the curriculum was a guidance curriculum in which teachers had little confidence. Frequently, teachers had little or no opportunity to buy in to the program, and they often perceived it as one more preparation in an already far too busy day. Consequently, for these and other reasons, the AA program has had far less success than other elements of the middle school concept such as the interdisciplinary team organization (Burns, 1996).

Burns says (1996, p. 1) of the experience teachers and students have had with advisories:

> They describe pervasive dissatisfaction with advisory experiences. Students rebuke advisory activities as contrived or "just lame." Teacher-advisors complain of confinement to "canned" activities while simultaneously being expected to form meaningful relationships with students they see for only a few minutes each day. To quote one seventh grade advisor, "I like the idea of ad-

visory, but I've come to the conclusion that 10–15 minutes a day of caring just isn't enough time to develop substantial relationships."

This sentiment seems to capture the dilemma faced by educators who seek to implement programs that strengthen the relationships between middle school teachers and their students. Most, if not all, of the educators involved are sympathetic with the need, but frustrated by the failures of many attempts, to formalize an advisory program. What do successful advisory programs look like, and what are the requirements for successful advisory programs?

Alternative Designs for Teacher-Based Guidance or Advisory Programs

Middle school advisory programs are of essentially two varieties, those that involve a daily meeting of the teacher with the same students and those that have a more variable schedule. The programs that emphasize a daily meeting with the same teacher and group of students tend to emphasize the sense of community, of group cohesiveness, that emerges, while those that do not involve a daily group meeting tend to stress the one-to-one relationship between the teacher and one student. Each type of program has its advantages.

Daily Large Group Programs

A daily advisor-advisee program has been functioning at Spring Hill Middle School, in High Springs, Florida, for more than three decades, since the opening of the school in 1970. In the 2001–2002 school year, advisory time is allocated every morning for 20 minutes. Under the pressures of standards-based reform in Florida, even the advisory has taken on more of an academic flavor. At Spring Hill, one of the advisory sessions is devoted to reading skills, one to mathematics, and a third is DEAR (Drop Everything and Read). The other two days of the program are up to the discretion of the teacher, based on the needs of the students in the group. Every certified teacher in the school has a group of advisees, and occasionally the school counselor has a group. As soon as the student arrives at school, the first experience is the advisor-advisee program. Homeroom and advisory responsibilities are combined, so that after the morning announcements and homeroom business, teachers are left with about 15 minutes for advisor-advisee activities. Variations of this program are now present in dozens, perhaps hundreds, of middle schools around the country.

At Oak View Middle School (OVMS), in Andover, Minnesota, a daily advisory program was a regular part of the block schedule that operated during the 2001–2002 school year. At OVMS, the day was divided into four 90-minute periods, and the students had an alternating day schedule. One of the blocks was split in two to accommodate exploratory classes and the advisory time. The schedule of a typical 6th grader for that year looked like this:

	A Day	B Day
Period 1	Family and consumer science	Science
Period 2	Mathematics	Social studies
Period 3a	Advisory (PRIDE)	Advisory (PRIDE)
Period 3b	Health	Music
Period 4	English	Reading

At Brandon Valley Middle School (BVMS), in Brandon, South Dakota, advisory is called B.E.S.T., an acronym for Becoming Exceptional Students and Teachers. At BVMS, advisory groups meet three days each week, for 20 minutes. The curriculum for the three days includes

- Weekend Wrap. Activities include journal writing, silent reading, individual teacher-student conferences, wellness plan check, study time, "spotlight on the student," homework or agenda book check, and locker clean-out.
- Personalized Education. Curriculum includes components consistent with human growth and development activities such as character education.
- Group Activities Period—G.A.P. Advisory groups challenge each other in appropriate levels of group competition and spirit building in games of interest to middle schoolers. A wide variety of citizenship-related activities such as service projects and group-building sessions such as sharing a meal and door decorating also takes place.

At Lewis and Clark Middle School, in Jefferson City, Missouri, during the 2001–2002 year, "Blazer Time" occurred for 20 minutes, also at the beginning of the day. All core team teachers have advisory groups that are built from within their teams. On Monday, groups focus on "Get Organized Day" activities such as organizing their folders, notebooks, and lockers. Tuesday is an activity day that involves more than one advisory group in minicourses, intramurals, and other activities. Wednesday is for silent reading, and Thursday is a second activity day. Friday is "Wrap Up Day" when students evaluate their goals for the week, preview next week, and engage in student assemblies and other culminating activities.

At Madison Middle School, in Seattle, Washington, a daily advisory time operates in a similar fashion. On Mondays, advisory groups meet at the end of the day, for organizational purposes similar to those at other middle schools. On the four following days, for a 25-minute period called "Team Time," students select an activity for three weeks. These activities include games, movies, art, anti-drug-abuse programs, student council, school clubs, study time, and teacher-student conference time. The Team Time is structured to be as appealing to students as possible, and the faculty use it as a privilege that can be denied if students have misbehaved.

Mt. Slesse Middle School (MSMS), in Chilliwack, British Columbia, had, during the 2001–2002 year, two advisory periods each day. The morning advisory time is 18 minutes in length and is usually devoted to group activities such as service projects, intramurals, and the like. The afternoon advisory lasts for 10 minutes and is connected to the lunchtime. Students are permitted to bring their lunches to their advisory room. At MSMS, advisories are multigraded and students stay with the same advisory teacher for the three years they attend the school.

At Heritage Middle School, near Orlando, Florida, in 2001, the "WINGS" program had this goal: "To promote student awareness and comfort with our school and with self, in the areas of social, emotional, and academic growth, in a small group setting." Students meet in a WINGS group each morning, working through a carefully designed curriculum and schedule. Monday is a "Team Day"; Tuesday and Wednesday are devoted to small group activities that are a part of the advisory curriculum; Thursday has clubs and other special interest activities; and Friday is an "Academic Review Day."

In midafternoon at New Smyrna Beach Middle School, in Volusia County, Florida, core academic team teachers meet with a group of 27–30 students from their team, whom they have in class at least one other period of the day. Two days a week are devoted to structured advisement activities. One day the advisors and advisees participate in intramural activities within the entire grade level house. The remaining two days include guided academic practice, in which students set goals for that period and advisors confer with individual students about academic or personal concerns, as their classmates work on their stated goal for the period.

At Chisholm Trail Middle School, in Round Rock, Texas, the CAT (Creative Advisory Time) program is based on the "belief that all students can learn when all the needed support systems are in place." A weekly schedule involves advisories in reading time, intramurals, tutorials, clubs, and the conduct of school business such as receiving and reacting to report cards.

At Broomfield Heights Middle School, in Broomfield, Colorado, the advisory period is the first thing that happens every day, lasting for about 25 minutes. Counselors prepare objectives and materials for monthly themes (e.g., decision-making) that are used in advisory groups two days each week. Teachers have the freedom to use the materials given to them by the counselors or to develop their own, but they must focus on the agreed-upon theme for the month during two days each week. A third day of advisory time is a silent day when students may read, write, or study quietly, while the advisor uses the time to interact with individual students. The other two advisory times of the week are up to the teacher and students to design. This advisory program operated under the supervision of principal Walt Grebing for nearly 20 years, a sign of the difference a commitment from the school leadership can make to the success of the program.

Such programs are not restricted to public schools on the North American continent. Private, American international schools have broadly adopted the advisory concept. At the Singapore American School, for example, a brief advisory time is held every morning and a 30-minute advisory every Friday. At the American School of Paris, advisory groups have operated for more than two decades, and at the relatively new American schools in Guangzhou, China, and Katmandu, Nepal, advisory groups are firmly in place.

One-on-One Programs

At Rusk Middle School, in Nacogdoches, Texas, a seven-period day permits the teachers in the school to have one planning period and one period of advisor-advisee time. Because the school is organized in interdisciplinary teams with common planning and advisor-advisee times, each team has its advisor-advisee period at a different time of the day. In addition, students on the teams are involved in physical education and unified arts when teachers have planning and advisor-advisee time. As a consequence, no attempt is made to build a sense of groupness. Instead, teachers are free to use the advisor-advisee time to focus on building strong one-to-one relationships with each of their advisees. Students are drawn out of either physical education or unified arts on whatever basis the advisor requires. The teacher usually works with one or two students at a time. The advisor-advisee period is also scheduled for parent conferences, in which the counselor assists the teacher. A unique feature of this program has been the effort of the school administration to secure the endorsement of the local chamber of commerce for the release of parents from work to attend a conference at the school.

Many middle schools, particularly those that follow this kind of schedule, use the advisor-advisee time for planning and conducting parent-student teacher conferences. At Westbrook Junior High School, in Omaha, Nebraska, the advisor assists in the conduct of such conferences on a quarterly basis as a substitute for the traditional report card. At Chaska Middle School, in Chaska, Minnesota, the faculty has found that the conduct of such conferences, through the advisor-advisee program, has provided a groundswell of parent support for that aspect of the program and for most other components of the school. Brookings Middle School, in Brookings, South Dakota, was the first middle school in that state to use the advisory program for developmental parent-student-teacher conferences as well. These triad conferences are held at the end of the first quarter, for the purpose of setting the student on a firm foundation for the remainder of the school year.

In the small group guidance program at Wakulla Middle School, in Crawfordville, Florida, only the academic team teachers have advisees. Each team teacher has about 30 advisees from the team. In much the same way as Rusk Middle in Nacogdoches, the teachers at Wakulla are organized in teams and operated, during the 2001–2002 year, on a seven-period day. The teachers have a planning period and an advisor-advisee period, which happens at different times during the day, depending on the team one is on.

At Wakulla, however, each teacher has a double planning period on Mondays, when all of the teacher's advisees go to physical education class. On Tuesday, during the time for advisor-advisee, most of each teacher's students go to physical education and one-third remain in the classroom for the small group. On Wednesday, 10 other students remain with the teacher while the majority are at physical education, and the same thing happens on Thursday. On Friday all students return to physical education. By the end of the week, then, the teacher has had a double planning period on Monday and Friday, and from Tuesday through Thursday has seen each of his or her advisees in a small group situation for an hour. Each student has had four periods of physical education and one period of small group guidance with his or her teacher.

This model allows teachers to experience relationships with a large number of students but to meet with them in unusually small groups. It also allows teachers to plan one activity for the week and repeat it often enough to minimize the burden on special planning for advisory programs. The program has lasted 25 years at Wakulla Middle School, and whenever an innovation manages to survive, even flourish, for that period of time, educators believe a substantial advantage must exist. The staff members at WMS point to the double planning period each Monday and Friday, to one period each Tuesday through Thursday during which the teacher has a small group of students, and the lack of need for a new daily preparation as factors that make this program easy for and popular with teachers. Given that the literature on effective advisors (Bushnell, 1992) has begun to stress the importance of the one-to-one relationship, organizational strategies such as those in Wakulla County take on additional attractiveness. The viability of this program, its endurance through difficult times in challenging situations, convinces us that school district planners who are interested in a relatively trouble-free and long-lived advisory program ought to look closely at the model operating in Wakulla County, Florida, middle schools.

The Shoreham-Wading River Middle School, in Shoreham, New York, has "built its entire program around the concept of an advisory system, a system that emphasizes consistency, support and advocacy for every child. The philosophy of the advisory system permeates the school day, influencing the children and the program at all times." The advisory arrangement is different from what is done at most places. It is a combination of small group and one-on-one advisement. Every morning, the advisor and a small group of advisees meet for 12 minutes, much like the conventional program. But, later in every day, the advisor meets with the group for another 15 minutes during lunch. They catch up with the happenings of the morning, discuss school issues, and so on. At Shoreham-Wading River, there is another component to the advisory program: All advisors have a conference period built into their schedules three days a week. This special period is held first thing in the morning, before school gets under way, and is specifically for meeting with advisees on an individual basis, to build relationships as well as work on problems. On a fourth morning, the group of advisory teachers meets to discuss students. Advisors also meet with parents, formally, three times each year. Few schools, in our experience, stress the advisory role of the teacher more than Shoreham-Wading River Middle. Few provide more opportunities for it to work.

Requirements for Successful Schoolwide Advisor-Advisee Programs

The advisor-advisee program is possibly the most attractive part of the entire middle school concept, but it seems to be the most difficult thing to implement successfully and to carry out effectively over a period of years (Johnston, 2001). Even after three decades of experience, many middle schools have begun with such programs only to find the idea scrapped after a year, sometimes in several months or even weeks. Schools that have managed to achieve some success with advisor-advisee programs report having learned a number of important lessons about doing it well. Here are some of the suggestions that have emerged from the last decade of experimentation and innovation.

First, and of crucial importance, is the need for the program to arise from a vision of the characteristics and needs of young adolescents that is shared by faculty members, school leaders, and parents. Such programs simply will not succeed if they are implemented as part of a checklist approach that comes from the need to be able to say that one's school has all of the characteristics of an exemplary middle school. A program must have a sufficient mass of commitment before it is designed (Galassi, Gulledge, & Cox, 1997).

Next in importance is the provision of staff development in advance of and accompanying the implementation of the program. Because the role of teacher as affective guide is an attractive and appealing one, it can sometimes seduce teachers into thinking that they are better prepared than they are. Often supervisors, administrators, and curriculum support people forget how much skill is required to operate such efforts effectively and, as a consequence, provide significantly less staff development than is necessary. Ironically, more staff development probably is required for an effectively functioning advisor-advisee program than any other aspect of the middle school concept. If no staff development time is available, putting off the AA program is probably better until there is.

Staff development does not, in the absence of a community consensus about the need for the program, guarantee effective implementation, even in the best of circumstances. In Orange County, Florida, the transition from junior high to middle school was accomplished unusually well, but staff development did not deliver an unblemished advisory program. Gene Pickler, director of secondary operations for the School District of Orange County, Florida, observes that

> although the staff development effort in Orange County was certainly as good as any other efforts with which I am familiar, I feel that the magnitude of change that would be required on the part of teachers and counselors was not fully appreciated. The staff development delivery model consisted of training school level teams of trainers, on the assumption that they would be able to go back to their schools and provide in-service for their faculties. Given the fact that these potential trainers, for the most part, had very limited experience in the use of facilitative teaching processes and literally no experience with an advisor-advisee program, their chance for success as trainers among their peers was in jeopardy from the start.
>
> Since the training was done in advance of the inaugural middle school year, certain assumptions about staffing levels were incorporated into the training and conveyed to the trainees. A model presuming teacher-student ratios of approximately 1:15 was described. This picture became indelibly etched into the minds of potential middle school teachers. As it turned out, the expectation that small advisory groups would be established was never realized. It is possible that such small groups may never be achieved. While this reality does not necessarily prevent refinement, redirection, and continuation of the program, it will probably continue to be a major weapon in the arsenal of teachers who are bent on its demise. (Pickler, 1991, p. 3)

Effective advisory staff development programs make clear that teachers are not being asked to engage in intense personal counseling and guidance with individual students. Staff development may, however, never be able to fully dispel the attitude (from teachers who wish to cling to it) that they are being asked to be counselors. Sometimes staff developers say one thing, but the materials and activities that they distribute make it difficult for traditionally trained teachers to internalize the message. In Orange County, for example,

> teachers developed a mind-set that it was a crisis centered guidance program and that they were not trained as guidance counselors. To this day, many teachers still use this argument for not attempting to use the scheduled IM-PACT period in any constructive manner—even when they may have other members of their faculties who are making excellent use of the time. While common sense would lead thoughtful persons to conclude that conducting personal counseling sessions in a public classroom is an unreasonable expectation that was never intended, dedicated non-adopters continue to cite this "inherent program flaw." (Pickler, 1991, p. 3)

Organizing the program so that the maximum number of faculty members participates, leading to groups that are as small as possible, is often thought to be equally important. If a school is so understaffed that advisors are asked to work with a daily group of 35 to 40 students, the program probably should be postponed until the numbers can be reduced. Sometimes certain faculty members are excused from having an advisor-advisee group in exchange for a school duty such as hall or cafeteria supervision. When this occurs, some of the best advisors (e.g., coaches) are lost to the program, groups are larger, and the morale of the other teachers in the program suffers because of the subtle message saying that the advisor-advisee responsibility is a lower priority than officially announced. Involving everyone, however, does not always work perfectly either, as Pickler says:

> School personnel such as media specialists and counselors were expected to be involved in the program even to the point of being assigned to an advisory group. (This proposal was consistent with implementation models from other districts.) The negative feedback received from some such personnel, coupled with a personal knowledge of their motivation for securing non-teaching positions, led me to conclude that they felt as if they had earned the right not to have to interact with students. The middle school concept shattered that perception of their role in the school. Given this high concentration of concern at the personal level of the change process, I doubt that such personnel can be counted on to embrace the concept in the future. (Pickler, 1991, p. 4)

We believe that if a faculty values a program, it will get onto the schedule of the school in a way that announces the significance attached to the activity. When school staff say, "Oh, yes, we act as advisors all day long" or "We do it in social studies," very little of that type of activity is likely being conducted in the school. Or when the comment "We schedule it when necessary" appears, it is usually safe to guess that the need for the program seldom appears. Schools that hope to develop any semblance of group feeling among their students need to think seriously about scheduling the activity on a daily basis. Schools that aim at the development of that special one-to-one relationship need to remember that this activity takes as much or more time to conduct.

Some important factors need to be considered in the realm of when the advisor-advisee time is scheduled. Practice seems to confirm the place of the advisor-advisee time at the beginning of the school day as best. In all the middle schools of Sarasota County, Florida, the advisory time was the first 30 minutes of the school day. A contest to name the program conducted among middle school teachers in the district resulted in the prize-winning "Prime Time" appellation. Slating the advisory program for the last time of the day is usually a reflection of the fact that it was barely scheduled on a daily basis at all and enjoys the lowest priority of any regularly scheduled activity. Few schools have been able to maintain the health of the advisor-advisee programs scheduled then, because the message that teachers and students perceive is that this is probably just one more of the stream of innovations that will come and go. Postponing an advisor-advisee program is probably better than scheduling it at the end of the day. While something has to be scheduled then, one of the required aspects of the curriculum is likely to suffer less in this slot than will the advisor-advisee program.

Scheduling an advisor-advisee period other than at the beginning or end of the day seems to depend for its success on how and why the program is being instituted. Filling a half hour before or after lunch, as a scheduling convenience, usually fails because students are either hungry or lethargic, depending on which schedule they have, and are in no mood to participate in advisor-advisee activities. It also conveys the only partly hidden message that placing the program thus was a device to fill the schedule and not all that important; and teachers and students usually act accordingly. Some schools are fortunate enough to have a regular period of the school day for the program. Whether a particular team in these schools has its advisor-advisee time during any special segment does not seem to matter, as long as the time is seen as an important piece of the school day and deserving of equal treatment by teachers and students alike.

The length of time devoted to the advisory period is important, too. For programs that require teachers to meet daily with the same group of students, 30 minutes seems about right. Three quarters of an hour is too long for most of the activity that one would expect to be conducted during advisor-advisee programs, and less than 20 minutes seems too short and is likely to turn into a homeroom, where little else than attendance is taken and announcements are made.

Teachers must be given a considerable amount of freedom in terms of the model of advisor that they attempt to emulate. Originally, many schools attempted to have each teacher follow a model that was almost identical to the Rogerian or client-centered therapy process, which should not be surprising given that many of the people who were implementing the programs saw guidance in the traditional sense as the heart of the program. In a short time following the beginning of those early programs, however, educators discovered that their expectations for teacher behavior were often incorrect. Given sharply restricted in-service education budgets that prevented teachers from receiving the type of intense training that might have made at least a portion of them capable of and comfortable with the Rogerian model, supervisors realized that achieving this goal was impossible. What is more, they came to realize that the goal was not appropriate. In a real sense, a good advisory program is what the old junior high school homeroom was intended to be, and the interpersonal skills of the teacher are simply extended into that homeroom setting.

Just as there is no one right way to teach, there is no right way to operate an advisory group. So long as teachers have a stated goal and can demonstrate that they are making progress toward that goal with their advisees, they may make the most progress when permitted to pursue that goal in ways that are most comfortable for them. Many teachers are comfortable with and effective when using a great deal of their advisory time for small group affective discussion; but many are not. For the program to succeed, teachers must see themselves as free to pursue their own activities in a mode that feels safe. Nonetheless, teachers also have to receive enough guidance in alternative methods of working with an advisor-advisee group that they actively pursue at least one model and do not respond to the freedom to be themselves by doing less than they might and merely substituting more of what they always do in a regular class for their advisor-advisee activities.

Teachers who have had success with the advisory role in the middle school offer a number of additional suggestions for teachers and others who are new to or are considering the adoption of such a program. The advisor should have a balance in the type of activity that is offered to the students during the advisor-advisee time. Seventeen straight days, let alone 17 straight weeks, of having one's values clarified is likely to be an unsuccessful advisor-advisee activity. Having the goals of the program clearly in mind as a teacher, and explaining the purpose of the advisor-advisee program to the students, will be an important part of the beginning of the program. Orienting parents to the activities conducted in each advisor-advisee group is an important step toward gathering parent support for the program. Having teachers share themselves in appropriate ways with the students at the beginning and throughout the year, adopt a nonmoralizing attitude to keep from projecting what is believed to be correct onto student behavior, and do a substantial amount of listening are all correlates of success in the operation of individual advisor-advisee groups.

Many times, in schools newly opened or reorganized as middle schools, the temptation is to move to an advisor-advisee program as the first step in implementing the new concept. This temptation is not difficult to understand: Consensus has been reached about the need for such a program, and organization and implementation seem simple. Not so. Schools that do not change from a departmentalized format, for example, but do implement an advisor-advisee program will find themselves involved in a situation in which teachers and students are together for that time but may never see each other again during the day. Under such circumstances, the advisor-advisee program will work much less effectively, because of the absence of repeated face-to-face contact between advisors and their advisees, which they would normally receive during class later in the day. If teachers have students in their advisory groups whom they do not have in other classes, and the advisor-advisee group activity is not graded (as it should not be), there is often considerably more reluctance on the part of students to participate fully in the activities of the group. Planners who fear the conflict that they believe will surround a change from departmentalized organization of teachers to an interdisciplinary framework, and who instead implement an advisor-advisee program in the hopes of satisfying the reorganization requirements, are often disappointed in the results, which usually include a failing advisor-advisee program.

The mutual support that the advisor-advisee program and the interdisciplinary organization of teachers offer to each other is another example of the synergism operating in the middle school program. Implementing one part of the program without the others results in a loss of efficiency and effectiveness of considerable proportions. As the heart of the middle school program, the interdisciplinary team organization model, when present, will make the advisor-advisee program much more likely to succeed.

The exemplary middle school is a balance between an enriched curriculum possible only in large schools and the sense of community that holds people together. A good middle school is, as Figure 5.2 illustrates, a creation of smallness inside of bigness, what looks like concentric circles of unity or building blocks of community. When the interdisciplinary team organization block or level is missing, the advisory program is at risk. When advisory programs are absent, the team is on less sure footing in its work with individual students. Both need to be present for the full functioning of each.

A number of other factors contribute to the success of an advisor-advisee program. Some school districts, such as Sarasota, Okaloosa, and Alachua

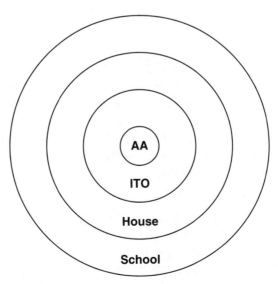

FIGURE **5.2**

LEVELS OF COMMUNITY IN MIDDLE SCHOOLS

Note: AA = advisor-advisee program; ITO = interdisciplinary team organization.

Counties, in Florida; Fort Campbell Middle Schools, in Kentucky; McCulloch Middle, in Highland Park, Texas; and many others, have found that preparing a handbook for teachers, which explains the purposes of the program, offers suggestions for organizing one's group, and contains a package of effective advisor-advisee activities, is a helpful project. A flexible but visible curriculum can add the right amount of structure to the program. The most comprehensive curriculum guide of this sort, prepared by a local school district, has been done, we think, by Putnam County Schools, in Winfield, West Virginia. Several resource guides for classroom advisory programs are available commercially, and groups such as Lions Club International have developed effective and successfully structured programs ("Skills for Adolescence") requiring a firm commitment to staff development. Several commercial advisory curriculum programs are also available.

The development of an advisory curriculum is, however, a mixed blessing. Teachers and others may stick to the book, regardless of the needs of a particular group of young adolescents. Gene Pickler found this to be the case. To prevent program failure and negative attitudes stemming from lack of a concrete basic resource, the district produced a three-volume (one for each grade level) advisory curriculum guide that "was equal in quality to similar resources form other school districts. In fact, it incorporated many refinements in format that made it considerably more 'user friendly'" (Pickler, 1991, p. 2). The use of the guide did not produce uniformly positive results, as Pickler reports.

> It is my belief that there was an understandable reluctance on the part of many administrators and teachers to vary from the printed curriculum in the first year of implementation. At that point in the middle school conversion process, there was natural apprehension about public acceptance of the advisor-advisee concept. The "values clarification" and "secular humanism" paranoia syndrome cannot be discounted. As a result, most schools took a "safe" route toward implementation. The norm quickly became a standardized, school-wide utilization of the activities in the IMPACT book. Teachers were, in effect, protected from having to confront their responsibilities for implementing IMPACT. This practice continues to a large degree in some schools today. (Pickler, 1991, p. 2)

A number of middle schools organize schoolwide monthly topics for the advisory program. At New Smyrna Beach Middle School, in Florida, staff members found success in doing so. There, teams of teachers determined which specific activities to use in implementing the selected unit. At Chinook Middle School, in Lacey, Washington, a group of teachers, counselors, and parents developed the following as monthly themes, with matching materials, for one school year.

| September: | "It's a Family Affair" | (transition and unity) |
| October: | "It's Not Just Talk" | (communication skills) |

November:	"Is There Life Outside of Homework?"	(life skills)
December:	"Partnership: It's Your School and Community"	(community involvement)
January:	"Hour of Destiny"	(goal setting)
February:	"Caring Is for Everyone"	(caring)
March:	"What I Think of Myself Matters"	(positive self-image)
April:	"Look and Think Before You Leap"	(decision-making)
May:	"Nobody Said It Was Easy"	(coping skills)
June:	"You Made It"	(transition again)

McCulloch Middle School, in Highland Park, Texas, offered a series of suggested (not required) themes for a school year, matched by a packet of materials to use in developing them.

September:	Classroom climate strategies
September:	Orientation and school rules
September:	Getting acquainted
October:	Study skills and time management
October:	Social skills
October and November:	School spirit
November and December:	Community service
November and December:	Holiday themes
January:	Decision-making
January:	Self-awareness
February:	Goal setting
February:	Educational and career planning
March:	Problem ownership
March:	Conflict management
March:	Accepting responsibility
April:	Communication
April:	Community service
May:	Appreciating and accepting diversity

East Grand Rapids Middle School, in Grand Rapids, Michigan, had the following monthly themes for one year.

September:	"What's Happening"	(getting acquainted with my school)
October:	"How Do I Fit In?"	(establishing myself in the group)
November:	"How Am I Doing as a Student?"	(developing academic responsibility)

December:	"How Can I Help Others?"	(giving to others and a sense of community)
January:	"Where Do I Go from Here?"	(self-assessment and goal setting)
February:	"How Do I Show I Care?"	(getting along with others)
March:	"Me? . . . Worry?"	(stress management)
April and May:	"Where Do I Stand?"	(peer pressure and assertiveness skills)
May and June:	"What's Ahead for the Summer?"	(exploring summer opportunities)

In a similar fashion, the first monthly newsletter to parents from Broomfield Heights Middle School, in Broomfield, Colorado, noted that the month of September, during the REACH program, was devoted to "Getting to Know You" in all grades. Topics for October were "What Is a 6th Grader?" for 6th grade, "Self-Concept: Who Am I?" for the 7th grade, and "What Kind of a Student Am I?" for the 8th grade. Other monthly topics would also be announced to parents in advance in this way. In one recent year, 8th graders at BHMS dealt with the following monthly topics, keyed specifically to their age group.

September:	"Groups and Their Process"
October:	"Ten Pressures and Social Situations"
November:	"Let's See—How Do We Communicate?"
December:	"The Holidays—Caring and Sharing"
January:	"Soon High School—Then What?"
February:	"Soon High School" (continued)
March:	"Transitions: Who, Where, Why, When?"
April:	"Career Awareness"
May:	"Middle School Is Over, Now What?"

At the same time, the students in 6th and 7th grades at Broomfield Heights Middle School had monthly themes of their own, with some overlap.

6TH GRADE

September:	"Getting to Know Our School"
October:	"On Becoming a 6th Grader"
November:	"Peers"
December:	"Holidays"
January:	"Safe in the Community"
February:	"Self-Control and the Art of Refusal"
March:	"Let's Talk"
April:	"Deciding to Decide"
May:	"Series Sampling"

7TH GRADE

September:	"Who's Who in Your REACH: Group Building"
October:	"Self-Concept"
November:	"Who's on First? What's On Second? I Don't Know's on Third" (communication skills)
December:	"Deck the Halls with Holiday Time"
January:	"What's Happening around Me?"
February:	". . . Walk Beside Me and Be My Friend"
March:	"Substance Abuse"
April:	"How to Make Choices"
May:	"How Time Flies When You're Having Fun—Welcome to the 8th Grade"

In a wise move calculated to defuse any misunderstanding of the value of the REACH curriculum or of the official endorsement by the school board, the Broomfield Heights Middle School staff explained how the advisory curriculum is an integral part of the total middle school curriculum for the Boulder Valley School District. A full page in the advisory curriculum guide detailed the topics of the advisory program (e.g., friendship), the place of that topic in the regular curriculum (e.g., health, home economics, and physical education), the grade levels at which it is taught in the regular curriculum, and the districtwide curriculum objectives and belief statements (e.g., personalization, equity, pervasive caring) to which it is related.

Other school staffs have found that keeping the same advisor and advisees together over a period of years is an effective practice, as is the case in the middle schools in Yakima, Washington. They believe that the objectives of their advisory program are far more effectively accomplished when advisors and advisees (and their parents) establish and maintain a three-year relationship unrelated to academic expectations. A considerable number of schools have used a parent orientation process at the beginning of every year and found that to be very helpful. Parents can be remarkably receptive to the advisor-advisee program if they are given the information they need to understand it.

Counselors play an important role, perhaps the most important, in the success or failure of the advisor-advisee program. When counselors see their role as including the success of the advisor-advisee program, they act in ways that provide support and enthusiasm to teachers. They become the school's team leader for guidance, acting as if the teachers were, in a sense, in their advisor-advisee group. When counselors mistakenly view the advisor-advisee program as a rebuke, perhaps as a result of the failure attributed to their counseling efforts by others, they react defensively and act in ways that undercut and lessen the chances for a successful activity. Counselors must be given the responsibility for the success of the advisor-advisee program and the freedom to accomplish the task. When counselors are used as assistant administrators, they will not have the time to fill other roles.

Nothing is more important, however, to the success of the advisor-advisee program than the understanding and spirited support of the school principal and other administrators. When administrators are enthusiastically in favor of a program and are willing to put themselves forward in support of it, the chances for success are good. When they are not, teachers will soon get the message, and those who are uncomfortable with the program will begin to lobby against it with the principal, will neglect their own advisor-advisee groups, and generally will seek to erode support for the program among other faculty members. Principals must be willing to treat teachers in the same way that they want teachers to respond to students. They must explain the goals of the program, show the teachers how they may succeed, encourage them to try, and let them know that the program is an important part of their day and that it is not an option.

One school principal with a long record of success with advisory programs—Walt Grebing, of Broomfield Heights Middle School, in Broomfield, Colorado—offered the following important suggestions for school leaders and the advisory program.

1. Be certain to reestablish the purpose and expectations of the advisory program, every year.
2. Provide prime time in the schedule for advisory.
3. Establish counselor and staff commitment to the program, especially with new staff members each year.
4. Be sure that advisory is not seen as a preparation for teachers.
5. Always be a role model of enthusiasm for the program: visit classes, attend staff development sessions, and so on.
6. Encourage continuous honest internal evaluation of the program.
7. Provide ongoing staff development.
8. Share successes among the staff members.
9. Evaluate staff members on their effectiveness as advisors.
10. Constantly explain and advocate the program to the external community and to other school and district personnel.

The National Resource Center for Middle Grades, at the University of South Florida, in Tampa, offers the following "Do's" and "Don'ts" for successful advisors. We endorse this list.

Do have a planned and regularly scheduled program.
Do inform your students why advisory is important.
Do share your own personal hopes, worries, and experiences when appropriate.
Do activities with the students, and not to them.

Do allow time for students to trust the program, the advisor, and each other.

Do lots of hands-on and interactive activities.

Do show your enthusiasm and commitment to the program.

Do initiate and maintain contact with your advisees' parents or guardians.

Do give advisees some ownership in the program through reasonable involvement in choices and decisions.

Do establish expected behavioral norms for advisory time.

Don't have unrealistic expectations.

Don't copy another district's program without customizing it to your students' needs.

Don't expect all students in your advisory group to like each other or you, especially at first.

Don't tolerate put-downs and "killer statements."

Don't forget to help other advisors be successful.

Don't cripple the program by complaining about it inappropriately.

Don't forget to have fun with your students.

The advisor-advisee program, properly organized and implemented, can be a bright place in the day of everyone involved. When all things were considered regarding the advisory program in Orange County, Florida, for example, the results were encouragingly positive. Pickler observed:

> Over the course of four years [1987–1991], interviews with interdisciplinary teams involved with IMPACT have revealed that teacher acceptance of and comfort with the concept is growing. More teachers report seeing value in the program and they are also able to cite more examples of ways in which they are personalizing the program to the needs of their students and engaging in collaborative efforts with their colleagues. This growth is admittedly slow, but after four years it is still evident. In schools where the leadership attaches significance to IMPACT and convey expectations as to its implementation, acceptance has grown and the program has begun to find a niche in the total school program.
>
> It should also be noted that parents generally support the concept of IMPACT. The majority of parents responding to the [middle school] program evaluation parent survey feel that the program has been beneficial for their children. School level administrators who have taken the time to articulate the goals and intent of the program to parents report that they tend to agree as to the need for such an effort on the part of the school. (Pickler, 1991, p. 5)

Reflecting on the process of implementing effective advisory programs in his district, Pickler (1991, pp. 6–7) offered several important recommendations.

1. Make an all-out effort to publicly dismiss the perception that the advisory program is a crisis-centered psychotherapy program. Stress that it is intended to address the normal development that [middle school]

students experience with or without adult guidance and direction. It is for mentally healthy children.

2. Accept the fact, from the beginning, that advisory groups will remain large, and develop a program that is congruent with this reality.

3. Dedicate the district to providing continuing in-service to teachers and administrators regarding the purpose and redesign of the program. Point out that the district has its own ideas of what works and what doesn't and that much has been learned since the initial implementation of the program, when planners were dependent on what they could learn from other districts.

4. Provide regular opportunities for schools to share successful practices.

5. Place primary responsibility for the program with curriculum people in the district, thus playing down the guidance function.

6. Revise the role of the school guidance department to ensure program involvement and support.

7. Keep the advisory program in the schools, no matter what. It belongs there. Many teachers are making good use of the time provided, and more can be encouraged to do so. "For those who staunchly refuse to do anything with it, it has its greater value in serving as a daily reminder to them that they may not be well suited for teaching at the middle school level."

When an advisory program is implemented incorrectly, it can be a glaring failure and a barrier to further progress. Educators who wish to implement the program but who cannot do so without risking its success should consider postponing the program. The advisor-advisee program is an excellent addition to the interdisciplinary team foundation, but it ought not be built in the absence of that foundation without extreme care.

Purposes of the Advisor-Advisee Program

Successful advisory programs are always found in schools with clarity, consensus, and commitment about the fundamental purposes of the program. Confusion, division, and vacillation regarding an advisory program are signs of impending doom.

According to the National Forum to Accelerate Middle-Grades Reform, exemplary middle schools offer programs that are developmentally responsive, which means "sensitive to the unique developmental challenges of early adolescence." Such schools create a "personalized environment," manifested in "small learning communities characterized by stable, close, and mutually respectful relationships." Such schools provide opportunities for students to have a "voice," to develop citizenship, and to engage in alliances with families (National Forum to Accelerate Middle-Grades Reform, 2001). All of this adds up to a powerful rationale for an advisory program.

The Fundamental Purpose The fundamental purpose of the advisor-advisee program, regardless of its design in any particular school, is to promote involvement between a teacher and the students in the advisory group. Every student needs to have a relationship with at least one adult in the school, which is characterized by warmth, concern, openness, and understanding. Such a program focuses on the fourth R, relationships—interpersonal relationships that produce growth for everyone involved. Good middle schools cannot be places where teacher and students pass by each other without recognition or attachment, like the stereotypical ships in the night.

Teachers may need this type of involvement with students no less than the students do. While mature, stable adults, teachers still need to be involved with students who show that they respect and care for them. But more directly, from the teachers' perspective, the most relevant personal reason for the advisor-advisee program is that in a school of a thousand or more students, or on a team that requires each teacher to meet as many as 150 students per day, developing the kind of relationships with students that allow teachers to make a significant difference in their lives is frequently impossible. Because most teachers seem to have a deeply felt need to make a significantly positive difference in the lives of their students, and the daily demands of the classroom often seem to make this difficult or impossible, the advisor-advisee program provides the teacher with an opportunity to get to know some manageable number of students in a meaningful way. In a middle school with an advisory program, says U.S. Representative Rosa DeLauro of Connecticut, those lessons "are every bit as important as the traditional classroom subjects. Second only to their own parents, the relationships our children make in school—with their teachers and classmates—will be the most important in their young lives" (DeLauro, 2000).

Other Purposes Education for personal and interpersonal competence is a closely related objective of the advisor-advisee program. The advisor-advisee program also attempts to offer an opportunity for social and emotional development. More than a quarter-century ago, Vance Packard (1972) described American society as "a nation of strangers," and in the early years of the 21st century, conditions seem much the same. Middle school students need a sense of community now more than ever. With the demise of the neighborhood school, the attempt to build a home base within the larger school takes on considerably more meaning. Middle school students are simply too immature to function well as complete individuals in an anonymous, amorphous institution of from 500 to 1,000 or more people. The advisor-advisee program continues where the homeroom left off, to work for an educational milieu in which students and teachers feel part of a group that students experience as supportive, safe, and familiar. This atmosphere is impossible on the level of the total school, and it is often difficult to achieve in even the most reasonably sized interdisciplinary teams.

The advisor-advisee program can also be a significant source of civic education. Given that the advisor-advisee group is usually a substitute for the homeroom or synonymous with it, decisions about student council representation, intramural competitions, and a host of related school issues can be discussed in a democratic manner that middle school students understand.

The advisor-advisee program is a source of guidance for the student, different from that available from the school counselor. While the guidance provided by the student's advisor will never replace that of the school counselor, it is a crucially important supplement to it. Teachers who not only act as advisors to students, but who teach those same students at least once each day, and possibly more often, have a knowledge of and a relationship with those students that school counselors, burdened as they are by a plethora of other duties, can never hope to have. Consequently, the advisor is likely to be aware of conditions in a student's life in or out of school that may influence his or her behavior and need to be handled. The advisor, as team teacher, will be well acquainted with the student's academic performance in every class. This knowledge of the students' lives, combined with the relationship that grows from the advisor-advisee program and the repeated contact that teachers have with the students during each day, is likely to make the advisor the first source of guidance.

Middle schools with effective advisor-advisee programs often report that classroom and school discipline situations improve as a result of the programs. Students who feel safe, accepted, and an important part of the school are much less likely to be disruptive. On numerous occasions, teachers have told us that students who have a place, time, and person to assist them in centering themselves, which encourages the appropriate expression of feelings of frustration, hurt, and sorrow, are much less likely to be found ventilating these feelings in regular classrooms. Teachers who know students well, and who have developed friendly relationships with them, are more able to deal effectively with them in regular classroom situations and to be a source of support and information to other teachers in the school when their advisees are involved in classroom discipline problems. The advisor-advisee group is, furthermore, a unique opportunity to teach the behaviors that students no longer seem to come to school already possessing but are essential to a productive school atmosphere. Teamwide advisor-advisee units that focus on issues such as theft, responsibility, rules, and so on are excellent advisor-advisee activities that have productive consequences for individual classrooms.

Mary Lane, principal of Hawkins Middle School (HMS), in Olympia, Washington, is one of many principals who report such positive results in behavior management and ascribe them to the success of the advisory program. At HMS, the "behavior management system has . . . been reworked to capitalize on the advisor-advisee relationship. The additional care and interest that results from such a program also wins much parent support. The data on the reduction of student behavioral referrals is impressive" (Mary Lane, personal communication, November 26, 2001).

The advisor-advisee group time is often used effectively as the organizational and informational hub of each team and of the school. Announcements are made there. Field trips are organized around the advisor-advisee group as the unit of responsibility during travel. School activities and projects, intramurals, and other unifying operations are appropriately assigned to the advisor-advisee group. This is not only because it is efficient to do so, but also because friendships form when people perform common day-to-day activities with each other as well as when they are involved in discussions that promote self-disclosure. Adults develop friendships with people they work with, study with, play bridge with, go to church with, and so on. Students and teachers become closer to each other as they participate in (and sometimes endure) the daily rituals and activities of the school.

Goals of the Advisory Program

At Connackamack Middle School (CMS), in Piscataway, New Jersey, the advisory program in the 2001–2002 school year had the following clearly articulated goals.

1. Foster an atmosphere characterized by concern, openness, and understanding.
2. Provide an environment and activities that allow students to feel accepted and valued by teachers and peers.
3. Promote the development of group and school spirit.
4. Allow students the opportunity to build self-esteem and social skills.

The mission statement for the same program at CMS was: "The Advisor/ Advisee program will foster a nurturing environment of honest communication and understanding for ALL STUDENTS while promoting social, emotional, and intellectual growth."

In an attempt to describe the essence and importance of the program in greater detail, educators at CMS put it this way.

> The program is an attempt to enhance the traditional role that teachers have always maintained as guides to their learners. Teachers have always worked with students in clarifying ideas, solving problems, and in lending a sympathetic ear to students in need. These activities usually have not been planned in a routine manner: as a result, some students who have had the need may not necessarily have received the help when needed. Also, some staff members have expressed the need for additional skills and time to help the students. In many cases, our middle school teachers have found themselves responding to students in crisis rather than working with them in a preventative and positive learning environment.

As middle school students are faced with a rapidly changing environment, they are in need of someone to trust who, in turn, knows them as individuals. The advisor/advisee approach allows students the opportunity to know an adult in the school environment who is truly caring, supportive and concerned about their academic and social growth. These students and their advisor will develop a relationship over time that will allow them to support each other as they attempt new tasks and share their successes and failures. The advisor and his/her students will form a team, which will make their middle school education a positive and productive experience. (Connackamack Middle School, 2001)

In our experience, the best advisory experiences are in schools such as these and in the classrooms of teachers who have, individually, thought through the purposes of their individual classroom advisory programs and developed their own list of goals. One such list, developed by Terri Stahlman while she was a teacher at Lincoln Middle School, in Gainesville, Florida, included the following objectives. The goal of the advisory program at Lincoln is to help students

- Make new friends in a new social setting.
- Assess their own personal and academic strengths and weaknesses.
- Make decisions in a logical, rational way.
- Work cooperatively with others.
- Develop a workable valuing process.
- Understanding courtesy, manners, and fair play.
- Develop effective study skills.
- Communicate effectively.
- Begin to build a philosophy of life, with goals, attitudes, and efforts.
- Develop self-understanding, self-acceptance, and self-discipline.

The list should not be thought of as complete, and others should not adopt it without thought. It is what one teacher set out to accomplish in her advisory program. Every teacher-advisor should attempt to establish his or her own goals.

Advisory programs are not unique to middle level schools in the United States. In Japan, many educators believe that early adolescents are at a unique point of readiness for learning about group involvement, loyalty, duty, responsibility, and citizenship. The development of these qualities among students is one of the central goals of the Japanese junior high school (George, 1989). George was surprised and pleased to discover, during a two-month study of these schools, that the schedules of the Japanese junior high schools, the most highly academic institutions in the world, involved almost 10 hours a week for activities and experiences designed to develop and enhance similar attitudes and values to those described by American educators. A dozen different sorts of activities were scheduled to involve homeroom students in community building: group competitions, charity drives, cleaning the school, and so on.

Teacher Roles

The advisory role of the middle school teacher is complex and multifaceted, and because advisor-advisee programs tend to vary at least slightly from school to school, the roles teachers fill also vary. Many schools take great care in spelling out to teachers, students, and parents what the roles played by the advisor in a specific school are likely to be. Combining the role descriptions of advisors provided by several middle schools, we summarize potential duties and responsibilities for advisors.

Academic Expert on Each Advisee   As the academic expert on each advisee, the advisor

- Assists the student in the planning of exploratory, extracurricular, independent study, and other academic choice activities; keeps a record of electives chosen by each advisee
- Communicates information about facilities, materials, and personnel to students and parents
- Maintains and utilizes cumulative records, personal profile sheets, and other information-gathering options
- Prepares and distributes report cards
- Assists students in studying and learning how to study
- Assists students in the process of developing and clarifying special interests and aptitudes
- Identifies and considers any physical handicaps the student may have
- Identifies and considers the reading level of the student and the mental and chronological ages of the student
- Contributes to the understanding of other staff members of the academic strengths, weaknesses, problems, and interests of each student
- Controls the student's overall academic schedule, assisting in decisions as to whom the student will study with, at what times, and in what groupings; assists in determining the degree of responsible independence each student can assume and what learning styles seem appropriate
- Prepares for and participates in parent conferences with reference to the student's academic progress

School Advocate and Guide for Each Student   As school advocate and guide of each advisee, the advisor

- Attempts to build a relationship with each student that is characterized by caring, trust, and honesty
- Is, in general, an available buffer between student, general faculty, administration, parent, and community
- Attempts to see that each student acquires an increasingly positive self-image during his or her enrollment time at the school

- Knows each student and his or her background as thoroughly as possible
- Contributes to and supports the school guidance program, especially in referring advisees to the counselor when appropriate
- Contributes to the other staff members' understanding of the personal strengths, weaknesses, problems, and interests of each advisee
- Is aware of the attendance record of the advisee
- Is responsible for parent-school communication and for participating in and planning for parent conferences concerning the personality and behavior of the advisee

Social and Emotional Educator of Advisees   As the person most directly responsible for the social and emotional education of a group of advisees and for assisting in the social and emotional maturation of each advisee, the advisor

- Attempts to create a sense of belonging and responsibility through participation in home-base activities
- Conducts activities during the advisor-advisee program that focus on increasing the social skills of advisees and on growth in personal and interpersonal understanding
- Assists students in clarifying their values and in developing more mature reasoning abilities
- Places increased emphasis on prevention of problems in the lives of the students
- Participates in outings, field trips, and after-school activities that promote opportunities for emotional and social education
- Helps students learn to work in a group and to realize the need for getting along with others to meet individual and group needs
- Assists students in the appreciation of individual differences
- Helps students develop appropriate attitudes toward competition and cooperation as the advisor-advisee group participates as a group in intraschool programs

Conducting an Advisor-Advisee Group

Conducting a successful advisor-advisee group, from a teacher's point of view, depends in large measure upon how the program is designed at the school level. If the program is designed primarily as a daily meeting of the teacher with the same group of advisees, the advisor proceeds differently than if the program is designed to focus sharply on the development of strong one-to-one relationships between the teacher and each of the advisees. Both practical objectives (group feeling and individual relationships) are important parts of each design, but each program design fosters one of the objectives more easily than the other. In the daily group, teachers must work harder to build strong relationships with students, because their time is obligated to a group.

In situations in which teachers do not meet with the same students on a daily basis, developing a sense of community is more difficult, but establishing meaningful one-to-one relationships with students is easier.

On the assumption that it is more difficult (but no less valuable) to function effectively in an advisor-advisee program that operates on the daily group design, and that many of the strategies a teacher pursues in this format can be adapted to the one-on-one design, this section will focus on suggestions for successful operation of the daily program. Daily group advisory programs are far more numerous than those that focus on the one-on-one approach. However, we do not prefer one type of advisor-advisee program to another. Experience has not yet been broad enough to indicate whether either design (daily group or one-on-one) is superior.

Faced with the task of meeting with a group of advisees on a daily basis, for about half an hour each time, many teachers are initially apprehensive about beginning. Although almost every teacher in junior high school or middle school wants to be effective in this role, few feel confident in pursuing it without some special training. Counselors can provide in-service training in basic facilitative skills such as active listening, asking open-ended questions, and so on. In addition, teachers who are hard-pressed to complete all the other assignments they are given in a new school situation often see the daily advisor-advisee group as an additional preparation they could do without, a burden they would rather not assume even if they believe themselves to be capable. Under these circumstances, teachers must realize that they are not being asked to replace the school counselor, and an advisor-advisee group can operate on a daily basis without rigorous preparations each night.

Teachers are not expected to be counselors or psychiatrists to be good advisors. Some districts, simply because of inexperience, have made the mistake of expecting teachers and middle school students to spend each day in intense encounter-like sensitivity sessions and, as a consequence, have had to endure a great deal of frustration from teachers, students, and parents. Teachers are not trained to conduct this type of activity, students are not ready for it, and parents will not support it. Advisor-advisee programs that insist on this type of format must expect to encounter serious difficulties in operation.

Teachers also should not think of themselves, in their advisory capacity, as replacing the home or the church. Teachers do deal with values on a daily basis. Humans cannot interact in educational settings without being involved with values. However, advisory programs are not established to compete with or usurp the values education students would, educators hope, encounter in healthy homes and churches. Teachers as advisors do, nevertheless, deal with values. They do so, in successful programs that have the support of parents and community members, by focusing on school-oriented values, those attitudes and predispositions that are essential for student success in school. Such values as honesty, cleanliness, punctuality, tolerance, friendliness, endurance, and loyalty are included in effective advisory programs. Rarely, in our experience, is the inculcation of such school-based values questioned by reasonable parents or community members or opposed by school board members.

Teachers are required, in their advisory role, only to be themselves. They must be able to display the same kind of characteristics that are found in good friendships, good teaching, and helping relationships in general. They must be able to accept the student and what he or she is experiencing and communicate that understanding clearly, without becoming a part of the problem or situation themselves to the extent that they need help, too. They must be able to communicate clearly to the student, so that what they say matches what they think and feel inside. Teachers must exhibit, to the degree possible and appropriate in a school setting, the characteristics of unconditional positive regard, empathy, and honesty in their interactions with their advisees. They are not asked to possess advanced training in psychology or psychiatry, but merely to be a helping adult school friend to the students they have in their advisor-advisee group (Galassi, Gulledge, & Cox, 1998).

Teachers need to develop plans for a schedule for their advisor-advisee program. These plans should not require continued daily reconfiguration. Middle school students seem to readily accept a planned schedule of advisor-advisee activities and are much less likely to balk at participating in an activity if it is what "educators always do on Tuesdays." Middle school students are often not, contrary to what an inexperienced layperson might believe, ready to talk about themselves and eager to engage in self-disclosing discussion without a great deal of encouragement. So a daily or weekly schedule helps. Teachers who are the most successful with advisor-advisee programs in exemplary middle schools almost always have a schedule that, while flexible, does provide structure and stability to the program and security to the students.

The advisor-advisee activity schedule should be well balanced, and it should proceed from a set of overall goals. Even though some middle schools provide teachers with a set of objectives for the advisor-advisee program on a schoolwide basis, the most effective advisors seem to give the program considerable additional thought and design their own activities on the basis of the goals that they have established, perhaps with their students, for their individual groups. Most advisory group activities are of the type that can be done one day a week for the entire year or for a week or so at a time without being repeated the remainder of the year. Beginning the year and the program with a schedule, modified by appropriate student input, will make the advisor-advisee time much more effective and much easier for the remainder of the year (Hoverstein, Doda, & Lounsbury, 1991).

The activities that the advisor chooses to include in the program will have a great effect on the success of the program. Advisors need to balance their advisor-advisee schedule with activities that require little or no daily planning, mixed in with some that do require additional thought and planning. Activities that happen regularly without extra effort on the teacher's part will prevent the teacher from becoming exhausted, and occasional things that do require new teacher effort will keep the program from becoming too stultifying by injecting fresh and invigorating approaches.

Successful Activities for Daily Advisory Programs

Most successful programs seem to have a schedule of advisory activities that occur regularly on different days of the week, in every group in the school. In schools that do not mandate such a weekly schedule and leave more discretion to the individual teacher, many teachers in exemplary middle schools, after 5 to 10 years of experience in the advisor-advisee program, have structured their advisories so that they have their own weekly schedule of different activities for different days of the week. Teachers have developed a number of activities that students enjoy but are relatively easy for the teacher to arrange.

Student of the Day or Week One day a week the teacher and the advisor-advisee group focus their attention on a different member of the group and this student becomes the teacher's pet for the week.

USSR, DEAR, and SURF Many teachers, teams, and whole schools use an activity called Uninterrupted Sustained Silent Reading (USSR), Drop Everything and Read (DEAR), or Silent Uninterrupted Reading for Fun (SURF). When the activity is used in conjunction with the advisor-advisee program, the teacher and all the advisees spend the greater part of the advisor-advisee time reading silently and individually.

Silent Writing Many teachers have discovered that students will write about themselves in ways that they will not talk about publicly, with or without a group. Using a period each week in the advisor-advisee group to engage in journal writing is an effective and appropriate use of student time together.

Academic Advisory Given that the teacher-advisor is as concerned as much with the academic success of each of the advisees as with their social and emotional maturation, if not more so, some advisory time should be used in an academic way. During the advisor-advisee time the advisor circulates from one student to another, gathering information about one student, encouraging another, counseling with a third, working with as many as possible during the time allotted.

Indoor and Outdoor Games Advisors can introduce a number of games into the advisor-advisee time. These games are fun for students, can be used to teach the group skills these students so desperately need, and require little preparation time from the teacher.

Story Time   Middle school students become engrossed in listening to the teacher or to other students read aloud, if the story has some relevance to their lives and the reader does the job well. Reading aloud has been brought back to the language arts classroom in the most modern approaches to reading and writing instruction at the middle level (Atwell, 1987).

Career Exploration   Another activity that fits with the nature of middle school students, which requires a little more teacher preparation, is devoting one advisory day each week to an investigation of adults and what careers they have pursued.

Goal-Setting Day   In some advisory groups, teachers use one day a week to help students take greater control of and responsibility for their lives, which is a popular task insofar as parents of middle schoolers are concerned. We believe that teachers who take 20 minutes a week to help students achieve more self-discipline will find parents as eager supporters of the effort.

Organization Day   In all six of the middle schools of Okaloosa County, Florida, the first day of the week in all advisory groups is "Organization Day." Advisors and students use a simple scheduling form to review the important tasks of the coming week, and time is set aside for getting lockers, agenda books, and other items ready for the week.

Magic Circle   Many skillful advisors report that arranging an opportunity for students to talk about what is on their minds results in powerfully important advisory time with little preparation required from the teacher. Such discussions, conducted in low-risk fashion on a once weekly basis, can lead to greater insights for the advisor into the interests and concerns of the students.

Joke and Riddle Day   Another teacher we know spends one day each week laughing and guffawing with his students over corny jokes and riddles they all contribute. Every Friday is "joke day" and everyone is required to bring a joke, a pun, a riddle, a story, or the like to contribute. Middle school students greatly appreciate a teacher with a sense of humor.

Clubs   Early adolescence is often a time for exploration, and this is true in the area of leisure-time interests and other club-oriented activities. Consequently, many exemplary middle schools have built club activities into their advisory programs, on a weekly basis.

Intramurals   At many middle schools, one day a week is devoted to intramural activity as a part of the advisory program. Here, again, participation is spirited, unity is developed, and advisors have very little preparation required of them.

A baker's dozen of advisory activities can be highly effective uses of advisory time with little preparation required by the teacher. We recommend a weekly schedule that incorporates as many of these as possible, so that teachers can see positive results from the program with as little effort on their part as possible.

Occasional Activities

Educators who build activities that can be used on a regular basis and that require little or no planning time into an advisor-advisee schedule find that the burden of daily lesson planning that they anticipated does not materialize to the extent expected. They may then find themselves willing to invest a little more time in planning activities that add a special flavor to the advisor-advisee group life.

Orientations   Teachers discover that a significant amount of their advisory time will often be consumed by activities that can best be described as orientation. Throughout the year a teacher can expect that a number of advisor-advisee periods will be used to orient students to state and national assessment and testing programs, dental and physical examinations and treatments, and so on.

Special Meals   Americans make friends by sharing meals together. It is a tradition formed during the hard years on the frontier. And adult social life almost always includes something to eat. Advisory groups that get together for a simple breakfast snack or bring their lunch trays back to their advisory classroom, once a month or so, find that students are left "with a good taste in their mouths."

Holiday Celebrations   Even in districts that sharply restrict the activities that can be conducted in the observance of religious holidays, or where teachers are concerned about the rights of religious minorities, dozens of secular holidays can be a great deal of fun and can produce both learning and community building opportunities.

Community Help Projects   Each community always has projects that need doing, for which there are few, if any, volunteers. A quick check with service clubs and a contact or two with some homes for the aging or the handicapped will turn up enough projects for an advisory group to do for years. This type of activity gives students a sense of contribution as well as helps to develop an advisor-advisee spirit that does a great deal to foster the feeling that "we are proud of us."

School Help Projects   The same situation exists for the school. One middle school we know has, throughout the school year, a rotating Pride Week project. Each advisor-advisee group in the school has one week of the year to conduct activities or plan projects that have as their goal the fostering of pride in the school. An advisor-advisee group might, for example, redo the hallway bulletin boards or clean up and repaint a particularly unsightly part of the building.

Field Trips While few schools are scheduled in a way that permits advisor-advisee groups to take regular field trips to places around the community, the advisor-advisee group can be used as the organizing center for such trips when taken by a whole team or part of a school. Walks to a local fast-food restaurant for a special lunch or breakfast are often popular in schools that are located near such spots.

Current Events Advisor-advisee time is well used to discuss current events, particularly if scheduled at the beginning of the day. Such an activity does require more preparation than other activities commonly do, but in schools where a great deal of stress is placed on the basic skills of reading and mathematics, this becomes a valid justification for the inclusion of the advisor-advisee time in the schedule of the day. Since September 11, 2001, few dismiss the need to have a time in the day for middle school students to review and react to current events.

These occasional activities are samples of the many different types of activities that are both possible and appropriate for the advisor-advisee period. Teachers may succeed best when they are able to design a schedule of activities that largely require a minimum of extra planning.

Research on the Advisory Program

One of the earliest carefully designed attempts to assess the effectiveness of an advisory program was during the spring of 1979, at Lincoln Middle School, in Gainesville, Florida. Conducted by a research team from the University of Florida, the study was part of a larger assessment of the affective (not effective) components of the Lincoln program.[1] A stratified random sampling procedure was used so that only one-third of the 900 students was required to evaluate any one aspect of the program, yet the results generalized to all students within the school. The evaluation team, the principal, and the Program Improvement Council worked together to specify the program's goals and objectives. They then developed instruments reflecting these goals and objectives. The instruments for both students and teachers were reviewed by a committee of teachers and modified as appropriate. To maximize the amount of information available to the school staff, the student data were analyzed by race, sex, team, and grade. The teacher data were analyzed only by team. The design was such that the anonymity of all respondents was maintained.

Students were asked questions that examined their relationship with and perceptions of their advisor-teachers and the related activities. The teachers

[1]Then associate professor Afesa Bell-Nathaniel and Sandra B. Damico, along with their students Charles Green, Wendy McClosky, and Nancy McGowan, conducted this study. The assistance of Bell-Nathaniel and Damico is gratefully acknowledged for producing this summary of the research.

were asked questions on the centrality of advisor-advisee programs to a middle school experience and the amount of teacher preparation required for an effective effort. In brief, all students

- Perceived their advisory teachers as caring for them and for the other students in their group
- Thought their group helped in their understanding of other people
- Differentiated between academic and personal problems; they indicated they would turn first to their advisor for help in solving an academic problem but would also seek out the guidance counselor for assistance with a personal problem
- Felt the advisor-advisee group provided skills for problem solving
- Differentiated between most important and favorite activities: the most important AA activities were USSR (silent reading) and study hall, while favorite activities were talking with a friend and free time
- Frequently listed the advisor-teacher as their favorite teacher or the teacher they knew best
- Agreed that their advisor-teachers were fair

Only a few significant differences emerged when the student data were analyzed by race, sex, team, and grade.

- African American students were more likely than whites to believe that their advisors cared about them and other students, helped them understand other people, and helped them learn how to solve problems.
- Females were more likely than males to believe that the advisory group helped them learn how to solve problems. They also identified more strongly with Lincoln Middle School than did the males.
- There were no differences in responses among students by grade.
- The only response on which a team difference emerged was: "I feel like an outsider in my group." While a majority of students indicated a strong sense of belonging to their group, some of the students on three of the teams were less positive on this item than were students on the other three teams.

The teacher findings were as follows:

- Teachers overwhelmingly endorsed the advisory concept for middle schools.
- Teachers were prepared to function in the advisor role, although about one-third believed that they needed more training for this role.
- Teachers indicated that they had long-range goals for their advisory groups.
- Teachers perceived the guidance counselor as playing an active role in the program.

- Half of the teachers indicated they prepared special activities for advisor-advisee time.
- Slightly less than half of the teachers reported having a value clarification type activity at least once a week.

All students, regardless of grade level, felt an integral part of the school and their advisory group. Failure to find grade level differences is probably a reflection of the impact of multiage grouping at Lincoln, but additional information would need to be collected to ensure this interpretation. Teachers at Lincoln Middle School should have been very pleased with the results of this evaluation. A critical step in developing an effective integrated school is for students to perceive their teachers as being fair and caring about them as individuals. This evaluation indicated that Lincoln had met this condition.

Another study of the advisor-advisee program at Lincoln Middle School was prompted by the Bell-Nathaniel and Damico study and by some chance remarks made by some high school teachers, who, at a district teacher's meeting, observed that students from Lincoln were more mature and easier to teach when they reached 9th grade than were students from several other schools in the district (Doda, 1979). After gathering considerable data from both questionnaires and interviews, Doda confirmed and extended the conclusions of the Bell-Nathaniel and Damico study. Among the significant conclusions were the following.

- Ninth grade students in the district's high schools felt good about their interpersonal relationships at school and attributed some of their successes in this area to the advisor-advisee program at the middle school.
- Students in the study believed that they understood themselves well and attributed this, in part, to the opportunities provided in the advisory program, particularly the extended relationships with a teacher who cared about them and the chance to talk about personal matters with peers.
- School survival skills appeared to be an area of weakness. Solving problems, using school time wisely, and meeting deadlines were perceived as unresolved difficulties by a significant portion of the students who had moved on to 9th grade.
- No special activities were mentioned by students as having been particularly helpful. A caring advisor and a special peer group were cited much more frequently as having been helpful.
- Males, and especially African American males, seemed less prepared and less successful in 9th grade than females.
- A small portion of youngsters believed that the advisory program was of no help or value at all. They tended to remark, "We did nothing in AA."

Comprehensively, however, this study came to the same positive conclusions about the advisory program at Lincoln Middle School, as did the first one.

Several more recent research projects have been reported widely. The Rochester experiment (Urbanski, 1991) indicates that, among the changes instituted in the wide-ranging reforms in that district, among the most successful has been the Home Base Guidance program in the new middle schools. Among the important outcomes in 1991, 73% of the parents reported that they had direct contact with their child's advisor by the middle of the school year, and 82% of the parents who had been contacted said that such contacts were helpful. Such home contacts were up 45% over the previous year.

Putbrese (1989) surveyed 3,400 7th grade students in middle and junior high schools with and without advisory programs. Of the 43 statements included in the survey, 29 were statistically significant in their results. From the data available, Putbrese drew the following conclusions. Advisory programs

Improve teacher-student relationships

Give students a feeling of more control over decisions

Promote an atmosphere of equality, especially according to girls

Provide opportunity for group work

Improve the sharing of feelings between students, especially girls (Three out of four boys refuse to share their deeper feelings with or without an advisory program.)

Help to maximize the altruistic nature of early adolescents

Reduce the incidence of smoking and alcohol use

Appear to make teachers more aware of or more attentive to student behavior, especially according to boys

Putbrese concluded that "reports of research on affective education clearly support the concept that advisory programs are necessary for the middle level school. Early adolescents need to feel known and recognized. The advisory program has the potential for attending to this need" (1989, p. 115).

Bergmann (1989) conducted a study of 115 boys and 66 girls, ages 11–16, in 20 middle level schools in urban, suburban, and rural settings. Students had all been identified by the principal as at-risk or having been frequently reported as discipline problems. Each was interviewed to determine the students' perceptions of discipline effectiveness, teaching strategies, and school climate. The overall purpose of the study was to identify instructional strategies that might assist such early adolescents to remain in school. All students "mentioned that this was the first time anyone had asked them their opinion about anything" (Bergmann, 1989, p. 3). Also "every student in the study mentioned at least once during the interview that they would like someone to listen to them" (p. 6).

Bergmann suggested that one way to achieve such an objective would be to design an advisory program that

1. Trained teachers in skills for listening, group dynamics, and parent conferencing

2. Encouraged teachers to take time to teach skills associated with students' decision-making, problem solving, and responsibility
3. Included health information
4. Informed and involved parents whenever appropriate

A study of 394 middle school students, by Buckner and Bickel (1990), reinforced the picture of desired personal qualities of teachers, especially when they act as advisors. The students indicated that the most desired quality is being respectful toward students, having an accepting attitude, and being easy to talk with. Students want teachers as advisors who are approachable and who, once approached, listen carefully, acceptingly, and respectfully to what the students say.

In 1997 a comprehensive review of the literature on advisory programs (Galassi et al., 1997) affirmed both the purposes and the difficulties of establishing effective advisory programs. Most important, the authors identified a substantial weakness of the research in this area to date—efforts to study such programs have not been strongly grounded in a theory base. The authors put it this way:

> Without a clear underlying theory to guide inquiry and suggest modifications for practice, it is not surprising that contemporary advisory programs, in many instances, are not much different from those that were advocated in the early days of the junior high movement, nor is it surprising that we still do not know a great deal about their effectiveness or their active ingredients. (1997, p. 327)

Social Support Theory   Fortunately, Galassi, Gulledge, and Cox go on to suggest such a theory from the world of social science research—social support theory—to help middle school educators in their attempts to understand and improve research and practice in advisory programs in all aspects of middle school organization. This social support theory is at the base of efforts by social scientists to understand how institutions and organizations are structured and operated so as to "protect people from the deleterious effects of stress" that come from living and working in the organization.

Basically, social support theory holds that every institution in America has a particular work to do, a unique set of tasks assigned by the society to those institutions. Schools, health care institutions, the corporation, the military, and the family—all have a unique set of tasks to perform for the society. But, just like in an automobile engine, work in human groups creates its own kind of friction, heat, and stress in the organization as it expends energy on its tasks. All human groups must have social support systems to maintain the organization so that it can continue to hold together and reduce the stress on its members while work is conducted. Otherwise, the group, the organization, the institution (and the individuals within) will collapse and be unable to continue.

All of this applies to middle schools. The work of the middle school, learning and academic achievement, must be conducted in an organization that has social support systems in place. The middle school concept utilizes several components directly as social support systems—advisory, interdisciplinary team organization, houses, heterogeneous grouping—so that students and teachers can keep at the work of the school without collapsing from friction and stress. Social support theory helps explain why such components are important to the education of young adolescents.

Recent research with this theory at its base has, we think, been very productive. For many years, Jacqueline Eccles and her colleagues (1991) have been studying the effects of various social support systems, or their absence in school environments, on middle school students' motivation, efficacy beliefs, and general self-esteem. Robert Felner and his associates (1997) suggest that the work of middle schools (higher academic achievement) can be conducted when important social support systems (advisory, interdisciplinary team organization, etc.) are in place. An important study of the relationship between social support systems and "academic press" (Lee & Smith, 1999), based upon data gathered from 30,000 middle school students, showed that both these factors must be present and balanced for a school to succeed in its work of academic achievement. Another comprehensive review of research (Osterman, 2000) confirmed that social support systems (such as that found in successful advisory programs) are essential to students' feeling of belonging and their sense of community at school.

We believe that social support theory is an important base from which to conduct research, and school improvement efforts, in several components of the middle school concept. We encourage advanced graduate students to explore this theory in detail as they prepare to conduct research, and we likewise encourage school leaders to utilize social support theory as they interpret the importance of various middle school components to their staffs and communities.

Guidance and Counseling in the Middle School

The advisor-advisee programs, and other elements of the middle school social support system, have not eliminated the need for school counselors. Counselors must perform so many other duties in a middle school (for example, staffing students into special programs, guiding new students, assisting in quasi-administrative duties and crisis intervention) that even the idea of eliminating or reducing their presence is unthinkable.

The position of counselor continues in middle schools much in the same role as in earlier junior high schools. The counselor is a student service person working in myriad ways to help in personal, educational, social, and other affairs of the students. Counselors are generally assigned duties that border on administration, with almost always too many students. Guidance activities grow from three central standards of effective school counseling programs identified by American School Counselor National Standards and state counseling standards. Academic development, career development, and personal or social development are, thus, the core of an effective middle school guidance program.

The guidance counselor is, in the best circumstances, concerned with the following activities that spring from these standards, as identified by Melinda Young, long-time counselor at Wakulla Middle School, in Crawfordville, Florida (personal communication, January 8, 2002).

Implement the guidance curriculum

Guide and counsel groups and individual students through the development of career and educational plans

Counsel small groups and individual students with personal problems

Consult with teachers, staff, and parents regarding the varying needs of students

Refer students/parents to community agencies as appropriate

Coordinate, conduct, and participate in activities that contribute to and celebrate student success (e.g., Wildcat Winners, a positive reward/incentive program that has been going on at the school for more than two decades)

Coordinate career activities like the 8th grade career day

Conduct new student orientations

Coordinate all transition activities for rising 5th graders and outgoing 8th graders

Evaluate and revise the guidance program

Administer the Exceptional Student Education program

Contribute to professional development programs

Schedule and participate in parent/teacher conferences

Coordinate schoolwide testing

The coordination of the school testing program is taking more of the counselors' time in middle schools across the country. Young looks at this development positively.

The counseling program at Wakulla Middle School is a comprehensive, developmental model that seeks to enhance student learning. Our accountability in today's world depends on assisting in increasing student performance.

The counseling team at Wantagh Middle School, in Wantagh, New York, describes the work of guidance personnel in a comprehensive program. Among the efforts regularly observable at Wantagh, and at the thousands of middle schools where similar professionals use their counseling skills, are individual and group counseling; the implementation of a developmental guidance curriculum that is different for each of the three grades; and a comprehensive orientation and transition program that includes parent and student orientation and visitation, counselors meeting with 5th grade students, and an introductory barbeque. Other indicators of a comprehensive counseling program include how counselors determine the direction of the child study team, facilitate grade level and team meetings focusing on students, lead parent conferences, devise educational plans for students, coach the peer mediation process, and serve as an advisor to the school's advisory program.

One promising direction in the work of middle school counselors is the growing trend to directly attach them to interdisciplinary teams. Educators in the middle schools of New Albany-Floyd County Consolidated School Corporation, for example, have reorganized the counseling process so that counselors are an integral part of several teams. Doing so, they assert, makes it much less likely that counselors will be involved in activities that weaken their impact in a middle school: discipline, attendance clerking, lunch duty, and covering classes when substitutes are not available. Counselors there either loop up to a new grade with their students or remain on the grade with the teams they have been serving.

Placing counselors in direct service to teams has, they assert, a number of other advantages. Counselors can advise teams on scheduling students and courses. They can receive referrals directly on site from the team. Counselors are more aware of curriculum and management issues and can advise the team and school leaders of needed changes. Counselors can develop programs to meet the needs of specific teams instead of for the school as a whole, and they can be a more effective liaison between the team and parents, the administration, and students. Counselors can work proactively with the team to forestall discipline problems, and they can work with the teams to integrate developmental guidance components directly into the curriculum of the teams with which they work (Perkins, Snider, & Bussaberger, 1998).

We believe that middle school counselors are busy and important people about whom many middle school educators know and, perhaps, appreciate, too little. One important new initiative at the middle level should certainly focus on the importance of guidance counselors in America's middle schools.

CONTENT SUMMARY

Young adolescents are passing through a time of life when aspects of their natural development pose challenges for teachers and others who work with them. In middle school, it is best for teachers to work together to, in a positive sense, gang up on the kids. Common team rules and routines, and a team discipline plan, can be important to managing student behavior. Mentoring the young adolescent is as important as it is challenging. Advisor-advisee programs are designed to help teachers connect more closely and positively to small groups of their students. Although advisory programs can be difficult to implement and sustain, when all the factors are in place, they can be wonderful experiences for both teacher and student. Counselors are important supports for the young adolescent in middle school.

CONNECTIONS TO OTHER CHAPTERS

The topic of teacher-student relationships in middle school connects naturally to a couple of other chapters. Chapter 1 focuses on the characteristics and needs of young adolescents. Dealing with these developmental changes requires close collaboration among teachers. Chapter 6 explains how teaming improves the capacity of teachers to positively influence student behavior. Teaming and advisory programs also fit together in important ways.

QUESTIONS FOR DISCUSSION

1. Middle school educators have sometimes been criticized for being too touchy-feely. What is the proper place of affective education in the schooling of young adolescents?
2. Does the phrase "ganging up on the kids" strike you as too negative? Why or why not?
3. What are the most important factors in why advisory programs have been so difficult to implement and to do successfully for any length of time?
4. Can you see yourself in the role of advisor? Would it be a pleasant responsibility or would you see it as a distracting imposition?
5. What do you believe are the most important attributes of an effective advisor? Are these different from the attributes required for effective classroom management at the middle school level?

ACTION STEPS

1. Investigate the circumstances surrounding the successful or unsuccessful attempt to implement a teacher-based guidance or advisory program. See if you can discover why the program ended up as it did.
2. Interview 10 young adolescents about their relationships with their teachers. Focus on factors such as how close they feel to their teachers, whether they feel their teachers trust them, whether they have at least one teacher they could tell a secret to, and the characteristics of their favorite teachers.

3. In a school that has a daily advisory program, poll five teachers about their attitudes toward the program and the ways in which they approach the use of time during the advisory period.

4. Survey a small group of parents of young adolescents about whether they believe taking time during the school day for an advisory program is something they would be positive about.

5. Design your own advisory calendar for a month. What regular activities would you include? What occasional activities would you build in? What would be the goals of your program?

SUGGESTIONS FOR FURTHER STUDY

Books

Angione, C., Giacobbe, M., & Bamberger, R. (1997). *Developing leadership potential and career choices microform: A report of the statewide conferences on Women Helping Girls with Choices: NYSAWA Women Helping Girls with Choices Project, July 1997.* Albany, NY: New York State Association for Women in Administration, and Washington, DC: U.S. Department of Education, Office of Educational Research and Improvement, Educational Resources Information Center.

Bemak, F., & Keys, S. (2000). *Violent and aggressive youth: Intervention and prevention strategies for changing times.* Thousand Oaks, CA: Corwin Press.

Blauvelt, P. (1999). *Making schools safe for students: Creating a proactive school safety plan.* Thousand Oaks, CA: Corwin Press.

Capozzoli, T., & McVey, S. (2000). *Kids killing kids: Managing violence and gangs in schools.* Boca Raton, FL: St. Lucie Press.

Cohen, J. (1999). *Educating minds and hearts: Social emotional learning and the passage into adolescence.* New York: Teachers College Press.

Dale, P. (1995). *Developing an effective advisor/advisee program.* Bloomington, IN: Phi Delta Kappa Educational Foundation.

Davis, T., & Osborn, C. (2000). *The solution-focused school counselor: Shaping professional practice.* Philadelphia, PA: Accelerated Development.

Dorsch, N. (1998). *Community, collaboration, and collegiality in school reform: An odyssey toward connections.* Albany, NY: State University of New York Press.

Dunkel, N., & Schuh, J. (1998). *Advising student groups and organizations.* San Francisco, CA: Jossey-Bass.

Ferguson, A. (2000). *Bad boys: Public schools in the making of black masculinity.* Ann Arbor, MI: University of Michigan Press.

Florida Bureau of Special Projects and Grant Development (1996). *Information age: Career cruiser: Career and educational information for middle school students.* Tallahassee, FL: Florida Department of Education, Bureau of Special Projects and Grant Development.

Hyman, I., & Snook, P. (1999). *Dangerous schools: What we can do about the physical and emotional abuse of our children.* San Francisco, CA: Jossey-Bass.

Montgomery, M. (1999). *Building bridges with parents: Tools and techniques for counselors.* Thousand Oaks, CA: Corwin Press.

Muro, J., & Kottman, T. (1995). *Guidance and counseling in the elementary and middle schools: A practical approach.* Madison, WI: Brown & Benchmark.

Salacuse, J. (2000). *The wise advisor: What every professional should know about consulting and counseling.* Westport, CT: Praeger.

Schwartz, W. (1996). *Preparing middle school students for a career.* New York: ERIC Clearinghouse on Urban Education.

Periodicals

Alder, N., & Moulton, M. (1998). Caring relationships: Perspectives from middle school students. *Research in Middle Level Education Quarterly, 21*(3), 15–32.

Alder, N., & Moulton, M. (1998). The eye of the beholder: Middle schoolers talk about caring. *Schools in the Middle, 7*(3), 6–7, 52–53.

Arigo, M., & Garland, V. (1996). A property poor district with a middle school mission. *Clearing House, 70*(1), 36–39.

Banks, S. (2000). Addressing violence in middle schools. *Clearing House, 73*(4), 209–210.

Barber, J., & Patin, D. (1997). Parent involvement: A two-way street. *Schools in the Middle, 6*(4), 31–33.

Baruth, L., & Manning, L. (2000). A call for multicultural counseling in middle schools. *Clearing House, 73*(4), 243–246.

Black, D., Tobler, N., & Sciacca, J. (1998). Peer helping/involvement: An efficacious way to meet the challenge of reducing alcohol, tobacco, and other drug use among youth. *Peer Facilitator Quarterly, 15*(4), 99–107.

Bobo, M., Durodoye, B., & Hildreth, B. (1998). Changing patterns in career choices among African-American, Hispanic, and Anglo children. *Professional School Counseling, 1*(4), 37–42.

Bowen, N., & Bowen, G. (1999). Effects of crime and violence in neighborhoods and schools on the school behavior and performance of adolescents. *Journal of Adolescent Research, 14*(3), 319–342.

Brown, D. (1999). The value of advisory sessions: Perceptions of young adolescents at an urban middle school. *Research in Middle Level Education Quarterly, 22*(4), 41–58.

Carpenter, S., King-Sears, M., & Keys, S. (1998). Counselors + educators + families as a transdisciplinary team = more effective inclusion for students with disabilities. *Professional School Counseling, 2*(1), 1–9.

Cooper, D., Paisley, P., & Phelps, R. (1998). Developing precollege programs for at-risk middle and high school students. *Journal of College Student Development, 39*(4), 387–388.

Corcoran, J. (1998). Solution-focused practice with middle and high school at-risk youths. *Social Work in Education, 20*(4), 232–243.

Crandell, P., & Sheldon, C. (1997). Making your programs work. *Schools in the Middle, 6*(4), 4–7.

Deck, M., Scarborough, J., Sferrazza, M., & Estill, D. (1999). Serving students with disabilities: Perspectives of three school counselors. *Intervention in School and Clinic, 34*(3), 150–155.

Desimone, L. (1999). Linking parent involvement with student achievement: Do race and income matter? *Journal of Educational Research, 93*(1), 11–30.

Fleischer, C., Hayes-Parvin, K., & King, J. (1999). Becoming proactive: The quiet revolution. *Voices from the Middle, 6*(3), 3–10.

Galassi, J., & Gulledge, S. (1997). The middle school counselor and teacher-advisor programs. *Professional School Counseling. 1*(2), 55–60.

Galassi, J., Gulledge, S., & Cox, N. (1997). Middle school advisories: Retrospect and prospect. *Review of Educational Research, 67*(3), 301–338.

Giles, R. (1998). At-risk students can succeed: A model program that meets special needs. *Schools in the Middle, 7*(3), 18–20.

Guichard, J., & Dosnon, O. (2000). Cognitive and social relevance of psycho-pedagogical methods in guidance. *Journal of Career Development, 26*(3), 161–173.

Hall, S., & Rueth, T. (1999). Counselors in the classroom: A developmental approach to student well-being. *NASSP Bulletin, 83*(603), 27–33.

Jesse, D. (1997). Increasing parental involvement: A key to student success. *Schools in the Middle, 7*(1), 21–23, 50–51.

Kaplan, L. (1997). Parents' rights: Are middle schools at risk? *Schools in the Middle, 7*(1), 35–38, 48.

Kareck, T. (1998). Making the time to counsel students. *Professional School Counseling, 1*(5), 56–57.

Manning, L. (2000). Child-centered middle schools: A position paper—Association for Childhood Education International. *Childhood Education, 76*(3), 154–159.

Manning, L. (2000). Developmentally responsive multicultural education for young adolescents. *Childhood Education, 76*(2), 82–87.

McGee, L., & Fauble-Erickson, T. (1995). The multifaceted role of guidance and counseling in the middle level school. *NASSP Bulletin, 79*(570), 16–19.

McGrath, D., & Kuriloff, P. (1999). The perils of parent involvement: Tracking, curriculum, and resource distortions in a middle school mathematics program. *Research in Middle Level Education Quarterly, 22*(3), 59–83.

McKnight-Taylor, M. (1997). Making education special for all young adolescents. *Childhood Education, 73*(5), 260–261.

Ost, N. (1999). Girls' class, infinite possibilities. *Journal of Family Life: A Quarterly for Empowering Families, 5*(1), 30–32.

Pietrzak, D., Petersen, G., & Speaker, K. (1998). Perceptions of school violence by elementary and middle school personnel. *Professional School Counseling, 1*(4), 23–29.

Shepard-Tew, D., & Forgione, J. (1999). A collaborative mentor-training program for learning-disabled middle-grade students. *Educational Forum, 64*(1), 75–81.

Vars, G. (1997). Creating options: Getting closer to middle level students: Options for teacher-adviser guidance programs. *Schools in the Middle, 6*(4), 16–22.

White, J., & Edmondson, J. (1998). A tutorial and counseling program: Helping students at risk of dropping out of school. *Professional School Counseling, 1*(4), 43–47.

White-Hood, M. (1996). Community spirit: Cluster schools redefine the school system. *Schools in the Middle, 5*(4), 9–12.

Willems, A., McConnell, R., & Willems, E. (1997). Middle school students, teachers, and parents contracting for success. *Journal of Instructional Psychology, 24*(4), 246–252.

Williams, W. (1998). Preventing violence in school: What can principals do? *NASSP Bulletin, 82*(602), 10–17.

Williamson, R., & Johnston, H. (1998). Responding to parent and public concerns about middle level schools. *NASSP Bulletin, 82*(599), 73–82.

Wood, K., & Jones, J. (1997). When affect informs instruction. *Childhood Education, 73*(5), 292–296.

Yonezawa, S., & Oakes, J. (1999). Making parents partners in the placement process. *Educational Leadership, 56*(7), 33–36.

ERIC

Anfara, V., & Brown, K. (1998). *Advisor-advisee programs in middle schools: Community building in a state of affective disorder* (ERIC document ED426987).

Bensman, D. (1999). *Open doors, closed doors: Home-school partnerships in a large Bronx elementary school* (ERIC document ED430695).

Braden, W. (1998). *Homies: Peer mentoring among African-American males* (ERIC document ED433411).

Carter, C. (1999). *Conflict mediation at school: Peace through avoidance?* (ERIC document ED433396).

Dykeman, C. (1998). *Maximizing school guidance program effectiveness: A guide for school administrators and program directors* (ERIC document ED421675).

Echevarria, P. (1998). *For all our daughters: How mentoring helps young women and girls master the art of growing up* (ERIC document ED426799).

Fitzgerald, D., & Bloodsworth, G. (1995). *Multicultural thematic instruction: One strategy for meeting middle learners' affective needs* (ERIC document ED390859).

Friedlaender, D. (1999). *The need for scaffolding parent support in an urban school* (ERIC document ED432654).

Gensemer, P. (2000). *Effectiveness of cross-age and peer mentoring programs* (ERIC document ED438267).

Georges, A. (1997). *Effects of access to counseling and family background on at-risk students* (ERIC document ED412441).

Gray, K. (2000). *Getting real: Helping teens find their future* (ERIC document ED433494).

Green, A. (1998). *Something to think about: A student generated project that reaches into the community* (ERIC document ED422467).

Grossman, S., Osterman, K., & Schmelkin, L. (1999). *Parent involvement: The relationship between beliefs and practices* (ERIC document ED433326).

Hansen, S. (1999). *Gender-based advocacy for equity and non-violence* (ERIC document ED435914).

Hu, P., & Wu, A. (1997). *Education and counseling on adolescent life* (ERIC document ED439356).

Juhnke, G. (2000). *Addressing school violence: Practical strategies and interventions* (ERIC document ED440313).

Kerka, S. (2000). *Career development specialties for the 21st century: Trends and issues* (ERIC document ED437555).

Kreps, R. (1999). *A behavioral peer group approach to combat truancy in the middle school* (ERIC document ED435875).

Landsverk, R. (1997). *Families, communities, schools—learning together.* (ERIC document ED414072).

Leland-Jones, P. (1998). *Improving the transition of sixth-grade students during the first year of middle school through a peer counselor mentor and tutoring program* (ERIC document ED424911).

Mackinnon, A. (1997). *Working together: Harnessing community resources to improve middle schools* (ERIC document ED414352).

Maddy-Bernstein, C., & Dare, D. (1997). *Career guidance for elementary and middle school students* (ERIC document ED415353).

Mizelle, N. (1999). *Helping middle school students make the transition into high school* (ERIC document ED432411).

Picklesimer, B., & Williams, J. (1999). *School violence in Japan and the United States: Sharing American practice with Japanese teacher educators* (ERIC document ED434088).

Riley, R. (1998). *Education first: Building America's future: The Fifth Annual State of American Education Speech, Seattle, Washington* (ERIC document ED416589).

Rios, H., Klanderman, J., Booth, W., Moreno, I., & Wiley, M. (1999). *Using collaborative planning to enhance instruction for all students* (ERIC document ED434292).

Schrumpf, F. (Ed.) (1993). *Life lessons for young adolescents: An advisory guide for teachers* (ERIC document ED395684).

Woo, A. (1998). *Lessons and challenges from a culture and gender responsive school-based youth program: Project Da Da Kidogo* (ERIC document ED421556).

Xu, J. (1999). *Reaching out to families from diverse backgrounds: A case study* (ERIC document ED437454).

Web Sites

California School Counselor Association
http://www.ca-schoolcounselor.org/
The mission of the California School Counselor Association (CSCA) "is to actively promote excellence in professional school counseling." Important site components include the following.

- Information about CSCA
- Links to resources: Related Organizations, California Resources, Special Topics for School Counselors, Violence Resources, Student Resources, CSCA Forum Share, Counseling Related Links, Violence Prevention, and Ethical Decision Making Model
- Publications

Pathways to School Improvement, North Central Regional Educational Laboratory
http://www.ncrel.org/sdrs/pathwayg.htm
Important site components include the following.

- Sources of updated information on critical issues in education in general and on specific subject areas
- North Central Regional Educational Laboratory Resource Center is a special library with a collection devoted exclusively to educational material
- Discussion groups and opportunities for offering suggestions for future issues

Six Seconds

http://www.6seconds.org/home.shtml

Six Seconds is a nonprofit educational service organization supporting the development of emotional intelligence for families, schools, communities, and corporations. Important site components include the following.

- Information about emotional intelligence
- Resources (emailing lists, links to organizations, and resources for emotional intelligence)
- Information about emotional intelligence training

National Forum to Accelerate Middle-Grades Reform

http://www.mgforum.org/

This group, made up mostly of middle grades reform leaders, promotes the academic performance and healthy development of young adolescents. "Through this forum, we hope to enhance the middle-level school movement by developing common goals and understandings, strengthening our individual efforts to improve middle-grades schools, collaborating across institutional and other boundaries, and working together to mobilize others in the larger middle-grades community." Important site components include the following.

- Schools to Watch
- The Southern Forum
- News and Updates
- Tools and Resources
- Schools and Policy

Family and Advocates Partnership for Education

http://www.fape.org

This project is aimed at informing and educating families and advocates about the Individuals with Disabilities Education Act of 1997 and related promising practices. It includes a news line and information on various special education topics. It may be useful for advisors of students with disabilities.

Black Families.com

http://www.blackfamilies.com

This site is focused on African American adults "who believe family is the most important thing in their lives." Information is available on health issues, finances, family relationships, and parenting. It may be useful to advisors interested in learning more about their African American students and their families.

The Guidance Channel

http://www.atrisk.com

The Guidance Channel is an educational publishing and media company. Its mission is to provide children, students, parents, adults, and professionals with tools that help them or their clients make critical life choices. This site could be a good source for advisors looking for materials and ideas for their advisory group time.

Interdisciplinary Team Organization

Mebane Middle School

Since the late 1960s, Mebane Middle School (MMS), in Alachua, Florida, one of America's first middle schools, has been organized into interdisciplinary teams. Over three decades as a middle school, the school organization has changed several times, but the focus on teaming and the strong commitment to shared responsibility for the education of a common group of students have never wavered. Teaming, at MMS, with nearly 600 students from predominantly low socioeconomic circumstances, means small teams of two or three teachers and 50 to 75 students working together in a long block schedule of four 83-minute periods. Teachers on teams have 85 minutes of common planning time each day. As a committed member of the Coalition of Essential Schools, MMS is dedicated to the implementation of an interdisciplinary curriculum on each small team. Each integrated curriculum unit "covers state standards, but is not standards driven," says principal Chet Sanders. In one recent school year, teams produced units with the following titles: U.S. Space Program, Careers, Genetic Engineering, Oregon Trail, Sound Waves and Music, Endangered Species, Pirates, Egypt, World Travel, Native Americans, Election 2000, and the U.S. Constitution. Quotes from student journals illustrate the effects of small teams, block schedule, and unit teaching at MMS.

"I like being taught with unit teaching. You can actually see what you're learning in action. Then it kind of makes it stick with you."

"We have more time for questions and they always get answered since we don't run out of time."

"I really like working like this. It's exciting! Bonding everything together is better than going to five different classes. I never thought school could be so much fun."

"I thought this unit was great. It didn't even seem like we were learning because we were having fun."

In 1998 MMS was a "C" school according to its scores on the state tests. Three years later, after the effects of the interdisciplinary team organization were beginning to be felt, the school earned an "A" on those same tests. Academic achievement and small teams go together.

WHAT YOU WILL LEARN IN CHAPTER 6

Interdisciplinary team organization is the heart and soul of an exemplary middle school. In this chapter, you will learn what a team is, how it is organized, the characteristics of effective teams, and how many different types of teams there are. You will learn about the phases of life on teams. You will take a close look at partner teams—small teams of two or three teachers. The advantages and precautions related to teaming are presented, along with the roles and responsibilities of team members.

INTERDISCIPLINARY TEAM ORGANIZATION: OPERATIONAL CORE OF THE MIDDLE SCHOOL CONCEPT

The interdisciplinary team organization has been the most significant contribution of the middle school concept to the process of schooling. In the early years of the 21st century, even high school educators have embraced the value of teaming (George, McEwin, & Jenkins, 2000). Over the preceding decade, middle school educators reached a consensus on the priority of the manner in which teachers and students are organized to learn. During the decade of the 1980s, a number of national organizations (e.g., Carnegie Council on Adolescent Development) and hundreds, if not thousands, of school districts recognized that the interdisciplinary organization of teachers was the most distinguishing feature of the middle school and the keystone of its structure. In the presence of a stable interdisciplinary team organization, other components of the middle school program function more smoothly. In the absence of the interdisciplinary team organization, they operate with considerably more difficulty, if they exist at all.

SHARING: THE BASIS FOR ORGANIZING THE MIDDLE SCHOOL FACULTY

What teachers share with one another is the basis for how they are organized, at all three levels of American education. The degree to which teachers share in teaching the same subject and the extent to which they share the same students determine, in most schools, the ways in which teachers are organized to deliver instruction. At each level, the phenomenon of teacher sharing has produced three distinct types of teacher organization for instruction.

In the elementary school, especially in the primary grades, the nature and needs of the students argue for little sharing between and among teachers. Elementary students need an almost exclusive relationship with one teacher. Consequently, the self-contained classroom has been the predominant mode of elementary school faculty organization throughout the history of American education. Teachers share few students with other teachers except specialists in music, physical education, and so on. They do not share the teaching of the same subject, because regular elementary level classroom teachers most often teach the basic academic program to their own students. In the decade of the 1990s, however, teachers, at least in the upper elementary years, seemed to have begun to do more sharing of the same subjects and students. Perhaps this was in recognition of the nature and needs of the students, but perhaps not.

At the high school level, (George & McEwin, 1999), teachers share few students but are committed to sharing the teaching of the same subject. High school teachers rarely teach in more than one academic discipline. Often they teach only one subject at one grade level. A teacher might, for example, teach only junior-level American history and never world history. Teachers see themselves as academic specialists, arguing that the sophistication of the subject matter at that level prohibits teachers from crossing disciplinary lines with ease. Released from a major concern with student relationships, the high school has maintained a steady focus on organizing to facilitate the delivery of what teachers are committed to, the academic disciplines.

High school teachers are still most often organized, therefore, into academic departments along the same lines as colleges and universities. Instead of one teacher generalist presenting virtually the whole world of knowledge to a specific group of small children, the high school teacher is usually responsible for an even smaller part (e.g., American history) of one of many areas (e.g., social studies) of the world of knowledge. Instead of working alone, the high school teacher often interacts with other teachers, but with the common focus being the subject area they share.

The goal of the middle school is to provide a program that ties the elementary school and the high school together in a smooth and continuous way. At the same time, the middle school seeks to provide a unique experience for the education of older children and young adolescents, a middle way between the elementary school self-contained classroom and the high school department. This middle way has come to be known as the interdisciplinary team organization, which focuses on teachers who share several important components of the school program. The need for planned gradualism as the key to K–12 articulation (identified several decades ago) remains and is met, in the exemplary middle school, through the interdisciplinary team organization.

The contributions of the interdisciplinary team to student success are not limited to middle and high school. In the late fall of 2001, an illustration of the power of interdisciplinary teaming at an even higher level was shared with one of the authors, while speaking casually over dinner with several students enrolled in the highly regarded University of Florida School of Law. Law school, at the University of Florida as elsewhere, is a highly pressurized atmosphere of intense intellectual challenge and academic diligence. Few school situations are more agonizingly stressful than finals time at a high-status law school. In the conversation, the exhausted, stressed, but persistent students shared what they perceived as an immensely satisfying afternoon with their instructors at the end of the semester, after the last class and prior to final exams.

At the end of their last class of the semester, at a prearranged signal, two professors marched into the classroom of a third with about 30 big pizza pies, as a surprise treat for the 100 law students in the room. The three professors distributed the pizzas and proceeded to tell the students that they were one of the best classes the team of law school professors had ever taught and how proud they were to be their instructors. The appreciation and pride that the author read in the comments and expressions of his young companions as they described the scene was similar to what might have happened in hundreds of middle school teams prior to the beginning of the holidays. The three law professors and the 100 students were an interdisciplinary team—the professors shared the same students, the same part of the building, the same schedule, and the responsibility for teaching the main courses of the semester to a common group of students. A warm sense of community had developed in what could have otherwise been one of the most competitive, even hostile, environments in all of education. As it turns out, even law students and their professors need and respond to the social support that an emerging sense of community can provide. How much more do middle school students need this social support?

THE NATURE OF THE INTERDISCIPLINARY TEAM ORGANIZATION

Considerably less misunderstanding and confusion now exists about the meaning of terms used to describe the organization for instruction in middle schools. Numerous terms that had been used previously as synonyms (*team teaching, interdisciplinary, intradisciplinary, multidisciplinary, cross-curriculum,* and several others) have given way, generally, to the use of the term *interdisciplinary team organization.* Few educators now use *team teaching* and *interdisciplinary team organization* synonymously.

About four decades ago, in one of the first books ever devoted entirely to the topic of teaming, Shaplin and Olds (1964) defined team teaching as "a type of instructional organization, involving teaching personnel and the students assigned to them, in which two or more teachers are given responsibility, working together, for all or a significant part of the instruction of the same group of students." With a few slight adjustments, this definition still works well for the exemplary middle school almost 40 years later (Arnold & Stevenson, 1998; Middle Grades Task Force, 2001).

Team teaching, as it was envisioned in the 1960s, was basically a hierarchical gradation of faculty members' roles and titles wherein a master teacher had major responsibilities for planning and presenting lessons to large groups of students, who were then dispersed to small seminar-size groups and led by presumably less competent faculty for discussion and review of the lesson presented by the master teacher. The impression is that the essence of teaming is expressed in the act of instruction. Such a model may work well for high schools and colleges. It rarely plays a major role in the exemplary middle school. Our impression is that the act of team teaching, as it was originally intended, is rarely practiced at any level of education.

By contrast, the term *organization* focuses on the structural requirements of the team. It highlights factors other than a particular style of large and small group instruction. Interdisciplinary team organization, the concept endorsed not only by us but also by the National Middle School Association and others, fits comfortably with Shaplin and Olds's definition. However, it goes further. We use the term *interdisciplinary team organization* to define "a way of organizing the faculty so that a group of teachers share (1) the same group of students; (2) the responsibility for planning, teaching, and evaluating curriculum and instruction in more than one academic area; (3) the same schedule; and (4) the same area of the building." These four factors are the necessary and sufficient elements of interdisciplinary teacher organization. When all four are present, nothing else is needed. When one or more elements is missing, the team organization is less than complete. Interdisciplinary team teaching is not a critical element of the exemplary middle school; interdisciplinary team organization is.

At McDonald Middle School, where teams have been in place for several decades, the 1999–2000 annual report states that

> research has shown that an effective middle school will lay the important foundation and preparation for the high school years. But, we must also be sensitive to our students' social/emotional needs as they depart elementary school. Thus, our academic teams are designed and scheduled specifically to meet the high academic expectations of East Lansing High School as well as being learning communities where students have an opportunity to develop positive friendships and experience different teaching styles.

FOUR PHASES OF INTERDISCIPLINARY TEAM LIFE

Earlier studies of the ways in which teachers and students work to accomplish the tasks of schooling more effectively and satisfactorily (George, 1982; Plodzik & George, 1989) indicated that teamwork is essential in four areas of middle school life: (1) organization, (2) community building, (3) instruction, and (4) governance. More recent work (Boyd, 2000; Dickinson, 2001) confirms these findings.

Phase One: Organization

Teamwork is virtually impossible unless several critical conditions are met. First, middle school teachers must share the same students, space, and schedule. Among the members of the team, at least two subjects must be taught. When these conditions exist, the interdisciplinary team organization is possible; when they are absent, teamwork is difficult. Once these requirements are satisfied, teamwork begins, even without planning. Almost immediately, teachers on the team realize the power inherent in their acting together. Time between classes becomes more closely supervised, as teachers begin to use the phrase "our students" more frequently. Teachers almost always report that the job becomes more satisfying and more productive.

Students begin to notice that they are in classes with others who have the same teachers at the same and different times of the day. Students observe that they do not travel as widely from one part of the building to another as frequently as they may have under prior arrangements, when teachers were organized by departments. Students will discover that they are moving around the school more often, if they have come from the self-contained classroom of the primary grades. Teachers, students will notice, begin to share the same academic and behavioral expectations. Even if the teachers have not told students of the existence of the team, they will begin to feel its effects.

Teachers respond to the new opportunities they discover. Teachers can take advantage of the new organization to design and implement common rules and procedures to govern student behavior. Time between classes can be shortened and more closely supervised. Team conferences with students, parents, and educational specialists become more productive. Teachers spend their planning time discussing what they have in common—their students. So they end up knowing their students better, perhaps, than they ever have before.

Middle school teachers discover that a number of essential organizational tasks must be performed in this phase of team life, if they are going to benefit from their work together. The teachers on the team must develop common team rules, which are consistently applied from one classroom to the next. Teachers can maintain their own individual classroom rules but collaborate on those that are important enough to justify their cooperation. Developing common procedures (e.g., headings for papers, test day, etc.) can also simplify life for students while it is made easier for teachers. Conferences with parents, students, and specialists, once done individually, now should be done as a team. Such meetings are almost always more satisfying for teachers when they go together. Finally, teachers can use their organizational time and skill to develop and redesign the schedules for their teams and for individual students on the team. Frequently, the schedule that they share permits teachers much greater latitude in such areas. Used properly, the interdisciplinary team organization affords teachers much greater leverage than they could possibly amass working independently.

Teachers on Team 6–N, at Wakulla Middle School (WMS), in Crawfordville, Florida, offered the following team rules in a letter home to parents in 1990.

1. Show up on time.
2. Be prepared for class.
3. Complete all assignments.
4. Talk only at appropriate times.
5. Help keep the room and school clean.
6. Be considerate and respectful of others.
7. Gum and candy are not allowed at school.

The team rules were followed by a list of team consequences for breaking the rules and rewards for following them. In addition, the teachers discussed positive aspects of team unity, special activities, and field trips. They expressed their hope that students and parents would realize that each student was a part of a team, no longer just an individual student on his or her own. In 2002, teams at WMS operate in the same fundamental way.

At Eggers Middle School, in Hammond, Indiana, teams assumed the sort of role in student discipline that is now duplicated in thousands of such schools. At Eggers, they engaged in

- Making phone calls and conducting parent conferences
- Making home visits when warranted
- Contacting parents when students accumulate three unexcused absences or tardies
- Notifying the principal of suspected "educational neglect" cases and filling out forms for all cases of potential abuse and neglect
- Developing and distributing learning community (team) rules to all students, and explaining rules during advisory time
- Handling the punishment of all offenses other than breaking specific school rules four or more times, fighting, verbal or physical threats to a teacher, possession of a weapon, or other similarly serious offenses
- Ensuring that disciplinary action issued by the team is fair and consistent, with parental involvement a priority

More evidence has accumulated indicating that the middle schools are frequently incorporating the interdisciplinary team approach and casting off the departmentalized organization. In California (Middle Grades Task Force, 2001), Washington (Washington State Middle Level Task Force, 2001), and many other states, state department of education task force groups have acknowledged the predominance of the interdisciplinary team organization at the middle level. Many other studies (e.g., Crow & Pounder, 2000; Flowers, 2000) confirm this strong trend.

Phase Two: Community Building

Once organized and operating somewhat collaboratively, teachers and students become more aware of the new arrangement and a sense of community becomes possible. The experience of many middle level educators is that both teachers and students yearn for this group identity, but teamwork is necessary to make it happen. The need must be clearly recognized. Goals must be set for its realization. Activities must be conducted with zeal. With teamwork, this component of the team organization can be powerfully productive. Furtwengler (1991, p. 7) demonstrated that the authentic involvement of students in the creation of team cultures could be an important factor in improving the ethos of the school as a whole. One student leader, involved in a number of community-building activities, remarked, "We blend in together now. Everyone has a say and works together. Our team members care about each other and they listen to what we have to say. Everyone, well not everyone, but most of the members of the team share the load, and we get the job done." Research (Lee & Smith, 1999) indicates that the potential of teams to build a sense of community, with a personal knowledge of students, is far greater than the high school-style department, but that in practice, this potential is, as yet, largely unrealized.

Young adolescents need, sometimes desperately, to belong to groups they admire. Middle school educators now know that teaming can help to bring students to a point of attachment to the school that might otherwise never occur. Wise teachers have, therefore, been organizing and operating their teams in ways that make this educational community attractive. Much of this activity centers on developing team names, colors, mottoes, songs, T-shirts, and other visible common possessions. At Desert Sky Middle School, in Glendale, Arizona, long-time principal Janet Altersitz has insisted that teams have names that invite student interest. Instead of simple, dull numbers for teams, for the 2001–2002 school year, Desert Sky teams were named Diamondbacks, Timber Wolves, Purple Thunder, Sharks, Coyotes, Wildcats, Grizzlies, Bobcats, and Dolphins. At East Lyme Middle School, in Niantic, Connecticut, in 2001–2002, the teams were named Navigators, Voyagers, Pathfinders, Explorers, Discovery, Nova, Trailblazers, Odyssey, and Quest.

At Mandarin Middle School, in Jacksonville, Florida, a large (2,400 students) school combines the house idea with appealing team life. At Mandarin, everyone is a Hawk. All students are then organized into three smaller houses (of 800 students each) with two teams each in grades 6–8: Jay Hawks, Silver

Hawks, and Black Hawks. The teams within each house also have a Hawk name, chosen by the students. In one recent year, there were Mo-Hawks, Astro Hawks, Fire Hawks, Awesome Hawks, Tomo Hawks, and Sky Hawks, among others. It is a big school that feels small, in part because of the sense of identity that comes from the careful and comprehensive use of teams.

For teachers, the sense of community can be the redeeming virtue of the interdisciplinary team organization (Knowles & Brown, 2000). Veteran educators frequently speak of the team arrangement as the factor that enabled them to continue teaching with a sense of joy and commitment that had long been absent from their lives in school. Students require this sense of community even more than the faculty. Older children and young adolescents are at a special time of readiness—to experience and learn the concepts of inclusion, group citizenship, responsibility, and duty. The team offers a turf to belong to and a group to join. Teamwork can make a major difference in the level of group feeling that exists on the team and the benefits that result from that feeling.

Once a sense of team identity has been established, other work that increases the feeling of community includes the following.

- Staging contests, special meals, meetings, field trips, intramurals, and a host of other group activities. People in all kinds of groups need to do things together. This is also true for young adolescents.
- Planning interdisciplinary curriculum units involving the whole team. In Chapter 3, we examine this in detail.
- Sending a memo or newsletter to parents informing them about the learning community. Team get-togethers, such as potluck dinners, can broaden the base of support for the team concept and bring parents to school in ways that are satisfying and effective.
- Establishing symbols, in addition to team names, to add to the sense of unity. Team colors, mottoes, constitutions, rules, songs, and other indications of team identity and spirit can be important.

At Longfellow Middle School, in La Crosse, Wisconsin, a team of teachers illustrated how this concept can be brought to fulfillment and can help in many ways (Frost, Olson, & Valiquette, 2000). A team of 8th grade teachers decided to create a nation among the students on their team. Building on the concepts of William Glasser, the teachers worked hard to help their students create a constitution for their team, along with laws that guided the behavior of all members of the nation. Wolf Pack Nation became "a good place to learn and a safe place to work on problems as they arose. We had very few serious discipline problems and when they arose, we found that we had a solid, positive ground on which to deal with them" (Frost et al., 2000, p. 35).

Other recent research indicates that proper use of the interdisciplinary team organization increases the sense of community experienced in important positive ways by middle school students (Lee & Smith, 1999). One careful earlier study (Arhar, 1990, p. 19), for example, concluded, "Interdisciplinary teaming does make a difference in student sense of social bonding to teachers and to school, and to a lesser extent, in student bonding to peers."

At Marshall Simonds Middle School, in 2000, educators expressed their middle school organizational philosophy in a way that emphasizes the development of this sort of bonding into a school community.

> All children have been placed on an interdisciplinary team. Teams are made up of four academic teachers from several content areas that share the responsibility for planning the instructional program for a group of students. A typical team includes a mathematics, language arts, social studies, and science teacher who work with between 90 and 100 students. The theory behind this type of team is to promote communication, coordination, and cooperation among subject matter specialists. This should provide students the benefit from instruction planned by specialists, but lacking the fragmentation that is typical of most departmentalized plans. Here again, it is the goal of Simonds to avoid a "subject-centered" high school type plan. (Richard Connors, personal communication, October 13, 2000)

Phase Three: Teamed Instruction

When teamwork has been successful in the first two phases, and teams are well organized and have a sense of unity, they are able to move to a new phase, a phase some teachers think of first. Teamed instruction, what used to be known as team teaching, is only one aspect of teamwork in middle grades education. It is an important part, but only a part, of the interdisciplinary team organization.

Teamed instruction requires a great deal of teamwork, in addition to the completion of the first two phases. Teamed instruction requires, first and foremost, a predisposition toward working together instructionally on the part of teachers on a team. They must want to plan and teach together. A great deal of planning is required, using time that is a precious commodity in most middle schools. Teamed instruction also requires more sophisticated communication skills than are necessary to function effectively in an isolated classroom. Finally, teamed instruction requires a different set of planning skills than are required for individual teaching situations. When the teamwork is moving smoothly, however, three exciting possibilities emerge.

1. Teams plan so that tests and major assignments are not due on the same days, so that field trips are scheduled when they are most appropriate, and so on.
2. Teachers make a serious effort to go further in their coordination of the curriculum, manipulating their individual plans so that matching topics, although from different subjects, are taught at the same time. Teams

plan for instruction so that such topics match across classes from time to time, perhaps even including a few joint assignments.

3. When coordination and parallel planning go well and when teachers have the time and energy, teamed instruction may enter an entirely new phase. Authentic interdisciplinary units may emerge when compatible people find the time available.

Phase Four: Governance

The evidence indicates that an additional phase of teamwork contributes greatly to the success of middle level education programs. Exemplary middle school programs are far too complex to be handled unilaterally by one or two people in the front office. Even if this were possible, it would not be preferable. Shared decision-making, in the team and across the school, is both the process and the product of fully functioning interdisciplinary team organizations.

Teachers, on teams, who successfully negotiate the first three phases of teamwork, frequently find themselves motivated to assume more responsibility for the decisions that affect their school lives and the school experiences of their students. Administrators who recognize the wisdom of a participative approach to leadership, and who possess the ego strength to implement it, help teams grow toward this area of teamwork.

Teamwork, in such situations, usually involves some form of representative government system. Often each team has a team leader who represents the other team members at weekly or biweekly meetings of a schoolwide group, such as a Program Improvement Council. This group engages in teamwork for the whole school. It establishes policies, makes decisions, and solves problems that affect more than one team. This school team may wrestle with important issues such as the master schedule, the budget, and promotion and retention or with mundane but no less important issues such as whether a school assembly will be held the last day before winter holidays.

Research indicates that the four phases appear in middle schools in more than one region of the country. But not all teams function fully. A study (Plodzik & George, 1989) including 159 middle school principals throughout New England, for example, concluded that the phases were observable in middle schools throughout that region and that various stages of team development could be determined when viewed in terms of the four-phase model.

Whether teams function fully in all four areas is determined by several factors. The availability of staff development for teachers was critical, as was the participation of the school principal in prior training in middle school education. The presence of effective teachers on a team was related to the degree to which teams became fully developed. Knowledge of procedures for grouping students for instruction and for interrelating curriculum also emerged as necessary skills for teachers functioning in well-developed teams.

In the Plodzik study, the amount of common planning time for teachers on teams did not show a relationship with whether or not teams functioned fully. More recent research (Erb, 2000a; Felner et al., 1997; Flowers, 2000) illustrates a close connection between the amount of planning time available to teachers and a host of desirable outcomes, including increased academic achievement.

Characteristics of Highly Effective Teams

Knowing the phases of team life should make it easier to identify teams that are operating, in all of these phases, in the most exemplary ways. Studies of the very best teams (George & Stevenson, 1989; Kain, 1998; Strahan, Bowles, Richardson, & Hanawald, 1997) indicate that, while no one formula determines the nature of highly effective teams, some distinctive trends deserve the attention of those attempting to implement or improve an interdisciplinary team organization.

When asked to describe the most effective teams in their schools, principals of some of the nation's better middle schools agreed on what might be called "team character." Teams that are identified as the best in the school, by the principal, tend to have the following seven attributes.

1. The team has an elementary flavor. Even the most experienced secondary administrators describe the best teams as those that have a student-centered style. Such teams are far more likely to have members with elementary teacher certification and experience. Rarely are the very best teams identified by school principals staffed entirely by teachers with secondary certification.

2. The team, while perhaps student-centered, is committed to academic outcomes. The members of the team value academic achievement and are committed to the success of their students in the subject areas teachers represent. Teachers see themselves as willing to do almost anything to help their students be more successful, academically and otherwise. Expectations are made clear to students and parents. Even small achievements are seen as worthy of recognition and reward. The team, as a whole, possesses a spirit of advocacy with regard to the students they share.

3. Distinctive academic climates are matched by equally distinctive team policies in regard to behavioral expectations and climate. Team members work out collaborative policies and establish systems of operation and accountability. A formal plan with rules and rule-making procedures is often in place. Reinforcement and emphasis upon good citizenship through recognition and reward are as important as more punitive restrictions and punishments.

4. The team works hard to develop and maintain a sense of community among the teachers, students, and parents of the team. Team names, mascots, logos, T-shirts, buttons, pins, and colors help signify belonging. The very best teams go beyond symbols, to specialized activities of an astounding number and variety, which build and nurture the sense of community on the team: town meetings, award and recognition assemblies, student-of the-month designations, camping trips, field days, competitions within and between teams, clubs, fairs, plays, musicals, parties, special suppers, and intramurals.

5. Exemplary teams develop unique and effective policies and procedures for communicating with parents. Good teams work to not only report their students' progress but also to involve parents in the educational processes that result in those progress reports. Teams use a variety of techniques with parents, including team newsletters and memos, progress reports, and team dinners and picnics. Most significantly, however, is that on these teams teachers saw themselves, as one principal described, as having a "customer orientation" and thought of themselves as providing a service to parents instead of doing them a favor.

6. A proactive posture is at the center of the nature of the very best teams. They do not wait to be told to contact parents. They initiate reward and recognition systems. They are willing to try something without being guaranteed ahead of time that it will be successful. They try, and when they fail, they examine their behavior and do not look for scapegoats.

7. With their peers, they attempt to remain diverse but unified. Teachers on the team recognize and celebrate, even joke about, their differences instead of attempting to eliminate them. They are, however, wise enough to know that a sense of unity requires the attention and effort of all of the members of the group. Principals describe such teams as characterized by a "healthy give and take," "accepting each other's shortcomings," and as "close professional friends, but not necessarily close personal friends" (George & Stevenson, 1989).

Alternative Types of Interdisciplinary Team Organization

Although interdisciplinary team organization is essential to the exemplary middle school, there is not only one acceptable model of such organization. Our study of exemplary middle schools reveals a variety of ways of organizing teachers in an interdisciplinary fashion.

Small, Partner Teams Teams vary in regard to size, roles and responsibilities of teachers, student composition, teacher autonomy, and the way time is structured. All of these variations, however, fully satisfy the four phases of interdisciplinary team life. Interdisciplinary team organization in the exemplary middle school varies considerably in the number of teachers and students who make up a separate team. Perhaps the most significant recent trends in interdisciplinary team organization have been in the area of team size. The range of size commonly encountered extends from teams of two teachers and 40–60 students to teams of six teachers and 150–190 students. Recent experience, however, has led more middle school leaders to favor smaller teams of two and three teachers.

History-making Boyce Middle School, in Upper St. Clair, Pennsylvania, for example, was one of the first middle schools in the country and continues to offer exemplary programs. Boyce, like many other exemplary middle schools, offers small two-teacher teams to students in the 5th and 6th grades. As leaders there described it in 1991:

> Because of our belief in nurturance, students are randomly placed in heterogeneously grouped two-teacher teams. A student spends approximately three hours a day with each academic teacher. This enables the teacher and student to develop a strong sense of bonding. One teacher is responsible for reading, language arts, and social studies. The other team member is responsible for math, science, and an exploratory component. Interdisciplinary teaming is strongly encouraged and, as a result, the team develops a strong sense of identity and pride. Because the skills and achievement levels of our learners are distributed across a broad continuum, different methods of instruction and strategies for grouping are used to adequately meet their academic needs. The homeroom size is approximately 28 and instructional groups vary from discipline to discipline and from time to time.

On the question of proper team size, we are in full agreement with Arnold and Stevenson (1998), two investigators who for years observed the advantages of smaller two- and three-teacher teams. Many advantages exist for what Arnold and Stevenson refer to as "partner teams." As a consequence of having fewer students:

- Teachers know each of their students better
- Closer teacher-student relationships prevail
- Students know each other better
- Teachers know parents better, and vice versa
- Teachers are able to require and assess more student products, such as writing
- Teachers are better able to build a curriculum that matches student needs
- All assessments can be more thorough and student-centered
- Classroom management and discipline can be less regimented and coercive
- Teachers can make decisions and come to agreement more easily
- Fewer personality conflicts emerge among teachers

- Teachers can be more flexible with the schedule and the curriculum
- An integrated curriculum is facilitated
- Formal and difficult teacher-based advisory programs are less necessary
- A more natural, personal teacher-based advisory process emerges
- More opportunities are available for student self-government, initiative, and responsibility

As Arnold and Stevenson (1998) state:

> In these smaller teams people get to know each other better and find agreement more easily. Because a two-teacher team has on average half as many students as a four-teacher team, there is a greater potential to create a strong spirit of belonging and community. Curriculum can be more easily attuned to students' interests and needs. Indeed, a great deal of the most innovative curriculum work we've seen has occurred in partner teams in which teachers and students apparently have been able to plan and organize their studies relatively easily. Comprehensive student-centered assessment appears to be more easily accomplished. Occurrences of student self-government are notably more frequent and more highly developed among smaller teams, and students appear to take initiative and accept responsibility more easily in these groupings. Discipline is also less external, rule-bound, and adversarial, and student advising appears to occur more naturally throughout the day. (p. 10)

A recent study indicates that when certain conditions are met, the small, partner team "provides a potentially powerful alternative to the interdisciplinary team format which is dominant in middle schools" (Bishop, 2000, p. 171). Teacher choice in team membership is important, as is sharing a belief system and common work ethic between team members. Complementary strengths and a positive personal relationship are essential to full functioning of small teams. When everything is in place, teachers experience a "heightened sense of professional efficacy and satisfaction . . . supported by increased collegial support, parent communication, modeling for students, added professional perspective, and risk-taking. . . . The overall enjoyment of teaching these teachers express suggests they also find a rare and high level of sustenance in their work" (Bishop, 2000, p. 171).

Perhaps as a consequence of these advantages, schools organized into small teams, of two and three teachers, are becoming more common around the nation. In Hillsborough County, Florida, one of the largest school districts in the country, educators have found great value in organizing each of its 34 middle schools so that all 6th graders in the district are members of two-teacher teams. Jackie Heard, assistant superintendent for middle schools, points to a lengthening series of higher scores on state tests for the district's 6th graders as evidence of the value of small teams (Personal communication, June 10, 2001).

The needs of the students, not the size of the school, often lead to small teams. At giant-sized Creekland Middle School (3,200 students), near Atlanta, Georgia, all 6th graders have two-teacher teams. At the other end of the continuum, at the highly advantaged and very small Duke School for Children Middle School, in Durham, North Carolina, small teams are also the norm, and consequently "each child is known personally in our intimate setting" (Cheryl Moody, personal communication, October 25, 2000).

Nor does location dictate team size, given that two-teacher teams are in place at dozens, perhaps hundreds, of other middle schools across the continent. All 21 middle schools in Guilford County, North Carolina, are organized so that two-teacher teams are the norm for all 6th graders. At Wantagh Middle School, in Wantagh, New York, 6th graders are organized into two-teacher teams, as they are at McDonald Middle School, in East Lansing, Michigan, and Batavia Middle School, in Batavia, Illinois. In California, two-teacher teams for 6th graders are the norm, such as at Dartmouth Middle School, in San Jose. In the province of British Columbia, small teams are also the norm. At George Bonner Middle School, in Mill Bay, British Columbia, the 7th grade, when students enter middle school, is organized into two-teacher teams. Two-teacher teams are also the norm in many middle schools in Washington State. Kevin Evoy, long-time middle school principal in Olympia, Washington, described the organization of small teams.

> The fundamental instructional unit at Marshal Middle School is the "core team" that brings together two teachers and 50–60 students for approximately five hours each day. One teacher in each pair is responsible for an integrated program of Language Arts, Reading, Social Studies, and Health (Humanities Core), while the other teacher provides an integrated program for Mathematics, Science, and Applied Technology (Technology Core). These two teachers share common planning time daily and are responsible for organizing the time students are with them based on the nature of their learning activities, rather than artificial school-wide "periods." This, it is highly likely—and highly desirable, in that it is the *curriculum* and not the clock that "drives" the schedule—that there may be variance in each team's use of their core time from day to day. (Kevin Evoy, personal communication, November 14, 1995)

Wakulla Middle School, in Crawfordville, Florida, one of the nation's most exemplary middle schools, has been organized into small teams for virtually all of its nearly 25-year history, for students in all grades 6 through 8. A high-scoring school when it comes to state and national tests, WMS tried larger, four-teacher teams during the beginning of one school year a decade ago, believing that it would make curriculum planning easier for teachers. Teachers saw so many of the benefits of small teams quickly disappear with the move to larger teams that they became eager to give up the advantages of teaching only one subject and to return to an organization that required them to teach two, three, or four subjects each day. By Christmas, teachers were clamoring for a return to smaller teams, a request that was honored the following January.

If the advantages of small teams are so clear, why are so many middle schools organized in other ways? Several reasons have been cited by Arnold and Stevenson (1998). Principals may believe that hiding a weak teacher in a small team arrangement is harder. Also, personality conflicts, when they occur, might be more destructive of both teacher efforts and student outcomes. Some principals believe that young adolescents benefit from regular contact with more adults.

Most important, perhaps, is that many secondary subject-oriented teachers are either unable or unwilling to teach two or more subjects daily. At Wakulla, however, teachers assert that when the number of students is drastically downsized, the number of preparations is far less important. When a teacher is faced with 150 or more students daily, it may be important to have only one subject to plan and teach. With small teams, a teacher may have only 45–50 students a day and may teach the same students two or three times during that day. Under these circumstances, experienced teachers say that subject preparation is not nearly the problem it is on larger teams. Certainly, no evidence shows that academic achievement suffers on small teams in which teachers teach more than one subject. We predict, therefore, that small teams will become more popular in the next decade of the evolution of middle schools, and we think this will be seen especially in school districts characterized by great ethnic diversity and substantial student poverty.

Many middle schools offer students teams of various sizes, and many of those who use two-teacher teams also use three- and four-teacher teams at grades 7 and 8. The middle schools in Guilford County, North Carolina, for example, each have teams of varied sizes, with teams of two, three, and four teachers with appropriate numbers of students. Two-teacher teams are placed in the 6th grades, three-teacher teams in the 7th, and four-teacher teams in the 8th. Educators in Guilford County believe that this progression provides incoming 6th graders with the supportive structure they need and gradually moves toward more teacher subject specialization as the students near the transition to high school. West Middle School, in Aurora, Colorado, has had teams of two, four, and five teachers, and MacDonald Middle School, in East Lansing, Michigan, has had teams of two, three, and four teachers each, for much the same reason as the Guilford County design.

Donnegal Middle School, in Mt. Joy, Pennsylvania, was designed to operate, when it opened in 1992, with teams of different sizes for each grade level. In the 6th grade, there are self-contained classes for the first nine weeks, then teams of two teachers and their students are created for the remainder of the year. Each 6th grade teacher teaches English and reading, dividing the remainder of the curriculum in an interdisciplinary fashion. The 7th grade has two three-teacher teams. Each teacher teaches English and reading, and mathematics, science, and social studies are divided among the three teachers. At the 8th grade level, two four-teacher teams exist, each teacher teaching one of the basic academic subjects, plus developmental reading through his or her own subject area.

Nipher Middle School, in Kirkwood, Missouri, another long-time high-quality middle school, is an excellent example of a school that has offered a variety of team designs. Sixth grade students and parents have been given the following choice (within the limits of staff flexibility): a modified self-contained classroom where one teacher will be responsible for teaching students the four basic subjects (language arts, social studies, science, and math); a two-teacher team in which one teacher is responsible for language arts and social studies, and another for math and science; a four-teacher team, students heterogeneously grouped, and each teacher responsible for one subject; or a two-teacher combined 6th and 7th grade team, multiage grouped, offering a two-year curriculum with a great deal of individualized instruction and student self-direction. Seventh grade students at Nipher have the same options, with the exception of the self-contained classroom, and 8th graders are all assigned to four-teacher teams. Nipher designs its teacher teams on the basis of student maturity, allowing for the greatest flexibility in the 6th grade and gradually moving toward the large four-teacher team for all students in the 8th grade.

Kinawa Middle School, in Okemos, Michigan, another of the better middle schools in America, has had a special method for organizing the faculty, in a basically interdisciplinary way, but with opportunities for other emphases as well. For most of its history (opened in 1969), Kinawa has organized its faculty into three different types of learning environments. As at Nipher, parents, students, and teachers have been given considerable latitude in choosing which academic environment they prefer. Sixth grade students may opt for two-teacher teams, in which they are taught the four basic subjects or they may choose the "Sixth, Seventh, and Eighth Grade House Program." Seventh and 8th grade students, and their parents, also have choices when it comes to team size. An organization of teachers, as it has been done at Kinawa, offers the maximum choice to everyone involved. It offers a situation that recognizes value in each person's preference for a learning environment. And it permits the design of a variety of alternatives that are possible without a prohibitive amount of staff development time and expense. This offers some explanation for Kinawa's successful long-term operation over a 30-year period.

Core Programs   For a number of years at Parker Junior High School, in Parker, Colorado, three very different designs were available. Within the same school, students could choose a traditional departmentalized option, a conventional middle school style interdisciplinary team organization, or an intensified core program. In the intensified core program, students learn in an interdisciplinary team context but concentrate on learning one academic subject at a time, remaining with the same teacher four to five periods every day for up to six weeks.

Many other exemplary middle schools, often on the West Coast, operate on what they also refer to as a core program. (See Chapter 7 for further details about core programs.) At Talent Middle School (TMS), in Talent, Oregon, for example, students are part of a multiage, multiyear core program. They stay with the same language arts and social studies teacher for all three years. During the 2000–2001 school year, some of the 6th grade students followed core or team long block schedules on an A/B schedule (see Chapter 8) that looked like this:

Blue Day	Silver Day
Health (75 minutes)	Band (75 minutes)
Mathematics (75 minutes)	Science and mathematics (75 minutes)
Homeroom (35 minutes)	Homeroom (35 minutes)
Lunch	Lunch
Physical education (75 minutes)	Core (150 minutes)
Core (75 minutes)	

On a Blue Day, the students were in language arts and social studies for 75 minutes. On the next, they were in these classes for 150 minutes. This is a substantial amount of time to be with one teacher, and continuing with that same teacher and student cohort for three years means that, at TMS, a significant personal bond can be created between teachers and students. At Sequoia Middle School, in Redlands, California, in 2001, 6th, 7th, and 8th grade students were organized into grade level core teams. Core teachers and students were together for three of the seven daily periods: reading, language arts, and social studies. The core teacher is also the advisor for the students in that group, so a great deal of intense teacher-student time is spent together during these multiple periods. Because each team has three core teachers (along with a mathematics and science teacher who has common planning time with the core teachers), each core teacher sees only 60 students per day.

Factors Influencing Team Size and Teaching Responsibilities Often, the variance in the size or design of the team stems from the existence of unequal numbers of students in schools using chronological age-graded grouping. A school may, for example, have an unusually large group of 7th graders compared with the numbers in the 6th or 8th grades, making it impossible to have teams of equal size. It may also be the design of the building that dictates the size of teams within the school. The middle school may have inherited an old junior or senior high school building not designed for team organization. The building may have little or no pattern to the way in which regular classrooms are grouped; for example, three classrooms together on one end of the hall, two at the other end, four in the center. The possibilities for grouping classrooms offered by older buildings seem infinite, while regularity seems almost nonexistent. School principals often demonstrate considerable creativity in making the most of their buildings, and varied team sizes are a common response.

For whatever reasons the size of a team varies, the number of teachers on a team usually sets limits on the number of different subjects each teacher teaches. And almost always, the four basic subjects are included, regardless of the number of teachers on the team. When two teachers form a team, as they do at Boyce, Guilford County, Wakulla, or in the 6th grades of the 34 middle schools in Hillsborough County, Florida, most often each teacher takes the major responsibility for planning and teaching at least two of the four basic academic subjects. Frequently, the teachers divide their responsibilities on the basis of personal preferences, desire for collaboration, or perceived subject matter compatibility as well as certification requirements.

The most frequent combinations for two-teacher teams, possibly a common holdover from the days of the core curriculum in the junior and senior high schools, are social studies and language arts and math and science. But there are other possibilities. Teachers could choose to share math and science and to assume individual responsibility for language arts and social studies. Teams can and do divide it differently: language arts and math or science and social studies. Rarely, however, do two-teacher teams at these schools opt to share all four of the basic academic subjects in a way that includes each person teaching all of the four.

Three-Teacher Teams   A number of middle schools have teams composed of three teachers. At Griffin Middle School, in Smyrna, Georgia; in two middle schools in Dothan, Alabama (based partially on the model at Griffin); and in many other middle schools, such as those in Guilford County, North Carolina, the three-teacher team has been the norm for many years. When a team of three teachers is assigned to teach the four basics (as is almost always the case), several possibilities for teaching responsibilities exist. Three teachers usually share the responsibilities for four subjects one of two ways: by having all three teachers teach all four subjects or by having each teacher responsible for one subject, while all three combine to teach the fourth.

Which path is chosen often depends on the number of elementary or secondary trained teachers on the team. In the 6th grade teams, where elementary trained teachers predominate, the pattern often displays the three teachers commonly planning and teaching all four subjects in a coordinated and collaborative way. In the 7th grade teams, teaching responsibilities seem split evenly between teams in which all teachers teach all subjects and those in which each teaches two subjects, one separately and one in common. In the 8th grade teams, the latter method predominates.

In many teams of three teachers at the 8th grade level, the teachers often plan and teach collaboratively those subjects that require their combined efforts to do well. An 8th grade team might, for example, be composed of three secondary trained teachers, with certification in language arts, social studies, and math, but not in science. Frequently, these teachers will choose to share the responsibility for science and teach the others individually. By pooling their expertise, they develop a science program that is respectable and maintain their individual specialties in the other areas. Schools that have opted for the three-teacher team have discovered that, by necessity, it produces a great deal of team planning in comparison with any other size team.

Four-Teacher Teams   Teams composed of four teachers are by far the most common, probably because the basic academic curriculum is most commonly thought of as having four distinct elements. Even in schools that would describe themselves as far from being exemplary, the four-teacher unit is often present. The four-teacher team organization is standard, but not necessarily better than other possibilities.

The four-teacher situation usually finds one teacher having special responsibility for one subject area. Each teacher is a resource person for one of the four basic areas, with state certification or college preparation or both in that particular area. This special responsibility can be handled, however, in several different ways. Each of these different ways is acceptable in terms of the definition of team organization.

The most common division of responsibilities on the four-teacher team assigns almost total responsibility for one subject area to each teacher. At the new Chain of Lakes Middle School, in Orlando, Florida, the team's math teacher plans and teaches all the math. The social studies, science, and language arts teachers each also plan and teach their individual subjects to the students on the team. Because they meet together regularly, however, teachers using this approach are likely to be aware of what is happening in the other academic areas and may contribute suggestions for improvements even though their formal responsibilities do not extend to teaching these other subjects.

A second, far less frequently found method for assigning teacher responsibilities on four-teacher teams follows the model known as Individually Guided Education (IGE), developed by the Institute for the Development of Educational Activities (IDEA), a creation of the Kettering Foundation. This model usually identified resource people in each of the special areas but expanded their teaching responsibilities to all four subjects.

At Spring Hill Middle School, in High Springs, Florida, teachers successfully followed the IGE model for a decade, perhaps longer. Each team had a resource teacher in each of the four areas. The resource person in math, for example, took the major role in planning the mathematics instruction for the students on the team. This involved many things: selecting objectives from the scope and sequence outlined in county and school curriculum guides, suggesting instructional activities, designing evaluative instruments, gathering materials and being certain that resources are ready, and many other activities. But when the math unit was ready to be taught, all members of the team were involved in the instruction.

All four teachers taught math, but all four teachers were not likely to be teaching for identical math objectives. The teacher on the team least comfortable with teaching math may, for instance, have taught remedial long division for six weeks, while two other teachers had different instructional assignments and the math resource teacher had the task of teaching the pre-algebra unit. The process was the same in the other three areas. All teachers on the team were involved in the planning and instruction of each unit, but in different ways. The same basic process has been followed, with some differences, at Oregon Middle School, in Oregon, Wisconsin; Glen Ridge Middle School, in Glenn Ridge, New Jersey; and Trotwood–Madison Middle School, in Trotwood, Ohio. We believe that, as middle school educators begin to search anew for more success in interdisciplinary curriculum work, the IGE process may regain a measure of its former popularity.

With this in mind, a third possibility exists for the four-teacher team, but because of several persistent challenges, it is often only partially implemented, even in the most exemplary middle schools. Teachers could integrate the four subjects into truly interdisciplinary units, thematic curriculum plans that weave together the several disciplines into coherent wholes. At Brown Barge Middle School, in Pensacola, Florida, teachers have engaged in this type of complex teaming since the early 1990s. At Brown Barge, all teachers and all students are engaged, all day, in a curriculum plan that integrates all subjects, all year, for all three years at the school. In this regard, Brown Barge Middle School may be unique.

Thematic interdisciplinary units appear more or less frequently in almost all good middle school programs. However, few middle schools (other than Brown Barge) seem to be able to sustain the use of thematic units as the curriculum of the basic instructional program for a majority of the day over a long period of several years or more. Recently, however, several schools have begun to emulate Brown Barge. King Middle School, in Portland, Maine, an exemplary middle school for many reasons, offers Expeditionary Learning, in which students engage in an integrated curriculum with an Outward Bound approach. At King, teams of teachers begin with state standards and proceed to plot a 9–12 week in-depth study that connects to the surrounding community through a service-learning component. Crabapple Middle School, in Fulton County, Georgia, in the fall of 2002 implemented the Expeditionary Learning approach as well. We discuss these approaches to integrated curriculum more in Chapter 3.

Gradewide Teams   A number of exemplary middle schools find themselves at the other end of the range in terms of size of team, with five-teacher teams relatively frequent and teams of six and seven teachers less frequent. Teams composed of 8–12 teachers are much less frequent and often can be described as gradewide teams, which break into smaller, informal subject-oriented groups composed of teachers in the same discipline who often do a great deal of team teaching. The large teams (more than six teachers) tend to subdivide, with each subdivision acting like a miniature subject-oriented department.

At Hand Middle School, in Columbia, South Carolina, teachers operate on what we call "gradewide teams." As many as a dozen teachers attempt to work together with all of the students at one grade level. In this situation, the teachers who teach the same subject operate as a miniature academic department. All of the teachers at the grade level, however, have common planning time and often spend that time on grade level concerns and activities.

Teams of five teachers usually resemble the four-teacher team in that they assign one subject to each teacher for both planning and teaching. The extra member usually comes, as at Glen Ridge Middle School in New Jersey, from the separation of reading from language arts, because of increased emphasis on reading skills now found in almost every school. At Glen Ridge this works out to about 45 minutes per day in each of the five subjects.

Lincoln Middle School, in Gainesville, Florida, has differed, in some years, from this pattern, using four teachers to teach five basic subjects. Having separated reading from the remainder of the language arts program, Lincoln staffers found themselves still heavily committed to other aspects of their program (advisor-advisee and exploratory courses). This commitment resulted in a four-person academic team in which one teacher had the responsibility for language arts, one for reading, one for math, and one for both science and social studies. This means at Lincoln, when this model was used, that students received a half-year of science and a half-year of social studies.

Based on the definition of team organization, all of the above descriptions are appropriate, although larger groups risk losing the many benefits that come with teaming. In the exemplary middle school, interdisciplinary team organization almost always means groups of from two to five teachers who share responsibility for planning and sometimes teaching curriculum in more than one academic area to the same group of students, with the same schedule, in the same part of the building. Teachers almost always represent strength in one particular subject, and they may teach only this subject to all the students on the team. Or they may teach two, three, or four different subjects in various collaborative arrangements with their team members. Frequently in some schools, and occasionally in almost all schools, teachers from various academic perspectives will combine their areas in thematic units. All of these efforts fall in the range of interdisciplinary team organization, and while some are more extensive in the amount of teaming done by the teachers, the greatest benefits of the interdisciplinary team organization accrue to both teachers and students in all of the various models described here.

ROLES AND RESPONSIBILITIES OF TEAMS AND THEIR MEMBERS

The roles and responsibilities of team members vary, depending upon the model of team organization followed. Virtually all exemplary middle schools, however, avoid complex hierarchical arrangements designating master teachers, regular teachers, and other, less qualified members. They instead are much more likely to use a model that assumes a much greater degree of equality of expertise on the team. Team leaders are often chosen and relied upon, but they are rarely given enough extra perquisites to make taking on the tasks worthwhile. Most often team leaders serve because they feel a sense of professional duty, or because they need the challenge of extra responsibility and the consequent opportunities for personal and professional growth. Almost always, team leaders work longer and harder than even they had believed possible.

What must teams, once organized, accomplish? When teams meet, what concerns are central? What decisions must be made? Members of a team in the exemplary middle school participate in decisions on many of the following: scheduling of classes and teacher assignments, student schedules, patterns of student grouping for instruction within the team, selection and development of curriculum plans and supportive materials, correlation of curriculum plans from different subject areas to ensure maximum effectiveness, space allocation, budget disbursement, use of blocks of time for planning and instruction, team teaching, selection of new staff members, parent contacts, placing students in special programs, orientation of new students, evaluation and in-service staff development of team members, and cooperation with special area teachers. Some teacher responsibilities are more important than others, and few decisions can be made without taking the whole school into account.

Teaching Responsibilities

In many exemplary middle schools the team decides on the teaching responsibilities for each member. The team must decide how many subjects each teacher will teach and what those subjects will be. Once the teams have been established, with the principal seeing to it that certification and related problems are resolved, the teams can be given the responsibility for staff-subject assignments. This is the case at Wakulla Middle School, in Crawfordville, Florida, and has been for 25 years. Once the teachers have been matched to be certain certification is properly covered, and the lunch and planning times have been established, teachers on teams are able to make the rest of the decisions as to what will be taught, by whom, when, and where.

Arranging the Physical Environment

Having been assigned the full complement of rooms or space in an appropriate area, the team must decide how these rooms should be used. Will space be assigned to individual teachers, in pairs, or some other combination? Will the space be assigned for the year, on a more temporary basis, or not at all? Will there be a planning room where each teacher will have a small space?

Structuring Academic Class Time

In most exemplary middle schools, teams are responsible for relatively large blocks of time to be devoted to instruction in the subjects for which the team has been given responsibility. Typically, the team is notified as to when their students will have certain activities such as lunch, physical education, and exploratory courses. Teams then decide what subjects will be taught at what times and often how much time will be devoted to each subject or how frequently the subject will be studied each week. The teams are responsible for establishing, evaluating, and reestablishing a daily schedule for subjects, teachers, and students. At Sarasota Middle School, in Sarasota, Florida, teams of teachers design virtually the total day, except for lunch, physical education, and unified arts.

Grouping Students

Often teams have some autonomy in the issue of student grouping for instruction within the team. The team may have to decide whether students will be grouped according to ability, and, if so, how they will be grouped. Some teams group heterogeneously in all classes, others group by ability for reading or math or both. Teams frequently attempt to have social studies, science, and exploratory classes grouped without reference to ability. Typically, however, teams that must group students according to ability for one or two subjects find it difficult to regroup heterogeneously for the other classes.

Scheduling Students

In the 21st century, computer programs have helped eliminate some of the most difficult chores of scheduling students on teams. Often, a team of teachers will receive a schedule that has groups of students built into every section taught by members of the team, with exploratory or unified arts options also built right in. While this new technology can make onerous tasks simpler, teacher autonomy and flexibility can be lost in the process.

Principals of exemplary middle schools sometimes discover that teams can do an outstanding job of scheduling students on their teams for their academic classes, with or without the use of technology to assist them. Teachers can quickly establish a method for assigning students to special programs, such as those for students with disabilities, and then parcel out students to different sections of academic subjects within the team. Teaming makes it possible for teachers to possess knowledge of students that enables them to decide which students should be grouped together and which ones should be separated. Teachers also find it frequently necessary to change a student's schedule, and when the team has this responsibility the task can be accomplished much more efficiently. Having teachers make decisions about who studies what, with whom, at what time also relieves the administrators of a tremendously time-consuming burden. This way teachers appreciate having an important role to play in the decisions that have a daily effect on their lives, and administrators, and sometimes counselors, are free for duties that they would otherwise be unable to perform. When teachers do the scheduling, their sense of control and their perceptions of their professional efficacy may benefit, even though the process takes a great deal of time.

One teacher from an exemplary middle school, experienced in the process of scheduling students, described the approach that worked in her school two decades ago. It still works this way in many schools.

> During pre-planning, each team of teachers (usually four academic teachers and three support teachers) sits as a group to "hand schedule" reading, math, language arts, and science/social studies (we offer a half year of each). Our first considerations are to those classes or programs with the least flexibility; classes for emotionally handicapped, educably mentally retarded, learning disabled and gifted students are scheduled first. These classes may only be offered two or three of the four possible times and therefore must be scheduled initially. Teachers of these specific classes present the teams with their time requirement for each individual student. These classes and other compensatory classes are offered throughout the day and can be scheduled as are the regular academic classes.
>
> Once these restrictive considerations are negotiated, the team teachers then continue by scheduling their own academics. Each team has the option of grouping homogeneously for one or two classes. For instance, if reading and math were to be ability grouped by a specific team, those classes would be scheduled first. Reading and math levels for each student would be determined (results from standardized tests), the students grouped, and then assigned to a class section. A student might be high in reading and low in math, so he/she would fall in a high reading class and a lower math class. Classes do not rotate as complete sections from one teacher to another. Students will have a new group of classmates in each class with only a few students following similar schedules. Classes that are randomly grouped are scheduled last. In this case, numbers of students are balanced to give each class an appropriate load.
>
> Changes from day to day can be made at the team's discretion. Our administrators leave the responsibility of this process up to the teams, with the team leader reporting back all difficulties or problems, and final decisions regarding grouping.
>
> Our exploratory program rotates every twelve weeks and students may select the classes they want to take. Each student makes a first, second and third choice. From this selection, the homeroom or advisory teacher assigns students to classes based on the students' choices and availability of classes. This same process repeats each time exploratories rotate.

Through this process of teachers scheduling their own students, the responsibility for developing appropriate learning activities and situations is left for teachers and teams to determine. We appreciate the opportunity of making these decisions and now perform this role automatically. (V. Childs, personal communication, March 4, 1980)

Selecting and Distributing Texts and Other Materials

Some middle schools follow a multitext approach to instruction, which permits teams to select the texts that best suit their students and the interests and teaching preferences of instructors. Almost all schools encourage team participation in decisions about texts or materials that the whole school must use. Some administrators turn over a portion of the operating budget of the school to each team. Teams at Fort Clarke Middle School, in Gainesville, Florida, for example, are given a budget of $10 per student at the beginning of the year, which amounts to about $1,500 per team. The teams apportion these funds as they determine their needs, but team budgets may include basic items such as a budget for copying, chalk, video rentals, and other items such as field trips, materials for special integrated curriculum units, and so on. This type of team budgeting enhances the teams' feelings of autonomy and frees the principal from the tiresome and sometimes demeaning role of keeper of the purse, doling out sometimes large, other times minuscule, amounts of money, but each time requiring a form or a response to a request.

Teamed Instruction

The complexity and diversity of the attempt to properly instruct middle school students have led teams of teachers in virtually every middle school in the nation to attempt, in one way or another, to combine their talents and their efforts to bring about a more effective educational program for the students they serve. The interdisciplinary teacher organization, as the foundation of the entire middle school program, recognizes, by its existence, the mandate to form team efforts to meet the needs of the students. While we have steadfastly maintained that interdisciplinary team organization and team teaching were not synonymous, and that the presence of the first does not always require or imply the presence of the second, it is hard to imagine an interdisciplinary unit that did not evolve from a team organization of at least rudimentary dimensions. It is also difficult to conceive of an interdisciplinary group of teachers who, having dealt effectively with the myriad problems that confront them regularly, did not at least discuss the possibility of coordinating their instructional efforts more closely. From this point to teamed instruction is a very small step.

Teams must deal with all of the team management issues that confront them, but teamed instruction is usually a much more voluntary practice, dependent upon several important conditions. A sufficient amount of common planning time, supplementing the planning time that individual teachers need, is probably the most important of the prerequisites to teamed instruction. Many exemplary middle schools are able to provide teachers with two planning periods per day, one for the team efforts and another for the individual teacher. Teamed instruction simply requires additional planning time, and without it few teams will be able to maintain the effort for long.

A second, and perhaps no less critical, requirement for the success of teamed instruction emerges from the nature of interpersonal communication (Arnold & Stevenson, 1998). Teaming resembles married life in several ways. When it is working well, it is beautiful; when it is not, it can be horrible. Much of the work of the team on a regular basis will require interpersonal skills and attitudes of the highest caliber. An especially large supply of patience and tolerance always is in demand. Much of the success of the team will depend on how well members communicate with each other: knowing how to listen so that others will talk to you, knowing how to talk so that others will listen to you, and knowing how to solve problems in a democratic fashion. Teachers who enjoy being with each other will seek opportunities to plan and teach together.

The third major component in successful teamed instruction deals with the level of proficiency among the team members in the area of planning thematic units (George, Lawrence, & Bushnell, 1998). Because team planning is different from the lesson planning that individual teachers must do, it will consume large portions of teacher time if the level of skill in planning as a team is not what it should be. Team members must know how to plan for instruction as a group.

The extent to which these three factors are satisfactorily resolved will determine the amount of teamed instruction that will occur. When time, predisposition, and skills are at a minimum, few effective interdisciplinary thematic units will be offered to the students. Minimally functioning teams will be consumed by the mechanics of team management and unable to find the necessary time or energy to engage in team teaching of the type most educators admire.

In most middle schools, teamed instruction is usually limited to an attempt, once or twice during a year, to plan and implement an interdisciplinary unit of a thematic nature, incorporating all of the teachers and subjects on the team. A few exemplary middle schools (e.g., Brown Barge, in Florida; King, in Maine; and Crabapple, in Georgia) have been able to move from this position to one that permits the frequent offering of interdisciplinary units throughout the school. Time, interpersonal skills, and planning skills are such that, in those schools, teams work together effectively and efficiently, offering an exciting thematic program to the students fortunate enough to be involved. The terms used to describe the typical effort at teamed instruction are many and varied: *core, multidisciplinary, interdisciplinary, thematic,* and so on. Most frequently, however, the process and the end product are similar, regardless of the name applied. Here, the term *teamed instruction* stands for all efforts of teachers from interdisciplinary groups who plan and teach together. See Chapter 3 for more on integrating the curriculum.

Given adequate time and the interpersonal resources to carry on, the planning process becomes extremely important. Teachers with experience in the design and implementation of teamed instruction suggest, and we agree, that, even under the most felicitous conditions, a team should try only two to four such units in the first year. It should use a planning cycle of six weeks followed by implementation of the unit on the seventh week. (See George et al., 1998, for extensive discussion and illustration of the team unit planning model.) Stressing the need to interpret the model flexibly, we offer the following seven-step process.

1. Week One: Choose an interdisciplinary theme by combining objectives from state or local standards or other documents that present required content in a separate subject format.
2. Week Two: Spell out clearly the subject area objectives that will be covered in the unit and exchange all of these materials among the members of the team.
3. Week Three: Team members work independently, gathering resources and developing learning activities to match them.
4. Week Four: Team members meet to examine the activities and materials developed by each teacher and to decide about the length of time to be set aside for the unit. A tentative schedule of events is produced at this meeting, tasks are divided, and the remainder of the week is spent in preparations related to these tasks.
5. Week Five: The final schedule for the unit is produced, with available resources, speakers, room schedules, student regrouping, and other details worked out.
6. Week Six: A meeting toward the end of the week helps teachers check on last-minute details and make emergency assignments and changes.
7. Week Seven: Implementation of the unit.

Considering the painstaking efforts required to develop and implement plans for teamed instruction that involve as many as five or more teachers and up to 200 students, it is little wonder that only a few such units are produced throughout a typical school year. We are aware, however, that many teachers in many schools seem to defy the laws of human effort in their determination to provide the best possible program for their students. Some schools have produced thematic units that were planned and taught involving the entire school. Others, such as Brown Barge, have thematic curriculum as the constant process in every team. More often, what emerges is the joint effort of the academic teachers on the team, supported and supplemented by specialists from other areas. One example of the thousands of fine interdisciplinary units that take place in middle schools everywhere occurred some years ago on "W Team" at Lincoln Middle School, in Gainesville, Florida.

Following a discussion about the need for greater team unity, the team teachers decided to "build some bridges," which led eventually to the theme for an interdisciplinary unit titled "Bridges." The teachers identified three general goals for the unit, in addition to the need for greater unity: to offer students a different, yet meaningful, experience in learning; to move team teaching from theory to practice on the team; and to strengthen parental involvement. Because this team was making its first attempt to produce such a unit, it was limited to one week's duration. Subsequent team meetings produced a series of learning objectives and a series of learning activities to match the objectives. Several of the teachers decided to venture into teaching areas other than their regular specialty. On the Saturday before the unit began, the team met at school to put up the props of the unit, and on Monday, following six weeks of intermittent planning, the unit was ready to go. To arouse student interest, the team posted riddles that hinted at the coming special unit and placed an advertisement in the school newspaper.

A variety of objectives and learning activities were offered in several subject areas: language arts, social studies, science, industrial arts, and the advisor-advisee program. The language arts teacher worked on the understanding of the literal and symbolic meanings of the word *bridge* upon exposure to "bridges" in different genres of literature and in offering the opportunity for creative writing. The social studies students were involved in locating famous bridges, reading about them, reviewing the historical development of bridge design, and investigating local bridges. In science, the teacher emphasized the physics of three types of bridge structures. In an exploratory model building class, the students worked in groups applying their knowledge and understanding of the physics of bridges to the construction of a model bridge. In the team's advisor-advisee groups, an emphasis was placed on building interpersonal bridges, using activities such as one called "The Friendship Bridge." One of the most exciting activities involved parents and students in the construction of a mural for each advisory group based on experiences that had "bridged the generation gap."

Both teachers and students felt excited and revitalized by the "Bridges" unit. A follow-up survey revealed that 82% of the students had enjoyed the unit, and a similar number wanted another such unit sometime during the remainder of the year. Parent feedback was generous and plentiful. As the teachers said, "For one week, teachers, students, and parents worked cooperatively towards a goal, but more importantly, we have laid a strong foundation for the bridges we have yet to build and cross."

Teams able to produce units like "Bridges" are often found in schools where the leadership has strongly encouraged teamed instruction and provided the training necessary for the fulfillment of the mandate to do so. Truly interdisciplinary teamed instruction of this sort, on a regular basis, in the context of today's middle schools, is simply a Herculean effort, usually beyond the capacity of all but the most dedicated staff members. Gordon Vars (2001) argued that the creation of a new curriculum of general education that rejects the standards-based, separate-subject, departmentalized version of contemporary middle school curriculum should be at the top of the agenda of the national middle school movement. We agree. We remain, however, pessimistic about the prospects for success in such an effort if the transformation of the curriculum must be done in the face of rebellion against standards-based reform. But it can be done.

Other Student Matters

Teams often need to spend time meeting with a counselor for the purpose of placing students into a program for exceptional children. They also find themselves frequently occupied with students leaving school or with new students transferring in from another school or, rarely, from another team in the same school. Teams also report a significant amount of time spent in conferences with parents of students on the team. The economy of time provided to parents by being able to speak with all their children's teachers at once makes this type of parent-team conference a popular item with teams that encourage it. Team consideration of the problems of an individual student is one of the major advantages of team organization.

Relating to Other Staff Members

Teams often need to act as a unit in collaboration with other school staff. The principal or the assistant principal would meet with a particular team for a special purpose many other times throughout the year. In addition to these administrators, teams confer with other staff members in dozens of instances. Many exemplary middle schools have a person who acts as the curriculum coordinator. This person frequently works closely with the teams, often serving as a type of overall team leader and ombudsman dealing separately with each team on issues, in-service opportunities, curriculum development, and so on. Just as often, teams meet with counselors, deans, or special education teachers regarding individual pupils or small groups of students from the team.

At Broomfield Heights Middle School, in Broomfield, Colorado, for example, each team spends one period each week in what they term their "Kid Meeting." A team of teachers meets with the counselor, who brings a list of students who need special attention from the teachers on the team. A student may be having problems at home that teachers need to know about. Another student may have been tested in some special way and teachers need to know the results to do a better job with that student. Two students may be having real difficulty getting along. Whatever the multitude of reasons for bringing these students to the special attention of the teachers on the team, academic teachers swear that the weekly "Kid Meeting" is the "most important 45 minutes of the week."

Team Planning

Experience in some middle schools indicates that matters related to the management of team affairs often consume the energy of the team members. While such a situation might seem, at first, to be less than ideal, all working groups function this way. Such day-to-day interaction helps solidify the bonds that unite the team. Given that agendas for team meetings reflect these concerns, an examination of what is discussed there should be instructive. One team had the following agenda for some of its meetings throughout one academic year.

October 11
Field trip plans
Media Center policies
Parent welcome letters
Team discipline issues

November 28
Retention policies and
 particulars
Christmas plans
Assemblies
Progress reports
Locker check for books

December 12
Use of machines
Budget allocation
Team population enrollment
Program
8th grade test scores
Teacher in-service workshop

February 20
Plans for desegregation
 workshop
Promotion and retention
 decisions
Hospitality
Reality Therapy Pilot
 Program
Intramural playoff plans

February 27
Miller analogy test (MAT)
Year-end field trips

November 14
Bilingual children's needs
Speech problems
Summer school
Grading practices and particulars

December 5
Duty stations
Team honor roll
Coffee sharing

January 4
Schedules for new students
Parent conference plans
Involvement in folk arts
Library books due
Time-out room

February 22
Discussion of goals
Professionalism
Schoolwide policies for new kids
Post-school planning

March 15
Sex education plans
5th grade orientation

| Possible early dismissal | Withdrawal forms |
| Title I problems | |

April 3 | *April 19*
Schedule for last three | Field trip plans
  school days |
Social Committee |

April 26 | *May 1*
Counselor input | Special assembly plans
Special media center unit | Money collection
Honor roll kids | Teachers appreciation week
8th grade testing |

Figure 6.1 illustrates the minutes from a 6th grade team (Frogtown) meeting, at Fort Clarke Middle School, in Gainesville, Florida. The topics at the meeting ranged widely: welcoming a university visitor for a week, Southern Association of Colleges and Schools (SACS) report, teacher appreciation breakfast sponsored by parents, field trip details, Citizens of the Month, orientation visits to the school by members of elementary school 5th graders ("tadpoles"), and a career education program that was conducted through the advisory program. "Frogtown" has been the name of the 6th grade team for more than 25 years, and the concerns evident at this meeting are typical of life on that team, and others like it, all through that period of time.

At Deltona Middle School, in Deltona, Florida, the minutes of a 7th grade house meeting show that the following topics were covered.

- Report cards
- Positive Recognition Forms
- Championship Friday (intramural playoff day)
- Conduct grades
- Upcoming Goal Setting meeting for the entire faculty
- Fundraisers
- Newsletter articles
- Candy Grams
- Interdisciplinary unit, one per semester, per team
- Team Notebooks due
- Concerns

At Nock Middle School, in Newburyport, Massachusetts, teams are provided with a set of guidelines for their meetings.

The time set aside for team planning each day should be used for that purpose.
    The meeting itself should take precedence over individual pursuits during that time.
1.   Team members will assume the responsibility of designating a team leader. This could be done on a rotating basis.

FROGTOWN TEAM MINUTES

May 14, 1991

Members present: Paul Burdick, Bob Carroll, Paul George, Clyde Graham, Vic Harrell, Willie Jackson, Bev Jones, Nancy McMillin, Amanda Searle, Jill Walters, Elaine White, Sara Zemlo.

Members in class: Mike Gibson, Anne Knight, Sally Rist and Sarla Ramayya.

Team Notes (🐸):

1. Welcome to Dr. Paul George who is visiting with us this week. We hope you have a profitable stay in Frogtown.

2. The SACS report was very positive. The administration, faculty, and support staff were all mentioned as being exceptional! Dr. Dixon expressed his thanks to all who contributed to the success of this review.

3. Teacher Appreciation Breakfast this morning at 8:05 in the bandroom.

4. Today (Wednesday, May 15) is the final day for collection of field trip money. Use extreme discretion in granting any waivers to this date, and then only after consulting with Vic.

5. We established a list of eight potential "no-goes." See Bob or Vic if you have any questions.

6. The Frogtown Citizens of the Month are as follows:

March	Ko-Shin Wang
	Mya Brumfield
April	Jeff Berryhill
	Shu-Ping Shen
May	Wendy Carlson
	Mindy Freedman

1

FIGURE **6.1**

FROGTOWN TEAM MINUTES

If any of these students are in your AA, please inform them of this honor, and request a good photo of them to be used on the bulletin board up front.

7. The tadpoles will be here next Tuesday, Wednesday, and Thursday. Vic will have a schedule posted for us later this week.

8. We decided to ask our students to sign up in groups of four as a means of offering a bit more protection while in Busch Gardens. While they will ride with their AA classes, students will be expected to stay with their group throughout the remainder of the day. One student in each group will be responsible for submitting a complete list of all four students and their AA teachers. This should be completed by next Tuesday (May 21) so that we can begin compiling a master list.

9. Thanks for your cooperation with the Career Education speakers on Tuesday morning. We will do it again on Thursday!

"Well, next time you invoke the muses, don't mumble."

2/84

2

FIGURE **6.1** (CONTINUED)

2. Team leaders will organize and conduct the team meetings.
3. Teachers might use planning time to explain and show what work they have planned for their classes for the purpose of planning interdisciplinary activities.
4. Suggested topics for discussions:
   a. Schedules and procedures
   b. Youngsters with particular problems; what can be done to solve them
   c. Re-grouping of students for teaching particular skills and concepts
   d. Evaluation of learning
   e. Making curriculum more appropriate
   f. Efforts to individualize teaching and learning
   g. Planning interdisciplinary ventures
   h. Parent conferences
5. The House Coordinator will take part in team meetings on a regular basis.

At East Cobb Middle School, in Marietta, Georgia, the two periods of team planning time came, as such time does everywhere, at a high cost. To ensure that this time is fully utilized, leaders at East Cobb Middle developed specifications for monitoring that planning to make sure that it is "used to promote cognitive, behavioral, and affective growth of students." Team planning, at East Cobb, is expected to provide evidence that

Plans are being made for individual student learning needs
Plans are being made for individual student behavior needs
Team spirit activities are planned
Plans are made to improve student affective growth
There is sharing of curriculum plans
Interdisciplinary units are being implemented
Learning and behavior goals are developed with and for the team as a whole and evaluated regularly
Time is being used flexibly
Grouping and regrouping are done appropriately
Available test information are used appropriately for individuals and groups
Parents are contacted as needed
There is a sharing of instructional strategies and materials
Conferences with other professionals are planned as needed
There is evidence of teacher collegiality

A "Team Planning Guide" for the teachers at East Cobb Middle introduced the expectation that teams of teachers, working together, would keep a "Team Log" that would be shared with the principal on a weekly basis.

This would be the place where teams would record the minutes of their meetings and the decisions that were made during that time. Among the matters to be included in the log at the beginning of the year were the following items.

Team student academic and behavior management plan
Room preparation and hall decoration plans
Strategies for achieving schoolwide goals on the team
Strategies for improving student attendance
Strategies for emphasizing interdisciplinary teaching
Strategies for improving team and school spirit
Strategies for recognition of student success
A first-day schedule for each team that will "make East Cobb the most inviting school in town"
Review of student grouping and scheduling to ensure correct placement

At MacDonald Middle School, in East Lansing, Michigan, teams are evaluated on a regular basis, on how they use their planning time as well as on a much broader scale. Comprehensive evaluations of intact teams occur every three years; new teams are evaluated within the first 10 weeks of the school year and then on a continuing basis. Detailed forms and procedures help to ensure that the evaluation is done carefully. The short form of the team evaluation instrument asks team members to help evaluate 26 factors in eight major areas: instruction, group composition, scheduling, expectations and rules, communications, support services, use of space, and miscellaneous. It should be extraordinarily clear to teachers on teams that planning and working together effectively, at MacDonald, is a high priority.

No middle school has been more specific in its detailing of the duties of team members than Olle Middle School, in Alief, Texas. The agenda of team activities (see Table 6.1) for the entire school year is introduced as follows:

Horizontal Grade Level Team Calendar
The suggested list of activities pertinent to team teaching is provided to give structure, continuity, and meaningfulness to our team meetings. While the list may seem formidable, it is in no way exhaustive.

This calendar, under the leadership and direction of the team captain, is to be used as a guide and as a checklist. Actually circle each activity that you have accomplished according to the given suggestions during each of the re- port periods.

It is also recommended that some flexibility be maintained regarding your involvement with each activity during the marking periods. Do not hes- itate to alter the sequence or extension of these activities or to suggest addi- tions or deletions to this list.

TABLE 6.1   HORIZONTAL TEAM ACTIVITIES, OLLE MIDDLE SCHOOL, IN ALIEF, TEXAS

Marking Period

1	2	3	Agenda of team activities
X			1. Select team captain, recorder, secretary and contact person.
X			2. Schedule students for English, social studies, math and science.
X			3. Team members review student orientation manual or handbook for new teachers on team prior to their use of the sequential material.
X			4. Obtain a schedule card for each section taught, and retain them in your classroom for your convenience in locating students.
X			5. Exchange copies of textbooks with other team members for teacher and student use in classroom discussions and correlating units of instruction.
X	X	X	6. Prior to conferences, check file for "Team Conference Cards" for information obtained from student and parental interviews in the past.
X			7. Develop a technique for phoning parents, greeting them when they arrive, opening and closing the conference. Refer to teacher's manual on hints for conducting a conference. Get to the point early and remember that information is held in strict confidence.
X			8. In addition to formal orientation program for sixth graders and new students, develop a thorough explanation of academic policies and procedures in each classroom
X			9. Distribute and explain the student handbook.
X			10. Check to find whether cumulative record folders are up-to-date and available for each pupil.
X	X	X	11. Disseminate information about children with special problems to teachers who are not familiar with these problems and who now teach these children.
X	X	X	12. Review the statistical data provided for each child in your team. Make full use of anecdotal records in folders.
X	X	X	13. Acquaint yourself with all sixth grade pupils to see whether they are adjusting to middle school. Help other teachers to understand pupils' backgrounds, abilities and achievement. Let the students know that you are going to be interested in them, in the results of their tests, in their work habits, and in their overall academic and social progress.
X			14. Homeroom teachers should schedule individual conference with each student.
X	X	X	15. Initiate a card file for all conferences (parent and student) giving sufficient information on results.
X			16. Prepare for PTO open house meeting.
X	X	X	17. Meet with the librarian and become familiar with her services as a curriculum resource person. Brief her on your courses of study, needs and expectations as the year progresses.
X	X	X	18. Review the district M.B.O.'s and make preparations to meet the guidelines as stated.

Marking Period

1	2	3	Agenda of team activities
X	X	X	19. When necessary, throughout the year discuss the merits of each student for resectioning purposes.
X	X	X	20. Throughout the year refer students who need individual counseling to guidance. Make referrals after the team has briefed the counselor on the need for such counsel.
X	X	X	21. Complete report cards.
X			22. Explain the reporting system to pupils.
X	X	X	23. Throughout the year acquaint nonteam teachers of areas covered by your team in classroom work.
X	X	X	24. Throughout the year check on transcripts of all new children for grades and other information. Designate one member to do this.
X	X	X	25. Coordinate the testing schedule so that pupils are not burdened with too many tests at one time.
X	X	X	26. Discuss the academic standards that will constitute achievement grades for each ability level. Try to arrive at some commonality within the team so that a particular grade has the same value of standards with each teacher.
X			27. Review guidance and discipline procedures in teacher's manual.
X	X	X	28. Review each pupil's disciplinary record and plan positive approaches to rectify this condition.
X	X	X	29. Compile lists of students not achieving at a reasonable level. Begin to confer with these students.
X	X	X	30. Prepare a list of those students who are having difficulties because of physical, social and emotional immaturity. Enlist the help of their teachers, and plan a program of counseling these students in conjunction with the guidance department. That these factors are passively understood is not sufficient. A planned program should be initiated.
X	X	X	31. Contact parents of children having academic, social or emotional difficulties for conferences with the team. Certify that the number of conferences required by M.B.O. has been met each quarter.
X	X	X	32. Confer with the art, music, industrial art and home economics teachers on correlating instruction in certain areas.
X	X	X	33. Exchange courses of study within the team to enable teachers to become familiar with the content of other subject areas. Give explanations to other team members.
X	X	X	34. Interview new students when they arrive.
X	X	X	35. Plan carefully for any large group–small group teaching and team or grade level assembly programs.
X	X	X	36. Distribute homework evenly.
X	X	X	37. Read and discuss current professional publications available in the media center.
X	X	X	38. Review grade distribution.
X	X	X	39. Prepare student progress reports.

(continues)

TABLE 6.1 HORIZONTAL TEAM ACTIVITIES, OLLE MIDDLE SCHOOL, IN ALIEF, TEXAS (CONTINUED)

Marking Period			
1	2	3	Agenda of team activities
X	X	X	40. Check with attendance office on reasons for excessive absenteeism. Enlist the aid of the office as patterns develop.
X	X	X	41. Confer with the Administration as trends in disciplinary incidents develop. Identify offenders and counsel them, or make referrals to the Guidance Department and Administration.
	X		42. Check your inventory and bulletins on future enrollment, and begin planning for preliminary budget considerations.
X	X	X	43. Continue to arrange parent conferences. Begin to conduct follow-up conferences when desirable. (Telephone, letter, note, personal, meeting, and so on.)
X	X	X	44. Explore the opportunities for joint participation in testing, group teaching, audio-visual work, and so on.
X	X	X	45. Maintain close contact with children who have been resectioned. Aid them in their adjustments to the new group.
X	X	X	46. Team check on progress of students in Physical Education, Practical Arts, Art and Music.
	X		47. Cousel those students who are failing through the first quarter. Inform them of the dangers of nonpromotion and plan a course of action for successful achievement.
X	X	X	48. Check the condition of all textbooks. Notify students that they are responsible for materials issued and must pay for all damaged and lost books.
	X	X	49. Continue to conduct parent conferences. Encourage parents of well-adjusted, talented students to come in for a conference.
		X	50. Make final check to see that all transcripts on new students have beem received.
		X	51. Submit a list of failures to the Principal. A notification of each student's status will be given to the parent.
		X	52. Organize team minutes in final form for the Principal.
		X	53. Complete report cards, cumulative folders, and other closing-of-school tasks.
		X	54. Begin final work on cumulative folders early in marking period.
		X	55. Review student orientation for next year.
		X	56. Check for lost and damaged books.
		X	57. Adhere carefully to schedule of responsibility in the closing-of-school bulletin.
		X	58. Review with team personnel procedures for determining condition of textbooks and assessments for lost, damaged or misused books.

The Team Leader

In most middle schools team leaders are formally identified, and in others no formal leader is designated. We estimate that formally designated team leaders are present in about 10 times as many cases as where they are not. No school is known to offer both alternatives. Schools featuring team leaders seem to depend strongly upon them; those without formal team leaders are often equally adamant about the reasons they consider that way is best.

Valley Middle School, in Rosemount, Minnesota; Twin Peaks Middle School, in Poway, California; Stoughton Middle School, in Stoughton, Wisconsin; and Louisville Middle School, in Louisville, Colorado, are four exemplary middle schools, out of many hundreds, that have used a formal approach to team leadership. Each has had a clearly written definition of the duties of team leader. Combining and editing the four lists yields a 23-item definition of a team leader's duties.

1. Function as the liaison between the administration and the team; individually, teachers are encouraged, however, to keep open communication lines with the principal, avoiding any unnecessary hierarchical elevation of the team leader to something in-between teacher and administrator.
2. Program coordination within the team; this is a task of consuming proportions, including a role in every activity of the team as described above. Together, items one and two here comprise a majority of the responsibilities of the typical team leader.

Other, more specific activities of the team leader spelled out in school materials, some of which fall within the scope of the first two above, include:

3. Coordinating between his or her team and other teams and teachers
4. Serving on and appointing team members to various committees
5. Scheduling and directing the utilization of teamwide criterion-referenced testing
6. Preparing the team budget and requisitions, supplies, textbooks, work books, films, and equipment
7. Familiarizing new teachers and substitute teachers with school programs and other pertinent information
8. Developing new approaches from within the team by coordinating new schoolwide programs, soliciting creative ideas from other members, and actively contributing suggestions for new team programs
9. Scheduling and conducting team meetings
10. Assisting in the selection of new team personnel
11. Directing aides assigned to the team
12. Identifying and encouraging the use, for the team, of other school and district personnel

13. Assisting in organizing volunteer and community resource activities
14. Coordinating reporting procedures and parent-teacher conferences
15. Promoting good home-school relationships
16. Assisting (in some schools) in a positive program of supervision of team personnel
17. Attempting to develop and maintain a high level of morale among team members
18. Facilitating communication between team members
19. Assuming responsibility for equipment, for instructional materials, and for their care and distribution
20. Assuming responsibility for the supervision of the work of student teachers
21. Recognizing and encouraging professional growth and initiative on the part of team members
22. Serving as a first recourse for team members who encounter classroom problems
23. Keeping abreast of trends and innovations in curriculum and instruction, and making recommendations to team members and principal and other staff

At Eggers Middle School, in Hammond, Indiana, larger multiage-grouped learning communities of about 250 students and 10 teachers have two learning community lead teachers. Their primary function is to "provide leadership to students and staff within their community and to serve as a liaison to the administration on matters relating to their learning community." Each leader also serves as a member of the school's leadership council. The lead teachers share some responsibilities and also have individual duties. The lead teacher for instructional development has responsibility for

- Coordinating teacher mentoring and peer networking within and among the communities
- Coordinating the development of interdisciplinary teaching units
- Supervising the planning of learning community field trips
- Coordinating testing
- Developing and coordinating staff development within the learning community
- Preparing a weekly instructional report for the principal

The lead teacher for pupil personnel services has responsibility for

- Establishing and maintaining an accurate student file system, which includes records on discipline, attendance, parental contacts, and other pertinent information
- Developing class schedules for students who are new or who require a program change

- Coordinating special education referrals and intervention
- Coordinating textbook and supply orders and inventories
- Preparing a weekly pupil personnel service report for the principal

The two lead teachers for each community share responsibility for

- Serving as a contact regarding student schedules
- Handling special requests directed to the community from other school personnel
- Facilitating the development and maintenance of the community's vision and goals
- Overseeing students' discipline and attendance
- Coordinating student discipline with the unified arts team and the school administration
- Preparing the community master schedule
- Facilitating and coordinating parent and student conferences
- Attending community leaders' meetings and other meetings as requested by the administration
- Coordinating activities related to student retention and placement
- Assisting in the planning of all meetings of the community and other school affiliates including parent and community groups
- Coordinating celebration activities and other special events of the learning community
- Engaging in daily communication regarding team meetings and activities

Six teachers at Lincoln Middle School, in Gainesville, Florida, most of whom have been successful team leaders for more than a decade, described good and ineffective team leaders as follows:

> Good team leaders have a number of important qualities. They are, first and foremost, good at organization and time management. They also possess excellent communication and interpersonal skills, since most of their power comes from the ability to influence and persuade their peers. They are able to keep their focus on the mission of the school and the team. They are skilled delegators, and also able to build and maintain the morale and cohesiveness of the team.
>
> Ineffective team leaders share a number of weaknesses. They are unable to represent the feelings of their team members in important school problem-solving discussions when the team's feelings are different from their own. They may feel, alternately, that "I have to do everything" or they are a "buck passer." Too often, the ineffective team leader "brings a negative approach to the table." They may not look for opportunities to build leadership skills in other members of their team. They may, lamentably, be unwilling or unable to invest "what it takes" to do the job.

These same team leaders also identified the ways in which regular team members perform their roles effectively and thus support the team leader. Such team members

Listen carefully and effectively
Take initiative appropriately
Compromise when the team needs a consensus
Support the team leader
Have a positive attitude
Support and implement the team's decisions
Use good verbal and nonverbal communication skills
Help make the team environment livable
Are unfailingly punctual
Give their undivided attention at meetings

PURPOSES AND POSSIBILITIES OF THE INTERDISCIPLINARY TEAM ORGANIZATION

Cecil Floyd, executive director of the Texas Middle School Association, described the advantages of the interdisciplinary team organization that accrued in his school when he was a principal.

Rewards for teaming seemed to multiply each year. Our discipline referrals declined by 50%; teachers had closer relationships with students and increased communication with parents; and instruction was enhanced by interdisciplinary planning and purpose. Team conferences with parents resulted in early intervention with at-risk students. A unity of purpose developed and was nurtured by the important adults in the student's life.

Advantages: Instructional

The advantages of the interdisciplinary team organization, cited by teachers and administrators of exemplary middle schools, fall into several categories. Many advantages of interdisciplinary team organization are claimed for the area of instruction, all of which emanate primarily from the combined knowledge, talents, and abilities of the team members.

Knowledge of Students   One such advantage lies in the team's comprehensive knowledge of student needs and the power this knowledge provides for educational planning of all kinds. The experience of the last three decades has convinced many middle school educators that increased knowledge of students leads directly to more positive feelings among the teachers on a team toward the students they share. These positive feelings lead to the teachers' willingness to act more readily in ways intended to benefit their students. Knowledge leads to positive affect that, in turn, leads to advocacy.

The interdisciplinary team organization also fits well and works synergistically with other elements of the middle school program, helping each component function more smoothly than it would alone. Advisor-advisee programs function much more effectively when the advisees of a particular teacher have an opportunity to interact with that teacher in a class situation another time in the day. When an advisor works with the other teachers of each of his advisees his knowledge of those students grows in a different way, and the teacher can share with his colleagues pertinent information about a particular child that only he, as advisor, may initially know (Arnold & Stevenson, 1998).

Intellectual Stimulation for Teachers   Another advantage is the increased intellectual stimulation for teachers that results from the interaction of people with different academic perspectives and professional points of view (Jackson & Davis, 2000). Certainly teachers who develop trust in each other will learn new methods from one another, and this is particularly so in regard to the use of the team in the introduction and orientation of faculty new to the school or to the profession. Particularly in the now-rare open-space schools, but not exclusively so, teacher-teacher interaction often leads to a knowledge of each other's teaching styles that produces improvement among less able or less enthusiastic teachers or permits the more able teachers to plan team operations to minimize the damage that might be done by the less skillful teacher. Teachers learn from working so closely together that even the most skillful and highly motivated teachers undergo periods of greater and lesser crises and stress, and the team organization permits colleagues to support each other with extra efforts during these periods (Erb & Dickinson, 1997).

Group Problem Solving   Other instructional advantages of the interdisciplinary team organization deal with the group's ability to plan and evaluate the instructional program. The superiority of group problem-solving efforts and greater integration of the curriculum, even in the absence of team teaching, seem to be sufficient reason in themselves for the commitment to the interdisciplinary team organization. A more extensive evaluation of course content may also emerge from the interdisciplinary situation, encouraging, as it does, a variety of perspectives. The territoriality sometimes associated with the departmental structure finds little sustenance in the interdisciplinary team organization, and this lack of territoriality, in turn, is more likely to develop better coordination of the curriculum within and across grade levels.

Teachers and administrators from exemplary middle schools remark about how dramatically the topics of discussion change—from the defense of a single subject and its place in the curriculum to a consideration of the students on the team and their varied curriculum needs—when teachers are organized in an interdisciplinary way and not in departments. As might be expected, teachers talk about what they have in common, and when the teachers share the same students instead of the same academic discipline, the students are at the center of discussion and program planning.

Evaluation of Students   Such a situation leads to a more balanced but comprehensive evaluation of individual student progress as well. The total group can know deficiencies a student may have in one area almost immediately. Students experiencing difficulties in more than one academic area can be identified, diagnosed, and prescribed for much more accurately and efficiently when, in an interdisciplinary team setting, teachers in all the academic areas are present for discussions.

Advantages: Affective and Behavioral

Teachers and administrators in exemplary middle schools refer much more frequently to the affective and behavioral potential of the interdisciplinary team organization, and they identify at least as large a number of benefits in this area as in instruction. The majority of the references focus on some aspect of group processes. Primary among the potentially positive group-oriented aspects of the interdisciplinary team organization is the development of a sense of community, with some models of the process referring to teams as learning communities. With dozens of scholars and quasi-scholars decrying the loss of this phenomenon in the larger society, the middle school, through the interdisciplinary team organization, attempts to move in the opposite direction.

Desmond Morris, author of *The Naked Ape,* has written of the agony produced in humans, essentially still tribal beings, by a modern society in which they are confronted by thousands of strangers masquerading as members of their tribe. Anonymity, amorphousness, and anomie seem to characterize contemporary society, and because the schools are in many ways a mirror of the society, these maladies infect the school as well.

The interdisciplinary team organization exercises an ameliorating effect on the degree to which these forces affect the middle school. Team organization has this effect first by limiting the number of people each student must learn with or from. Instead of an amorphous group of 1,500 students and as many as a dozen teachers to get to know, the exemplary middle school is designed so that students are members of a team of 150 or fewer, often with a maximum of six teachers or as few as two. The dimensions of the group that students must deal with are reduced dramatically, ninefold in this example. The team of students moves together, in various combinations, throughout most of the day. Further, the group spends most of the time in the same part of the building. As a consequence, both numbers and movements of students are reduced to appropriate levels, comfortably between the exclusivity of the self-contained classroom and departmentalized anonymity.

Jay Hertzog, dean of the School of Education at Slippery Rock University of Pennsylvania, has been studying these issues for years. Hertzog says, "When four teachers get to know 130 students really well, they can start sensing who is a loner, who is angry, and who needs more help." Such efforts belong at the heart of both middle and high school programs (Education Update, 2001). Hertzog argues that the best proof of the efficacy of teaming at the middle school level is the fact that many high schools are now organizing in the same way. When advisor-advisee programs and multiage grouping are combined with the interdisciplinary team organization, the result is repeated face-to-face interactions between and among the same teachers and students during the day, in several contexts, and over a period of several years. Identity of person, place, and time becomes possible. A student knows that he or she is a member of a specific team, even a specific advisory group, and these structures have dimensions that early adolescents can manage.

In a similar way the interdisciplinary team organization helps the middle school achieve a precarious but precious balance between the demand for a specialized, enriched curriculum and the need for in-depth, enriched interpersonal knowledge among the teachers and students involved in the process of schooling. School size has been a perennial problem of American education. The burden of large schools has, in recent years, been a terrifying anonymity. This has been contrasted with the blessing of size: an economy of scale permitting a stimulating and exciting range of course offerings sufficient to involve the most able students and support the least able. The challenge to the middle school is to develop an exciting array of curriculum plans within a context of schooling where students are known as persons and a sense of community exists (George & Lounsbury, 2000).

Teams can identify and recognize individual students in ways that schools without teams simply cannot. At Wassom Middle School, in Fort Campbell, Kentucky, the Cosmic Kids team engaged in a Student of the Month program that had an effect on students' feeling known and accepted (see Figure 6.2). With six teams in a school, six times as many students can be so identified. Someone will probably keep a letter home from the principal, for a lifetime. Fortunately, such recognition activities are becoming a more integral part of life on such teams.

The junior high school emerged, originally, as an attempt to satisfy two goals: a richer curriculum than the elementary school was able to offer and a more personal atmosphere than the high school was able to develop, although it might be argued that the junior high school has failed to achieve the second. Educators in the middle school seem aware of the need to accomplish both. The interdisciplinary team organization can be the answer.

This sense of community can extend beyond the school, involving parents in new and different ways. The interdisciplinary team organization permits the middle school staff to assemble and present knowledge about students to

WASSOM MIDDLE SCHOOL
Forrest and Gorgas Avenue
Fort Campbell, Kentucky 42223

February 13, 1990

Mr. and Mrs. Larry K. Fisher
4949-D Hammond Heights
Ft. Campbell, Kentucky 42223

Dear Mr. and Mrs. Fisher:

Your son has been chosen as one of the outstanding students of the month for February. Ronnie's teachers described his selection as follows:

The Cosmic Kid team has selected Ronnie Fisher as its Student of the Month for February.

Ronnie is well-mannered, cooperative, and always strives to do his best.

He has excelled in all academic areas, and the teachers are very proud that he has advanced to a higher reading level.

We are proud to have Ronnie as a member of the team!

We are proud of Ronnie's accomplishments. We know that it is your help and support that makes him an outstanding student.

Sincerely,

Carolyn C. Dove

rj

FIGURE **6.2**

STUDENT OF THE MONTH LETTER

parents in a comprehensive and efficient manner. Parent-teacher conferences take on a wholly different character when they become parent-team conferences, a situation in which a lack of information, leading to misunderstanding, is rare. As time passes, parents begin to realize that students, not subjects, come first with teachers. As a result, a new spirit of cooperation and understanding often develops.

Cooperation and understanding are not restricted to relationships with parents. It seems clear that the interdisciplinary team organization develops an esprit de corps among teachers and on the team as well. Teachers on teams show evidence of a higher morale, report greater job satisfaction, and go on to seek higher levels of professional responsibility than do teachers who work alone (Erb & Doda, 1989). In the last three decades, few teachers involved in an effective interdisciplinary team organization have chosen to return to the self-contained classroom or the departmental structure, and an amazingly few schools, having experienced the interdisciplinary team organization, depart from it.

One of us sat in on a team meeting at a nearby middle school where he was on temporary assignment. The team leader began the meeting, proudly, reading a letter that she had received from a parent. It reflects the sense of community fostered by the interdisciplinary team organization.

> Dear "M" Team,
>
> Just wanted to let you all know how much I appreciate your efforts with Barry. His attitude towards learning is changing and I really believe it is due to your attitude toward teaching. Barry said, "This is the best team I have ever been on; they don't just care about me, but they are friends with each other."
> I think this statement sums up what team teaching should be.
>
> Lucky will be the students that get on "M" Team next year.
> Sincerely,
> Delores Evans

Student Behavior Educators frequently report that the interdisciplinary team organization generally leads to an improved standard of student behavior. Certainly, the reduction in individual anonymity and group amorphousness, with the consequent development of identity in students, is a significant factor in improved student behavior.

Other educators point out that the interdisciplinary team organization, as opposed to the department, cuts back drastically on the amount of movement of students back and forth from one area of the building to the other. Because students remain in the same general area during their study of all four basic academic subjects, time and distance involved in movement are reduced by about half. Students have less time to encounter problems in the halls, and they do not often find themselves in parts of the building where they are unfamiliar to teachers. Minutes gained from reduced passing time can be applied to advisory programs, special interest activities, or academics.

The cohesiveness of the teachers on the team also encourages the development of a degree of consensus about student behavior, which leads to a more rational, well-planned, and consistent set of rules for students on the team. This consistency itself makes even further behavior improvement likely. Too, team cohesiveness permits the development of a clearer and more complete picture of student behavior in response to rules than the observations possible by teachers working alone.

The consistency of the rule-making and enforcement process so essential to good classroom and school discipline is firmly reinforced by the interdisciplinary team organization. Students are more likely to know that they are cared about and that they have an opportunity to succeed. They can, therefore, accept rules more readily. The teachers on the team can determine whether a particular rule is reasonable by their collective awareness of whether most students follow the rule, whether the best students follow it, and whether the rule requires heavy enforcement to make it work.

The team teachers may also be able to model effective group behavior, encouraging imitation among the students. Early adolescents need to see adults working together cooperatively. If the school does not have an interdisciplinary team organization, young people may not witness collaborative relationships among adults at all. The team is also able, functioning as a learning community, to involve students in directly experiencing the group life, sharing in the decision-making process with teachers and their peers.

Such experience can come about only when the interdisciplinary team organization is functioning fully as a real learning community, and it requires that the teachers have a measure of autonomy found only infrequently outside the interdisciplinary team organization. When school principals share power with teams, teams are free to share power among themselves and with the students on the team. A measure of professional autonomy is necessary to the success of the interdisciplinary team organization, and successful teams tend to produce even more autonomous behavior on the part of the teachers on the team. Teachers need to be given the opportunity to make some of the decisions about their team life, regarding the use of time, scheduling of students, distribution and use of funds, and a number of other issues. Working together, they can and will make these decisions and carry out such tasks effectively. In Chapter 5, we discuss, in more depth, how teams of teachers can influence student behavior.

A letter to one of the authors from a veteran team leader spelled out the advantages of the interdisciplinary team organization in detail.

> I think the team organization is "the only way to go." Of the 13 years of teaching middle school reading, only the past 2 were in a team. Is there ever a difference! Without it I really think I'd be quitting. In fact, a teammate is 60 and was going to retire until she teamed up with the mighty Orca's—and she's staying on at least 3 more years now—a total of 6 beyond what she'd planned to do.

Obviously teaming is better for *the child*—any child, whether gifted and talented or remedial. The communication among the teachers results in much better planning for all students. In our daily team meetings, we highlight positives for all of us to reinforce, and also target negatives that we'll all work to extinguish. Oh, I'm sure there are some teams somewhere who don't function as effectively, but for us it works miracles!

A child's parents see an organized group of adults ready and willing to help. Parent conferences used to be a fiasco-time—a bunch of teachers blurting out the bad things the kid had done and none (or very few) offering solutions. Now we call the parents in most times, and we've already set up the agenda, with the emphasis on problem-solving. Usually the counselor sits at the table and says little, and problems get solved. Most of our parents think we're the greatest things walking! We've structured several night activities— potlucks usually—for the parents and all their kids—sometimes with a talent (?) show and a "getting to know you" theme at the first of the year. We even did a Christmas play (guess who directed) with a 7th grade team this past December, and presented it at night, with parents bringing desserts for afterward. It results in the parents knowing us better, us knowing the kids and their parents better, and all of us working together for the child's benefit. Does it take more time? Of course! But can we see rewards?? OF COURSE! When the environment is so positive (as it is in our team), you almost don't mind the extra work!

Finally, three very professional, previously very successful teachers have each other! Teaching in the public schools is lonely. You think you're the only one with problems; when you're down it seems others are anxious to see you crumble; but in a good-working team, your mates boost you up, or shoulder part of your load if you're hurting. We inspire each other, add ideas to one another's projects—always causing more work, of course! When we began teaming we had a total of 70 or so years of successful experience, so we weren't new, or naively enthusiastic about any project. In fact, we were skeptical about our district's support—and with good reason! But we have weathered other teams' jealousy (lots of that), and a principal who on one hand would like to tell us to "rein in," but who doesn't dare because our parents are so happy about what's going on, and an assistant principal who is—well, an assistant principal!

If you didn't know me, you'd think this was just so much euphoric crap! But you know me! I work damned hard—and with the team I'm able to achieve far more with our students. I suspect that you even know that I'm not the easiest person in the world to work with—but all three of us on the Orca's are similar in those qualities—and somehow we haven't killed each other. In fact, we've grown closer, more efficient, and surely more effective.

Because it's summer and I'm trying not to give my district any free "mind time" until August, I just don't have specific examples on my brain. I'm sorry about that. But either come to our session [at the national conference], or have someone tape it for you—and you'll hear that it's not just me! We love it!!!

P.S. And I'm just as enthusiastic about teaching reading in the heterogeneous middle school classroom!

We bet she is.

Precautions

It would be a less than total exploration of the interdisciplinary team organization if no reference is made to the difficulties encountered by the staffers of even exemplary middle schools as they attempt to establish workable interdisciplinary team operations. That the same difficulties appear in almost every situation should make caution considerably more important. Several conditions are crucial to the success of the interdisciplinary team organization, regardless of the particular model followed.

Balanced Teams

Early in the evolution of the contemporary middle school movement, one team leader in an exemplary middle school identified the factors she believed to be basic to the existence of authentic interdisciplinary teams (Doda, 1976). More than a quarter-century later, these factors remain at the center of effective team organization. Balanced teacher and student populations, so that each team is a microcosm of the school, are crucial: teachers balanced according to complementing strengths, personal styles, instructional expertise and experience, as well as race, sex, and age; students balanced according to sex, achievement, race, exceptionalities, and age. Schools that have severely imbalanced teams in terms of the student membership will be likely to find the situation difficult to manage.

Proximity   Other basics include the need for physical identity—that is, having the members of the team housed in adjacent or nearly adjacent classroom areas. In this way each team has a separate and distinct territory. Without this closeness teams may function only minimally, because teams of any kind (sports, academic, or otherwise) must play on the same field. Another aspect of the physical space needs has to do with the team planning room. Most advocates of the interdisciplinary team organization (e.g., Arnold & Stevenson, 1998) see the planning room as highly desirable for effective planning, for the storing of materials, and for the maintenance of personal relationships.

Common Planning Time   In addition to place, time together is essential. Some time each week must be designated as team time, allowing regular team meetings and planning sessions to occur (Jackson & Davis, 2000). Interdisciplinary team organization does take more teacher time, because teachers require the same amount of time for their individual efforts and additional time for whatever team activities require. Little wonder that early attempts at teaming were frequently disappointing, as team members were expected to teach together as well as work on teams together. The two were seen as synonymous, when, in fact, they are not. Teams that are asked to produce exciting thematic units or integrated lessons all day, every day, require at least 50% more planning time than teams that do not focus on team teaching. Fortunately, many of the benefits of team organization can be had without team teaching.

Recent experiences in the field and from research (Felner et al., 1997; Jackson & Davis, 2000) testify to the importance of planning time. In the early 1990s, in dozens of school districts, two periods of planning time out of a seven-period day were recognized as the minimum for effective teaming and effective individual teaching. Teachers need a daily planning time to prepare for their own individual lessons and to take a well-earned break from time to time. If much is to be expected from the team organization, in terms of parent conferences, field trips, or other team activities, a second daily planning time is virtually essential. With the advent of the long block schedule, common and individual planning times remain indispensable.

This planning time was recognized as so essential and desirable that, at Westwood and Fort Clarke Middle Schools, in Gainesville, Florida, teachers voted to achieve the two-planning-period situation by increasing the number of students in their other five classes. So, in these two schools, class sizes went from about 25 students per class to about 30 students. No one believed that it was good to increase class size by so much, but no one voted to eliminate it in later school years.

Autonomy   In addition to time, teams need autonomy to function well. Given the opportunity, teams can and will assist the school principal with scheduling, budgeting, curriculum, evaluation, long-range planning, and dozens of other concerns vital to school progress. Administrators of exemplary middle schools find it essential to involve teams in participatory decision-making (Husband, 1994). Given balance, time, place, and autonomy, most teams move forward. Without the proper skills and attitudes, however, forward movement will be minimal. The interdisciplinary team organization requires skills that are slightly different and considerably more sophisticated than those required by non-teaming teachers: planning skills and communication skills.

Interpersonal Skills   Teachers who do not know how to plan as a group will not do so. Teachers whose interpersonal communication skills are minimal will find their team functioning at a minimal level. Any group that is together regularly and intensely, as in an interdisciplinary team organization, soon discovers that it must devote almost as much time and effort to the interpersonal side of the process as it does to the more work-oriented tasks. This effort requires extra amounts of cooperative spirit and creativity.

In attempting to answer the question "What really makes a team work?" Erb and Doda (1989) identify six important ingredients: (1) establishing clear expectations among the members of the team; (2) careful attention to team meetings; (3) building team identity and spirit with team names and so on, fostered by regular spirit-building activities such as projects, field trips, honor rolls, and special gatherings; (4) constant and effective team communication and conferences between and among teachers, students, parents, and administrators; (5) a team approach to discipline; and (6) when possible, a measure of totally teamed instruction.

The teacher handbook of West Middle School, in Aurora, Colorado, deals with team functions and describes six keys to success.

1. These are our students—not my students.
2. There are many ways and not just my way.
3. There are goals to achieve and plans to implement the goals, including long-range as well as short-range plans and goals.
4. The team must evaluate what happened last week before planning for next week.
5. The team must be willing to change a plan if it appears to be going wrong.
6. Team members should remember that disagreements are normal but can and should be resolved.

At Olle Middle School, in Alief, Texas, the teachers' handbook listed 13 keys to successful interdisciplinary team teaching.

1. A tactful honesty and a willingness to work and plan together on an idea
2. A utilization of the differences, as well as the similarities, among team members
3. The ability to accept and recognize failure and a desire to try again
4. The realization on each teacher's part that his or her subject is of no more or less importance than the other subjects
5. A recognition of new and better avenues to a definite goal (Don't think "subject matter," just . . . THINK!)
6. An awareness of how student interest can be employed in teaching the required curriculum
7. A knowledge that students recognize "busy work" and respect work pertinent to the topic
8. The realization that ability grouping may not be compatible with interdisciplinary team teaching
9. A flexibility among team members in individual scheduling to meet a particular student's needs
10. A knowledge that interdisciplinary thinking complements individual instruction

11.   An interest in (not necessarily an understanding of) the other academic subjects

12.   A sensitivity to the feelings of the other team members; an elimination of petty or personal gripes that may interfere with the primary objective . . . interdisciplinary team-teaching

13.   The awareness that interdisciplinary topics may not include all four disciplines and may, in fact, encompass some electives

Ten Commandments of Teaming

During the 20-year period from 1981 through 2001, we assembled the collective wisdom of hundreds of experienced middle school educators into what we describe as the "ten commandments of interdisciplinary team organization at its very best."

1.   Interpersonal compatibility. Most school leaders of our acquaintance argue that interpersonal compatibility is more important than any other factor, even having team members' rooms in close proximity. Arranging teams so that members are comfortable with one another is critical. Using personality inventories such as the Myers-Briggs Type Indicator, sociograms, and other methods of team design can be helpful. Once achieved, however, team compatibility must be constantly nurtured.

2.   Balance. In so many ways, balance is crucial to teamwork: subject strengths, personality style, ethnic background, sex, age, certification, and many others. The key is to have teams balanced in as many ways as possible, in terms of both teachers and students on the team.

3.   Planning time. Teamwork depends upon having the time to plan together and using it effectively. At least one common planning time per day is required for full operation. Two planning periods (out of a seven-period day) makes planning possible, because team members can have their own time as well as one period for teamwork.

4.   Team leadership. Almost all effective teams have a skilled team leader. Whether selected by the team or the school principal, the team leader must be able to work with both teachers and administrators. The team leader coordinates team meetings, serves as liaison between the team and the school principal, and performs many other duties for the team. The good leader is "well-liked, trusted, efficient, and task-centered."

5.   Personal characteristics of members. For teamwork at its best, individual members must like teaching at this level and enjoy their role as team member. They must be optimistic as persons, about themselves, their students, and the process of teamwork. Having common belief systems and work ethics helps, as does humor, flexibility, and commitment to the team. Maturity, in terms of patience and tolerance, is high on the list.

6. Attitudes toward students. Effective teamwork grows from a pro-student attitude. Teachers are committed to their students' success, and team members explore every alternative to improve the educational process. On these teams the students are not blamed. They even treat kids as clients. "Don't give up if the students are not properly appreciative" is advice given by seasoned practitioners. Motivating students is part of the process.

7. Attitudes toward teammates. Teamwork depends on team members who fit the expression "diverse but unified." All good teams possess a variety of interests, values, and instructional styles that they recognize as potentially divisive. Good teams, however, accept these differences and work hard to preserve the team. They listen respectfully. They are willing to compromise. Agreement about school and team philosophy provides the foundation for resolving incidental disagreements. Team members do their best to show appreciation for each other on a regular basis, even to the point of institutionalizing certain team rituals such as "Secret Santas," monthly breakfasts, and others. Effective teams welcome new members, regular and substitute.

8. Relative autonomy. Teamwork depends upon reasonable room for teams to create their own policies, schedules, activities, curriculum plans, and systems for monitoring student behavior and academic performance, and for ensuring parent involvement. Teams are not, however, thrown into situations they are unable to handle.

9. Principal involvement. School principals must, in the language of one of them, "keep a tight grip on loose reins." They attend as many team meetings as possible, playing the role of observer and consultant—not chairperson. Principals help teamwork grow by listening to teams' ideas and focusing on teams' concerns, by modeling the behaviors expected in teachers' relationships with students and with each other. Encouraging innovation in teamwork also enhances team development. Walt Grebing, of Broomfield Heights Middle School, lists the following as central to the principal's involvement in team effectiveness.
   - Develop individual team expectations and goals with teams each year.
   - Allow teams to help in the selection of new members.
   - Provide as much common planning time as possible.
   - Require teams to make decisions.
   - Provide continuous staff development for teams and team leaders.
   - Teach flexibility in use of the block schedule.
   - Encourage and expect interdisciplinary teaching.
   - Give teams a budget.
   - Require all staff members to be a member of a team.
   - Evaluate teams on their effectiveness and the contributions that individual teachers make to the life of the team.

10. Professional development. Teacher and team involvement in training sessions aimed at their interests and concerns supports the refinement and extension of teamwork. When this education is the result of planning by the team, the team leader, and the principal, it can be most effective. Training in interpersonal communications skills and in the conduct of effective meetings are important topics, as well as the whole concept of interdisciplinary team organization, the nature of middle school students, and so on.

At Conway Middle School, in Orlando, Florida, 50 teachers who have participated in the teaming process for several years gave the following suggestions in response to the question "What advice would you give the members of a brand-new team?"

Keep the needs of the students first on your list when planning.
Go all out for your team identity.
Get to know one another and become friends.
Always be supportive of each other.
Work and plan together every day.
Share responsibilities.
Share the decision-making of the team.
Provide new members with training on the concept of the interdisciplinary team.
Know each other's personality types and capitalize on those strengths.
Develop a team discipline plan and be consistent.
Plan activities involving each other's curriculum.
Plan advisory activities together.
Maintain a positive attitude and a sense of humor.
Be prepared to devote the time it takes to be a team.

Teams and Team Meetings: Problems to Avoid

Experience in the last several decades indicates that teams of teachers need to be able to function together effectively during team meetings for the work of the team to move smoothly. Teachers spend most of their days in their own rooms working with their students. This is what they know best and what they feel most comfortable continuing. Hence, when problems arise with team meetings, fewer meetings are held, less is planned, less is accomplished, and a sense of failure and discouragement permeates the team members. There are several ways in which problems are likely to appear in connection with team meetings.

Being aware of problems with team meetings may help team members avoid them. First, and most difficult, is the reluctance of one or more members to participate. Team teachers who are unfamiliar or uncomfortable with working directly with other adults may simply avoid team meetings if they can. Other teachers may not accept the need for teamwork, or they may disagree with the goals of the team or even of the middle school concept. They may come late, if at all. They may come to the meeting but spend the session on other tasks that they consider more important, such as grading their papers or chatting with other team members. They also could find other ways of sending the message that they do not want to be involved in the team's meetings.

Faced with such lack of interest or open opposition, some team leaders are tempted to throw up their hands. This is a critical problem that cannot be ignored and will not go away if it is. Once the team and its leader have exhausted all the efforts they can think of, including straightforward but skillful confrontation of the problem with the team member, it takes a real commitment from the principal, most often, to bring reluctant members into full participation with the team. Team leaders should not hesitate to ask for the help of the school administrator, if and when they have tried all they can think of to get the reluctant participant involved.

A lack of clarity or agreement on the agenda may cause team meetings to go awry. No agenda at all will bring a meeting's progress to a screeching halt. It is the task of the team leader to formulate the agenda for the team meetings and to be certain that it contains the items that are central to the goals of the team and its members.

Too much dependence on the leader can result in eventual team breakdown. Enthusiastic and energetic team leadership is important, but martyrdom is not. All team members must share the burdens of teamwork. What the team leader does must be different but not more than what other members contribute, even in situations in which team leaders are modestly compensated for their duties. We have never seen a salary adjustment that adequately compensated team leaders for what they contribute to the school.

Sloppy communication during the meeting can damage both the personal and pedagogical outcomes. Teachers on teams need training in listening, problem solving, assertiveness, and many other interpersonal and communication skills. It cannot be left to chance, even though most middle school teachers demonstrate a remarkably high degree of skill in their interpersonal relationships.

Hidden feelings that surface only after the meeting, and outside it, can damage the trust between members as well as the honesty and reality of the meeting itself. Negative reactions, unexpressed fears, and jealousies—all of these feelings may result in a growing distance and unproductive formality between and among team members. One clue to the existence of such feelings is often the degree of formality in the way team members address each other and work together interpersonally. If team members refer to each other in formal ways, as Mister or Ms, for example, indicating that they either do not know each other's first names or are uncomfortable using them, then not much trust, honesty, reality, and productivity are likely to be present in team meetings involving such strangers.

Unclear decision-making procedures and the absence of action plans that throw too much weight on the team leader can also lead the best-laid plans awry. Keeping notes of commitments of who, what, when, and how regarding team plans and regularly reviewing those commitments at the beginning of meetings will help move plans toward fruition.

PLANNING FOR AN INTERDISCIPLINARY TEAM ORGANIZATION IN THE NEW MIDDLE SCHOOL

Educators involved in or contemplating the move to an interdisciplinary team organization should look forward confidently to the outcome, given attention to several factors. Decisions need to be made regarding the size of teams, the teaching assignments of each member, and the place in the school where each team will be located. Teachers new to this process should be helped to see that they would not be required to make major changes in the type of teaching they have always done. Unless a considerable amount of staff development money and time, as well as an excess of planning time, is available, teachers ought not be expected to produce any significant amount of team teaching. The effort required to make the team organization work will be considerable, and the results of effective teams reward enough. When provided with some tutoring in conducting team meetings and in scheduling their own students, most teams will function smoothly, provided the interpersonal mix is right and the communication skills are what they should be. Combine this with a proper location and a comfortable division of teaching responsibilities and things should operate without major problems.

CONTENT SUMMARY

Teaming is about teachers who share the same students, the same area of the building, the same planning time, and the responsibility for teaching the academic program to students on the team. There are four phases to life on teams: organization, community building, instruction, and governance. Teaming allows teachers to develop mutual support systems, impact student behavior together, and teach in more exciting ways. Small, partner teams often turn out to be the most effective. Teaming does take a considerable amount of work, plenty of positive enthusiasm, and a willingness to use good interpersonal skills in working together.

CONNECTIONS TO OTHER CHAPTERS

As the core of the middle school, teaming is connected to almost everything else. Teaming is especially and closely connected to scheduling (Chapter 8), grouping (Chapter 7), developing relationships with students (Chapter 5), curriculum (Chapter 3), and teaching (Chapter 4). References to teaming are found in each of these chapters.

QUESTIONS FOR DISCUSSION

1. How persuasive are the arguments about the strengths of small, partner teams? Would you find the advantages of such teams more than compensation for teaching more than one subject?
2. Which of the many requirements for effective teaming do you find to be most essential, those that deal with arrangements such as common planning time or those that deal with interpersonal relationships?
3. How can interdisciplinary teams best assist their students to respond to the demands of standards-based reform?
4. How important is the school principal to the success of interdisciplinary teams? What are the most important aspects of the interaction of principal and teams?
5. Do you expect teaming to spread even further into the high schools? Why or why not? What about teaming in the elementary school—is it preferable to self-contained classrooms at that level?

ACTION STEPS

1. Visit a school where small teams are known to be functioning fully. Find out firsthand whether the purported advantages are present in the lives of students and teachers on these teams.
2. Attend a local, state, or national conference where a team of teachers is making a presentation about their program. These teachers tend to be creative and energetic educators from whom much can be learned about teaming and relating to young adolescents. The annual conference of the National Middle School Association, now numbering 30,000 members, is a great place to learn about teams.
3. Read John Arnold and Chris Stevenson's book about teaming—*Teacher's Teaming Handbook: A Middle Level Planning Guide,* published by Harcourt Brace (1998). These authors know a great deal about the principles

and practices of effective teams and have squeezed a great deal of knowledge into a small and readable book.

4. Read Chapter 9, "Interdisciplinary Planning and Support Skills," in George, Lawrence, and Bushnell, *Handbook for Middle School Teaching* (2nd ed.), published by Longman (1998). It will teach you how to plan together to create effective integrated curriculum for teams.

5. Look in the library for the work of these middle school educators, well known for their work with interdisciplinary team organization: James Beane, Tom Erb, Nancy Doda, Heidi Hayes Jacobs, and Gordon Vars.

SUGGESTIONS FOR FURTHER STUDY

Books

Arnold, J., & Stevenson, C. (1998). *Teachers' teaming handbook: A middle level planning guide.* Fort Worth, TX: Harcourt Brace College Publishers.

Bess, J. (2000). *Teaching alone, teaching together: Transforming the structure of teams for teaching.* San Francisco, CA: Jossey-Bass Publishers.

Brock, B., & Grady, M. (1997). *From first-year to first-rate: Principals guiding beginning teachers.* Thousand Oaks, CA: Corwin Press.

Davis, J. (1995). *Interdisciplinary courses and team teaching: New arrangements for learning.* Phoenix, AZ: American Council on Education and Oryx Press.

Dickinson, T., & Erb, T. (1997). *We gain more than we give: Teaming in middle schools.* Columbus, OH: National Middle School Association.

Donaldson, G., & Sanderson, D. (1996). *Working together in schools: A guide for educators.* Thousand Oaks, CA: Corwin Press.

Fishbaugh, M. (1997). *Models of collaboration.* Boston, MA: Allyn and Bacon.

Fleming, P. (2000). *The art of middle management in secondary schools: A guide to effective subject and team leadership.* London: David Fulton.

Graham, P. (Ed.) (1999). *Teacher/mentor: A dialogue for collaborative learning.* New York: Teachers College Press.

Kain, D. (1998). *Camel-makers: Building effective teacher teams together: A modern fable for educators.* Columbus, OH: National Middle School Association.

Kruse, S., & Seashore Louis, K. (1995). *Teacher teaming: Opportunities and dilemmas.* Madison, WI: Center on Organization and Restructuring of Schools, and Washington, DC: U.S. Department of Education, Office of Educational Research and Improvement, Educational Resources Information Center.

Maeroff, G. (1993). *Team building for school change: Equipping teachers for new roles.* New York: Teachers College Press.

Periodicals

Alspaugh, J., & Harting, R. (1998). Interdisciplinary team teaching versus departmentalization in middle schools. *Research in Middle Level Education Quarterly, 21*(4), 31–42.

Alvoid, K. (1999). Leadership: A function of teamwork. *High School Magazine, 7*(3), 16–21.

Arguelles, M., Hughes, M., & Schumm, J. (2000). Co-teaching: A different approach to inclusion. *Principal, 79*(4), 48, 50–51.

Clark, S., & Clark, D. (1997). Exploring the possibilities of interdisciplinary teaming. *Childhood Education, 73*(5), 267–271.

DeRouen, D. (1998). Maybe it's not the children: Eliminating some middle school problems through block support and team scheduling. *Clearing House, 71*(3), 146–148.

Erb, T. (1997). Meeting the needs of young adolescents on interdisciplinary teams: Reviews of research. *Childhood Education, 73*(5), 309–311.

Gable, R., & Manning, L. (1999). Interdisciplinary teaming: Solution to instructing heterogeneous groups of students. *Clearing House, 72*(3), 182–185.

Giba, M. (1998). Empowering teachers to lead. *Principal, 78*(1), 49–50, 52–53.

Gutheinz-Pierce, D., & Whoolery, K. (1995). The reality of early adolescence: Using what we know to guide our classroom practices. *Middle School Journal, 26*(4), 61–64.

Kain, D. (1996). Recipes or dialogue? A middle school team conceptualizes "curricular integration." *Journal of Curriculum and Supervision, 11*(2), 163–187.

Kain, D. (1997). Critical incidents in teacher collaboration on interdisciplinary teams. *Research in Middle Level Education Quarterly, 21*(1), 1–29.

Pounder, D. (1999). Teacher teams: Exploring job characteristics and work-related outcomes of work group enhancement. *Educational Administration, 35*(3), 317–348.

Roth, W., & Boyd, N. (1999). Coteaching, as colearning, is praxis. *Research in Science Education, 29*(1), 51–67.

Rottier, J. (1996). The principal and teaming: Unleashing the power of collaboration. *Schools in the Middle, 5*(4), 31–36.

Rottier, J. (2000). Teaming in the middle school: Improve it or lose it. *Clearing House, 73*(4), 214–216.

Russell, J., Jarmin, H., & Reiser, M. (1997). Interdisciplinary teaming in the middle school: The relationship of implementation to teachers' attitudes over time. *ERS Spectrum, 15*(4), 32–33.

Trimble, S., & Miller, J. (1998). Principals' and teachers' perceptions of the work of teaming teachers in restructured middle schools. *Research in Middle Level Education Quarterly, 21*(3), 1–13.

Warren, L., & Payne, B. (1997). Impact of middle grades' organization on teacher efficacy and environmental perceptions. *Journal of Educational Research, 90*(5), 301–308.

ERIC

Brown, J., & Sheppard, B. (1999). *Leadership, organizational learning, and classroom change* (ERIC document ED431230).

Buckley, F. (2000). *Team teaching: What, why, and how?* (ERIC document ED435764).

Cramer, S. (1998). *Collaboration: A success strategy for special educators* (ERIC document ED436878).

Ediger, M. (2000). *The teacher, reading, and parents* (ERIC document ED439387).

Ehman, L. (1995). *Interdisciplinary teacher teams: A first year's experience in a restructuring middle school* (ERIC document ED3908).

Frana, B. (1998). *High school culture and (mis)perceptions of support: A case study of success and failure for interdisciplinary team teaching* (ERIC document ED421476).

Gullatt, D. (1995). *Effective leadership in the middle school classroom* (ERIC document ED388454).

Husband, R., & Short, P. (1994). *Middle school interdisciplinary teams: An avenue to greater teacher empowerment* (ERIC document ED372043).

Kruse, S., & Louis, K. (1995). *Teacher teaming—opportunities and dilemmas* (ERIC document ED383082).

Saad, A., Uskov, V., Cedercreutz, K., Geonetta, S., Spille, J., & Able, D. (1999). *Faculty collaboration on multidisciplinary Web-based education* (ERIC document ED436124).

Trimble, S., & Peterson, G. (1998). *A multitrait-multimethod framework to assess team leadership and team functioning* (ERIC document ED420710).

Trimble, S., & Peterson, G. (1999). *Beyond the process of teaming: Administrative support, classroom practices, and student learning* (ERIC document ED438601).

Trimble, S., & Rottier, J. (1998). *Assessing team performance* (ERIC document ED422305).

Wallace, M. (1998). *Synergy through teamwork: Sharing primary school leadership* (ERIC document ED423606).

Web Sites

Flexible Scheduling Program
http://www.flex.org/
This Web site is for Seaholm High School's Flexible Scheduling program.

The program is interdisciplinary, combining language arts and social studies in a college preparatory setting. It is based on the idea that some people learn best when they can connect different things and learn about them as a whole.

CENTERFOCUS: Teacher Collaboration in Secondary Schools
http://ncrve.berkeley.edu/CenterFocus/CF2.html
This article written by Morton Inger argues that reforms in teacher preparation and the integration of academic and vocational education demand collaboration among teachers.

Teacher-to-Teacher Collaboration
http://teachnet.edb.utexas.edu/~lynda_abbot/teacher2teacher.html
"The primary focus of this Web site is to note sites that support teacher-to-teacher collaboration, particularly teacher-to-teacher exchanges focused on professional development 'of teachers, by teachers, and for teachers.'"

GROUPING STUDENTS IN THE MIDDLE SCHOOL

CREEKLAND MIDDLE SCHOOL

Creekland Middle School, in suburban Atlanta, Georgia, is one of America's largest middle schools, with 3,200 students (including 141 on Ritalin), 274 staff members, 38 portables, and 70 busses. With so many students in grades 6–8 housed in one place, it might also have been one of the most unproductive situations in all of middle level education. Under the spirited leadership of founding principal Joan Akin, however, Creekland Middle engineered a successful effort to make this big school feel small. Using the school-within-school process, Akin organized Creekland into five smaller learning communities of 600–650 students, each with its share of 6th, 7th, and 8th graders. Each community, or house, has its own assistant principal, counselor, and clerk in that area of the building; each house has its own computer lab. In each house, teachers and students are organized into interdisciplinary teams—small teams of two teachers in the 6th grade; and two-, three-, and four-teacher teams in the 7th grade; and four-teacher teams in the 8th grade. Each house, and classes within each house, is grouped heterogeneously. Gifted students are not all placed in one house or team within a house. Siblings are placed in the same house, for family convenience and for the family feeling it brings to the house. A long block schedule of 80-minute periods facilitates the sort of instruction that helps students feel known by their teachers. The combination of these organizational factors (houses, small teams, heterogeneous grouping, block schedule) makes Creekland Middle School feel much smaller than it is.

WHAT YOU WILL LEARN IN CHAPTER 7

Because young adolescents vary greatly from one another, in terms of their development, grouping them for instruction can be a sizable problem. We will compare the grouping issue at the middle level with the elementary and high school levels. The advantages and disadvantages of various grouping strategies will be catalogued. We will take a close look at two particular grouping strategies: inclusion of exceptional students and ability grouping.

ORGANIZING STUDENTS FOR INSTRUCTION

Perhaps more than any other aspect of the exemplary middle school, strategies for grouping students are or should be strongly influenced by the characteristics of the learner. Variability and dissimilarity among students in the middle school, the central developmental features of this group of learners, require schools attempting to implement an effectively unique but transitional education program to consider a variety of alternative methods of student grouping. The special nature of the young adolescent is recognized most clearly by educators attempting to design ways of grouping students that accommodate this age group.

Organization in Elementary and High School

Developmentally, students in the primary grades are strikingly similar. Most students in the first three or four grades will be at or below the stage of concrete mental operations in Piagetian terms. Most, if not all, will be sexually immature, not having experienced puberty. Few will have had to deal with the consequences of the early adolescent growth spurt. These elementary school pupils are children, in that they respond to peers, to parents, and to other adults in ways that do not reflect the changes they will experience as early adolescents. Mentally, sexually, physically, emotionally, socially, they are developmentally similar.

When chronological age is a reliable guide to the characteristics of the learners, as is the case in the primary grades, it is reasonable to have students grouped for instruction in a manner that reflects this. If 6-year-olds are almost all alike, developmentally, it makes good sense to group them in a way that capitalizes on this similarity.

Chronological age-graded grouping in the elementary school years appears to have considerable validity, particularly in the earliest years. However, flexibility is important even here. During the primary school years, similarity in academic achievement is at the highest level it will ever be. That is, during the first few years of school, students are more homogeneous in what they have achieved scholastically than during any later period of school. Academically, as well as developmentally, relative similarity is the rule, so grouping students chronologically by grades seems acceptable. Acceptable or not, this is the common practice.

Students in the elementary school can be thought of as being at an early and vulnerable stage of development as learners. They have not established a record of success as students. In all too many instances, they come from homes and communities torn by poverty, divorce, crime, drug abuse, and other varieties of discord. They may enter schools that are immensely larger than any other setting they have ever been in. The responsibility of the elementary school has been, therefore, to provide great amounts of supportive interpersonal structure, usually in the form of an exclusive relationship with a warm and supportive teacher in a self-contained classroom. The nature of this supportive interpersonal structure, in the early years of the elementary school, was memorialized in the Latin phrase *in loco parentis,* the teacher takes the place of the parent.

At the high school, the developmental and academic characteristics of the learners also suggest strategies for grouping for instruction. Especially in the later years of high school, learners have matured as persons. They have established records of some academic success or, at least, stability. Many less successful learners have, unfortunately, dropped out. High school students are also returning to a position of developmental similarity, one to another, that parallels the situation in the early years of the elementary school. Many high school students have matured mentally, one hopes, to the stage of formal operations described by Piaget. Puberty has been negotiated. Physical size and strength reflect the experience of the growth spurt during early adolescence. Much of the stereotypical turmoil of the social and emotional changes is past. Developmentally, high school students are reentering a position of considerable maturity and similarity.

Academically, however, the situation is different. By the high school years, the students who remain have reached a point where differences in academic achievement levels and areas of interest are at a maximum. As each year has passed, the differences have become more marked. Consequently, strategies for grouping students for instruction in high school reflect this developmental and academic situation.

Given that variability among students is low developmentally and high academically, the typical high school has responded by grouping students according to their interests in and their achievement of academic goals. Students, historically, select one of three subject matter pathways: general, academic college preparatory, or vocational. Students choose courses (e.g., world history) with little regard to grade level, and students from several ages and grade levels are commonly found in a particular class. Grouping is accomplished primarily by the student's choice of, or ability in, a particular subject or group of subjects.

At the high school, because students select their programs in this way, and because they have achieved a substantial degree of developmental maturity, the amount of supportive interpersonal structure they require for academic success is likely to be much less than they needed as children in the early elementary grades. Consequently, at the high school, teachers are organized to deliver instruction in a way that is almost totally based on subject matter specialization. This results in the familiar departmental organization similar to that experienced in virtually all colleges and universities.

Organizing Students at the Middle Level

The exemplary middle school, too, attempts to group students for instruction to accommodate the special developmental characteristics of the students it serves, but the situation is different in a couple of ways. First, middle school students are dramatically different developmentally from both elementary school and high school students. Second, developmental similarity has been replaced, at the middle level, by great variability. Middle school students seem to have little in common with each other developmentally, except that they have so little in common. Rapid, pervasive, powerful, unpredictable, personal change is the rule, often so much so that describing a typical 13-year-old is almost impossible. Middle school students may be mature mentally; they may not be. They may have already passed through puberty; they may not have yet begun. They may be 6 feet tall or 4 feet tall. They may still act like children, they may often seem like adults, or they may range unpredictably from one end of the continuum to the other. Chronological age is frequently not a completely reliable guide to identifying the characteristics of such students and, hence, not the only guide to grouping students for instruction.

Academically, middle school students seem far more variable than their elementary school counterparts but less than they will be as high school students. They may, however, come to the middle school from very different academic experiences in the elementary school. Some will have been successful. Some, unfortunately a rapidly growing number, must be characterized as abject failures. Others will be in-between. So that the experiences of the elementary school are not simply made permanent, especially in the case of those who are unsuccessful, the middle school staff must organize the students for learning in ways that supply the proper positive structure for success.

Organizing all students in middle schools according to subject matter choices, as if they were all ready for a high-school-style learning experience, would be arbitrary, capricious, and contrary to the spirit of organizing the program on the basis of the developmental characteristics of the students. It would also be against the best interest of many students. Most middle school students need less supportive interpersonal structure than elementary students, but more than they will require when they reach the high school. In the same way, middle school students can benefit from a considerably greater degree of subject specialization on the part of their teachers, but much less so than is the case for high school students. Consequently, the balance of these factors must be different at the middle level that it is at either the elementary or the high school level.

If chronological age grouping and subject matter choices are not totally effective means of grouping middle school students for instruction, is there an organizational strategy that more closely considers the development and maturation of the students? Do exemplary middle schools often choose alternatives to the traditional organizational procedures? If the middle school is unique in its attempt to focus on the special characteristics of the learners within, are some methods more likely to be congruent with student development than others? As the middle school aims at a program that is different from that of the elementary school and the high school but leads smoothly in transition from one to the other, a middle way with school organization and grouping must exist, too.

For nearly a century, the evolving middle level concept has been based on the often fervently held conviction that middle school age students, as a developmental-age group, are unique in their characteristics and needs. Rarely will a meeting of any group of middle level educators pass without pointed references to the special nature of the students. Some evidence shows that establishing and maintaining high-quality middle schools depends, in several ways, on the recognition of the special qualities of these learners and the willingness to tailor programs to their needs (George & Anderson, 1989).

Just as in the case of the United States Postal Service, therefore, the nature of specific school addresses should be determined by who lives there, educationally speaking. The nature and needs of the residents of a particular educational place should determine the specific design and operation of that individual program. The students and their developmental needs should determine more than just the general guidelines of generic middle level education. The specific needs of a single population of early adolescent learners should be the foundation upon which the unique features of any particular middle level school are constructed.

But which student development characteristics should be most carefully considered when designing the school and its program? Which features of the school program should be fine-tuned to those developmental characteristics?

STUDENT DEVELOPMENT AND SCHOOL ORGANIZATION

Student developmental characteristics have always been a factor in school organization, at all three levels. We have argued here that the nature of the elementary school child requires a school organized with an emphasis on smallness and a supportive interpersonal structure (SIS) provided by teachers who specialize in a group of students instead of a particular subject. Teacher subject specialization (TSS), in an academic department organization similar to universities, characterizes the large American comprehensive high school. This is congruent with the belief that high school students are far more developmentally mature. Because of their position between elementary and high school, middle level educators have struggled for almost a century to establish a balancing point between supportive interpersonal structure and teacher subject specialization, which should characterize all middle level schools, and the corresponding expectation that all interdisciplinary teams be identical.

This was a mistake. SIS and TSS are both important to every middle level school, but not in the same proportions or balance. The interdisciplinary team organization is an important part, if not the most distinguishing characteristic, of the middle school zip code. But it should not be the same at every address. Every school's interdisciplinary team organization should reflect the characteristics and needs of the students who live at that specific school. Every middle level school must balance SIS and TSS in the way that the needs of the particular student population require.

One fundamental question, then, facing those who seek to develop an exemplary middle level school, a school carefully tailored to fit the dimensions of those who inhabit it, is this: "What do the developmental characteristics of our particular students suggest for the grouping of teachers and students in our school?" Another way of asking this question is "What special type of student grouping, within the context of the interdisciplinary team organization, will be right for our students?"

These types of questions must be asked in every individual middle level school. One answer will not do for all schools, or perhaps for all time in any one school, just like one address will not fit every family's needs. One size, in this case, does not fit all. The correct answer to such questions, asked in individual settings, will result in the appropriate balance of SIS and TSS, the combination of the two that is most effective for the particular students in a particular school.

A Model of Student Development and School Organization

A model can be envisioned that integrates the factors of student development and middle school organization to indicate the balancing point of SIS and TSS that is appropriate for particular populations of young adolescent students. Such a model should be helpful in the design of new buildings and programs, in the reorganization of existing facilities and programs, in more effective deployment of teachers into various sorts of interdisciplinary collaboration, in the evaluation of middle level schools, and in prediction and solution of problems that are traceable to organizational roots.

The basic thesis that supports the model presented in Figure 7.1 is that the most effective grouping strategy for a particular population of students is dependent upon the specific characteristics and needs of the students in that school. Effective grouping (and teacher organization) is, in this model, defined as the appropriate balance of supportive interpersonal structure and teacher subject specialization. The higher the level of student development, the more the school organization can, theoretically, effectively emphasize teacher subject specialization. The less highly developed the students in the school, the greater the amount of supportive interpersonal structure required to meet the goals of the school.

The apex of teacher subject specialization in the public schools comes in the upper grades of the large comprehensive high school. Organized in academic departments much like universities, teachers specialize in teaching one small part of an academic discipline, usually at one grade level and often to one ability level. A teacher might, for example, teach only 9th grade honors algebra 1. Another might teach only Advanced Placement Spanish, and so on. One teacher teaching one small part of a small part of the world of knowledge to a small portion of the school population is the sort of assignment that is often regarded as highly desirable.

Supportive interpersonal structure is most crisply illustrated at the other end of the educational continuum. It is the hallmark of the elementary school. In the early years of the primary school, during the first few years following their departure from home, students need all the supportive interpersonal structure the school can provide. A further example can be found in the old

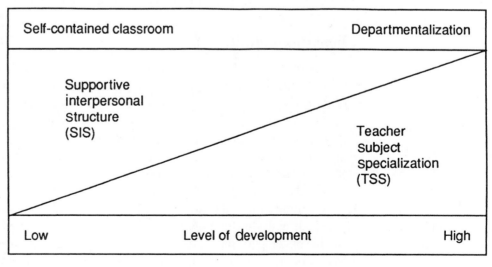

FIGURE **7.1**

A MODEL OF STUDENT DEVELOPMENT AND SCHOOL ORGANIZATION

one-room schoolhouse, where one teacher forged an exclusive relationship with a group of students ranging from kindergarten to 8th grade. Typically, one teacher taught many subjects to one group of students, often over more than one grade level. In that one-room schoolhouse, and in the early years of primary school today, teacher subject specialization is virtually absent. Those not involved in departmentalization often deplore its encroachment down into the upper grades of the elementary school.

Middle school educators seek to balance these two factors when grouping students and teachers on teams. Each middle school must find the most appropriate best fit for its particular student population. The best fit (derived from a knowledge of the characteristics of the students) between SIS and TSS determines, according to the model in Figure 7.1, the best grouping strategy for a particular middle level school. An important question, then, is "What special characteristics and needs of the students are to be considered in arriving at the concept of best fit?"

In a real sense, student development during the early adolescent years is hard to capture in generalities. These students are often described as having little in common but the fact of changing development itself. Nevertheless, we believe useful generalizations can be made about total school populations, so long as the tentative nature of this process is clear from the outset. Generalizations can be made about the age range of the students, their socioeconomic levels, their success in elementary school, and the extent of their heterogeneity as a group. Some accurate statements also can be made about the school environment: the size of the school, the distance students must travel, the attrition rates, the resources available to the school for the education of its youth, whether the school is public or private, and so on.

Departmentalization

Putting together a composite of these factors yields the once typical small town midwestern junior high school. Such schools were often populated by students in grades 7–9, ranging from 12 to 15 years in age. The students often came to junior high school having been successful in elementary school. Frequently the students came from majority culture, middle- or upper-middle-income families, traditional in their makeup and stable in their structure. Many of these schools tended to be considerably smaller than their counterparts today. In comparison with middle level schools in the 21st century, there were a number of important differences in student development.

Such a student population is defined here, according to the model, as "highly developed" or "mature." "Advantaged" might be an accurate synonym. Such a population, we argue, might have been successful in reaching the goals of the school when learning within the traditional junior high school organizational model. This forerunner of today's middle level school, consequently, stressed a high degree of teacher subject specialization and little emphasis on supportive interpersonal structure.

Individual teachers in such schools, perhaps a majority of them, were known to care deeply about their students. But little attention was paid to structuring the school in any formal way to provide more interpersonal support. Teachers often saw themselves as subject matter specialists with little responsibility for the personal lives of their students. They might have argued that students did not need such attention from them and that to organize in ways that would produce it might be counterproductive in terms of academic achievement. They may have been right—for that time and those students. Beaver Cleaver probably attended such a school.

With these sorts of student development factors in mind, educators charged with organizing an effective learning environment might have been correct in their almost exclusive emphasis on TSS. Because the students were significantly younger than those in the high school, however, a few important adjustments were usually made. The junior high school was usually smaller than the high school. Competition may have been muted, by comparison to the senior version. Teacher tolerance for their students' relative lack of maturity might have been higher. By and large, however, such schools were "junior" high schools.

A number of such schools still exist, although the name, "junior high school," has almost disappeared by 2002. Compared with other school districts, student populations attending these schools today tend to be majority culture and middle and upper-middle class. These students have, on the whole, successful elementary school experiences, and the assumption is, at least until recently, that they come from stable and resilient home environments. State and national achievement tests support the belief that the schools they attend are productive, at least in terms of standardized tests.

Are these schools bad? Should they abandon their current grouping model for something else? When the faculties and administrations of such schools question the merits of alternatives for their students, are they wrong? It depends.

We would argue, on the basis of the model, that it depends on whether the students are achieving all three of the goals that the schools pursue. Are academic outcomes at the level they should be for these students? Are most students growing as persons, experiencing success, and feeling positively about themselves? Is the school capitalizing upon the natural early adolescent readiness for group involvement in positive and socially productive ways?

In 2000 the National Forum to Accelerate Middle-Grades Reform identified three similar criteria to be used to judge the degree to which a school has attained high-performing status. We think these three criteria can also be used to judge the need for change in a school's grouping strategies. To what degree, the forum asks, is the school academically excellent? To what extent are school programs developmentally responsive? And is the school operating in a way that is socially equitable?

When a school is populated with highly developed students and organized to enable a high degree of teacher subject specialization and the minimum of supportive interpersonal structure, and the students experience positive outcomes in the attainment of the goals, it must be considered effective. It is effective if it can supply valid and reliable evidence that it has fulfilled all three criteria for a high-performing middle school.

Consider such a school called School G, located at an address called Departmentalized within the middle level zip code (see Figure 7.2). The school placed just inside the middle level area, only a short distance from the high school zip code. Its program, organization, and emphasis are oriented toward the secondary location: heavy emphasis on TSS and little SIS.

Gradewide Interdisciplinary Teams

One position inside the middle level zip code, moving away from the high school area, is the address of schools organized into gradewide interdisciplinary teams. In School F, students tend to be high on the developmental criteria, but in grades 6 to 8, they are younger than those in the traditional junior high school and, thus, need a bit more supportive interpersonal structure. In such schools, teachers cannot act as if their students were completely without need for SIS. We have found, over the years, that such schools are also often physically located in upper-middle-class suburban areas, even though their population may be more diverse than it has been in years past.

Schools organized into gradewide teams usually use the terms *team* and *grade level* synonymously. Teachers think of themselves as working with a team of other teachers who serve, in limited ways, the students from the entire grade level. Terms such as *6th grade team* or *7th grade team* are commonly used. As many as a dozen or more teachers may work with a grade level of 300 or more students. Students may have a grade level mascot, colors, and so forth. The teachers and students will be organized by grade levels in differ-

School A	School B	School C	School D	School E	School F	School G
Modified Core program	Developmental age grouping	School-within-school	Long term teams	Grade level team	Grade-wide teams	Departmentalized

More elementary   More secondary

FIGURE **7.2**

THE MIDDLE SCHOOL ZIP CODE

ent wings of the school—6th grade occupying one wing, 7th another, and the 8th grade still another. Teachers design special activities of considerable variety, work together with parents when they have students in common, develop grade level rules and procedures, interact together with school and district specialists, and perform many other activities and duties commonly associated with the interdisciplinary team organization concept. They enjoy their students and seek regular opportunities to support their development. They believe, however, that most students can succeed fairly well in school without further emphasis on supportive interpersonal structure, and the teachers often see no need for and resist attempts to design smaller interdisciplinary teams with only one teacher assigned for each subject. They enjoy working with one or two other teachers in the grade level from the same subject.

In this gradewide team grouping situation, however, one vital concept of the interdisciplinary team will be missing: Most of the teachers will not share the same students. More often, teachers of the same subject, at the same grade level, will work together in what amounts to a small grade level department. Teacher planning will be focused, for the most part, on single subject curriculum, even when teachers work together. The emphasis will be on teacher subject specialization, but not to the total exclusion of supportive interpersonal structure.

Kanapaha Middle School (KMS), in Gainesville, Florida, offers an example of the gradewide team organization. An innovative school in many ways, KMS was, for example, one of the first middle schools, in the 1990s, to utilize a long block schedule (see Chapter 8). Faculty at KMS have worked hard to implement interdisciplinary units and to sustain a teacher-based advisory program. In the fall of 2001, though, the faculty opted to move from two teams per grade level to one gradewide team at each level. Each gradewide team continued with a team name, color, and motto. Many team activities were also conducted. The faculty was convinced, however, that the gradewide team organization was much easier for the teachers than smaller teams might have been. In a time of declining resources, disappearing planning time, pressure to increase ability grouping, and inexperienced leadership, such logic can often be persuasive, whether or not the solution is developmentally appropriate for students. At Northwestern Lehigh Middle School, in New Tripoli, Pennsylvania, 7th and 8th graders and their teachers are organized into gradewide teams like those at KMS. In the two earliest grades in this 5–8 middle school, teachers and students are organized into partner teams of two or three teachers and their students. These 5th and 6th grade partner teams operate much like core-style programs.

Core-Style Grouping

At the other end of the continuum of student development are those students who are defined as the least highly developed, the least mature. Without going far in time or distance, most educators can imagine such a school situation. For purposes of illustration, assume that a particular school population contains students in grades 5–8, with ages ranging from 10 to 14—50% younger as a school population than those in the traditional junior high school. The school is located in a large urban area, in an extremely multicultural situation. (We are familiar with one such school where 97 languages and dialects were reported to be spoken in students' homes.) The students come from predominantly lower middle and lower income homes, and their entrance into the middle level school is not often marked by measures of great success in the primary schools they attended. The students, as a group, have experienced a great deal of delayed development, manifested in academic failure and low self-esteem, and their cohesiveness as a group leaves much to be desired. The school is large for this age group—perhaps as large as 2,100 students at the same school site. (We know of two such schools just opening in one school district.)

What would be the best fit between SIS and TSS for the organization of this school? What do these students need to attain the three goals posited? Even though they attend a middle level school, should it be organized like School G? If it is, what is likely to happen to the academic achievement, personal development, and group citizenship goals of the school? Will the school be academically excellent, developmentally responsive, and socially equitable?

In an actual school much like the composite (School A), the existing balance between SIS and TSS is very different. The staff believes that the transition from primary to middle level school is an extremely vulnerable process for the students. Entry into the first year of the middle level school must be handled very carefully (i.e., with a great deal of supportive interpersonal structure). This organizational address is a core-style program.

At School A, the 5th grades are arrayed in predominantly self-contained classrooms. Fifth grade students spend almost all day with their homeroom teacher and their peers in the homeroom group. Homeroom teachers are responsible for teaching all of the academic subjects. Students leave the homeroom only for lunch and one other period a day. The teacher-student interpersonal relationship is very highly structured. The teacher and the students spend almost all day, all year, together in a small group much like an elementary class.

Fifth grade teachers' assignments at School A are the antithesis of subject specialization. Many fifth grade faculty members argue, however, that multiple lesson preparations in connection with a small daily student load (e.g., 25) are different from teaching four or five subjects to as many as 150 students each day. Teachers with experience in such a situation argue that while such an assignment may not be easier than a more subject specialized one, it is often more satisfying in terms of relationships with students and parents.

At this school, the best fit emphasizes supportive interpersonal structure almost exclusively in the 5th grade. It permits the teacher to concentrate on one group of students, instead of on one subject in the curriculum. Gradually, however, SIS and TSS strike different balances as the developmental level of the students at School A increases, especially in terms of age. In the 6th grade, the students still stay with their homeroom teacher for 70% of the day, moving out of the homeroom to one class with another 6th grade teacher on the interdisciplinary team (as they have defined it) and for an elective class. In the 7th grade, students spend 50% of the day with the homeroom teacher and group. In the 8th, the students spend 40% of their day with their homeroom teacher and the remainder of the day with other teachers from the team and with elective teachers.

The faculty of this school believes that the developmental level of their students requires a different mix of SIS and TSS than one would find in the traditional junior high school. Are they right? They are if they can demonstrate that they are more effective in reaching their goals than they might otherwise be. What might happen to academic achievement, personal development, and group citizenship if the school were organized with an exclusive emphasis on teacher subject specialization as in School G? School A's placement is, most logically, near the border of the elementary zip code.

Middle schools in many districts approximate the grouping strategy employed in the composite example. In the school district of Volusia County (Daytona Beach), Florida, for example, planners were so concerned about the developmental immaturity of incoming 6th graders that they organized all of the nearly one dozen middle schools so that 6th graders are in largely self-contained classroom settings. For most of the school day, the students learn from one teacher. In many of the middle schools of Washington State, all students in grades 6–8 were organized into a block program. It features extended daily relationships with one teacher, the homeroom teacher, balanced by learning from a much smaller number of other teachers who work together in interdisciplinary teams.

Talent Middle School (TMS), in Talent, Oregon, offers a contemporary example of the core-style organization in action. In the fall of 2002, faculty and students at TMS were organized so that every student was a part of a multi-age, multisubject core class group. Each of the four core teachers at TMS provided a heterogeneous group of 6th, 7th, and 8th grade students with their language arts, reading, and social studies. Students were part of the same core class for three years, remaining with this cohort of students the entire time. Several different types of core groupings were possible, with grades 6 and 7 and grades 7 and 8 the most popular. Core classes met daily for the equivalent of three out of the six periods in the day. Students left the core to attend classes in mathematics, health, science, and electives. In contrast to the core, students were grouped for mathematics in five different levels, through algebra 1 and advanced students could attend the high school for geometry. Interviews with the students in TMS core classes indicated that students prized the core experience for its "home-like atmosphere," the "variety of people," the friends they make, and the fact that, when students go on to the high school, they will "already know someone there."

The core, or block-type organization, remains popular in the West Coast states of California, Oregon, and Washington, with many schools organized this way in the early years of the 21st century. Many West Coast middle school educators are persuaded that the intensive block program offers many benefits to all middle school students, not just those whose special needs require greater increments of supportive interpersonal structure. California, Oregon, and Washington middle school educators argue that all middle school students profit from this organization, but they are particularly persuaded it is best for the youngest students in the school. Principal Kevin Evoy stated that students at his middle school achieved "greater concentration in the basic subjects, integration of subject matter" and developed a "student-teacher relationship similar to the elementary school setting" (Personal communication, November 1990).

Between school grouping placements such as these (Schools A, F, and G), within the middle level zip code, are many special addresses, unique balancing points of SIS and TSS. Theoretically, an infinite number of such points exists, each depending on the developmental level of the students. Only a few of the possibilities are now implemented in functioning middle level schools.

Grade Level Interdisciplinary Teams

By far the most popular address in the middle level zip code is two steps inside it, at the spot indicated by School E, with the gradewide team and the traditional junior high school separating it from the high school zip code. Alexander and McEwin (1989) estimated that approximately one-third of all operating middle level schools organize teachers and students into the conventional grade level interdisciplinary team program. A study by Connors and Gill (1991) revealed that upward of 88% of middle schools identified as "Schools of Excellence" by the U.S. Department of Education organized in this interdisciplinary manner. Many of the exemplary middle schools identified in this textbook are organized in this basic grouping strategy.

At the address of School E, and at thousands of others, the best fit is at that point where one teacher teaches one subject to one grade level. Instead of being organized together with others who share that subject, as in the traditional junior high school program, however, the teachers are organized according to the students they have in common. This pattern has been recommended as the most appropriate middle school address and has been adopted by increasingly greater numbers of school faculties.

Middle school educators know, now, that when teachers share the same students, schedule, building area, and responsibility for planning the majority of the academic subjects students study, the amount of SIS is often substantially increased in comparison to the traditional junior high school. Frequently, it is the best fit, balancing TSS and SIS to permit teachers to concentrate on one or two teaching areas with a smaller group of other teachers who share the same students. In recent years, educators have learned a great deal about the advantages of organizing middle level schools in this way (Dickinson & Erb,

1997; Dickinson, 2001; Felner et al., 1997). Teachers may teach what they have always taught, in the manner in which they have always taught it, if the subject and the teaching strategy made sense in the first place. They maintain a comfortable level of TSS. At the same time, by working closely with others who teach the same students, they can increase the consistency, the knowledge of students, and the degree of careful planning that permits them to reach middle school goals more effectively.

Marshall Simonds Middle School (MSMS), in Burlington, Massachusetts, is a good example of the long-term viability of the standard interdisciplinary team model. Under the continuing leadership of principal Richard Connors, grade level teaming has been in place at MSMS for 30 years, from 1972 until 2002. Each of the three grade levels at MSMS has three interdisciplinary teams, complete with common planning time, heterogeneous grouping, team leaders, and flexible scheduling. Common planning time is also available to teachers in all subject areas to meet by grade levels to coordinate their curriculum. MSMS is an example of an exemplary middle school that has stood the test of time and, as a consequence, validated the concept of the interdisciplinary grade level team.

We believe that the conventional interdisciplinary grade level team organization, as illustrated by Marshall Simonds Middle School, may be the most appropriate balance between SIS and TSS for many, perhaps for even the majority of, middle level schools. But we are now convinced that a consideration of the facts of student development at many middle level schools would indicate that important modifications might be necessary for the students to achieve the goals of the school. If the students in a particular middle level school are less highly developed, then some alteration of the standard team process will be important. The model suggests that, under such circumstances, some new balancing point would be appropriate, one that involves substantially more supportive interpersonal structure for the students. In the last two decades, several successful alternatives have emerged.

Long-Term Teams

Several strategies for organizing middle school teams allow teachers and students to spend more than one year together. Multiage grouping (MAG), looping, and the school-within-school (SWS) models are becoming more popular. Many middle school educators seem to have arrived at consensus that teachers and students benefit in many ways when they are able to spend two or three years together on the same team.

Multiage-Grouped Teams   Multiage grouping is, by far, the least common of the three major versions of long-term teams. Relatively few schools are organized in complete MAG structures, even though the variability in development of young adolescents makes MAG logical. Brown Barge Middle School (BBMS), in Pensacola, Florida, is one of the few contemporary examples.

At BBMS, in 2001, 6th, 7th, and 8th grade students were placed in multi-age teams as a result of the curriculum choices the students made. Students and teachers at BBMS are involved in a comprehensive program of both integrated curriculum and MAG (see Chapter 3). Students choose three different, trimester-length curriculum streams to be a part of every year, and these choices dictate the grade levels of the students who are involved. The Flight stream, for example, might be composed of equal numbers of 6th, 7th, and 8th graders or some other pattern reflecting student interests and choices. Each 12 weeks, students make new curriculum choices, and a new MAG structure emerges to fit those choices. This pattern has been in successful operation at BBMS for more than a decade, indicating the viability of such an atypical arrangement.

At Lincoln Middle School, in Gainesville, Florida, for the first 10 years of its existence as a middle school, all six interdisciplinary teams were organized so that students from three grade levels remained not only in the same house or on the same team but also with the same team of students and teachers for three years. Students almost always began and ended their middle school careers on the same team.

Each of the six teams at Lincoln contained five teachers and approximately 150 students, 50 each from the 6th, 7th, and 8th grades. Each teacher taught one subject, but to students on the team from three grade levels. The teachers and students remained together for three years. Each year the 8th graders were replaced by a new group of 6th graders. Each team reflected the composition of the total school population; that is, each team was a Lincoln in microcosm.

In mathematics, reading, and language arts, students were diagnosed, placed, and taught via a form of cross-grade ability grouping for the three years they were on the team. In social studies and science, a three-year cycle ensured that every student received all three elements of the curriculum in each subject by the time they departed for the high school. Meanwhile, the cross-grade ability grouping worked so that teachers were confronted with a reasonable range on achievement levels in each of their classes. This appears to be one version of the few grouping processes that generally defy the negative outcomes to which most variations of tracking are prone (Slavin, 1987).

At Lincoln Middle School, the balance of SIS and TSS struck through multiage grouping appeared to have fit the students and the faculty extremely well. To insist on the fit that worked for the traditional junior high school would have been, we believe, irresponsible folly. To force traditional secondary teachers to employ a process similar to School A most likely would have been unsuccessful. Multiage-grouped teams were an important new and appropriate organizational pattern for the teachers and students at Lincoln.

Some curriculum adaptations are necessary for MAG to function smoothly, but MAG does not require that each teacher teach three different grade level lessons in each class each day. Some teachers recoil at the thought of being responsible for teaching world history, American history, and geography in the same class to three different groups. This is not what happened.

The basic academic program at Lincoln, and at most other schools that have implemented a similar grouping pattern, was modified in two ways. Mathematics, language arts, and reading were individualized so that students worked independently or in small ad hoc learning groups on specific objectives or tasks that were appropriate for them. Students moved from objective to objective or from skill to skill as they demonstrated mastery or completed a particular set of activities. This way, students could have joined a team in 6th grade, or at any other point, and moved along as quickly as possible from one year to the next.

In social studies and science, the curriculum was arranged on a three-year cycle. Based on the credible assumption that there is little inherent sequence in learning either of these two subjects, entire teams of students studied a particular aspect of the curriculum during the same year, regardless of the age or grade of the students. In social studies, students on two teams might have, for example, studied American history during year one, world history during year two, and geography during year three of the cycle. Two other teams would study world history during year one, and the final two teams would study geography during year one. In science, the rotation of the cycle would be similar. Table 7.1 illustrates how the cycle revolves in these two areas.

For new students, placement on a long-term team usually was not difficult. Because everything major in the curriculum was always being taught on some team in the school, students were placed on the team that most nearly matched the program they had been following in their previous school. This situation also prevented excessive strain on library and other resources for any particular subject.

Mebane Middle School, in Alachua, Florida, may have been, at one time, the most flexibly grouped middle school in America. In operation since 1970, during most of the decade from 1975 to 1985 Mebane had approximately 460 students in grades 5 through 8. The school had three multiage-grouped teams,

TABLE 7.1 **THREE-YEAR CURRICULUM CYCLE, LINCOLN MIDDLE SCHOOL, IN GAINESVILLE, FLORIDA**

Years	Teams B and C	Teams D and M	Teams T and W
One	American history Earth science	World history Life science	Geography Physical science
Two	Geography Physical science	American history Earth science	World history Life science
Three	World history Life science	Geography Physical science	American history Earth science

each containing approximately 40 students from every grade level, 5 through 8. Students remained on the team for four years.

At Mebane the student population on each team changed by one quarter each year. The 8th graders moved on to the high school, and new 5th graders moved up from the elementary school. The team or learning community remained about 75% whole each year. Within each team at Mebane, special grouping for instruction further accommodated the characteristics of the students on the team.

In reading and mathematics, students on the teams at Mebane were divided by ability into two large groups. One group was composed of middle- to high-ability students, the second contained middle- to low-ability students. Half of the students studied the basic skills in the morning, half in the afternoon. Because the grouping disregarded grade levels, students from at least three grade levels commonly were together in class. Such a program permitted regrouping for mathematics in much the same way grouping is done for reading.

In science and social studies, and in physical education and prevocational classes, the students were grouped without rigid ability or achievement level criteria, but with an attempt to reduce the instructional range. Within each team, students were grouped as follows: 5th and 6th graders, 6th and 7th, 7th and 8th, and occasionally at least three grade levels are in class together if the student characteristics or needs suggested it. Curriculum units were repeated every other year, avoiding duplication for students. Mebane seemed to be able to combine both MAG and developmental-age grouping into an efficient and effective overall grouping strategy.

Nipher Middle School, in Kirkwood, Missouri, has been an exemplary middle school for many years. Parents and students have been offered a variety of choices in a school containing grades 6 through 8. A self-contained 6th grade option is available, as well as two- and four-teacher teams. Eighth graders all work in interdisciplinary teams. In between, the option is available of a two-year 6th to 7th grade multiage-grouped situation. Materials distributed to parents by the principal explain that the 6th to 7th grade team is a two-year curriculum incorporating materials from both years and students would be expected to be on the team for two years.

At Noe Middle School, in Louisville, Kentucky, the practice of MAG was introduced to the school gradually, one team at a time. Everyone involved, and particularly teachers, had a chance to become familiar with the concept of having 6th, 7th, and 8th graders on the same team. Initially, the students in the school were grouped entirely according to age and grade level. Then a team of volunteer teachers and a selected group of students became a multiage-grouped unit. After a year's successful operation, a second team switched to the multiage format, and the next year a third team changed over. Eventually, all teams were multiage. Over a period of years, changes again transpired such that, a decade later, multiage grouping operated on only one team.

Sarasota Middle School (SMS), in Sarasota, Florida, is another example of a school offering choices that include MAG. A large but always exemplary school, in the 2000–2001 school year, SMS had 15 teams. For a decade, three of the teams were multiaged. Each of the three grade 6–8 teams has 110 students and four teachers. Each team offers the full range of curriculum through algebra 1, and gifted students are dispersed through all teams. At SMS, teachers on teams arrange their own grouping strategies, within school-based guidelines, informing the administration of the decisions they have made. Further demonstrating the flexibility for which educators in exemplary middle schools are famous, one of the MAG teams adopted a long block schedule while the other 14 teams remained on a traditional schedule. Teachers on the MAG teams love it, they report, and students enjoy the fact that when they get to high school they "have older friends waiting there."

Looping   Looping is the arrangement of classes and teams so that students and teachers move together from one grade level to another, staying together as a learning unit for two or three years. By 2001, looping had become very popular, even faddish, in both elementary schools and middle schools. In a national survey of middle schools engaged in looping, conducted in 1996, George and Lounsbury (2000) identified several dozen schools engaged in a form of looping. We estimate that, as of mid-2002, several hundred middle schools, perhaps more, are using looping in some way. The use of looping is not limited to any geographic region. Pittsford Middle School, in Pittsford, New York; Manatee Middle School, in Naples, Florida; Westview Middle School, in Longmont, Colorado; Hutchins Middle School, in Detroit, Michigan; and Skowhegan Middle School, in Skowhegan, Maine, are dramatically different locations, with different student demographics, where educators decided that the looping version of long-term team worked for them and their students.

Skowhegan Middle, containing only grades 7 and 8, has five teams of teachers and students. Each team stays together for the two years the students are in the school. Each team is heterogeneously grouped, and all special education and gifted students are mainstreamed on these teams. In an evaluation of the two-year relationship, the following conclusions were reported (Lynch, 1990).

- Ninety-two percent of the staff agreed or strongly agreed that this approach results in our students receiving a better education.
- Ninety-six percent of the staff agreed or strongly agreed that this approach resulted in the team having a better understanding of the individual student.
- Ninety-six percent of the staff agreed or strongly agreed that this approach resulted in better parent communication and cooperation.
- Ninety-one percent of the staff agreed or strongly agreed that these organizational changes have made our students more enthusiastic about learning.

Westview Middle School may have been the first middle school to implement the looping program in a brand-new building and program, doing so during the 1991–1992 school year. Bob Moderhak, principal of Westview, cited David and Roger Johnson (1989, 4:24–26) for support for the looping program.

> School has to be more than a series of "ship-board romances" that last for only a semester or year.
>
> In this and a number of other ways schools act as if relationships are unimportant. Each semester or year, students get a new set of classmates and a new teacher. The assumption seems to be that classmates and teachers are replaceable parts and any classmate or any teacher will do. The result is that students have a temporary one-semester or one-year relationship with classmates and the teacher.
>
> Relationships do matter. Caring and committed relationships are a major key to school effectiveness, especially for at-risk students who often are alienated from their families and society. . . . Classrooms and schools need to be caring communities in which students care about each other and are committed to each other's well-being. . . . Some of the relationships developed in school need to be permanent. . . . When students know that they will spend several years within the same cooperative base group, students know that they have to find ways to motivate and encourage their group mates.
>
> Teacher relationships can also be permanent. If teachers followed students through the grades, continuity in learning and caring could be maintained. Better to be taught 9th grade English by a 7th-grade English teacher who knows and cares for the students than by an excellent 9th-grade English teacher who does not know and/or care about the students.

For the last 10 years, Mandarin Middle School, in Jacksonville, Florida, has used looping to make a large school (2,400 students) feel small. The school is organized into three houses of approximately 800 students, each with two 6th, 7th, and 8th grade teams. Teachers and parents are given the option of teaching or having their students learning on a looping team or a regular grade level, nonlooping team. Even with this freedom to choose, 85% of teachers and parents have opted to belong to looping teams.

At the Manatee Education Center, in Naples, Florida, principal Santo Pino extended the practice of looping to its natural conclusion. A middle school and an elementary school share the same large campus. On the elementary campus, teachers and students loop from grades 1 to 2 and 3 to 4. Then, the teachers of 5th graders move with their students to the middle school at the beginning of the 6th grade year. Teams of students and teachers also loop in grades 7–8. Manatee Center has few elementary-to-middle school transition problems, communication has improved between the faculties of the two schools, and the scope and sequence of the curriculum can be easily managed.

The survey reported by George and Lounsbury (2000) revealed that teachers, administrators, parents, and students all supported the practice, citing a number of advantages. Classroom management improved. Students felt a heightened sense of group involvement and cohesiveness. Teachers believed that they knew students better, more accurately diagnosed the needs of their students, and were more committed to providing an extra effort that an accurate diagnosis revealed. Teacher-parent relationships were more positive, because extended time allowed both to see that each had the students' best interests at heart. No substantial problems were revealed. The survey also showed that the fears of some parents (that their child would have a bad teacher for more than one year) were rarely realized in practice. Long-term teams work well, and we expect that the coming years will reveal more schools implementing these strategies.

School-within-School   At School C in the model, the school-within-school approach to student grouping usually retains the basic format of the conventional grade level teams but adds a significant and increasingly popular organizational modification. In the SWS approach, each school is divided into houses, pods, or villages, which are subschools representative of the larger school. A growing number of exemplary middle schools utilize this method of grouping students for instruction, and the staff members and students of schools using an SWS approach cite several objectives.

Attesting to the viability of the school-within-school model, Wakulla Middle School, near Crawfordville, Florida, has been grouping students and teachers this way for about 25 years. The student population of approximately 750 students in grades 6–8 is composed of a predominantly rural, majority culture, lower middle income group, characterized by a greater degree of respect for adult authority if not for education itself. These students require a different balance between SIS and TSS. Here, and at a growing number of middle schools across the nation, staff and students are organized according to the school-within-school process. Also a version of the interdisciplinary team process, SWS combines elements of several options.

The hallmark of the SWS process at Wakulla Middle School, and elsewhere, is that each house contains an interdisciplinary team from each grade level. The school is not organized by subject departments as in the traditional junior high school or by grade level teams as in the conventional middle school. "C" House at WMS, for example, contains a team of teachers and students in each of the 6th, 7th, and 8th grades. Students spend three years in one house, but not with just one set of teachers. Wakulla Middle has only eight academic classrooms on each wing. This would have been perfect for grade level wings, but Roger Stokely, the principal who designed and implemented the program in the early 1980s, was dedicated to the school-within-school approach. He adjusted to the number of classrooms by creating smaller teams of two and three teachers. This means that each house has all three grade levels, in smaller teams than would have been the case if the teachers and students had simply been placed in grade level wings, one for each grade.

This simple alteration of the physical placement of teachers and the number of teachers and students on each team had a tremendous effect on the culture of the school over the last quarter-century and leveraged the resulting popularity of the program in the district and the state. Smaller teams (discussed in detail in Chapter 6) mean that teachers, students, and their parents have much more personal relationships. Teams of two and three teachers must work together to deliver the five-pronged curriculum. Teachers have more subjects to teach, but far fewer students to whom they must be taught. Teachers interact with from 50 to 90 students daily, which is as much as 100 fewer students each day. The students' movement around the school is dramatically reduced by this arrangement, meaning that students spend almost all of their day in one set of two or three classrooms and almost all of their three years in one wing of the building.

The placement of teams in houses, as it is done at Wakulla, means that incoming 6th graders quickly learn not only who their teachers are for the current year, but also who they will be for the next year and the next. Knowing this, do the 6th graders in "T" House pay closer attention to what the 7th and 8th grade teachers in that house say to them about their behavior? They certainly do. Do the 7th graders in a house care what 6th and 8th grade teachers think? Yes, they do, because they had them last year or will have them next year. Students move within the house, from one year to the next.

The SWS approach at Wakulla Middle School has many advantages. Students generally know, from the beginning of their time at the school, who their teachers will be for the next three years, and the teachers can, likewise, accurately forecast who will be in their classes one or two years hence. For example, members of 8th grade teams in each house (students and teachers alike) regularly inquire about members of 7th and 6th grade teams from their peers on those teams. Sixth grade students care what 8th grade teachers in their house have to say about behavior in the hallways. Eighth grade students care what their former 6th grade teachers think of them. Seventh graders have to look both ways on everything. It is a three-year positive structure without either the intensity or the complexity of the processes that have emerged at the point of School D (Lincoln Middle School) on the continuum balancing SIS and TSS. The school-within-school model also lacks the power of the three-year intensity, but the staff argues that the developmental level of the students at Wakulla Middle School does not require that sort of intensity.

At Wakulla Middle School, teachers may teach several subjects, but to only one grade level. This permits a comforting level of TSS for the secondary teachers on the staff, while deriving the benefits of more SIS for the students and parents. Wakulla Middle offers an example of a highly successful version of SWS. A decade of experience there indicates a number of positive outcomes associated with fitting this model to the corresponding degree of student development.

A school publication at pioneering Brookhaven Middle School, in Decatur, Alabama, referred to the concern for the students' sense of identity that resulted, years ago, in the design for a school that allowed the students to relate to a relatively small component of the total school. At Brookhaven, the staff believed that students' sense of security is fostered and a spirit of loyalty and pride is developed in a situation small enough for middle school students. As one 8th grader at Brookhaven said, "I feel more loyal to Winter House than I am to the school."

Understanding the developmental level of most middle schoolers, this can be understood as a very positive statement. Student loyalty to larger institutions such as the total school can result from a prior sense of belonging located in the smaller house. School loyalty, the concern of many teachers and administrators, is not compromised by loyalty to the smaller group; it is enhanced.

The staff at Nock Middle School, in Newburyport, Massachusetts, expressed well this important concept of balancing SIS and TSS, and the students must have come to understand its benefits early. Over a decade ago, in "Middle Unmuddle," the student handbook, students explained their conception of the SWS concept, concluding that it was designed "so that we students don't get lost in such a large school."

HOUSE, SWEET HOUSE

Our Middle School is divided into thirds. These divisions are referred to as the Red, White, and Blue Houses. Each house is to some degree a "school-within-a-school" and every effort has been made to give each house an identity so that we students don't get "lost" in such a large school. The head of each house is the House Coordinator who is, in effect, the "principal" of a school-within-a-school. In each house there are four teams of teachers. Each team of teachers works together to teach us all of our subjects. Sometimes we may have only one teacher in a class; at other times there may be several. Each of us is assigned to a certain house and within that house we are assigned to a certain team of teachers. Our basic subjects (language arts, social studies, science, and math) will be taught in a block of modes and then there will be other modes set aside for special subjects. This includes art, music, guidance, skill centers, and the SPARK [Service, Participation, Activity, Recreation, and Knowledge] block. The team to which we are assigned will decide what our schedule will be for each day during the basic block.

The SWS approach also attempts to assist in the process of articulation on a K–12 basis, as do all such efforts to balance SIS and TSS. The SWS permits students to enter the middle school from an elementary school and, depending upon developmental maturity, experience a range of options from self-contained classrooms to grade level teams. In the ensuing years, within the same house, students move smoothly and steadily to a more advanced interdisciplinary milieu that will help to prepare them for the first years of high school. Having students spend their entire middle school experience in the same house permits the house faculty to design each student's learning experience much more personally.

At Nock Middle School, the house identity receives slightly more emphasis. Twelve hundred students in grades 5 through 8 are divided into smaller units. Three houses (Red, White, and Blue) are assigned approximately 400 students each. Each house has its own educational leader (team coordinator or house director) who, while a master teacher, also assists in the guidance function. Each house is encouraged to develop a feeling of uniqueness, and the design of the school (with specially colored carpeting for each house, for example) invites this feeling. Oaklea Middle School, in Junction City, Oregon, operates in much the same ways, identifying its houses by naming them after prominent rivers in Oregon.

At Jamesville-Dewitt Middle School, in Jamesville, New York, approximately 625 students are arranged into three houses of 210 students, about 50 students in each grade level (5th, 6th, 7th, and 8th grades). Each house has 12 classrooms, a guidance suite, and a team conference room. The students are randomly assigned to each house and heterogeneously grouped on each grade level team. Each house has a complement of academic teachers, with foreign language teachers, a counselor, and a secretary also serving the students of the house. At Jamesville-Dewitt Middle School the counselor also serves as the house educational leader, who is not so much an administrator but, reflecting the school's child-centered philosophy, a counselor to the students, consultant to the house teachers, and coordinator and liaison between the house and other adults in and out of the school.

Farnsworth Middle School, in Guilderland, New York, is entering its third decade of excellence. There, the SWS approach is "an attempt at harmonizing the best of both worlds—one of which is small enough to foster a leveling of concern for the individual student, and one which is large enough to offer the varied resources necessary to meet the needs and interests of preadolescent and early adolescent youngsters." Farnsworth Middle School named its three houses Hiawatha, Mohawk, and Tawasentha (Indian tribes that once inhabited the general area), achieving a measure of identity, vicarious distinction, and pride for its students. In this large school (1,650 students in grades 5, 6, 7, and 8), each of the three houses contains approximately 550 students in four or five interdisciplinary team organizations of 110 to 115 students per team. While separate house identities are encouraged, every team and house is connected both physically and programmatically to the rest of the school. Houses are formed by random assignment of students, but within each house both homogeneous and heterogeneous ability grouping are found. At Farnsworth, each house is directed by its own principal, and in addition to the regular team teachers, each house has its own secretary, counselor, reading teacher, foreign language teachers, and learning workshop teacher.

As an illustration of the way in which the SWS assists in articulation, the 5th grades in each house at Farnsworth Middle School are relatively self-contained. The house principal and the 5th grade teachers provide the close attention and counseling that they believe the 5th graders require. The house counselors focus their efforts on the students in the 6th, 7th, and 8th grades, and they assist the teachers who are working in the 5th grade. Because the students remain in the same minischool setting for the four years, the interpersonal knowledge required for truly supportive interpersonal structure is assured.

Thematic Houses One particular version of the school-within-school strategy has appeared with more frequency in recent years. Combining an interdisciplinary, integrated curriculum, or thematic approach along with the school-within-school model, thematic houses offer a great deal to young adolescent learners.

At Venice Area Middle School, in Venice, Florida, principal Gary Wetherill in 2001 was planning a large school divided into two houses, grades 6–8. Within each house, he envisioned three smaller learning communities, each with a theme. Each of the three teams in each of the two houses would represent one of these themes: technology, service learning, and an arts-oriented interdisciplinary program. Each team or learning community would have four content area teachers, one learning strategies teacher (exceptional education teacher for inclusion purposes), and two elective teachers connected to the theme of the team. For example, the technology team in each house would have two technology teachers attached to it. The arts team would have two to three arts, such as ceramics, drawing, and drama. The service learning community or team would have industrial technology, careers, or business teachers.

At Longfellow Middle School (LMS), in La Cross, Wisconsin, exemplary middle school practices have been in place for two decades. While technically not organized into houses, the teams, like those at Venice Area Middle School, are all thematically designated, integrated curriculum programs. Sixth graders at LMS are organized on one of three interdisciplinary teams, three teachers on each team. "When students are ready for the 7th grade, they choose from three different types of programs. Those programs are named School on the River, School in the Coulee, and Shakespeare Pod" (Glen Jenkins, personal communication, January 2001). The School on the River is a seamless two-year school-within-school program that focuses on the theme of the Mississippi River watershed. This house has been in existence for nearly a decade. The School in the Coulee program is a 7th grade curriculum with a year-long theme centering on another aspect of the geography of the area, with a strong emphasis on involvement in the life of the community outside the school. The Shakespeare Pod follows a fairly traditional curriculum, with special emphasis on the study and dramatization of Shakespeare's writings. The culminating event of the year for this group is the Shakespeare Festival.

In the 8th grade at LMS, students on one team become citizens of the Nation Pod, three teachers and 75 students whose unifying focus is the teaching of early American history. Students experience the nation-building process themselves as they struggle to create a sense of community in the pod that parallels the experience of nationhood in American and in Native American communities (Frost, Olson, & Valiquette, 2000). In alternate years, the students and teachers in the Nation Pod produce a living history stage show called "The Mississippi River Chautauqua," based on the students' research on the history of their city and the river. Several hundred students are involved in the process and the production. Several thousand parents and community members have seen the show.

Demonstrating the flexibility necessary to meet the needs of all the school's students, however, means that the other 8th grade team is a traditional one. "We have found that some of our parents feel more comfortable with a traditional approach to the children's learning, and that makes this offering needed. These teachers provide a solid educational experience for their students" (Glen Jenkins, personal communication, January 2001).

Finally, LMS offers an educational alternative middle school housed at the school, but serving young adolescent students from across the district. The School of Technology and the Arts is a small program capped at 53 students. The program is based on five constructs: multiaged, continuous progress classrooms; assessment by performance, product, or demonstration; individualized programs of study; emphasis on the arts and technology; and joint student-parent-staff governance.

More versions of the SWS approach appear on the middle level scene, as each new school year begins. More new buildings are being designed and constructed with the SWS concept in mind. It is, in our opinion, the most popular schoolwide grouping concept in middle level education and promises to become even more so.

Developmental-Age Grouping

Donald H. Eichhorn (1966) advocated a strategy of grouping students based on selected developmental characteristics of the learner. First implemented at the middle level in 1969 in Boyce and Ft. Couch schools in Upper St. Clair, Pennsylvania, following an extensive medical and psychological analysis of the students in those schools, the process came to be known as developmental or developmental-age grouping. Based on an index of social, physical, mental, and academic maturity, students were placed in three cross-age groups. The first group was composed largely of prepubescents (ages 10–12), the second of pubescent youngsters (ages 11–13), and the third of adolescents (ages 12–14). The results were substantially positive, yielding continued increases in academic achievement and self-esteem when compared with Upper St. Clair students from earlier years and with students from comparable districts in Pennsylvania. The procedure has continued there, with refinements, since that time. Perhaps because such a program appears to require a great deal of time and effort, few school districts have followed Upper St. Clair's lead.

School B in the middle school zip code offers yet another version of the interdisciplinary team organization, one that again shifts the balance away from TSS toward more SIS. The School B option, although rare, was practiced for more than two decades at Spring Hill Middle School, in High Springs, Florida. Students were developmentally far less mature than the traditional junior high school process demands. They were much younger; they were from Southern rural areas and small towns and primarily middle and lower middle income families; and they were bimodally distributed in terms of their success in elementary school. About 20% of the students were from a minority culture. For the entire history of the school, the staff has been committed to a much greater degree of SIS.

At the School B point on the grouping continuum, Spring Hill students from four grade levels are distributed into three teams according to an index of developmental factors that added chronological age to those originally identified by Eichhorn. Three interdisciplinary multiage teams each contained students from two grade levels. Unit One, for example, contained four teachers and 120 students, ages 9–11 (90 from the 5th grade and 30 developmentally less mature students from the 6th grade). Unit Two contained an equal number of teachers and students from the 6th and 7th grades, ages 11–13 (60 of the more mature 6th graders and 60 of the less mature 7th graders). Unit Three contained 30 advanced 7th graders and 90 8th graders, ages 12–14.

Teaching assignments at Spring Hill varied from unit to unit. Teachers in Unit One each taught all five basic academic subjects to some portion of the students on the team, grouped according to how the teachers felt most able to deliver instruction. Typically, there would be three sections of each subject from the 5th grade and one from the 6th grade. In Unit Two, each teacher taught three academic subjects, and in Unit Three, each instructor was responsible for only one or two academic subjects. Students in each unit were grouped and regrouped by the teachers within the unit.

Because the school had four grades, but only three teams, each student had to spend two years on one of the teams. Hence, students were also grouped each year, according to the judgment of teachers, counselor, administrator, and parents, on the team that fit them best developmentally. Students receive the appropriate balance of SIS and TSS within the team (see Table 7.2).

Spring Hill Middle School and the schools of Upper St. Clair have not been the only schools grouping students in this way, although only a few schools have opted for this design. Another school that chose this process was Glen Ridge Middle School (GRMS), in Glen Ridge, New Jersey. GRMS demonstrated that such a design could be implemented to fit diverse school sizes. With a population of about 575 students, GRMS was well over 50%

TABLE 7.2	GROUPING AT SPRING HILL MIDDLE SCHOOL, HIGH SPRINGS, FLORIDA		
Grouping Category	Unit One	Unit Two	Unit Three
Grade level	5–6	6–7	7–8
Student age	9–11	11–13	12–14
Level of development	Prepubescent	Pubescent	Adolescent

larger than Spring Hill, but it used the same grouping strategy. The school was arranged into five teams (compared with three in Spring Hill) of approximately 115 students, five teachers, and an aide. Each team at Glen Ridge includes two grade levels: two teams cover grades 5 and 6; one team contains grades 6 and 7; and two teams are composed of grades 7 and 8.

Many other options and combinations of options can be used to create special addresses on the continuum representing the middle school zip code. The precise placement of each one at some specific point would be somewhat arbitrary and arguable. Shelburne Middle School, in Shelburne, Vermont, for example, has for 25 years offered students, parents, and teachers a multiage-grouped team option. Students from grades 5 to 8 may choose this multiyear, integrated curriculum option. The Alpha Program at Shelburne involves advisory groups and regular and frequent "community time" sessions in which all members of the team "share projects and writings, listen to a guest speaker, solve group problems, and participate in other group activities." Each week, a community time session becomes a "class meeting," where the group discusses and solves problems that face the Alpha community, a process modeled after the Vermont town meeting. Each June, the group takes a week-long camping trip. Each year, the Alpha Program participants produce their own musical "extravaganza" and engage in major interdisciplinary units and projects of a great variety. All of this is possible, Shelburne educators believe, at least in part because of the unusually lengthy (four years) teacher-student relationship.

Parker Intensive Core Program

Parker Junior High School, in Parker, Colorado, offers three grouping possibilities to parents, teachers, and students. Within a large middle level school, Parker Junior High School offers a traditional junior high school option, a conventional interdisciplinary team option, and the Intensive Core Program (ICP). Every attempt is made to place students in the program that makes the most educational sense for them.

The Intensive Core Program at Parker was, we believe, unique. Within this version of the interdisciplinary team program, students concentrated on one academic subject each six weeks, while teachers concentrated on teaching that subject to only one small group of students. Students took only one academic subject per day, for four periods of the day, for the entire six weeks of the grading period. A student might, for example, have social studies four periods a day for six weeks. The teacher would have only one group, perhaps 25 students, for six weeks, and had only one subject for which to prepare. At the end of the six weeks, students moved to another subject, and the teacher repeated the six-week plan to a new group of 25 students.

The staff at Parker reported a number of advantages from this constellation of options. Parents were pleased to be able to choose the option they thought best fit their individual child. Teachers also had some choice about the way in which they balanced SIS and TSS in their own professional lives. Students were, theoretically, matched with the balance they need.

Within the Intensified Core Program, further advantages were found, reported the staff members of Parker. Teachers could give far more attention to individual students where it is particularly needed, in mathematics, for example. Restraints stemming from the ringing of the bell were forgotten, permitting a much more flexible use of instructional time. Passing time was virtually eliminated. This, they said, resulted in much more of a thematic unit type of lesson planning. Parents and students had only one academic teacher to work with. Students never had homework or assignments in more than one academic subject. The last six weeks of the year was devoted to a regular schedule, with the traditional one period per day for each subject, permitting review and consolidation of the learning for the year. There were additional advantages, causing the staff to be enthusiastic about the long-term future of this option.

How teachers and students at Parker were organized could be modified and adapted in any number of ways. This is also true of virtually all varieties of the interdisciplinary organization, no matter what balance of SIS and TSS students may need or teachers may prefer. The Parker model, furthermore, did not need to be the way in which students in all middle level schools are organized. Nor should any other version be acceptable in all situations. That is the point of the model we have elaborated here.

The model of student development and school organization presented in this chapter asserts that there is no one right way to group all students in all middle level schools. The correct way to achieve a balance between SIS and TSS for a particular population of students depends on the developmental level of those students and no others. What is required for younger, less highly developed, diverse populations, in large urban schools, for example, may be different from what makes pedagogical sense in a junior high school in a small midwestern town.

In some schools, even today, an exceptionally high level of student development may indicate the effectiveness of a high degree of TSS, with little attention to SIS. (However, we have not visited such a school.) In other schools, the opposite is likely to be the case. The best fit in any particular school should be determined by examining the developmental level of the students in the school, not solely by the strongly felt and firmly voiced preferences of some vocal portion of the faculty.

We believe that the experience of the last several decades of middle school education suggest that it is wholly undesirable to defer, in the organization of middle level schools, to the strongly expressed preferences of a faculty or a segment of the community for an exclusive emphasis on subject specialization and to omit a careful consideration of the affective and social needs of the students (Felner et al., 1997). Our belief is that a careful study and testing of the model presented here will indicate that errors in middle level school organization occur, far more often, in the omission of degrees of SIS that students need than in the inclusion of too little TSS.

All too often, this results in the failure of a substantial number of schools around the nation to achieve the goals to which middle level schools are dedicated. We believe that an exploration of the model will indicate that, generally, excessive reliance on TSS, to the exclusion of SIS, results in lower levels of academic achievement, less positive personal development, and less of a sense of group citizenship than the next generation needs. Recent research (Lee & Smith, 1999) supports our assumption.

Middle school educators have reached a point of widespread professional consensus, where considerable confidence is felt about the existence of a middle level zip code (National Middle School Association, 1995). The general concepts and practices of middle level education are often accepted as the most effective way for thousands of middle level schools to achieve important goals in the education of millions of older children and early adolescents. This increased clarity in middle level education now enables educators to more accurately make important organizational decisions for individual middle level schools, based on knowledge of the development of the students within them. In Ann Arbor, Michigan, for example, the districtwide standards for the implementation of the middle school concept established the importance of the concept of "smallness within bigness" for all the middle level schools in that district. Small teaching units or houses were a requirement. These standards were, however, designed so that "each middle school could develop a plan for program implementation. This permits site-based decisions about what serves each school community. Each school may determine the house structure appropriate for that school. This resulted in schools with grade level houses and schools with multigrade houses, 6, 7, 8, in each of three houses" (R. Williamson, personal communication, January 1991). This district was developing standards for all its middle schools based on the known generic needs of early adolescents but making it possible for the educators in each school site to establish the organizational framework, to fine-tune the structure of each school, on the basis of the particular characteristics of the student populations of those schools.

We hope that the model of student development and school organization presented here, when adequately tested by research and the experiences of districts such as Ann Arbor, will move middle level education further in the direction of conceptual clarity regarding how students should be grouped on interdisciplinary teams.

ADVANTAGES AND DISADVANTAGES OF ALTERNATIVES TO AGE-GRADE GROUPING

Advantages

The thrust of this chapter might be described as the case for more flexible, learner-oriented methods of schoolwide grouping, balancing supportive interpersonal structure with the traditional teacher subject specialization. It is not so much that the traditional process is bad, but that the alternatives seem so much better, in light of changing demographic patterns.

Most important is that these alternatives more nearly satisfy the other twin criteria of offering a unique program to middle school learners and at the same time moving toward continuous progress from the elementary school through the middle grades on to the high school. But there are many more advantages.

Continuous Progress   These alternatives, from SWS through MAG, looping, and others, offer increasing opportunities for continuous progress. Yet each preserves the structure and accompanying economy, efficiency, and popularity of group (even grade level group) learning.

In the SWS situation, for example, teachers are familiar with their colleagues in the contiguous grade levels and may consult with them frequently about the progress or problems of past, present, or future students. Records may often be kept in a common planning area. Counselors can serve the same students year after year. The scope and sequence of the curriculum and its development in each subject area can be carefully designed and scrutinized by vertical committees composed of teachers within the house who teach the same subject. The SWS retains all of the advantages of grade level grouping while providing significant opportunities for continuous progress for the students involved.

Conversely, MAG and looping provide maximum opportunities for continuous progress learning while permitting grade leveling to occur whenever necessary. Students may begin their studies at whatever point they are when they enter an MAG or looping situation and continue uninterrupted for two, three, or four years or until they move on to high school. For as long as they are in the school there are few, if any, important grade level barriers to learning. Both MAG and looping would seem to offer the advantages of both so well that it is astonishing that these practices are not more widespread.

Community   All of these alternatives offer the promise of continuous progress and also deliver what continuous progress, as a single goal, would prevent—a

strong sense of community. This sense of community, the feeling of membership, of ownership, may be the most important advantage of all. Middle school
students, because of their nature and because of the character of contemporary society, need a place to belong, a place away from home that feels safe and
supportive. An increasing core of research confirms the effectiveness of providing middle school students with this social support, in terms of student academic achievement (Lee & Smith, 1999).

The presence of a sense of community can be observed most dramatically
in middle schools practicing extensive MAG and looping. Where teachers and
students work together for up to four years, one teacher writes, important
parts of the lives of each are invested in the others: "Powerful human bonds
are formed and sealed."

In a society that has become, in Vance Packard's words, "a nation of
strangers," stability and continuity in human relationships become more important in every endeavor. Schools are not exceptions. Loneliness and a feeling of disconnectedness drain the psychic energy from many of the society's efforts, and the middle school suffers in direct proportion. As a poster on the
wall of one middle school proclaimed, "True friendship is a plant of slow
growth." Relationships that are growth producing do not develop overnight,
and the results of such relationships cannot be produced in their absence.
There is no substitute for the human factor.

It has long been common knowledge that schools learn a great deal from
the military, and that much that occurs in schools has been borrowed from the
armed services. It is also the case regarding the power of interpersonal relationships in human motivation. Long ago the military learned that interpersonal bonds were a more important source of motivation than coercion. Men
could be motivated to kill and die for their friends, because of the incredible
bonds that their common experiences had forged. The sense of community
that this produced was more effective than the fear of death. If the armed
forces have changed from force to relationships to accomplish their most difficult tasks, surely the schools can do no less. If interpersonal bonds can motivate grown men, and now women, to risk their lives, the same kind of interpersonal power can motivate students to learn.

Discipline   The strength that derives from the sense of community produced
by a group of teachers and students spending several years together is evidenced in a number of different spheres, but school discipline and classroom
management appear to have significant benefits (George & Lounsbury, 2000).
In comparison to single grade centers, which are at the opposite end of the
continuum from long-term relationships, statistics on factors such as vandalism, expulsions, suspensions, and office discipline referrals appear to be significantly lower. In the single grade center, as many as 1,500 new students arrive in the fall, knowing no one and possessing no feelings of loyalty or school
spirit. In the spring these same students are transferred to a new school, leav-

ing the wreckage they have created behind, and 1,500 new students are delivered to finish the job the first group began.

Effective discipline and classroom management depend in large measure upon a positive relationship between the teacher and the students. These relationships take time. In a middle school with core-style programs, SWS, MAG, or looping, the time is readily available. At many middle schools utilizing looping, for example, at the beginning of each new school year, 95% of the students return from the previous year and only a handful of the students are new. The entire first grading period of the year, so often wasted in other schools with rule setting, rule testing, and a host of other activities, can be devoted to real academic effort. The teachers and students in looping schools have, by contrast, been together for as long as three years prior to the beginning of the year.

At the end of the year, the teachers and students in schools with long-term teams find themselves, again, in a totally different situation. Instead of being desperately in need of release from one another, the 8th graders and their teachers discover that they have come to know and care about each other deeply over the preceding three or four years. Instead of yells of joy, an observer is often confounded by tears produced by the sorrow of separation in the eyes of both students and teachers. Other students in earlier grades, realizing that they will be returning to the same situation next year, are much less likely to give up on academics and more frequently are found challenging themselves with their efforts to stay on task in spite of the heat. Teachers, also realizing that the large majority of their students from this year will be their students again next year, often find themselves possessed of considerably more creativity than might be typical at the end of the year in other school situations.

Based on our observations of MAG, looping, SWS, and other models in action over a period of years, we believe that school discipline and classroom management problems are considerably reduced. Teachers and administrators from such schools confirm this belief (George & Lounsbury, 2000).

Diagnosis and Prescription   Alternatives to traditional schoolwide grouping strategies simplify the processes of diagnosis and prescription in the program of personalizing instruction, the ultimate goal of the middle school. Students who return to the same academic circumstances of the previous year(s) can begin where they left off. New students, because they may be a small fraction of the total team, can have their learning needs analyzed much more immediately, extensively, and carefully than would otherwise be possible. The efficiency benefits the students in more than one way. Because teachers can devote their attention and their energies to directing instruction, instead of to the seemingly endless routines of beginning and ending the year with new groups of students, much more time is likely to be spent in academically direct efforts.

Individualized Perception   In traditional circumstances, in a worst-case scenario, an individual teacher may face as many as 150 students a day, 300 a year, and up to as many as 900 in a three-year period. In such circumstances, the chances of being able to see students as individuals may be slight. New grouping alternatives, however, have the capacity to substantially reduce the number of different students a teacher has to get to know and with whom they must develop positive and productive relationships. Teachers may see 66% fewer students. With such major reductions in numbers, teachers likely are able to get to know students, and their needs, in individual ways. Here are results from one study of students on a three-year team organized as looping. As each year passed, the strength of students' responses increased. Nine hundred students responded to the following statements (George, 1987).

Statement	Percent of affirmative responses		
	6th graders	7th graders	8th graders
My teachers . . .			
Believe in me	73	80	83
Care about me as a student	75	80	88
Care about me as a person	73	84	86
Trust me	69	89	90
Have patience with me	67	66	77
Expect more from me		80	81
I feel . . .			
Pride in my team	72	78	82
Self-confident	65	67	75
I have more friends	74	78	77
I belong	70	81	80
I can be a friend with all kinds of people	58	64	71

Parental Relationships   The years together strengthen the bonds between teachers and students, as well as between teachers and parents and among the students. Teachers and parents have time to discover that both have the best interests of the students in mind. They have time to discover trust, empathy, and friendship. Barriers fall. Bonds grow.

Peer Relationships   Students also learn that their peers are okay, that older students need not be feared so terribly, that students from other ethnic groups can be valued friends, and that younger students are also tolerable.

Positive peer modeling and peer teaching are much more likely to occur in grouping situations where several ages and grade levels are combined in some way. Cross-age friendships, made possible by a grade-free grouping strategy, allow students to seek support from other students who are similar to them in development, regardless of age or grade level. Teachers who have had experience with MAG, looping, and SWS report that the older students often seem less hurried in their attempts to act like high school students and that younger students are more likely to imitate the admirable traits of their older classmates than they are the less desirable ones. For some unknown reason, parents and other adults unfamiliar with alternatives to standard chronological age grouping often assume that putting older and younger students together will result in something socially undesirable. Experiences with these alternatives do not confirm these fears; the opposite is much more likely.

Synergism   One of the most important advantages of the alternative grouping strategies is that they act in a synergistic fashion, strengthening the other programs with which they interact. The advisor-advisee program and the interdisciplinary team are both much more effective, for example, in combination with a grouping plan that extends the life of the team or the advisory group. When teacher and students remain in the same advisory group for two, three, or four years, all of the goals of the process become much more realizable. The interdisciplinary team, and all of the advantages connected with it, is significantly enhanced. Without this built-in increase in supportive interpersonal structure, these programs achieve significantly less than they might with the multiplier effect of the grouping strategy utilized.

Innovation   The grouping alternatives have a similar effect on innovation in curriculum and instruction. When teachers and students stay together for several years, repetition of the same units and instructional strategies becomes counterproductive, if not embarrassing. Teachers are, therefore, more frequently found in an innovative mode, searching for the most effective and most motivating instructional strategies and curriculum units. This innovative trend is most strikingly noticed during the spring. Weeks before the end of school, teachers, recognizing that many of the same students will be returning in the fall, implement plans that they hope will not only motivate the students for the remaining weeks, but also bring them back with pleasant memories and eager anticipation in the new school year.

Teacher Investment in Students   Conventional wisdom holds that close interpersonal relationships are more likely to encourage one person to spend time and energy contributing to the welfare of another. Research in education, in the area of school effectiveness, for example, indicates that academic achievement is related to the capacity of the teacher to make this kind of more intense investment in their students. Within the context of long-term relationships, teachers more clearly recognize the special needs of particular students and, more important, are able to summon the psychic energy necessary to persist in attempting to meet those needs.

Teachers believed that, because they knew students more thoroughly, they were likely to take their students' successes and failures more personally. The teachers were more likely to persist in working through problems with students instead of avoiding the problems or giving up as quickly as they might have had they not had three years to spend with the same students (George, 1987, p. 12).

Academic Achievement   We believe that, when all the advantages are manifested, increased academic achievement results. Furthermore, for individual students, failure and retention do not carry the social stigma that they might. Because, with these alternatives, students are frequently less aware of the grade other students are in, and because they were together last year, students often presume that it is normal that they should be together again. To date, however, the paucity of research in this area makes it impossible to firmly substantiate such professional judgments.

Moral Reasoning   Some logical support exists for the likelihood that the development of moral reasoning, as described by Lawrence Kohlberg (see Chapter 1), may be enhanced in situations where MAG or related practices are implemented. When students of varying maturity rates are together frequently enough to learn to value each other, exposure to more mature moral reasoning should enhance growth in these areas among less mature students. The attachment to small groups such as the advisory group and the team, strengthened over time by MAG, probably should encourage students in the first two stages of moral development to move continuously closer to stage three, where they differentiate between right and wrong on the basis of the norms of the face-to-face groups to which they belong.

Disadvantages

While the advantages of alternatives to chronological age grouping far outweigh the disadvantages, no program is without trade-offs. Implementing some of these alternative grouping strategies requires a significant departure from previous structure and some program disruption will occur, usually fading after the first year. Most frequently, some stress is experienced as a result of the curricular adjustments required when continuous progress or cyclical curriculum designs replace the graded program. Student turnover and teacher attrition can cause an erosion of the benefits of the program, to the extent that such turnover and attrition occur. In schools where teachers are already burdened by excessive demands coupled with insufficient funds, the flexibility and innovation required by multiage grouping and developmental-age grouping may demand more energy than teachers have to give. Finally, we believe that these alternatives to traditional schoolwide grouping strategies throw teachers into situations where they get to know and care more about their students. As a result, the teachers work harder, and such work, unusually rewarding though it may be, is exhausting.

Requirements for Success

With any new, alternative program, educators (in schools using an alternative program) must be able to explain it clearly to parents and other community members. In the area of middle school student grouping, this need appears to be doubly so, for while parents seem able to accept such practices in the elementary school or high school, they do not appear to accept them with equal ease in the middle grades. Perhaps parents are anxious because they are witnessing their children changing into adolescents, and these changes indicate changes in their own lives they find difficult to accept. Perhaps it is only because they have enjoyed their children as children that they are reluctant to have them grouped with students who seem older and more mature. For whatever reason, patience and a willingness to take the necessary time to explain, and explain again, in simple and concrete language, are absolute requirements. School leaders should be especially well prepared to articulate clearly and with conviction the rationale behind the benefits to be received by such a plan. Parents will listen and be supportive if they believe that educators are competent and concerned. After planning carefully and providing ready explanations to new parents, most educators using grouping alternatives find the large majority of parents at ease and in full support of such practices. Educators involved in grouping students differently must be thoroughly convinced of the validity of their own efforts when dealing with students, in the same way as with parents.

Initially, during the first year or two at the most, older students involved in a transition from chronological grades to an alternative may feel demoted. When 7th graders become 8th graders in a new multiage-grouped team and find themselves with younger students, they may initially resent what has happened. After one year, however, when these students have moved on to the high school, and the only students left are those who have known no other way, most of the complaints will have disappeared. Almost every school using an alternative form of grouping has experienced this pressure from older students but, having resisted it for at least a year, find the problem disappearing with their first group of graduates.

Staff development is as important here as in other aspects of the middle school program. But with grouping (in contrast to advisory, exploratory, or teaming components), the emphasis on staff development should be aimed primarily at curriculum development. As the school moves into its second, third, or fourth years, the benefits of the grouping plan will become increasingly obvious, as the need for curriculum adjustments becomes proportionately less.

INCLUSION: GROUPING STUDENTS WITH LEARNING PROBLEMS IN THE MIDDLE SCHOOL

Middle school educators easily embrace the idea of including exceptional students in the life of the team and classroom. Many alternative strategies are evolving, but problems of implementation remain.

Schoolwide Arrangements

The identification of exceptional students and the provision of special programs for those students have been important themes in American education for decades. Because middle school educators have always focused on the characteristics and needs of students, attention to exceptional students has come naturally (Kilgore, Griffin, Sindelar, & Webb, 2002). It may be difficult to believe, but prior to the first half of the 20th century, students with exceptionalities were often excluded from school entirely. By mid-century, however, educators became increasingly aware of the inappropriateness of the continued exclusion of exceptional children from the schools. By the early 1960s, these children had been welcomed into the schools, and special classes had become the nearly universal method for educating exceptional students. Concurrently with the development of special classes, research was begun to assess its effectiveness and, by the middle of the 1970s, was found to not conclusively support the special class process as being superior to other methods. Until November 1976, however, most middle school educators had only an academic interest in the question of the most appropriate method for educating exceptional children. When President Gerald R. Ford in 1975 signed Public Law 94-142, which provided for public school education for the handicapped, professional interest became widespread and practical strategies became considerably more important. *Mainstreaming* became the term used to describe the process of moving special education students back into the regular classroom in the least restrictive environment.

The term *mainstreaming* has lost currency in the 21st century, and *inclusion* is the term most often used to describe contemporary attempts to meet the mandates of newer legislation and broader thinking. Inclusive education means that "all students in a school, regardless of their strengths or weaknesses in any area, become part of the school community. They are included in the feeling of belonging among other students, teachers, and support staff" (Alper, 2001, p. 1). Even this term, however, has been subject to widely varying interpretations and definitions. For purposes of considering its utility in the middle school, in this discussion it is intended to mean the educational placement closest to the normal classroom in which the child can succeed—that is, the least restrictive educational environment. But beyond that, in the 21st century, the emphasis is on accepting all learners as deserving of involvement in the normal activities of the school and finding ways to make that happen without perceiving of exceptional students as a burden on the school. In the past, the placement options for the education of exceptional students were limited to the special classroom. Children were often diagnosed, placed in a special classroom out of the sight of, and out of the mind of, all but special education personnel. Today, with changes to the Individuals with Disabilities Education Act made in 1997, middle school educators are urged to make maximum use of regular school facilities and programs, adapting them to the needs of exceptional students whenever possible.

Inclusion has several objectives. Special educators hope that putting the exceptional child into the regular program will continue to remove the stigma associated with special class placement and that it will enhance the social status of the disabled with their so-called normal peers. Educators expect that inclusion will provide a more stimulating environment for cognitive growth and that contact with the regular classroom will facilitate the modeling of appropriate behavior by their peers within it. Such an environment is intended to provide students with just manageable difficulty in areas and activities that must eventually be faced in out-of-school environments, such as competition and self-evaluation. Inclusion is touted as being more cost-effective, more flexible in terms of the delivery of services to students in need, and more acceptable to the parents of exceptional children. Finally, in the new century, educators assume that all students have gifts to bring to the classroom and that all students, exceptional and not, can make positive contributions to the learning experience of everyone. Inclusion is an ambitious and potentially far-reaching innovation in American education, and educators in exemplary middle schools have made substantial headway in developing inclusion as a regular part of the school experience.

In the late 1970s, the Council for Exceptional Children (CEC), a professional organization for special educators, identified four major components of inclusion that remain current.

1. Providing the most appropriate education for each child in the least restrictive setting
2. Looking at the educational needs of children instead of clinical or diagnostic labels such as mentally handicapped, hearing impaired, or gifted
3. Looking for and creating alternatives that will help general educators serve children with learning or adjustment problems in the regular setting. Some approaches being used to help achieve this are consulting teachers, methods and materials specialists, itinerant teachers, and resource room teachers.
4. Uniting the skills of general education and special education so that all children may have equal educational opportunity

The CEC has also identified four common misinterpretations of inclusion. Inclusion is not

1. Wholesale return of all exceptional children in special classes to regular classes
2. Permitting children with special needs to remain in regular classrooms without the support services that they need
3. Ignoring the need of some children for a more specialized program than can be provided in the general education program

4. Less costly than serving children in special self-contained class-rooms (West, Bates, & Schmeil, 1979, pp. 8–10).

Middle school educators must deal effectively with the critical question of the students to be placed in these least restrictive environments. Federal legislation defines the disabled considered in the law (deaf, deaf-blind, hard of hearing, mentally retarded, multihandicapped, orthopedically impaired, other health impaired, seriously emotionally disturbed, specific learning disability, speech impaired, and visually handicapped). However, special educators maintain that, all things equal, these students have far more in common with so-called normal students than they have differences. It is a matter of degree, because no one is perfect. While some children are handicapped, disabled, or otherwise exceptional and need attention predominantly from specially trained teachers within resource room environments, these are few in comparison to the numbers that can be served effectively in the general education system (Mercer & Mercer, 2001).

A second question, for middle school educators, follows from the first. If much of inclusion is a matter of the degree of the disability, what are the various degrees of least restrictive environments that are appropriate? Figure 7.3 represents a time-honored continuum of placement options that are now available in many school systems, and it has direct application in the middle school program. A version of this chart originally published in 1962 (Reynolds, 1962) has been adapted and discussed in countless inquiries on the nature of effective placement of exceptional children since that time. On the chart, it is critical to remember the importance of fluidity (versus rigidity) in classification and treatment of children in and between various levels of the continuum. In essence, children should only be moved as far up the ladder as necessary, and they should be returned to a more normal environment whenever they are prepared to function there.

Figure 7.3 illustrates that at one end of the continuum the regular classroom teacher is almost totally responsible for the education of all the children in the classroom, no matter what may be the degree of variation in exceptionality. From that point on, the amount of assistance to the classroom teacher increases until the students identified have little or no contact with regular classes or even regular schools. For most middle schools, when help is available to classroom teachers, functioning at the first four levels on the bottom of the figure, it comes in increasing increments from special teachers, consultants, school counselors, school psychologists, nurses, social workers, and the principal.

Resource Rooms

For many middle schools, however, when inclusion is discussed, the major vehicle for implementation is the combination of resource room and regular classroom. Students are scheduled to attend the special education resource room on the basis of those skills, subjects, or situations that can be best handled there. Time spent in the resource room varies with the degree of excep-

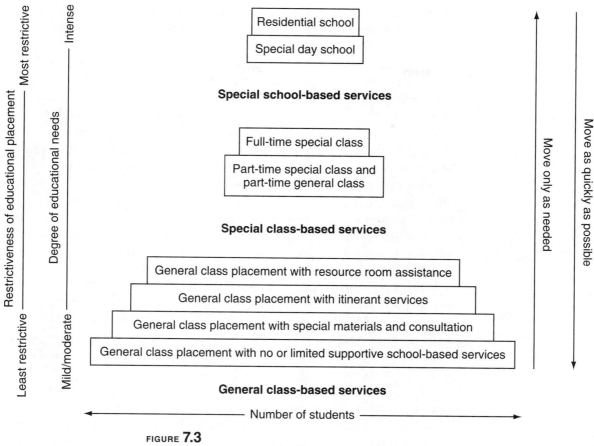

FIGURE **7.3**

CONTINUUM OF EDUCATIONAL PLACEMENTS FOR STUDENTS WITH DISABILITIES

From *Teaching Students with Learning Problems,* 6/e by C.D. Mercer and A.R. Mercer, © 2001. Reprinted by permission of Pearson Education, Inc., Upper Saddle River, NJ.

tionality of the student and with the progress being made by the child. Some students spend as little as one hour per week in the resource room, while others spend as much as three quarters of each day there. The use of the resource room exemplifies the commitment of many middle schools that the needs of the individual student will take precedence over the convenience of the delivery system, as in the now outmoded special education classroom to which exceptional students were formerly exiled.

Years ago, educators at Farnsworth Middle School, in Guilderland, New York, modernized the concept of the resource room and called it the Learning Workshop. Clearly committed to the integration of all children into the total school program, the school ensures that each student, regardless of disability, is a member of a regular team with an assigned homeroom and is entitled to all services offered within the building. The Learning Workshop was developed to aid teachers in responding to as many individual differences among students as possible, drawing upon the services of four professional educators and seven teacher aides.

The majority of the students who are served by the Learning Workshop are divided into two general categories: those who are two to three years below their grade level and those who are more than three years below their grade level. The Learning Workshop staff at Farnsworth has created two special programs for dealing with these youth. The Curriculum Adaptation Program provides students in the first category with the supplementary instruction, support, and materials that permit them to participate in almost all regular classroom tasks—that is, adaptation, modification, and enrichment through alternative teaching methods designed for learning-handicapped children. Children who fall into the second category are generally guided to the Basic Skills Instruction program created by the staff of the resource room to provide intensive small group prescriptive instruction in language arts, mathematics, basic sight vocabulary, and occupational education.

The Learning Workshop staff at Farnsworth places special emphasis on occupational education in realistic settings. The program is aimed at developing positive work habits, personal responsibility, positive peer interactions, and exposure to as many areas of the world of work as possible. Many such opportunities exist within the school setting, which involve community volunteers and stress vocational skills in demand in the economy.

Each Learning Workshop teacher must work closely with the teaching teams. Weekly meetings take place with each team to discuss the progress of Learning Workshop students in each academic area, and joint plans are developed to encourage additional learning. Learning Workshop teachers are not assigned to homeroom tasks or other morning duties, so that they will be free for consultation with individual teachers. To further assist this cooperation with teams and within houses, resource room staff operates from small rooms located in each house and utilizes one other regular size classroom for centralized functions. Table 7.3 illustrates a typical day for a Learning Workshop teacher at Farnsworth Middle School.

At Oaklea Middle School, in Junction City, Oregon, the resource room functions in a similar way to meet the needs of handicapped learners. The stated goal of the Resource Center at Oaklea Middle was to increase a student's participation in the regular program as much as possible, through instruction provided directly to the child or indirectly through consultation with the teacher. The center also offered services such as program preparation and diagnostic testing. The center provided services to middle school students who are functioning at least 1.5 years below grade level and who need special services to learn most effectively. The Resource Center, staffed by one full-time resource teacher, one math teacher, two Title I reading teachers, and three full-time aides, provided intensive instruction to students after referral by regular classroom teachers.

TABLE 7.3 **MODEL LEARNING WORKSHOP TEACHER SCHEDULE, FARNSWORTH MIDDLE SCHOOL, IN GUILDERLAND, NEW YORK**

	MOD time	Class
1.	9:05–9:30	Vince Leon 8th graders
2.	9:30–9:45	Stan et al. curriculum assistance
3.	9:45–10:00	Basic Skills Math Class
4.	10:00–10:15	4 students
5.	10:15–10:30	Peter curriculum 6th
6.	10:30–10:45	Todd assistance graders
7.	10:45–11:00	Barry Red Brian White; Silas–math reinforcement
8.	11:00–11:15	Mark Day Vince Day
9.	11:15–11:30	Ed
		John–curriculum assistance
10.	11:30–11:45	LUNCH—Teacher Consultation
11.	11:45–12:00	
12.	12:00–12:15	Basic Skills Math Class
13.	12:15–12:30	4 students
14.	12:30–12:45	
15.	12:45–1:00	Teacher (Team) Consultation Time
16.	1:00–1:15	(Guidance, parents, etc.)
17.	1:15–1:30	Todd Harvey; Harry–math assistance
18.	1:30–1:45	Gary
19.	1:45–2:00	Peter curriculum assistance
20.	2:00–2:15	Basic Skills Math Class
21.	2:15–2:30	5 students
22.	2:30–2:45	Team Consultation–8th grade
23.	2:45–3:00	Harry } curriculum assistance; Don–math assistance
24.	3:00–3:15	Kevin } curriculum assistance; Peter–math assistance
25.	3:15–3:30	Linda } curriculum assistance

At Oaklea, a special section of the Resource Center handled both remedial and gifted math students, and the staff at Oaklea developed special programs for gifted students as well as those with deficiencies. Most middle schools offer programs for the gifted, often structured in much the same way as the resource center for problem learners, except that the activities and the curriculum are geared for acceleration, independence, and in-depth work.

The referral procedure for the Resource Center at Oaklea Middle School seems fairly representative. Nine steps were followed.

1. Teacher becomes aware of specific problem.
2. Teacher fills out top of referral form in as much detail as possible and notifies parents that child is being referred to Resource Center for individual testing.
3. Teacher places referral in the appropriate Resource teacher's box. Resource Center will get parent permission for individual testing.
4. Resource Center will do individual testing in specific skill areas and notify referring teacher of test results.
5. Resource Center teacher will set up time for staffing if test results indicate a skill deficiency.
6. Staffing will be held including resource teachers, referring teacher, counselor, and parent. Resource teachers will present program plan based on test results.
7. Recommendations will be made on the basis of the staffing.
8. If approved for entry in Resource Center, student will begin individual program.
9. If not approved, conference will be held with the referring teacher to determine alternative programs to be utilized in regular classroom.

Once the referral process is complete, for either a disabled or gifted student, an Individualized Education Plan (IEP), required by law, is developed and implemented. Such plans are then subject to periodic review. Table 7.4 is an example of the form used at Oaklea Middle School to record the analysis of the plan.

Inclusion and the Interdisciplinary Team

In the last decade, many middle school educators moved beyond the resource room as the central focus of the education of students with disabilities. Inclusion has come to mean more central involvement of students in the life of the school, primarily through their membership in the interdisciplinary team. The program at Canandaigua Middle School (CMS), in Canandaigua, New York, exemplifies the strategy now frequently encountered in exemplary middle schools, in the early years of the 21st century. At CMS, in the early 1990s, we encountered the inclusion team process for the first time in a fully functioning program. At CMS, in the 2001–2002 school year, the process implemented a decade earlier remains virtually intact, testifying to its utility and validity. We believe that, school revenues permitting, the process in place at CMS will become the norm in middle schools across the nation.

At CMS, every student, including all students with exceptionalities, is a full-fledged member of an interdisciplinary team. A large school in the former high school building, CMS is organized into three houses, each containing three teams, one each at the 6th, 7th, and 8th grades. Each team has teachers

TABLE 7.4   INDIVIDUALIZED EDUCATION PLAN REVIEW, SPECIAL SERVICES, OAKLEA MIDDLE SCHOOL, IN JUNCTION CITY, OREGON

			Explain If Unmet					Action	
STUDENT NAME:	SCHOOL:		Lack Pre-requisite Skill	Objective Too Difficult	Activity Inappropriate	Materials Unavailable	Other	Carry Over Objective	Deep Objective

Annual Goal Code Number	Objective Number:	Comments:	PERFORMANCE Met As Stated	Not Met As Stated	Lack Pre-requisite Skill	Objective Too Difficult	Activity Inappropriate	Materials Unavailable	Other	Carry Over Objective	Deep Objective

RECOMMENDATIONS FOR FOLLOWING YEAR:

Teacher:_____   Parent: _____

_____   _____

_____   _____

_____   _____

TEACHER SIGNATURE   DATE   PARENT SIGNATURE   DATE

White: Permanent File   Yellow: Teacher   Pink: Parent

in mathematics, science, social studies, language arts—and inclusion. Every team, not just one at each grade level, has an inclusion teacher. The inclusion teacher and a group of exceptional education students are completely integrated into the life of the team. The inclusion teacher is just as much a part of the team at CMS as any of the other teacher team members, and so are the exceptional students served on the team. Every subject and every class is influenced by the presence of the inclusion teacher on the team. Common planning time offers all members of the team, with the inclusion teacher, opportunities to discuss the needs of the team's students and plan instruction that meets these needs.

At Collins Middle School, in Salem, Massachusetts, the organizational strategy is similar to that at CMS. At Collins, 1,100 students are organized into three houses (called "wharves" in honor of Salem's maritime history), each containing grades 6–8. Within each wharf are teams of 100 students and two language arts and social studies teachers, two mathematics and science teachers, one world language teacher, and one inclusion teacher. A three-period-long block schedule is also in place. Students with learning problems are as much a part of the wharf and team as any other student.

At CMS, Collins, and other schools using the inclusion team model, some students need special attention, in a smaller setting such as a resource room. Students whose capacity to learn is profoundly limited, or who have fragile medical conditions or emotional states, need a more sheltered classroom environment. At CMS, inclusion teachers and their teacher assistants plan for the needs of such students across the house or the school as a whole and organize, schedule, and staff the resource room as necessary. The emphasis is, nevertheless, always to help students to succeed in the larger environment of the team.

In the 2001–2002 school year, schools in many different states have implemented a similar process. At Monroe Junior High School, in Omaha, Nebraska, teams at the 7th and 8th grades have five members, including an inclusion teacher. At Monroe, inclusion teachers are expected to influence the team in many ways: creating a focus on individual students, shaping the curriculum, overseeing behavior management, bringing an objectivity to discussions of the needs of special students, and leading the team in creating accommodations and interventions to help students to succeed. The inclusion teacher at Monroe might help his or her peers to present information in different ways or might assist them with the use of learning contracts for students on the team. The inclusion teacher helps with a daily check-in process with special students on the team to make sure they are organized for the day's work. The inclusion teacher assists other teachers with the design of extra-credit activities that build on the particular strengths of special students. The inclusion teacher on the team would lead the design and implementation of behavioral interventions for students or identify students who might need to be referred for special services in the school or elsewhere. When instruction is included in these duties, inclusion teachers are very busy.

A slightly different model is in place at Mt. Slesse Middle School (MSMS), an exemplary middle school in Chilliwack, British Columbia. The school covers grades 7–9 but is organized on the middle school concept. The students and teachers are organized in a school-within-school model they call "pods." Students remain in a pod for their three years, moving through membership in two multiage teams (7th and 8th grades, 8th and 9th grades). In each pod, teachers on the teams work closely with another teacher who takes on a dual role of inclusion teacher and counselor. Each pod contains a "Learning Assistance Center" that "becomes the hub from which the pod operates" (Robert Patterson, personal communication, January 2001).

At Pawtuxent Valley Middle School, in Jessup, Maryland, yet another variation of the inclusion team is in place, combining cooperative learning, integrated curriculum, block scheduling, and inclusion. Teachers in the 6th grade implemented a sophisticated inclusion program that yields an engaging educational experience for all students. In a daily block of time that lasts for 126 minutes, science, mathematics, service learning, and technology are combined to produce an integrated, inclusive learning program designed around the use of learning centers or stations. All stations are focused on a theme, such as these past examples: Acid Rain, Travel to the Planet Xenar, the Fish Police Project, and Voyage of the Mimi.

At the beginning of each daily block, all students report to one of several mathematics classrooms organized around "identified instructional needs, be they remedial, developmental, or enrichment." Specific requirements of exceptional students, gifted students, or those in the general education program are addressed in this first time period. At the conclusion of this period, three days a week, all teachers in eight classrooms place a station rotation transparency up for students to see their station assignments. The integrative performance lesson then proceeds, with students in heterogeneous, cooperative groups working at stations and engaging in a problem-based learning curriculum. Groups of students move from station to station. All students are expected to successfully complete all of the stations in any particular unit. See Figure 7.4 for a graphic illustration of the structure.

Middle schools in virtually every state are now moving to implement an inclusion team process similar to that pioneered at CMS and other early adopters of the model. At MacDonald Middle School, in East Lansing, Michigan, one of the first exemplary middle schools in the nation, inclusion teams are now in operation. At Haltom Middle School (HMS), in Haltom, Texas, a pervasive inclusiveness shapes the whole school. The HMS inclusion philosophy "embraces children educated equally in all facets of school life in order to provide readiness for the future—through improving self-esteem, discovering independence, promoting survival skills, and building a desire for the continuation of learning" (Carol Glinsky, personal communication, November 1, 2000). To illustrate how the concept is spreading, other exemplary middle schools using the inclusion team model are Canyon Vista Middle School, in

SNAPSHOT OF THE WEEK - MATH/SCIENCE/SERVICE BLOCK (blue crew)

	MONDAY	TUESDAY	WEDNESDAY	THURSDAY	FRIDAY
1ST PERIOD OF BLOCK (42 minutes)	ADVISORY Schoolwide theme activities or Portfolio assessment/ academic support	MATH FUNDAMENTALS ⟷ G/T and Systems I math classes meet as homogeneous groups			
2ND PERIOD OF BLOCK (42 minutes)	Current events or non-fiction READING (all classes). or Student Government Caucus Group Meetings	READING in the content area. Lesson will be completed with reading teacher.	INTEGRATED STATION PROJECTS Problem solving applications/activities meeting math and science curriculum objectives. (heterogeneous groups that are changed weekly) These are called integrated performance units.		
3RD PERIOD OF BLOCK (42 minutes)		All students rotate through 3 classes over 2 days 2 student service project/ student government activities with math, science and reading curriculum objectives included. 1st semester will be the P.I.N.E.S. Environmental Center service course (see syllabus).	3 STATIONS Cooperative Learning Station ⟷ (All students rotate through each station over a 3 day period) NOTE: All stations are supported with technology tools	Integrated Laboratory	Knowledge Stop

FIGURE **7.4**

6TH GRADE WEEKLY SCHEDULE, PAWTUXENT MIDDLE SCHOOL, IN JESSUP, MARYLAND

Austin, Texas; Carrington Middle School, in Durham, North Carolina; Northport Middle School, in Northport, New York; and Cleveland Middle School, in Tulsa, Oklahoma.

In many other middle schools, funding limits the extent to which the inclusion team process can be implemented and, in those schools, it works a little differently. A school without the financial capability to place an inclusion teacher on every team instead may have an inclusion team at every grade level where most, but never all, of the exceptional students are served. At Wantagh Middle School, in Wantagh, New York, teams of three adults work within a smaller regular education classroom to provide services to a wide range of regular and exceptional students. At Fairfield Woods Middle School, in Fairfield, Connecticut, two special education teachers per grade level support inclusion, on teams, for students with the full range of learning or physical disabilities. Many variations of the process are in place, but most educators in exemplary middle schools aspire to implement an inclusion team model of some sort.

Inclusion and the Regular Teacher

Special educators stress that the methods that regular classroom teachers should use with the exceptional students who are included in their classrooms and teams are the methods used by all efficient, well-trained teachers (Kilgore et al., 2002). Little separates the effective special education teacher and the effective regular classroom teacher. Again, it becomes a matter of degree. Nonetheless, several suggestions are often cited as particularly important when considering students with special needs. Here is one such list, indicating the time-tested nature of these suggestions.

- Accept the child as he/she comes to you. Guard against the formation of negative expectations based on appearance, smell or verbal behavior.
- Realize that every child can do better than he/she is now doing.
- Learn as much as you can about the specific characteristics of the students who will be in your class.
- Survey your resources carefully, within and beyond the school.
- Respect the opinions of other professionals.
- Carefully determine the role and preparation of classroom assistants when available.
- Involve parents realistically.
- Offer a workable, practical curriculum broken down into subunits.
- Do not be overly rigid in your plans for grouping students for instruction.
- Make use of behavior modification and contingency management techniques. Be especially careful to function consistently with special students. Plan to reduce the child's dependence on you. (Department of Special Education, 1975)

Other helpful hints for regular classroom teachers working with students with learning problems in the regular classroom can be more concrete. Much of what is recommended to the regular classroom teacher seems to be based on the primacy of attention deficits among such students. When these deficits are added to the makeup of the young adolescent student in general, supportive instructional structure is very important in the classroom lives of these students. Consider a few of the items on one list of recommendations to the regular classroom teacher when mildly disabled students are present in some numbers (B. Commandy, personal communication, December 1990).

Post a calendar on the front board for assignments, color-coded by class.
Provide monthly calendars to students for long-range planning.

Provide a weekly assignment sheet, for students' or parents' use in keeping up with assignments or results.

Write important, timely announcements on the board.

Post a homework chart somewhere in the room to record receipt of work.

Design opportunities for "breaks": pencil sharpening, trash deposits, passing papers; these build in "legal" opportunities for moving and talking.

Acquire a second set of textbooks, or permission to share for those who forget.

Develop tapes for poor readers.

Give two grades, one for content and one for spelling.

Give frequent quizzes rather than large examinations.

In math, color code steps, and use graph paper to keep columns and rows straight.

Give lots of extra credit.

Provide as many checklists as possible for students to use as guidelines (e.g., a proofreading checklist).

Additional suggestions are developing strategies for giving students time to think about their answers to teacher questions; providing students with study guides; using graphic organizers; including alternatives to writing, such as the use of video or audio recorders; giving students paper on which they can doodle, because some students with disabilities seem to think better when they doodle; occasionally giving tests orally; and using multiple choice instead of fill-in-the-blank questions (Kolstad, Wilkinson, & Briggs, 1997).

TRACKING AND ABILITY GROUPING: WHICH WAY FOR THE MIDDLE SCHOOL?

The National Forum to Accelerate Middle-Grades Reform established, as its first policy statement, that exemplary middle schools combine heterogeneous classrooms and high standards and that ability grouping is a barrier to social equity (Norton & Lewis, 2000). The forum underlined the obligation of middle school educators to emphasize programs and practices that are socially equitable. Socially equitable middle schools make fair student classroom assignments and ensure that every student is taught to high standards, with challenging and relevant materials of the highest quality. "In high-performing schools, heterogeneous assignment of students is the norm" (Norton & Lewis, 2000, p. 10). Unfortunately, the opposite practice, ability grouping or tracking, is still far more frequently utilized in large numbers of middle schools (Gamoran & Weinstein, 1998). Not only is this practice of ability grouping, or tracking, a widespread activity, but it is also controversial. In the last 50 years, tracking has been the subject of more research studies (well over 500) than almost any other educational practice. And never have educational research and common school district practices been at greater variance. The great preponderance of the evidence weighs against tracking, while the great majority of school districts utilize it comprehensively (George, Renzulli, & Reis, 1997). Tracking, certainly at the middle level, may be the single most important unresolved issue in education.

Tracking seems like such a sensible idea. It ought to be possible to accurately identify and arrange students by ability or achievement. Reducing class heterogeneity should then make it possible for teachers to more accurately target their instruction, to meet more students' needs more often. Students should learn better and feel more positive about themselves as a consequence. Teachers should be able to accomplish their tasks with greater efficiency and ease. In practice, however, tracking does not seem to work out quite as sensibly, for the great majority of the students.

Synthesis of Research on Ability Grouping

An enormous amount of evidence testifies to the failure of ability grouping to deliver the expected benefits (Gamoran & Weinstein, 1998; George et al., 1997). Oakes made it clear, in her landmark 1985 work on the subject, *Keeping Track: How Schools Structure Inequality*, that identifying students accurately and fairly is extremely difficult and that all too often students are grouped so that income, social class, and race are most highly correlated with the so-called ability groups. Virtually all reviews of research (Slavin, 1987, 1990; Gamoran & Berends, 1987) indicate that the expected gains in academic achievement simply do not materialize. There is also good reason to believe that virtually no positive social or personal effects are produced by between-class ability grouping at the middle level school (Good & Brophy, 2000). As Anne Wheelock states, "As schools make greater use of ability grouping and tracking as students move from the fifth to ninth grades, students risk not only depressed achievement but also reduced motivation to learn" (1998, p. 110).

Why Tracking and Ability Grouping Fail

Between-class ability grouping, or tracking, is supposed to reduce student heterogeneity so that teachers can plan and deliver lessons that more nearly match the needs of the class in terms of the pace and the level of the lesson. This practice is supposed to improve student self-esteem and increase academic achievement. But apparently it does so, if at all, only for the upper 10% in the elementary setting and for the college bound in the high school.

Ability grouping may fail for several important reasons. First, a stigma results from negative labels and placements. Second, when students are tracked for most or all of the day, the power of expectations acts on teachers and students in ways that lead both to settle for less for low-track classes. Third, students are exposed to dramatically different curriculum. Fourth, teaching assignments, in many middle level schools, are not made randomly and equitably; often the more experienced teachers are assigned to high-track classes and unproven or inexpert teachers are given the low sections. Fifth, less successful students, continually placed together year after year, become, at the middle level, like an "anti-school camp" (Gamoran & Berends, 1987).

In our minds, the most stinging indictment of ability grouping is that in many districts it results in the de facto racial and social class resegregation of what were intended to be integrated schools. In many such middle level schools, three schools are in one building: a smaller honors or advanced track of higher income, majority culture students who also mostly are in the school's gifted and talented programs; an increasingly larger low track, composed primarily of poor and minority culture students, who also have a higher number of students in remedial and special education programs; and an increasingly ignored regular class of students whose educational experience is lacking in any special qualities. Even if ability grouping delivered tremendous benefits in academic achievement, educators would have to reject the practice, if it resulted in the racial, ethnic, and social class segregation of the public schools.

Which Way for the Middle School?

Middle school educators like to think of themselves as both familiar and comfortable with the diversity of their students. Good middle school teachers are described as being student-centered—that is, willing to meet their students where they are and carry the students forward as far as time and effort will permit. Exemplary middle schools are described as schools "willing to adapt all school practices to the individual differences in intellectual, biological, and social maturation of their students" (Lipsitz, 1984, p. 167). Such schools ought to be places where the abuses of tracking and ability grouping are found far less frequently.

In fact, this appears to be so. The evidence suggests that schools identified as exemplary middle schools engage in considerably less tracking than other middle level schools (George, 1988). In a study of 154 of some of the nation's best middle schools, virtually all of the respondents indicated that their schools were organized so that each student in the school was a member of a heterogeneously grouped interdisciplinary team, with each team a microcosm of the school as a whole. The survey also indicated that fully one-third of these exemplary middle schools rejected the practice of tracking, except insofar as they must serve students with identified special needs. Other schools grouped students on the teams for math or language arts, but rarely for more than two subjects. Most important, perhaps, the great majority of survey respondents indicated that they would like to move even further away from rigid between-class ability grouping.

At the beginning of the 21st century, we think that the great majority of middle school educators prefer heterogeneous grouping and seek to organize their schools into teams representing all of the variation within the school's student body. We believe that far fewer schools are organized into rigid ability levels, as might have been the case several decades ago. Virtually all of the middle schools identified in this textbook are committed to heterogeneous grouping. The evidence indicates that ability grouping has little educational value at the middle level; that educators in exemplary middle schools already do substantially less such grouping than is practiced in other schools; and that many, if not most, middle level educators would like to move even further away from ability grouping. Yet, the pressures for continuing the practice of ability grouping, from parents and teachers, continue (Kohn, 1998). New state and national standards, high-stakes tests, and harsh accountability programs threaten to reinstall ability grouping in many schools (George, 2000/2001).

Strategies for "De-Tracking"

Educators have not been successful, in large numbers, with "de-tracking" middle level schools. Some of this persistent failure may be the result of haste and poor planning.

Proceed with Caution and a Long-Term Plan   Practitioners engaged in de-tracking must begin with the recognition that the tracking process has been deeply embedded in their schools for generations. It has a tremendous hold in the public schools. Furthermore, tracking is unlikely to wither tomorrow or next year, in spite of the seemingly overwhelming amount of evidence against its use or the most earnest efforts of those who seek to eliminate it. De-tracking efforts may even result in the withdrawal of substantial numbers of middle- and upper-middle-class majority culture families from the school population. De-tracking must not be taken lightly.

To protect the interests of everyone involved, and the success of the de-tracking effort itself, a strategic planning process is needed that establishes a clearly desirable future state for the organization of the school or schools, identifies tactics required for success, and employs an action plan to achieve it all. Such a plan ought to involve a variety of efforts over a period of several years.

The worst possible results should be expected in situations where middle school leaders, even for the best of reasons, take unilateral and impulsive action to end tracking in their school or district. When this happens, practitioners with such experiences report that parents and policy-makers in and outside the school react angrily and noisily. Many teachers will find such plans difficult to implement successfully and will feel frustrated and discontented. Such efforts rarely lead to complete success, and more often the program, the participants, and the leadership suffer.

Secure Involvement and Representation of All Groups   Educational change of any sort is always at least partially political. In the case of tracking and ability grouping at the middle level, it is very political. The attempt to alter current grouping arrangements will surely go awry, practitioners say, unless all of those affected are involved to some extent.

This may be particularly the case with two groups of parents: those who believe that the current situation benefits their children and those who believe that it is inequitable. The first group must be persuaded that their children's educational experience will not be sacrificed on the altar of educational experimentation. They must be helped to see that educational excellence will not suffer as a result of capricious social engineering. They must be assisted to learn that the research suggests that high-ability, high-achieving students do well, academically, in virtually any setting.

Parents are often already anxious about their children moving from the more protective, and often monocultural, atmosphere of the smaller elementary school to a larger, multicultural, and often far less personal middle level school. When this transition also includes the potential for heterogeneous classes, anxieties of middle class majority culture parents can reach a potentially explosive peak. These parents must be convinced that their children will be challenged academically but not threatened personally.

Other parents, initially less well informed perhaps, must learn how important class placements are for the success of their children. They must come to see how important peer group influences are, especially for less successful learners. They must understand how important one teacher can be in the lives of their children, even at the middle level. They must be willing to speak out against what they believe to be unjust and unfair practices. They must be encouraged to insist on equity in the assignment of students, teachers, and school resources.

Policy-making school board members must become acquainted with the research. They must be helped to see that current arrangements may not meet the test of being fair or effective for all of the students in their schools. They must see that it can be politically safe to change.

Practitioners who have de-tracked successfully have frequently utilized a task force or steering committee of educators, parents, community members, and representatives from the board. Such groups become informed, participate in the design of the alternative, and, in doing so, become more committed to the implementation of alternatives to current practice.

Conduct a Local Self-Study   Practitioners say that research based on national studies is unlikely to convince the local professionals, parents, and policy-makers who most need to be persuaded. The national research must be reinforced with a study of the grouping practices in the local school or schools in question. The study must focus on real children known, at least in general, to those who will read the findings. One such study, conducted in a school on the east coast of Maryland, sought answers to the following 10 questions from educators in that school (H. Martin, personal communication, June 28, 1990).

1.   How careful are we in the way we place students in ability-grouped classes? Do we rely on a single measure? Do we use student behavior as an important criterion? Are all parents informed about the place-

ment of their students in sufficient time for them to explore the ramifications? Can we be confident that students are placed accurately and fairly?

2. What are the results of our identification and placement processes? Are the high track classes populated primarily by students from higher income home situations? Are minority group children underrepresented in high track classes or over-represented in low track classes?

3. What are the results, in terms of academic achievement? Can we say with confidence that the results are not skewed in terms of ethnic group or family income? That is, do we have an "effective school" in the sense that no identifiable groups of students can be predicted to have either generally lower or higher academic achievement? Are the ranges of higher academic achievement the almost exclusive province of majority culture upper middle class children? Are the bottom levels of achievement populated by predominantly children from families that are characterized as lower income and minority culture?

4. How flexible are our grouping strategies? How much mobility do our plans permit, from day to day, and from year to year? Do students spend most of the day, most of the year, and most of their tenure in the school in one ability group?

5. How does the current situation affect students' perceptions of themselves? Do high-track students, for example, have an advantage in terms of self-concept? Might positive self-perceptions of high track students be unjustifiably inflated, leading to an unreasonable sort of elitism? Do low track students feel good about themselves and about school?

6. How do high track and low track students feel about school and about each other? Is there a sense of community in the school such that students all enjoy being there? Do members of different ethnic and income groups evaluate school, and each other, positively? Is there a substantial amount of voluntary integration, in terms of seating in classes and elsewhere, choice of friends, etc.?

7. Is there a relationship between track placement and student behavior in school? For example, do most of the referrals to the office, for discipline reasons, come from the lower track students? Most of the suspensions? Do high track students represent most of the participation in school extracurricular activities of an academic nature?

8. How do teachers respond to the current arrangements? Does faculty support for maintaining ability grouping come primarily from teachers assigned to high-track classes? Are such assignments made fairly? That is, do all teachers share in the teaching of both high and low track groups? Is the teaching "talent" in the school dispersed evenly over all ability groups? Given an opportunity, would most teachers honestly prefer to teach high-track classes?

9. Do teachers actually prepare different lessons for different ability groups, or do both groups get the same content with substantially different expectations for mastery? Do teachers actually use different instructional strategies with high and low track classes, or are both groups expected to learn the same way?

10. Does parental support of and involvement in school programs come from a broad spectrum of the school population, or is it primarily a middle class, middle-income phenomenon?

If most of the answers to these questions result in a positive evaluation of the school organization, then little need may exist for the potentially upsetting changes that de-tracking could cause. If, however, the results of the self-study call the current situation into question, the data are likely to be much more persuasive than the results of national studies referenced by an outside expert.

Engage in Information Dissemination before Attempting Change   The results of both national and local research efforts need to be widely publicized, and stakeholders need time to process the information. Practitioners assert that opposition to proposed changes, on the part of parents and board members, can be substantially allayed by reliance on data and logic.

One middle level principal evolved a strategy for the frequent one-on-one sessions with parents and policy-makers in which he found himself prior to the decision to move to more heterogeneity in the social organization of the school that he led. Step one was to permit the concerned visitor a period of ventilation without interruption. Step two was to ask: "Do your concerns come from intuition or knowledge?" Inevitably, the answer given by the visitor was "intuition." Step three was to make this statement: "I'm using knowledge. Here are some of the resources and information I've been consulting. Please take it with you and read it carefully. Then let's talk again." According to this principal, a follow-up session was never needed.

Admittedly, the parents in this middle school population may have been exceptionally fair-minded and responsive to reason; other leaders may not be so fortunate. Efforts to alter the current grouping patterns will, however, be likely to proceed much more smoothly when a constant attempt is made to provide data where previously only intuition or bias prevailed.

Policy-makers, responsible for all of the children in the district, must be helped to see the wisdom in John Dewey's remark: "What the best and wisest parents want for their children, that must the community want for all its children." The change-oriented practitioner must take responsibility to see that board members and others have all of the information they need for reasoned, balanced decisions, not just what they hear on the telephone from a smaller number of parents or others with more narrowly focused vested interests.

Change to Heterogeneity in Grouping at the Lower Grades   The conventional wisdom suggests that, in efforts to change the patterns in a whole district, the early years of elementary education are the place to begin. Practitioners advised that, for a single school, try to change the first grade or two in the school. In a 6–8 middle level situation, for example, start in the 6th grade; in a 7–9 junior high school, attempt to change the 7th grade first.

Whether or not these suggestions are completely valid and reliable, a reasonable bit of folk wisdom is involved. Our own experience with change in middle schools over the last three decades squares with this contemporary advice. Organizations and hierarchies could evolve to a point where, for one reason or another, those members most resistant to change are found in the higher grades of a school or upper school levels in a district.

Make No Moves without Staff Development   Those who will be expected to successfully implement any proposed changes in the way students are grouped in a school or district must be prepared and confident. Including teachers in the research and decision-making that result in proposals for change is not enough, although doing so is essential. Teachers must be prepared to deal with a potentially different mix of learners. And the evidence suggests that simply moving to greater heterogeneity in grouping patterns does not automatically result in greater differentiation of instruction (Gamoran & Weinstein, 1998).

Practitioners suggest that several important components to staff development programs successfully prepare teachers for heterogeneous classrooms. Teachers must have an opportunity to think through the philosophical rationale that supports more flexibility in grouping. They must have a chance to study the research, both from the national and the local perspectives. These staff development sessions will enable teachers to come to decisions about the moral issues involved, but more will be required for a successful transition to heterogeneous classes.

Teachers must be acquainted with the skills that are characteristic of their peers who are effective in managing and instructing such classes. Training and assistance in applying the strategies of effective classroom behavior management will be required. Techniques for giving in-class assistance to less successful students and for challenging more successful students will need to be developed. Alternative models of grading, emphasizing individual progress and de-emphasizing the normal curve, must become part of the teachers' repertoire. Techniques for providing choice and diversity in homework and major assignments will be necessary. Every district has teachers who are or could quickly become effective in heterogeneous classrooms. Effective professionals can comprise these staff development cadres.

Staff development in effective instructional strategies will be essential. Training in cooperative learning is both popular and potent. Other strategies also lend themselves to heterogeneous classes; mastery learning models and varieties of individualized instruction will help teachers cope successfully. Two other important instructional strategies are the reading and writing workshop approach, and consultation and co-teaching (see Chapter 4). Differentiating instruction is the hallmark of an effectively de-tracked classroom (Tomlinson, 2000).

As with the consultation and co-teaching strategies, educators trained to deal with exceptional students may have much to offer. Many middle level practitioners say that one high-quality, low-cost, staff development resource for helping regular classroom teachers enjoy the heterogeneous classroom is the special educators in the building. Inviting these teachers to provide staff development for their regular classroom peers (e.g., on how to deal effectively with learning disabled students) may be credible, welcome, and inexpensive.

Some practitioners are using another strategy. These school-building leaders are less than confident about being able to spontaneously design and deliver adequate staff development to their teachers, but they are nevertheless feeling a sense of urgency to do something about tracking. Their approach is to say to their teachers, "Just do your best with the slow students." The school leader, in these situations, appears to be saying to the teachers, "I know there's only so much you can do with the slower students. Do your best with them, but I won't expect you to accomplish miracles."

We believe this advice is based on the assumption, held by many middle school practitioners, that slower students moved out of basic or compensatory classes and integrated into higher sections will be likely to do no worse and perhaps considerably better on some criteria than they would have done in those ability-grouped lower level sections. Without probing all the assumptions and implications of this sort of advice, and the outcomes to which they might lead, we think that, at the least, such statements might encourage some anxious teachers to agree to increasing the heterogeneity of their classes. So long as the sort of staff development that would permit the teacher to deal effectively with that heterogeneity follows this temporary situation, it seems, to us, a sensible stopgap measure.

Impose More Rigorous Identification Procedures Whether or not the school or district grouping strategies are amended, practitioners agree that virtually all procedures for the identification and placement of students into ability-grouped classes can profit from being closely examined and evaluated.

A number of suggestions apply here. Because of the nature and vulnerability of standardized instruments, educators in many districts are reluctant to place students in any program on the basis of only one such test or evaluation. In other schools, placement procedures are careful to avoid placing students in low sections solely because of the classroom behavior they exhibit. In still others, educators take pains to explain the potential ramifications of placement to parents prior to finalizing the process. As more middle level educators move "off the track," new and improved strategies for doing so effectively should emerge.

Getting Off the Track: Options and Alternatives

More than a dozen options and alternatives are available to rigid ability grouping currently being practiced in middle schools around the nation. Most appear to be congruent with research on tracking and ability grouping. Others seem promising and deserve to be implemented on a trial basis. Careful evaluation of any attempt to de-track should benefit all educators. All grouping patterns that attempt to account for differing abilities, however, should conform to the following characteristics (Slavin, 1987).

- Students should spend most of their day in heterogeneous situations, being grouped only in specific skill areas that might benefit from such a sharp focus (e.g., reading or mathematics).
- Grouped classes should be shaped on the basis of specific skills, not just on the basis of an IQ [intelligence quotient] measurement or overall achievement.
- Frequent reassessment of student placement should be a high priority.
- Flexible reassignment should be an easy thing for teachers to accomplish.
- Instruction should actually vary by pace and level to fit the real needs of the students in the groups.
- Within classes, the number of smaller ability groups should be small.

Joplin-Style Plans Grouping students for specific skills, across grade levels, appears to make instructional groups more manageable in terms of the range of achievement but mitigate the worst effects of traditional ability grouping. In this strategy, students are grouped, on multiage teams, by achievement in reading or math or both without regard for grade level. A math class might have any number of 6th graders, 7th graders, and 8th graders, or some other combination that would constitute a group of students who all needed the same math or reading skills. In this way the range of ability levels that the teacher had to accommodate is much narrower, permitting the teacher to engage in much more large group, teacher-directed instruction and to spend less time in arranging the traditional three reading groups. Students are grouped and regrouped as time permits, depending entirely on the progress they made in their respective classes.

Such a school organization can produce a variety of possible positive outcomes, all of which are potentially related to academic achievement. The three-year team made diagnosis and placement of students, for example, a much more data-based process. Home-school connections became firm earlier and grew more positive as the years passed. Peer relationships were far more positive than the school demographics would have led one to expect. Time on task was easier to achieve in the fall of the year and sustain throughout the spring.

Similar designs have also been used, at different times and places, in elementary schools. Currently, the Success for All/Roots and Wings programs (Slavin & Madden, 2000) used a model for the reform of urban education that includes a substantial measure of Joplin-style school organization. Children in an inner-city elementary school are grouped for reading across grade levels one, two, and three. The students spend most of their day in grade level heterogeneous classes, but in reading they are grouped by skill level regardless of grade. This permits the teacher, once again, to utilize a great deal more teacher-directed large group instruction, because the range of achievement is much narrower. We are convinced that Joplin-plan organizational strategies, which are combined with effective efforts to develop a real sense of community through team and school-within-school operations, have a great deal to offer middle level schools.

Partial De-Tracking   It may be politically unwise, pedagogically difficult, or possibly illegal to completely dismantle current grouping arrangements in many middle schools. State and national regulations may demand that certain identified student populations be served in narrowly prescribed patterns. Parents of certain students may exert intense pressure to maintain separate arrangements. And advocacy groups may throw up barriers of various kinds. But some of the levels of grouping or some of the subjects in which students are grouped can almost always be eliminated.

If students in a particular middle school or district are grouped, for example, in five levels per subject, in five academic subjects, the number of levels could be cut to three, or the number of subjects in which students are grouped to two or three. Pressure from parents and teachers of students in gifted, honors, and advanced classes, for example, may make it impossible to eliminate those sections. As a result, most middle level practitioners do not touch them.

Practitioners argue that, instead of fighting an endless and costly battle to eliminate all tracking and ability grouping, cut back where it is easiest. Make a case to eliminate the lowest sections, or eliminate grouping totally in classes where the subject matter is anything but hierarchical (e.g., social studies). Eliminating a substantial degree of tracking may also be the path of greatest fairness, because the final truth may not yet be known on ability grouping, especially for the gifted and in subjects such as mathematics and foreign language.

Teacher Autonomy   Many practitioners report that when they are unable to develop a consensus among the faculty for a major move away from ability grouping, another more moderate strategy is to empower teams of teachers to make the decisions. In any one school, a policy on grouping can be developed that says, in effect, all students are taught in instructional configurations that represent the way in which their team of teachers believe that they can best deliver instruction to that student or group. The school leaders thus are in a positive position of being able to say that every student in the school is receiving instruction in the way that teachers believe they can be most effective.

There are a number of possibilities, depending on the level of the school. In the elementary school, for example, teachers who work in self-contained classrooms can often make major modifications in the degree of heterogeneity within learning groups. Small groups of teachers working as a grade level group can do the same for the students they have in common. At the middle school, teachers on interdisciplinary teams can agree to group students for achievement, for example, by reading and math, reading only, math only, or all academic subjects, or they may designate no ability grouping whatsoever. The strategies they choose need not affect any other teacher in the school if the schedule is done carefully.

Before- and After-School Acceleration   A number of middle school programs are being redesigned to shift funding for remedial programs away from the official school day to early morning, late afternoon, and Saturday sessions. This is combined with the elimination of compensatory or other bottom-rung basic sections that, in the opinion of many practitioners, are extremely ineffective as they are now operated.

Whether or not these changes will make a measurable difference is yet to be determined, but some precedent exists for feeling positive about them: The Japanese do it that way (George, 1989). Emphasizing effort instead of ability, the Japanese encourage those who are not being successful to try harder, to study more, to "gambare" (endure with effort). In the Japanese junior high schools, contrary to many Americans' beliefs, very little ability grouping has taken place. The Japanese junior high schools are basically drawn from adjoining neighborhoods, and classroom groups are almost entirely heterogeneous.

Students who are behind are encouraged to enroll in mostly private after-school remedial and acceleration programs called "juku." Many Japanese junior high school students spend one or two hours, one or two afternoons a week, at such private schools. No insurmountable reason exists that many American children could not do more of the same, especially if the costs are borne by the school system.

Split-Level Grouping (Winchester Plan)   Some middle schools are organizing to both maintain and minimize ability grouping in an attempt to get the best of both educational worlds. At Conkwright Junior High School, in Winchester, Kentucky, students and teachers are organized into grade level team-type groups, each of which contains about 125 students. All students on a team are placed into one of five ability levels (see Figure 7.5): low (K, H), low average (W, T), average (C, R), high average (N, G), and high (O, I). Each of these groups is further subdivided into two equal size groups of 12 or 13 students, yielding 10 ability groups, two each at five levels. This grouping arrangement makes it possible for teachers to be assigned students from all five levels but never to have more than two ability levels in class at any one time. More important, perhaps, is that students travel with a group of peers of the same approximate ability, but they never spend the whole day with any one ability group. All students mix with students of all ability groups throughout the day.

Consider a sample group of low-ability students, subgroup K. The students in this group begin their day with math, grouped with students from subgroup R, an average subgroup. Second period is completely heterogeneous in elective and exploratory classes, while the academic teachers have a common planning time. Then group K has English with the other low group, group H, followed by reading with the same group. During lunch and physical education (team planning), students from group K are in mixed groups. In

Subject

		Math	English	Reading	Social Studies	Science
	1	CW	RT	OI	NG	KH
	2	Elective classes, Planning time				
	3	NG	OI	KH	CR	WT
Period	4	Lunch				
	5	Team planning				
	6	KR	NC	WT	OH	IG
	7	OI	KH	CG	WT	NR
	8	TH	WG	NR	IK	CO

Note: Ability levels: low (K, H), low average (W, T), average (G, R), high average (N, G), and high (O, I).

FIGURE 7.5

WINCHESTER PLAN, CONKWRIGHT JUNIOR HIGH SCHOOL, IN WINCHESTER, KENTUCKY

social studies, they learn side by side with the students from high group I. During the last period of the day they recombine with group H for science.

The teachers' experience is similar. The greatest homogeneity may be in subjects that are the most hierarchical, but no teacher must endure an unreasonable range for much of the day. For most of the day, the groups are probably much more homogeneous than necessary. Depending on the desires of the school or team, far more mixture could be injected in the grouping. Teachers and administrators say that this process has passed the test of time with them.

Administrative or Student Choice A number of middle level schools permit individuals to have their established placement altered for unofficial reasons. Some schools permit students to make the choice of the level or section they desire. Many middle level principals have been known to engage in administrative placement for a variety of reasons. Sometimes it is because of the power or persuasiveness of a parent, but in many schools it is because of the positive attitude and behavior of one or more students. These are students identified as good bets—students who may not have the IQ or the test score but who seem to the administrator to be capable of success in a more advanced section or group.

In many parts of the country, the racial and ethnic balances in school classrooms can be substantially and constructively altered. By selecting as good bets minority group students whose re-placement will at least partially correct the imbalance in formerly all-majority culture classrooms, the resegregation of American schools inside the school building can be at least somewhat mitigated. In a school of 1,000 students, for example, identifying 50 students for administrative reassignment can make a big difference in the composition of high level classes. Most practitioners say that such reassignments are almost always successful.

Repackaging the Curriculum   One wily middle school administrator reports solving the honors math conundrum by requiring every student in the school to take regular grade level mathematics. Honors mathematics is placed on the exploratory wheel and may be chosen by students at every grade level, every year. This way, students get two periods of math a day, not an unpopular option with parents.

Consultation and Co-Teaching   In many school districts, practitioners are pleased with two other instructional delivery models: consultation and co-teaching. Teachers of exceptional children and general education teachers collaborate, to various degrees, to bring greater numbers of exceptional students and their regular classroom peers together for instruction. In the consultation model, the general education teacher consults with and is regularly coached by the teacher of exceptional education. In co-teaching situations, the two teachers may regularly work together in the same classroom with the same heterogeneous group of students. Practitioners report increasing satisfaction with such efforts, with greater numbers of students with learning disabilities being served effectively in the regular classroom. Educators with experience in this practice express their optimism but also stress that these procedures work only when they are voluntary, when careful training is a prerequisite, and when adequate common planning time is available.

Consultation and co-teaching models are primarily a consequence of the inclusion movement and focus most often on students with learning disabilities. Educators in an increasing number of school districts are, however, discovering that the two models can work equally well when gifted and talented students are the focus. There is little to prevent regular classroom teachers and teachers of the gifted from working closely together. Moving gifted and talented students back into the regular classroom, where they can continue to have their specific needs met, ought, in our judgment, to assume a high priority in districts struggling to resolve the inequities and inefficiencies of rigid tracking and ability grouping.

We predict that the dialogue surrounding ability grouping, middle school concepts, and the effective education of the gifted and talented students will continue to assume a position of great significance among educators and parents. Advocates for gifted and talented programs will contend with those who support less emphasis on those programs in favor of more interdisciplinary and heterogeneous efforts (George et al., 1997). All children will suffer if adequate answers to these issues are not developed.

Pilot Programs   Many educators agree that, almost inevitably, a sizable number of teachers in every middle school are willing to try virtually anything that they believe will improve the program. That is at least part of the secret of good middle level schools. Typically, practitioners assert, these same teachers usually possess the energy, dedication, and effectiveness to be successful at whatever they attempt. Consequently, many educators seeking alternatives to tracking are encouraging individuals and small groups of teachers to pilot heterogeneous grouping in one or more parts of a school.

Guidelines to successful pilot programs commonly suggest collecting benchmark data for later comparison purposes. Most practitioners have been satisfied that teacher responses are positive enough to persuade others in the building to consider doing the same, because the opinions of professional peers carry more weight than virtually anything else. Other data might also be helpful in attempts to encourage parents and policy-makers to consider supporting further change: student responses, achievement scores, counts on school behavior problems such as referrals to the office, and positive interaction between majority and minority culture students.

The evidence against tracking and between-class ability grouping continues to mount (Mallery & Mallery, 1999). Yet, the practices persist almost everywhere. Middle school educators must make a concerted effort to invent effective alternatives, proceed cautiously, and give each option a careful public trial. Only then will American middle schools be able to de-track.

Good middle schools have often led the way instructionally in the last 35 years. With tracking, too, this appears to be the case. Among the very best middle schools, tracking is less often a part of the experience of teachers and students. Additional research ought to show how these educators have resisted the use of tracking and the details of the effective alternatives that they utilize. Which way for the middle school? Once again, middle school educators more often choose a different path.

CONTENT SUMMARY

In this chapter, we examined the connection between student development and school organization, suggesting that a relationship should exist between student maturity and the amount of social support and teacher specialization the students experience. We looked at several examples of school organizational practices: core-style, school-within-school, multiage grouping, and looping. We studied the process of inclusion and the contemporary practice of inclusion teams. Finally, the practices of tracking and ability grouping were examined and alternatives proposed.

CONNECTIONS TO OTHER CHAPTERS

How students and teachers are grouped for teaching and learning has definite and direct implications for other chapters, especially those dealing with curriculum (Chapter 3), instruction (Chapter 4), teaming (Chapter 6), and scheduling (Chapter 8). Much in these chapters relates to how grouping occurs. How should instruction occur in inclusive and heterogeneously grouped classes? What kinds of schedules work best for different organizational strategies? How does grouping affect the curriculum and vice versa? Chapter 6 discusses how closely the interdisciplinary team organization and grouping strategies must be aligned.

QUESTIONS FOR DISCUSSION

1. How has standards-based reform (see Chapter 3) affected the grouping practices occurring in contemporary middle schools?
2. How do the concepts of equity and fairness relate to a school's decisions to adopt one grouping strategy or another?
3. What are the primary concerns voiced by parents when school leaders propose changes in the way the school is organized for teaching and learning?
4. What percentage of teachers do you believe to be fully capable of differentiating instruction in their heterogeneous classrooms?
5. How does the number of content preparations teachers may have interact with the attempt to create smaller, more personal organizational strategies?

ACTION STEPS

1. Conduct a series of interviews with three teachers who are engaged in teaching more than one subject during the day. What are the advantages of seeing fewer students but having more preparations? What concerns do the teachers mention? Is their current situation to their liking, or would they opt for another arrangement if they could do so?
2. Use InfoTrac® College Edition or some other database to conduct a review of recent research on tracking and ability grouping over the last three to five years. How many studies can you locate? Is recent research consistent with earlier evidence? Are there newly important findings? What are your conclusions regarding this complex and important topic, as a result of your review?
3. Conduct a shadow study of a student involved in an inclusion team. First, secure permission from a school to do so. Be sure to ask permission to shadow the student without his or her knowledge. Then, acquire the student's schedule for a day. Arrive at the school before the first period, locate the student, and do your best to stay with the student,

without his or her knowledge, for as much of the day as you can devote to the observation. Using your own ideas, describe the experience of that student, and contrast it to what you think might have happened if the student were not on an inclusion team.

SUGGESTIONS FOR FURTHER STUDY

Books

Bauer, A., & Shea, T. (1999). *Inclusion 101: How to teach all learners.* Baltimore, MD: Paul H. Brookes Publishers.

Booth, T., & Ainscow, M. (1998). *From them to us: An international study of inclusion in education.* New York: Routledge.

Brownlie, F., & King, J. (2000). *Learning in safe schools: Creating classrooms where all students belong.* Markham, Ontario: Pembroke Publishers.

Capper, C., Frattura, E., & Keyes, M. (2000). *Meeting the needs of students of all abilities: How leaders go beyond inclusion.* Thousand Oaks, CA: Corwin Press.

Cohen, E., & Lotan, R. (1997). *Working for equity in heterogeneous classrooms: Sociological theory in practice.* New York: Teachers College Press.

George, P., & Lounsbury, J. (2000). *Making big schools feel small: Looping, multiage grouping, and school-within-school.* Columbus, OH: National Middle School Association.

George, P., Renzulli, J., & Reis, S. (1997). *Dilemmas in talent development in the middle grades: Two views.* Columbus, OH: National Middle School Association.

Harris, K., Graham, S., & Deshler, D. (1998). *Teaching every child every day: Learning in diverse schools and classrooms.* Cambridge, MA: Brookline Books.

Jones, C. (2000). *Curriculum development for students with mild disabilities: Academic and social skills for inclusion IEPs.* Springfield, IL: C. C. Thomas.

Kochhar, C., West, L., & Taymans, J. (2000). *Successful inclusion: Practical strategies for a shared responsibility.* Upper Saddle River, NJ: Merrill.

McLaughlin, M. (1996). *Appropriate inclusion and paraprofessionals: Changing roles and expectations.* Washington, DC: National Education Association.

Putnam, J. (1998). *Cooperative learning and strategies for inclusion: Celebrating diversity in the classroom.* Baltimore, MD: P. H. Brookes Publishers.

Ryan, K., & DeStefano, L. (2000). *Evaluation as a democratic process: Promoting inclusion, dialogue, and deliberation.* San Francisco, CA: Jossey-Bass.

Smith, D. (1998). *Inclusion: Schools for all students.* Belmont, CA: Wadsworth Publishing Co.

Tharp, R., Estrada, P., & Dalton, S. (2000). *Teaching transformed: Achieving excellence, fairness, inclusion, and harmony.* Boulder, CO: Westview Press.

Tiegerman-Farber, E., & Radziewicz, C. (1998). *Collaborative decision making: The pathway to inclusion.* Upper Saddle River, NJ: Merrill.

Tilstone, C., Florian, L., & Rose, R. (1998). *Promoting inclusive practice.* New York: Routledge.

Tomlinson, C. (1999). *The differentiated classroom: Responding to the needs of all learners.* Alexandria, VA: Association for Supervision and Curriculum Development.

Zionts, P. (1997). *Inclusion strategies for students with learning and behavior problems: Perspectives, experiences, and best practices.* Austin, TX: Pro-Ed.

Periodicals

Arguelles, M., Hughes, M., & Schumm, J. (2000). Co-teaching: A different approach to inclusion. *Principal, 79*(4), 48, 50–51.

Betts, J., & Shkolnik, J. (2000). The effects of ability grouping on student achievement and resource allocation in secondary schools. *Economics of Education Review, 19*(1), 1–15.

deBettencourt, L. (1999). General educators' attitudes toward students with mild disabilities and their use of instructional strategies: Implications for training. *Remedial and Special Education, 20*(1), 27–35.

Burns, M. (1999). Effectiveness of special education personnel in the Intervention Assistance Team Model. *Journal of Educational Research, 92*(6), 354–356.

Callahan, K., Rademacher, J., & Hildreth, B. (1998). The effect of parent participation in strategies to improve the homework performance of students who are at risk. *Remedial and Special Education, 19*(3), 131–141.

Carpenter, S., King-Sears, M., & Keys, S. (1998). Counselors + educators + families as a transdisciplinary team = more effective inclusion for students with disabilities. *Professional School Counseling, 2*(1), 1–9.

Duchardt, B., Marlow, L., Inman, D., Christensen, P., & Reeves, M. (1999). Collaboration and co-teaching: General and special education faculty. *Clearing House, 72*(3), 186–190.

Elliott, D., & McKenney, M. (1998). Four inclusion models that work. *Teaching Exceptional Children, 30*(4), 54–58.

Gibb, G., Ingram, C., Dyches, T., Allred, K., Egan, M., & Young, J. (1998). Developing and evaluating an inclusion program for junior high students with disabilities: A collaborative team approach. *B.C. Journal of Special Education, 21*(3), 33–44.

Giles, R. (1998). At-risk students can succeed: A model program that meets special needs. *Schools in the Middle, 7*(3), 18–20.

Hendershott, T. (1997). Under observation: Critical areas of school effectiveness. *Schools in the Middle, 6*(4), 34–36.

Hewitt, M. (1999). Inclusion from a general educator's perspective. *Preventing School Failure, 43*(3), 133–134.

Jitendra, A., Hoff, K., & Beck, M. (1999). Teaching middle school students with learning disabilities to solve word problems using a schema-based approach. *Remedial and Special Education, 20*(1), 50–64.

Kaiser, J. (1997). Advocate for your adolescent: Encouraging special needs parents to get involved. *Schools in the Middle, 7*(1), 33–34, 52.

Karnes, F., & Stephens, K. (2000). State definitions for the gifted and talented revisited. *Exceptional Children, 66*(2), 219–238.

Langone, J. (1998). Managing inclusive instructional settings: Technology, cooperative planning, and team-based organization. *Focus on Exceptional Children, 30*(8), 1–15.

Prom, M. (1999). Measuring perceptions about inclusion. *Teaching Exceptional Children, 31*(5), 38–42.

Rees, D., Brewer, D., & Argys, L. (2000). How should we measure the effect of ability grouping on student performance? *Economics of Education Review, 19*(1), 17–20.

Renzulli, J., & Richards, S. (2000). Meeting the enrichment needs of middle school students. *Principal, 79*(4), 62–63.

Richardson, D. (1998). Eric's journey: A restructured school's inclusion program and a student with disabilities. *NASSP Bulletin, 82*(594), 74–80.

Rochester, M. (1998). What's it all about, Alfie? A parent/educator's response to Alfie Kohn. *Phi Delta Kappan, 80*(2), 165–169.

Shore, K. (2000). Teaching the gifted student. *Principal, 79*(4), 37–39, 42.

Sobel, D., & Vaughn, N. (1999). Here comes the SUN Team! Collaborative inclusion at work. *Teaching Exceptional Children, 32*(2) 4–12.

Sprague, M., & Pennell, D. (2000). The power of partners: Preparing preservice teachers for inclusion. *Clearing House, 73*(3), 168–170.

Stanovich, P. (1999). Conversations about inclusion. *Teaching Exceptional Children, 31*(6), 54–58.

ERIC

Demchak, M. (1999). *Facilitating effective inclusion through staff development* (ERIC document ED429769).

Gensemer, P. (2000). *Effectiveness of cross-age and peer mentoring programs* (ERIC document ED438267).

Gibb, S., Gibb, G., Randall, E., & Hite, S. (1999). *From "I" to "we": Reflections about leadership* (ERIC document ED432059).

Gilberts, G. (2000). *The effects of peer-delivered self-monitoring strategies on the participation of students with disabilities in general education classrooms* (ERIC document ED439871).

Hammond, H. (1999). *Developing prereferral teams in your schools and keeping them there!* (ERIC document ED429744).

Irvin, J. (1997). *What current research says to the middle level practitioner* (ERIC document ED427847).

Levison, L., & St. Onge, I. (1999). *Disability awareness in the classroom: A resource tool for teachers and students* (ERIC document ED432101).

Markham, R., & Shelly, P. (1996). *Coming from behind: A "catch-up" philosophy in education: The story of Carver Middle School* (ERIC document ED402071).

Mills, R. (1998). *Grouping students for instruction in middle schools* (ERIC document ED419631).

Mitchem, K., & Benyo, J. (2000). *A classwide peer-assisted self-management program all teachers can use: Adaptations and implications for rural educators* (ERIC document ED439868).

Mortimore, P. (2000). *Globalisation, effectiveness, and improvement* (ERIC document ED440448).

Pedroza, A., Mueller, G., & Whitley, J. (1998). *Reconstructing special education services in middle school: Success for All* (ERIC document ED425580).

Power-deFur, L., & Orelove, F. (1997). *Inclusive education: Practical implementation of the least restrictive environment* (ERIC document ED401682).

Rice, D., & Zigmond, N. (1999). *Co-teaching in secondary schools: Teacher reports of developments in Australian and American classrooms* (ERIC document ED432558).

Seferian, R. (1999). *Design and implementation of a social-skills program for middle school students with learning and behavioral disabilities* (ERIC document ED436863).

Taylor, G., & Harrington, F. (1998). *Inclusion: Panacea or delusion* (ERIC document ED423225).

Trimble, S., & Peterson, G. (1999). *Beyond the process of teaming: Administrative support, classroom practices, and student learning* (ERIC document ED438601).

Web Sites

Alternatives to Ability Grouping: Still Unanswered Questions
http://www.ed.gov/databases/ERIC_Digests/ed390947.html
This article for ERIC/CUE Digest (no. 111, December 1995) written by Gary Burnett, discusses several de-tracking alternatives such as cooperative learning, within-class ability grouping, interest grouping, and restructured vocational education. Burnett suggests that further research is needed into the impact and effectiveness of specific de-tracking efforts.

The Tracking and Ability Grouping Debate
http://www.edexcellence.net/library/track.html
Research on tracking conducted by Dr. Thomas Loveless is presented on this site. The research was sponsored by the Thomas B. Fordham Foundation.

Ability Grouping

http://www.indiana.edu/~eric_rec/ieo/bibs/ability.html

This Web site has a collection of materials about ability grouping. The collection "was assembled from various resources on the World Wide Web, bookstores, libraries and others. Included materials were selected to provide a balanced, cursory picture of current research and practices."

Northport Middle School

http://northport.k12.ny.us/~nms/index.html

The site includes a presentation of the school's team organization and its full inclusion program.

Education Policy Analysis Archives

http://olam.ed.asu.edu/epaa/v4n19.html

"Inclusive Education in the United States: Beliefs and Practices among Middle School Principals and Teachers," by C. Kenneth Tanner, Deborah Jan Vaughn, and Susan Allan Galis presents the findings of a study in which "a total of 714 randomly selected middle school principals and teachers responded to concerns about inclusion, 'degree of change needed in' and 'importance of' collaborative strategies of teaching, perceived barriers to inclusion, and supportive activities and concepts for inclusive education."

The Consortium on Inclusive Schooling Practices

http://www.asri.edu/cfsp/brochure/abtcons.htm

"The Consortium on Inclusive Schooling Practices represents a collaborative effort to build the capacity of state and local education agencies to serve children and youth with and without disabilities in school and community settings." Important site components include the following.

- Information about the activities of the consortium
- Electronic Catalog of Products from Funded Projects
- Access to the National Statewide Systems Change Network (SWSCNet) Listserv
- Full-text copies of reports from the consortium's research studies
- Links to other sites related to inclusion

Inclusive Education

http://www.uni.edu/coe/inclusion/index.html

The Web site is "designed for general education teachers, special education teachers, parents, and school staff to help provide some answers about how inclusive education can be accomplished. Resources for making accommodations are included as well as links to other web sites and resource lists for learning more about inclusive education."

ORGANIZING TIME AND SPACE IN THE MIDDLE SCHOOL

BATAVIA MIDDLE SCHOOL

Batavia Middle School, in Batavia, Illinois, has successfully implemented many components of the middle school concept. Over the years, it has transformed the traditional junior high school program into one focused on the characteristics and needs of the young adolescent. Rigid tracking, for example, has been abandoned in favor of heterogeneous grouping—including a team-based gifted program—focusing on differentiating instruction instead of a pullout program. Teams of two to three teachers work with 6th graders; teams of three to four teachers work with 7th graders; teams of four to five teachers work with 8th graders. Advisory is scheduled every day, for one period, within each team's block of time. The school's schedule is a classic example of a flexible block schedule, with large blocks of time under the control of teams of teachers.

WHAT YOU WILL LEARN IN CHAPTER 8

School leaders and others charged with the responsibility for organizing and operating middle schools frequently discover that the successful implementation of advisory programs, interdisciplinary teaming, or an exciting curriculum depends largely on the effectiveness of the schedule and the creative use of the school building. Factors that, in the past, were thought to be separate enterprises are now recognized as having an important, sometimes all-important, bearing on the success of curriculum and teaching efforts. Few middle schools have been able to overcome the barriers erected by a poor schedule or restrictive environment. This chapter focuses on two central factors: the use of time and space to facilitate important goals of the middle school program.

ORGANIZING TIME IN THE MIDDLE SCHOOL

Organizing time in the middle school follows the same mandate to provide a unique and transitional approach, as does every other component of the middle school concept. Because the programs of the elementary school and the high school differ from each other as well as from the program in-between, the methods of scheduling not surprisingly also differ. The middle school schedule attempts to lead from that of the elementary school to that of the high school, while reflecting the special program provided for the students in the middle grades. While several varieties of scheduling are appropriate for the middle school, for the schedule to be congruent with the program it serves, it must accommodate the team organization. One teacher cannot be working alone and making all the decisions about scheduling his or her students; and one massive schedule cannot be determined by the office and operated by the bell without any teacher input. The middle school schedule is designed to be controlled by groups of teachers organized into teams in collaboration with the office, a unique and transitional type of schedule for a special type of program. Teachers from several different subject areas, working together to create and operate a comprehensive academic program for the students they serve, need a schedule with flexibility and structure. Any schedule that removes the team's ability to manipulate the daily time frame to suit the objectives of its planning is clearly inappropriate for the middle school.

THE FLEXIBLE BLOCK

The schedule for 2000–2001 at Batavia Middle School, in Batavia, Illinois, illustrates well the flexible block schedule that has come to be identified with the middle school concept. Ten much smaller periods are organized into large blocks of time controlled by teachers on teams. Try to match what principal Harold Wolff describes with the schedule in Table 8.1.

> Our schedule provides for academic and exploratory blocks of time "owned" by the team. There are no bells that occur in our academic wings since each team may be operating on a different schedule and the schedule may vary from day to day. Longer/shorter classes are an option at any time. We work very hard to make the *team* the focal point of the school and not have other issues (band, special education, gifted, algebra) impact the ability of teams to flexibly use their block time. Since we are a large school, student movement *could* be an issue. It is *not* an issue in our building due to our schedule. [This is because] grade levels are dismissed to exploratory and lunch times minutes before the next grade level is in the hall. This allows us to never have students in the halls going in two directions. It works great! (Personal communication, January 8, 2000)

Implementation of the Middle School Concept

The 2000–2001 schedule at Wakulla Middle School (WMS), in Crawfordville, Florida, is another good example of the type of schedule that has been characteristic of hundreds, if not thousands, of exemplary middle schools during the last several decades (see Table 8.2). The recent team schedule at WMS is

TABLE 8.1 2000–2001 MASTER SCHEDULE, BATAVIA MIDDLE SCHOOL, IN BATAVIA, ILLINOIS

	1	2	3	4	5	6	7	8	9	10
Grade	8:00 a.m.–8:39 a.m.	8:41 a.m.–9:20 a.m.	9:22 a.m.–10:01 a.m.	10:05 a.m.–10:45 a.m.	10:47 a.m.–11:27 a.m.	11:31 a.m.–12:07 p.m.	12:11 p.m.–12:52 p.m.	12:54 p.m.–1:35 p.m.	1:37 p.m.–2:17 p.m.	2:19 p.m.–3:00 p.m.
6th grade	Explore	Explore	Explore	Block	Block	Lunch	Block	Block	Block	Block
	8:00 a.m.–8:40 a.m.	8:42 a.m.–9:22 a.m.	9:24 a.m.–10:04 a.m.	10:08 a.m.–10:48 a.m.	10:50 a.m.–11:29 a.m.	11:31 a.m.–12:10 p.m.	12:14 p.m.–12:50 p.m.	12:54 p.m.–1:36 p.m.	1:38 p.m.–2:18 p.m.	2:20 p.m.–3:00 p.m.
7th grade	Block	Block	Block	Explore	Explore	Explore	Lunch	Block	Block	Block
	8:00 a.m.–8:40 a.m.	8:42 a.m.–9:21 a.m.	9:23 a.m.–10:02 a.m.	10:04 a.m.–10:43 a.m.	10:47 a.m.–11:24 a.m.	11:28 a.m.–12:10 p.m.	12:12 p.m.–12:53 p.m.	12:57 p.m.–1:36 p.m.	1:38 p.m.–2:17 p.m.	2:19 p.m.–2:58 p.m.
8th grade	Block	Block	Block	Block	Lunch	Block	Block	Explore	Explore	Explore

TABLE 8.2 **2000–2001 MASTER SCHEDULE, WAKULLA MIDDLE SCHOOL, IN CRAWFORDVILLE, FLORIDA**

First Bell—7:35 a.m. Homeroom 7:40 a.m.–7:50 a.m. Team	7:55 a.m. 1	8:45 a.m. 2	9:35 a.m. 3	10:25 a.m. 4	5	12:40 p.m. 6	1:30 p.m.–2:20 p.m. 7
Cheetahs 126—Barwick 130—Strickland	Academics	Academics	Academics	Academics	Lunch 11:18 a.m.–11:48 a.m.	U.A.	P.E.
Lions 127—Busen 129—Hill	Academics	Academics	Academics	Academics	5th 11:50 a.m.–12:40 p.m.	U.A.	P.E.
Tigers 196—Byars 194—Coyle	Academics	Academics	Academics	Academics		P.E.	U.A.
Leopards 125—Edwards 124—Price 122—Graham	Academics	Academics	U.A.	P.E.	5th 11:15 a.m.–12:00 p.m.	Academics	Academics
Bobcats 134—Commander 132—Stringer	Academics	Academics	U.A.	P.E.	Lunch 12:05 p.m.–12:35 p.m.	Academics	Academics
Panthers 207—DuBois 210—Newland	Academics	Academics	P.E.	U.A.		Academics	Academics
Jaguars 136—Anderson 137—Fielder 140—Johnson	U.A.	P.E.	Academics	Academics	5th 11:15 a.m.–12:00 p.m.	Lunch 12:50 p.m.–1:30 p.m.	Academics
Lynx 205—Glisson 198—Spivey 200—Thomas	P.E.	U.A.	Academics	Academics	6th 12:00 p.m.–12:50 p.m. Academics		Academics
Pumas 149—Masterson 147—Webster	Academics P.E.	Academics U.A.	P.E. Academics	U.A. Academics	Lunch 12:50 p.m.–1:20 p.m. 12:05 p.m.–12:35 p.m.	Academics Academics	Academics Academics

Note: U.A. = unified arts; P.E. = physical education. Lunch time: Chrestensen—11:15 a.m.–11:48 a.m.; Jump—12:05 p.m.–12:35 p.m.; Price—11:15 a.m.–11:48 a.m.; Shipley—12:50 p.m.–1:20 p.m.; Stringham—12:05 p.m.–12:35 p.m.

only a slight variation of the schedule that has operated effectively at the school since the early 1970s and in many other schools for the same duration. It has been called the flexible block because it offers teachers numerous choices and options, because it can be a traditional seven-period day, or because it can be reorganized into one or more much larger blocks of time. Such a schedule has been common, and consummately durable, in exemplary middle schools around the nation, precisely because it affords the maximum opportunity to implement components of the middle school concept.

The flexible block schedule facilitates the implementation of virtually every component of the middle school concept, although simply looking at the schedule does not reveal some of these features. Teachers and students are organized on teams (Cheetahs, Leopards, Jaguars, etc.). The school is also organized into multigrade houses, with teams of 6th, 7th, and 8th graders in each house, although the schedule is organized around grade levels. This means, for example, that all 6th graders have physical education together, even though they are in houses with 7th and 8th graders. The schedule provides the teaming teachers with common planning time when their students are at unified arts and physical education. All 6th grade teachers (and 7th and 8th) in the building have common grade level planning time, so grade level concerns can be dealt with whenever necessary. Students have daily physical education and exploratory classes, in addition to five academics. No bells are necessary. An advisory program that has worked well for 25 years is offered daily, although it is not obvious on the schedule because it takes place at the same time as physical education. (See Chapter 5 for a detailed description of the advisory program at WMS.)

The schedule at WMS offers increments of flexibility and autonomy for teaching teams not found in other scheduling arrangements. Teachers at WMS (and the hundreds of other middle schools using a similar schedule) have control over their time. They can treat the schedule as a seven-period day or as one long block to be divided how and when teachers on teams see the need. If they wish to stick closely to a traditional schedule, each teacher on the team can teach his or her own class five separate times each day. If, however, the Cheetahs team wished to take a field trip to the locally famous deep freshwater spring, it can be gone from 7:35 a.m. until 12:40 p.m. without having to secure the cooperation of anyone else in the building. It could spend every day of a particular week there, as the lesson plans require.

If the teachers on the Cheetahs team (or any other) wanted to use their schedule in the format of the long block, they could take that same time period and carve it up, say, into three blocks of 85 minutes, with different subjects meeting for that length of time on alternating days. If the team wanted to create a two-week interdisciplinary unit (which is often the case at WMS), the Cheetahs could suspend the meeting of separate subjects for whatever number of days the team wished to do so.

At Wakulla Middle School, the school leadership places even more confidence in the teaching teams. After firmly fixing the times for physical education, lunch, and exploratory classes for each team, the principal empowers the teachers to decide when particular classes will be taught, how students will be grouped within the team, and which subjects will be taught by each teacher. Teachers at Wakulla Middle have the maximum amount of leverage in the decisions that affect their immediate professional lives at school, especially regarding the schedule.

At WMS, the administration goes through a series of steps each year to make certain a balanced group is delivered to each team and house, thus making later scheduling easier for teachers and administrators. The process begins in the late spring when the information about rising 6th graders is received from the elementary schools. Students are identified according to a number of criteria: Exceptional Student Education (ESE) status, math and reading recommendations from 5th grade teachers, alternative education recommendations, retentions, teachers' comments, special requests, and student identification by gender, race, and socioeconomic status. Each 6th grade team, and homerooms within the team, then is set up to receive the same number of students according to these criteria. Sixth grade teams are then assigned a physical education period, a unified arts period, and lunch; the rest is up to the team. For 7th and 8th graders, the process is much the same, except that compromises must be accepted in the assignment of band and chorus students.

The teachers at Wakulla decide how the responsibility for the curriculum will be divided among the teachers on the team. Each teacher may teach every subject or may specialize according to his or her strengths and preferences. A schedule for academic instruction within the team is devised. Students are grouped in whatever configurations the teachers on that team believe will promote the most successful learning for that particular team of students. Other teams in the same school may group students differently or arrange responsibilities for the curriculum in dissimilar ways. The professionals closest to the action, the teachers on the team, make these decisions.

The continued excellence of the middle school program in Wakulla County, nearly 25 years later, is a testimony not only to the persistent commitment of the middle school educators but also to the effectiveness of the components as they implemented them, including the schedule. The WMS schedule, with its flexible blocks of time, provides much needed flexibility to teams of teachers. The schedule could be rotated each trimester (12 weeks) if the staff at the school chose, so that over the year everyone would experience the most and least desirable aspects of the schedule. Typically, however, 6th graders have most of their academic time in the morning and their physical education and exploratory time in the afternoon. This, educators there testify, provides a much smoother transition into the middle school for those young adolescents. Seventh and 8th graders, who presumably have greater stamina than 6th graders, have academics later in the day.

The Flexible Block Responds to Clearly Established Priorities

A flexible schedule is like a budget—used to maximize the satisfaction of basic needs and the desire for luxury items. Just as few human beings are able to satisfy all their needs and wants in terms of the financial budget, acquiring enough time and apportioning it wisely enough to accomplish all that a school program can offer is often impossible. Choices must be made and priorities must be set.

There is never enough money or time to accomplish all of one's wishes. Scarcity of money requires the ordering of financial priorities and making some difficult choices among competing options. Money, for example, must always be divided between necessities and luxuries. One might wish to spend a great portion of one's income on trips to the beach, but at some point such expenditures will have to be limited. Spending money on necessities tends to be required, simply by definition. The same is true in arranging time—in the life of an individual and in the life of a middle school.

Priorities emerge from values, and values are the results of a philosophy, a sense of purpose, and a commitment to a certain set of goals. These will be different, in some way, in virtually every school, even though each middle level school ought to begin with a commitment to responding to the characteristics and needs of older children and early adolescents.

Broomfield Heights Middle School (BHMS), in Broomfield, Colorado, is another school with a long tradition of excellence in middle school education. During one typical year at BHMS, the priorities for consideration in the development of the master schedule were the following.

1. An advisory program of at least 15 minutes will be scheduled daily.
2. Common planning time will be available for teams of teachers.
3. All teachers will be members of only one academic team.
4. No more than 150 students will be allowed per team.
5. Students will be able to choose exploratory classes.
6. A co-curricular program will exist.
7. Electives and academic classes will be scheduled on a trimester basis.
8. Multiage grouping will be permitted in electives.
9. Lunch periods will be scheduled at reasonable times.
10. A school-within-school model will be feasible.
11. The schedule will permit a pilot team of two grades, 7th and 8th.

As the process of schedule development proceeded, the scheduling team at BHMS committed itself to attending to these priorities and to achieving as many as possible, starting at the top of the list and working down. The best schedule for that year, at that school, would be the one that permitted the maximum number of priorities to be included. The priorities of any one school will be different from those of other schools, and priorities at a particular school will be different from year to year. Starting the scheduling process without a clear sense of the priorities, however, may introduce a fatal flaw at the outset. Just like an automobile tire that goes flat far down the road from the point at which the leak began, the scheduling process can suffer, at the end, from confused or conflicting priorities that were unresolved at the beginning of the process.

Just because scheduling priorities are not publicly listed does not mean that such priorities do not exist. Too often, we have worked with school administrators who have claimed to be unable to implement one program or another (e.g., pure interdisciplinary teams) because of scheduling difficulties. In many cases, the difficulties experienced by these administrators are tied to unannounced, perhaps even unconscious, but very real scheduling priorities. When certain priority programs from earlier years are assumed to continue unchanged, and these assumptions are unspoken, the hidden priorities may skew the scheduling process in unsatisfying directions. When programs for special small groups, in particular, are allowed to assume priority in the curriculum, they will also assume priority in the schedule. When gifted and talented programs, journalism, or athletic activities are placed at the top of the school philosophy, in a spoken or unspoken way, they must be satisfied first when it comes to scheduling. Satisfactory scheduling processes depend upon the open, public, and honest discussion of school curriculum philosophy and the establishment of priorities in the same way. Schedules always reflect the school philosophy, the real school philosophy.

Table 8.3 is an example of the schedule that emerged from the philosophical and programmatic consensus among the staff members of BHMS. The school entered the scheduling process after first developing a firm philosophical consensus achieved by a combination of spirited leadership and dedicated professionalism in the classroom. That consensus at BHMS included an advisory program, interdisciplinary teams, exploratory curriculum, a block schedule with common planning time, and a belief in heterogeneous grouping—that is, the basic foundation components of an exemplary middle school design.

As one can see from studying the left side of the schedule, it is both a flexible block schedule and a seven-period day, just like the schedule at Wakulla. This feature offers stability and structure while preserving the flexibility so desirable when it is required. The day begins with a 20-minute advisory time, called "Reach" at Broomfield Heights Middle School. Each grade level is divided into two interdisciplinary teams; each team is named (e.g., Blue Flames, Jetsons). The 6th grade academic block lasts from 8:19 a.m. until 12:52 p.m., with time out for lunch. Similar blocks are constructed for the 7th and 8th grade teams.

Not quite so obvious in the master schedule is the strong commitment to heterogeneous grouping at Broomfield Heights. In the 6th grade, where teacher subject specialization is less, teachers can group and regroup their own students without much reference to the master schedule. In the 7th and 8th grade, the only ability grouping option included is a high-level math group, one

TABLE 8.3 MASTER SCHEDULE, BROOMFIELD HEIGHTS MIDDLE SCHOOL, IN BROOMFIELD, COLORADO

Time	Pd.	Team Name	6th grade: Blue Flame	6th grade: F-16 Fighting Falcons	7th grade: Rolling Thunderbolts	7th grade: Phalanx	8th grade: Legal Eagles	8th grade: Jetsons
7:55–8:15	0	REACH Advisory Period						
8:19–9:07	1		Lang. Arts / Science / Reading / Social Studies / Math	Math	Lang. Arts / Science / Geography — Math / Elective	Lang. Arts / Science / Geography — Math / Elective	P.E./Health	Science / Lang. Arts / American Studies — Math / Elective
9:11–9:55	2		Team	Science / Social Studies / Lang. Arts / Reading	Team — Math / Elective	Team — Math (H) / Elective	Lang. Arts / Science / American Studies — Math / Elective	P.E./Health — Math (H) / Elective
9:59–10:43	3		Team	Team	Team — Math / Elective	P.E./Health	Team — Math (H) / Elective	Team — Math (H) / Elective
10:47–11:17 / 11:21–12:04 / 10:47–11:30 / 11:34–12:04	4		Lunch / Team	Lunch / Team	Lunch / Team — Math / Elective	Team — Math / Elective / Lunch	Team — Math / Elective	Team — Math / Elective / Lunch
12:08–12:52	5		Team	Team	Team	Team / Lunch	Lunch / Team — Math / Elective	Lunch / Team — Math / Elective
12:56–1:40	6		Art / Industrial Arts / Mini-Society / Computing / Foreign Cultures / P.E. / Music / Band / Orchestra	P.E. / Music / Band / Orchestra	Team — Math (H) / Elective	Team — Math / Elective	Team — Math / Elective	Team — Math / Elective
1:44–2:30	7		Mini-Society / Computing / Foreign Cultures / P.E. / Music / Band	Mini-Society / Home Economics / Art / Computing / Foreign Cultures	Team — Math / Elective	Team — Math / Elective	Team — Math / Elective	Team — Math / Elective

Note: P.E. = physical education; H = honors.

on each team (labeled H). This is achieved without grouping the students all day long by dividing each team into two groups of about 75 students. On the Rolling Thunderbolts, for example, one half of the team (75 students) takes language arts, science, and geography, while the other half takes mathematics and two electives. This is reversed during the afternoon. A particular student might, if he or she were an able math student, have the following schedule on most days. Not all able mathematics students would travel together all day. This one mathematics class is the only time they are grouped for instruction.

Period 1: Language arts
Period 2: Science
Period 3: Geography
Period 4: Elective
Period 5: Physical education and health
Period 6: High math
Period 7: Elective

The schedule at BHMS did not simply happen. It was constructed after a carefully crafted consensus emerged surrounding program priorities. Then, educators at the school spent their time allotments according to the program they were committed to implementing. Were the faculty members satisfied that they achieved as much as they could of the things they desired? Probably so. Did they get everything they wanted? Probably not. That is the nature of budgeting, with time or money. It is also, therefore, the nature of the scheduling process. Start with being clear about your priorities and the rest of the process should flow more smoothly, especially with a flexible block schedule.

The Flexible Block Schedule Yields Instructional Responsiveness

In addition to accommodating the essentials of an effective middle school program, flexible block scheduling offers several other reasons for its use. Chief among these is that a flexible block schedule, like those at Batavia Middle School, Wakulla Middle School, and Broomfield Heights Middle School, allows teachers in teams to influence the process. These schedules give teachers the opportunity to make judgments about how much time should be given to each of the subjects under their jurisdiction, considering the characteristics of the students in their charge. Effective schedules permit teachers to vary the time given to different subjects on separate days. A team may decide, for example, to devote the first half of every day for an entire week to a review of basic math skills prior to the administering of standardized achievement tests. Another team might decide to teach a thematic unit that required a different schedule for as long as four to six weeks. Or one teacher may simply request a few additional minutes to complete a lesson on a particular day. Flexible block schedules, tuned to team decision-making, permit these and many other modifications of the time assigned to each subject in the curriculum.

The flexible block schedule, when utilized effectively, permits the use of variable instructional strategies as well. Teams can manage their time to accommodate large group functions, laboratory experiments, individualized and independent study, and regular and small group classes. When a particular subject or skill requires a special method or grouping, the flexible block schedule permits it. The properly designed and utilized schedule can be thought of as an educational blueprint similar in many ways to the architect's work in preparation for the construction of a new building. It arranges for a variety of instructional opportunities but mandates none.

Flexible schedules that offer a greater selection of academic opportunities to students, provide unstructured time when desired, increase teacher influence on school programs, and break the monotony of the traditional daily period schedule are now much more easily implemented. With the removal of the 9th grade to the high schools, middle school schedule builders are no longer constrained by the Carnegie unit, college preparation, and the standardization required for keeping track of credits for graduating from high school. Having gone beyond the grip of the computerized schedule, many administrators are discovering that flexible block schedules can be implemented with lower cost, fewer irrevocable errors, increased options, and greater flexibility.

THE NEW LONG BLOCK SCHEDULE

Flexible block scheduling has been one of the central components of the middle school concept. For decades, in conventional middle school settings across the nation, school leaders have designed their schedule in this way (George & Alexander, 1993). In doing so, most leaders appear to have been designing a school day aimed at providing teachers and teams with the maximum amount of flexibility. All too frequently, however, the exciting options made possible by the flexible block schedule have been too rarely exercised and the potentially flexible aspects of the schedule went unrealized. Blocks of time tended, in many middle schools, to be divided into four or five separate and equal periods, with students moving from class to class in ways little different from the junior or senior high school approach. Flexible block schedules have been available but dramatically underutilized, except in the most exemplary of middle schools, where they continue to be implemented as they were intended and with wonderful results. In many others, however, flexibility is only a possibility, and the instructional and learning climate most often remains unchanged. This, perhaps, helps explain why the response to the new long block schedule has been so dramatically positive.

The new long block schedule or, more simply, block scheduling (as the term is now most frequently used) is a major restructuring effort that organizes the daily school schedule into longer blocks of class periods. It is intended primarily to encourage more diverse and meaningful instructional activities aimed at enhancing student learning. This type of scheduling has already become popular in American high schools (George & Dow, 1997). Block scheduling is a relatively new concept at the middle level, but we believe that variations of this strategy will be implemented in great numbers of middle schools as the 21st century moves ahead. Few innovations have captured secondary education so quickly and comprehensively as this new scheduling format.

Varieties of Long Block Schedules

Long block schedules have burst onto the middle school scene with incredible speed and dazzling variety. Perhaps at least a half dozen major versions of the long block schedule are in place in hundreds of schools. One of the first, but now least common, is the Copernican Plan.

The Copernican Plan   Research on block scheduling indicates that a number of models exist, as well as a multitude of perceived benefits. Joseph Carroll (1994) was one of the first to challenge the traditional structure of school schedules when he discovered the positive effects of four-hour macro-classes during a nonremedial summer school program. From then, Carroll promoted the Copernican Plan that radically changed the way many secondary schools use time. Carroll (1990) believed that students and teachers need extended time to learn subjects and information in depth, as opposed to the traditional method of covering material that encourages lectures and passive learning. Teachers report that the longer blocks of class time allow students to construct meaning by engaging in such activities as conducting experiments, taking measurements, collecting data, analyzing findings, completing a rough draft, going to the library to begin research, and asking and answering questions (Gallagher, 1999). Carroll (1990) recommended an alternative schedule in which students enrolled in only one four-hour class each day for 30 days. Each student would enroll in six of these classes each year.

Following the advent of the Copernican Plan, a number of block scheduling variations have appeared, with classes meeting for 90 minutes, two hours, or four hours per day, or for only part of the school year. George and Dow (1997) found that some high schools implemented a Copernican-style schedule using trimesters, with students attending each of the three daily classes for about two hours and five minutes. Teachers taught only two of the class periods and used the other as a planning period. Substantial benefits seemed to follow implementation, such as classroom environments with improved relationships between teachers and students and more manageable workloads for both.

Copernican-Style Macro-Class   Few middle schools utilize the true Copernican schedule with its extremely long blocks of time. The pure concept of the Copernican Plan allows students to concentrate on one or two subjects at a time, perhaps for as long as six weeks; then another subject or two are studied, in depth, for a whole grading period, and so on throughout the year. A few middle school educators have implemented similar and fascinating models, including the concept of macro-classes (Carroll, 1994). The macro-class consists of much longer periods of class time of two or more hours. One school offers a schedule in which a student might enroll in four extended courses, offered in two blocks each day—a math and science block in the morning, and a social studies and language arts block in the afternoon. Another school provided a schedule in which students are on a 3 × 3 Alternate Day Schedule (A/B), with two 2-hour academic blocks and one 87-minute elective daily. Another principal reported that the school's schedule is divided into two 2½-hour blocks, or two blocks of 150 minutes, every day. The first block consists of an integrated curriculum of language arts, reading, critical thinking, and social studies. The second block consists of integrated math, science, and critical thinking. We find these schedule variations to be intriguing and potentially dramatic alterations in the use of time in middle schools.

Woodlands Middle School, in Lake Worth, Florida, offers an example of the possibilities inherent in the macro block. Using an alternating day format, students take three courses per day; academic classes meet every other day for 132 minutes, while electives are scheduled for 84 minutes. Core teachers teach two 132-minute classes, with one 84-minute planning time daily, and exploratory teachers teach three 84-minute classes, with two 42-minute planning times daily.

At Richmond Heights Middle School (RHMS), in Dade County, Florida, a Copernican-style schedule was in place during the 2001–2002 school year (see Table 8.4). At RHMS, three long blocks meet daily for 110 minutes each. The school operates on a schedule that includes a total of seven courses, but only four meet each day. A student would take language arts, social studies, reading, mathematics, science, and an elective throughout the year, meeting on alternating days for 110 minutes each. The homeroom or advisory time is the daily period, meeting each day after the first block. At RHMS, large classes require a substantial amount of time for homeroom duties and the school's

TABLE 8.4 1999–2000 BELL SCHEDULE, RICHMOND HEIGHTS MIDDLE SCHOOL, IN DADE COUNTY, FLORIDA

9:00–10:50	BLOCK I
10:25–11:20	H.R./AA
11:25–1:45	BLOCK II/LUNCH
1:50–3:40	BLOCK III

Class Period	110 minutes
Advisement	25 minutes

- 30-minute lunch built into Block II
- Five-minute class changes

commitment to the middle school concept includes the daily advisory program. The length of academic periods is more than twice the length of typical class periods in many middle schools, where the time frame for class periods has traditionally been from 45 to 50 minutes, but the schedule has been in place for several years and has become popular there. This schedule is a dramatic departure from the traditional. In most cases, however, the extremely long classes of the Copernican-style schedule have not proved to be common in contemporary middle schools.

Alternating Day Schedule Other models, less drastically altering the length of time for classes, have been more frequently implemented. The two most popular models are the Alternate Day, or A/B, Schedule and the 4 × 4 Semester Plan (Canady & Rettig, 1996; Hackman & Valentine, 1998). The Alternate Day Schedule, such as at RHMS, divides the traditional schedule in half, with classes meeting every other day. Three or four classes meet one day and three or four different classes meet the next day, alternating throughout the year. Classes on a three-period day meet for 100–122 minutes and classes on a four-period day may meet for 85–100 minutes, with the second, shorter, version being much more common (George & Dow, 1997). This schedule is most commonly referred to as A/B, but Odd/Even and Day 1/Day 2 also apply to this schedule (Canady & Rettig, 1996).

Crabapple Middle School (CMS), an exemplary middle school in Fulton County, Georgia, utilizes an A/B schedule similar to that at Richmond Heights. The CMS schedule for 2001–2002 is illustrated in Table 8.5. Students at CMS enroll in what amounts to an eight-period program of studies. Four classes meet daily, including those designated as Academic Blocks 1, 2, and 3, meeting on A day and Academic Blocks 4, 5, and 6 meeting on B day. These two scheduled days then rotate, ad infinitum, throughout the school year. Sixth grade students at CMS might have mathematics, language arts, and social studies on A day and science, reading, and what the school calls "Focus" on B day. The schedules for 7th and 8th graders are only slightly different.

At CMS, courses in the exploratory or unified arts and physical education curriculum are called "Connections" classes, reflecting the faculty's attempt to "connect to the real world" through these courses. These courses meet for 83 minutes, also alternating daily, so a student might have 83 minutes of physical education one day and a class of the same length in art the next. Teachers have their planning periods during the Connections period. Band and chorus classes meet daily for 40 minutes, reflecting the priorities of suburban middle school parents.

A/B/T Schedule In many other schools using the Alternating Day Schedule, administrators add a traditional schedule one day a week when all classes meet. Some educators choose to use a traditional schedule on Monday, for example, when all classes would meet, and then have three or four classes meet Tuesday, with three or four different classes meeting on Wednesday. The same

TABLE 8.5   2001–2002 A/B SCHEDULE, CRABAPPLE MIDDLE SCHOOL, IN FULTON COUNTY, GEORGIA

6th grade, A Day	6th grade, B day	7th grade, A day	7th grade, B day	8th grade, A day	8th grade, B day
8:45 a.m.–8:50 a.m. Homeroom	8:45 a.m.–8:50 a.m. Homeroom	8:45 a.m.–8:50 a.m. Homeroom	8:45 a.m.–8:50 a.m. Homeroom	8:45 a.m.–8:50 a.m. Homeroom	8:45 a.m.–8:50 a.m. Homeroom
8:50 a.m.–10:30 a.m. Academic Block 1	8:50 a.m.–10:30 a.m. Academic Block 4	8:50 a.m.–10:30 a.m. Academic Block 1	8:50 a.m.–10:30 a.m. Academic Block 4	8:50 a.m.–10:30 a.m. Academic Block 1	8:50 a.m.–10:30 a.m. Academic Block 4
10:33 a.m.–12:43 a.m. Academic Block 2 Lunch	10:33 a.m.–12:43 a.m. Academic Block 5 Lunch	10:33 a.m.–12:43 a.m. Academic Block 2 Lunch	10:33 a.m.–12:43 a.m. Academic Block 5 Lunch	10:33 a.m.–11:56 a.m. Connections A	10:33 a.m.–11:56 a.m. Connections B
12:46 p.m.–2:09 p.m. Connections A	12:46 p.m.–2:09 p.m. Connections A	12:46 p.m.–2:09 p.m. Academic Block 3	12:46 p.m.–2:09 p.m. Academic Block 6	11:59 a.m.–2:09 p.m. Academic Block 2 Lunch	11:59 a.m.–2:09 p.m. Academic Block 5 Lunch
2:12 p.m.–3:55 p.m. Academic Block 3	2:12 p.m.–3:55 p.m. Academic Block 6	2:12 p.m.–3:55 p.m. Connections A	2:12 p.m.–3:55 p.m. Connections B	2:12 p.m.–3:55 p.m. Academic Block 3	2:12 p.m.–3:55 p.m. Academic Block 6
3:55 p.m. Dismissal	3:55 p.m. Dismissal	3:55 p.m. Dismissal	3:55 p.m. Dismissal	3:55 p.m. Dismissal	3:55 p.m. Dismissal

classes that meet on Tuesday meet on Thursday, and the same classes that meet on Wednesday meet again on Friday. Some school principals report Wednesday, others Friday, as their traditional day during the week. This variation is called A/B/ T. An example is provided in Table 8.6.

A/B-Rotation   One more variation on the Alternating Day Schedule deals with a rotation system. Schools using this schedule rotate the class meeting several times each day. For example, on a Monday, first, third, and fifth periods might meet, in that order. On Tuesday, second, fourth, and sixth periods meet in that order. On Wednesday, the schedule changes. Third, fifth, and then first period meet, in that order. On Thursday, fourth, sixth, and second periods meet, in that order, and so on until all classes meet at different times. An apt title for this variation is A/B-Rotation. See Table 8.7 for an illustration.

TABLE 8.6   **EXAMPLE OF AN A/B/T BLOCK SCHEDULE**

Monday A	Tuesday B	Wednesday A	Thursday B	Friday A
1	2	1	1	2
		2		
3	4	3	3	4
		4		
5	6	5	5	6
		6		

4 × 4 Schedules   The 4 × 4 Semester Plan, sometimes called the accelerated schedule, is the other main configuration of the block schedule used in secondary schools. Teachers may teach six or seven classes in one year, but only three or four per day, every day, for a semester, instead of every other day for the whole year. Students may take four 90-minute classes for a whole semester and then take another four 90-minute classes the second semester (Canady & Rettig, 1996). This allows what were formerly year-long courses to be completed in one semester, and semester courses can be completed in nine weeks. One high school study found that students agreed they had more learning time, more time to work with other students, and more individual help from their teachers in the 4 × 4 schedule than in the traditional seven-period day. This same study found that teachers used more peer tutoring, more hands-on activities, more small group activities, and a wider variety of teaching strategies (Liu & Dye, 1998).

Far fewer middle schools report using the pure 4 × 4 Semester Plan, a circumstance markedly different from high school preferences. Many middle

TABLE 8.7   **EXAMPLE OF AN A/B ROTATION SCHEDULE**

Day 1 A	Day 2 B	Day 3 A	Day 4 B	Day 5 A	Day 6 B
1	2	3	4	5	6
3	4	5	6	1	2
5	6	1	2	3	4

TABLE 8.8 **EXAMPLE OF A 4 × 4 Semester Plan**

Fall semester Team 1	Spring Semester Team 2
Math	Science
Social studies	Physical education
Exploratory	Language arts
Spanish	Computer and keyboard skills

schools do, however, use variations of the 4 × 4. Schedules in 4 × 4 schools are arranged so that four subjects meet for, say, 90 minutes each, every day for a whole semester or term, August through December or January through May. A student's schedule might look like the one in Table 8.8

3 × 3 Semester Plan   Administrators in a few schools on the semester schedule further reduce the number of classes students attend per day and lengthen the time for each class period. Instead of four 90-minute classes as in the 4 × 4 Semester Plan, educators implement three 120-minute classes. This results in a 3 × 3 Semester Plan. We believe this type of schedule offers many advantages, especially to small teams intent on curriculum integration. We also acknowledge the problems raised by the lack of continuing study of the subjects throughout the year. A student's schedule, in the 3 × 3 Semester Plan, may look like the one in Table 8.9.

The Kanapaha Model   Educators in some schools concerned with students' retention of knowledge from one semester to the next have made adjustments to the 4 × 4 Semester Plan. Because emerging accountability measures in many states result in assessment of mathematics and language arts in the spring of

TABLE 8.9 **EXAMPLE OF A 3 × 3 Semester Plan**

Fall semester Team 1	Spring Semester Team 2
Math	Science
Social studies	Language arts
Physical education	Elective

the year, teachers and parents fear that students taking either of those two subjects in the fall would not retain adequate knowledge to perform (and compete) on the standardized tests given in February, March, or April. Putting both subjects in the spring semester, however, raised the problem of not introducing or teaching enough content material before the tests. To remedy this dilemma, educators in some middle schools constructed a schedule that offers a compromise in the 4 × 4 schedule—including daily teaching of language arts and math. We call this schedule the "Kanapaha model" after the name of the middle school where we first encountered it in the mid-1990s.

In these schools, the basic format of the 4 × 4 Semester Plan is retained, but with major adjustments. In such schools, science meets every day for one semester and students take social studies the other semester. Each class meets daily for approximately twice the amount of time the class might meet during a traditional seven-period day. Students would also take physical education daily, for one semester, and electives the other. Physical education might meet for 90 minutes; each of two exploratory classes might meet for 45 minutes each. Alternately, physical education and exploratory classes might meet every other day for 90 minutes each, throughout the year.

A student's schedule may look like the one in Table 8.10, a 2001–2002 schedule for Kanapaha Middle School (KMS), in Gainesville, Florida. Only two bells are rung during the day, to signal the beginning and the end of the school day. A 15-minute advisory starts the morning, then four blocks arrange the rest of the day. A student might have a schedule during the first semester that included blocks of language arts, mathematics, science, and a daily exploratory class. In the spring, social studies would replace science and physi-

TABLE 8.10   **2001–2002 BELL SCHEDULE, KANAPAHA MIDDLE SCHOOL, IN GAINESVILLE, FLORIDA**

				Warning Bell
8:50				Warning Bell
8:55–9:10				AA
9:15–10:35				1st Block

6th Grade		7th Grade		8th Grade	
10:40–11:15	2nd Block A	10:40–12:00	2nd Block	10:40–12:00	2nd Block
11:15–11:45	Lunch				
11:45–12:30	2nd Block B	12:00–12:30	Lunch	12:05–12:45	3rd Block A
				12:45–1:15	Lunch
12:35–1:55	3rd Block	12:35–1:55	3rd Block	1:15–1:55	3rd Block B
2:00–3:20				4th Block	

Note: AA = advisor-advisee program

cal education would replace the exploratory class. Teachers would teach three blocks and have one 90-minute block for planning each day.

The main change from the 4 × 4 model to the Kanapaha model occurs with math and language arts. Math and language arts each met every day for 90 minutes, throughout the entire school year. The total number of minutes allocated was doubled for those two subject areas per school year. Experience with the schedule has validated the belief, among the designers of this schedule, that it would have positive effects on the test scores for mathematics and science. Recent state tests have indicated that scores in these areas at KMS have accelerated substantially.

Combination Schedules Another common schedule type is the combination schedule, which combines elements of long and short blocks of class time (Dental & George, 1999). Educators at some schools may combine aspects of the 4 × 4 with traditional aspects, such as keeping the long blocks of class time for some courses meeting in the mornings for only one semester, while other 50-minute classes meet after lunch time for both semesters (George & Dow, 1997). Other educators may choose to modify a traditional schedule by keeping three days of the week when all six 50-minute classes meet and adding an A/B schedule two days of the week, when only three 100-minute classes meet. A combination schedule may also appear when a school's faculty decides to make a gradual transition from a traditional schedule to a block schedule. It usually reflects a degree of uncertainty or apprehension among the faculty members and provides them with a sense of security that at least one day will be traditional.

The resulting combination schedule might include any of the models (4 × 4 Semester, Kanapaha, Alternate Day, etc.) matched with parts of the day or week on a traditional schedule. The design in a particular setting is usually crafted to fit the needs of the individual school. Some administrators report practices as varied as using a traditional six-period schedule on Monday, Thursday, and Friday and blocking the first three periods on Tuesday and the second three periods on Wednesday.

Another principal used a similar formulation of the schedule, blocking only two days of the week. For example, on Wednesday students met with the core academic classes such as reading and social studies only, and on Thursday students met with only math and science. The rest of the week consisted of six periods including exploratory courses and physical education. Other school administrators report blocking only social studies and science on alternating days throughout the school year with the remaining subjects meeting on a traditional schedule.

Other principals use block scheduling to target certain populations or certain subjects. Drop-out prevention programs, special education, and gifted classes are often targeted as areas for use of blocks inside otherwise regular schedules. In some schools, only one grade level may use block scheduling. The subject areas that are most often targeted for blocking are usually core subjects, including reading, language arts, math, science, and social studies. In most of these schools, block schedules appear to be a small portion of the overall school program and as a result do not benefit from as many advantages reported by schools where most or all students have fewer classes for longer periods of time.

Reasons for Adopting a Long Block Schedule

When asked about the reasons for moving to a block schedule, many leaders point first to the opportunity to implement greater increments of best practices for teaching and learning. Others agree that their chief reason for moving to a block was to raise students' academic achievement through emphasis on certain curricula, as in the example of the Kanapaha schedule and its emphasis on mathematics. Other leaders attempted to encourage teachers to use different instructional strategies, to provide teachers with more flexible time frames, and to improve student behavior. Some principals asserted that reducing the number of students taught daily by teachers was an important reason, while others were thinking of changing the traditional impersonal, factory-type school climate as the reason they moved to the block in their school. In the long block schedule, teachers may work with fewer students per day and have longer class periods. The number of times students change classes each day is also reduced, which increases the amount of class time available. Fewer classes and fewer students may help teachers develop stronger relationships with their students and enable teachers to more closely monitor student learning (Canady & Rettig, 1996; Liu & Dye, 1998).

Some school leaders suggested other reasons for adopting a block schedule: to have more instructional time, to lessen the number of daily class changes, to reduce students' skipping classes, to reduce stress on students and teachers, and to improve the learning environment. The ability to offer a greater variety of activities and to offer more electives, as a consequence of having up to eight course selections, also appeals to educators in many schools.

Results from several studies (George & Dow, 1997; Hamdy & Urich, 1998; Mistretta & Polansky, 1997) report that effective block schedules may help to produce positive outcomes in these areas at the high school level. Whether similar benefits pertain to middle schools remains to be verified. One potential benefit of block schedules over traditional schedules, at the middle school level, is that they may support a more appropriate curriculum and better quality instruction through expanded and flexible uses of time. One middle school teacher (Wormelli, 1999) wrote, "I now have the time to teach to the rhythm of my training and experience instead of to the tick of the classroom clock." Also, block schedules may promote students' academic development through a greater variety of learning activities and more in-depth, supportive relationships with teachers and other students as a result of spending concentrated time with them (Liu & Dye, 1998). In addition, the block schedules seem to foster quality teacher collaboration, professional growth, and teacher empowerment (George & Dow, 1997; Mistretta & Polansky, 1997).

Although block schedule structures can encourage more active learning opportunities and less lecturing by teachers, some teachers are not always prepared to take advantage of the extended class periods effectively. Teachers may find it difficult to maintain students' attention for 90 to 120 minutes unless they vary the learning strategies they use and involve more active learning opportunities (Rettig & Canady, 1996; Gallagher, 1999). Rettig and Canady (1996) recommend implementing a block schedule only when appropriate staff development activities are provided.

Reported Outcomes of the New Long Block Schedules

Practitioners and researchers seem divided about the outcomes of new long block schedules. Practitioners seem more enthusiastic about positive results. Here are some of the outcomes most frequently mentioned by practitioners.

Better Teaching   The most frequently reported outcome across all models is "more creative and innovative teaching methods." With longer class time, teachers may have greater opportunity for extensive projects and can break away from solely relying on lectures and textbook-based activities. Some principals report an "increase in hands-on activities" and "active learning." Others state that the block schedule allows "better presentation of the curriculum, and more time for labs and writing assignments." Also, with fewer classes per day, teachers may devote more planning time to those classes, allowing time for more thoughtful and in-depth instruction (Dental & George, 1999).

Positive Teacher-Student Relationships   Other middle school educators with block scheduling experience report more positive relationships between teachers and students as an important outcome. Positive relationships appear to have more time to grow as teachers and students have more time to learn more about one another. Also, teachers see fewer students each day, allowing teachers to better focus on the uniqueness of each student's personality.

Revitalizing Teachers   A third outcome reported by many leaders is the revitalization of some of the teaching staff. With a new structure in place, veteran teachers have the opportunity to refocus their teaching methods to reflect best practices. Others indicate "high teacher morale," "an increase in teachers' daily attendance," and "an increased interest in staff development" as outcomes of the new long schedule (Dental & George, 1999).

Better Discipline   Many educators see, with the advent of the new long block schedule, a decline in the number of students referred to the office for discipline. This could be related to a number of factors, such as the stronger relationships between teachers and students and less movement in the hallways from fewer class changes. Other factors could be less frustration experienced by young adolescent students with fewer classes to concentrate on or less misbehavior by students who are now more engaged in class activities.

Higher Test Scores   Standardized test scores seem to factor into many restructuring initiatives, and block schedules are no exception. Many educators attest to an increase in their students' test scores, especially when the new schedule devotes more time to areas such as mathematics (e.g., Kanapaha model). Other middle school leaders believe that the new schedule can result in more motivated students, which may be a result of more interesting or varied instruction. However, little evidence has been gathered from carefully designed quantitative studies to support the claims that block scheduling leads to increased academic achievement (McLeland, 2001).

Better Hallway Situations   Some educators correlate their new schedule with cleaner classrooms and hallways, perhaps as a result of fewer class changes. Some schools experience "less hallway traffic and better hallway behavior," and a few indicate increased daily attendance rates. One school with which we are familiar claimed the "highest attendance rate and lowest out-of-school suspension rate of secondary schools in the county since using the block schedule."

Higher Grades   Principals often report that students' grades improve as the result of the block schedules, particularly a decrease in the number of failures. Reasons for fewer failures could be "less stress on students" or teachers' increased ability to know students and identify students who are falling behind. At least one reason for this may be connected to the tendency for students to get started on their independent practice (homework) during class, thereby avoiding the classic middle school student problem of not completing or turning in homework. Coincidentally, with the decrease in class failures, the number of students on the honor roll may increase. With an increase in the number of students on the honor roll, schools may experience an increase in the average student grade point average (GPA) or in the number of "A's" on students' report cards. Two other outcomes may occasionally result from the use of the new block schedule: increase in enrollment in foreign language courses or in the number of students enrolled in electives. Both of these factors are of greater significance for high school students, however, who have more opportunities to enroll in a number of foreign languages and diverse electives.

Sometimes, however, the outcomes are not as positive. Some teachers and students have "experienced frustration over which day it was," A or B, block or traditional. Others point out that when a student is absent, she or he "missed too much coursework," because of the double period they miss. There are other problems with new long schedules.

Problems and Concerns Surrounding Block Schedules

While the overall experience of middle school educators with the block schedule, thus far, seems to demonstrate that block schedules address and may have helped to overcome some important pedagogical issues that plague middle level schools, nothing works perfectly. Persistent concerns are associated with the adoption of long block schedules.

Knowledge Retention   The first concern centers on whether students are able to retain content knowledge from one semester to the next. Students' ability to remember and apply what they have learned is an age-old concern in middle schools, not unique to block schedules, but some schedules seem to be more conducive than others in assisting students to retain knowledge long enough for standardized tests. The ability of students to retain knowledge from one semester or year to the next does not seem to be a concern for faculty in most schools using an Alternate Day Schedule (which includes A/B, A/B/T, and A/B-Rotation).

Amount of Time   Another issue has to do with the amount of time allotted per course. Implementing a schedule with four daily periods, eight for the year, may mean that fewer minutes can be devoted to each course. When a student takes eight courses instead of six or seven, there is no magic way to increase the time, unless a school moves to a longer day, which is the way some schools have dealt with this issue. Because most of the schedules allow for more efficient use of time throughout the day, however, few educators consider fewer minutes per course a major concern.

Curriculum Pacing   Particularly with 4×4 models, including the Kanapaha model (with social studies and science), pacing the curriculum effectively—covering the material required for the total year in any particular class—can be a real concern. Teachers and students may feel rushed, so nonessential but high-interest curriculum may have to be eliminated. Sometimes the nature of the schedule, with its increased class time, creates problems with "getting teachers to effectively use the 80 minutes."

Effective and Active Teaching   All block schedule types seem to raise a concern for the ability and willingness of teachers to use teaching strategies appropriate for the long block. School leaders may lament that the new schedule frees the best teachers to do even better, but it does nothing to improve the more mediocre instructors in the school. Students consistently report that their only complaint about the block schedule is that some teachers continue to lecture on and on. Clearly, training for teachers is an essential component of implementing a new block schedule. Even with training, however, questions remain about the extent to which the average teacher can effectively implement new and complex teaching strategies on a regular basis.

The change in instructional methods is not always easy or simple. An adjustment period may be necessary to allow school personnel to make necessary changes in their traditional routines. Teachers need more time and support to continue to fine-tune their instruction and adapt to a new way of schooling children. Many principals assert that their staff members needed considerable help in adapting their instructional strategies. This can be done by effective staff development and by having teachers sharing their successes in overcoming some of the challenges.

No particular block schedule seems to stand out as having an advantage with regard to teachers' instructional strategies. Each block schedule faces similar challenges and responses from teachers. The effectiveness of the new schedule is, however, clearly and directly related to whether teachers use better and more appropriate instructional strategies and embrace the block schedule philosophy. Fortunately, many administrators assert that, in their new scheduling situations, the majority of teachers have made changes in the instructional methods they use. Staff development opportunities appear to have been effective in motivating teachers and assisting them in developing new instructional methods. Leaders agree that cooperative learning, projects, and other student-centered methods are now more widely used.

Daily Practice   A number of components in the middle school curriculum are based on the assumption that daily short practice is more effective than longer, more widely spaced, practice. In fact, "spaced" practice has long been known to be superior to "massed" practice. Music teachers, for example, are likely to believe that daily instruction and practice with instruments is essential for students to progress and develop their musical skills. Block schedule proponents, as a result, often encounter opposition from music teachers and parents. Teachers of mathematics and foreign language may voice the same concerns, arguing that even an every-other-day schedule is too infrequent for mastery of their lesson.

Course Sequencing   For some courses, such as foreign languages, sequencing is especially important. Students in Spanish classes advance from beginning Spanish to Spanish II to Spanish III. Others advance from algebra I to geometry or algebra II. Students who have algebra I in the beginning of one year and geometry in the second semester of the next year may experience substantial loss in the interim. Changing the traditional schedule can, therefore, affect which classes students attend and which courses schools continue to offer.

Resistance to the Long Block Schedule   One major factor related to rate of change in schools is resistance by the faculty to buy into a proposed initiative, whatever it may be. Block schedules are no different. Some teachers find the block schedule to be more conducive to their content area and are more open to rearranging the way class time was spent. Other teachers, however, see little reason to fiddle with the schedule, seeing block schedule as one more in a long line of educational fads.

Science teachers appear most likely to take the lead in adapting the block schedule, with language arts, or English, and social studies teachers often found to be supportive of block schedule efforts. Mathematics teachers and teachers of electives are reported to be less supportive, with special area teachers, such as band, physical education, and music, often mentioned as resistant.

Transfer Students   Moving from one school to another is difficult enough for many middle school students. Because not all middle schools are using the same type of schedule, students transferring in and out of school can experience a rough transition and may not complete the classes they started. A student transferring into a 3 × 3 semester schedule, from a traditional seven-period schedule, after winter holidays, for example, will be placed in only three classes, classes in which she or he may have already completed half of the content. Equally as bad would be the three or four courses in which the student covered only half of the material at the former school that she or he would not be able to complete. Many educators claim that this was not a problem or a concern when students transferred to their schools. It may be that, because students are not counting Carnegie units at the middle school level, concerns about transfers are reduced, compared with the high school level. It may also be that transfer and transition are always problems for middle school students, regardless of the type of schedule.

In the two decades since the first edition of this text was published, in 1981, no alteration to the framework of the exemplary middle school has swept in with the drama and speed of this new approach to the organization of time. We expect this pace to continue during the decade to come.

TEN STEPS TO DESIGNING AN EFFECTIVE MIDDLE SCHOOL SCHEDULE

Regardless of the type of schedule used in a school, important considerations must always accompany the design and implementation of the schedule. First is constructing the match between school priorities and the schedule. Nothing is more important than achieving congruence between the mission of the school and the schedule that serves that mission. This means that, in an exemplary middle school, the schedule accommodates an interdisciplinary team organization and provides the autonomy and flexibility that teaming teachers require—again, regardless of the kind of schedule. Beyond these essential elements, other factors contribute to the successful implementation of a schedule that serves the needs of students and teachers.

Master or Servant?

Perhaps, then, the master schedule should be called the "servant schedule," given that the purpose of the organization of time in a middle school is to facilitate the accomplishment of other components—team organization, advisory programs, curriculum plans, planning time, and others. Consequently, the schedule must be made to mold itself to the other priorities identified by the staff and the district, and not the reverse.

This means, among other things, that the computer services and software packages for scheduling, available from the district office or commercially, are unlikely to meet all the needs of a particular middle school and must be used with trepidation. Such services may have, as their priorities, the efficient packaging and movement of faceless masses across the entire district, not an unimportant task. But every middle school schedule is unique, or it should be. It is highly desirable, as well as highly improbable, that the developers of computer scheduling packages understand the priorities of the middle school program, in general, or the priorities of a particular school. It is much more likely that the standard computer scheduling services are driven by the needs of the larger schools in the district, the high schools. Course numbers seem, sometimes, to assume greater weight in such situations than the priorities of the school staff. The computer is not an evil thing. It is simply not the answer to every middle school scheduling need.

Steps in Designing the Master Schedule

There is no single step-by-step correct order to the process of constructing the best schedule. The popularity of the new long block schedule complicates the process even more. In every school, exceptions will make the process unique in that place. Nonetheless, certain steps must be included at one point or another. Here, we detail the process as it unfolds in many contemporary exemplary middle schools.

Step One: Establish the Curriculum   The school curriculum must be in place before students can be scheduled into it. Curriculum decisions will influence the schedule almost as comprehensively as the decisions made about teacher and student organization. Because no school day can contain all the demands of parents, state departments of education, and so on, a considerable amount of the frustration in the final scheduling process is the result of preestablished curriculum priorities. Knowing how many curriculum components will make up the basic day for each student is a crucial prerequisite to schedule development. Will reading and language arts be offered together or separately? Will there be daily physical education? Will there be an advisor-advisee program? What kind of exploratory emphasis will the curriculum offer? Will instrumental music be offered in a grade level format (e.g., 6th grade band) or skill levels (e.g., advanced band)? All these questions, and many others, need to be answered before the final stages of developing the master schedule can begin.

Ideally, the school scheduling team will be able to make many of these decisions themselves, in collaboration with the rest of the staff. In practice, however, these decisions and many others come to the staff as givens, decided for them by others beyond the school. Even the unit of time into which the school day is divided (flexible block, long block, or traditional periods) may have been previously determined along with the number of units in a daily schedule. Regardless of where these decisions are made, those who schedule must incorporate these data into the process.

Additional decisions will have to be made: How much passing time will be permitted between classes? What length of time will be required for each of the parts of the curriculum each day or week? Are there restrictions that arise from the nature of the school building, from the student-teacher ratio, or from funding concerns? Answers to these questions, and others unique to each school, must be clearly known before scheduling can begin; otherwise, barriers will arise during and after the construction of the schedule. Neophytes in the scheduling process may feel exhausted or discouraged, in the face of all these prerequisites, even before they begin, but in most situations, schedulers can emerge from the process with much of what they hoped for included in the final schedule.

No two school schedules are exactly alike, because no two schools have exactly the same curriculum. The most important steps in the scheduling process, it should now be more than obvious, are those that precede the design of the master schedule. Schedules are only a reflection of the decisions that have already been made with regard to curriculum and the instructional organization of teachers and students. Firm commitments to advisory programs, to team organization, and to particular methods of grouping students will inevitably and irrevocably shape the schedule that eventually emerges.

Veteran schedule builders continue, from this point, with equal amounts of humility and determination. Accepting that all the school's priorities cannot be achieved is as important as the dogged determination to achieve them in spite of the impossible nature of the task. The objective of the scheduling process becomes the struggle to achieve as much as possible from the list of priorities with which one begins.

Step Two: Begin with Collaboration   The process of time budgeting that results in a school schedule is, in many ways, a process of prioritizing. Because achieving all of the priorities of all of the constituents is rare, prioritizing, to be successful, must be a collaborative process, a process of maximum involvement leading to a broad consensus. The final schedule also requires considerable compromise from a number of stakeholders. Willingness to compromise rarely comes from situations in which decisions are announced as undebatable, from the district office or the school administrative suite.

This process must be a collaborative effort for one other reason: Rarely is one person skilled enough to be able to unilaterally produce the most effective master schedule for a school of a thousand or more students and teachers. Rarely can one perspective, either teaching or administration, capture all of the important concerns that should shape a middle school schedule. Some middle school educators argue that few persons are able to be effective in all the necessary areas of school leadership and that, frequently, the ability to schedule is one skill missing from the repertoire. Furthermore, experience in developing schedules for elementary, high school, and junior high contributes very little to one's skill at scheduling the middle school. It may even be counterproductive. So, a scheduling team made up of a variety of people possessing necessary skills and important insights is likely to produce the most satisfactory, long-lasting product, after numerous revisions have been attempted.

Step Three: Determine the Number of Students to Be Served and Make a Survey of Curriculum Options   Once the curriculum has been determined, and the scheduler knows, for example, that family and consumer science will be a part of the exploratory program, then he or she can proceed to matching student numbers and curriculum offerings. How many students, for example, will want family and consumer science in the 7th grade? How many 6th graders want to be in band? How many want an exploratory wheel experience instead? A letter may be sent to elementary schools to determine the number of rising 6th graders who will need each choice, especially some choices, such as instrumental music, which may have to be rationed. Experienced schedulers recommend using a waiting list process for popular classes such as band, if necessary.

The scheduler gets a printout of the registration form from the appropriate clerk or assistant principal, depending on the size of the school. The students' choices are entered either individually or via mass loading (e.g., all 6th graders take physical education first period). At one school in 2001, 900 students' names were entered into the computer for each of eight courses.

Step Four: Match the Curriculum with the Teaching Staff   Teams now begin to emerge in the schedule. The basic school relationship for middle school students is with their academic interdisciplinary team of teachers and fellow students. This team is their school family. This is where the students spend most of their school day. The process of organizing teams begins but only after the components of the curriculum have been determined. The interdisciplinary team organization is, however, as important as the curriculum program in its influence on the scheduling process.

The scheduler determines the degree to which a good match has been made between the desired curriculum and the number of teachers who will be grouped into interdisciplinary teams. The scheduler translates information from step two into the number of sections needed for each basic course on each team. This information must be checked against the number of teacher units available to teach these sections, to see if the teachers available match the students' needs. The question is deceptively simple: "Do I have enough teachers to teach what has to be taught?" The correct answer may be more difficult to determine, especially when designing an A/B or 4 × 4 schedule. With some modifications for the long block schedule, the process usually involves the following steps.

- Divide the number of students to be served by the number of students per class. This calculation gives the number of sections needed for each required class to be taught daily or in the alternating day cycle. In a school of 900, for example, where the student-teacher ratio is 30:1, 30 sections are needed of every basic, regularly taught class. The school, in this case, would need to offer 30 sections of social studies, 30 of science, 30 of mathematics, and 30 of language arts—if these were the basic components of the schedule.

- Next, divide the number of sections needed for each subject (e.g., 30) by the number of periods that each teacher will teach. If the schedule had seven periods, either daily or alternating from day to day on a long block, and the teachers all taught five out of the seven, then the scheduler would divide 5 into 30. The result is the approximate number of teachers required to serve the school's students in each of the required subjects. The example school would need about six teachers in every one of the basic subjects to get the job done.
- Form the teachers into teams, configurations depending upon the number of students at each grade level. Teams may be different sizes at the same grade level, if the numbers of students are uneven.
- Establish a room use chart. Academic teams and others are placed so that teachers are closest to the other teachers who share the same students, not the same subject. This has often been true in exploratory areas and now has become the preferred practice with academic teachers on teams.

Step Five: Add Special Features Special interest programs, advisory programs, schoolwide silent reading, and other special features next take their place in the schedule. Here, too, the scheduler, together with others, will have to make decisions about classes with small numbers, such as algebra and geometry, honors sections, or different sorts of band and orchestra. If no natural match exists, then school leaders will find more teachers, consider cross-teaming, crowd more students into existing classes, or operate on a first come, first served basis and deny some students enrollment in classes that are over-enrolled. Knowledge of faculty preferences comes into play, because a teacher may say, "I'll take four large classes in algebra I and regular math, if I get an algebra II class with eight kids in it."

In the 6th grade at one school, social studies and science classes were organized so that all students in one teacher's social studies classes have the same teacher in science. This provides much flexibility for the teachers as they attempt to work together, integrate the curriculum, and so on. In the 7th grade at Westwood Middle School, in Gainesville, Florida, another special feature was that one teacher taught language arts and reading to the same group of 25–30 students for a double period each day, providing a 90-minute time that they believe works remarkably better. The scheduler tells the computer to tie the two classes together to achieve this arrangement. This is also necessary for semester classes that contain the same students, but in different semesters—for example, when students take an exploratory class that lasts for one semester and go to physical education as a group the next semester during the same period of the day.

Step Six: Looking for Big Conflicts A conflict matrix determines the number of students whose schedules, if nothing is done, will be in conflict. They may, for example, be assigned to several singleton (those offered only once) sections that are offered at the same time. The operative question, then, is "Where are the biggest conflicts?" Singletons and doubletons are scheduled first, while dealing with part-time teachers and other known constraints. As an example, if algebra is going to be offered during the first and second periods, the only section of Spanish I should not be scheduled at the same time. Compensatory reading programs and compensatory math programs, for the same reason, cannot be easily offered at the same period for the same grade level. Schedulers should work in the special compensatory classes as early as possible, although it will often be difficult to do so. In a school of 900 students, during any one period, the scheduler must accommodate those 900 students, so naturally small classes have to be balanced with larger ones.

Step Seven: Schedule the Planning Times for Teachers on Interdisciplinary Teams Planning times for teachers on interdisciplinary teams can often be kept constant from year to year, by building the rest of the schedule around them. In virtually every schedule, regardless of type, planning time for teams of teachers takes place when their students are at their exploratory or physical education classes. After all, someone must be teaching their students when they are not.

Step Eight: Enter the Master Schedule into the Computer Entering the master schedule into the computer begins by putting in the teachers' names and their numbers (e.g., Social Security, certification number, etc.). Then, for each period, course and number are entered. The section number must be put in so that it does not produce duplication, because many state funding formulas are tied to student attendance and monitored through these registration data. The maximum number of students in each section (whether it is a semester or a year-long course) must be noted, and the period, the room number, and the teacher number identified. If the school has adopted an A/B schedule of four daily block-length periods, for every teacher, there must be eight entries (their classes, including planning times). Every night, the computer program provides a feedback run, which can be examined the next day to determine progress and difficulties remaining.

Step Nine: Build the Data into a Scheduling Program The computer program will schedule students into classes and teams according to the choices they have made. A printout will reveal which students could not be scheduled and why (e.g., class load limits, conflict with a singleton, etc.). Transfer students, coming in from other schools, must also be anticipated, and experience in some schools indicates that transfer students who come to school for the first time on the first day of school are frequently remedial students who will need singleton compensatory sections.

Teams of teachers can take over the task of scheduling the students on their team, instead of utilizing a computer scheduling program any further.

Step Ten: Make Final Tweaks   The schedule, and the needs of individual students and teachers, must again come to the fore. The schedule must be "massaged and massaged" so that individual needs can be met. For example, in a school with a number of compensatory or remedial classes, those classes should be spread out through the day so that students do not experience so many back-to-back classes together that tracking becomes a worse problem than it already is. If ability groups are involved, one scheduler's advice is to "always change kids up, when changing their place in the schedule, in terms of ability groups, rather than down, since they almost always do well and the higher sections can hold more students."

Teachers and teams who want to change students after the first week of school must, if a computer program is used, bring those changes to the scheduler for entry. This usually entails dozens of hours of rescheduling time. The assistant principal or other scheduler works closely with teachers to move students from one class to another. Students who do not belong together, awkward imbalances in the size or demographics of classes, and so on must be corrected individually, even with the use of a computer program for that purpose. Sometimes, many hours of the first three weeks of school are used for this purpose and lamentably so, we think, because an assistant principal for curriculum ought to be able to be doing other things at this critical point of the year. Schools that are able to employ scheduling clerks may enjoy quite a luxury. Schools where teams of teachers do not have to report every schedule change may be in the best position.

No Single Right Way to Schedule a Middle School

There is no right way to organize the middle school day, except insofar as the schedule facilitates or interferes with the program of the school. We believe that a seven-period day (organized in a flexible block) often can, if designed correctly, accommodate the programs of a middle school equally as well as a long block schedule. Furthermore, the staff of a school does not need to feel either self-satisfied with one type of schedule or ashamed with another. Individual teams inside a regular flexible schedule can decide whether to block their classes or not. The question is not "What kind of schedule is best?" The question is "How can we schedule our day to facilitate the priorities we have established?" Misunderstanding this basic concept has led to scheduling controversies that are bitter and divisive.

All schedules, no matter what variety, are arbitrary divisions of the total school day into smaller units. The only major differences are in the size of the smaller units and in who influences or controls the manipulation of those units. In the middle school, the size of the time unit is more varied than it often is in either the elementary school or the high school. Any way in which time is divided is arbitrary. Whether one chooses periods or blocks, the most important decisions will deal with assigning fixed times to the priorities that emerge in discussions of curriculum priorities. School day time, however organized, must be divided between necessities and luxuries. Even among the requirements, there are often more than a comfortable number of such necessities, each clamoring for its share of time during the day. Each luxury has its spirited advocates, enthusiastically claiming that the subject or topic is actually a necessity and ought to be required of all middle school students on a daily basis. This shortage of time, compared with the plethora of possible subjects that might be included in the day, causes a number of serious conflicts for middle school leaders.

Scheduling in Perspective

Few aspects of the exemplary middle school are both as fraught with difficulties and as crucial to the success of the program as the process of scheduling. Most middle school leaders recognize that an effective schedule is the fulcrum upon which the remainder of the program is moved. Yet the scheduling process has probably received less attention from research and development than any other item. Training in the skills necessary for effective schedule construction is still inadequate. The emergence of the new long block schedule complicates the process further. Much remains to be done.

ORGANIZING SPACE IN THE MIDDLE SCHOOL

For those attempting to implement the best practices associated with an exemplary middle school, the building in which the program is housed may be either a burden or a blessing. School buildings, by their nature, can block, or permit, or facilitate desired teaching or curriculum options.

The Middle School Building

The famous aphorism "We shape our buildings; thereafter they shape us," attributed to Winston Churchill, applies directly to the discussion of middle school buildings. Often placed in the position of inheriting old high school or junior high school buildings, middle school educators find themselves in possession of a building designed for purposes and programs that are, at best, foreign to those the middle school advocates. During the 1980s and early 1990s, when declining enrollments dominated school demographics, middle school educators who pinned their hopes for a fully functioning school on the opportunity to design a new building to fit their program could be destined to be disappointed. In the last decade, however, many new middle school buildings have been designed, constructed, and opened. The good news is that many of these new middle school buildings are being designed with the middle school concept in mind. This was not the case for the previous several decades, but in dozens of districts across the country, old secondary schools are being razed and new ones erected in their place. Population increases have also required dozens, if not hundreds, of new middle schools to be built. By some estimates, the nation is expected to spend $500 billion on new schools over the next decade (Zernicke, 2001). However, exemplary middle schools can function effectively in all kinds of physical plants.

Given that, in architecture, form should follow function, comments on the most appropriate organization of space in middle schools must be accompanied by the familiar requirement to provide a unique and transitional approach. What the middle school building looks like and how it is organized should depend upon the type of program; that is, the building should be designed to serve the program. Consequently, building construction should follow program design. Organization of space in existing facilities that become the site of newly organized middle school programs should follow the acceptance of program changes. All too often, however, this does not happen.

Middle School Buildings: Unique and Transitional   Middle school buildings should be different from elementary and high school buildings. In the elementary school, where the emphasis is upon close relationships built in self-contained classrooms or those that are nearly so, where the curriculum focuses on skill development of the most basic kinds, and where teachers frequently work alone, the building is designed to accommodate this style. In spite of some recent changes in the construction of elementary schools, a building that focuses on single classrooms remains the model structure at that level. Many elementary schools seem to be a series of single classrooms strung together for reasons that are difficult to determine. Because of the nature of the children they serve and the programs they offer, elementary schools also tend to be smaller and less expensive than middle schools.

The high school building also reflects the program within it. Committed to the departmentalized organization of teachers, high schools are almost inevitably organized to reflect this design. The science department is housed in one wing, the mathematics department in another, the English department in a third, and the social studies in a fourth. Subject specialization is the key to high school programs, and the building reflects it with a myriad of special rooms, equipment, and areas. High schools, because of this focus on specialization, and the increased costs that accompany it, tend to be much larger and much more expensive than middle schools.

Middle schools serve a kind of student and offer a kind of program that fits somewhere between the elementary and secondary positions. Middle schools attempt to provide a middle way, balancing the twin goals of personalized climate and enriched curriculum, or supportive interpersonal structure and teacher subject specialization. Most middle school students would be lost in buildings housing between 3,000 and 5,000 students, which is, lamentably, the size of some high schools. The limited programs that very small schools can afford would often challenge these same students less than optimally.

The middle school building must be large enough to hold the number of students necessary to justify the inclusion of expensive special programs so essential for effective early adolescent education. The cost of computerized instruction, industrial arts, agriculture, music, art, home economics, technology, and other expensive programs places them beyond the reach of the elementary school, which, because of the young children involved, must remain small and connected with the neighborhoods it serves. The number of students required to offer high school programs, however, produces a school building and student body large enough to drown the average middle schooler in a sea of anonymity and amorphousness. Recent experiences with school violence make this clearly undesirable.

The challenge of the middle school building, thus, is to be large enough to hold a number of students that will justify the expenditure of funds necessary for the exploratory and physical education programs that educators believe these students require. At the same time, however, the middle school building must be organized in a manner that ensures a sense of community and a personalized educational experience for each student. This is no simple task—designing smallness within bigness (George & Lounsbury, 2000).

It is not an impossible task, however, even though, until the last decade, it has been made more difficult by the frequent need to implement middle school programs in buildings designed initially as elementary, junior high school, or high school facilities. Middle schools can be designed originally or modified later to accommodate advisory programs, the interdisciplinary organization of teachers, just about any type of schoolwide student grouping pattern, enlarged library and media facilities, new programs in the unified arts, and more complex and sophisticated opportunities for physical education and, if preferred, sports. These same schools can be organized to permit the development of close personal relationships with teachers and a sense of community that leads students safely away from the protective atmosphere of the elementary school (George & Lounsbury, 2000). Middle schools are the most effective way to educate older children and young adolescents, in part because they allow educators to offer stimulating programs and enriched educational experiences without sacrificing the atmosphere most conducive to growth-producing interpersonal relationships. Neither program nor school climate needs to be subjugated to the other in an exemplary middle school.

Flexibility   No single type of physical facility is required for the implementation of the middle school program, just as no one schedule is appropriate for all. Programs are influenced by the buildings they inhabit, but they are not completely determined by those buildings. A program can be exemplary in an old motel-style high school building, a converted elementary school, an open-space school, or a structure built around pods of one kind or another. What one asks of a building matters most.

Open-Space Buildings   Much earlier in the life of the middle school movement, near the end of the decade of the 1960s, some educators seem to have been convinced that middle school and open-space facilities were synonymous, that open-space buildings were required for effective middle school programs. Many exemplary middle schools have been housed in open-space facilities, originally designed in the 1960s and 1970s to accommodate programs also described as open and featuring the centrality of "individualized instruction" and "team teaching," catchphrases of that period. These schools featured large open spaces without internal walls or windows to the outside. Many such schools were designed to hold entire teams of students in one large room.

Following three decades of painful illumination about the relationship between form and function, however, most open-space schools have been modified in major ways. A substantial amount of evidence suggests that, while open-space schools may have been less expensive to construct, and even designed to facilitate teaming and differentiating instruction, academic achievement suffers in buildings where most classrooms have no windows or daylight (Zernicke, 2001). The experience of middle school educators over the last several decades also testifies to the high noise levels in such schools, and this, too, is confirmed by research as a very negative factor (Zernicke, 2001). Noise, the absence of natural sunlight, and the generic tendency toward distraction of the young adolescent do not go well together. When schools are designed, in addition, to permit eyes to roam over a dozen classrooms simultaneously, the formula for educational disaster is nearly complete. Consequently, open-space schools are no longer thought desirable and should be avoided in the construction of new facilities for middle schools.

Luckily, just as educators seem to have realized that the middle school concept is not totally dependent on a particular instructional strategy (for example, individualized instruction or cooperative learning), so, too, they understand that many kinds of school buildings can be made to serve the middle school concept and almost no building can prevent the concept from developing. Almost every type of building has its strengths and weaknesses. The key to the use of the facility resides in using the strengths of a particular building to enhance the program offered within.

No more effective demonstration of the truth of these comments could be found than the simple fact that, of the many exemplary school programs described in this volume, few are housed in facilities that are exactly alike. Outstanding programs are found in old buildings and new, large and small, pod-style and conventional. Some of the schools had the buildings designed especially for the programs; others took old high school, junior high school, or elementary school buildings and modified them for new programs in highly effective ways. Equally true, in our opinion, is that sterile, unimaginative, and ineffective programs can be found in buildings that were designed to accommodate much more than they do. A reasonably flexible school plant is necessary for a good program but is far from being sufficient to guarantee that program.

Adapting Older Buildings

Perhaps because establishing an exemplary middle school program may be easier in a new building designed specifically for that purpose, fewer schools that might be labeled exemplary are found, in our experience, in older buildings that have been adapted. This is certainly influenced by the likelihood of being able to assemble a new faculty, specially selected for the middle school program, whenever one opens a new middle school building. While new faculties can be assigned to older buildings, doing so is almost mandatory in a new facility, because the staff has never been there before the building opened—unless, that is, the faculty moved to the new building, en masse, from earlier quarters. Most middle school administrators in our acquaintance assert that it is many times more difficult to change from an existing junior high school to a middle school program than it is to begin a middle school program where no prior school existed. While the faculty makeup can be the most important factor, the building itself is important in determining the ease with which the new program is established. The simple fact that older buildings were almost always designed for other purposes and, therefore, require adaptations creates a measure of additional difficulty.

Sometimes middle schools inherited their space from elementary schools, but more frequently the program moved into a plant that housed a high school or, even more frequently, a junior high school. In the relatively infrequent instances in which the middle school took over space from an elementary school, the major problem stemmed from inadequate space and from facilities that did not contain areas or equipment to house the unified arts and other new programs that may have been in the planning. Because these enrichment areas were central to the middle school concept, their absence was serious. Accommodations for these programs usually came in the form of portable buildings or additions to the existing facilities, or they did not come at all. Schools fortunate enough to convince district planners to add the space had a new chance to excel. Those that were refused were forced to accept severe limitations in the program they offered to their students.

Middle school programs that inherited their space from older secondary programs were more fortunate, or at least their problems were of a different nature. Moving into an older secondary school building usually meant that the enlarged library and media space was there, even if the books and the equipment were not. The areas where the unified arts had been offered were still there, even if the spaces looked like vacant airplane hangers. Inheriting a high school building has usually also meant more space of all kinds—offices, cafeteria, hallways, lockers, study areas, auditorium, laboratories, and larger classrooms. High schools, simply, were bigger. So, the problems were not connected with having enough space to put all the program components.

The major problem with inheriting the high school or junior high school building was related to the differing practices of organizing teachers for instruction. Most secondary schools have operated on the departmentalized model of curriculum and teacher organization. In addition, in the headlong rush to erect buildings large enough to offer expanded, comprehensive programs—and consolidating (read eliminating) the smaller schools in the process—few architects or school planners gave any thought to the need to design the new structures to preserve the sense of community that existed in the smaller schools. New middle school programs in older secondary buildings, thus, found themselves with space that was often difficult to adapt to new needs.

Most older secondary school buildings were constructed so that classrooms were not grouped together in any type of recognizable pattern, except in the case of the science program. The department concept and, perhaps at the time, cost of construction required the science laboratories to be grouped in the same area. This simple construction decision has caused an endless round of difficulties for middle school planners as they have attempted to adapt the buildings to the pattern of interdisciplinary teacher organization. Finding convenient groups of classrooms, and surmounting the science department problem so that team members could be close to each other in the middle school, presents a major stumbling block to establishing effective new programs in old school buildings. Once these problems are solved, the rest seems to be relatively easy.

Consider the floor plans for Deland Junior High School, in Volusia County, Florida, for the school year 1986–1987 and for the middle school that inherited the same facility in the school year 1991–1992. The organization of the building when it housed the junior high school program illustrates the centrality of academic disciplines and electives (see Figure 8.1). Figure 8.2 demonstrates the challenge of reorganization: moving grade level teams into a school originally designed with a subject-centered facility. The location of the science labs and, thus, the science teachers posed distinct challenges for the effective operation of interdisciplinary teams.

Educators who must implement middle school programs in older buildings choose one of several ways to deal with the need to make the science area more flexible. Some planners organize the day and the teams so that teams are able to schedule the time in the available science laboratory areas, avoiding major conflicts. With some notable exceptions, many middle school science programs seem to be relatively independent of the need for constant access to a science laboratory, and being able to schedule special lab time when necessary often seems to be enough. Other schools have found that portable

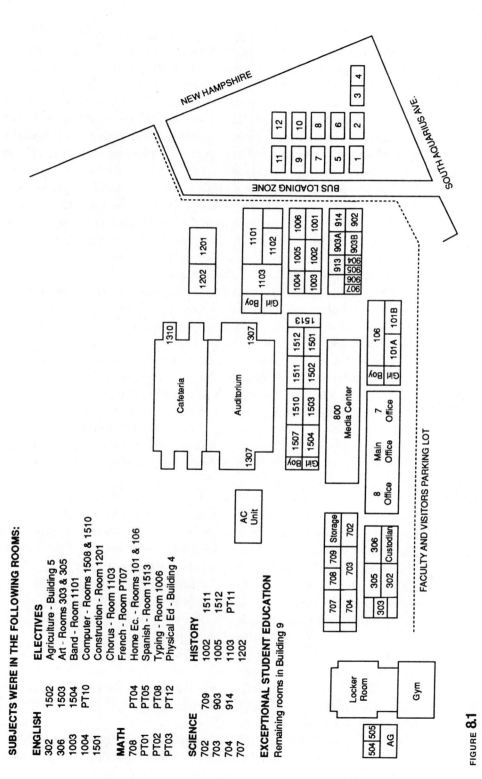

SUBJECTS WERE IN THE FOLLOWING ROOMS:

ENGLISH

302	1502
306	1503
1003	1504
1004	PT10
1501	

ELECTIVES

Agriculture - Building 5
Art - Rooms 303 & 305
Band - Room 1101
Computer - Rooms 1508 & 1510
Construction - Room 1201
Chorus - Room 1103
French - Room PT07
Home Ec. - Rooms 101 & 106
Spanish - Room 1513
Typing - Room 1006
Physical Ed - Building 4

MATH

708	PT04
PT01	PT05
PT02	PT08
PT03	PT12

SCIENCE

702	709
703	903
704	914
707	

HISTORY

1002	1511
1005	1512
1103	PT11
1202	

EXCEPTIONAL STUDENT EDUCATION

Remaining rooms in Building 9

FIGURE **8.1**

DELAND JUNIOR HIGH SCHOOL, IN VOLUSIA COUNTY, FLORIDA, 1986–1987

GRADE LEVELS LOCATED IN THE FOLLOWING:

SIXTH GRADE
Building 16
Building 17
Portables 1, 2 & 3

SEVENTH GRADE
Rooms:
303 & 305, 504
1504, 1510, 1511
& 1512
Portables 5, 8, 9, 11 & 12

EIGHTH GRADE
Rooms:
101A & 101B
902 & 914
1001, 1002, 1003, 1004
& 1005
1501, 1502 & 1503

ELECTIVES
Agriculture - Room 505
Art - Rooms 302 & 305
Band - Room 1101
Computer - Room 1508
Construction - Room 1201
Home Ec. - Room 106
Physical Ed - Building 4
Spanish - Room 1202

SCIENCE LABS FOR 7th & 8th Grades
located in Building 7

EXCEPTIONAL STUDENT EDUCATION
Remaining rooms in Building 9
Portables 4 & 7

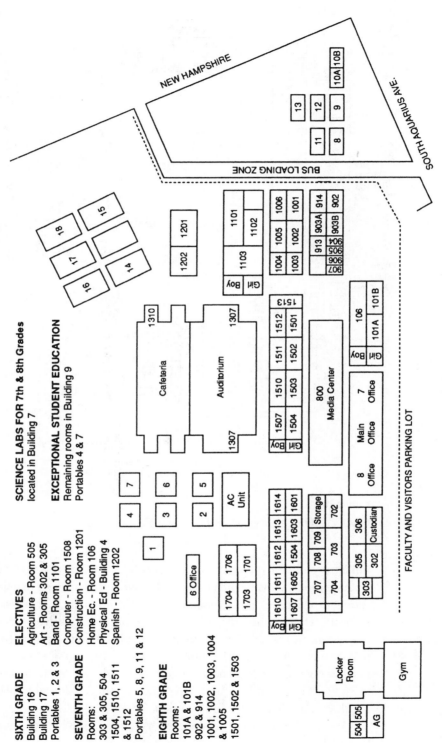

FIGURE **8.2**

DELAND MIDDLE SCHOOL, IN VOLUSIA COUNTY, FLORIDA, 1991–1992

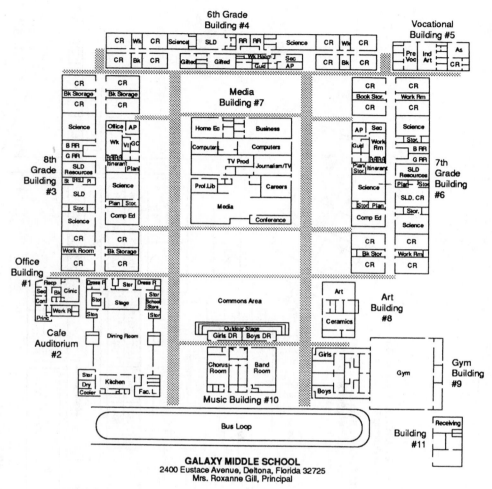

FIGURE 8.3

GALAXY MIDDLE SCHOOL, IN DELTONA, FLORIDA, 1991

miniature labs or demonstration tables often suffice. Still others are able to arrange their teams in the space so that while the science teachers have their rooms in what was the science department, interdisciplinary groups are still close together. Some other schools have found themselves so stymied by the placement of the science rooms that they have had to resort to interdisciplinary teams composed of mathematics, social studies, and language arts teachers, leaving the science teachers together in a department. We believe that this is the least acceptable option, but that it is still considerably better than having the entire faculty remain in a departmentalized structure.

We also believe that, in almost every case, these science area problems can be resolved without sacrificing the interdisciplinary team concept. Faculties that find it difficult to do so may be philosophically resistant instead of spatially troubled. Because the experience of 40 years of middle school development from 1960 to 2000 so strongly supports the idea that the interdisciplinary team concept is central and must come first in the development of an exemplary middle school, time must be taken to help the staff see the need to make both the philosophical and the territorial changes.

A new middle school, opened in the fall of 1991 in Deltona, Florida, illustrates how that same district (Volusia County) responded with new facilities to match new middle school programs (see Figure 8.3). Middle school interdisciplinary teams operate with considerably greater ease, effectiveness, and efficiency in this building than in the older building for Deland Middle School in the same district, where adaptation had to be the rule.

One school that has done an outstanding job of adapting an older secondary school building to the middle school program is Lincoln Middle School, in Gainesville, Florida. Lincoln inherited a building that had a history as a racially segregated high school for several decades, followed by a period of vacant idleness after schools in the district were integrated in 1970. Opened several years later as a vocational school, it was changed to a middle school in 1974. Figure 8.4 is a floor plan of Lincoln drawn in 1973, prior to the opening of the middle school program there.

In 2001 Lincoln housed approximately 1,000 students in a building intended to hold considerably more, when it was designed several decades earlier. A glance at the floor plan will show that the school was not intended as a middle school when built, but that the Lincoln staff made the necessary adaptations to convert it to serve the team concept well. Believing that teams work better when located in contiguous classrooms, and having inherited enough space to give each team a planning area, the school was organized in 1974 along these lines. Each of the six teams at Lincoln were assigned to team areas: C team was given rooms 25 to 28 as classrooms and room 15 as a team planning space; B team was given rooms 31 to 34 as classrooms and room 13 as its planning area; D team was given rooms 44 to 47 as classrooms and room 40 as a team planning room; W team was housed in rooms 48 to 51, with 42 as a planning room; G team had rooms 52 to 55 as teaching areas, with 56 as the planning room; M team was located in rooms 87 to 89, 90, and 91, with its planning space in room 88, which had been an automotive mechanics shop during the years the high school had been there. Six teams operated in six areas. Other rooms and areas in the school are used conventionally.

Gymnasium 76	Special education resource rooms 12 to 17
Cafeteria 19 to 24	Computer lab 18
Auditorium 62	Family and consumer science 39, 41
Technology lab 93	Offices 1 to 8
Media center 67 to 68	

Since the opening of school that first year, three decades ago, many changes have occurred at Lincoln. New programs that affected the entire district, in

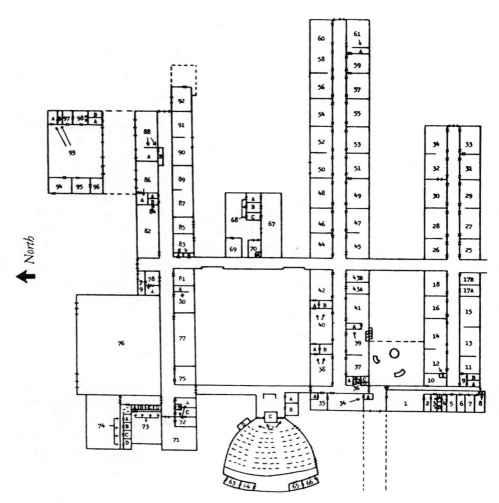

FIGURE **8.4**

LINCOLN MIDDLE SCHOOL, IN GAINESVILLE, FLORIDA, 1973

areas such as bilingual education, deaf education, and so on, have been located there. Enrollment fluctuations and other factors have required space to be adjusted, but the concept of team areas and planning spaces has been guarded jealously and sacrificed only when there was no other choice. As a result of this, Lincoln was still an exemplary middle school in the 2001–2002 school year, 30 years after it was opened. Separate team planning rooms have virtually disappeared as enrollment has grown, special science labs have been added to each team, and computer and technology labs now dot the school, but team organization and planning have continued.

The simple fact of Lincoln Middle School's continued existence as an exemplary middle school should add confidence to those new to the concept, especially as they explore ways of adapting old buildings to new programs. The experience of most middle school educators, in the 21st century, is that leadership and professional commitment sustain programs for decades, not buildings or money.

Many other middle schools have made creative adjustments to their inherited space in ways that have allowed them to develop and maintain outstanding programs. But some school districts, more than most others, seem to exemplify the ability to make creative programs develop and prosper in school settings of widely varying types. The district of Dothan, Alabama, is such a place.

In early 1974, the school district of Dothan, Alabama, began to implement a well-planned project, with funding assistance from several sources, to close three junior high schools in the city and open four middle schools in the fall of 1977. Two of the four junior high school buildings were to be used as middle schools, and two new middle school buildings were to be built. The plan included a commitment to almost identical programs in each of the four middle schools, but the buildings that were intended to house these programs were radically different from one another. Two were to be brand-new, flexibly spaced, pod-type structures. One was a relatively modern junior high school of conventional classroom design, built about 20 years previous to the middle school plan, and the fourth was a building that needed monumental renovation to make it acceptable to members of that community. Because the middle school plan also included a total reassignment of teachers throughout the district's middle level, the teachers had a vested interest in the building construction and renovation.

As it turned out, the programs for the four schools were, and remained as of 2002, virtually indistinguishable from each other, with talented faculties operating within nearly identical team designs. Advisory programs function in each school, along with exploratory curriculum plans that should be the envy of neighboring districts. The most interesting thing about the program, in this respect, is that all four middle schools function with roughly identical schedules as well. The schedule for Beverlye Road Middle School is almost exactly like the schedules of sister middle schools Honeysuckle, Girard, and Carver regardless of the dramatic differences that exist in the facilities that house the programs.

AN EMERGING CONSENSUS ON THE NATURE OF FACILITIES FOR THE EXEMPLARY MIDDLE SCHOOL

The building that contains the program for Wakulla Middle School (see Figure 5.1) demonstrates the profound interaction between building and program that is required in the exemplary middle school. We discuss this interaction in detail in Chapter 7, on grouping. A review of this interaction conducted by an architect 10 years after the opening of the building (Peterson, 1991) examined the results and found that the building's design did effectively enhance the implementation of the middle school concept. Peterson's conclusions are fascinating.

> The Wakulla Middle School functions very successfully in its established framework of philosophies and curriculum concepts of a middle school. There has been an apparent commitment to those concepts by the faculty and staff since the inception. Most conflicts that have arisen over the ten years have been overcome through adaptation in policy or change in spacial usage. The optimum operation of a middle school as defined by the Wakulla facility demands a specific building type to support the curriculum concepts and organizational philosophies. Although the Wakulla Middle School was designed as such a building type, there are a number of aspects that have not proven optimum. The continued operational success is in large part attributable to the personnel and their goal commitment rather than the physical form. (Peterson, 1991, p. 129)

A decade later, in 2000, educators in Wakulla County needed to open an additional middle school to serve the needs of young adolescents in their growing district. Over the previous two decades, educators in Wakulla County had learned much about the interaction of school buildings and the program of the school. Furthermore, the school district had been devoted to the middle school concept throughout this whole period. So, when the time came to design the new Riversprings Middle School, educators in the county had identified some important things that came to bear on the new facility. Robert Myhre, a longtime leader in the middle school and district, had this to say about the design of the new school:

> The challenge in life is not to repeat previous mistakes but to learn from them and constantly improve. This should be true in school construction where many times educational settings are built with one criterion overriding all others—cost. After 17 years at a great middle school (WMS), I had the opportunity to be a part of the design and construction of a new middle school. . . . The lessons that I learned at WMS led to these ten suggestions for constructing a middle school that can provide a quality learning environment and also addresses certain middle school student behaviors.
>
> 1. The design should allow for easy supervision by a small number of personnel. Having the new school built in an "X" pattern allows two people to supervise all hallways in the main building. The traditional "H" pattern has many corners to hide behind. Also, there should be no "gang" type restrooms where groups can be out of sight. The design should also reflect the scheduling pattern of the school so that students have minimal distances to travel between classes.
> 2. Administrative and student service areas (guidance, clinic, etc.) should be totally separate. When the guidance counselor's office is next to the

principal's or assistant principal's office, they are often viewed as a part of the administration and many middle school students are uncomfortable being around these office areas.

3. The classrooms should be as versatile as possible (i.e., folding walls to create team space, sinks and water in all rooms, a tiled area in each room for messy projects and large display areas for student work). The more versatile the room, the easier it is for teachers to provide interdisciplinary instruction.

4. All classrooms should have some natural lighting, but windows should be placed above eye level when students are seated. Outside distractions are not good for middle school students.

5. Lockers should only be large enough to hold the books that are issued. Large lockers encourage large book bags that are havens for contraband.

6. Middle schoolers are hard on flooring. Carpets are great in the classroom but tile in the hallways is much easier to maintain.

7. Cafetoriums should be separate buildings from the main campus. There is nothing more rambunctious than a middle schooler on the way to lunch or coming back from lunch. Allowing them access to the outside reduces the need to try to quiet them all the way there and back.

8. If the school has a band or chorus program, these should be directly adjacent to the stage where the students will perform. This provides less travel time with instruments, music stands, and other things that may need to be transported for performances.

9. If the school has a gymnasium, the boys and girls locker rooms should be on opposite sides of the building. Putting middle school boys and girls on the same side of a building where dressing and undressing occurs is asking for trouble.

10. The common areas of the school should be central to all buildings so that it appears to students that eyes could be on them at all times.

There is probably no perfect middle school design, and every district faces different challenges in school construction. However, after one year at Riversprings Middle School, the teachers and administrators who have transferred there and have experience in both buildings report that the changes that have been made have had a positive impact on the students' learning environment and on general student control. (Robert Myhre, personal communication, October 4, 2001).

Pods, Team Areas, and Houses

Middle school educators across the nation seem to have learned these lessons, given that the great majority of new middle school buildings opened during the period between 1981 and 2002 were pod-style facilities. Pod-type construction seems particularly suited to the middle school program, accommodating the

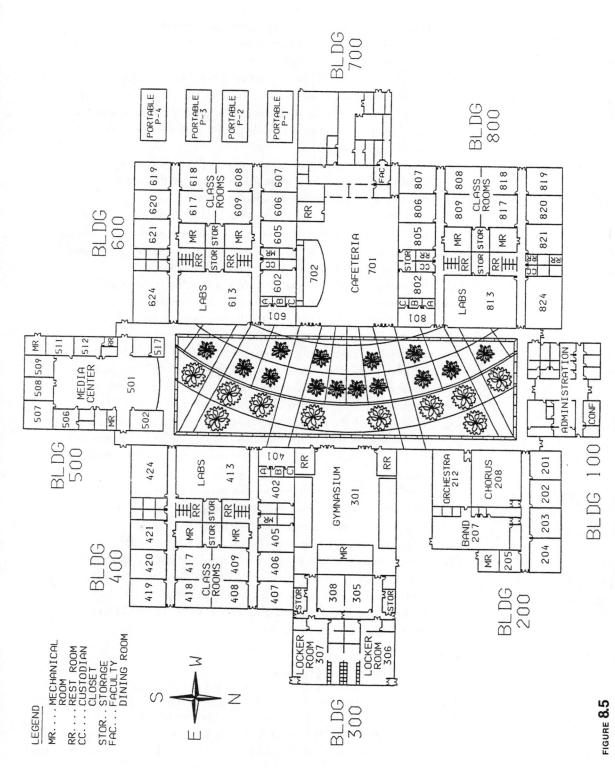

FIGURE **8.5**

CHAIN OF LAKES MIDDLE SCHOOL, IN ORANGE COUNTY, FLORIDA, 2000

interdisciplinary team organization in a special way and offering the maximum amount of flexibility to leaders when program priorities shift. An analysis of the floor plan of the Chain of Lakes Middle School (CLMS), in Orange County, Florida, a school opened in 2000, illustrates the typical features of the modern middle school design (see Figure 8.5).

CLMS houses approximately 1,200 students in grades 6 through 8. The program is almost identical to the program in the other 25 middle schools in the Orange County school district, in spite of the radically different physical facilities of the separate schools. John Meinecke, longtime middle school principal who led the district into the creation of 20 middle schools in the 1980s, designed CLMS. Meinecke ensured that the school was designed with a middle school program in mind and with the realization that the interdisciplinary team organization was the heart of the program. The school building, therefore, is especially facilitative of the team and its community. At CLMS, each grade level is housed in a separate pod (400, 600, 800). There can be two teams for each pod, with up to four to five teachers on each team, and each pod contains part of the school's exceptional students and other classes. "There is no more separate wing for exceptional students," says Meinecke forcefully. The school can also be organized in three houses, with grades 6–8 in each. The design of CLMS also illustrates, with the placement of science and tech facilities, the commitment of the district to the interdisciplinary team organization. Every pod has its own science labs.

CLMS can offer an opportunity for an extensive exploratory program, with such a large number of students to support it, potentially including almost anything: physical education, vocal and instrumental music, drama, business education, family and consumer science, arts and crafts, and technology. The building can accommodate these programs beautifully, and classes that are likely to need buffering space for the sound they may make are, for the most part, separated from academic areas.

The design of the building, with a large enclosed courtyard space, allows a gradual transition from the surrounding neighborhood. The courtyard at CLMS functions as a circulation, congregating, outdoor assembly area for teams and as an area for overspill events. All student cross-school, out of team, movements occur within the perimeter of the courtyards, enhancing security measures. Team-based corridors allow great visibility and help students move quickly from class to class. The commons area radically expands the instructional space available to teachers and, therefore, contributes flexibility to the academic program that is far beyond the capacity of schools without this design. Architects designed the building as a prototype for a countywide system of new middle school buildings.

The CLMS plant also illustrates the flexibility that permits a number of program modifications to be installed without major plant renovation. The design at CLMS, for example, permits educators to organize teachers and students for instruction in a variety of ways. The staff in CLMS decided to remain with the standard chronological grade level pattern when the school opened for the 2000–2001 school year, with two four-person teams of teachers in each of three buildings. But educators in CLMS could also have chosen to organize in other ways. Should there have been a decision to move to a school-within-school program, for example, it could easily have been accomplished with this building. Even a move to complete multiage grouping could have been accommodated without plant modifications, simply establishing six or seven such teams. These choices can still be made.

A new middle school for the school district of Cleveland, Tennessee, opened in the fall of 2001, further illustrates the power of new pod-style facilities to effectively accommodate the needs of the middle school concept. Cleveland Middle School is designed so that it can house three separate grade level pods, one of which is illustrated in Figure 8.6, but it is flexible enough to be used in other ways. First, the school could easily be organized to accommodate a school-within-school design, with a 6th, 7th, and 8th grade team in each of the three houses. Principal Ashley Smith writes, "In the future, we may go to communities of 6th, 7th, and 8th grades in each wing" (personal communication, June 10, 2001). It is also possible to return, at some future time, to a departmentalized approach in each pod, because the science facilities are located together. This is so, even though each science room faces the rest of the classrooms of the interdisciplinary team of which it is a member. We find few building designs to be more flexible and, simultaneously, more accommodating of middle school concepts than that of the new Cleveland Middle School plant. We recommend it for consideration by planners investigating new middle school designs.

In the Cleveland building, several items are of particular note, in addition to the overall match with middle school concepts.

- Three regular computer labs are housed in the media and technology center, which also houses a communications and technology lab and an additional lab for mathematics and science applications in technology.
- Each classroom wing is identical to the other two.
- Each classroom wing has five movable walls that can be opened for team activities.
- Science storage space is available in each pod.
- Dining, physical education, and chorus and band facilities are at the opposite end of the building from academic programs.
- Classrooms for exceptional students and some exploratory classes are integrated into the academic team wings.
- Bus loading and automobile loading are, for the sake of safety, located at opposite sides of the building.
- Underneath the bleacher area in the gymnasium, not visible on the floor plan, are two additional basketball courts.

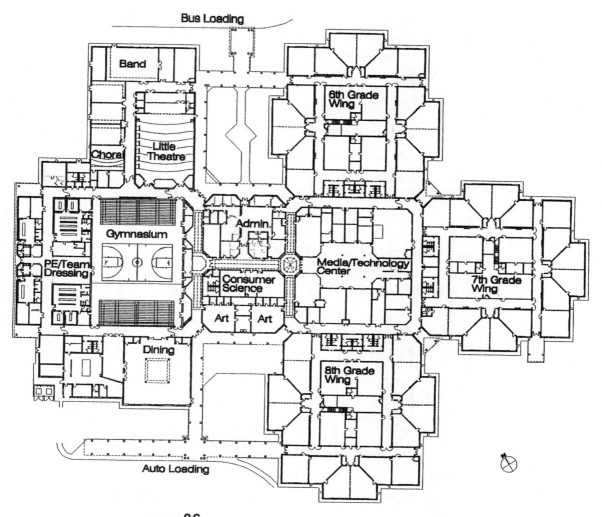

FIGURE **8.6**

CLEVELAND MIDDLE SCHOOL, IN CLEVELAND, TENNESEE, 2001

- A little theatre, a great place for presentations, productions, and team affairs, is provided.
- Bathrooms inside each team area make long, unmonitored trips to those facilities unnecessary.

In the close-up of the classroom pod at CMS (see Figure 8.7), several team configurations can be put in place, depending on the vision of the school leaders. The arrangement could be four teams of three teachers each, three teams of four teachers each, or six two-teacher teams. The pod could house several two-teacher and three-teacher teams. Combine that with the possibility of

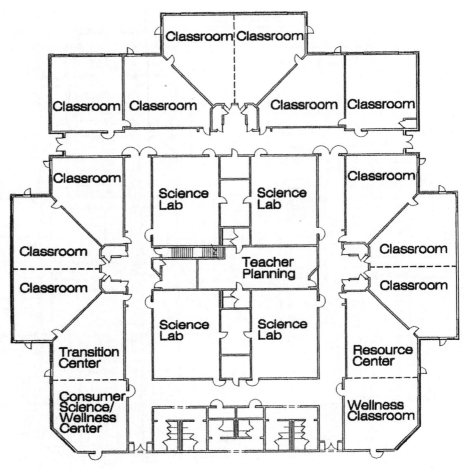

FIGURE 8.7

CLASSROOM POD, CLEVELAND MIDDLE SCHOOL, IN CLEVELAND, TENNESSEE, 2001

school-within-school and multiage designs, and the options allow for maximum flexibility. A large teacher planning room in the center of the pod accommodates whatever teaming arrangements are implemented. Flexible walls allow for team activities, and internal doors connect classrooms to each other, making for easy communication and collaboration among team members. The new Cleveland Middle School building offers the best in current middle school building design.

The new facility (opened in 2000) for the Blue Valley Middle School (BVMS), in Stilwell, Kansas (see Figure 8.8), while geographically distant from Tennessee or Florida, illustrates the common building design emerging for middle schools across the nation. These geographically distant schools have buildings with much in common. This commonality in design is based on the widespread consensus on what is best for the education of young

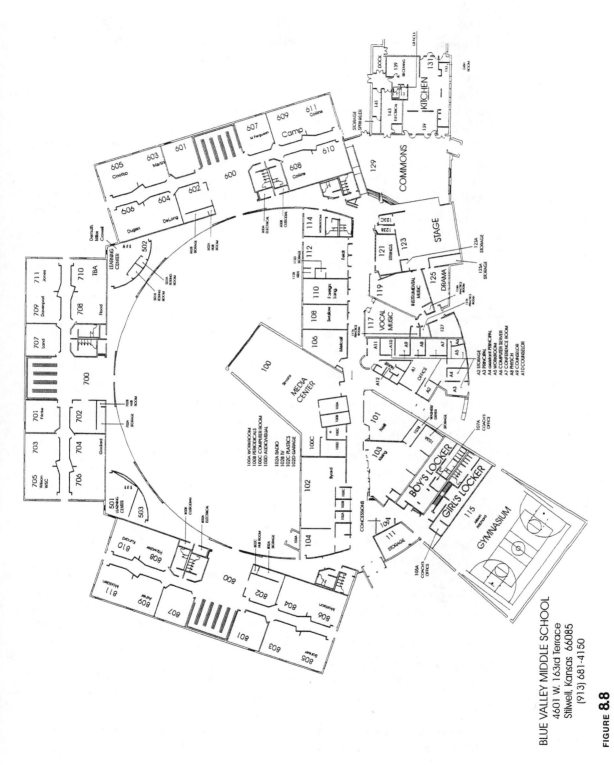

BLUE VALLEY MIDDLE SCHOOL
4601 W. 163rd Terrace
Stilwell, Kansas 66085
(913) 681-4150

FIGURE 8.8

BLUE VALLEY MIDDLE SCHOOL, IN STILWELL, KANSAS, 2000

adolescents—and the nature of facilities that serve them well. BVMS features the flexible placement of science laboratories, academic wings designed to hold two interdisciplinary teams at each grade level or three 6–8 schools-within-schools, and a strong commitment to the unified arts and physical education, including the performing arts. Areas that produce high levels of noise are located at a distance from academic programs, just as in the other new schools illustrated here.

The new building for the Mt. Slesse Middle School (MSMS), in Chilliwack, British Columbia, Canada, illustrates the now international consensus on programs and buildings designed for young adolescents (see Figure 8.9). One hour east of Vancouver, MSMS serves approximately 750 students, grades 7–9, fully implementing the middle school concept in a building designed for that purpose, even though the grade structure would have, in an earlier era, implied a traditional junior high school. Three pods are organized in a school-within-school model, with equal numbers of 7th, 8th, and 9th graders in each. Also, within each pod are two multiage teams, a grade 7 and 8 team and a grade 8 and 9 team. Students stay in one pod during the three years they are enrolled at MSMS.

At MSMS, each pod also has one teacher who takes on the dual role of counselor and learning assistance teacher, an inclusion teacher with counseling responsibilities. This person, located at the center of each pod's suite labeled LA/Counselling, attends to the affective concerns of all students and to the special academic needs of exceptional students in the pod. This, we think, is a forceful combination of inclusion and affective education. Educators at MSMS assert that the LA/Counselling suite becomes the hub from which the pod operates. This allows the two teams of teachers to work closely with their learning assistance teacher or counselor colleague and the students upon which they focus. Over the period of the three years that students (and parents) stay together in the same pod, the connections become "extremely strong." This closeness is enhanced by the presence of 12 advisory groups that meet in each pod; each is multigraded, 7–9. Teacher planning rooms are also a part of each pod.

The CLMS plant, Blue Valley Middle School, Mt. Slesse, and dozens of other pod-style facilities in schools elsewhere (for example, three-decade-old Beverlye Road Middle School, in Dothan, Alabama; Jamesville-DeWitt Middle School, in Jamesville, New York; and Nock Middle School, in Newburyport, Massachusetts) offer the maximum flexibility to middle school programs. A number of schools described in this volume can reasonably be described as pod-type schools, even though their physical plant may or may not have been designed with this purpose initially in mind. For example, Farnsworth Middle School, in Guilderland, New York, has been an exemplary middle school for decades. We suppose that a building that has matched the programs beautifully has assisted this success. Figures 8.10 and 8.11 illustrate both the first and sec-

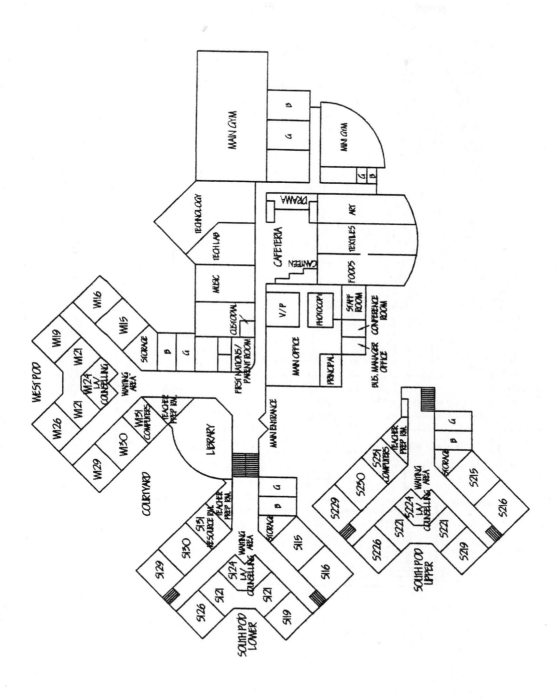

FIGURE 8.9

MT. SLESSE MIDDLE SCHOOL, IN CHILLIWACK, BRITISH COLUMBIA, CANADA, 2001

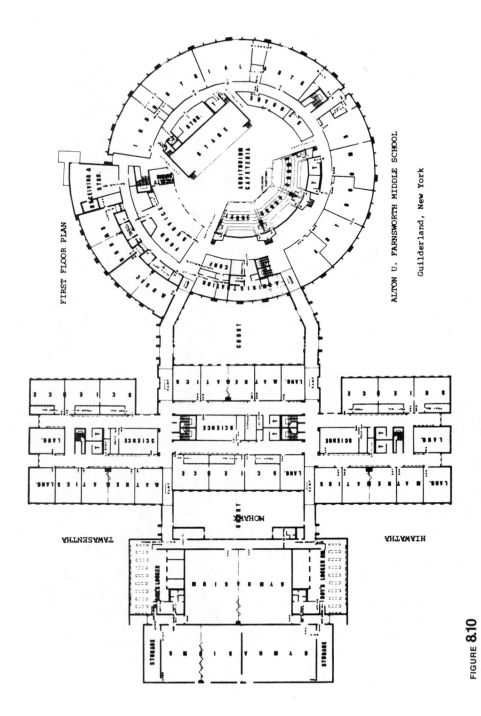

FIRST FLOOR PLAN

ALTON U. FARNSWORTH MIDDLE SCHOOL

Guilderland, New York

FIGURE 8.10
FIRST-FLOOR PLAN, FARNSWORTH MIDDLE SCHOOL, IN GUILDERLAND, NEW YORK

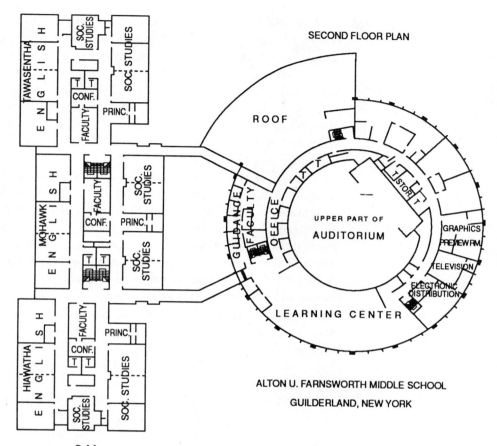

FIGURE **8.11**

SECOND-FLOOR PLAN, FARNSWORTH MIDDLE SCHOOL, IN GUILDERLAND, NEW YORK

ond floors at Farnsworth, where each house extends over both levels. Designed to accommodate 1,650 students, each house consists of four or five interdisciplinary teams, including grades 6 through 8. The staff members at Farnsworth express their commitment to "harmonizing the best of two worlds, one which is small enough to foster a feeling of concern for the individual student and one which is large enough to offer the varied resources necessary to meet the needs and interests of preadolescent and early adolescent youngsters."

Examining the floor plan at Farnsworth creates an excited expectation that this type of program is possible there. One of the authors visited the school in the spring of 1991 to participate in the community celebration of 20 years of outstanding middle school education. The design of the building has contributed to that exemplary program, now for over three decades, as of 2002—something worth celebrating.

One final example of the emerging consensus on middle school buildings: Oak Hill Middle School (OHMS), in Milledgeville, Georgia (see Figures 8.12 and 8.13). OHMS was carefully designed over a period of several years to combine a complete middle school program with an elegant building that would match and facilitate the program. Local resident and longtime middle school leader John Lounsbury consulted with founding principal Marion Payne (a past president of the National Middle School Association) to conceive both program and building design in a community that had not had an exemplary middle school prior to this time.

Opened in August 2000, OHMS was designed as a large school, intended to house all 1,500 young adolescents in the district in one large building. The large number of students makes it financially efficient to provide two technology labs for the school as a whole and a large gymnasium with classrooms for instruction in physical education. A sizable, state-of-the-art Discovery Center features a 30-station computerized research and publishing lab, as well as all of the print materials that would be needed to meet the needs of young adolescent readers and researchers. As is now the case in new middle school buildings, noisy areas such as music and physical education are located at a distance from academic classrooms. A separate staff development suite is unique, in our experience, and the theater is large enough to hold almost all of the students from one house. OHMS is a large facility and, as such, provides the opportunity for rich and robust curriculum experiences.

Program designers were, however, well aware of the need to organize the building with a sense of smallness, a school where young adolescents felt known and cared for. Hence, the school-within-school design prevailed. A perusal of the four schools of Oak Hill indicates much that is similar to other exemplary middle school facilities. Team planning and teacher workrooms are placed in each house. Science facilities are located in the center of each house, much like those at Cleveland Middle School. A guidance center contains each subschool's counseling area. Computer labs, all with Internet access, are located in each house, for the specific use of students and teachers in each place. Because each house has its own principal, these offices are located there as well, along with the secretary for each of the four schools.

In a studied attempt to make this large school seem smaller, each of the four schools-within-schools was designed to be a microcosm of the larger school. This includes four leaders, counselors, and secretaries. It also includes separate identities for each of the places in which students will spend their three years at OHMS: Historic Piedmont, Mystic Mountains, Coastal Plains, and Golden Isles. All of the names are drawn from important parts of the geography of the state of Georgia. Supplemented by teams at each grade level, and teacher-based advisory programs within each team, the building shapes the education of young adolescents much in the way that Winston Churchill must have had in mind.

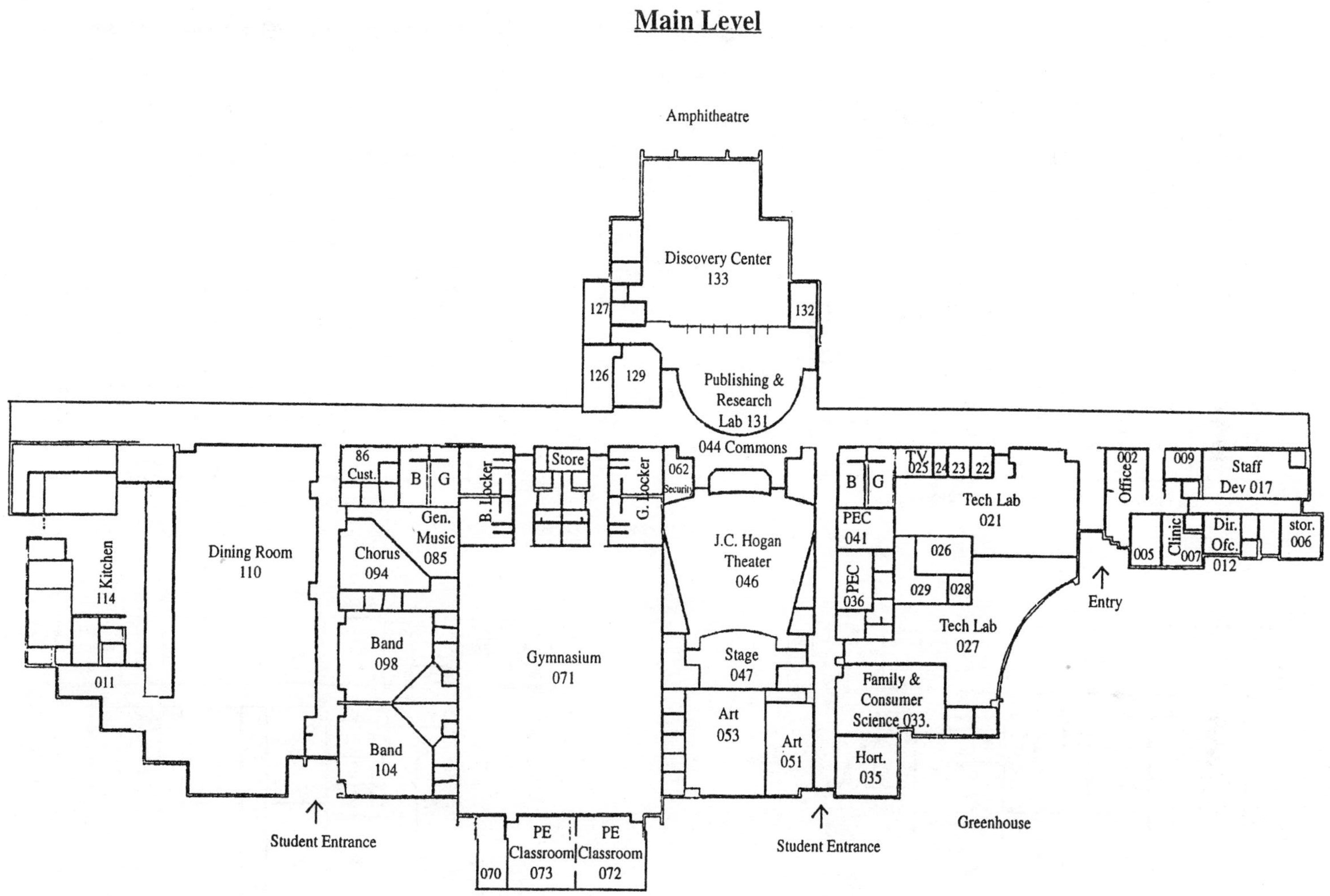

Main Level

FIGURE 8.12

OAK HILL MIDDLE SCHOOL, IN MILLEDGEVILLE, GEORGIA, 2000

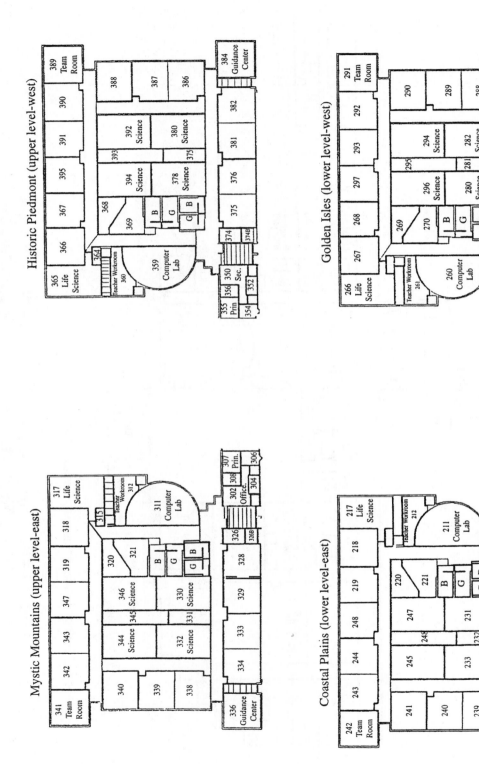

FIGURE 8.13

THE FOUR SCHOOLS OF OAK HILL MIDDLE SCHOOL, IN MILLEDGEVILLE, GEORGIA, 2000

General Considerations for Specifications for New Buildings

Following three decades of adapting old buildings and erecting new ones, most school leaders have agreed on several principles that should be considered by the next generation of middle school facility planners.

1. Size is an important factor. Schools with fewer than 800 students, while desirable for many reasons, quickly become expensive propositions when planners attempt to build in a full core of opportunities beyond regular classrooms. Physical education facilities cannot be halved. Libraries and media centers should not be made so small that they make later expansion of the facilities difficult. However, schools substantially larger than 1,000 students quickly begin to lose the economy of scale that they gain by their size. This is true in terms of the physical facility and also regarding the management of the program.

2. The larger the school, the more important it becomes to place assistant administrators and counselors in academic wings of the school, instead of in administrative suites. Direct delivery of their services to teachers and students can be done much more efficiently. In small schools, where there are no assistants, this cannot be done.

3. Administrative and counseling areas should always be separated. Again, this is a result of considering whom the counselor is serving. The recipient of counselor services, ideally, ought to be the students and not the school administrators. This separation is likely to enhance the services as they were intended.

4. In line with the inclusion movement, co-teaching, and other considerations for exceptional students, areas for these students should be dispersed throughout the academic wings, not clustered together in the rear of the facility. This is particularly so in the case of learning disabled students, generally considered the best candidates for complete inclusion. But other exceptional students have a right to be considered a part of the school as a whole, and their placement should reflect it.

5. New schools should be designed to minimize student movement around the building, which recommends the house plan or school-within-school model where students remain in the same part of the building for the whole day and for the whole tenure of their time in middle school. Schools such as Wakulla, Mt. Slesse, and Oak Hill are flexible enough to be used in this way or in more traditional grade level wing groupings.

6. These schools also offer the sort of flexibility that is clearly desirable for the schools of the 21st century. Arranged as they are, they can be changed to reflect new insights into middle level education, changing demographics, or other factors that might influence the way in which a building should be used. The placement of the science facilities in buildings like those we have illustrated testifies to the flexibility that a

new generation may appreciate. Other plans should make future expansion a possibility.

7.   The placement of driveways for parents and busses is also important. Experience indicates that separate areas should be made available for parents and busses picking up students at the end of the day. And new facilities should be planned so that the busses deposit students at an entrance near the cafeteria, because so many students now eat their breakfast at school.

8.   Teachers on teams engage in a large number of parent conferences. Experienced middle school educators recommend that several big conference rooms be placed near the entrance of the school to facilitate the efficient conduct of such conferences. This placement makes it unnecessary for parents to wander through the school in search of a teacher planning room or for administrators to accompany them to a distant destination.

9.   Security of the school plant and school site should be considered in initial planning. Landscape designs should harmonize with building security, as in the internal courtyards at the Chain of Lakes Middle School. Blind corners, dead-end corridors, and areas difficult to supervise should be excluded whenever possible. Smooth exterior areas, large glass panels, or other features that will provide for graffiti or other types of vandalism are not in the best interests of new middle schools. Adequate night lighting should plan for evening uses of the facility for community education programs and the like.

10. Perhaps nothing is more important than daylight and windows in the classroom. Recent studies have demonstrated that the amount of daylight in classrooms is more closely related to increased academic achievement than sex, class size, or whether the students come from single-family households (Zernicke, 2001). Students in windowless classrooms such as those in the open-space buildings of the 1970s do distinctly less well than their peers in classrooms with bright outside light.

CONCLUDING COMMENTS

The effective use of time and space in the middle school is absolutely critical to the successful implementation of the other portions of the middle school program. If a component of the middle school program cannot be scheduled, it cannot be offered to the students. If no space can be adapted to the use of a program part, that part will be unlikely to become a regular component of the program. In a sense, the organization of time and space stands as the ultimate restriction on the type of program possible in any particular middle school. But in the opposition sense, properly designed, these two factors represent a liberating opportunity for the expansion and enrichment of complex yet community-building school programs.

School planners interested in helping the staff of a middle school program get the most from the schedule and the building they use must foster the development of several important skills. For administrators, a clear understanding of the program priorities and the knowledge of the steps involved in the construction of a master schedule to accommodate team organization are crucial. The ability and commitment to place teams together within the building seems almost as important. For teachers, directors of staff development programs will assist most directly when they help teachers learn how to use the schedule to their own advantage, to schedule their own students and special activities within the schedule, and to turn the design of the plant, however constructed, to the enhancement of the life of the interdisciplinary team.

CONTENT SUMMARY

Both the schedule and the building must serve the academic program. In the 21st century, distinct changes in both schedules and buildings for middle schools have made their appearance. A new long block schedule has begun to organize the school day into periods or blocks ranging from 60 to 120 minutes, with three or four blocks per day, usually alternating to offer a seven- or eight-course schedule. New middle school buildings are becoming more alike, designed to facilitate interdisciplinary teams, exploratory programs, and school-within-school designs. Making big schools feel small has become an important objective of both schedule developers and building designers.

CONNECTIONS TO OTHER CHAPTERS

Schedules and buildings influence everything, but connecting the way in which time and space are organized to several factors is particularly important. For example, how students are grouped for teaching and learning (Chapter 7) and the connection to the interdisciplinary team organization (Chapter 6) are critical. Every exemplary middle school must find ways to harmonize these four central factors: schedule, building, grouping, and teaming.

QUESTIONS FOR DISCUSSION

1. How does the teacher education one receives (either elementary or secondary level) have an influence on one's attitude toward the attractiveness of the new long block schedule? To what extent does a teacher's subject specialization affect his or her level of comfort with a much longer class period?

2. If a team is creative, is it absolutely necessary to have a long block schedule to derive the benefits such a schedule offers? How can a team create such a situation for themselves?

3. How many different types of middle school schedule, in the districts near to you, do you know about? What types are most common?

4. In your opinion, how important is the type of building to determining the quality of the academic program?

5. If you were taking over the leadership of a school in an older building originally intended for other purposes, what would you want to do first?

6. What kind of building housed the middle school program you attended as a young adolescent? What do you remember about its effect on your experience?

ACTION STEPS

1. Conduct a telephone poll of 10 middle schools in your area to determine (1) the type of schedules and (2) the type of buildings that house the programs. You should be able to get this information from the school secretary. Summarize the data in a brief report on "The Status of Time and Space in Local Middle Schools."

2. Conduct a Web search for information on scheduling and facilities. Identify the Web sites for 10 schools in 10 different states, sites that include information about the schedules and buildings for each school. Determine the current status of scheduling and buildings in these schools and produce a brief report on "The Status of Time and Space in Middle Schools in 10 States."

3. Visit a school that uses a long block schedule. Determine the type of schedule in the school. Interview leaders and teachers about their opinions on the value of the schedule. Compare your information with others who visit different schools.

4. Call the central office headquarters in four or five nearby school districts to determine which middle school is the newest building. Visit the school, tour the building, and compare what you see with the buildings described in this chapter. Are we correct about the emerging consensus on the best buildings for middle school programs?

SUGGESTIONS FOR FURTHER STUDY

Books

Adams, D., & Salvaterra, M. (1997). *Block scheduling: Pathways to success.* Lancaster, PA: Technomic Publishing Co.

Ball, W., & Brewer, P. (2000). *Socratic seminars in the block.* Larchmont, NY: Eye on Education.

Bevevino, M. (1999). *An educator's guide to block scheduling: Decision making, curriculum design, and lesson planning strategies.* Boston, MA: Allyn and Bacon.

Conti-D'Antonio, M., Bertrando, R., & Eisenberger, J. (1998). *Supporting students with learning needs in the block.* Larchmont, NY: Eye on Education.

Erlandson, D., Stark, P., & Ward, S. (1996). *Organizational oversight: Planning and scheduling for effectiveness.* Princeton, NJ: Eye on Education.

Flinders, D. (2000). *Block scheduling: Restructuring the school day.* Bloomington, IN: Phi Delta Phi.

Hottenstein, D. (1998). *Intensive scheduling: Restructuring America's secondary schools through time management.* Thousand Oaks, CA: Corwin Press.

Hoy, W., Sabo, D., Barnes, K., Hannum, J., & Hoffman, J. (1998). *Quality middle schools: Open and healthy.* Thousand Oaks, CA: Sage Publications.

Kennedy, R., & Witcher, A. (1998). *Time and learning: Scheduling for success.* Bloomington, IN: Phi Delta Kappa International.

Lybbert, B. (1998). *Transforming learning with block scheduling: A guide for principals.* Thousand Oaks, CA: Corwin Press.

Queen, A., & Isenhour, K. (1998). *The 4 × 4 block schedule.* Larchmont, NY: Eye on Education.

Raebeck, B. (1998). *Transforming middle schools: A guide to whole-school change.* Lancaster, PA: Technomic Publishing Co.

Rettig, M., & Canady, R. (2000). *Scheduling strategies for middle schools.* Larchmont, NY: Eye on Education.

Robbins, P., Gregory, G., & Herndon, L. (2000). *Thinking inside the block schedule: Strategies for teaching in extended periods of time.* Thousand Oaks, CA: Corwin.

Strzepek, J., Newton, J., & Walker, D. (2000). *Teaching English in the block.* Larchmont, NY: Eye on Education.

Williamson, R. (1998). *Scheduling middle level schools: Tools for improved student achievement.* Reston, VA: National Association of Secondary School Principals.

Winn, D., Menlove, R., & Zsiray, S. (1997). *Rethinking the scheduling of school time.* Bloomington, IN: Phi Delta Kappa Educational Foundation.

Periodicals

Baker, B. (1997). Architecture for the whole child: Celebrating change! *Schools in the Middle, 7*(2), 22–27.

Bullock, A., & Foster-Harrison, E. (1997). Making the best decisions: Designing for excellence! *Schools in the Middle, 7*(2), 37–39, 60–61.

Chan, T., & Ledbetter, D. (1998). Do planning ideas work? A look back. *School Business Affairs, 64*(6), 36–40.

DeRouen, D. (1998). Maybe it's not the children: Eliminating some middle school problems through block support and team scheduling. *Clearing House, 71*(3), 146–148.

DiBiase, W., & Queen, A. (1999). Middle school social studies on the block. *Clearing House, 72*(6), 377–384.

DiRocco, M. (1999). How an alternating-day schedule empowers teachers. *Educational Leadership, 56*(4), 82–84.

Hackmann, D. (1995). Improving school climate: Alternating-day block schedule. *Schools in the Middle, 5*(1), 28–33.

Hendershott, T. (1997). Under observation: Critical areas of school effectiveness. *Schools in the Middle, 6*(4), 34–36.

Hill, F. (1997). Harmony in design: It's a people process! *Schools in the Middle, 7*(2), 34–36.

Pantano, P. (1999). Flexible spaces that work: Renovating today for tomorrow's needs. *School Planning and Management, 38,* 74–75.

ERIC

Gilkey, S., & Hunt, C. (1998). *Teaching mathematics in the block: Teaching in the block series* (ERIC document ED431780).

Miller, E., Graves-Desai, K., & Maloney, K. (1996). *The Harvard Education Letter* (ERIC document ED433115).

Schroth, G. (1997). *Fundamentals of school scheduling* (ERIC document ED413672).

The Jefferson County School District (Denver, Colorado). (1998*). Middle school educational specifications: Facilities planning standards* (ERIC document ED436934).

Whitman, N. (1999). *The Japanese middle schools: A reflection on practices, issues, and trends* (ERIC document ED434094).

Williamson, R. (1998). *Scheduling middle level schools: Tools for improved student achievement* (ERIC document ED434407).

Web Sites

Design Share
http://www.designshare.com
The site discusses the characteristics necessary for an ideal middle school building and their importance in supporting student learning. It includes many award-winning floor plans.

National School Board Association
http://www.nsba.org
This site discusses the characteristics necessary for middle school buildings and schedules. Floor plans are included.

Middle School Partnership
http://www.middleschool.com
This site, developed by private consultants seeking clients, contains more than 50 documents on school facility planning and management, and it offers resources on block scheduling.

The Case against Block Scheduling
http://www.jefflindsay.com/block.shtml
This site is devoted to the decimation of block scheduling and should be consulted with the recognition that the case against the practice is presented.

Block Scheduling
http://www.education.umn.edu/carei/blockscheduling
The College of Education at the University of Minnesota offers research and information, addresses of schools using block scheduling, and other resources, including a listserv on the topic.

PLANNING AND EVALUATING THE EXEMPLARY MIDDLE SCHOOL

OAK HILL MIDDLE SCHOOL

Oak Hill Middle School, in Milledgeville, Georgia, which opened in August 2000, was planned very carefully. The design and development of the school plan took several years. John Lounsbury, a resident of the community, was a middle school consultant involved from the beginning. Long before the building was completed, or any other decisions made about staff or curriculum, Marion Payne, an experienced leader and past president of the National Middle School Association, was hired as the director of the school. The new, large building would accommodate all of the young adolescents in the district. Early on, the formation of numerous study groups invited widespread participation of teachers, parents, and community members in developing a vision for the school. Questions and concerns were dealt with promptly and continuously through these study groups. Eventually a vision for the school included houses, teams, advisory groups, integrated curriculum, active instruction, and involvement and support of parents and the community. A newsletter, Oak Hill News, *began publication before the study groups were formed, continued while the steering committee did its work, and appeared up through the opening of the school. The newsletter was widely, and repeatedly (more than 13 issues prior to opening), sent to teachers, parents, and community members. Additional school leaders and teachers were hired, and a summer full of training preceded the opening date, which arrived with great anticipation among all concerned. With all of this exceptionally careful planning, the first year was a positive one, but not without challenges that required program revision and personnel retraining. By the beginning of the second year, Oak Hill Middle School was functioning as a lighthouse middle school for the state and the region. Careful planning pays off, even if it is no guarantee of long-term stability.*

WHAT YOU WILL LEARN IN CHAPTER 9

In this chapter we discuss planning and evaluating new middle schools and the revitalization of existing ones. We will examine the components that must be addressed in planning and revitalization. The chapter will highlight the importance of staff development and strategies for maximizing its effectiveness. Practical tools are available for use in the formative and summative evaluation of middle schools.

EXEMPLARY MIDDLE SCHOOLS FOLLOW SIMILAR PLANNING PATHWAYS

Hundreds of school districts have reorganized their grade level configurations over the last 40 years. In the decade of the 1990s and in the 21st century, rising student populations have required school leaders to add new middle schools to their district rosters. Some of these reorganized or new schools have been designed and developed to produce middle schools with high-quality programs that have been sustained over long periods. In many other districts, high-quality programs were either never established or, once established, were allowed to quickly erode, so that few traces of the earlier efforts remained, save for the changes in grade levels that accomplished other purposes for the district and were thus sustained for other reasons. The difference in these two experiences has a great deal to do, we believe, with the degree of understanding and skill (i.e., leadership) with which the reorganization effort was planned and managed.

Dozens of additional school districts now appear primed to launch reorganization efforts, open additional new middle schools, or install authentic middle school components in existing middle level schools that have never reached exemplary status. To do so effectively, we believe (based on our experiences), a number of important planning tasks must be accomplished. We offer the steps and tasks described below as a relatively complete catalog of planning decisions that must be made during a district level reorganization. Decisions that we believe are essential to the development and maintenance of quality middle school programs are related to the recommendations of groups such as the National Middle School Association and the Carnegie Council on Adolescent Development (Jackson & Davis, 2000).

Six-Step Middle School Implementation Plan

In our 30 years of experience working with school districts changing to middle school, we have discerned, in the most ideal situations, what amounts to a six-step planning and implementation process. In the most ideal circumstances, each step is equivalent to a year. Even in districts where planners and implementers may not consciously employ a six-year model, it seems to evolve this way. Here the term *step* indicates that, however long the time period, the process is essentially the same.

Step One: Need   Planners determine that a move to middle school, or a new middle school, may meet one or more important needs manifested by students or schools in the district.

Step Two: Study   Planners study the middle school concept and its implications for the district or the new school.

Step Three: Plan   Specific guidelines, programs, and action plans are developed to translate the middle school concept into real school programs.

Step Four: Open   New middle school programs are implemented and evaluated formatively.

Step Five: Fix   Efforts are extended to make certain that mistakes are corrected and revisions implemented to bring the original intentions to fruition.

Step Six: Evaluate   Summative evaluations determine the extent to which the new middle school programs produce the desired outcomes that manifested themselves as needs during the initial year.

Strategic Planning for Middle School Implementation

Plans will be made most knowledgeably and implemented most effectively throughout the entire implementation cycle when involvement of stakeholders is as complete as possible. Involvement is the key, whether the change affects a whole district or a single new middle school. Our experience has been that the process works best when a strategic planning model is followed carefully, including the in-depth and continuing involvement of the district superintendent, board members, parents, teachers, other school building leaders, and outside consultants. A steering committee representing these groups, and smaller task groups for each assignment, should study and develop a consensus. A carefully written planning document that will guide the implementation of exemplary middle schools should result from deliberations on 14 important planning areas.

1. Middle School Philosophy   Few exemplary middle schools are implemented without attention to developing a school or district middle school philosophy as a part of the initial planning process. The philosophy must spell out the district's (or school faculty's) beliefs about the characteristics and needs of its young adolescent students, based on an analysis of the specific demographics students present. Among questions for which planners need answers are these:

- How many students of what ages and grades are to be served?
- What are the characteristics of the school community to be served? Socioeconomic status? Mobility or stability? Racial, religious, cultural backgrounds?

- What is the age or grade distribution of the population? What factors explain any unusual age variations (e.g., overage students)?
- What data as to the distribution of mental ability are available? What do they show?
- What data as to academic achievement, especially reading levels, are available? What do they show?
- What generalizations can be made from available data regarding previous students in this school community as to such factors as continuation in high school, college attendance, and career choices?

Additional insight regarding the needs of the school community and the student population may be gained from examination of data that are available or can be gathered on such items as these:

- Occupations of the parents of students who attend the school
- Attitudes of parents toward schooling
- Stability of families
- Presence of both parents in the home

The middle school philosophy also relates to affirmations about schools that are responsive to the needs of the students. This might include comments about the goals and objectives of the overall middle school program to be planned for students with the special characteristics that have been identified. Details of these program components will enter the plan at a later point, but the purpose of such components can be spelled out in the philosophical statement, alerting readers and planners that a different sort of school experience is intended. Over the years, many school leaders have leaned on two documents for assistance with developing a middle school philosophy: *This We Believe,* by the National Middle School Association (National Middle School Association, 1995); and *Turning Points,* by the Carnegie Council on Adolescent Development (1989) and, now, *Turning Points 2000* (Jackson & Davis, 2000). We hope that earlier editions of this textbook have also been helpful in this area.

This section of the planning document should include a statement that clarifies the extent to which the district guidelines are to be interpreted flexibly by individual schools. If substantial differences are evident in the demographic patterns for students attending middle schools in different areas of the same district, a statement should be included that encourages flexibility in the implementation of the middle school plan. To do otherwise would abandon the commitment to build the school around the characteristics and needs of a specific group of students. In the real world of schools, many districts are characterized by schools in one area of the district serving majority culture, upper-middle-class students, while schools in another area of the same district serve primarily poor and minority children. To ignore such important differences in the implementation of middle schools is to ignore the uniqueness of each school population. This does not mean that there are no districtwide guidelines; it means that such guidelines should be implemented with specific groups of students in mind. All schools in the district, for example, might be committed to the interdisciplinary team organization without specifying exactly what sort of teams might be implemented in each school.

A middle school philosophy can also be sharpened into a mission, or vision, statement. The 2001 "Vision in Progress," from Rachel Carson Middle School, in Fairfax County, Virginia, is an example of a brief statement that is clear in its focus and appropriate for a school population of upper-middle-class, high-achieving, but multicultural, students.

> Within a safe and nurturing community, students, staff, and parents of Rachel Carson Middle School seek to foster personal and academic excellence, treat one another with dignity, respect our environment, embrace diversity, and develop character which merits trust and honor. We encourage positive risk taking and perseverance in the pursuit of our goals.

Desert Sky Middle School, in Glendale, Arizona, was named one of the top 10 schools in Arizona in 1990. It was still among the nationally prominent middle schools in 2001. The mission statement may have contributed to that long run of excellence.

> The faculty and staff believe in the self worth of each individual at Desert Sky Middle School. Our curriculum and instruction are organized to match the unique developmental characteristic of middle level students and to create a sense of belonging for all. Our focus is to integrate academic, explorative, and thematic learning. It is our emphasis to prepare our middle level students in cooperative and critical thinking skills to enhance their success in our informative society. Students at Desert Sky will possess a receptiveness for new learning and carry with them Thunderbolt Pride.

In the first edition of this textbook (Alexander & George, 1981), the statement of philosophy from MacDonald Middle School, in East Lansing, Michigan, from the late 1970s, was as follows:

> Regardless of the organizational structure, the ultimate goal of the MacDonald Middle School is in human relationships. Humanizing education can be accomplished when each person involved in the process recognizes and cares about the needs of each individual student. It is the goals of the middle school to help transescents meet and effectively deal with the challenges confronting them. Thus, all personnel—students, teachers, administration, parents, community members, and other school related personnel—have responsibilities toward this end.

The mission statement at the same school, with the same leadership, 20 years later, was as follows (S. DiFranco, personal communication, December 1990):

> The staff at MacDonald Middle School is committed to the belief that all children, regardless of gender, race, socio-economic status or previous

academic performance, can realize their potential. Our purpose is to teach skills, thinking processes, and concepts while fostering positive social and emotional growth. Therefore, we eagerly accept this obligation with the confidence that our combined efforts will prepare students to function as responsible and contributing members of society.

Student participation does not need to be omitted from this process. When Broomfield Heights Middle School, in Broomfield, Colorado, was being established, the students were helped to develop a student philosophy that was permanently inscribed and displayed in the school foyer. The student philosophy stated:

> Broomfield Heights Middle School is a good place to learn. It is a clean, bright, safe, comfortable and peaceful place where we can learn and work. We will get a good education so we can go to high school while at the same time enjoying our school and its activities. [BHMS] is a place where we can:
> Work hard, be helpful, friendly and meet new friends.
> Take basic subjects.
> Study new and different subjects, learn new things and participate in different activities.
> Have many choices.
> Have many things going on so that learning will be done in many different ways.
> Develop personal pride and cooperate with the rules and standards of the school.
> Find out about careers and learn skills that may help us get a job.
> Have volunteers and parents in our school helping us.
> Have good todays and better tomorrows.

A faculty's philosophical statement can profit from knowledge of what the students seek from their middle school experience. A quarter-century of excellence at BHMS proves it.

2. Organization of Teachers and Students for Learning   In many ways, the uniqueness of the middle school concept, up to the first years of the new century, relates to the way in which teachers and students are organized, not in how teachers teach or what students learn. School planners must develop two important plans: How will teachers be organized to deliver instruction? How will students be organized to receive it? Planners must use their knowledge of student needs to decide the degree of subject specialization that should enter into the way in which teachers are organized. Although some variability will exist among middle schools in large and diverse districts, the planning document for a new middle school must address the specific question of how many subjects teachers will be expected to teach and to how many students per day.

Planners will also want to highlight the importance of the teacher-student relationship in the district's schools and the strategies that will be used to build those relationships. Questions such as the amount of time that the same team of teachers and students should spend together each day must be answered. In many districts, long-term teacher-student relationships will be important, requiring the same group of teachers and students to stay together for more than one year; in other schools this will not be nearly so important. Balancing these two factors (subject specialization and teacher-student relationships) will yield information for planning the sort of interdisciplinary team organization that is implied for a particular school within the district and for the particular address for a school within the middle school zip code. Will the school(s) have gradewide teams, a school-within-school plan, looping, or some other design?

3. *Curriculum* Planners will be required to outline the nature of the daily curriculum offered to middle school students. While standards-based reform has intruded on the independence once possessed by curriculum planners, much discretion remains. Plans must be made for both daily required subjects and additional curriculum opportunities that will be available in the form of exploratory, unified arts, or elective classes. One district (Richland District #1, in Columbia, South Carolina), for example, committed itself in 2001 to an exploratory program that included each of the following in all nine of its middle schools: art, band, chorus, dance, drama, French, home economics, keyboarding, orchestra, physical education, and Spanish. Even schools with fewer than 500 students were guaranteed these options. This takes both planning and commitment. Furthermore, even in a district with this many options, the role student choice should play must also be considered.

4. *Co-curriculum* Planners must arrange for an exciting array of activities in which all students can experience success. Planned policies must ensure that middle school activities will be appropriate for young adolescents and that high school activities and experiences will be saved for high school. Controversies in these areas must be faced and resolved. We discuss many of these issues in Chapter 3.

5. *Advisory Programs* Plans must be laid so that every student will have at least one supportive adult in the school. Steps must be taken to ensure that such a program will have the support of all members of the school and community. The staff at Wakulla Middle School (WMS), in Wakulla County, Florida, did its level best to maximize community understanding and acceptance of the implementation of its advisory program in 1982. It involved church groups, community agencies, and parent representatives in the steering committee that reviewed the plans for the new advisory curriculum. Even then, fringe groups interested in advocating special positions on a narrow range of issues found room to criticize it, much to the disappointment of hard-working planners. Nonetheless, in 2001 the advisory program at WMS remained one of the best in the nation and one of the strongest components of the program in the school.

6. Instruction   A comprehensive plan for moving to a middle school, or opening a new one, will include encouraging instructional strategies that are the most appropriate and effective for the education of young adolescents. Methods of grouping for instruction within each classroom must be arranged. The most acceptable mix of heterogeneous and homogeneous grouping must be woven into the fabric of the new school(s). The most heated discussions will occur with this issue, even more so than those surrounding the advisory program or interscholastic sports. Planners must be well prepared if they want a positive response from parents. It can be done, even in the most difficult situations. In Ann Arbor, Michigan, for example, middle schools were successfully implemented in the early 1990s with a maximum amount of heterogeneous grouping because of the assiduously careful planning that preceded the transition.

7. Schedule   Planners must arrive at the most effective design for the use of time for implementation of the middle school program: Will it be a new long block schedule or the traditional middle school flexible block tied to the interdisciplinary team organization? Will teachers have the sort of planning time they need? A copious number of questions will have to be answered by school planners before individual school leaders will be able to implement an effective schedule. Every district must also be clear about the roles that will be played, in the scheduling process, by the principal, the teacher teams, the central office, and, most notably, the computer services.

8. Leadership   Planners have, all too often, left leadership untouched in the last three decades of middle school development. Middle school principals are still too frequently recruited from the ranks of high school assistant principals. New roles for teachers and accompanying staff development have been common, but little has been done to clarify new roles for the middle school leader or to prepare leaders to acquire the knowledge, skills, and attitudes to go with those roles. Special roles must be developed for various school leaders: team leaders, subject area coordinators, committee chairs, and so on. Processes for choosing and supporting such persons must be installed in the plans for the new schools. A preferred model of collaborative administrator-teacher decision-making must be established in the district's middle schools.

9. Special Programs   Plans must be drawn up to ensure that the needs of exceptional students will be attended to in the new middle schools. Such efforts must be coordinated with the model of interdisciplinary team organization. Will there be inclusion teams? Programs such as those for the gifted and talented, foreign language, Chapter 1, and so on must be accommodated in the new program.

10. Staffing and Staff Development   The district must establish, as early as possible, a career mobility plan to ensure that the administrators and teachers most appropriate for that assignment staff the new middle schools. Staff members must have informed opportunities for making career choices that may involve moving from one school or school level to another. In Orange County, Florida, the career mobility plan included job fairs held several times during the year prior to the opening of the new schools. On several evenings, high school principals convened in a school library and interviewed any junior high teacher who wanted to transfer to high school instead of becoming a part of the new middle school. A parallel program was scheduled for elementary teachers who wished to move to the middle. As a result of these fairs, and other components of the career mobility plan, Orange County middle school planners were able to say that, on the day the new middle level schools opened, 98% of the teachers in Orange County were teaching at the school level they desired and the others were on a waiting list for the first available openings at the level of their choice. Such results go a long way toward the sort of positive professional morale that leads to commitment to implement difficult new designs. Such staffing effectiveness lifts a considerable burden from the staff development needs.

Districts must, nevertheless, plan for training opportunities that ensure that the staff members who do come to the new middle schools possess the appropriate knowledge, skills, and attitudes for launching and maintaining the new middle schools. Special training experiences will be required in knowledge of the characteristics of young adolescents, effective classroom strategies, working on and with interdisciplinary teams, acting as an advisor, and being a part of collaborative decision-making groups.

11. New Buildings or Adjustments and Modifications to Buildings and Articulation Programs   The implementation of middle schools is not simply a middle level project. It is extremely critical to the success of district level reorganization that those responsible understand and act on the knowledge that all students and every school in the district will be affected by the reorganization effort. In one stroke, virtually all of the schools in the district will become younger. The elementary school will lose the older students, the middle level will be one-third younger, and the high school will house a student body that will be 25% younger. This means that every administrator, teacher, student, and parent in the district will be involved. "Business as usual" at any level, when the schools will have much younger student bodies, will court disaster. A task group must be assigned the responsibility for planning what communications tactics will be pursued to inform both the internal and external publics of the purposes and programs associated with middle level reorganization.

These planners must ensure that teachers and administrators at the elementary and high school levels will be informed and involved and that parents and community members will also be informed. The same group must confront the question of the adjustments in programs that will be necessary for the elementary and high schools in the district. They must figure out how the high school staff members will be involved in preparing for the changes that will be necessary to effectively accommodate the arrival of 9th graders. Failure to do so will cause substantial disappointment among 9th grade parents and frustration among the faculty and students. Plans must be made for adjustments to school buildings, at all three levels, to accommodate the new middle school programs and to the effects that new groups of students will have on high schools.

In New Hanover County, North Carolina, for example, planners implemented "Passport," a transition program that prepares students moving from 5th to 6th grade and from 8th to 9th grade. Developed by counselors at all grade levels, each spring students in the appropriate grade levels are involved in a program that is like going to a new country. Students receive "travel brochures, maps, travel kits, travel videos, pen pals, and other items that orient them to their new school." Each spring, student "ambassadors" from the new schools travel with counselors to meet the rising groups.

In Panama City, Florida, the district established districtwide articulation committees for elementary-to-middle transitions and for middle-to-high school transitions. Videos of middle and high schools were developed for every school in the district. Students from middle and high schools return to their middle or elementary schools for visits in which they share their experiences and give advice. Each 8th grader in the district is given a booklet, "Into the Future," which helps them get registered in the correct high school programs.

In Randolph Township, New Jersey, planners established a "Passages and Transitions" program to deal with articulation between the middle and the elementary and high schools. The program includes more than 50 ideas for making these transitions smooth and effective: orientation visits of all types; contacts between teachers, administrators, and counselors at the three levels; evening programs for parents; summer mailings and social activities; joint meetings of the middle school and high school student governments; peer leader programs; and more. Perhaps the most interesting-sounding articulation program in Randolph County, however, is Project SMILE (Society for Making Incoming Learners at Ease), a peer leadership program focusing on the orientation process.

Redwood Middle School, in Napa, California, had a "Road Show," which is the name for the team of middle level educators that visits feeder elementary school faculty and attends parent meetings. The purpose of Road Show sessions is primarily to answer questions and dispel misconceptions. The district also holds "Teacher Transition Workshops" for teachers in the elementary schools, to help them help their students get ready for middle school.

The district may be involved in programs or organizational strategies that, if not in direct conflict with the middle school concept, could make implementation of the middle school more difficult. The "Year-Round School" is one such program. Educators in some districts have found that integrating the interdisciplinary team organization into a Year-Round School is challenging. At Cache County Public Schools, in North Logan, Utah, for example, bringing both interdisciplinary teams and year-round school to fruition simultaneously has been difficult. Difficult, but not impossible, because that district has made determined efforts to do just that. In the 1992–1993 school year, each of four middle level schools was organized into four-teacher interdisciplinary teams. Even at this point, however, one track of students will always be out on vacation so that teachers can never engage all students in team activities simultaneously. We, however, see this as a minor complaint, and we wager that the interdisciplinary team organization will become a more important part of year-round school efforts, especially at the middle school level. To do so most effectively, however, district planners must build in such intentions at the beginning.

12. Communication Plans The district must set out to inform all stakeholders of the concepts involved and the planning stages that the district will pass through. Communications must be targeted at both internal and external publics, as soon as clarity can be ensured, to quash any misinformation that might lead to misunderstanding and opposition. In Orange County, Florida, the communications plan involved a variety of strategies matching the stage of development of plans for the new middle schools. Early on, for example, bookmarks announcing "Coming Soon—America's Best Middle Schools" were distributed by the thousands. This simple message let everyone know that planners were convinced the change would be a positive one. Posters saying "6–7–8—Middle School Is Great" came later and appeared in all schools and all over the district. Students were given the opportunity to write letters to their middle level principals about concerns they might have about the new school; thousands of such letters were received. Parents received a letter from the superintendent and a middle school brochure. They read articles about middle schools published in school district and community newspapers. Dozens of orientations were held. An equally rigorous communications campaign focused on teachers and their concerns. All of these plans came out of the committee on communications.

In Ann Arbor, Michigan, another district with a reputation for having accomplished a difficult transition well, the communication plans were very important, because during "the early stages of the transition to middle schools there was not a broad base of community support" (R. Williamson, personal communication, January 1991). The community information effort that resulted had three major components: surveying and gathering information from the staff and community; distribution of a newsletter to build a shared base of information; and inclusion of all constituencies in the planning, including "known dissenters." We believe that this last strategy, including persons who are initially opposed to the transition, is as important as it is difficult. In districts with the courage to involve such opponents, the transition that eventually takes place is almost always smoother. The temptation to attempt to exclude such dissenters, while appealing in the short term, is usually disastrous in the long haul. As Ron Williamson, of Ann Arbor, expressed it:

> Many school constituencies were included in the planning committees. The committees included staff, parents, and community members without children in the schools, senior citizens, an adolescent psychologist, business

people and others. This broad base of involvement contributed to our successful planning. One additional critical component was the inclusion of known "dissenters" on planning committees. The district acknowledged their concern and recognized that the issues they raised would either be addressed during the planning or at a later date. It is particularly powerful when a known "dissenter" endorses the recommendations for a middle school program.

13. Evaluation   Planners must identify which evaluation strategies must be pursued and what data are to be collected for the district staff to be able to judge the extent to which the middle school program has been implemented as planned. (This is called formative evaluation.) They must also identify the outcomes of the reorganization that should be measured to determine the degree to which the middle school program has improved education in the district. (This is called summative evaluation.)

14. Action Plans   Ultimately, subcommittees contribute recommendations that become a part of a school or district action plan for conversion to, or construction and organization of, the middle school. Excellent examples of such plans abound and can easily be acquired from school districts mentioned in this textbook (especially valuable are those from Orange County, Florida; Ann Arbor, Michigan; and Guilford County, North Carolina) and from districts near one's own that have made a successful transition. The Middle School Action Plan from Orange County, Florida, emerged from long months of careful study, and it contained 31 basic standards, with matching activities that would guarantee the implementation of those program standards, persons responsible, and the date for the standards to be achieved. Standards identified components of the middle school concept that Orange County had chosen to implement. The plan became the guide that moved 18 junior high schools toward a successful transition to middle schools, implementing all 31 standards in 1988. In 2002 the district boasted 25 middle schools all dedicated to serving the needs of the young adolescent.

Individual schools must have their own action plans. And, as an indication of how far the middle school movement had spread by 1990, the Singapore American School Program Planning Guide, 1990–1991, serves as a good example of such a plan for an individual school. In 2001 the middle school concept is still securely in place in the Singapore American School, testifying to the efficacy of the original action plan. The action plan for the school identified eight basic steps in the transition process, with accompanying assignments of personnel, start and due dates, and the date completed to be filled in. The major steps were (1) development of a steering committee, (2) needs assessment, (3) development of questionnaires and surveys for research and study purposes, (4) school visitations, (5) professional development and staff development, (6) establishment of a professional library, (7) development of a written philosophy to be the driving force for program improvement, and (8) establishment of subcommittees for developing recommendations to the steering committee in these areas: academics, professional development, guidance and human relations, student evaluation, extracurricular activities, community awareness, and facilities. The title of this overall action plan for the Singapore American School was "We will research, develop, and implement an exemplary middle school program." The resolve to do so is now evident in many distant places, in American international schools and Department of Defense Dependent Schools in many parts of Europe, Saudi Arabia, India, Japan, Africa, Indonesia, and the Philippines—virtually everywhere.

Assessing the odds for a successful conversion from junior high schools to middle schools, or in reinventing existing ones, is an important part of planning. Gene Pickler, senior administrator for secondary operations in Orange County, Florida, shares important questions that can help estimate the odds.

1. What is the history of middle level education in your district?
2. What is the real momentum behind your district's conversion plan?
3. Is there a district level commitment to the change process?
4. Is your district willing to commit its own resources (human, money, and time) toward your conversion process?
5. Does your conversion effort involve a broad base of participants?
6. What is your public relations plan?
7. How will you monitor your change process?
8. What is your staff development plan?
9. Will you convert all of your schools at the same time or in phases and pilots?
10. How will you staff your middle schools?
11. Is your superintendent elected or appointed?
12. Do you have any "good schools" in your district, those likely to resist change of any kind?
13. Will your contract permit you to begin pilot programs prior to implementation?
14. How will you evaluate your effort?

In Baldwin County, Georgia, when Oak Hill Middle School was being planned for opening in the fall of 2000, the members of the steering committee had followed a planning process that had seven discrete and important stages (John Lounsbury, personal communication, June 2000).

1. Identify and clarify the condition that needs changing. Give it visibility, and communicate the rationale for making the change.
2. Establish a task force that involves a leadership group with enough "clout" and representation to lead the way. Build a team spirit within this group.
3. Develop a vision to direct the change effort, and secure the involvement of others in developing that vision.

4. Communicate the vision through several means, especially to stakehold-ers who will be most directly affected. Provide plenty of opportunities for dialogue and discussion.

5. Empower leadership to act. Identify obstacles and determine ways they could be neutralized. Encourage risk taking and discussion of nontradi-tional ideas and activities. Take visible actions to demonstrate that the proposed change will become a reality.

6. Consolidate gains and initiate more change. Use the group's increasing credibility to change some system, structure, or policy that inhibits the proposed change. Hire, promote, and develop people who can assume leadership in the change. Launch some new project or activity that will build positive attitudes and involve others.

7. Implement the new structure with full recognition that it is a work in progress. Continue public relations efforts. Develop means to ensure leadership development and succession. Focus staff development ef-forts on concerns of teachers.

The steering committee in Baldwin County did its best to stick to that planning process. As a result, Oak Hill Middle School had every chance of be-coming one of the best middle schools in the region if not the nation. Unfor-tunately, recent events related to standards-based reform may have redirected the focus at Oak Hill. Sadly, political events often force educators to accept less than what they believe is best for young adolescent learners.

REVITALIZING EXISTING MIDDLE SCHOOLS

In many school districts, the implementation and operation of middle schools may have had much in common with the building of sand castles (Tye, 1985). The transition to middle school and the construction of sand castles both re-quire a great deal of effort and planning, inspire a great deal of enthusiasm, generate high levels of creativity, involve many people often working together in teams, and frequently produce new structures and strategies that are excit-ing to behold. Creation of such structures, whether sand castles or middle schools, can be great fun.

Unfortunately, in too many school districts the creation of middle schools has eventually yielded to the educational equivalents of wind, pounding waves, marauding teenagers, and too little attention to maintenance after the excite-ment of creation passes. In dozens of districts, the result has been the even-tual erosion of the components of the middle school concept and the reap-pearance of an organization and school program that resemble older and less effective educational structures. Like a half-finished and abandoned sand cas-tle whose creators have turned, too soon, to other activities, the transition to middle schools in many districts may never have been effectively completed during the initial implementation process.

The outcome is that, while nearly 15,000 schools carried the designation of middle school by the beginning of the 21st century, far fewer are likely to exhibit the core traits that make them effective learning environments for young adolescents. Sadly, this situation has occurred at the very time when impressive evidence to support the effectiveness of the middle school concept continues to accumulate (e.g., Felner et al., 1997; George & Shewey, 1994).

Another exceedingly important factor influencing the development and maintenance of high-quality middle school programs, and pointing to the need for careful revitalization efforts, is that a large number of the 12,000 to 15,000 middle schools in America are contained within the 130 largest school districts (National Center for Education Statistics, 1997). A relatively small number of middle school and district office leaders, therefore, has influenced, positively and negatively, the education of millions of young adolescents. While the quality of programs in many so-called middle schools in these districts may have been subject to erosion over the last decade, or may have never been implemented effectively, a relatively few well-designed efforts to revitalize middle schools in these large school districts could have dramatically positive effects on great numbers of young adolescents.

Much of the most difficult aspects of the transition to middle schools, the educational infrastructure of middle school, has already been accomplished in these large districts. The enormously high costs of school reorganization efforts that are required when reorganizing and moving entire grade levels within a district, for example, have already been paid. The remodeling of dozens of buildings; the reassignment of large numbers of staff members; the redesign of transportation plans, report cards, and computer services; the shifting of library and media services; and the shuffling of textbooks and learning materials—all of this has been completed. The costs associated with garnering both public and professional support for the transition have been paid.

The costs of such basic transition efforts (financial and human) in many large districts have been so high that this fact, in itself, may have contributed heavily to the lack of additional funds and energy for the staff development and other activities that were necessary for full and effective implementation of the middle school concept. With millions of dollars spent on the logistics of transition, few districts may have had the resources to complete the transition effectively.

With such a phenomenally high investment already made in the transition to middle schools around the nation, however, educators in those districts must ensure that the components of effective middle school programs are implemented broadly and permanently. Fortunately, the evidence for the effectiveness of middle school concepts suggests that such a second effort, an attempt to revitalize middle schools in large school districts, can provide an extremely high return on the initial investment.

Revitalizing Middle Schools: A Case Study

Educators in Guilford County, North Carolina, the nation's 60th largest school district, have taken middle school revitalization seriously and provide a good case study of an effort to revitalize middle schools in a large district. Over a period of seven years, educators in Guilford County outlined and implemented a series of strategies that brought new life to all of the middle schools in that district. In the spring of 1995, the Board of Education of Guilford County Schools adopted a plan and approved a timeline for assessing and revitalizing its middle schools. By 2001, significant results had been achieved, and the results offer both hope and a successful pathway to others who seek to do the same in their own districts.

Revitalization Strategy One: Form a Middle School Task Force   Achieving a common vision for the start of the revitalization process required lengthy discussions among members of the community and school system. The Board of Education had called for the creation of a Middle School Task Force two years earlier that included teachers, administrators, and parents. Considerable time was spent in staff development for the members of the task force, focusing upon the middle school concept as well as emerging trends in areas of education that would affect middle level schools. Achievement patterns in each school and across the district were examined and probed for underlying factors. Numerous periodicals and books were reviewed, with subsequent discussions regarding equity and access for all students to a rigorous curriculum. A commitment to balancing equity and opportunities for excellence began to emerge. Various models of school organization, schedules, and components (e.g., advisory) were examined. In particular, considerable time and energy focused upon the pros and cons of curriculum tracking and ability grouping.

Revitalization Strategy Two: Develop a Middle School Revitalization Plan   After several months of intense dialogue and debate among the members of the task force, a common vision statement was adopted. That vision for all 17 Guilford County middle schools was, it turns out, an affirmation of the central components of the middle school concept (Jackson & Davis, 2000). In another district, the central components of revitalization might have a different look, but in Guilford County, the plan included seven central elements.

1. Focus on academic achievement in the core curriculum
2. Daily teacher advisory
3. Team organization at every grade
4. Flexible block scheduling

5. An expanded menu of electives and student activities (cultural arts, athletics, and intramurals)
6. Differentiated instruction
7. Heterogeneous grouping in science and social studies in all schools

Academic Achievement.   Increased student academic achievement was to be the primary objective of middle school revitalization efforts. It had already become the central focus of the superintendent and the board. Standards-based reform had arrived in North Carolina, and test scores in the district were lower than anyone wanted them to be. Furthermore, the scores were distributed across the district in a way that correlated far too closely with the socioeconomic status of the students attending particular schools. The superintendent, the school board, and middle school educators in the district were committed to increasing student achievement and decreasing the variability of academic achievement on the basis of socioeconomic status within the district. Every component of the middle school concept in Guilford County was, therefore, expected to focus on, support, or at least not to detract from the emphasis on increasing academic achievement for all students.

The extent to which the other six components of the new plan were already in place in 1995 was difficult to describe, as it is in many large districts. The teacher advisory program was absent in some schools, in place only in name and time in others. Interdisciplinary teams were organized in most schools so that teachers on teams shared a common group of students, in the same area of the building, and had a common schedule allowing for team planning. But teams seemed to be accomplishing little else. Few teams worked together to improve student behavior management; few attempted to create a sense of community on their teams; and fewer worked together to integrate the curriculum. Flexible, team-controlled schedules were in place in a number of the schools, but few teams made any attempts to modify or adapt the schedule to student-oriented uses.

The district did have a time-honored commitment to a rich and exciting unified arts, or exploratory, curriculum, but questions arose about the extent to which this aspect of the curriculum was contributing to increased academic achievement. Educators there, as elsewhere, struggled with the tension between a curriculum focused on the needs of the young adolescent and a curriculum dictated by standards-based reform. Differentiated instruction may have been discussed, but traditional secondary large group, whole class, teacher-directed instruction was the norm. And, in a number of the middle schools, a rigid ability-grouping plan was as dominant as it ever had been.

The establishment of these seven common components for all 17 schools was, given the immense diversity of the district, a bold and courageous move, both pedagogically and politically. As always, leadership was a crucial, and complicated, factor in determining the extent to which a new vision becomes reality. The new superintendent brought a fierce and uncompromising commitment to the creation of district unity, a non-negotiable demand for increased student achievement, and an unwavering insistence on new fiscal responsibility. In the district office and within the middle schools in each of the three former districts that made up Guilford County, however, a sizable group of professional educators, as a result of years of experience with middle level education, were deeply committed to that concept.

Such situations have created volatile mismatches in other districts, where unresolved conflicts have led to the collapse of momentum for change. In Guilford County, the vision of the board and the superintendent coalesced with the deeply felt and knowledgeable commitment to middle school education and to the specific components of the middle school plan. This happened in a way that created an even sharper focus on needs at the middle level, brought a commitment of resources for revitalization, and heightened the sense of importance and accountability that gave force to the revitalization effort.

Tracking and Ability Grouping. An incident connected to the early efforts at implementation of the new middle school plan, specifically the component of heterogeneous grouping, brought an increased sense of urgency to the revitalization effort. As a part of the development of the new vision by the school board, a review of instructional grouping practices had brought the members of the board and the superintendent's staff to an endorsement of increased heterogeneous grouping in all of the district's middle schools (Wheelock, 1992). A sense of the importance of equity accompanied the new board's realization of the immense diversity that the new district represented.

As a result of earlier attempts at implementation of the middle school concept, all but three of the new district's middle schools had tried a considerable amount of heterogeneous grouping. Three schools representing historically high-achieving areas of the district had not yet been de-tracked. Unfortunately, in a classically bi-modal distribution of achievement, high achievement growth in these schools had been restricted to the upper range of the ability grouping classes, and students in low tracks maintained a level of comparatively low achievement. Furthermore, the three schools were caught up in a grouping plan that resulted in having the upper tracks composed predominantly of white, upper-middle-class students and lower tracks composed mainly of children from minority, lower socioeconomic groups. Thus, the schools were in a potentially combustible situation when asked to begin the de-tracking process.

When the district commitment to increased heterogeneous grouping in the middle school was announced, teachers and parents of students in high-track classes in these three traditional, racially diverse schools were less than enthusiastic about the change. One of the three school principals embraced the change to heterogeneous science and social studies classes; two others kept a low profile, hoping, perhaps, that this might be one more dictate that they could eventually ignore.

Eventually, rumors mixed with district guidelines to the point that a group of parents of advanced students at one school, where the principal supported the changes, became alarmed at what they believed might be the elimination of gifted programs at that site. A relatively impromptu public meeting held at the school drew a group of nearly 500 concerned parents, teachers, students, and community members. During the meeting, angry, nearly physical, confrontations occurred between advocates for various positions as audience members wrestled for the microphone. The local media became involved, and alarming reports of the meeting spread quickly throughout the district. Board members immediately received dozens of phone calls from alarmed citizens and educators representing both sides of the grouping issue.

School board members, having made a public commitment to equity in all of the district's school programs and having endorsed the middle school grouping strategies related to it, became openly concerned about the divisions within the community over ability grouping. Individual board members' clarity about what "the research" said seemed less certain in the midst of public furor. The members of the board were also concerned about whether teachers and school leaders had the "instructional prowess" to implement the new grouping policy effectively. Instructional grouping was clearly as political a component of the revitalization plan as it was a pedagogical one.

Nevertheless, the district leaders and the board maintained their commitment to de-tracking in science and social studies. That decision was not capricious or made too quickly, and it entailed extensive staff development for decision-makers. Effective implementation of more heterogeneous grouping would also require extensive staff development for those who would implement it in schools and classrooms. In addition to workshops, district leaders contracted with two universities to deliver additional services, including a course from High Point University leading to certification in teaching the academically gifted. Professors from the School of Education at the University of North Carolina–Greensboro also observed in classrooms and offered assistance in the area of multiple intelligences. Other prominent national consultants also visited teachers in their classrooms to offer specific strategies and increase confidence in this area.

Parental understanding was just as crucial. Several public forums were conducted. These forums focused upon the characteristics and needs of adolescent learners, elements of exemplary middle schools, and differentiated learning. A luncheon meeting with PTA (Parent-Teacher Association) presidents was typical of the opportunity for discussion and dialogue with parents.

Ultimately, public communication and staff development made it possible to keep the commitment to increased heterogeneous grouping. Staff development was supported by central office members' in-depth knowledge of the political maneuvers required to increase acceptance of heterogeneous grouping by members of the school and the community. School board members were pleased that heterogeneous grouping would focus primarily on science and social studies classes, not language arts or mathematics. They were also pleased to learn that grouping within classes could occur when appropriate and that gifted programs would not be dismantled.

Teachers were relieved when staff development workshops centered on the skills for differentiating instruction that they would need to be successful in heterogeneous classrooms. Parents were pleased when they learned that their bright children would not be held back or that their children would not be relegated to a school-based underclass. Eventually, test scores would affirm the effort.

Having experienced the positive resolution to the grouping incident produced by the combination of effective staff development and determined, skillful leadership, central office leaders moved ahead with the implementation of the other components of the new middle school revitalization plan. A common understanding and effective programmatic implementation of teacher advisory, interdisciplinary team organization, flexible scheduling, curriculum enrichment, and differentiated instruction became the next targets. Increased academic achievement would be the most important measure of the successful implementation of these program components. Staff development and a comprehensive model of program evaluation became centerpieces in the strategy to implement the revitalization plan.

Revitalization Strategy Three: Provide Staff Development   Comprehensive staff development was and continues to be necessary in middle level education, because middle schools are truly emergent, developing, and evolving as time passes.[1] Staff development for middle school educators in Guilford County focused sharply on the seven components of the middle school revitalization effort, constantly keeping in mind the goal of restoring public confidence through increasing academic achievement. Professional development activity was characterized by variety and involvement, important elements for teachers and principals as well as students. Teachers and principals are adults; as adult learners, staff developers presumed, they must have variety as well as relevancy embedded within their staff development.

In the Guilford County School System, staff developers worked to make this premise an operational reality. Each middle school leader was required to submit a detailed staff development plan that included participation in systemwide initiatives as well as in building-level staff development directly related to the seven components of the middle school revitalization plan. In addition, teams of teachers and principals formed a task force that has planned and delivered several summer institutes.

---

[1]William Alexander, generally recognized as the "father" of the middle school concept, intentionally used the term *emergent* in the title of the first book he coauthored on the subject, *The Emergent Middle School,* published in New York, in 1968, by Holt, Rinehart, and Winston. He believed that effective middle schools must always be undergoing revitalization or they would cease to be live, growing, and meaningful places for learning.

These institutes focused upon strategies for strengthening and revitalizing Guilford County middle schools by the renewing of everyone's understanding of fundamental elements. In many cases, teachers and principals have led or presented at these sessions. In other cases, a university partnership afforded an expanded menu of consultants and services. Teams of local educators, formed at the institutes, assumed leadership for subsequent training in their respective buildings. They had a common understanding and the necessary commitment, developed as a result of the district efforts. Their colleagues were receptive to training provided by teachers from the classroom next door or down the hall.

Quadrant Meetings.　Following the initial summer institutes, in 1995 and 1996, the district was divided into quadrants for further training in new middle school initiatives. Each quadrant was made up of at least two of the three former districts. In this way some degree of districtwide uniformity would emerge along with overall middle school revitalization. Informal meetings of middle school teachers and administrators from each quadrant allowed them to continue to cement their knowledge of the pace of program implementation and permitted them to share their knowledge, concerns, and best practices with each other. These quadrant meetings were well attended and afforded another opportunity for sharing and building a districtwide sense of momentum regarding the implementation of the components of the middle school plan.

Revitalization Strategy Four: Focus on the Principalship　Sooner or later, every middle school takes on the characteristics of its leadership (George & Anderson, 1989). Numerous sources cite the unparalleled importance of the principals' leadership on the establishment and maintenance of long-term high-quality school programs. Because the middle school movement is uniquely based on the characteristics and needs of young adolescents, effective leadership in those schools is predicated upon a continuing understanding and commitment to the middle school concept and to young adolescents these schools serve.

In many school districts, however, quality middle school programs may fail to survive over the long term because dedicated school leaders who initially establish middle school programs are eventually replaced by principals who have no training, have little experience, or lack long-term career interest in middle school leadership. As soon as five to seven years after establishing middle schools, a school district may find itself with a whole new leadership team in place, a group of principals who may have come from the elementary principalship or high school assistant principalship. In either case, too many of these new middle school leaders have never had the opportunity to learn about the uniqueness of young adolescence or the special nature of the middle school.

Succession planning in large school districts too rarely includes selection and training procedures that guarantee that new middle school leaders have what it takes to maintain high-quality programs. School district leaders in Guilford County understood that middle school revitalization simply would not occur without the right kind of leadership in every school.

The Courage to Act.   The initial and crucial step was for central office leaders to realize, themselves, the importance of selection and training of new middle school principals and to commit to fashioning the selection process in several ways. First, central office leaders conducted a careful and confidential assessment of school principals in place at the beginning of the revitalization effort. As a result, more than a third of the middle schools received new leadership within the first year of the revitalization process. The message to those who remained was that the school district was committed to the middle school concept and to retaining only those principals who fit the middle school well. New middle school principals would no longer be selected on the basis of time served in elementary or high school buildings.

Staff Development for Principals.   To achieve a new level of understanding and commitment to the revitalization effort among principals required more than careful selection. Regular, frequent, and sharply focused principals' meetings became another important source of staff development. Beginning in 1995, and extending through each month of 1996 and 1997, a major portion of the district middle school principals' meetings focused upon components of exemplary middle schools, the accompanying research findings, and the implications for school leaders in Guilford County. Most important, these sessions were an opportunity for the district superintendent and other highly placed central office leaders to voice their firm commitment to the middle school concept and to endorse the direction in which the district was moving to implement the seven central components of the middle school plan. There was no doubt about where schools were expected to go and who was expected to lead them there.

Examples of topics from district principals' meetings during the 1995–1996 school year include:

September:	The Middle School Student: Implications for Curriculum, Organization, and Instruction
October:	Team Organization: Effective Practices
November:	Teacher Advisory: Building Relationships and Character Education
December:	Differentiated Instruction
January:	Explorations and Encore
February:	Assessment and Evaluation

Jawboning.   Large group meetings of middle school principals are necessary but not sufficient. In our experience, central office leaders also must engage in a considerable amount of what President Lyndon B. Johnson called "jawboning." To jawbone, in this situation, is to meet one-on-one, face-to-face, with individual school leaders to reinforce the message and to make eminently clear that one's current position and possible future in district leadership is related to the degree to which the principal can bring his or her school into compliance with the district commitments. Over a period of two years, several middle schools experienced additional changes in leadership when the principal could not or would not exert the sort of leadership that was necessary to bring about the revitalization happening elsewhere in the district. Education is always and everywhere a complex dance between the pedagogical and the political, and middle school revitalization efforts clearly reveal this truism.

Revitalization Strategy Five: Evaluate the Middle Schools   As a part of the middle school revitalization plan, the Board of Education committed the district to an annual evaluation of its middle schools, in part because members were anxious to determine that effective implementation of the revitalization plan was occurring and in part because they believed that frequent feedback from such an evaluation would spur additional efforts to succeed. Considerable time and effort were required to develop what has become a comprehensive survey instrument for middle school teachers, parents, and students (Ward, 1998). A combined effort by the district Office of Assessment and Evaluation as well as the Office of Curriculum and Instruction produced a comprehensive evaluation system that provided feedback for annual school improvement plans. This assessment effort included a careful examination of academic achievement in each school and a comprehensive survey of parents, students, and teachers.

Annual Publication of Achievement Scores.   An important part of the evaluation process included the annual publication of how each individual middle school has fared academically. Not only were the data made available to school board members and the local media, but colorful posters depicting the academic progress of each middle school, and of all the middle schools as a whole group, also were displayed for weeks in the district office and in the chambers of the school board. Public attention and knowledge of progress, or the lack of it, have had a significant effect on the speed and energy devoted to curriculum alignment in Guilford County middle schools. Fortunately, the result has been steady upward annual growth of achievement in all areas measured by the state. In 2001 Guilford County middle schools exceeded state averages in every area.

The Middle School Survey.   The district's instrument for the annual middle school survey is comprehensive, focusing on all seven of the central elements of the new middle school plan (Ward, 1998). It included these components:

- Questions about the middle school concept—advisory, flexible block scheduling, thematic and interdisciplinary curriculum and instruction, team organization, electives, and intramurals
- Questions about instruction and learning—expectations, effort, diversity and equity, student success, use of technology and media, and differentiated instruction
- Questions about school climate—safety, discipline, behavior, respect and caring, support programs, and building cleanliness

- Questions about parental involvement
- An opportunity for respondents to grade the school

Using Results of the Surveys.   As with the achievement test scores, each year's survey results for each middle school, and for the middle schools as a group, were compiled and made public. The first two years of survey results revealed that the basic components of the middle school concept were in place in Guilford County middle schools but that much remained to be done, particularly in the area of differentiation of instruction. The central office staff used the survey data to plan annual summer middle school professional development institutes that aimed to provide teachers with the skills they need to arrange for a heterogeneous group of learners in virtually every class. High Point University, located in the district, developed and delivered specially designed courses on the topic of differentiated instruction. The district developed a *Handbook on Differentiated Instruction* and distributed copies to all middle school teachers, as well as a systemwide curriculum resource guide for the teacher advisory program.

Survey Data and Continuous School Improvement.   Every one of the 17 middle school principals studied the data from each annual survey and then came to the central office for a school improvement planning conference. Prior to the conference, principals identified, along with their school leadership teams, goals and objectives for school improvement and a plan for addressing those aims. Plans differed from school to school, but there was often common focus.

Data from this survey process have enabled the school district to create a cycle of continuous improvement in almost every area of the middle school. For example, team effectiveness has been enhanced. The data revealed the need for a curriculum guide in the area of teacher advisory. The purposes of advisory needed to be clarified. Subsequent staff and curriculum development led to improvements in this area. The data from the surveys has also revealed the need for closer working relationships between core and encore (related arts) teachers. Consequently a districtwide goal was developed to improve the collaboration that occurred between both of these areas.

A major thrust has been to provide teachers with the knowledge and skills that are essential in working with student diversity. Numerous workshops have been offered in differentiated instruction. In addition, teachers have been given the opportunity to pursue licensure in academically giftedness with little expense.

The revitalization of middle schools in Guilford County is a work in progress. The seven goals of revitalization in Guilford County middle schools have been approached, if not fully achieved. The good news in 2001 was that academic achievement was climbing higher each year, and the results of the most recent annual survey were very positive. In that survey, better than 88% of the middle school teachers continued to assert their belief that educators in their school are effectively implementing the middle school concept. Ninety percent of middle school teachers agreed that their schools deserve a grade of "C" or better; 80% awarded their school an "A" or "B."

Even better, perhaps, is that 91% of parents agreed that their child's middle school deserved a grade of "C" or better, with approximately two-thirds saying that they would give the school an "A" or "B." The students were not far behind, with 81% giving their school a "C" or better; 52% gave their school an "A" or "B."

Generally, public confidence in the schools of Guilford County has risen, perhaps because of the open, candid nature of the district's revitalization effort. The district has received positive notice in national journals, local media are much more generous in their praise, and members of the school board are pleased. Local school leaders have begun to talk about a revitalization of the high schools in the district as a next step. What more positive evidence could there be?

We hope this case study, with its detailed description of the process in one district, illustrates the successful implementation of strategies aimed at revitalization of existing middle schools. We hope that many more districts choose a similar path in the years to come.

STAFF DEVELOPMENT FOR MIDDLE SCHOOLS: GUIDELINES AND ROLES

At its core the middle school movement has been a reconceptualization and reorganization of the ways in which people work with each other to facilitate the learning process. As such, the success of efforts at revitalization in places such as Guilford County can be interpreted as the result of their ability to respond to the need to prepare people for this new way of being together professionally. We believe that effective staff development is the key to comprehensive program implementation, whether in a new or revitalized middle school. When this is acknowledged and planned, effective programs emerge; when it is not, changes are almost never more than cosmetic. Even the most carefully designed multiyear plan cannot overcome the deficiencies imposed by inadequate staff development.

Staff development efforts will, we believe, almost always be more successful when, as a prerequisite, the commitment of the central administration to the middle school is clearly perceived and easily discussed by those who are asked to undergo the training to equip them for the move to the new school organization. Teachers and others at the school level have learned to measure the commitment of others farther up in the district hierarchy by, among other things, the amount of visible time that central office personnel and school administrators devote to participation in the fundamental efforts of retraining. People allocate their time to projects to which they assign value. When central office staff members are seldom seen at the staff development activities or when teachers and others never have an opportunity to listen to these persons articulate their interest in or support for the reorganization effort, enthusiasm and effort wane. Modeling is an important tool for stimulating learning, even at such an advanced professional level.

In the school district of Okaloosa County, Florida, for example, over a two-year period of staff development leading to the implementation of middle school in 1990, rarely a single session went by without an appearance, even if just for a few minutes, by the district superintendent. The district had the highest test scores in the state, the lowest drop-out rate, and very popular football programs in its junior high schools during most of the decade of the 1980s. Consequently, many parents and patrons of the district were adamantly opposed to the middle school concept, and the transition could have been an unpleasant and unsuccessful process. It was, on the contrary, highly successful, at least in part because of the willingness of several central office staff members to attend frequent and time-consuming planning and staff development sessions.

Similarly, staff development efforts are enhanced whenever those involved have the opportunity to hear school board members demonstrate their understanding of and commitment to the reorganization effort. Early efforts to inform and advise the school board almost always, we believe, result in increased personal and financial support for professional staff development efforts when they become necessary. The adoption of a wait-and-see attitude by board members often seems to almost guarantee less than optimal success in retraining the professional staff. In Okaloosa County, staff development time and funds were available in unprecedented amounts because of the direct involvement of school board members. Unpaid, after-school teacher training was, therefore, held to a minimum. In the spring of 1990, consequently, a formative evaluation of the new middle school program revealed that the planned program had been effectively implemented. In 2001 middle schools still thrive in that district.

A second prerequisite to effective staff development is the appointment of a coordinator for the retraining effort. One person must be the central figure responsible for the professional development education of those who will be a part of the new or revitalized middle school(s). Spreading the responsibilities around will only dilute their power to change the schools. The coordinator should, ideally, have training and experience at both the elementary and secondary levels, in addition to an in-depth exposure to the middle school movement. Such a broad perspective is important to the design of appropriate components of the staff development program. Without such a broad background, the staff development program will likely take on a character that reflects the narrower perspectives of educators wearing professional blinders. It is only human to design programs, staff development or otherwise, that reflect one's own experience and training.

The design of a comprehensive staff development program is, however, too complex to be left entirely to one or two people. Consequently, another prerequisite to effective efforts is the presence of a broadly based staff development committee to assist the coordinator. There should be representatives from administration, curriculum, and the potential faculty of the school(s), ensuring a balance between organizational and programmatic concerns. Such a committee should find it possible to prepare an acceptable rationale for extensive staff development and to articulate a sensible long-range plan of such activities, complete with timelines, learning experiences, funding requirements, and identification of participants. The committee should be able, further, to assist the district in escaping the trap of expecting too much too soon. Permanent change requires careful and realistic planning.

Effective staff development for a new middle school depends on the early identification of participants. Teachers, we believe, are not inherently opposed to change or even anxious to avoid extra duties. They are, however, likely to perceive the opening of a new middle school as a positive one for them to the extent that they are provided with early opportunities for information and involvement. Kept in the dark about the future of the school, and especially about their own place in the future, teachers will have difficulty concentrating on the purely professional aspects of the impending changes (Hall & Hord, 1987). Given that the majority of teachers care deeply about children, a great deal can be gained by extending to them the earliest possible opportunity to assimilate the meaning of the changes and the chance to opt for inclusion in or exclusion from any further participation. In our experience, a direct connection seems to exist between voluntary participation in the change to middle school and the success of the staff development efforts that accompany it.

In Columbia Heights, Minnesota, the faculty of the middle school was selected and informed 18 months before the school was to open. Each faculty member was asked to give a first and second priority as to preferred level of teaching: elementary, middle, or high. In all but a few cases, even in a district with severely declining enrollments, teachers were given the choice they preferred. The faculty was, in addition, given a central role in the development of the local rationale and the unique components of the program to come. In Orange County, Florida, the process worked in virtually the same way, although it happened a decade later, in the late 1980s, and in a district that was 10 times larger.

Successful Staff Development Strategies: Eight Recommendations

A great deal of research on the characteristics of successful staff development programs is now beginning to surface, and the cautious will review this literature carefully before embarking on any program of this nature. The entire field of organizational development is relevant to the effort to reorganize the middle grades, under almost any circumstances. The few suggestions made here come primarily from the testing ground of our experiences in middle school staff development efforts. With these disclaimers, here they are.

1. Operate on a 90/10 Philosophy   With the limited funds and time that almost inevitably accompany staff development activities, spend 90% of the funds available on 10% of the people. Permanent change comes when the staff is changed permanently, and this means that some of the faculty and administration must undergo a training experience that is sufficient to alter their ways of thinking and acting, professionally, forever. When staff members with the commitment, desire, and talent are also provided with the skills necessary to do the tasks required for implementation, we believe that these persons will train those with whom they work on a daily basis. A small cadre of expertly trained personnel can grow; a large group of confused and unskilled faculty members, no matter how professional in their attitude, can only grow smaller.

Spend 10% of the staff development money before the school is opened, and 90% afterward. Providing answers for questions that the staff does not yet have is a highly inefficient use of time and money, and the same amounts of time and money will bring much higher yields of understanding and skill development when applied as the needs become evident. Only the most alert and farsighted educators are able to suspend present needs to attend to issues not yet faced, and most members of this group are so highly professional that the training is almost unnecessary for them in the first place.

Another way of expressing this principle of expending staff development funds is to think in terms of pyramids. That is, when funds for staff development are limited, expend the funds with an inverted pyramid in mind. See that the majority of the opportunities are offered to those who will bear the greatest responsibilities when the reorganization arrives: school administrators, team leaders, and counselors, for example. When in rare cases such as a special grant, a significantly greater amount of money is available. The luxury of making enriched staff development opportunities available for the majority of those who will be involved is possible. In these instances, using the model of the pyramid (with the greatest effort at the base) becomes logical.

A unique approach to staff development utilizing this philosophy is employed by the Pittsburgh, Pennsylvania, public schools, in the Greenway Middle School Teacher Center. Greenway Middle School is a functioning middle school, the educational home for 800 students. It is also a unique staff development center geared specifically to the needs of middle school teachers. The school acts as a model middle school for the district, containing as much of an exemplary middle school program as possible. Greenway Middle is a two-house school, with grades 6–8 in each of the two houses. It features interdisciplinary teaming and advisory programs, as well as cooperative learning, shared decision-making, special schedules, special programs for specific student groups, and a host of other attractive programs.

Over the life of the center, Pittsburgh educators say, it will offer special middle school staff development to more than 500 teachers and administrators, each of whom will spend five-and-a-half weeks at Greenway Middle. Replacement teachers are used to teach the students of visiting teachers while the latter attend the center's staff development program. Teachers develop personal action plans to guide their time there. Each visiting teacher is assigned to work closely with a clinical resident teacher, who assists in planning the personalized staff development for the teacher. These resident teachers also act as observers of and critics for the visiting teacher. Four separate but interrelated strands of staff development opportunities are available at the center: The Middle School Child, Middle School Programs, Instructional Practices, and Personal and Professional Enrichment. The program includes phases that begin before a teacher leaves the home middle school and continues with follow-through plans and new goals after the teacher returns. From our experience with such programs, we find them extremely effective.

2. Be Prepared to Make Difficult Choices about Staff Development Activities   While it may sound somewhat Machiavellian, a person who has been designated as the coordinator of the middle school reorganization plan must develop leadership that will last, with the most efficient and economical expenditure of scarce resources. It may not even be too farfetched to suggest that coordinators take a page from the book of French battlefield medicine, investigating the usefulness of the concept of triage as applied to the development effort. Confronted with inadequate time and medical supplies, in the midst of a battle that would not stop, French physicians would divide the casualties into three groups: those who would die regardless of the amount of help they received; those who would get well without help; and those who would recover only with help from the physician. The physician then spent the time and scarce supplies where they would do the most good, in essence applying the principle of the greatest good for the greatest number. The middle school revitalization coordinator may want to think in similar ways. Some teachers and administrators need little, if any, assistance in making the transition successfully, and many of them can be used to assist in the training of others less able or ready. Some teachers and administrators, no matter what opportunities are afforded them, will never be able to make the adjustment but may make superb professionals at other levels. They should be helped to do so. Another, larger group of teachers and administrators will guarantee the success of the reorganization effort if they are able to receive the training opportunities that will allow them to develop the required insights and skills. Concentrating a greater proportion of available opportunities for growth on this third group likely will result in the most effective deployment of meager staff development funds.

3. Develop a Multiyear Staff Development Plan   Based on the time-honored principle that spaced practice assists learning more effectively than does massed practice, having a long-term staff development plan that initiates different components at different times following the implementation of the middle school reorganization effort would be advantageous. A program component (for example, an advisor-advisee program) could be introduced one year, with a full-blown professional development effort, followed periodically during the next several years by supportive services that take new faculty into account and that solve new problems as they arise. Haste is the enemy of effective middle school staff development.

Some elements of the middle school program appear to be prerequisites to others. We believe that the firmly established interdisciplinary organization of teachers must come before other program changes are attempted. Furthermore, the basic organizational effort, from departmental or self-contained to interdisciplinary, requires much less staff development than do other components of the new program. Teachers can be organized in an interdisciplinary fashion without being asked to perform dramatically new or different tasks. The teacher who, for example, has been teaching math for 20 years in a departmentalized junior high school can continue to do much the same sort of thing in an interdisciplinary organization. Because it makes all the other programs easier to establish and maintain, and because it can be implemented with the minimum of staff development, interdisciplinary team organization should come first.

Consider arranging the remainder of the programs in terms of the difficulty of implementing them with a minimum of professional development education, so that the most difficult are last to be brought on line. Doing so would probably result in a decision to prioritize the grouping of students for learning in some way that would go beyond simple chronological age grouping, because only the most extreme forms of multiage grouping require a significant amount of retraining of the staff or redesigning of the curriculum. This might be followed, in a wisely designed staff development plan, by an attempt to structure the curriculum to permit the infusion of a more exploratory type of program. A more flexible schedule, if it emerges from the effort to regroup teachers and students, will follow naturally. Only when all of the above components of the program have been effectively planned and implemented will it be wise to implement an advisor-advisee program of teacher-student guidance, because this program requires more staff development than possibly all of the others together. Changing from a completely tracked and rigidly grouped, departmentalized setup to a completely heterogeneous grouping plan requires phenomenal amounts of planning and staff development, so doing so might be saved for last. All the components of the middle school program are not equal, in terms of the amount of staff development time and effort required for successful implementation, and the sequence in which each is introduced should be carefully planned.

4. Seek Assistance in Arranging and Conducting the Staff Development Program   The first middle schools established during the 1960s and early 1970s were largely on their own. A few guidelines had been suggested, but fewer school systems had established successful and long-running programs to which new middle school educators could turn. It was a time of experimentation and innovation in the middle grades and, fortunately for middle school educators, for the nation in general. A plethora of new programs were attempted, some surviving, others failing. Given that the middle school movement shows little sign of slackening, as the 21st century dawns, it is fortunate that nearly 40 years of experimentation and innovation will now pay dividends in the coin of knowledge that can be relied upon. Whereas in 1960 there were few, if any, educators who could boast of years of experience in middle schools, this is no longer true. Educators seeking to establish a new program in the middle grades of their school systems can now reach out for assistance from hundreds of experienced educators who, remembering their own eager first efforts, are pleased to help in any way they can.

Consultant help can often be important to the success of a middle level reorganization effort. Chosen carefully, outside consultants can help a school district in the decision-making and planning phases of the move to a middle school. But, more often, consultants are needed to assist in the development of local expertise, leadership, and skills. Because most districts need help in the area of leadership in the daily operation of middle schools, consultant help should be chosen on the basis of demonstrated successful experience in the areas in question. Many districts report that the combination of university and public school personnel into a small consultant team leads to both a clear conceptualization of the needed skills and the credibility that makes the tasks acceptable to local teachers and faculty. The best clue to the potential effectiveness of any particular consultant would seem to be whether or not close proximity to and involvement with one or more exemplary middle schools is a prominent part of that person's regular professional experience. When districts are clear about the needs they have and select a consultant on the basis of demonstrated experience with effective programs related to those needs, a satisfactory relationship is more likely to develop.

5. Develop and Maintain a High Degree of Local Leadership Expertise No consultant, regardless of how expert, can substitute for the existence of local school district employees who have developed a commitment to and the skills necessary for the implementation of an exemplary middle school program. The consultant's effectiveness depends in part upon the availability of an alter ego in the district or school who sets the stage and follows through, before and after the consultant. We believe that the performance of many programs depends in large part upon the emergence of strong local leadership. Staff development efforts should begin at this point. If at all possible, these persons (curriculum coordinators, school principals, team leaders) should be given the opportunity to participate in a mini-internship in a middle school away from home, a school that has the characteristics that the local district wishes to build into its program. Hearing about the middle school concept, studying about it, even having participated in intensive workshops on how to do it are simply not enough for the development of exemplary programs that will last a decade or more.

In our experience, the most permanently successful programs are those that were built upon the resources that created an opportunity for direct involvement of the local leadership in fully functioning middle schools elsewhere. Implementing a middle school program guarantees that, no matter how well it is done, a great deal of anxiety, doubts, and new pressures will result. School leaders who have had an opportunity to experience a successful program directly will be much more likely to bear up under those pressures and see the program through to a successful future. Team leaders who have both seen it and made it happen elsewhere will be confident that it can happen in their own schools and will be able to bring it about. The funds required to provide such opportunities are so well spent that it seems impossible to mount an effective argument to the contrary. So many good middle schools are available for such assistance that it might be foolish to proceed without it.

6. Realize That Revitalizing a Middle School Is Much More Difficult Than Implementing a New Middle School Program When a new faculty is being gathered, and perhaps a new school building being opened, innovative programs are much more readily implemented. When a faculty and building with a heritage remain and only the program is to be changed, one might be led to think that the tasks would be even easier, but such is not the case. Such transitions seem infinitely more difficult.

When faced with the task of revitalizing a middle school with an existing faculty within a facility that will not be changed, the approach must be more deliberate and will often be more costly. Interpersonal loyalties and differences, subject matter preferences, established ways of doing things and working together, and pure inertia interact to make this sort of transition one of the most difficult processes in the educational profession. The task ought not be taken on lightly. For those who find themselves involved in a revitalization project, several factors are important for planning the staff development program.

Plan for the transition to take about twice as long as you might have expected.

Plan for a staff development budget that will be about twice as much as you expected, for each program component implemented.

Plan to include, from the outset, those faculty members who are experienced and who have shown their leadership ability within the faculty over previous years. A real advantage to having a sizable number of experienced teachers (more than 20 years of teaching) is that one can be certain that whatever they agree to implement will work and will last.

Plan to involve a great deal more visitations to exemplary schools, to attend more conferences, and to cut back drastically on the number of expert led after-school workshops.

Refuse to yield, when staff development funds are minuscule compared with the needs, to the temptation to implement the programs without the professional development. Very little else will contaminate future change efforts more than the taint of badly managed present failures.

Be prepared to insist that the change from departmentalized organization of teachers to a truly interdisciplinary grouping take place. Without this change, nothing else is likely to be successful for long. Teachers who have taught in one subject and in one grade level for many years may still do so with the interdisciplinary framework. Several years of becoming accommodated to the interdisciplinary organization may be necessary before any additional program components can be easily brought on line. Once comfortable with and acclimated to the interdisciplinary organization, the faculty is likely to view other new programs much more favorably.

7. *Pay Attention to the Concept of Synergism* The programs of the middle school (for example, interdisciplinary organization, advisor-advisee, and so on) are complementary; the presence of one strengthens the others. So it is with staff development. Working on one component of the middle school program will contribute to the improvement of the others.

8. *Tie Staff Development to State Certification in Middle School Education* An increasing number of states, perhaps as many as 35, have middle level certification procedures. Staff development that delivers a new or broader license, enhancing a teacher's employment opportunities, will be greeted with much more enthusiasm. Simply earning points for certificate renewal is better than nothing. In Florida, for example, middle school certification has been available through district level professional development education for many years. New regulations, released in 2001, both expanded the coverage under middle grades and increased the desirability of such certification by narrowing the elementary and high school certificates so that the middle level certificate was more necessary.

The Focus of Middle School Staff Development: Skills

While allowing ample opportunity and time for the development of proper attitudes toward the change effort is important, behavioral psychologists have long maintained that changes in attitudes often follow changes in behavior. When behavior changes (in other words, when new skills are developed and used), changes in attitudes are close behind. With this in mind, staff development planners may be wise to focus on the new skills that will be required in the new organizational framework, on the assumption that with skills mastered will come confidence and assurance, followed by increasingly positive attitudes toward the coming new programs. Specific skills are necessary for both school administrators and the faculty.

Staff development for school administrators will usually focus on two different areas: knowledge of the new program and organizational development expertise. Principals need to understand the team organization, the advisory program, the curriculum plan, the grouping strategies, and other elements of the planned changes so that they can assist teachers in implementing those programs. Principals need the knowledge so that they can effectively communicate the purposes and the structure of the program to parents and community members who will have dozens of questions that will need to be answered. Principals need this knowledge to bolster their own confidence in the efficacy of the proposed changes and to give them the courage to venture into areas that the district has not yet attempted.

Most of all, school principals need to know how to use the building and the daily schedule to accomplish the demands of the new program without placing unreasonable stress on the faculty and students. If a place in the building is not available for an activity, that activity will not occur. If the schedule allows no time for the program, there will be no program. And, given that many new middle school principals come from a secondary background, having often served successfully as an assistant principal in a high school, it cannot be assumed that the necessary skills were learned prior to assuming the leadership of the new middle school. Some unlearning of certain skills, which may lie at cross-purposes with the new duties at the middle school, is likely.

In addition, because the middle school will be an adventure in new relationships of all kinds and in new patterns of teaching and learning, school principals must be skilled at helping people solve the problems that these new patterns create. They must also be able to assist in the process of ongoing change and adjustment that any dynamic organization will encounter. And principals must, whenever possible, represent an unwavering source of support and enthusiasm for the staff and for their involvement in decision-making. These are behaviors that can be learned (Schmuck & Runkel, 1985).

Teachers, whether team leaders or not, will need dozens of new skills when the revitalization is complete. Several are worth emphasizing. To make the team organization function at its optimum, teachers need to be effective communicators and problem solvers with each other. They also need help in planning and managing a program for a large group of students: ordering supplies, planning activities, conducting parent conferences, arranging student schedules, team budgeting, reporting pupil progress, and many other management activities. They need to learn how to schedule an advisor-advisee program so that they are not involved in making new lesson preparations for each new day of the week. They need to be helped to discover activities for advisory programs that can be repeated on a once weekly basis and activities that require little or no teacher planning but deliver considerable power to the advisor-advisee relationship. Teachers will require curriculum adjustment assistance if alternatives to chronological age grouping are implemented on a schoolwide basis. No one should consider eliminating ability grouping capriciously, without providing teachers with the training they require to diversify instruction. Exciting exploratory programs require creativity and high levels of energy from teachers, but assistance in learning how to develop and conduct an exploratory minicourse that students will enjoy can go a long way toward releasing that creativity and energy. Teachers must be helped to develop a repertoire of instructional skills and the knowledge of when each is effective.

Above all, many would say, teachers must understand the characteristics and needs of the students they serve and be able to respond to those needs in ways that are satisfying for both student and teacher.

The selection of effective school leaders and outstanding classroom teachers will help ensure the success of the new middle school program, but it is not sufficient. Staff development, even with the most outstanding recruits, is essential. Just as no corporation would introduce a major new product without assigning and carefully training some of its most talented staff, no school system can afford to introduce a major reorganization without a similar effort. Product knowledge is essential in private enterprise and in education. Remember, sooner or later every middle school takes on the characteristics of its leadership.

Special Planning Concerns for Exploratory Teachers and Their Programs

Many school district planners have discovered that, even after planning as carefully as possible, several unanticipated problems crop up. One of the most serious, in our judgment, is the situation that tends to develop with exploratory teachers after the interdisciplinary teams begin functioning fully. Many exploratory teachers feel left out, like second-class citizens, in a traditional middle level school. Often this changes very little during the transition to a more modern middle school program.

In many middle schools, morale among exploratory teachers will be lower than it is for academic teachers, in the same buildings, teaching the same students. This has probably been the case since report card procedures, credit counting, and general school practices established a hierarchy in the earliest junior high schools. New efforts in interdisciplinary team organization frequently bring a new sense of unity and purpose to the academic staff, while exploratory teachers ask, "What about us?" Sometimes the academic teachers, as a consequence of their agreement to work as a team, receive an additional planning period during the day. When this happens, in some circumstances, exploratory teachers do not receive the additional planning time, which sends morale among them spiraling even lower.

In one middle school, teachers in physical education and the elective areas were identified in school communications by joining together the letters *PE* and *EL,* into the word *PEEL,* while the so-called academic teachers in the building were referred to as *CORE.* One exploratory teacher in this school asked, "How would you feel being the 'peel' rather than the 'core' of an apple?" Designations such as "core" and "encore" are not much improvement.

Such a situation is particularly ironic, because exploration and enrichment were important reasons supporting the establishment of both the junior high school and the middle school. In a sense, the middle level school was created because of the exploratory teachers and their exciting new curriculum. The junior high was created to offer curriculum that went beyond the simple academic basics: home economics and family studies; foreign language instruction; industrial arts, business, and technology education; music education of all kinds; art; and now, computer education. Small elementary schools, or one-room schools, simply did not have enough students to make the cost of such programs effective. To afford such enrichment in the curriculum, larger schools were created. And, yet, as the end of a century of middle level education approaches, many exploratory teachers still feel pushed aside from the mainstream of the school into a curriculum backwater.

Many contemporary middle school leaders recognize the need to plan to change this clearly undesirable situation, but few completely satisfactory arrangements have emerged. Virtually all middle level schools need some creative thinking in this area. What follows is a list of ideas that some middle school educators have found useful, although not perfect, in narrowing the gap between exploratory teachers and their academic colleagues (Doda & George, 1999).

1. Have all exploratory teachers assigned as members of interdisciplinary teams. Each team would still have "core" members, most likely, made up of academic teachers, and an "extended team," which would include the academic teachers and a representative of the exploratory teachers, special education teachers, and the physical education staff. Exploratory teachers would have advisees from that team, and be a member of the team for school decision-making purposes. Sometimes, exploratory teachers, rather than having their own advisory group, fare better when they co-advise a group with a member of the academic team.

2. Schedule weekly, biweekly, or monthly team meetings before students arrive for school, so that all teachers can attend their respective team meetings. When academic teachers have their planning time at the time their students are being taught by the exploratory teachers, it makes communication between the two groups of teachers virtually impossible, without a regular meeting held when students are not present.

3. Hold these team meetings in the exploratory areas of the building on a regular basis, so that exploratory teachers are not always the ones traveling to the meetings. No one should feel like they are always on foreign soil when they attend such meetings.

4. Rotate the responsibility for setting the agendas for the team meetings so that exploratory teachers have an equal opportunity to see their concerns discussed on a regular and equal basis. Academic teachers are often unaware of the perspective that exploratory teachers can add to their own. Similarly, they may be unaware of the concerns with which exploratory teachers are dealing.

5. Have the school administration monitor the agendas of team meetings and larger faculty meetings to make sure that the items to be discussed include the specific concerns of exploratory teachers. The school administrative team might also have exploratory teachers as advisors to their process.

6. Encourage each interdisciplinary team to create at least one truly thematic unit each year, a unit that would include exploratory teachers in the planning and teaching process. The sort of excitement that such units can contribute can be greatly enhanced by the participation of exploratory staff members.

7. Involve exploratory teachers, in a similar way, in the planning and conduct of field trips. Scheduling arrangements can often be made more efficiently if exploratory teachers are involved. In fact, academic teachers should always, always seek the permission of the exploratory teachers in advance, or at least explain in detail why such actions are necessary, before pulling students out of exploratory classes for trips or any other purpose. The principal's permission is not sufficient.

8. Experiment with rotating the assignment of exploratory teachers from one team to another, according to grading periods, so that by the end of the year the exploratory teacher has been attached to every team in the school. Richview Middle School, in Clarksville, Tennessee, has six interdisciplinary teams and six exploratory teachers, a not uncommon situation. At this school, the art teacher teaches art to two sixth grade teams, for six weeks each. Then the art teacher teaches art to two seventh grade teams, for six weeks each. The process is repeated for the eighth grade teams, and by the end of the year, the art teacher has been a member of every team, teaching only students from that team for the grading period. This pattern is followed at another school, King Middle, in Portland, Maine, where music and computer teachers are each assigned to two sixth grade teams for one semester each, health and art teachers work with the seventh grade teams, and technology education and home economics teachers are members of eighth grade teams for a semester each. In the much larger district of Orange County, Florida, the process works this way in a dozen of the district's middle schools.

9. Have exploratory teachers serve as team leaders whenever it is appropriate and can be organized effectively. Even though they may teach students from other teams, the process has worked in several schools that have tried it.

10. Articulate, on a regular basis, for all staff members, the purposes of the interdisciplinary team organization and the extra work that it requires of academic teachers, so that all of this is clear to the exploratory teachers. Otherwise, it is natural for exploratory staff members to feel mistreated.

11. Appoint core team members to serve as liaisons with all non-core team groups.

12. Facilitate the development of a team approach among the exploratory teachers in the school. At Godwin Middle School, in Manassas, Virginia, for example, the exploratory teachers named themselves the G.R.E.A.T. team, which stood for Godwin Related Exploratory Arts Team.

13. Be very careful about grading systems that reveal beliefs about the value of exploratory courses, by grading academic courses with one set of letter grades (A to F) and exploratory courses with another (S, N, U). While this practice was initiated to allow students to explore related arts programs without so much fear of grades, it also often communicates to everyone involved that exploratory courses are not as valuable as others. Exploratory teachers, consequently, can feel less valuable as members of the faculty.

14. Celebrate the whole concept of multiple intelligences developed by Howard Gardner (1983). At the Middle School of the Kennebunks, in Kennebunkport, Maine, principal Sandra Caldwell initiated the use of multiple intelligences in guiding students in their choice of exploratory courses, in modifying exploratory courses to reflect the multiple intelligences concepts, and in encouraging teachers in academic courses to recognize and utilize tools developed in exploratory courses in their own classes.

Special attention to the role and importance of exploratory teachers, in the planning stages, can save a great deal of difficulty in the first months and years of new middle level schools. Planners ignore such issues to their peril.

EVALUATION OF THE MIDDLE SCHOOL

Inevitably, schools are accountable for their results, and middle schools are no different. Perhaps the middle school movement ought to be more accountable, because the change to middle schools in America has involved many millions of dollars, an equivalent amount of human time and energy, and the adjustment of the school experiences of an entire generation. Patrons, parents, school board members, teachers, and students deserve to know that the money, time, energy, and adjustments involved were worth it. This sort of evaluation, the process whereby results are determined and judged, is a leadership responsibility.

Purposes and Scope of Evaluating Middle Schools Two types of evaluation are common; both are applicable to the evaluation of middle school programs. Formative evaluation, in regard to middle school programs, is the process used to determine whether plans and intentions have been effectively implemented. It includes those processes that evaluate the school's progress in an ongoing program. Generally, formative data can serve as feedback to make corrections in faulty or incomplete plans as school life continues. Formative evaluation should be thought of as an important continuation of the planning process. Simply put, it answers the question "Are we doing what we said we wanted to do in our new middle schools?"

Summative evaluation includes those processes involved in reaching a decision about the value of a program that has been implemented. It has to do with outcomes, not implementation. Summative data are used to determine how well the new school programs have met expectations. Comparisons may be made with earlier programs to determine if the changes worked well enough to continue them. Summative evaluation of middle schools, done correctly, provides answers to the question "Is the middle school better?"

Generally, during the early years of the middle school movement, formative evaluation was done poorly and summative evaluation was not done at all. Many middle schools were opened to accomplish other important goals such as school desegregation, effective use of school buildings, and so on. School leaders and policy-makers could content themselves with observing the outcomes in those areas, and so long as the middle school program was not an unavoidable disaster, it could be safely ignored while other, more urgent needs were attended. And so it was.

Few districts devoted much in the way of resources, during the last three decades, to formative or summative evaluation. Consequently middle school educators were often left without sufficient data to determine whether middle school programs that were planned actually were implemented. Nor did they know whether such programs, assuming they were functioning fully and effectively, performed as they had hoped. Such a state of affairs is understandable, but lamentable, because middle school educators have had to endure endless accusations of soft-mindedness (e.g., Bradley & Manzo, 2000). We hope that the next generation of middle school educators improves upon the evaluation procedures of the last.

Formative Evaluation of a Middle School

District and school leaders engage in formative evaluation of a middle school when they wish to know how well plans have been implemented and how fully the middle school concept is functioning. The outcomes of the change to a middle school cannot be evaluated without first being able to demonstrate that the plans made for the middle school are in place and functioning as intended.

As a consequence of our experience with middle schools during the last 35 years, we have developed "Twenty Questions for Exemplary Middle Schools" (see Table 9.1), reflecting a combination of the concepts of the effective schools movement and the middle school concept. When we have been invited to participate in a district's formative evaluation of a middle school program,

TABLE 9.1	TWENTY QUESTIONS FOR EXEMPLARY MIDDLE SCHOOLS

Part One: Is there a vital philosophy that serves as the driving force behind the program of the school?

1. Is there evidence, written or otherwise, indicating that the staff has developed a consensus regarding the proposed goals of the school?

2. Is there evidence that this mission relates directly to the characteristics and needs of early adolescent learners?

3. Is there evidence of a school learning climate that encourages increased academic achievement for all students? From the faculty? From the administration? From the students?

Part Two: Is there a curriculum alignment and assessment process that implements the school goals and objectives?

4. Are there written documents that clearly define specific course or grade level objectives that students are expected to accomplish with clear standards for mastery?

5. Are the curriculum documents easy for teachers to use in daily planning for instruction, with textbooks and other materials matched to the objectives of the school?

6. Is effective assessment of student achievement a central, regular, comprehensive, and public part of the process of curriculum implementation providing specific feedback for program improvements?

Part Three: Is classroom instruction congruent with the philosophy and the curriculum of the school?

7. Is there evidence that teachers hold high expectations for all students?

8. Can classroom climate be described as high in on-task behavior of students and low in teacher negative affect?

9. Are teachers clearly matching their classroom curriculum with the overall curriculum plan of the school?

10. Are students presented with instruction that can be characterized as active (for both the teacher and students) and varied?

11. Do most students spend the greater part of their school day learning in heterogeneous groupings?

12. Do the teachers plan whole class instruction on a unit basis, in a style that fits the teachers' and the learners' strengths, with opportunities for remediation and enrichment where needed?

Part Four: Is the school organized in a manner that maximizes opportunities for group involvement for both teachers and students?

13. Is there evidence that the members of the school staff recognize and support the need for group involvement, for a sense of unity and belonging, among the students?

14. Do smaller advisory groups have the opportunity to meet regularly and often?

15. Is the interdisciplinary team group the central organizing unit of the school?

16. Is the team process chosen by the school organized in an appropriate balance, for the needs of the particular students in the school, of teacher subject specialization and supportive interpersonal structure?

17. Does the administration and faculty arrange for a maximum number of activities that enhance group involvement for students? For teachers?

Part Five: Is there evidence of the necessary balance between spirited leadership and faculty involvement in the governance of the school?

18. Is there evidence that school leaders are continuously engaged in the process of clarifying the mission of the middle school as a regular part of their school activity?

19. Is there evidence that the leaders in the school act in ways that can be described as "instructional leadership"?

20. Is there evidence that authentic, regular, and systematic shared decision-making is the mode for school level problem solving and policy development?

one version or another of this simple instrument has proven useful in guiding the process of data gathering and analysis. Most recently, we have used these and other questions in formative evaluations of school programs in Guilford County, North Carolina (1997), Charlotte-Mecklenburg, North Carolina (1998), Savannah, Georgia (1999), Talent, Oregon (2000), and Columbia, South Carolina (2001). If 5 points were awarded to every question that evaluators consider to be answerable with a "confident positive" and if the points were withheld from questions that cannot be so answered, the total points out of a possible 100 yield a rough estimate of the degree to which a particular school is functioning in an exemplary way. It is an instrument to be used solely as formative evaluation, and we suggest that educators modify and adapt the questions to fit their own particular middle school programs. We offer our version for whatever unofficial purposes readers may find it useful.

Another device that we have used in formative evaluation situations is the "Exemplary Middle School Checklist" (see Table 9.2). The checklist is a summary of what we believe to be the 15 most important attributes of a fully functioning exemplary middle school program. The items are not listed in any order of importance. Once again, we offer the device for the reader's use in unofficial situations where formative evaluation of a middle school program is called for. We find it useful, also, in workshops and faculty meetings where staff members can be productively engaged in a review of their school's programs. Respondents can be asked to report their scores for a group total or to work toward a consensus with another small group of two or three persons that then shares its consensus. An analysis of the findings of a complete faculty group can yield important formative data that will be useful in planning staff development and program improvement activities designed to bring the middle school closer to exemplary status.

A substantially more comprehensive approach to the evaluation of middle school programs has been undertaken in several regions of the nation. In Carrboro, North Carolina, at the Center for the Study of Early Adolescence, educators developed the Middle Grades Assessment Program (MGAP) that has been used successfully in many parts of the country. The New England League of Middle Schools (NELMS) has also developed its own evaluation. Based on 10 core middle school concepts about which much national agreement exists, the NELMS program involves three major phases: consultation and school-generated reports, on-site visits by representatives of the NELMS group, and a post-evaluation audit based on another visit at a later time. The evaluation examines

- Educators' knowledge and commitment to early adolescents
- Balanced curriculum based on the needs of early adolescents
- Organizational arrangements
- Instructional strategies
- Exploratory programs

TABLE 9.2 EXEMPLARY MIDDLE SCHOOL CHECKLIST

Directions: Each of the following items should be ranked in the following manner: (1) present and up to standard, (2) present but in need of substantial improvement, or (3) absent or in need of complete revision.

___ A. Flexible (perhaps block) scheduling within the classroom and across the school

___ B. A real school philosophy firmly based on characteristics and needs of developing adolescents

___ C. A building and facilities designed especially for the middle school program

___ D. Flexible grouping strategies, primarily heterogeneous, within the classroom and across the school

___ E. Active instruction based on the learning styles of developing adolescents

___ F. A curriculum characterized by both a core academic focus and a broad range of exploratory opportunities

___ G. A smooth and continuous program of staff development, renewal, and school improvement focused on the unique concerns of middle school education

___ H. A smooth and continuous transition between the elementary and the high school program permitting uniqueness at the middle level

___ I. A shared decision-making model that is formal, regular, systematic, providing authentic collaboration between and among teachers, administrators, parents, and students

___ J. An extracurricular program based on the needs of early adolescents, providing regular success experiences for all students

___ K. Teachers and administrators trained and selected especially for educating the developing adolescent

___ L. Organizational arrangements that encourage long-term teacher-student relationships (e.g., multiage grouping, school-within-school, etc.)

___ M. A teacher-based guidance or homeroom program

___ N. A school program focused on three overall goals: academic learning, personal development, and group citizenship

___ O. An interdisciplinary team organization with teachers sharing students, space, and schedule

- Advisory and counseling programs
- Evaluation procedures based on nature of early adolescents
- Cooperative planning
- Positive school climate
- Continuous progress for students

Formative Evaluation of Specific Middle School Components Most middle school educators believe that the interdisciplinary team organization is the heart of a good middle school, the single most important factor in distinguishing between an effective and an ineffective middle level school. It is, typically, also the component of the middle school program that receives the most attention at the time of middle school implementation. Consequently, formative evaluation of the middle school program often centers on the question of the successful implementation of the team organization. We offer, therefore, one additional checklist (see Table 9.3) for those interested in formative evaluation of the interdisciplinary team process. Answers to these questions will help the evaluator gauge how well the team process is working in a particular middle school. By awarding each "yes" answer 5 points, the total out of 100 gives a grade to the team implementation process. If a school's teamwork scores an 85 and an 85 is a "B," then the faculty will have a rough estimate of how well the teams are working. Answers that receive a "no" response will provide a set of goals for establishing more effective teamwork in the future, which is a central purpose of formative evaluation.

In Orange County, Florida, the formative evaluation following the implementation of middle schools was conducted over a two-year period, and among other components of the extraordinarily comprehensive process was a series of interviews conducted with every interdisciplinary team in every one of the district's 18 middle schools. Interviews examined the extent to which the teams were functioning as they were intended: organizationally, developing a sense of community, and instructionally. The interviews also investigated the degree to

TABLE 9.3   TEAMWORK: TWENTY QUESTIONS

____ 1. Are teams organized so that teachers share the same students, space in the school, and schedule?

____ 2. Does the membership on the team represent all the basic academic subjects?

____ 3. Does the team have some common rules, procedures, and expectations?

____ 4. Do the students recognize and feel a sense of belonging to the team?

____ 5. Do the teachers work together to develop and implement activities that heighten the students' sense of community?

____ 6. Do the teachers on the team develop a sense of commitment to each other and draw professional and personal support from each other?

____ 7. Do teams have frequent parent conferences and good home-school relationships?

____ 8. Is there adequate planning time and a planning space used by the team members for their work?

____ 9. Do the teachers on the team use the time and the place for teamwork?

____10. Do teachers work on interrelating their separate subjects, coordinating major assignments, correlating major units, and so on?

____11. Do the teachers provide, on the average, a special teamwide activity (e.g., a recognition assembly) during each grading period?

____12. Do teachers take turns in assuming leadership for different activities within the team when appropriate to individual strengths and interests?

____13. Do teachers meet to discuss their students, at least weekly?

____14. Do team teachers develop and carry out joint strategies in an attempt to resolve students' problems?

____15. Do one or more team members talk with the substitute teacher about team expectations and encourage the substitute to contact the nearest team member for any assistance needed?

____16. Do teams have carefully selected team leaders?

____17. Do teams have at least some control over items such as the schedule, the budget, and the curriculum?

____18. Is there a formal group and process for shared decision-making, composed of teacher, administrators, and others who meet regularly and frequently?

____19. Does the principal work with individual teams regularly and frequently?

____20. Do team members, generally, feel a sense of success and satisfaction about their work together?

which the district's advisory program had been effectively implemented. Information was collected by the middle school coordinators but analyzed and synthesized by the district's excellent Testing and Program Evaluation Section.

Other interview checklists and similar devices can easily be constructed for additional components of the middle school program that need to be subject to a formative evaluation. The advisory program stands out in this regard, but the curriculum, instructional practices, decision-making, and staff development practices can be evaluated formatively in the foregoing manner. Until such formative evaluation practices are conducted, as they were in Guilford County, and leaders are satisfied that the planned program is in place as it was intended, summative evaluation will be relatively disappointing.

Self-Study Programs: School Improvement and Accreditation

Self-study programs are a more frequently used, comprehensive effort to evaluate a middle school. Self-study programs can be used for either formative or summative evaluation purposes. In recent years, legislation in many states has mandated the completion of annual School Improvement Plans for every school, in every district in a state. The other type of self-study most often encountered is that conducted as part of the accreditation or re-accreditation process associated with a regional association of schools, such as the Southern Association of Colleges and Schools (SACS). There are many types of such studies, ranging from a fairly cursory compilation of faculty responses to a questionnaire (such as those in the foregoing section on formative evaluation) or in a group evaluation session to a complete analysis of each aspect of the school by the faculty followed by the review of a visiting team or committee. The complete, accreditation-style review has the most possibilities, we believe, for affecting program development and school quality, and we give it primary attention here. Less comprehensive self-studies could be done for almost any aspect of the school by the designation of study committees and guides for the aspect(s) concerned, with the use of visiting individuals or committees also possible.

Purposes of the Self-Study Programs Two overlapping purposes dominate self-study programs: (1) to evaluate the school to improve it and (2) to satisfy accreditation requirements of the regional and state accrediting agency. These purposes should not conflict because accrediting agencies require self-studies so that the schools may improve, but the immediate goal of accreditation can overshadow the long-range goal of improvement.

Accreditation of a middle school by the state department of education or any agency designated by the state is essential for public schools in most states, although the requirements for accreditation vary widely in the 50 states. The requirement of a periodic self-study program is a sensible means for the school to determine its status and maintain improvement as well as an effective way for the agency to have data basic to accreditation. Regional accreditation is an option for the school. Being accredited by the regional association is recognition for status purposes desired by some school boards, faculties, and patrons. Both purposes of the self-study program are stated in the following illustrative excerpts from the superintendent's foreword to the 1990–1991 self-study report of the Powell Middle School, in Brooksville, Florida.

> The self-study process afforded us an opportunity to critically re-examine our philosophy, mission, and goals. Our collective vision for our school is now more focused. With the completion of this report we have taken an introspective look at our school and its program. We now have a better understanding of where we have been as well as a clearer picture of where we want to go. . . .
>
> Often, everyone involved in a self-study, sponsored by a group such as the Southern Association of Colleges and Schools (SACS), benefits from the experience. The involvement required by self-evaluation can provide insight that will result in a stronger program and improved learning experiences for boys and girls.

A major problem in accreditation standards and processes for middle schools, until recently, had been the tendency of accrediting agencies to expect the middle schools to use guidelines developed for secondary schools or elementary schools or both that may not provide for unique elements of the middle school. By 2000, however, the SACS group (see www.sacs.org) and others like it, had developed special standards unique to middle schools. These accreditation standards required educators involved in a middle school self-study to look carefully at parent education relating to the characteristics and needs of young adolescents, exploratory curriculum opportunities, the central place of interdisciplinary teams, the importance of integrated curriculum, the necessity of effective counseling and guidance efforts, and other areas central to the middle school concept. The standards also required middle schools to demonstrate that their students were faring well on local, state, or national standardized tests. This modernization of SACS standards is a welcome improvement.

Summative Evaluation and the Middle School

Summative evaluation is an attempt to determine whether the middle school program has achieved the outcomes that were desired. When the desired outcomes are incidental to the central focus of the middle school concept (e.g., school desegregation, facility usage, conformity to state legislation), summative evaluation has rarely been conducted in any comprehensive manner. In the same way, if formative evaluation has failed to confirm the effective implementation of middle school components (which is usually the case), summative evaluation is frequently disappointing.

As a result, until recently, research regarding the middle school concept has been difficult to accumulate (Felner et al., 1997). Too often, poorly implemented programs have been compared with prior programs that also failed to be designed to the needs of young adolescents. Such research has, consequently, ended up comparing similar treatments and, thus, has failed to demonstrate any significant differences. During the 1970s and 1980s, misinterpretations of this sort of research led some to conclude that the middle school made no difference in the lives of learners. In the 1990s, fortunately, the situation slowly began to change. Reliable research can be conducted only when careful formative evaluation and descriptive studies have first demonstrated that substantially different programs have been successfully implemented.

District leaders may be pressed to present evidence to decision-makers and policy-makers that the move to the middle school, and away from some prior arrangement or design (e.g., junior high school), has been worth the investment of time and money. In such situations, the leader's first response should be to ask for a three-year grace period to ensure the effective implementation of the program, to be followed by a formative evaluation. After conducting a careful formative evaluation and ascertaining that the implementation has been successful, it may be necessary, if not desirable, to engage in summative evaluation. If a formative evaluation is rejected, or if the results are negative, leaders must have the courage to point out the frailties and inappropriateness of a summative evaluation. However, a summative evaluation may be either appropriate or unavoidable. Under those circumstances, we offer the following comments about summative evaluation of the middle school.

Use of Single Criteria Any use of achievement data, alone, for school evaluation purposes is an example of the unwise misuse of a single criterion. Nonetheless, evaluation of a middle school on the basis of achievement test results in a particular area such as reading or mathematics has become more common with the rapid spread of standards-based reform and, as such, threatens to replace more comprehensive, broad-based evaluation strategies (Vars, 2001; Weilbacher, 2001).

The use of a single criterion alone can be least helpful in identifying strengths, weaknesses, and needs for improvement of a school. Data regarding many specific criteria are needed and may be gathered singly or in combination as is feasible but should be used in concert so that the school is not labeled good or bad, an "A" or "F" school, on any single testing, opinion poll, visit of an evaluator, or other one aspect. The current practice of giving schools a letter grade based on the students' achievement on state-mandated tests is a clear example of the shocking misuse of such data.

Nevertheless, in some exemplary school districts, the summative evaluation of the middle school program is done painstakingly and with positive results, even when focusing on the single variable of academic achievement. In Orange County, Florida, for example, in the spring of 1991, a memo from the director of testing and evaluation reported one part of the five-year evaluation of the middle school design (including many other components as well as the interviews described above): a longitudinal assessment of the results of student achievement on the California Test of Basic Skills. The memo stated:

> One conclusion that can be warranted is that the middle school cohort seems to have at least held its own and in some cases outperformed the junior high school cohorts.

Program developers in Orange County, and school board members, were pleased with these results. In central Florida, in the early 1990s, funds were low, new enrollments threatened to swamp the districts with new students, and social conditions were difficult. If the new middle schools had simply held their own, in terms of achievement, it could have been considered a victory. Under the circumstances faced by these educators, for achievement to rise substantially was something to be excited about, and they were. When such analyses are conducted on a large scale (e.g., Felner et al., 1997), the results are also strikingly positive in regard to the connection between the middle school concept and increased academic achievement.

Focus of Summative Evaluation   Eighteen hypotheses were proposed in the evaluation chapter of one of the first textbooks about middle school education, *The Emergent Middle School* (Alexander, Williams, Compton, Hines, & Prescott, 1968), as some of the possible bases for summative studies of and more formal research on middle schools. They are still valid in the 21st century.

1. Pupils in the middle school will become more self-directed learners than pupils in the control schools.
2. Pupils in the middle school will have fewer or less intense social and psychological problems than pupils in conventional schools.
3. Achievement of middle school pupils on standardized tests will equal or exceed that of pupils in conventional schools.
4. Middle school pupils will equal or exceed pupils in conventional schools on standard measures of physical fitness and health.
5. Pupils in the middle school will have more favorable attitudes toward school than will pupils in conventional schools.
6. Middle school pupils will hold more adequate self-concepts than will pupils in the conventional schools.
7. Social acceptance among middle school pupils will be higher than among those in conventional schools.
8. The average daily attendance of middle school pupils will exceed the attendance of pupils in conventional schools.
9. Measures of creativity among middle school pupils will show an increase during middle school years.
10. Middle school graduates will compile better academic records in 9th grade than will 9th graders from the control schools.
11. Middle school graduates will drop out of senior high school less frequently than pupils who follow the traditional pattern.

12. Middle school teachers will more often use best practices that experts generally recommend as superior.
13. Teachers in the middle school will experience a higher degree of professional fulfillment and self-satisfaction than teachers in conventional schools.
14. Teachers in the middle school will utilize a greater variety of learning media than will teachers in conventional schools.
15. Teacher turnover will be lower in the middle school than in conventional schools.
16. Teachers in the middle school will be more open to change.
17. Patrons of the middle school will hold more positive attitudes toward objectives and procedures of the school than patrons of conventional schools.
18. Principals of experimental and control schools will have similar operating patterns within each school system.

· To our knowledge, no school district has attempted to test all of these hypotheses, nor did the authors of *The Emergent Middle School* suggest such a large-scale evaluation in a single district. Note this suggestion, which seems still a very useful one that school districts and state and regional, even national, groups might utilize.

> Obviously, a thorough evaluation in which even the hypotheses to be listed in this section were tested would strain or be beyond the resources of most school systems. However, with state or federal help, a single system could give evidence on many or most of the hypotheses. It would be better, however, from the standpoints of both economy and sound research if a number of systems were to cooperate in testing these and perhaps additional hypotheses. If a dozen schools were involved, and if there were eighteen major hypotheses to be tested, then each school might test six of the eighteen. In this way, the opportunity to generalize results would be greatly increased, for each hypothesis would be tested four times in different schools.

Many of these hypotheses have been at least partially tested singly or in some combination as self-studies, while other summative evaluations have collected and analyzed data relevant to the hypotheses (e.g., Felner et al., 1997). Many doctoral dissertations have used certain hypotheses for researching the effects of middle schools, and in most cases, the results support the use of the middle school concept. For example, a comprehensive meta-analysis of 30 studies by Hartzler (2000, p. vii) concluded:

> Students in integrated curriculum programs consistently out-performed students in traditional classes on national standardized tests, on statewide testing programs, and on program developed assessment. Integrated curriculum has been shown to be a viable alternative to traditional subject-centered programs without fear of student failure or declining standardized test scores.

In school districts approaching the transition to middle school education from some other organizational structure, decision-makers are bound to want evidence that the process has desirable outcomes. In such cases, they are interested in research studies from other settings prior to approving the reorganization, but afterward, they will be interested in outcomes in their own district. Wise planners will anticipate the need to respond to these concerns by capturing benchmark data from the years preceding the transition to middle school. In this way, presentations can be made to the school board, for example, comparing certain outcomes in the new middle schools with prior years and organizational formats. In our judgment, a number of factors will respond favorably to the change to middle school, if the transition is done in an exemplary way. We suggest that program developers in districts moving to middle school immediately capture benchmark data in the following areas.

- Standardized test scores
- School climate measures
- Ethnic relationships
- Suspension and expulsion rates
- Faculty morale
- High school performance in the 10th grade
- Parent support and approval
- Discipline referrals to the office
- Attendance by students and teachers
- Grade point average
- High school drop-out rate
- Self-concept
- Truancy

Other factors also may be at play. If the district has no data on the above items, planners will be in the uncomfortable position, a few years later, of being unable to prove the middle school is better than prior plans. If data on the above items are not now regularly collected, designing a few simple items to measure them with will be well worth the effort. At least, planners should be able to demonstrate, in later years, that important outcomes did not suffer as a result of moving to middle school. Even if things just stay the same, in the new century, with educational conditions becoming more challenging every week, holding steady is a victory of sorts.

EVALUATING THE MIDDLE SCHOOL MOVEMENT

Although statements are frequently made in journals and speeches about the success (Jackson & Davis, 2000) or failure (Bradley & Manzo, 2000) of the middle school movement, insufficient evidence is available to support such statements. Furthermore, making any categorical assessment of the earliest middle level school, the junior high school, is equally impossible and unwise. We know of no comprehensive study justifying categorical statements as to the efficacy of any one pattern of school unit organization, elementary, secondary, or otherwise. For one reason, controlling the other variables in experimental comparisons of different school organizations is difficult, if not impossible. Nevertheless, the middle school movement is a sufficient departure from the prior 8–4 and 6–3–3 school organizations as to need such critical examination if possible.

Several types of studies can be made, and a few have been successfully conducted (Felner et al., 1997). Comparisons of the status of middle schools with regard to practices relevant to the goals of the movement can be made at different periods. We reviewed in Chapter 2 the several surveys that showed the numerical growth of middle schools. Given that three of these surveys (Alexander, 1968; Brooks & Edwards, 1978; and Alexander & McEwin, 1989) used some identical questions, some comparative data could be drawn out regarding program and organizational features of the middle schools. In addition to such repeated benchmark surveys, national collection and publication of local research studies and school evaluations (e.g., George & Shewey, 1994) can help to provide state-of-the-art information and perhaps stimulate additional studies in neglected and critical areas. Also, statewide studies such as *Caught in the Middle* (Superintendent's Middle Grade Task Force, 1987) and *Middle Level Strategies for School Improvement* (Washington State Middle Level Task Force, 2001), sponsored by leagues of middle schools or state agencies, are useful as surveys and also as comparisons of different school organizations.

We believe that one very promising area of research that is often underutilized is dissertation research for the doctoral degree. Hence, we list at the end of the chapter a few of the more than 1,500 such studies, completed between 1981 and 2001, that relate to middle school education. When and if basic research or full school evaluations reveal how best to organize a school and provide a program therein that will produce students with the most interests and skills in continued learning, then educators, administrators, parents, and students will have full confidence in such a school. Even though we believe that the profession has drawn much closer to increased certainty about effective programs and practices (e.g., Epstein, 1990; Felner et al., 1997; Jackson & Davis, 2000), our own opinion is that such comprehensive and conclusive research studies and findings are as yet insufficient to quell the constant criticism of student-focused educational programs such as the middle school concept. Perhaps it will always be so.

CONTENT SUMMARY

Middle schools do not spring forth fully formed like Athena from the forehead of Zeus. They require much planning and development. Staff development is the core of the change process in both new and revitalized middle schools. Evaluating middle schools can be an important part of both the creation and renewal of middle schools.

CONNECTIONS TO OTHER CHAPTERS

An automobile tire rarely goes flat at the moment of puncture; usually the tire loses its pressure and its effectiveness further down the road. So it is with exemplary middle schools. Program failures can almost always be traced back to planning errors or to the absence of careful evaluation. Hence, planning and evaluation relate especially to strategies developed for advisory programs (Chapter 5), teaming (Chapter 6), group strategies (Chapter 7), and school schedules and buildings (Chapter 8).

QUESTIONS FOR DISCUSSION

1. If you were to be involved in the creation of a new middle school, where would you begin? What would be the sequence of steps that would be essential parts of the planning process for your school?
2. Is it more difficult to plan a new middle school or to revitalize an existing middle school? Explain your choice.
3. In revitalizing a middle school, are there factors to look out for that are not a part of implementing a new middle school? If so, what are they? If not, why not?
4. Think of the middle school or system of middle schools with which you are most familiar. Are you aware of any comprehensive evaluation of those schools in recent years? Have there been any attempts to revitalize these schools?
5. If you are familiar with a middle school that has opened in the last five years, what do you know about the planning process that preceded the new school?

ACTION STEPS

1. Volunteer to serve on a school evaluation committee. It might be for one of the regional accrediting associations such as the Southern Association of Colleges and Schools, or it could be with a local effort to improve middle school programs. Share what you learn from this experience with members of your team or study group.
2. Seek permission of a middle school principal to conduct an informal evaluation of a middle school. Using the materials from this book, and

particularly those from this chapter, engage in a one-person evaluation team or join together with a small group of others. Visit the school, talk with teachers, examine documents, interview students, and question the school leaders. Look carefully at the schedule and the teacher and student organization patterns. Visit classes to get a sense of the type of instruction that is taking place. Then pull all the data together, analyze it carefully, and report a series of commendations and recommendations to the principal. He or she may want to discuss it with you. You may be asked to share it with a group of teachers.

SUGGESTIONS FOR FURTHER STUDY

Books and Monographs

Epstein, J., & Mac Iver, D. (1990). *Education in the middle grades: National practices and trends.* Columbus, OH: National Middle School Association.

Fouts, J. (1999). *School restructuring and student achievement in Washington state: Research findings on the effects of House Bill 1209 and school restructuring on western Washington schools.* Seattle, WA: Seattle Pacific University School of Education.

Fuhrman, S. (Ed.). (2001). *From the capitol to the classroom: Standards-based reform in the states.* Chicago: National Society for the Study of Education.

Knapp, M. S., & Shields, P. M. (1991). *Better schooling for the children of poverty.* Berkeley, CA: McCutchan Publishing Co.

Kohut, S. (1988). *The middle school: A bridge between elementary and high schools* (2nd ed.). Washington, DC: National Education Association.

Leithwood, K., Aitken, R., & Jantzi, D. (2001). *Making schools smarter: A system for monitoring school and district progress* (2nd ed.). Thousand Oaks, CA: Corwin Press.

McEwin, C., Dickinson, T., & Jenkins, D. (1996). *America's middle schools: Practices and progress—A 25 year perspective.* Columbus, OH: National Middle School Association.

NASSP's Council on Middle Level Education (1988). *Assessing excellence: A guide for studying the middle level school.* Reston, VA: National Association of Secondary School Principals.

Wheelock, A. (1998). *Safe to be smart: Building a culture for standards-based reform in the middle grades.* Columbus, OH: National Middle School Association.

Williamson, R. (1991). *Planning for success: Successful implementation of middle level reorganization.* Reston, VA: National Association of Secondary School Principals.

Periodicals

Fashola, O., & Slavin, R. (1997). Promising programs for elementary and middle schools: Evidence of effectiveness and replicability. *Journal of Education for Students Placed at Risk, 2*(3), 251–307.

Lipsitz, J., & Felner, R. (Eds.) (1997). Middle grades research: A Phi Delta Kappan Special Report. *Phi Delta Kappan, 78*(7), 517–556.

McElroy, C. (2000). Middle school programs that work. *Phi Delta Kappan, 82*(4), 277–279.

Mc Laughlin, H., Watts, C., & Beard, M. (2000). Just because it's happening doesn't mean it's working: Using action research to improve practice in middle schools. *Phi Delta Kappan, 82*(4), 284–290.

Merrill, A. B. (1991). Planning for the end of the year at a middle school. *Middle School Journal, 22*(5), 4–9.

Norton, J. (2000, June). Important developments in middle-grades reform. *Phi Delta Kappan On-line Articles, 81*(10), k1–k4 (www.pdkintl.org/kappanklew0006.htm).

Norton, J., & Lewis, A. (2000). Middle grades reform: A Kappan special report. *Phi Delta Kappan, 8*(10), k1–k20.

ERIC

Baer, V. E. (1987, October). *An information and "cultural" exchange between two middle schools* (ERIC document ED295158).

California State Department of Education (1989). *Quality criteria for middle grades: Planning, implementing, self-study, and program quality review* (ERIC document ED308636).

Christie, S. (1989). *A report on opinion surveys of parents, students, and staff of four-track year-round schools in Cajon Valley, 1987–1988* (ERIC document ED303 888).

Clark, T. A. (1989, April). *District-based and community-wide planning to address student dropout prevention: A discussion paper* (ERIC document ED302596)

Dewalt, M. W., et al. (1990, February). *Lunch at Sams: A cooperative community and school program* (ERIC document ED317605).

Foody, M., et al. (1990). *Developing a plan for multicultural education* (ERIC document ED327605).

Mac Iver, D. J. (1990). *A national description of report card entries in the middle grades* (ERIC document ED324124).

Martinez, M. P. (1987). *Music program evaluation, 1985–1986*. Albuquerque, NM: Albuquerque Public Schools (ERIC document ED294792).

Mitchell, S., & Hansen, J. B. (1989). *The use of evaluative data for instructional planning and decision making in the Portland public schools* (ERIC document ED312275).

National Association of Elementary School Principals (1990). *Standards for quality elementary & middle schools, kindergarten through eighth grade* (Rev. ed.) (ERIC document ED322639).

O'Sullivan, R. G. (1990, April). *Evaluating a model middle school dropout prevention program for at-risk students* (ERIC document ED317928).

Schine, J. (1989). *Young adolescents and community service* (ERIC document ED325206).

Shefelbine, J. (1990). *Parents sharing books: Motivation and reading* (ERIC document ED324662).

Dissertations and Dissertation Abstracts

Burke, A. (1990). Junior high to middle school transition in Washington State: A survey and three case studies (Doctoral dissertation, University of Washington, 1990).

Coburn, T. A. W. (1989). The effects of diagnostic information on teacher planning and student achievement (Doctoral dissertation, Texas A&M University, 1989). *Dissertation Abstracts International,* 51 (01a), 65.

Duthoy, R. J. (1989). An evaluation of middle school excellence by California school districts that have implemented a school program (Doctoral dissertation, United States International University, 1989). *Dissertation Abstracts International,* 50 (05a), 1152.

Fine, R. (1989). A program evaluation of one school district's out of district placement program (Doctoral dissertation, Rutgers, the State University of New Jersey, 1989). *Dissertation Abstracts International,* 50 (10a), 3117.

Haboush, K. L. (1989). An evaluation of student learning outcomes under a critical thinking–social studies program (Doctoral dissertation, Rutgers, the State University of New Jersey, 1989). *Dissertation Abstracts International,* 50 (10a), 3185.

Kane, C. C. (1988). Toward an expanded middle school philosophy: An analysis of philosophy and practice in middle level education (Doctoral dissertation, Florida State University, 1988). *Dissertation Abstracts International,* 49 (12a), 3652.

Knight, R. W. (1989). Program evaluation as a catalyst for instructional change: A study of teachers evaluating the effects of a computer-assisted writing-to-learn initiative (Doctoral dissertation, University of Louisville, 1989). *Dissertation Abstracts International,* 51 (04a), 1100.

Lee, Y. (1988). On the improvement of the middle school programs: The impact of north central association visiting team recommendations on junior high/middle schools in Iowa (Doctoral dissertation, University of Iowa, 1988). *Dissertation Abstracts International,* 50 (04a), 865.

Smith, P. D. (1990). Planning, implementing, and maintaining a middle school program: A case study of excellence in a North Carolina school (Doctoral dissertation, North Carolina State University, 1990). *Dissertation Abstracts International,* 51 (04a), 1076.

Twiest, M. M. (1988). Construction and validation of a test of basic process skills for the elementary and middle grades using different methods of test administration (Doctoral dissertation, University of Georgia, 1988). *Dissertation Abstracts International,* 50 (02a), 423.

Web Sites

National Education Association

http://www.nea.org

This site represents the home of the largest association of educators in the world—2.6 million. It is a large and complex site with dozens of links potentially helpful to those with an interest in revitalizing middle schools. The site alerts readers to resources, grant opportunities, educational events, and important news.

Wallace-Reader's Digest Funds

http://www.wallacefunds.org

This site is hosted by a wealthy foundation dedicated to educational improvement. The site offers information about many grants available from the foundation for school revitalization.

Research for Action

http://www.researchforaction.org/index.html

Research for Action is a nonprofit organization based in Philadelphia. It is dedicated to assisting educators in bringing about change and improvement in their schools. The group focuses on conducting research and promoting reform through assisting educators with using new tools and identifying new directions.

MIDDLE SCHOOL LEADERSHIP

LINCOLN MIDDLE SCHOOL

Lincoln Middle School, in Gainesville, Florida, was an exemplary middle school the day it opened in the autumn of 1974. In 2002, more than a quarter-century later, the staff of Lincoln remained dedicated to providing a quality program for the young adolescent. Particular leaders have come and gone, programs and priorities have changed, and heated controversies have captured the spirit of the school from time to time. District and state priorities have forced the school to cater to agendas the faculty has not chosen. Nonetheless, the essential character of the school, one unwaveringly dedicated to young adolescent students, has remained constant. In particular, teachers and students at Lincoln have been organized in interdisciplinary teams for 27 years. Teachers and students continue to identify, first, with their team. In addition, teacher-based guidance has never completely disappeared and efforts at integrated curriculum continue. What accounts for this extraordinary stability? The series of school principals at Lincoln has come almost entirely from the ranks of teachers in the building, which provided a continuous commitment to the school's vision. At least as important is that shared decision-making— faculty and administrators working together to establish policies and solve problems—has been so long a part of the school that two generations of staff members have felt ownership in the life of the school and have been willing to work hard to maintain the program. Educators who aspire to provide long years of high-quality education to the young adolescent must attend to leadership.

WHAT YOU WILL LEARN IN CHAPTER 10

The passage of time has helped middle school educators appreciate the critical importance of spirited school leadership. The ability to formulate and inculcate a clear vision for one's school seems paramount. The capacity to involve staff members in the decisions that affect their professional lives is central. In the 21st century, spirited leaders are challenged daily, particularly by the national popularity of standards-based reform. Other challenges and new directions are emerging that require the attention and skill of middle school leaders.

CORE COMPONENTS OF MIDDLE SCHOOL LEADERSHIP

Middle schools are affected by many factors as they seek to become exemplary, but none is more significant than the quality of their leadership. Theory, research, and experience all attest to the great importance of the leadership of the school principal and of the many other individuals who may at one time or another have roles as leaders (Kilgore, Griffin, Sindelar, & Webb, 2002). More specifically, we believe that effective middle school leadership is composed of the following three sets of global behaviors.

1. Possessing a compelling vision of middle school education based upon a clear understanding of the characteristics and needs of young adolescents.
2. Planning the school program and developing effective implementation strategies to create a unique and effective learning environment based on the characteristics of young adolescents, and evaluating the success of the school in achieving its objectives.
3. Engaging the stakeholders (teachers, parents, students, board members, and central office staff) in a process of shared decision-making that has, as its aim, the continued long-term maintenance and improvement of the school(s).

We believe that the carefully balanced presence of these factors—spirited leadership, a clear vision, and authentic involvement of all the stakeholders—is the catalyst leading to long-term success of high-quality middle schools. Without spirited, visionary leadership, there is no direction; without authentic involvement, there is no follow-through.

MIDDLE SCHOOL LEADERSHIP AND VISION

Leadership has the responsibility to "craft a clear, concise, and bold declaration that defines the school's mission—its purpose for existing" (Jackson &

Davis, 2000, p. 152). A study of the long-term survival of high-quality middle school programs (George & Anderson, 1989) linked the longevity of quality middle school programs to this heightened sense of mission and the resulting clarity about the nature of the school, shared by the members of the school leadership team. Understanding the purpose of the middle school, and the school's commitment to the personal and educational needs of youngsters from ages 10 to 15, plays an important role both prior to and following the implementation of quality programs at the middle level.

In the 1989 George and Anderson study (pp. 4–5), respondents identified

> the establishment of quality programs, and their continued existence over a long period of time, as resting on a bedrock of a leadership group which understands and demonstrates commitment to the needs of young adolescents. Exemplary programs are never established in the first place without this understanding; continued excellence in the education of early adolescents is impossible, say survey participants, when there is no clarity about or commitment to the needs of the early adolescent age group.

Sometimes a written philosophical statement based on the nature and needs of the students is the filter through which successful program deliberations pass. Constant reference to this written school philosophy (and the refusal to ignore it) when making decisions about curriculum, organization, schedule, and other program components can be more important than almost anything else in the preservation of high-quality middle schools. Written documents are worth little unless they accurately reflect the degree of school leadership commitment to the needs of young adolescents and the extent to which that commitment is dispersed among the staff members of the school, the district, and its patrons. If this student-centered mission is critical to the duration of high-quality programs, then careful selection of school leaders and their involvement in effective staff development programs seem to be crucial activities.

MAINTAINING THE MIDDLE SCHOOL: SHARED DECISION-MAKING

Establishing an exemplary middle school is a wonderful thing, but maintaining an exemplary program for two decades or more has been extremely arduous. At this point in the middle school movement, however, we believe that the long-term maintenance, and the revitalization, of high-quality programs should be of the utmost concern, because educators already know how to begin them. The profession seems to know a great deal less about how to maintain or revitalize an exemplary middle school, and this may be the most important aspect of leadership of all.

Many leadership factors contribute to the long-term health of an exemplary middle school. A study of these factors (George & Anderson, 1989) identified as many as a dozen. Among the more significant were

- Support of the central office and of colleagues in other schools
- A focus on continuing improvement
- Establishing the most exemplary program possible at the start
- Carefully planned staff development, without expecting miracles

Two factors explain a great deal more of the long-term success of high-quality middle schools. The first is a schoolwide vision built solidly on a compassionate understanding of the characteristics and needs of young adolescents. The second is at least as important as the first, if not more so. Few middle school programs achieve exemplary status and fewer still are able to maintain that status for long periods of time in the absence of a regular, honest, systematic, frequent problem-solving, decision-making, policy-setting, collaborative group that brings together leaders from the administration, the classroom, and other areas of the school community. Without real shared decision-making, exemplary middle school programs do not appear to be viable for long periods of time.

We believe that the very best middle schools (and of this number, those that last) are characterized by a dynamic tension between spirited, visionary leadership and authentic, effective involvement of as many members of the school community as possible. Without leadership of this sort, there is no direction, no mission; without involvement, there is no continuing comprehensive momentum toward completion. How does this involvement come about in the exemplary middle school?

The Program Improvement Council or Building Leadership Team

In our experience, viable exemplary middle school programs are so complex, and their mission so challenging, that they require constant midcourse corrections to help them continue toward the realization of important goals. Authoritarian, control-oriented leadership has been shown to have a negative effect on the ways in which teachers and administrators work toward maintaining an exemplary middle school (Blase, 1990). Spirited, visionary leadership is necessary, even critical, but not sufficient. Some broader, schoolwide group of leaders, by whatever name, must be the locus of control for the decisions that provide the continuing momentum to the school program. This is achieved by shared decision-making. We call this the Program Improvement Council (PIC), but there are many other names for such groups. The BLT (Building Leadership Team) is one of our favorite appellations.

When the shared decision-making process works effectively, the process is the same, regardless of the name of the group. With the principal as its chair, the decision-making group (e.g., PIC, BLT) establishes schoolwide policy and oversees the many wide-ranging aspects of the total program. Teacher leaders, who make up the balance of the PIC membership, have teaching and advising as well as administrative duties in their teams. They combine a thorough understanding of team operations and problems with an overall appreciation of the task of implementing effective programs throughout the school.

More than 30 years ago, middle school leaders in Alachua County, Florida, adopted a version of the Program Improvement Council to meet the needs of their middle school programs. It was and continues to be a practical and effective way to combine leadership and involvement to provide continuing energy and enthusiasm to middle school education. The way it works in Alachua County's middle schools (of which Lincoln is one) need not be the way it works everywhere, but it has proven to be both effective and hardy in the form it is utilized there. Consequently, middle level education has been at least minimally effective in Alachua County throughout most of the last three decades.

For most of these many years, the process has begun on Monday morning, on a weekly or biweekly basis, when the principal posts the tentative agenda for the PIC meeting to be held that afternoon, when the students have departed. Posted near the faculty sign-in area, anyone can add an item to the tentative agenda. Sometime near mid-morning the principal takes down the tentative agenda, goes back to the office, and makes out the final agenda for the afternoon meeting. Then at, say, 2:55 p.m., all of the staff members who wish to attend the PIC meeting move to the library, where the meetings are always held.

PIC has regular members. All of the team leaders in the school are members, as are those in the school administration. In addition, there are representatives from unified arts, physical education, and special education. A counselor will also be a member. In some schools, in other districts, parents and students also have representatives. Only regular members can vote, if a vote becomes necessary.

Staff members are allowed to attend, and they are encouraged to do so, even if they cannot vote. Sometimes teachers come to advocate a particular position or to ask for special permission for an activity that will affect the whole school. At certain times, issues may be so important to the life of the school that substantial numbers of the staff will attend just to fishbowl, to observe the deliberations closely. New staff members are encouraged to attend PIC meetings, for staff development purposes, because these gatherings are the closest one can get to the heartbeat of the school culture and new staff members can get in touch with the mission of the school in record time. Meetings are not held in secret, behind closed doors in the principal's office.

At PIC, decisions are made openly and with authentic shared decision-making, but school leaders do not give away the store. Items that are brought up for discussion and decision-making are carefully planned and selected as well as widely known. When the process is done correctly, school leaders know before the meeting that they can live with whatever decision is made. This does not mean, however, that decisions are foregone conclusions and that the

PIC group is simply a rubber stamp for the principal. The substance of the PIC group's deliberations is recognized as concerns that require everyone's input and commitment to decide correctly and implement effectively.

Items for discussion and decision-making at PIC are, consequently, selected from a specific, albeit wide-ranging, area. PIC members do not discuss items beyond their control, such as the total monies allocated to the school or changes they would like to see in the school board contract or state legislature. They do not discuss items such as teacher evaluations or problems within one team. Nor do they discuss the myriad items that bore teachers to death during traditional faculty meetings and that administrators can manage with their knowledge and permission but without their involvement.

PIC agendas are composed of the schoolwide issues, problems, and decisions that most concern the staff as a whole. Here are the items that appeared on the November 26, 1990, agenda for the PIC meeting at Lincoln Middle School.

1. "Steppers (a singing and dancing group)" will be out Monday, December 10, at the Village Retirement Home. They will also be out Thursday and Friday. All work must be made up. If this does not happen, let Hannah know.
2. Sixth grade chorus students will be out Friday, December 14, at Alley Katz, as a reward for performing two shows.
3. Be careful of scheduling parent conferences during special activity time.
4. Dance Party video? Too many concerns and not enough support. Not this year.
5. Teacher-student football game.
6. C Team teachers will provide a special "hospitality time" for the rest of the faculty on Wednesday morning at 8:00 a.m.
7. The Recycling Program.
8. Christmas Party at Don's house.
9. Monday night's School Advisory Council.
10. Report Cards.
11. Alachua County Council of Middle School Educators meeting.
12. IBM workshop for reading and writing teachers.
13. Comments for D, F, or U grades on interim reports.

As an indicator of consistency, among the items on the PIC agenda at Lincoln, on August 30, 2000, a full decade later, were the following items.

1. Attendance issues
2. Team conferences
3. Services of the new school psychologist
4. The $98,079.00 award for gaining "A" school status—brainstorming ideas for the money
5. T-team trip to Animal Kingdom

6. Yearbook sales begin already
7. Concerns about AA (Teacher-based advisory)
8. Need Team Citizens of the Month ASAP
9. Team supply dollars

Nothing is done carelessly regarding PIC; even the physical set-up is carefully designed. The meeting takes place in public, not in the privacy of the principal's office where everything is expected to go one way. Participants sit in a circle, and seats change every week so that cliques do not form. The moderator's role changes on a regular basis. The recorder's role also rotates. At the end of each meeting, the recorder makes copies of the minutes of the meeting and places them in each staff member's mailbox.

At 7:45 a.m. the next morning, the first information each faculty member receives is the record of what happened at PIC the previous afternoon. At 7:50 a.m., each staff member reports to one of the team meetings that are scheduled, with the school administrators circulating from meeting to meeting to ensure that all are present and that the meetings are moving along as intended.

The first item on the agenda of every weekly team meeting in the school is the record from PIC, so that the concerns about which the faculty cares most are instantly communicated schoolwide. Faculty members react to the decisions and decide how they will be implemented on their team. However, they may also inform their team leader if they cannot live with a particular PIC decision and why. The team leader brings this feedback to the next PIC meeting and at least asks for a reconsideration of the issue.

Life in schools in major urban areas, such as those in Miami/Dade County, Florida, can be challenging, and even the PIC concept can be difficult to implement smoothly. At Campbell Drive Middle School, in Dade County, Florida, the PIC process reflected both the high profile of the teachers union (United Teachers of Dade) and the district's commitment to school-based management. The members of the faculty and administration worked out and agreed to a carefully designed "PIC Contract." Among the provisions of the contract were the following.

1. Attendance is mandatory to vote. One must attend the previous meeting to vote at a current one and must be present the entire meeting.
2. Meetings will follow a formal written agenda; late items will be placed on subsequent agendas.
3. Length of the meetings, to be held after school twice monthly, will be determined by the agenda.
4. The chairperson of the group will be determined by majority vote.
5. The principal has one vote, and no veto—only the right to table a motion.

The process can work beautifully, but not simply or easily. When the process is in place, increased ownership of decisions is frequent. Effectiveness and consistency of implementation are common. Morale improves. Working with young adolescents, a consummately challenging task, takes on a more positive momentum. But shared decision-making can be faked, and it can be fumbled. Authentic, effective, shared decision-making takes both commitment and skill on the part of the leaders and other participants involved (Spindler & George, 1984).

RAISING ACADEMIC ACHIEVEMENT: THE MIDDLE SCHOOL LEADER'S CHALLENGE

In a special supplement titled "Middle Grades: Feeling the Squeeze," the editors of *Education Week* magazine echoed the voices of other contemporary critics by charging that "many middle schools have created shallow, fragmented, unchallenging curricula" (Manzo, 2000, p. 15). Middle school educators, the authors declared, have made real progress in areas such as organizational structure and school climate, and even in the area of differentiating instruction. The authors agreed, however, that little progress had been made in developing a coherent curriculum or in raising academic achievement as measured by standard assessment. Whether or not such a judgment is accurate, the majority of policy-makers and the media accept it.

In the early years of the 21st century, therefore, middle school leadership requires special attention to one particular aspect of the educational program—curriculum and instruction. Standards-based reform, with high-stakes testing and the harsh accountability measures that are part of the process in many states, has compelled school leaders to pay increasingly greater attention to academic achievement as measured by standardized tests. Kaplan and Owings (2001) observed that, by 2000, 49 states had implemented comprehensive programs of standards-based reform, 48 states had testing programs to match state standards, 19 states required students to pass an exam to earn a high school diploma, and 26 states planned to implement tests for high school graduation by 2003. Most of the responsibility for responding effectively to these new and rigorous challenges falls into the lap of the middle school principal, and so instructional leadership has become the central role played by middle school leaders.

With this situation in mind, in the spring of 2000 we conducted a study of 50 middle school principals under pressure to ensure that academic achievement scores went up in their schools. The goal of the study was to identify strategies for raising academic achievement. Ten such strategies emerged. Not every identified strategy was being utilized in every middle school, but as the pressure to improve test scores intensifies, middle school leaders are finding it necessary to use more of these tactics. We share them here because you, too, likely will find yourself in a middle school where raising academic achievement is a high-stakes priority. Our experience in many states convinces us that middle school principals around the nation, under pressure to increase scores on standardized tests, are utilizing similar strategies.

Strategy #1: Utilizing a Breakthrough Planning Process

In schools that seem to be heading toward real improvement with standards, leaders utilize a planning process that focuses, first, on tasks that are urgent, compelling, and immediate—tasks that everyone agrees on. The tasks that are identified in this breakthrough process tend to be those that have a standards-focused goal achievable in weeks, or a few months, not years. The goals of the project tend to have concrete and measurable results, these days most often in terms of success with state standards. The project or tasks are those that the faculty feels ready to accomplish. And the tasks of such breakthrough planning are achievable with available resources and authority. Hard-pressed school leaders know that, rightly or wrongly, they are under pressure to make identifiable progress almost immediately. A series of low school grades could, and does, result in the removal of the principal.

In the schools in our study, breakthrough planning begins with the annual School Improvement Plan and includes a great deal of department involvement and team input—planning, monitoring, and adjusting curriculum, instruction, and programs. This process takes different forms and moves at different paces in the hands of many different leaders. But schools that are making substantial progress are clearly being led by principals who know that standards-based planning cannot be haphazard or spontaneous. They know that they need attention, help, and linkages with the larger school system. They recognize that the work plan must be flexible and visible. They know that they cannot be successful without internal participation, trust, and problem-solving skills and procedures. And they know they cannot do it alone. Consequently, the first steps usually taken by turnaround principals are concerned with strengthening school climate, building faculty cohesiveness, and improving student behavior management.

Strategy #2: Improving School Climate, Faculty Cohesiveness, and Student Behavior Management

In middle schools faced with challenges from standards-based reform, new principals frequently begin the turnaround to higher academic achievement with simultaneous work in two areas. First, they foster faculty cohesiveness—establishing a climate of collaboration and trust. Second, they correct both faculty and public perceptions about the seriousness of purpose regarding implementation of standards-based reform at the school.

Such efforts are almost always undertaken in collaboration with teachers who are team, grade level, or department leaders. The first step is to develop a feeling of cohesiveness and commitment among this small group of leaders and to strengthen their loyalty to school leaders. Eating meals together, attending conferences as a group, and going on weekend retreats are the kinds of things that help develop this sense of community. Reorganizing a school's strategy for decision-making so that greater value is given to the input of these teacher leaders is another way that contributes to the faculty's sense of empowerment and involvement in what is to come. Teacher leaders must be on board before the turnaround train goes farther down the track.

When the principal is convinced that a strong sense of team unity exists within this group, and between the principal and the group, the next steps can be taken. But too little may be accomplished if planning moves forward without first establishing this team spirit. Eventually, the principal and team leaders plan retreats, parties, and other activities that begin to build a sense of community within the faculty as a whole and within groups such as teams, grade levels, and departments. Continued expansion of shared decision-making and faculty empowerment is an important aspect of this strategy. These activities are especially important in low-scoring schools because faculty turnover is often high and morale is frequently very low. In such schools, the effort to build faculty cohesiveness, spirit, and commitment is never over.

After achieving a satisfactory level of faculty cohesiveness, principals can begin to work on faculty members' views of student potential for achievement. Developing committees devoted to examining problem situations is a good step. These committees may begin with efforts to examine data on achievement, student behavior, and other areas. At one school in the process of being turned around, every teacher served on one of three committees in line with the annual School Improvement Plan—safety, staff development, and student performance.

Sometimes, however, a few members of the faculty seem to need more vigorous reminders about the new seriousness of focusing on state standards in a school. Reinstating semester exams, or a new discipline plan, may not be all that is necessary to awaken the most complacent teachers. In the schools one of the authors has visited, leaders, even though they did not enjoy it, spoke of their willingness to go head-to-head with teachers who seemed less than eager to do their part in a renewed school mission.

So, when faculty cohesiveness and school climate improve, and only then, the principal can confidently take additional steps to implement standards-based reform, as evidenced by rising academic achievement. When teachers see that school climate and faculty cohesiveness have begun to change for the better, and that everyone is expected to do their part, their confidence in the principal will encourage them to support additional steps toward standards-based reform in the school. Frequently, the new strategy selected by many principals focuses on the strategic use of school achievement data.

Strategy #3: Strategic Use of School Achievement Data

Adapting the work of G. Edwards Deming and the quality movement from the corporate world (George, 1983), middle school principals have become data-driven organizational leaders. In many schools, virtually every decision that may affect educational outcomes appears to be made only after careful consideration of all relevant information. In the most effective schools, regular and skilled analysis of student achievement data has become a critical step in understanding how to break through the barriers of low achievement and low expectations.

Shared Dissatisfaction   In a number of middle schools, where students have been performing at lower levels on measures of state standards, new principals have been assigned to serve as a catalyst for school improvement. In such schools, teachers have often become discouraged and many believe that their students are not capable of substantial academic improvement. In such circumstances, effective principals have used school achievement data to develop what one leader described as "shared dissatisfaction" among the staff. A principal might, for example, use data from test results at the state and district level to compare with the school level, relying on teachers' pride to help develop a core of teachers ready to work for change. They might use data from the SAT to show that students have more ability than their achievement indicates, helping teachers develop the confidence that the students can do better.

Disaggregating Data   Assessment veterans recommend that principals interested in using data to promote school improvement acquire student performance data disaggregated by race, gender, socioeconomic level, subject, and grade level. The disaggregation of data for different ethnic groups is particularly important in focusing attention on the achievement of minority students, now an essential element of many state accountability programs.

In some middle schools, data from elementary and high school levels are also used to provide guidance to school improvement efforts. Middle school educators use data from elementary schools to adapt grouping, curriculum, and instruction in the first year of middle school. Data from 9th grade assessments are used to analyze the strengths and weaknesses of the 8th grade program regarding successful implementation of standards-based curriculum and instruction.

Some principals hold weekly data analysis meetings with department chairs and team leaders, usually after school hours. Data are shared in department meetings, and then team meetings; eventually it all comes to the School Advisory Council. All of a school's stakeholders are involved in data analysis. This sort of data analysis can help in changing the negative attitudes of discouraged teachers who may be resistant to contributing new increments of energy and time to the change process.

Many schools also have training sessions for parents and school advisory councils to be sure they understand school data and the academic standards, assessment, and accountability that figure in. In many middle schools, everyone is involved in the analysis of achievement related data. A school's effectiveness in achieving educational outcomes is no longer a secret. It is well-publicized news.

Strategy #4: Enhancing Professional Development

Educators have concluded that effective professional development, training that demonstrably connects to standards-based reform, has several crucial qualities. It is based on the strategic use of achievement data; it is data-driven. Student achievement data point out professional development needs for different subject areas, individual schools, and individual teachers.

As a result, a great deal of training focuses on various aspects of state standards and tests. Virtually every district has conducted training regarding the state standards, the accountability program, the theory and implementation of the state test, holistic scoring procedures, and how to model good short-answer and extended response questions. Most districts have offered training on writing test questions, on selecting and using effective test preparation materials, and on how teachers from every subject area can make a contribution to improved scores. For example, science and social studies teachers, in many districts, are receiving training to help them customize class and test questions to the test format. Teachers in all subjects are being trained in how to use the textbooks in their classrooms to teach test skills such as marginal and two-column notes and reading strategies such as visualizing, asking questions, and predicting. Teams in many middle schools are regularly given vocabulary lists of test terms and jargon to infuse in all areas of the subjects on the teams.

Professional development has taken center stage in the effort to improve standards-based reform. Where in-service education was once a casual, even lazy, affair, it now takes on a sense of urgency. The three essential elements of middle school leaders' influence on teacher learning are creating a learning community, exerting instructional leadership, and fostering conditions necessary to support teacher learning.

Where once the content of professional development programs in the state might have ranged across dozens of widely differing topics, the focus is much more sharply on training that will lead unarguably and directly to improved test scores. The biggest change in professional development, however, may have to do with a new and pressing interest in higher order thinking skills for students. Because many new tests focus on application and higher levels of Bloom's taxonomy, middle school leaders are doing everything possible to prepare teachers to gear curriculum and teaching to levels of thinking that go beyond memorization and recall of factual knowledge. Bloom training is everywhere.

Strategy #5: Curriculum Alignment

Curriculum alignment, historically, has been the process of determining that the curriculum that is planned, taught, and tested in the school fits carefully into the goals and priorities of educators, parents, and community members. In today's context, however, curriculum alignment has come to mean a high degree of congruence between state standards, state and national assessments, and what is taught in the classroom. It is certainly not news, and probably not controversial, to identify careful curriculum planning as a crucial part of achievement-oriented middle schools, but in high-achieving schools, the role played by standards-focused planning stands out even more clearly. And the degree to which curriculum alignment has narrowed the curriculum to a strict attention to what appears on standardized assessments has certainly become controversial. The statement "Every activity has been reviewed with regard to how it impacts the test" is, for better or worse, likely to be heard in the majority of middle schools in our study.

School leaders are extremely busy with the monitoring and coaching necessary for effective curriculum alignment. At one middle school, counselors examine each student's schedule for the year to see if he or she is taking enough of a rigorous program. Many students were rescheduled into more rigorous work. In other schools, teachers must include specific plans for preparing for the state test in their lesson plans. New curriculum materials, in many schools, are selected only if they fit state standards and tests.

Observation of classes and monitoring of lesson plans for standards happen far more frequently than outsiders may realize. Department chairs, team leaders, assistant principals, and principals all monitor lesson plans to ensure that standards are addressed. Lesson plans might first be submitted to a team leader or department head who then reports on the team's or department's progress to the principal. In other schools, the principal may be the one who checks lesson plans directly. Some principals use random unannounced classroom visits to check on the lesson plan and whether it focuses on standards. In one school, three administrators are responsible for approximately 16 teacher classroom visits per week.

Departments meet more regularly than in the past, discussing school goals and implementation of standards as critical aspects of curriculum alignment. Teachers meet as teams and departments during the summer to write curriculum for specific target areas, especially mathematics and language arts. District curriculum alignment manuals in mathematics and language arts are common.

Administrators confer frequently and closely with teachers who need help with curriculum alignment. In some districts, school principals then meet monthly with the area superintendent or their direct supervisor to engage in an examination of curriculum alignment at a schoolwide level. So the curriculum alignment process is monitored at several levels.

Strategy #6: Finding Additional Time for Learning

As the pressure for increased test scores grows, creative ways of finding more learning time proliferate. One of the most common, and perhaps least desirable, methods for increasing the amount of time devoted to tested subjects is to decrease the amount of time devoted to those subjects not currently tested. In many schools, exploratory curriculum and advisory programs have been co-opted for basic academic purposes. Science and social studies may suffer.

Other strategies for finding time to devote to academics abound: required reading at home; adopting a block schedule that doubles the amount of daily and yearly time devoted to mathematics; creating an advisory period combining lunch and study hall so that students who need help in particular areas can meet with teachers; counseling students who are identified as low-scoring to substitute an additional mathematics or language arts class for an exploratory course; and canceling science and social studies classes for severely low achieving students whose regular curriculum is suspended until practice skills improve adequately.

School time is being focused more sharply on test preparation in numerous ways. Tutoring, for example, is everywhere; silent reading periods are common. One school replaced an elective class with test strategies for the entire 8th grade. Many schools keep the library open during the summer for the Accelerated Reader program. In one district, the entire month of January is devoted to test preparation for 8th graders, and no other curriculum is taught, no clubs meet. In the same district, throughout the whole year, every Wednesday is devoted to test practice in all three grades. Some schools are initiating a Saturday Academy where students, referred by the counselor, attend with their parents. The state's accountability program funds the academy; high school students come to tutor; and counselors also attend to work with parents.

In one county, all of the middle schools have a 50-minute period daily for what is called ACE—Academic and Curriculum Extension—during which students do remedial work, independent study, additional exploratory, silent reading, and so on. Another county requires a critical thinking elective in all 34 of its middle schools for a full year in 7th and 8th grades. The curriculum includes language arts, organizational skills, and assessment strategies. Several school leaders pay teachers to give their planning time to remediate and to tutor at its Saturday school. Many middle schools have nine weeks of reading required at every grade level, for students of all ability levels. Time, as the resource for increased academic achievement, is being spent much more narrowly in middle schools across the state.

Strategy #7: Implementing Special Standards-Based Curriculum Programs and Instructional Strategies

Middle school curriculum plans for improving accountability outcomes tend to utilize three different sorts of efforts: state-produced, commercial, and local curriculum materials. Many schools use commercial materials or those prepared by the state's department of education designed specifically for new state standards and test preparation. Among commercially produced curriculum programs and materials, several are very popular. CRISS (Creating Independence through Student-owned Strategies) and Accelerated Reader (and

Accelerated Mathematics) are clearly favored by the majority of leaders and teachers. CRISS supports students with a variety of tactics such as webbing, KWL, and other independent study techniques that can be used in many different subject areas. It is not uncommon to visit middle schools and see walls covered with the results of students working with CRISS strategies.

Accelerated Reader is so popular that some schools use it in homeroom every day for 45 minutes. Because students read books appropriate to their identified literacy levels, they can improve and earn recognition without being compared with students who have greater or lesser skills. Motivated students with limited literacy skills can and do make it to the top of the list. It was nearly impossible to visit a middle school in our study without encountering CRISS or Accelerated Reader or both. There are many other popular, mostly computer-based, programs with pretest, prescription, and posttest, often for a whole class.

Other strategies are common. Some are creative, some more straightforward. A school has developed a special Web site with math problems for summer work. In another, students contribute to daily journals based on books they have chosen to read. In the same school, the first 10 minutes of every math class is devoted to solving a math word problem on the board. Students put the problems in their math journal. Once a week, the problem is a state test problem. Students turn in the solved problems on Friday.

Working with scoring rubrics has also become ubiquitous. Virtually every middle school educator understands what a grading rubric is and how it relates to state standards and accountability. Now most students do, too. Teachers use rubrics routinely, in most classes. Many schools hang reading rubric posters in each language arts classroom.

In spite of all of these efforts, troubling questions remain. Is it possible that the majority of middle school teachers continue to rely on lecture, question and answer, and worksheets tied to a textbook that may or may not be aligned with the standards of the state? Are the standards-based efforts undertaken in many schools so highly prescriptive and unimaginative that some of the best teachers are being driven away? How are standards, testing, and the accountability measures influencing the quality of curriculum experiences encountered by students?

Strategy #8: Components of the Middle School Concept

In many middle schools, leaders were quick to point out that they believed that they were able to maintain a healthy middle school program while they attempted to respond to standards-based reform. School leaders claimed that the interdisciplinary team organization of teachers and students is particularly indispensable to the attempt to do so. Teams often meet weekly, sometimes daily, to allow teachers to compare evaluations of student work and to set team standards for consistency.

In one school where test scores have been going up steadily for the last three years, the principal claimed that departments are virtually nonexistent in his school, compared with the importance of teams. He attributed the rapidly rising test scores to the collaborative work that teams of teachers do on the implementation of standards-based curriculum and teaching. In this school, teams constantly meet to explore curriculum together and to find ways of reinforcing each other as regularly and efficiently as possible. In a number of schools, leaders meet formally with teams at the beginning and end of the school year to set goals, discuss growth, and evaluate the year. In others, the continuous presence of new data allows principals to talk with teams about each period's group scores on an almost weekly basis. Without teams, such focused efforts would be difficult, if not impossible. Teams are also at the center of efforts to promote the test, stressing the test by way of contests, brain bowls, and so on. Interdisciplinary teams are clearly much more than a tool for getting to know students better.

The long-term effects of continuing standards-based reform on the middle school concept, however, are not clear. In some schools, educators claim that the middle school concept is the core of their response to these pressures. In other schools, educators claim that the middle school concept has been badly damaged by standards, test pressures, and the accountability program. In these latter schools, educators claim that standards-based reform has disabled teacher-based advisory programs, which have, they claim, become absorbed into the testing effort as additional teaching time. These educators also assert that exploratory curriculum programs have been badly weakened, as schools replace exploratory teachers with additional mathematics and reading teachers and replace exploratory curriculum with additional basic mathematics and reading courses. Ability grouping is seen, in many middle schools, as an indispensable part of the effort to implement standards-based reform, in spite of decades of evidence suggesting the ineffectiveness of such practices.

Strategy #9: Promoting the Test

School leaders are attempting to raise scores by promoting the test. In many schools, students, teachers, and parents are the targets of what are best described as public relations efforts to persuade them of the overwhelming importance of standards and testing and of the contribution each person can make to the school's overall success. Special efforts to motivate students toward improved performance, through incentives, are also common. Finally, efforts to bring community and business partners in to support school achievement have begun to increase.

One school, for example, has a comprehensive recognition program connected with test scores, with different prizes for different levels of achievement. Students get prizes for moving to a higher score level on the test (the school gave out 300 teddy bears) or maintaining a high score. The test identifies five levels of scores, from nonperformance to the highest level, so students at this school who score at the highest level receive a limousine ride to a luncheon destination of the students' choice. "Most improved" students get new bikes. Students with very poor scores can be retained.

In many schools, the daily TV show features a set of math problems, with prizes for completion. In one school, three times a week a student reads a Math Problem of the Day over the public address (PA) system. Homerooms ring the office with their answers and the classrooms with the correct answer are given recognition via the PA. The homeroom with the highest amount of correct answers is given special recognition.

Leaders in a few schools have attempted to reach out to community and business partnerships for support for standards-based reform. Some solicit help from churches, synagogues, mosques, and community organizations to increase family involvement in school. Others conduct outreach meetings at local churches and civic organizations. Leaders in one school left flyers at grocery stores near the school and put them on car windshields. Several schools have developed Web pages containing information about the test, practice tests, and important dates.

Strategy #10: Changing School Leadership Style

Across the country, middle school principals now see themselves as instructional leaders. Everything else is viewed as an irritating distraction from their responsibility for instruction. While the best leaders have always cared deeply about instruction, standards-based reform measures initiated by the state government have mandated this change: Instructional leadership is now a professional survival strategy as well as the desirably central aspect of middle school leadership. Athletic programs, for example, are scarcely noticeable if not totally absent in the language of middle school leaders who now speak with great familiarity regarding state standards, what each teacher in the building is teaching, and how well they are performing.

However, standards-based reform seems to have driven many middle school principals beyond instructional leadership, to an all-consuming preoccupation with academic achievement. This is certainly so in California, Florida, Nevada, North Carolina, South Carolina, and dozens of other states. In many schools today, nothing matters as much as state assessments and the school grades that are attached to the process. Many principals speak candidly about their need to balance the needs of the state and its insistence on academic achievement at any cost, with their own beliefs about education and what is developmentally appropriate for young adolescents. As a consequence, many factors related to achievement aspects of curriculum and instruction (e.g., vision development, teacher training, teacher motivation, modeling important behaviors, and supporting teacher efforts to meet new expectations) have taken on new importance for school leaders.

Concerns about Standards-Based Reforms in Middle Schools

Middle school principals are struggling to meet the challenges of their state's standards-based accountability program, and they are working diligently to raise academic achievement scores in their schools. However, many principals note that, in spite of their best efforts, they believe that the state's standards-based program is deeply flawed and damaging to their best efforts to provide a developmentally appropriate education for their students.

The first and most frequently mentioned concern has to do with what many principals believe to be an exceedingly narrow definition of school success. They see this definition as resulting in an abnormal and inappropriately skewed curriculum plan, one that emphasizes test scores in narrow areas where state standards are tested and excludes much of the remainder of the curriculum required for a balanced educational program. Curriculum based on the felt needs of students is imperiled. Principals lament the sacrifice of advisory programs, exploratory curriculum, integrated curriculum activities, enrichment programs for gifted students, and the downgrading of social studies, science, and foreign language study. They worry about whether their students are receiving an educational experience that is in any way based on the needs of those students.

The second major concern of middle school principals has to do with the tremendous pressure brought on schools, principals, teachers, and students by standards, testing, and school grades. Many principals report that teacher morale has never been lower, especially for 8th grade teachers who believe their jobs are on the line.

In low-scoring schools, those graded "D" and "F" (or the equivalent), many of the best teachers are reported to be leaving as soon as possible for employment in other schools or in other districts. Even in high-scoring schools, principals report that high stress levels have become a major problem for teachers. In one school, for example, a local hospital's free comprehensive physical exams for teachers at its partner middle school determined that 60% of the teachers who were examined exhibited medically high levels of physical and emotional stress—and this was an "A" school.

This says nothing about the stress on students. Recess, physical education, advisory, interdisciplinary, and exploratory courses disappear. Basic curriculum work prevails in all classes, and homework time increases dramatically. Social promotion is ended, without first installing effective alternatives. Simultaneously, the drop-out rates of poor and minority students increase in states where accountability measures are the most punitive. Students do less well in the development of social skills, the rate of obesity increased by 50% in the last decade, and more students are murdering their peers and teachers than ever before.

The third major concern expressed by school principals deals with the perceived inequities of the standards-based reform process as it is unfolding. One administrator expressed it with this example from his district: "School 1 raised its students' scores from the 18th to the 46th percentile, and got an 'F.' School

2 raised its scores from the 51st to the 56th percentile and got $80,000 in bonus money." Another pointed to research that suggests that grades earned by schools are directly correlated to aspects of socioeconomic status: the number of students in the school on free and reduced-price lunch, the percentage of gifted students in the school, the number of students who move during the school year, and the size of the school. One leader expressed his cynicism by asserting that test scores related more closely to the square footage of homes in his school's attendance area than to anything else. Another leader stated that test scores correlated more with the number of students in a school fitted with orthodontia than with other factors.

In many low-performing schools, the regular curriculum has been replaced with test preparation workbooks and other materials that have little value for the student beyond practicing for the tests. Scores may go up in these classrooms, but the academic quality can go down. The result may be a growing, instead of a narrowing, gap between the educational experience of poor, minority students and their majority culture middle-class peers. This is just the opposite of what state accountability systems are supposed to create (McNeil, 2000).

A middle school leader from one large, urban district stated that she believed her state's accountability program had been "a terrible experiment. Students threw up; parents are irate. It destroys everyone's self-esteem and morale, and produces more stress than I have seen in 27 years as an educator." She is not alone in expressing such sentiments.

Only the benefit of hindsight, provided by the vantage point of several years of experience with standards-based reform, will inform educators as to the effects of the program on school leaders, their staff members, students, and parents. Eventually, every member of the American community will all experience the consequences.

OTHER CHALLENGES FOR LEADERS OF THE MIDDLE SCHOOL MOVEMENT

The middle school movement has faced many challenges in the last four decades, with standards-based reform the most recent and tenacious. Many solid accomplishments have been achieved, but many real challenges remain to be faced. In these final pages, we catalogue what we believe those accomplishments and challenges to be.

What the Middle School Movement Has Accomplished

Legend has it that, toward the end of the Constitutional Convention some 200 years ago, Benjamin Franklin was buttonholed on a Philadelphia street corner by a colonial matron as he emerged from the final planning session on the new

Constitution. Running up to Franklin from the center of the crowd milling about in the street, she inquired anxiously, "Well, Dr. Franklin, what have we got?" Franklin replied, "A republic, madam, if you can keep it!"

The implications of Franklin's insightful and prophetic remark are still significant for a crisis society such as America's. Leaders concerned particularly about the quality of schooling for young adolescents in the 21st century must answer two questions: "What is the middle school that now exists?" and "What must be done to keep it as it should be?"

Looking back over the last 40 years, we think that it is safe to say, and immensely satisfying to see, that the people working in the middle school movement have done a wonderful job of maintaining the middle school concept against tremendous odds. The middle school movement is, consequently, the most successful grassroots movement in American educational history. It has stimulated three decades of national focus on the young adolescent, in education, science, medicine, and elsewhere. Local, state, and national organizations such as the National Science Foundation and a dozen others now acknowledge the critical importance for human development of the period surrounding puberty. These youngsters will never again, as Joan Lipsitz once lamented, "grow up forgotten."

Middle level leaders have transformed what was the most stagnant, unproductive, and unsatisfactory level of education, the junior high school, into the most innovative, dynamic, and successful. They have established the middle school as the most long-lasting, comprehensive, and successful innovation in the history of American education. Middle school educators have struck a dramatic new balance between elementary and secondary education, allowing both curriculum and community to count in the educational lives of the students within.

Educators in the middle school movement have arranged a marriage of bigness and smallness that helps schools that are big enough to have a rich and rigorous curriculum still feel small enough for students to be known and cared about. To do so, middle school educators invented almost totally new forms of educational organization: teacher-based advisory programs, interdisciplinary team organization, heterogeneous grouping, looping, schools-within-schools, and others.

They have established an equilibrium between educational equity and opportunities for excellence, awakening at least some Americans to the realization that public schools must be a place where success is available to every student and where no student's education is sacrificed to others whose parents are more available, influential, or articulate.

Middle school educators have helped to stimulate a new energy and enthusiasm for change and improvement at the high school level. The saying goes that imitation is the sincerest form of flattery. Much of the core of contemporary high school restructuring was invented and implemented first at the middle school level. And that fact is deeply and profoundly satisfying to those who endured years of biting criticism and predictions of failure from the very people who now enthusiastically discover the merit of those practices for themselves.

Middle level leaders have helped pioneer a combination of spirited school leadership and authentic involvement of teachers in truly shared governance. The middle school movement has always been a unique coalition of equals focused on the characteristics and needs of the students they share. The National Middle School Association (NMSA), for example, is not a role group such as composed of just principals, or just counselors, or just teachers. It is a group of 25,000 educators concerned about the education of the young adolescent.

The middle school movement that achieved these benchmarks is the only true movement in the history of American education, even though Americans are a nation of major historical movements. A close examination would show that the middle school movement has much in common with the many other areas of American culture that have witnessed movements in the past 40 years. These movements have exerted powerful changes on various phases of the national life: civil rights, women's rights, gay rights, peace movements, religious movements, and the environmental movement. But, with the possible exception of the Progressive education experience in the early 20th century, the middle school movement is it for education—not just now, but ever. The middle school concept is now effectively embedded in dozens of program components in schools in all 50 states, in hundreds of school districts, thousands of schools, and a hundred thousand classrooms. The middle school movement is affecting millions of students, this week.

In the face of all these accomplishments, especially considering what the American society and education system have been through, middle level leaders might be forgiven for thinking that it is time to take it easy, to congratulate themselves and rest on their laurels. However, at this point, you probably recognize that much more needs to be done.

What More Must Be Done?

William Alexander gave the first book on middle school education the title *The Emergent Middle School* (1968) because somehow he understood that the school in the middle would always be facing important challenges. He knew that to be alive as a person or a concept means to change, to always face challenges. Some readers may disagree with our assessment of the challenges that remain. This is acceptable, even necessary, because middle school people have never failed to wrestle with controversial issues. Middle level leaders have never claimed they had the final answer. They insisted, however, that whatever they did had to be developmentally appropriate for older children and younger adolescents. In that spirit of mutual inquiry, we would like to share what we think are the crucial challenges for leaders of the middle school movement in the 21st century.

Urban Middle School Revitalization   The first important challenge to be faced by middle school leaders, for the middle school to be safely secured for the 21st century, is to recognize that many critics have been correct when they say that, after all of this time, in hundreds of so-called middle schools only the name or the grade level has changed. Visits to the majority of America's middle schools would still find that teams function minimally if at all; advisory programs are bankrupt; rigid ability grouping is locked into place; curriculum is anything but integrated; and instruction anything but differentiated.

Most of the research on the status of the middle school concept (McEwin, Dickinson, & Jenkins, 1996) does show that effective implementation of the middle school concept has grown steadily over the last quarter-century. But as of 2002, only half of the schools that are named middle schools demonstrate an effective and comprehensive implementation of the middle school concept. Our own experience is that this is especially true in large, urban school districts.

Over the last three decades, we have had the opportunity to work as consultants in dozens of the largest 150 school districts in America. The unfortunate reality is that one could count the number of exemplary middle schools, in all of those districts, on one hand. The good news is that these large school districts are fertile soil for the revitalization of exemplary middle schools for the new century.

Fortunately, the evidence for the effectiveness of middle school concepts, in urban circumstances, gathered by Robert Felner and others (1997), suggests that such a second effort, perhaps through an organized, high-profile attempt by NMSA to revitalize middle schools in the nation's large school districts, could provide an extremely high return on that initial investment. The work of the Edna McConnell Clark Foundation and the Kellogg Foundation illustrates that it is difficult, but that it can be done. We have had recent and very positive experiences with school districts, for example, in Charlotte-Mecklenburg and Guilford County, North Carolina, and Savannah, Georgia, demonstrating that the energy and resources required to revitalize urban middle schools can be accessed. We urge the next generation of middle school educators to move on to the establishment of high-performing middle schools in the largest urban school districts in America.

The 9th Grade   We urge the next generation of middle school leaders to help to save the 9th grade. The middle school concept has, too often, not been able to fulfill its announced intention to make the transition to high school a smooth and successful experience. The transition to high school has never been more treacherous, and the consequences have never been more personally disastrous for so many. All over America, thousands of 9th graders are and have been painfully failing.

In just one district with which we are familiar, the director of high schools recently estimated that one-third of all of the current 9th graders will fail for the year. In just this district, this means hundreds, perhaps several thousand, students. How many millions of 9th graders in the nation are failing to make enough progress to move to the 10th grade? Will these students conclude that they will not be able to accumulate enough credits to graduate and, so, drop out? The life costs for those students, and for all Americans, are much too high to pay.

Many high school educators in every school district are finally ready to stop blaming middle school educators for not doing the job. Many high school teachers have stopped believing, or at least saying out loud, that the solution to the 9th grade problem is "to keep students at the middle school until they are ready for 9th grade." Many high school teachers have begun to realize that an attitude of "We'll show them they're not in middle school anymore!" is, at the very least, counterproductive.

Perhaps this new mood among high school educators is because many new school and classroom leaders at the high school level have moved there following successful years in good middle schools. We suspect that a group of undercover middle school people may now be beginning to lead American high schools. High school people may not know what they are in for.

High school educators are, nonetheless, eager for the very first time to step up and take responsibility for the success of the 9th graders in their building. Many may be too proud to ask, but they are ready for help, if it can be made available skillfully and tactfully. Visit them, meet with them, and enlist the support of 8th grade parents. Confront and challenge anyone who says that the best way to educate 9th graders is to fail them and watch them drop out. Go to the school board. Insist that the 9th grade be saved. All the good work done in middle schools cannot be permitted to evaporate in the first six weeks of high school.

Middle School Teacher Education   We urge the next generation of middle school leaders to redouble efforts toward the establishment of many more college and university middle school teacher education programs. At one time we believed that first there had to be good middle schools where university students could receive their training. We believed that the profession ought to put its energy into ensuring the emergence of such exemplary middle schools. This strategy was wrong. Much more attention needed to be paid to producing new teachers and school leaders to take the place of the early innovators. The movement badly needed middle school teacher education then, and it is desperately needed now.

Teacher-Based Advisory   The failure of teacher-based guidance, or advisory, programs has too often brought discredit on middle school efforts as a whole. The general public is certainly skeptical of advisory programs. Parents of every stripe continue to question the validity of advisory efforts. In many schools, a majority of the faculty rejects the programs either outright or by the silent sabotage that results from allowing inadequate programs to be implemented. School leaders too rarely and with little fervor act as advocates for advisory programs. A curriculum has never been developed. Those without real experience have frequently trained teachers. Assessment of outcomes has been almost nonexistent.

Yet, we believe that it is impossible to find a successful 9th grade student whose positive experience in high school was not preceded by a warm and positive relationship with at least one middle school teacher. We suspect that readers also believe that nothing is as important as close and caring teacher-student relationships and a warm and supportive group of peers. The attempt to create nurturing relationships through the traditional advisory-advisee (AA) programs except in rare situations, however, has simply failed. Therefore, we urge the next generation of middle school educators to find new ways to make advisor-advisee relationships and programs work well, so well that teachers, parents, and community members acknowledge the centrality of advisory programs to a complete middle school education.

Alternative Grade Configurations   We urge the next generation of middle school leaders to investigate alternative grade configurations for schools educating young adolescents. We do not believe that the middle school envisioned by its pioneers either dictates or is bound, in any way, to a particular grade level, such as the currently popular 6–8 configuration. The original model from *The Emergent Middle School* (Alexander, Williams, Compton, Hines, & Prescott, 1968) was 4–4–4, with the middle level including grades 5–8. In the more than 1,000 middle schools that we have visited over the last 30 years, we have discovered that we can always predict more complete middle school implementation in 5–8 middle schools than in other grade configurations. We want to go further, to go on record as favoring a reexamination of the value of the K–8 school model—what some educators are now calling "ele-middle schools." We would even favor a reexamination of the potential for K–12 schools.

The sacredness of the 6–8 configuration must be questioned, because we believe that the influence of secondary education on the development of true middle schools has all too often been profoundly negative. In spite of recent efforts to reform the high school, in the last 25 years the 6–8 configuration, as did the 7–9 junior high school earlier, has allowed the influence of secondary education's demand for subject specialization to block true middle school restructuring in so many places.

While many exceptions exist, we have found that too many secondary education majors choose to enter the profession not because they love students or love teaching, but because they love their subject discipline. The love of the secondary person for their subject too often dooms them, we believe, to continued disappointment, because they spend their lives with students who do not love that subject as they do. Consequently, we have observed that many secondary people, marooned in a middle school, seem to always be angry with their students, disdainful of the level of sophistication of what they teach, disgruntled with components of the middle school such as advisory and interdisciplinary team organization, and secretly (often not so secretly) wishing they could move to the high school if only they were better prepared in their subject area.

Secondary subject-centered educators have, in innumerable districts, so vigorously insisted on a traditional curriculum taught in traditional ways that it has been impossible to establish anything but large and impersonal teams or traditional high-school-style departments that permit teachers to focus on a single subject. Secondary educators have long refused to let go of the curriculum put in place by the Committee of Ten in 1892, making it difficult, in many schools, to even attempt, let alone succeed in, integrated curriculum, looping, multiage grouping, heterogeneous grouping, differentiated instruction, or alternative assessment. We have, as a result of observing such circumstances for almost four decades, come to believe that in many areas of life beyond education, excessive specialization is the enemy of creativity, growth, vitality, insight, health, strength, and flexibility.

We are persuaded that almost everyone has had experiences with the negative effects of specialization, whether in health care, the government, or business. When was the last time you called a government office or corporate number, or tried to make an airline reservation, and got a human being who made sure your need was met? Excessive size and specialization are too often the bane of quality of life in today's world.

Subject specialization may be necessary at the high school level, but inside the middle school, size and the rigid subject specialization that comes with it have caused endless problems. In spite of wonderfully creative efforts in making big schools feel smaller, the trend toward ever-larger 6–8 middle schools worries us greatly.

Freed of the presence of the traditional secondary school model of specialization, and allied with the person-centered perspective of elementary school educators, the K–8 school could give new energy and freedom to the education of young adolescents. Further, we are convinced that academic achievement scores would be higher in such schools and that student personal development and group citizenship would be more positive.

We believe that, after all is said and done, the character of the human relationship defines the quality of the educational experience for all those involved. As opposed to single grade centers, 5–8, K–8, and K–12 schools have often been able to simultaneously achieve the economy of scale sought by those who favor large schools and maintain the immensely positive quality of personal relationships as a result of the many years that teachers, parents, and students shared the same school. Even now, parochial, private, and university laboratory schools seem to elevate the quality of interpersonal life by making long-term human interaction the rule instead of the rarity. We believe that human beings were intended to spend long periods of time together and that the potential value, for young adolescents, of grade level plans that make possible these long-term relationships must be recognized.

Embrace Diversity   We urge the next generation of middle school leaders to keep the true spirit of the middle school concept alive by continuing to proudly teach and equally serve whoever attends a school. Middle school educators launched the most successful innovation in the history of education because leaders were uniquely willing to put young adolescent students first.

Middle level educators' commitment was to the needs of kids, all the kids, every one of them, and leaders have held unwaveringly to that commitment for 35 years. Middle school leaders have rarely embraced choice, vouchers, charters, or any other method for circumventing the challenge to teach every child well. They have rejected elitist practices in sports and other areas of school life. They rejected the intrusion of inappropriate high school programs and curriculum. They also have rejected the more recent demands of affluent parents to organize and operate the middle school so that their children receive undue attention and inappropriate shares of the school's resources for learning.

The harsh choice for middle school leaders in the years to come will focus on whether, to ensure that a substantial group of affluent majority culture children is retained in the school population, leaders will permit one group of students, those from the upper-middle-class, affluent majority, including the gifted, to gain and retain such a favored foothold on school opportunity and success that schools become divided in the same way society is moving. Middle level leaders reject the idea that Americans' treasured democratic way of life can long exist in communities where a few small islands of plenty dwell amidst a surging, angry sea of poverty, discouragement, and dismay. Neither can middle schools exist for long as leaders have designed them if they have within their walls places where small, endangered islands of educational excellence are surrounded by the sad surging seas of failure.

Leaders have done a wonderful job of designing schools where all students, including the gifted, can be successful. Many districts have made it clear that, even in the most challenging circumstances, schools can be designed to meet the needs of every child, not just the so-called average child.

Wanting to succeed with every child is where it begins. Unfortunately, these efforts may not be good enough. Educators may soon, lamentably, have done everything possible to persuade parents of the affluent to keep their children in the public schools. Affluent parents may demand that educators abandon the commitment to proudly teach and equally serve everyone. Educators may feel pressured to organize what will turn out to be private academies for the gifted and affluent inside middle schools. We hope this will not be done.

We believe that an honest examination of the performance of public schools in general, and middle schools in particular, must conclude that the overwhelming evidence shows that most American schools, not just middle schools, are much better than ever. Consulting the government's long-buried Sandia Report (Carson, Huelskamp, & Woodall, 1992) or Berliner and Biddle's *The Manufactured Crisis* (1995) will demonstrate that academic achievement, as measured by the National Assessment of Educational Progress, as just one example, has been rising steadily every year since the early 1970s. American schools compare much more favorably with schools in other developed nations than the newspaper would have readers believe, and any reasonable comparison between public and private middle schools always shows public schools in a favorable light.

Some schools have problems, for certain, but the problem is not declining test scores, poor teachers, or inadequate school leadership. The problem is plain and simple. The problem is child poverty. The United States has the highest rate of child poverty of any industrialized, developed nation. In 2001 nearly 25% of middle school students lived in poverty, and the statistical correlation between child poverty and academic achievement is .7, which means that virtually everywhere child poverty is found, low academic achievement is also present.

Funding for middle school education varies wildly from state to state and from one district to another within the state. In many states, funding for education ranges from $3,000 to $15,000 per student per year. In many states, the amount of money spent for a student's education in one district can, therefore, be five times as much as in another district in that state. We believe that the promise of an equitable education is a basic civil right in America and that millions of students are being denied that right. That is the problem with these schools.

Sadly, if leaders hold to their commitments, in the next decades the demographic composition of the students who come to their classrooms and schools will more greatly reflect the devastating impact of poverty and the consequences of lives wounded by divorce, scarred by violence, clouded by substance abuse, drowned in discouragement, and condemned to failure. The good news is that middle school educators have demonstrated that they can and will be successful even in the face of such challenges. Teaching young adolescents well has never been easy. Unlike private and parochial schools, and the charter, choice, and voucher schools that will soon be seen in increasing numbers, middle school educators have never dictated what kinds of students can walk through the school doors. Middle school educators have made history by proudly teaching and equally serving whoever comes. Twenty-five years from today, we hope that educators then will say that the middle school movement never compromised on its commitment to socially equitable middle schools, to teach all the children well.

Differentiate Instruction Nothing is more important than the teaching and learning experience, so our last two recommendations for leaders deal with those areas. First, there is the need for differentiated instruction. As research by Robert Felner and his colleagues (1997) indicates, even when a high level of implementation of the middle school concept has been achieved, the teaching and learning experience may still be what Rip Van Winkle would recognize. Middle level educators have done a great job on teaming, have shown good work on the implementation of the integrated curriculum, and have made a stand on heterogeneous grouping.

But in the great majority of classrooms we observed, teaching and learning are still conducted as if the heart of the instructional process consisted of the teacher filling empty vessels with the knowledge from his or her own jar. In most classrooms, in most middle schools, in the early years of the 21st century, the teaching and learning experience is unchanged—oral presentations by the teacher and seatwork by the students dominates many class sessions. In some miracle middle schools such as Brown Barge in Pensacola, teaching and learning have leapt into the new century, but these examples are rare. The new block schedule may help move teachers toward differentiated instruction, but it is too soon to tell.

Good teaching is important to middle level leaders, too, and consequently we are optimistic about the future of classroom instruction. Middle school educators have made positive changes almost everywhere else, except down deep in the daily experience of instruction in the classroom. Because leaders have been able to accomplish all that they have over the last 35 years, we believe that they will find ways to surmount one of the last two barriers to complete implementation of the middle school concept—differentiation of instruction on a regular and widespread basis.

Needs-Based Curriculum Finally, we urge the next generation of middle school leaders to fight to establish a curriculum that is truly based on the living concerns of the youth who experience it. Leaders must not be seduced or intimidated by the cacophony of local, state, and national voices constantly condemning public schools in general and middle schools in particular. Similar voices have always shouted their carping criticisms, and it will always be this way. Middle school leaders are not in a popularity contest. They must follow school board dictates, but they must not surrender to or seek the favor or approval of those who clamor for a singular focus curriculum aligned in lockstep with standardized tests of academic achievement. Such surrender, as tempting as it might be, will not help America keep the middle school it needs.

At the close of the 20th century, a student in Wyoming was beaten and hung on a fence to die because he was gay. A man was dragged to his death in Texas because he was black. A candidate for office was murdered in Tennessee because he was a Democrat. A sniper assassinated a doctor because he was pro-choice. And students in their schools murdered a dozen middle and high school teachers and classmates. There is still too much hatred and not enough tolerance; too much religion and not enough faith; too much greed and not enough charity. Too little attention is being paid to the rage that seems to underlie life in America at the beginning of the 21st century; too much attention to symptoms and blame. And too little energy is being devoted to solving the real problems.

Middle school students most certainly will not learn about these concerns from the curriculum standards and high-stakes tests and punitive consequences now substituting for real curriculum in state after state. A national curriculum will not do it, certainly not one that bows to the influence of the corporate invaders and business interests that seek to control or destroy public schools under the ill-concealed camouflage of so-called local partnerships or state and national committees stacked with those committed to the destruction of the public school system. Reading, writing, and retailing are not the three R's that students need most. A school where all the students learn well the things that do not matter will not be the place William Alexander envisioned.

If middle level leaders allow private corporations to purchase the public school curriculum in exchange for free TV sets, computers, and soda machines, or dinners and retreats for the faculty, they will have turned their backs on the living concerns of youth and mortgaged students' futures and everyone else's. The core of the curriculum must include the truth about the clear-cutting of the national forests, the destruction of the middle class, the collapse of the family, the concentration of wealth in fewer hands, the disappearance of safe tap water after seven decades of corporate pollution, and the investigation of a dozen other topics that are usually censored by local Chambers of Commerce.

Leaders must follow school board policy. Academic achievement as measured by standardized tests is a legitimate objective. Leaders may have to do what they are told. But they do not have to believe it is what students need, and they do not have to stop advocating for more enlightened educational experiences for young adolescents.

We think William Alexander would agree that exemplary middle schools, 25 years from now, must be more than the narrowly focused test score mills they are in danger of becoming. As a group of educators from New York have said, if the emergent middle school is to be retained, middle schools must become exciting places—more like newsrooms, galleries, debating halls, studios, laboratories, field sites, and workshops. Students in such schools would feel connected to other people and supported in taking risks, launching investigations, and thinking independently. They would be engaged in initiating their own projects, assessing their own effectiveness, assisting others, and learning to respect their own work and the work of others.

Teachers in such schools will act more like coaches, mentors, research associates, wise advisors, and guides instead of purveyors of prepackaged, teacher-proof curriculum, lecturers, test administrators, or classroom police. Such teachers will engineer bridges between challenging curriculum and students' unique needs, talents, and characteristics. Such teachers would continue learning because they teach in schools where everyone would be glad to be a student or a teacher—where everyone would want to be, and could be, both.

We know this sounds idealistic. It is. But the middle school movement has been driven by 35 years of idealism. The eight challenges we have identified here are not the only ones. Leaders know there are many more. Middle school leaders once thought there would be a finish line. They believed that once there were no more junior high schools, once interdisciplinary teams were established, once a desegregated student body or an integrated curriculum was in place, the process would be complete. Not so. Clearly, middle school leadership is not finished.

Life-long radical I. F. Stone once wrote, "If you expect an answer to your question in your lifetime, you have not asked a big enough question." If middle school leaders expect to soon cross the finish line now that the 21st century has dawned, maybe they have not set their goals as high as they should.

THE GENERATIVE SCHOOL

Research in the application of systems theory in the world of organizational behavior (Senge, 1990) indicates that schools, as organizations, may come in three types. The Reactive School is a place without spirited leadership and that leadership's vision or involvement, where staff members have no direction or capacity to deal with problems in a systematic way. In difficult periods, life in such schools may be a process of hurtling from crisis to crisis. Principals and teachers feel as if they have no control over their professional lives. Eventually, many, especially those who are deeply committed to education, burn out. Cynicism pervades the school.

In the Responsive School, a visionary leader may help the school to respond more positively because of his or her capacity to see causes and events or because the leader can help the school react to emerging trends. In such schools, the climate is less reactive, life is less crisis-oriented. But a school's capacity to respond is limited by the lack of involvement and the lack of commitment on the part of the staff as a whole. Or a Responsive School may have a systematic approach to solving problems, with a high degree of involvement of teachers and administrators working together collaboratively, but does not have a sense of mission produced by a driving vision of a school based on the characteristics and needs of young adolescents. In such Responsive Schools, problems are solved, but the solutions are likely to be short term. Goals may atrophy. Direction is imposed from outside the school. In such situations, certainly more positive than in a Reactive School, faculties may feel less failure but experience little success. Cynicism may not be all-pervasive, but authentic professional satisfaction may be elusive.

In a Generative School, spirited, visionary leadership combines with authentic involvement to produce a possible future for the school, and for the individuals within it, that engages all staff members. Administrators and teachers possess a shared vision and the skills to make the continuous adjustments and improvements required to progress toward the goals of the school. They feel pride in their short-term accomplishments, energized by their progress, and satisfied with their achievements. The work is hard, the tasks are exhausting, and the challenges are daunting. But everyone knows they are involved in an endeavor that gives meaning and purpose to their lives as educators. This is the exemplary middle school.

CONTENT SUMMARY

Leadership is the critical feature of the exemplary middle school. Two central tasks of middle school leadership are (1) establishing and communicating a vision based on the young adolescent and (2) engaging the faculty in shared decision-making. National movements toward standards-based reform, including harsh accountability measures, have increased the necessity for middle school principals to engage in instructional leadership. Many important challenges remain if the middle school movement is to continue to be the positive force in American education that it has been in the past 40 years.

CONNECTIONS TO OTHER CHAPTERS

Leadership, we believe, is the most important component of the 40-year-old middle school movement. No aspect of the middle school concept can be effectively implemented without skillful, spirited leadership. Therefore, what you have learned in Chapter 10 is related to every other chapter in this book. Leadership affects curriculum (Chapter 3), instruction (Chapter 4), the life of teams (Chapter 6), and the way students are grouped (Chapter 7) and scheduled (Chapter 8). Planning and evaluation (Chapter 9) are impossible without good leadership.

QUESTIONS FOR DISCUSSION

1. How does a middle school leader develop a vision for a school that is authentically based on the characteristics and needs of young adolescents?
2. How can educators from elementary school and high school levels develop a valid vision for the middle school level?

3. What are the risks associated with attempting to implement a shared decision-making process in a middle school? What are the risks associated with failing to implement such a process?

4. How can middle school educators effectively balance the needs for responding to standards-based reform and for maintaining the middle school concept?

5. Which of the challenges identified in this chapter do you consider to be the most important? Why?

6. Is there anything more important to the implementation and maintenance of the middle school concept than effective leadership? Why is this the case?

ACTION STEP

1. Nearly 40 years ago, middle school pioneer John Lounsbury and his colleague Jean Marani (1964) developed a unique tool called the shadow study for an evaluative study of the junior high school. This distinctive brand of action research has been utilized many times since then (Lounsbury & Clark, 1990; Lounsbury & Johnston, 1985; Lounsbury, Marani, & Compton, 1980). On the same day and at the same time, dozens of educators across the nation visited a number of schools, making observations that gave a picture of what was going on in the schools that day.

    If you are working or learning with a group of at least three people, a similar approach might yield interesting insights into the nature of middle school leadership. You might identify a group of leaders in the middle schools of a single district, or you might wish to broaden your investigation to several districts. This might depend on how many observers are involved. One person can also conduct a shadow study of a single middle school leader or of several leaders done over a period of time.

    We recommend that you follow some of these steps. Select the qualities and characteristics of middle school leadership that you wish to look for. Identify a school leader who is willing to have you conduct the study with him or her. Meet with that person to converse about the nature of the study. Arrive early on the day of the study and wait for the leader to arrive at the school. Then spend the entire day with that person. During the day, you could note the activities in which the principal is involved, the persons with whom the principal interacts and the focus of that involvement, the aspects of the middle school concept that are connected to the day, and other pertinent aspects of the leader's role. At the end of the day, conduct a debriefing session with the principal, conversing about the day and asking final questions stimulated by the experience you have had. You may want to submit the final shadow study evaluation to the instructor of the course in which you are enrolled if such is the case.

SUGGESTIONS FOR FURTHER STUDY

Books and Monographs

Blase, J., & Kirby, P. (2000). *Bringing out the best in teachers: What effective principals do* (2nd ed.). Thousand Oaks, CA: Corwin Press.

Glatthorn, A. A. (2000). *The principal as curriculum leader: A guide to leadership* (2nd ed.). Thousand Oaks, CA: Corwin Press.

McEwan, E. (1998). *The principal's guide to raising reading achievement.* Thousand Oaks, CA: Corwin Press.

Seyfarth, J. (1999). *The principalship: New leaders for new challenges.* Upper Saddle River, NJ: Merrill.

Ubben, G. (2001). *The principal: Creative leadership for effective schools* (4th ed.). Boston: Allyn and Bacon.

Periodicals

Calderwood, P. (1999). The decision dance: Staff decision making in a restructuring urban middle school. *Urban Review, 31*(4), 385–417.

George, P. (2001, January). The evolution of middle schools. *Educational Leadership, 58*(4), 40–45.

Felner, R., Jackson, A., Kasak, D., Mulhall, P., Brand, S., & Flowers, N. (1997, March). The impact of school reform for the middle school years. *Phi Delta Kappan, 78*(7), 528–532, 541–550.

Lipsitz, J., Mizell, H., Jackson, A., & Austin, L. (1997, March). Speaking with one voice: A manifesto for middle grades reform. *Phi Delta Kappan, 78*(7,) 533–540.

Livingston, M., Slate, J., & Gibbs, A. (1999, Fall). Shared decision making: Beliefs and practices of rural school principals. *Rural Educator, 21*(1), 20–26.

McNeil, L. (2000, June). Creating new inequalities: Contradictions of reform. *Phi Delta Kappan, 81*(10), 728–734.

Norton, J., & Lewis, A. (2000, June) Kappan special report—middle grades reform. *Phi Delta Kappan, 81*(10), K1–K20.

Sherman, L. (2000, Spring). Sharing the lead. *Northwest Education, 5*(3), 2–10.

Short, P. (1998, Winter). Empowering leadership. *Contemporary Education, 69*(2), 70–72.

ERIC

Anfara, V., Brown, K., Mills, R., Hartman, K., & Mahar, R. (2000). *Middle level leadership for the 21st century: Principal's views on essential skills and knowledge: Implications for successful preparation* (ERIC document ED442205).

Cobb, O., Lindle, J., & Rinehart, J. (1998). *How does a principal use Kentucky's high stakes assessment to monitor and improve student learning?* (ERIC document ED424637).

Correa, J., & Bauch, P. (1999). *Teacher perceptions of parent and teacher participation in shared decision-making* (ERIC document ED438245).

Marsh, D. (1997). *Educational leadership for the 21st century: Integrating three emerging models* (ERIC document ED408699).

O'Donoghue, R., & Ragland, M. (1998). *Collaborative models to promote equity and excellence for all children* (ERIC document ED419877).

Dissertations and Dissertation Abstracts

Bengler, A. (2000). How one middle school began to plan for instruction: An action research journey (Doctoral dissertation, Virginia Polytechnic Institute and State University). *Dissertation Abstracts International,* 61 (06A), 2161.

Demopolous-Roberts, N. (2000). Teachers' and principals' perceptions of principal influence on teacher learning (Doctoral dissertation, University of Florida, 2000).

Richards, P. (2000). Shared decision-making: Principals' facilitative leadership and teacher sense of efficacy (Doctoral dissertation, State University of New York at Albany). *Dissertation Abstracts International,* 61 (06A), 2133.

Kessler, S. (2000). The roles of the principal and teachers in the development of collegiality among a middle school faculty: A case study (Doctoral dissertation, Peabody College for Teachers of Vanderbilt University). *Dissertation Abstracts International,* 61 (06A), 2125.

McLeod, C. (2000). The principal's impact on student achievement through culture-enhanced leadership behaviors (Doctoral dissertation, Clemson University). *Dissertation Abstracts International,* 61 (06A), 2129.

Murphy, C. (2000). Caught in the middle: Surveying school principals' beliefs, stakeholder support, and their actions in school management (Doctoral dissertation, Fordham University). *Dissertation Abstracts International,* 61 (06A), 2131.

Web Sites

National Association of Secondary School Principals
http://www.nassp.com
The National Association of Secondary School Principals (NASSP) is composed of leaders in middle and high school education. Over the years, NASSP has tended to emphasize high school programs, but it has also supported the middle school movement.

Association for Supervision and Curriculum Development
http://www.ascd.com
Association for Supervision and Curriculum Development is the nation's largest group of curriculum development people and general supervisors in schools of all kinds and in school district offices. It offers important resources to middle school educators in the areas of curriculum and instruction.

National Middle School Association
http://www.nmsa.org
National Middle School Association is the nation's largest group of educators devoted to the education of young adolescents. With more than 30,000 members, the association offers an array of services, resources, national conferences, journals, and other support for middle school educators.

References

The Adolescent Years: Sexual Activity (n.d.). *Columbia University College of Physicians and Surgeons.* Retrieved December 27, 2001, from http://cpmcnet.columbia.edu/texts/guide/hmg08_0002.html #8.13.

Alexander, W. (1968). *A survey of organizational patterns of reorganized middle schools* (Cooperative Research Project No. 7–D–026). Washington, DC: U.S. Department of Education.

Alexander, W., & George, P. (1981). *The exemplary middle school.* New York: Holt, Rinehart, and Winston.

Alexander, W., & McEwin, C. K. (1989a). *Earmarks of schools in the middle: A research report.* Boone, NC: Appalachian State University.

Alexander, W., & McEwin, C. K. (1989b). *Schools in the middle: Status and progress.* Columbus, OH: National Middle School Association.

Alexander, W., & Williams, E. (1965). Schools for the middle school years. *Educational Leadership, 23*(3), 217–223.

Alexander, W., Williams, E., Compton, M., Hines, V., & Prescott, D. (1968). *The emergent middle school.* New York: Holt, Rinehart, and Winston.

Allen, L., & McEwin, C. K. (2001). Reinventing middle level teacher preparation via professional development schools. In T. Dickinson (Ed.), *Reinventing the middle school* (pp. 302–320). New York: Routledge/Falmer.

Alper, S. (2001, Fall). *Inclusion: Children who learn together live together.* Retrieved from http://www.uni.edu/coe/inclusion/index.html.

Apple, M., & Beane, J. (1995). *Democratic schools.* Alexandria, VA: Association for Supervision and Curriculum Development.

Arhar, J. (1990). *The effects of interdisciplinary teaming on social bonding of middle level students.* Unpublished manuscript. See also Arhar, J. (1990, July). The effects of teaming on students. *Middle School Journal, 20,* 24–27.

Arnold, J. (1990). *Visions of teaching and learning: 80 exemplary middle level projects.* Columbus, OH: National Middle School Association.

Arnold, J., & Stevenson, C. (1998). *Teacher's teaming handbook: A middle level planning guide.* Fort Worth, TX: Harcourt Brace.

Arnold, W., Silcox, E., & Springer, M. (1998). *Watershed: A whole learning program.* Wayne, PA: Radnor Middle School.

Association for Supervision and Curriculum Development (1954). *Developing programs for young adolescents.* Washington, DC: Author.

Atwell, N. (1987). *In the middle: Writing, reading, and learning with adolescents.* Portsmouth, NH: Boynton/Cook.

Beane, J. (1993). *A middle school curriculum: From rhetoric to reality* (2nd ed.). Columbus, OH: National Middle School Association.

Beane, J. (1996). On the shoulders of giants! The case for curriculum integration. *Middle School Journal, 28*(1), 6–11.

Beane, J. (1997). *Curriculum integration: Designing the core of democratic education.* New York: Teacher's College Press.

Belkin, L. (2000, December 24). The making of an 8-year-old woman. *New York Times Magazine,* 38–43.

Bengston, J. (1996, October). *Draft position paper for initiating program design: An educational view of pre and early adolescent development.* Paper presented to the faculty of the University of Florida, College of Education, Gainesville, FL.

Bennett, D., & King, T. (1991). The Saturn School of Tomorrow. *Educational Leadership, 48*(8), 41–44.

Bergmann, S. (1989). *Discipline and guidance: A thin line in the middle level school.* Reston, VA: National Association of Secondary School Principals.

Berliner, D., & Biddle, B. (1995). *The manufactured crisis: Myths, fraud, and the attack on American public schools.* Reading, MA: Addison-Wesley.

Bishop, P. (2000). Portraits of partnership: The relational work of effective middle level partner teams. *Dissertation Abstracts International, 61* (09A), 171.

Black, S. (2001). Ask me a question: How teachers use inquiry in a classroom. *American School Board Journal, 188*(5), 43–45.

Blase, J. (1990). Some negative effects of principle's control-oriented and protective political behavior. *American Educational Research Journal, 27*(4), 727–753.

Boyd, J. (2000). The nature of interdisciplinary organization on two teams at W. T. Chipman Middle School. *Dissertation Abstracts International, 61* (03A), 203.

Bradley, A., & Manzo, K. (2000, October 4). The weak link: In today's standards-driven environment, the middle grades are under pressure—and ill-equipped to deliver. *Education Week,* 3–8.

Branigan, C. (2001a, May). Research team develops free software for handhelds. *eSchool News, 4,* 24.

Branigan, C. (2001b, May). School districts in five states are first to get Internet2. *eSchool News, 4,* 10.

Brevino, M., Snodgrass, D., Adams, K., & Dengel, J. (1999). *An educator's guide to block scheduling.* Boston: Allyn and Bacon.

Brimfield, R., Masci, F., & DeFiore, D. (2002). Differentiating instruction: Teaching to all learners. *Middle School Journal, 33*(3), 14–18.

Brooks, J., & Brooks, M. (1993). *In search of understanding: The case for constructivist classrooms.* Alexandria, VA: Association for Supervision and Curriculum Development.

Brooks, K., & Edwards, F. (1978). *The middle school in transition: A research report on the status of the middle school movement.* Lexington, KY: University of Kentucky, College of Education.

Brophy, J. (1979). Teacher behavior and student learning. *Educational Leadership, 37*(1), 33–38.

Brophy, J., & Good, T. (1986). Teacher behavior and student achievement. In Wittrock, M., *Handbook of research on teaching* (3rd ed.). New York: Macmillan.

Buckner, J., & Bickel, F. (1990). *Teaching in the middle: Given 'em what they want while providing what they need.* Paper presented at the annual conference of the National Middle School Association, Long Beach, CA.

Burns, J. (1996, Fall). The five attributes of satisfying advisories. *New England League of Middle Schools Journal.* Retrieved December 18, 2001, from http://www.vla.com/idesign/attributes2.html.

Bush, G. W. (2001). *No child left behind: Communication from the President of the United States transmitting a report for nationwide education reform entitled: No child left behind.* Washington, DC: U.S. Government Printing Office.

Bushnell, D. (1992). *Middle school teachers as effective advisors: Student and teacher perceptions.* Unpublished doctoral dissertation, University of Florida, Gainesville.

Caissy, G. (1994). *Early adolescence: Understanding the 10 to 15 year old.* New York: Plenum Press.

Canady, R. L., & Rettig, M. (1996). Models of block scheduling. *The School Administrator, 53*(8), 14.

Canter, L., & Canter, M. (1976). *Assertive discipline: A take-charge approach for today's educator.* Seal Beach, CA: Lee Canter and Associates.

Carnegie Council on Adolescent Development (1989). *Turning points: Preparing youth for the 21st century.* New York: Carnegie Corporation of New York.

Carnegie Council on Adolescent Development (1996). *Great transitions: Preparing adolescents for a new century.* New York: Carnegie Council on Adolescent Development.

Carroll, J. M. (1990). The Copernican Plan: Restructuring the American high school. *Phi Delta Kappan, 71*(5), 358–365.

Carroll, J. M. (1994). The Copernican Plan evaluated: The evolution of a revolution. *Phi Delta Kappan, 10*(2), 105–113.

Carson, C. C., Huelskamp, R. M., & Woodall, T. D. (1992, April). Perspectives on education in America (The Sandia Report). Reprinted in the *Journal of Educational Research, 86*(5), 259–310.

Cawelti, G. (1989). Designing high schools for the future. *Educational Leadership, 47*(5), 30–35.

Clemetson, L. (2000, May 8). Color my world: The promise and perils of life in the new multiracial mainstream. *Newsweek,* 70–74.

Cobb, N. (2001). *Adolescence: Continuity, change, and diversity* (4th ed.). Mountain View, CA: Mayfield.

The College Board (2001). *Florida Partnership.* Retrieved from http://www.college-board.org/floridapartnership/about/index000.html.

Connackamack Middle School (2001). *Program goals—Connackamack Middle School.* Retrieved on December 19, 2001, from http://www.myschoolonline.com/page/0,1871,34749-36934-38-55954,00.html.

Conners, N., & Gill, J. (1991, March/April). Middle-schoolness and the federal school recognition program. *T.E.A.M.: The Early Adolescent Magazine, 4,* 44–48.

Costa, A. (1995). Process is as important as content. *Educational Leadership, 52*(6), 23.

Cotton, N. (1985). The development of self-esteem and self-esteem regulation. In J. Mack & S. Ablon (Eds.), *The development and sustaining of self-esteem in childhood* (pp. 122–150). New York: International Universities Press.

Crow, G., & Pounder, D. (2000). Interdisciplinary teams: Context, design, and process. *Educational Administration Quarterly, 36*(2), 216–254.

Cuban, L., Kirkpatrick, H., & Peck, C. (2001). High access and low use of technologies in high school classrooms: Explaining an apparent paradox. *American Educational Research Journal, 38*(4), 813–834.

Cuff, W. (1967). Middle schools on the march. *NASSP Bulletin, 51*(40), 82–86.

Daniels, H., & Bizar, M. (1998). *Methods that matter: Six structures for best practice classrooms.* York, ME: Stenhouse Publishers.

DeLauro, R. (2000). *Congresswoman Rosa L. DeLauro, press release.* Retrieved on December 19, 2001, from http://www.house.gov/press/2000/ed_values_event_9-12-00.html.

Dental, K., & George, P. (1999, Spring). Survey of block scheduling in Florida middle schools. *Journal of the Florida League of Middle Schools, 2*(1), 3–24.

Department of Special Education (1975). *Instructional settings for exceptional children: A continuum of services.* Unpublished manuscript, University of Florida, Gainesville.

de Rosenroll, D. A. (1987, Winter). Early adolescent egotism: A review of six articles. *Adolescence, 22,* 791–802.

Dickens, W., Kane, T., & Schultze, C. (1995). Does "The Bell Curve" ring true? *Brookings Review, 13*(3), 18.

Dickinson, T. (Ed.). (2001). *Reinventing the middle school.* New York: Routledge/Farmer.

Dickinson, T., & Erb, T. (1997). *We get more than we give: Teaming in middle schools.* Columbus, OH: National Middle School Association.

Doda, N. (1976). Teacher to teacher. *Middle School Journal, 7*(3), 9.

Doda, N. (1979). *Advisor-advisee and high school preparation: An evaluation report on student perception.* Mimeograph, University of Florida, Gainesville.

Doda, N., & George, P. (1999). Building whole middle school communities: Closing the gap between exploratory and core. *Middle School Journal, 30*(5), 32–39.

Dodge, B. (1995). WebQuests: A technique for Internet-based learning. *Distance Educator, 1*(2), 10–13.

Doherty, K. (2001, January 11). Poll supports standards—with hesitation. *Education Week,* 20.

Dryfoos, J. G. (1990). *Adolescents at risk: Prevalence and prevention.* New York: Oxford University Press. Quoted in R. Roeser, J. Eccles, & A. Sameroff (2000). School as a context of early adolescents' academic and social-emotional development: A summary of research findings. *Elementary School Journal, 100*(5), 443–471.

Duke, B. (1986). *The Japanese school.* New York: Praeger.

Eccles, J., Lord, S., & Midgely, C. (1991). What are we doing to early adolescents? The impact of educational contexts on early adolescents. *American Journal of Education, 99*(4), 521–542.

Eccles, J. S., & Midgely, C. (1989). Stage—Environment fit: Developmentally appropriate classrooms for young adolescents. In R. Ames & C. Ames (Eds.), *Research on motivation in education. Vol. 3. Goals and cognitions* (pp. 139–186). Orlando, FL: Academic Press.

Education Update (2001). Passages to learning. *Education Update, 43*(7), 1, 3, 6.

Eichhorn, D. (1966). *The middle school.* New York: Center for Applied Research in Education.

Elkind, D. (1981). *The hurried child.* Reading, MA: Addison-Wesley.

Elkind, D. (1984). *All grown up and no place to go: Teenagers in crisis.* Reading, MA: Addison-Wesley.

Epstein, J. L. (1990). What matters in the middle grades—grade span or practices? *Phi Delta Kappan, 71*(6), 438–444.

Erb, T. (2000). Do middle school reforms really make a difference? *Clearing House, 73*(4), 521–542.

Erb, T., & Dickinson, T. (1997). The future of teaming. In T. Dickinson & T. Erb (Eds.), *We get more than we give: Teaming in middle schools* (pp. 525–540). Columbus, OH: National Middle School Association.

Erb, T., & Doda, N. (1989). *Team organization: Promises—practices and possibilities.* Washington, DC: National Education Association.

Erikson, E. H. (1963). *Childhood and society* (2nd ed.). New York: Norton.

Erikson, E. H. (1968). *Identity, youth and crisis.* New York: Norton.

Eson, M. E., & Walmsley, S. A. (1980). Promoting cognitive and psycholinguistic development. In Johnson, M. (Ed.), *Toward adolescence: The middle school years; Seventy-ninth yearbook of the National Society for the Study of Education, Part I.* Chicago: University of Chicago Press.

Feldman, S., & Eliott, G. (Eds.) (1990). *At the threshold: The developing adolescent.* Cambridge, MA: Harvard University Press.

Felner, R., Jackson, A., Kasak, D., Mulhall, P., Brand, S., & Flowers, N. (1997). The impact of school reform for the middle years: Longitudinal study of a network engaged in *Turning Points*–based comprehensive school transformation. *Phi Delta Kappan, 78*(7), 528–532, 541–550.

Feuerstein, R., & Kozulin, A. (1995). "The Bell Curve": Getting the facts straight. *Educational Leadership, 52*(7), 71–74.

Florida Department of Education (n.d.). *Sunshine state standards: Grades 6–8.* Tallahassee, FL: Department of Education.

Flowers, N. (2000). What makes interdisciplinary teams effective? Research on middle school renewal. *Middle School Journal, 31*(4), 53–56.

Forte, I., & Schurr, S. (1994). *Interdisciplinary units and projects for thematic instruction for middle grade success.* Nashville, TN: Incentive Press.

Fraser, S. (Ed.) (1995). *The bell curve wars: Race, intelligence, and the future.* New York: Basic Books.

Frost, R., Olson, E., & Valiquette, L. (2000). The wolf pack: Power shared and power earned—building a middle school nation. *Middle School Journal, 31*(5), 30–36.

Furtwengler, W. (1991). *Reducing student misbehavior through student involvement in school restructuring processes.* Paper presented at the conference of the American Educational Research Association, Chicago, IL.

Galassi, J., Gulledge, S., & Cox, N. (1997). Middle school advisories: Retrospect and prospect. *Review of Educational Research, 67*(3), 301–338.

Galassi, J., Gulledge, S., & Cox, N. (1998). *Advisory: Definitions, descriptions, decisions, directions.* Columbus, OH: National Middle School Association.

Gallagher, J. (1999, February). Teaching in the block: Flexible scheduling helps staffs repackage the school day. *Middle Ground, 2*(3), 10–15.

Gamoran, A., & Berends, M. (1987). The effect of stratification is secondary schools: Synthesis of survey and ethnographic research. *Review of Educational Research, 57*(4), 415–435.

Gamoran, A., & Weinstein, M. (1998, May). Differentiation and opportunity in restructured schools. *American Journal of Education, 106*(3), 385–431.

Gardner, H. (1983). *Frames of mind: The theory of multiple intelligences.* New York: Basic Books.

Gardner, H. (1991). *The unschooled mind: How children learn and how schools should teach.* New York: Basic Books.

Gardner, H. (1993). *Multiple intelligences: The theory in practice.* New York: Basic Books.

Garrod, A., Smulyan, L., Powers, S. I., & Kilkenny, R. (1992). *Adolescent portraits: Identity, relationships and challenges.* Needham Heights, MA: Allyn and Bacon.

Garvin, J. (1987). What do parents expect from middle level schools? *Middle School Journal, 19*, 3–4.

Gately, S., & Gately, F. (2001). Understanding co-teaching components. *Teaching Exceptional Children, 33*(4), 40–47.

George, P. (1980). Discipline, moral development, and levels of schooling. *Educational Forum, 45*(1), 57–67.

George, P. (1982). Interdisciplinary team organization: Four operational phases. *Middle School Journal, 3*(4), 10–13.

George, P. (1983). *The "theory z" school.* Columbus, OH: National Middle School Association.

George, P. (1987). Teambuilding without tears. *Personnel Journal, 66*(11), 122–129.

George, P. (1988). Tracking and ability grouping: Which way for the middle school? *Middle School Journal, 20*(1), 21–28.

George, P. (1989). *The Japanese junior high school.* Columbus, OH: National Middle School Association.

George, P. (1999, Spring). Survey of block scheduling in Florida middle schools. *Florida League of Middle Schools Journal, 2*(1), 3–25.

George, P. (2000, December/2001, January). The evolution of middle schools. *Educational Leadership, 58*(4), 40–44.

George, P., & Alexander, W. (1993). *The exemplary middle school* (2nd ed.). Fort Worth, TX: Harcourt Brace.

George, P., & Anderson, W. G. (1989). Maintaining the middle school: A national survey. *NASSP Bulletin, 73*(521), 67–74.

George, P., & Dow, J. (1997). The building blocks of school reform: An investigation into the use of block scheduling in Florida. *Research Bulletin, 24*(1–2).

George, P., Lawrence, G., & Bushnell, D. (1998). *Handbook for middle school teaching* (2nd ed.). New York: Longman.

George, P., & Lounsbury, J. (2000). *Making big schools feel small.* Columbus, OH: National Middle School Association.

George, P., & McEwin, K. (1999). High schools for a new century: Why is the high school changing? *NASSP Bulletin, 83*(606), 10–25.

George, P., McEwin, K., & Jenkins. J. (2000). *The exemplary high school.* Fort Worth, TX: Harcourt Brace.

George, P., & Oldaker, L. L. (1985). *Evidence for the middle school.* Columbus, OH: National Middle School Association.

George, P., Renzulli, J., & Reis, S. (1997). *Dilemmas in talent development: Two views.* Columbus, OH: National Middle School Association.

George, P., & Shewey, K. (1994). *New evidence for the middle schoool.* Columbus, OH: National Middle School Association.

George, P., & Stevenson, C. (1989). The "very best teams" in the "very best" middle schools as described by middle school principals. *T.E.A.M., 3*(1), 6–17.

George, P., Weast, J., Jones, L., Priddy, M., & Allred, L. (2000, January). Revitalizing middle schools: The Guilford County process. *Middle School Journal, 31*(3), 3–10.

George, P. (with Evan George). (1995). *The Japanese secondary school: A closer look.* Columbus, OH: National Middle School Association.

Gilardino, N. (2000, April). The magic of mini-courses. *Middle Ground, 3*(5), 36–37.

Gilligan, C. (1982). *In a different voice: Psychological theory and women's development.* Cambridge, MA: Harvard University Press.

Glasser, W. (1965). *Reality therapy: A new approach to psychology.* New York: Harper and Row.

Glasser, W. (1972). *The identity society.* New York: Harper and Row.

Glasser, W. (1985). *Control theory.* New York: Harper and Row.

Glasser, W. (1990). *The quality school: Managing students without coercion.* New York: Harper and Row.

Glickman, C. (2001). Holding sacred ground: The impact of standardization. *Educational Leadership, 58*(4), 46–51.

Goldberg, M. (2001). A concern with disadvantaged students: An interview with Harry Levin. *Phi Delta Kappan, 821*(8), 632–634.

Goleman, D. (1995). *Emotional intelligence.* New York: Bantam Books.

Good, T., & Brophy, J. (2000). *Looking in classrooms* (8th ed.). New York: Longman.

Goodenow, C., & Espin, O. M. (1993). Identity choices in immigrant adolescent females. *Adolescence, 28*(109), 173–184.

Greeson, L., & Williams, R. (1986). Social implications of music videos for youth. *Youth and Society, 18*(2), 177–189.

Gruhn, W., & Douglas, H. (1947). *The modern junior high school.* New York: Ronald Press.

Hackman, D. G., & Valentine, J. W. (1998). Designing an effective middle level schedule. *Middle School Journal, 29*(5), 3–13.

Hall, G., & Hord, S. (1987). *Change in schools: Facilitating the process.* Albany, NY: State University Press.

Hamdy, M., & Urich, T. (1998). Principals' perceptions of block scheduling. *American Secondary Education, 26*(3), 8–12.

Hardy, L. (2000, September). The trouble with standards. *ASBJ.com.* Retrieved from http://www.asbj.com/2000/09/09coverstory.html.

Hartzler, D. (2000). A meta-analysis of studies conducted on integrated curriculum programs and their effects on student achievement. *Dissertation Abstracts International,* A, 61 (03).

Havighurst, R. J. (1972). *Developmental tasks and education.* New York: David McKay.

Hechinger, F. M. (1992). *Fateful choices: Healthy youth for the 21st century.* New York: Hill and Wang.

Heistad, D. (1999, April 19–23). *Teachers who beat the odds: Value-added reading instruction in Minneapolis 2nd grade classrooms.* Paper presented at the annual meeting of the American Educational Research Association, Montreal, Canada.

Herrnstein, R. (1973). *I.Q. in the meritocracy.* Boston: Little, Brown, and Co.

Herrnstein, R., & Murray, C. (1995). *The bell curve: Intelligence and class structure in America.* New York: Free Press.

Hirsch, E. D. (1987). *Cultural literacy: What every American needs to know.* Boston: Houghton Mifflin.

Hodgkinson, H. (2001). Educational demographics: What teachers should know. *Educational Leadership, 58*(4), 6–11.

Honig, W. (1987). Foreword. In Superintendent's Middle Grade Task Force, *Caught in the middle: Educational reform for young adolescents in California public schools.* Sacramento: California State Department of Education.

Hoverstein, C., Doda, N., & Lounsbury, J. (1991). *Treasure chest: A teacher advisory source book.* Columbus, OH: National Middle School Association.

Hunter, M. (2000, June). *Applied education reform: Observations and lessons from the business community.* Paper presented at the annual leadership conference of the Florida League of Middle Schools, Marco Island, FL.

Husband, R. (1994). Teacher empowerment in departmental and interdisciplinary team middle-level education programs. *Dissertation Abstracts International,* 55 (10A).

Ianni, F. A. J. (1989). Providing a structure for adolescent development. *Phi Delta Kappan, 70*(9), 673–682.

Jackson, A., & Davis, G. (2000). *Turning points 2000: Educating adolescents in the 21st century.* New York: Teachers College Press.

Jacobsen, D., Eggen, P., & Kauchak, D. (2002). *Methods for teaching: Promoting student learning.* Upper Saddle River, NJ: Merrill/Prentice Hall.

Jensen, A. (1969). How much can we boost IQ and scholastic achievement? *Harvard Education Review, 69*(39), 1–123.

Johnson, D., & Johnson, R. (1989). *Leading the cooperative school.* Edina, MN: Interaction Book.

Johnson, D., Johnson, R., & Holubec, E. (1998). *Cooperation in the classroom* (7th ed.). Edina, MN: Interaction Book.

Johnston, H. (2001). *From advisory programs to restructured adult-student relationships: Restoring purpose to the guidance function of the middle level school.* Retrieved on December 18, 2001, from http://www/middleweb.com/johnston.html.

Jones, F. (1987). *Positive classroom discipline.* New York: McGraw-Hill.

Joyce, B., Weil, M., & Calhoun, E. (2000). *Models of teaching* (6th ed.). Boston: Allyn and Bacon.

Kagan, S. (1994). *Cooperative learning.* San Juan Capistrano, CA: Kagan Cooperative Learning.

Kain, D. (1998). Teaming in the middle school: A review of recent literature. In P. S. Hlebowitsh & W. G. Wraga (Eds.), *Annual review of research for school leaders 1998* (pp. 51–75). New York: Simon and Schuster, Macmillan.

Kanter, R. M. (1983). *The change masters: Innovation for productivity in the American corporation.* New York: Simon and Schuster.

Kaplan, L. S., & Owings, W. (2001). How principals can help teachers with high-stakes testing: One survey's findings with national implications. *NASSP Bulletin, 85*(622), 15–23.

Kearns, D., & Harvey., J. (2000). *A legacy of learning: Your stake in standards and new kinds of public schools.* Washington, DC: Brookings Institution Press.

Kilgore, K., Griffin, C., Sindelar, P., & Webb, R. (2002). Restructuring for inclusion: Changing teaching practices (Part 2). *Middle School Journal, 33*(3), 7–13.

Knowles, T., & Brown, D. (2000). *What every middle school teacher should know.* Portsmouth, NH: Heineman.

Kohlberg, L. (1981). *The philosophy of moral development: Moral stages and the idea of justice.* San Francisco: Harper and Row.

Kohn, A. (1986). *No contest: The case against competition.* Boston: Houghton Mifflin.

Kohn, A. (1991). Caring kids: The role of the school. *Phi Delta Kappan, 72*(7), 496–506.

Kohn, A. (1998). Only for *my* kid: How privileged parents undermine school reform. *Phi Delta Kappan, 79*(8), 569–577.

Kohn, A. (2000). *The case against standardized testing: Raise the scores, ruin the schools.* Portsmouth, NH: Heineman.

Kolstad, B., Wilkinson, M., & Briggs, L. (1997, Spring). Inclusion programs for learning disabled students in middle schools. *Education, 117*(3), 419–427.

Kozol, J. (1991). *Savage inequalities: Children in America's schools.* New York: Crown.

Lee, V., & Smith, J. (1999, Winter). Social support and achievement for young adolescents in Chicago: The role of school academic press. *American Educational Research Journal, 36*(4), 907–945.

Lenssen, S., Doreleijers, T., Van Dijk, M., & Hartman, C. (2000). Girls in detention: What are their characteristics? *Journal of Adolescence, 23*(3), 287–303.

Levinson, D. (1978). *Seasons of a man's life.* New York: Balantine Books.

Lewis, A. (1999). *Figuring it out: Standards-based reform in urban middle grades.* New York: Edna McConnell Clark Foundation.

Lindsay, D. (2000, April 5). Contest. *Education Week,* 30–37.

Lipsitz, J. (1980). The age group. In M. Johnson (Ed.), *Toward adolescence: The middle school years: Seventy-ninth yearbook of the National Society for the Study of Education, Part 1.* Chicago: University of Chicago Press.

Lipsitz, J. (1984). *Successful schools for young adolescents.* New Brunswick, NJ: Transaction Books.

Lipsitz, J., Mizell, H., Jackson, A., & Austin, L. (1997). Speaking with one voice: A manifesto for middle-grades reform. *Phi Delta Kappan, 78*(7), 533–540.

Liu, J., & Dye, J. F. (1998). Teacher and student attitudes toward block scheduling in a rural school district. *American Secondary Education, 26*(3), 1–7.

Lounsbury, J., & Clark, D. (1990). *Inside eighth grade: From apathy to excitement.* Reston, VA: National Association of Secondary School Principals.

Lounsbury, J., & Johnston, H. (1985). *How fares the ninth grade?* Reston, VA: National Association of Secondary School Principals.

Lounsbury, J., & Marani, J. (1964). *The junior high school we saw: One day in the eighth grade.* Washington, DC: Association for Supervision and Curriculum Development.

Lounsbury, J., Marani, J., & Compton, M. (1980). *The middle school in profile: A day in the seventh grade.* Columbus, OH: National Middle School Association.

Luker, R., & Johnston, J. (1988). TV and teens: Television in adolescent social development. *Social Education, 52*(5), 350–353.

Lynch, J. (1990). *Evaluation report for Skowhegan Area Middle School.* Skowhegan, ME: School District #54.

MacIver, D. (1990). Meeting the needs of young adolescents: Advisory groups, interdisciplinary teaching teams, and school transition programs. *Phi Delta Kappan, 71*(6), 458–464.

Mallery, J., & Mallery, J. (1999, Fall). The American legacy of ability grouping: Tracking reconsidered. *Multicultural Education, 7*(1), 13–15.

Manzo, K. (2000, October 4). Missed opportunities. *Education Week,* 15–19.

Maryland Task Force on the Middle Learning Years (1989). *What matters in the middle grades: Recommendations for Maryland middle grades education.* Baltimore: Maryland State Department of Education.

Marzano, R., Pickering, D., & Pollock, J. (2001). *Classroom instruction that works: Research-based strategies for increasing student achievement.* Alexandria, VA: Association for Supervision and Curriculum Development.

McEwin, C., Dickinson, T., & Jenkins, D. (1996). *America's middle schools: Practices and progress—A 25 year perspective.* Columbus, OH: National Middle School Association.

McLeland, Bradley. (2001). *Block scheduling and academic achievement.* Unpublished doctoral dissertation, University of Florida, Gainesville.

McNeil, L. (2000, June). Creating new inequalities: Contradictions of reform. *Phi Delta Kappan, 81*(10), 728–735.

Meier, D. (2000). *Will standards save public education?* Boston: Beacon Press.

Mercer, C., & Mercer, A. (2001). *Teaching students with learning problems* (6th ed.). Upper Saddle River, NJ: Merrill Prentice Hall.

Middle Grades Task Force (2001). *Taking center stage: A commitment to standards-based education for California's middle grades students.* Sacramento: California Department of Education.

Miller, B. (1980). *Achievement of ninth grade students in science curricula emphasizing concrete and formal reasoning.* Unpublished doctoral dissertation, University of Florida, Gainesville.

Mills, G. (1961). The how and why of public schools. *Nation's Schools, 68,* 6.

Mistretta, G. M., & Polansky, H. B. (1997). Prisoners of time: Implementing a block schedule in the high school. *NASSP Bulletin, 81*(593), 23–31.

Mizell, H., & Gonzalez, E. (1991). *Disadvantaged youth: Program update.* New York: Edna McConnell Clark Foundation.

Murphy, J. (1965). *Middle schools.* New York: Educational Facilities Laboratories.

National Association for Core Curriculum (2000). *A bibliography of research on the effectiveness of block-time, core, and interdisciplinary team teaching programs.* Kent, OH: Author.

National Center for Education Statistics (1997, September). *Elementary and secondary school districts: Common core of data survey.* Washington, DC: U.S. Department of Education.

National Commission on Excellence in Education (1983, April 27). An open letter to the American people; A nation at risk: The imperative for educational reform. Washington, DC: U.S. Government Printing Office.

National Forum to Accelerate Middle-Grades Reform (2001). *Developmental Responsiveness.* Retrieved on December 18, 2001, from a site created by the Education Development Center with funding from the Edna McConnell Clark Foundation. Available at http://www.schoolstowatch.org/criteria/develp.html.

National Middle School Association (1977). Report of the NMSA Committee on Future Goals and Directions. *Middle School Journal, 8*(3), 16.

National Middle School Association (1991). *Position statement: Preliminary draft.* Columbus, OH: Author.

National Middle School Association (1995). *This we believe.* Columbus, OH: Author.

Norton, J., & Lewis, A. (2000). Middle grades reform. *Phi Delta Kappan, 81*(10), k1–k20.

Oakes, J. (1985). *Keeping track: How schools structure inequality.* New Haven: Yale University Press.

Oliner, P. M. (1986). Legitimating and implementing prosocial education. *Humboldt Journal of Social Relations, 13,* 391–410.

Osterman, K. (2000). Students' need for belonging in the school community. *Review of Educational Research, 70*(3), 323–368.

Packard, V. (1972). *A nation of strangers.* New York: David McKay.

Perkins, D. (1999). The many faces of constructivism. *Educational Leadership, 57*(3), 6–11.

Perkins, T., Snider, C., & Bussaberger, M. (1998, November 6). *Catch the team spirit: Restructuring the middle school counselor's role.* Paper presented at the annual conference of the National Middle School Association, St. Louis, MO.

Peshkin, A., & White, C. J. (1990). Four African-American students: Coming of age in a multi-ethnic high school. *Teachers College Record, 92*(1), 21–38.

Peterson, J. (1991). *A post occupancy evaluation: Wakulla Middle School.* Master's project, Florida A & M University, School of Architecture, Tallahassee, FL.

Piaget, J. (1977). *The essential Piaget.* New York: Basic Books.

Pickler, G. (1991). *IMPACT: The Orange County middle school advisement program.* Unpublished manuscript.

Plodzik, K., & George, P. (1989). Interdisciplinary team organization. *Middle School Journal, 20*(5), 15–19.

Public Agenda (1997). *Getting by: What American teenagers really think about their schools.* New York: Author.

Pulliam, J., & Van Patten, J. (1995). *History of education in America.* Englewood Cliffs, NJ: Prentice Hall.

Putbrese, L. (1989). Advisory programs at the middle level—the student's response. *National Association of Secondary School Principals Bulletin, 73*(584), 514.

Renzulli, J. (2001). Academies of inquiry and talent development (Part 2). *Middle School Journal, 32*(3), 7–14.

Rettig, M., & Canady, R. L. (1996). All around the block: The benefits and challenges of a non-traditional school schedule. *The School Administrator, 53*(8), 8–14.

Reynolds, M. (1962). A framework for considering some issues in special education. *Exceptional Children, 28,* 368.

Rice, D., & Zigmond, N. (2000). Co-teaching in secondary classrooms. *Learning Disabilities: Research and Practice, 15*(4), 190–197.

Roberts, P., & Kellough, R. (2000). *A guide for developing interdisciplinary thematic units* (2nd ed.). Columbus, OH: Merrill.

Roche, T. (2001, May 21). Wired for the future. *Time,* 75.

Roeser, R. W., Eccles, J. S., & Sameroff, A. J. (2000, May). School as a context of early adolescents' academic and social-emotional development: A summary of research findings. *The Elementary School Journal, 100*(5), 443–472.

Romano, N., & Timmers, N. (1978). Middle school athletics—intramurals or interscholastics. *Middle School Journal, 9*(6), 16.

Rosenshine, B., & Stevens, R. (1986). Teaching functions. In M. Wittrock, *Handbook of research on teaching* (3rd ed.) (pp. 376–391). New York: Macmillan.

Roth, J., & Brooks-Gunn, J. (1999). Implications of individual difference theories for enhancing adolescent development. In R. Boniface (Ed.), *Collected papers from the OERI conference on adolescence: Designing developmentally appropriate middle schools* (pp. 60–92). Reston, VA: National Association of Secondary School Principals.

Rutter, M., Maughan, B., Mortimore, P., & Ouston, J. (1979). *Fifteen thousand hours: Secondary schools and their effects on children.* Cambridge, MA: Harvard University Press.

Sanders, W. L. (1998). Value-added assessment. *School Administrator, 11*(55), 24–27.

Sanders, W. L. (2000). Annual CREATE Jason Williams memorial lecture: "Value-added assessment from student achievement data: Opportunities and hurdles." *Journal of Personnel Evaluation in Education, 14*(4), 329–339.

Scheidlinger, S. (1984). The adolescent peer group revisited: Turbulence or adaptation? *Small Group Behavior, 15,* 387–397.

Schmoker, M. (2000). Standards versus sentimentality: Reckoning—successfully—with the most promising movement in modern education. *NASSP Bulletin, 84*(620), 49–60.

Schmuch, R., & Runkel, P. (1985). *The handbook of organization development in schools* (3rd ed.). Prospect Heights, IL: Waveland Press.

Schurr, S., Lewis, S., LaMorte, K., & Shewey, K. (1996). *Signaling student success: Thematic learning stations and integrated units.* Columbus, OH: National Middle School Association.

Schwartz, G., Merten, D., & Bursik, R. (1987). Teaching styles and performance values in junior high school: The impersonal, nonpersonal, and personal. *American Journal of Education, 95*(2), 346–370.

Secretary's Commission on Achieving Necessary Skills (SCANS) (1991). *What work requires of schools.* Washington, DC: U.S. Department of Labor.

Senge, P. (1990). *The fifth discipline: The art and practice of the learning organization.* New York: Doubleday.

Shaplin, J., & Olds, H. (Eds.). (1964). *Team teaching.* New York: Harper and Row.

Shave, D., & Shave, B. (1989). *Early adolescence and the search for self: A developmental perspective.* New York: Praeger.

Simmons, R. G., & Blyth, D. A. (1987). *Moving into adolescence.* New York: Aldine de Gruyter.

Slavin, R. E. (1987). Mastery learning reconsidered. *Review of educational research, 57*(2), 175–213.

Slavin, R. E. (1990). Achievement effects of ability grouping in secondary schools: A best-evidence synthesis. *Review of Educational Research, 60,* 471–500.

Slavin, R. E. (1991). Synthesis of research on cooperative learning. *Educational Leadership, 48*(5), 71–82.

Slavin, R. (2001). Expecting excellence. *American School Board Journal, 188*(2), 22–25.

Slavin, R., & Madden, N. (2000). Roots and Wings: Effects of whole school reform on student achievement. *Journal of Education for Students Placed at Risk, 5*(1), 109–136.

Speaker's Task Force (1984). *The forgotten years: Report of the speaker's task force on middle childhood education.* Tallahassee: Florida House of Representatives.

Spindler, J., & George, P. (1984). Participatory leadership in the middle school. *The Clearing House, 57,* 293–295.

Steinberg, L., & Levine, A. (1997). *You and your adolescent: A parent's guide for ages 10–20.* New York: Harper Collins.

Stevenson, C. (1992). *Teaching ten to fourteen year olds.* New York: Longman.

Strahan, D., Bowles, N., Richardson, V., & Hanawald, S. (1997). Research on teaming: Insights from selected studies. In T. S. Dickinson & T. O. Erb (Eds.), *We get more than we give: Teaming in middle schools* (pp. 359–384). Columbus, OH: National Middle School Association.

Superintendent's Middle Grade Task Force (1987). *Caught in the middle: Educational reform for young adolescents in California public schools.* Sacramento: California State Department of Education.

Talent Development Middle Schools (2000). *Johns Hopkins University.* Retrieved from http://www.csos.jhu.edu/talent/middleold.html.

Tapscott, D. (1995). Educating the "Net Generation." *Educational Leadership, 56*(5), 6–11.

Texas Education Agency (1999). *Texas social studies framework, kindergarten–grade 12: Research and resources for designing a social studies curriculum.* Austin: Author.

Thomas, R., Pickler, G., & Sevick, M. J. (1990). *Middle school instructional practices scale.* Unpublished manuscript, Orange County Public Schools, Orlando, FL.

Toepfer, C. F., Jr. (1980). Brain growth periodization data: Some suggestions for reorganizing middle grades education. *The High School Journal, 63*(6), 224–226.

Tomlinson, C. A. (1993). Independent study: A flexible tool for encouraging academic and personal growth. *Middle School Journal, 25*(1), 55–59.

Tomlinson, C. (2000). Reconcilable differences: Standards-based teaching and differentiation. *Educational Leadership, 58*(1), 6–13.

Tomlinson, C. A. (2001). Grading for success. *Educational Leadership, 58*(6), 12–15.

Tye, K. (1985). *The junior high: School in search of a mission.* Lanham, MD: University Press of America.

Urbanski, A. (1991, October 25). Real change is real hard: Lessons learned in Rochester. *Education Week,* 29.

Urdan, T., & Klein, S. (1999). Early adolescence: A review of the literature. In R. Boniface (Ed.), *Collected papers from the OERI conference on adolescence: Designing developmentally appropriate middle schools* (pp. 27–59). Reston, VA: National Association of Secondary School Principals.

U.S. Department of Education, Office of Educational Research and Improvement, Educational Resources Information Center (1999). *Highlights from TIMMS: Overview and key findings across grade levels.* Washington, DC: National Center for Education Statistics.

Van Til, W., Vars, G., & Lounsbury, J. (1961). *Modern education for the junior high school years.* Indianapolis, IN: Bobbs-Merrill.

Vars, G. (1997). Student concerns and standards too: This we believe and now we must act. *Middle School Journal, 28*(4), 44–49.

Vars, G. (2000, Summer). Editor's comment. *The Core Teacher, 50*(1), 7.

Vars, G. (2001). Can curriculum integration survive in an era of high-stakes testing? *Middle School Journal, 33*(2), 7–17.

Vars, G., & Beane, J. (2000, June). *Integrative curriculum in a standards-based world.* Urbana-Champaign, IL: University of Illinois. (ERIC Document Reproduction Service No. ED441618).

Walberg, H. (1986). Synthesis of research on teaching. In M. Wittrock, *Handbook of research on teaching* (3rd ed.). New York: Macmillan.

Ward, M. (1998, April). *A systems approach to middle school evaluation: Guilford County Schools Formative Approach.* Paper presented at the annual conference of the American Educational Research Association, San Diego, CA.

Washington State Middle Level Task Force (2001). *Middle level strategies for school improvement.* Olympia, WA: Office of the Superintendent of Public Instruction.

Webb, N., & Farivar, S. (1994). Promoting helping behavior in cooperative small groups in middle school mathematics. *American Educational Research Journal, 31*(2), 369–395.

Weilbacher, G. (2001). Is curriculum integration an endangered species? *Middle School Journal, 33*(2), 18–27.

West, T., Bates, P., & Schmeil, R. (1979). *Mainstreaming: Problems, potentials, and perspectives.* Minneapolis, MN: National Support Systems Project.

Wheelock, A. (1992). *Crossing the tracks.* New York: New Press.

Wheelock, A. (1998). *Safe to be smart: Building a culture for standards-based reform in the middle grades.* Columbus, OH: National Middle School Association.

Winebrenner, S. (1992). *Teaching gifted kids in the regular classroom: Strategies and techniques every teacher can use to meet the academic needs of the gifted and talented.* Minneapolis, MN: Free Spirit.

Winton, J. (1989). *Shelburne Middle School.* Unpublished manuscript.

Wittrock, M. (1986). *Handbook of research on teaching* (3rd ed.). New York: Macmillan.

Wolfgang, C., & Kelsey, K. (1991). Discipline and today's students: They're sure not what they used to be. *Contemporary Education, 62*(3), 150–156.

Wormelli, R. (1999, February 2). One teacher to another: Block classes change instructional practice—carpe diem! *Middle Ground,* 17–19.

Yair, G. (2000). Educational battlefields: The tug-of-war over students' engagement with instruction. *Sociology of Education, 73*(4), 247–269.

Ysseldyke, J. (2001). Reflections on a research career: Generalizations from 25 years of research on assessment and instructional decision-making. *Exceptional Children, 67*(3), 295–309.

Zernicke, K. (2001, August 5). The feng shui of schools. *New York Times, Education Life,* 20–22.

Ziegler, M. J. (2000a, Winter). Standards are our friends. *The Core Teacher, 50*(1), 4–6.

Ziegler, M. J. (2000b, Summer). Standards are our friends. *The Core Teacher, 50*(1), 5–6.

Roster of Middle Schools

Many exemplary schools are not on this list. However, because of their level of excellence, the schools included have become known to researchers and practitioners on a local, state, national, or international basis. We know some of them well, for a long period of time; for others, our knowledge of their programs is limited to reputation only. While we do not endorse their efforts by listing them here, we are certain that each school on this list has endeavored to shape its organization and program to meet the needs of middle school students. We believe that each school on the list, however incomplete it may be, offers much to learn. We struggled with whether to list the principals of the schools, because we know and respect so many of them, but we decided that to do so would render the list out-of-date almost immediately. Hence, we have not recorded the names of school leaders, even though exemplary programs depend upon the presence of spirited leaders. We apologize to those leaders, and to the many others who play important roles in exemplary schools that are not included here. We invite educators involved in exemplary programs that have been omitted to inform us of their efforts.

Alabama

Beverlye Road Middle School
427 S. Beverlye Rd.
Dothan, AL 36301

Brookhaven Middle School
1300 5th Ave. SW
Decatur, AL 35601

Girard Middle School
600 Girard Ave.
Dothan, AL 36303

Honeysuckle Girard Middle
  School
1665 Honeysuckle Rd.
Dothan, AL 36305

Saint James Middle School
6010 Vaughn Rd.
Montgomery, AL 36116

Alaska

Homer Junior High School
500 Sterling Hwy.
Homer, AK 99603

Marie Drake Middle School
10014 Crazy Horse Dr.
Juneau, AK 99801

Arizona

Desert Sky Middle School
5130 West Grovers
Glendale, AZ 85308

Osborn Middle School
1102 West Highland
Phoenix, AZ 85013

California

Burlingame Intermediate School
1715 Quesada Way
Burlingame, CA 94010

Dartmouth Middle School
5575 Dartmouth Dr.
San Jose, CA 95118

Redwood Middle School
3600 Oxford St.
Napa, CA 94558

Rogers Middle School
4835 Doyle Rd.
San Jose, CA 95129

Sequoia Middle School
1805 Sequoia St.
Redding, CA 96001

Taylor Middle School
850 Taylor Blvd.
Millbrae, CA 94030

Twin Peaks Middle School
14640 Tierra Bonita Rd.
Poway, CA 92064

Union School District
2130 Los Gatos at Almaden Rd.
San Jose, CA 95124

Valley Junior High School
801 Pine Ave.
Carlsbad, CA 92008

Colorado
Broomfield Heights Middle School
1555 Daphne St.
Broomfield Heights, CO 80020

Challenger Middle School
10215 Lexington Dr.
Colorado Springs, CO 80920

Louisville Middle School
1341 Main St.
Louisville, CO 80027

Mountain Ridge Middle School
9150 Lexington Dr.
Colorado Springs, CO 80920

Parker Junior High School
6651 Pine Lane Ave.
Parker, CO 80134

Thunder Ridge Middle School
5250 South Piccadilly St.
Aurora, CO 80015

West Middle School
10100 E. 13th St.
Aurora, CO 80010

Westview Middle School
11651 N. 85th St.
Longmont, CO 80503

Connecticut
Dodd Middle School
100 Park Pl.
Cheshire, CT 06410

East Lyme Middle School
25 Society Dr.
Niantic, CT 06340

Fairfield Woods Middle School
1115 Fairfield Woods Rd.
Fairfield, CT 06432

Timothy Edwards Middle School
100 Arnold Way
South Windsor, CT 06074

Tolland Middle School
104 Old Post Rd.
Tolland, CT 06084

Florida
Brown Barge Middle School
151 East Fairfield Dr.
Pensacola, FL 32503

Campbell Drive Middle School
900 NE 23rd Ave.
Homestead, FL 33033

Chain of Lakes Middle School
8700 Conroy-Windermere Rd.
Orlando, FL 32835

Conway Middle School
4600 Anderson Rd.
Orlando, FL 32806

DeLand Middle School
1400 S. Aquarius Ave.
DeLand, FL 32724

Deltona Middle School
250 Enterprise Rd.
Deltona, FL 32725

Fort Clarke Middle School
9301 NW 23rd Blvd.
Gainesville, FL 32606

Fort King Middle School
545 NE 17th Ave.
Ocala, FL 32670

Haile Middle School
9501 State Rd. 64E
Bradenton, FL 34202

Heritage Middle School
1001 Parnell Ct.
Deltona, FL 32738

Jackson Heights Middle School
141 Academy Dr.
Oviedo, FL 32765

Kanapaha Middle School
5005 SW 75th St.
Gainesville, FL 32608

Lincoln Middle School
1001 SE 12th St.
Gainesville, FL 32601

Logger's Run Middle School
11584 West Palmetto Park Rd.
Boca Raton, FL 33428

Manatee Middle School
1920 Manatee Rd.
Naples, FL 34114

Mandarin Middle School
5100 Hood Rd.
Jacksonville, FL 32257

Mebane Middle School
Rte. 1, Box 4
Alachua, FL 32615

Nautilus Middle School
21211 NE 23rd Ave.
North Miami Beach, FL 33180

New Smyrna Beach Middle School
1200 S. Myrtle Ave.
New Smyrna Beach, FL 32069

Okaloosa County School District
120 Lowery Pl., SE
Ft. Walton Beach, FL 32548

Orange County Public Schools
445 W. Amelia St.
Orlando, FL 32801

Paul W. Bell Middle School
11800 NW 2nd St.
Miami, FL 33182

P. K. Yonge Middle School
1080 SW 11th St.
Gainesville, FL 32601

Powell Middle School
4100 Barclay Ave.
Brooksville, FL 34609

Richmond Heights Middle School
15015 Southwest 103rd Ave.
Miami, FL 33176

Riversprings Middle School
800 Spring Creek Hwy.
Crawfordville, FL 32327

Sarasota Middle School
4826 Ashton Rd.
Sarasota, FL 34233

Sebastian Middle School
2955 Lewis Speedway
St. Augustine, FL 32095

Sebastian River Middle School
9400 CR 512
Sebastian, FL 32958

Silver Sands Middle School
1300 Herbert St.
Port Orange, FL 32119

Spring Hill Middle School
1015 North Main St.
High Springs, FL 32643

Venice Area Middle School
1900 Center Rd.
Venice, FL 34292

Volusia County School District
DeLand Administrative Complex
P.O. Box 2118
DeLand, FL 32721

Wakulla County Middle School
Rte. 2, Box 526
Crawfordville, FL 32327

Woodlands Middle School
5200 Lyons Rd.
Lake Worth, FL 33462

Georgia
Coastal Middle School
170 White Marsh Island Rd.
Savannah, GA 31401

Crabapple Middle School
10700 Crabapple Rd.
Roswell, GA 30075

Creekland Middle School
170 Russell Rd.
Lawrenceville, GA 30043

East Cobb Middle School
380 Holt Rd.
Marietta, GA 30065

Faith Middle School
1375 Ingersoll St.
Fort Benning, GA 31905

Fulton County Middle Schools
786 Cleveland Ave. SW
Atlanta, GA 30315

Griffin Middle School
4010 King Spring Rd.
Smyrna, GA 30082

Oak Hill Middle School
356 Blandy Rd.
Milledgeville, GA 31061

North Hall Middle School
4856 Rilla Rd.
Gainesville, GA 30505

Southwest Middle School
6030 Ogeechee Rd.
Savannah, GA 31419

Towns Middle School
1400 U.S. Hwy. 76E
Hiawassee, GA 30546

Troup County Schools
200 Mooty Bridge Rd.
La Grange, GA 30240

West Chatham Middle School
800 Pine Barren Rd.
Pooler, GA 31322

West Side Magnet School
301 Forrest Ave.
La Grange, GA 30240

Illinois
Batavia Middle School
10 S. Batavia Ave.
Batavia, IL 60510

Jefferson Middle School
1115 South Crescent Dr.
Champaign, IL 61821

Julian Junior High School
416 S. Ridgeland Ave.
Oak Park, IL 60302

Lake Bluff Middle School
31 E. Sheridan Pl.
Lake Bluff, IL 60044

Stokie Junior High School
520 Glendale Ave.
Winnetka, IL 60093

Indiana
Barker Middle School
319 Barker Rd.
Michigan City, IN 46360

Eggers Middle School
5825 Blaine Ave.
Hammond, IN 46320

Hazelwood Junior High School
1021 Hazelwood Ave.
New Albany, IN 47150

New Albany Floyd County Consolidated School Corporation
2813 Grant Line Rd.
New Albany, IN 47151

Kansas
Blue Valley Middle School
7500 W. 149th Ter.
Overland Park, KS 66223

Leawood Middle School
2410 W. 123rd St.
Leawood, KS 66209

Kentucky
Barren County Middle School
555 Trojan Trail
Glasgow, KY 42141

Brown Middle School
546 South First St.
Louisville, KY 40202

Conkwright Middle School
360 Mt. Sterling Rd.
Winchester, KY 40391

East Jessamine Middle School
851 Wilmore Rd.
Nicholasville, KY 40356

Fort Campbell Middle Schools
Education Center
Fort Campbell, KY 42223

Noe Middle School
121 W. Lee St.
Louisville, KY 40208

Wassom Middle School
Forrest Rd. and Gorgas Ave.
Fort Campbell, KY 42223-5000

Louisiana
Cope Junior High School
4814 Shed Rd.
Bossier City, LA 71111

Maine
King Middle School
92 Deering Ave.
Portland, ME 04102

Middle School of the Kennebunks
87 Fletcher St.
Kennebunk, ME 04043

Skowhegan Middle School
Willow St.
Skowhegan, ME 04976

Maryland
Pawtuxent Middle School
9151 Vollnerhausen Rd.
Jessup, MD 20794

West Middle School
60 Monroe St.
Westminster, MD 21157

Massachusetts
Amherst Regional Middle School
170 Chestnut St.
Amherst, MA 01002

Collins Middle School
29 Highland Ave.
Salem, MA 01970

Marshall Simonds Middle School
114 Winn St.
Burlington, MA 01803

Rupert A. Nock Middle School
70 Low St.
Newburyport, MA 01950

Michigan
East Grand Rapids Middle School
2425 Lake Dr. SE
Grand Rapids, MI 49506

Graveraet Middle School
611 N. Front St.
Marquette, MI 49855

Hutchins Middle School
8820 Woodrow Wilson
Detroit, MI 48206

Kinawa Middle School
1900 Kinawa Dr.
Okemos, MI 48864

MacDonald Middle School
1601 Burcham Dr.
East Lansing, MI 48823

Minnesota
Centennial Middle School
399 Elm St.
Lino Lakes, MN 55014

Chaska Middle School
1750 Chestnut St.
Chaska, MN 55318

Oak View Middle School
15400 Hanson Blvd.
Andover, MN 55304

Saturn School of Tomorrow
65 E. Kellogg Blvd.
St. Paul, MN 55101

Scott Highlands Middle School
1411 Pilot Knob Rd.
Apple Valley, MN 55124

Valley Middle School
900 Gardenview Dr.
Apple Valley, MN 55124

Missouri
Brentwood Middle School
2221 High School Dr.
Brentwood, MO 63144

Lewis and Clark Middle School
325 Lewis and Clark Dr.
Jefferson City, MO 65101

Margaret Buerkle Middle School
623 Buckley Rd.
St. Louis, MO 63125

Nipher Middle School
700 S. Kirkwood Rd.
Kirkwood, MO 63122

Rockwood School District
111 East North St.
Eureka, MO 63025

Nebraska
Monroe Junior High School
5105 Bedford Ave.
Omaha, NE 68104

Westbrook Junior High School
1312 Robertson Dr.
Omaha, NE 68114

Nevada
Becker Middle School
9151 Pinewood Hills Dr.
Las Vegas, NV 89134

Thurman White Junior High
School
1661 Galleria Dr.
Henderson, NV 89014

New Jersey
Beck Middle School
950 Cropwell Rd.
Cherry Hill, NJ 08003

Conackamack Middle School
5205 Witherspoon St.
Piscataway, NJ 08854

Glen Ridge Middle School
235 Ridgewood Ave.
Glen Ridge, NJ 07028

Mount Hebron Middle School of
Science and Technology
173 Bellevue Ave.
Upper Montclair, NJ 07043

New Mexico
Vista Middle School
4465 Elks Rd.
Las Cruces, NM 88005

New York
Ballston Spa Middle School
210 Ballston Ave.
Ballston Spa, NY 12020

Canandaigua Middle School
Granger St.
Canandaigua, NY 14424

Farnsworth Middle School
State Farm Rd.
Guilderland, NY 12084

The Fox Lane Middle School
Rte. 172
Bedford, NY 10506

Jamesville-DeWitt Middle School
Randall Rd.
Jamesville, NY 13078

Louis Armstrong Middle School
32-02 Junction Blvd.
East Elmhurst, NY 11369

Northport Middle School
P.O. Box 210
Northport, NY 11768

Pittsford Middle School
Barker Rd.
Pittsford, NY 14534

Pleasantville Middle School
40 Romer Ave.
Pleasantville, NY 10570

Robert E. Bell Middle School
50 Senter St.
Chappaqua, NY 10514

Shoreham-Wading River Middle
School
Randall Rd.
Shoreham, NY 11786-9745

Southampton Public Schools
141 Narrow Ln.
Southampton, NY 11968

Wantagh Middle School
3299 Beltagh Ave.
Wantagh, NY 11793

North Carolina
Carrington Middle School
227 Milton Rd.
Durham, NC 27712

Duke School for Children Middle
School
3716 Old Erwin Rd.
Durham, NC 27705

Guilford County Schools
712 North Eugene St.
Greensboro, NC 27401

Northeast Guilford Middle School
6720 McLeansville Rd.
McLeansville, NC 27301

Southeast Guilford Middle School
4825 Woody Mill Rd.
Greensboro, NC 27406

Westover Middle School
275 Bonanza Dr.
Fayetteville, NC 28303

Ohio
Green Middle School
1711 Steese Rd.
P.O. Box 218
Green, OH 44232

Independence Middle School
6565 Brecksville Rd.
Independence, OH 44131

Richmond Heights Middle School
447 Richmond Rd.
Richmond Heights, OH 44143

Stanton Middle School
1175 Hudson Rd.
Kent, OH 44240

Trotwood-Madison Junior High
3594 Snyder Rd.
Trotwood, OH 45426

Oklahoma
Cleveland Middle School
724 N. Birmingham Ave.
Tulsa, OK 74110

Oregon
Oaklea Middle School
1515 Rose St.
Junction City, OR 97448

Talent Middle School
102 Christian Ave.
P.O. Box 359
Talent, OR 97540

Pennsylvania
Boyce Middle School
1500 Boyce Rd.
Upper St. Clair, PA 15241

Donegal Middle School
1175 River Rd.
Marietta, PA 17547

Fort Couch Middle School
3326 Elmdale Dr.
Bethel Park, PA 15102

Greenway Middle School Teacher
Center
1400 Crucible St.
Pittsburgh, PA 15205

Jay Cooke Middle School
13th and Louden St.
Philadelphia, PA 19141

Northwestern Lehigh Middle
School
6636 Northwest Rd.
New Tripoli, PA 18066

Radnor Middle School
131 South Wayne Ave.
Wayne, PA 19087

South Carolina
Hand Middle School
2600 Wheat St.
Columbia, SC 29205

Richland School District Two
6831 Brookfield Rd.
Columbia, SC 29206

Southeast Middle School
731 Horrell Hill Rd.
Hopkins, SC 29061

South Dakota
Brandon Valley Middle School
700 E. Holly Blvd.
Brandon, SD 57005

Brookings Middle School
601 4th St.
Brookings, SD 57006

Tennessee
Richview Middle School
2350 Memorial Dr.
Clarksville, TN 37043

Texas
Canyon Vista Middle School
8455 Spicewood Springs Rd.
Austin, TX 78759

Chisholm Trail Middle School
500 Oak Ridge Dr.
Round Rock, TX 78681

Dallas Independent School
  District
3700 Ross Ave.
Dallas, TX 75204

Haltom Middle School
5000 Hires Ln.
Haltom, TX 76117

McCulloch Middle School
3520 Normandy
Dallas, TX 75205

Olle Middle School
9200 Boone Rd.
Alief, TX 77099

Rusk Middle School
411 N. Mound
Nacogdoches, TX 75961

Terrell Middle School
701 Town North Dr.
Terrell, TX 75160

West Ridge Middle School
9201 Scenic Bluff Dr.
Austin, TX 78733

Utah
Cache County Public Schools
2063 N. 1200 E.
Logan, UT 84341

Dixon Middle School
750 West 200 N.
Provo, UT 84601

Vermont
Shelburne Middle School
Harbor Rd.
Shelburne, VT 05482

Virginia
Carl Sandburg Middle School
8428 Fort Hunt Rd.
Alexandria, VA 22308

Godwin Middle School
14800 Darbydale Ave.
Woodbridge, VA 22193

Rachel Carson Middle School
13618 McLearen Rd.
Herndon, VA 20171

Washington
Chinook Middle School
4301 NE 6th Ave.
Lacey, WA 98506

College Place Middle School
7501 208th St. SW
Lynnwood, WA 98036

Hawkins Middle School
Box 167 E. 50 N. Mason
Belfair, WA 98528

Madison Middle School
3429 45th Ave. SW
Seattle, WA 98116

Marshall Middle School
1113 Legion Way SE
Olympia, WA 98501

McLoughlin Middle School
5802 MacArthur Blvd.
Vancouver, WA 98661

Thurgood Marshall Middle School
3939 20th Ave. NW
Olympia, WA 98502

Yakima Middle Schools
104 North 4th Ave.
Yakima, WA 98907

West Virginia
Putnam County Schools
9 Courthouse Dr.
Winfield, WV 25213

Wisconsin
Longfellow Middle School
1900 Denton St.
La Crosse, WI 54601

Oregon Middle School
200 N. Main St.
Oregon, WI 53575-1499

Sherman Middle School
1610 Ruskin St.
Madison, WI 53704

Stoughton Middle School
220 North St.
Stoughton, WI 53589

Canada
Constable Neil Bruce Middle
  School
2010 Daimler Rd.
Kelowna, BC VIZ 3Y4

George Bonner Middle School
3060 Cobble Hill Rd.
Mill Bay, BC VOR 2P0

Mt. Slesse Middle School
5871 Tyson Rd.
Chilliwack, BC V2R 3N9

China
American School
No. 55 Hua Yang St.
Ti Yu Road East
Tianhe District
Guangzhou, People's Republic of
  China
510620

France
American School of Paris Middle
  School
41 rue Pasteur–B.P.82-32216
Saint-Cloud CEDEX-France

Nepal
Lincoln American School
P.O. Box 2673
Rabi Bhawan
Kathmandu, Nepal

Singapore
Singapore American Middle
  School
40 Woodlands St. 41
Singapore 738547

Author Index

A

Adams, K., 190–191
Alexander, W., 43, 48, 78, 254, 378, 504, 546, 549, 575, 578
Allen, L., 213
Allred, L., 576
Alper, S., 402
Anderson, W., 2, 369, 557
Arhar, J., 310
Arnold, J., 305, 314–315, 317, 328, 345, 352
Atwell, N., 200

B

Bates, P., 404
Beane, J., 74, 87, 93–95, 100–102
Bengston, J., 20–21
Bennett, D., 132
Berends, M., 416
Bergmann, S., 287
Berliner, D., 88, 581
Bickle, F., 288
Biddle, B., 88, 581
Bishop, P., 315
Bizar, M., 200
Black, S., 174
Blase, J., 558
Blyth, D., 5, 9
Bowles, N., 312
Boyd, J., 306
Bradley, A., 548
Brannigan, C., 140
Brevino, M., 190–191
Briggs, L., 414
Brimfield, R., 167

Brooks, J., 11
Brooks, K., 549
Brooks, M., 11
Brooks-Gunn, J., 7, 25, 30
Brophy, J., 159, 160, 162, 163, 415
Brown, D., 5, 154, 309
Buckner, J., 288
Burns, J., 254
Bursik, R., 23
Bush, G., 75
Bushnell, D., 328
Bussaberger, M., 291

C

Calhoun, E., 193
Canady, R. L., 448, 450, 454–455
Canter, L., 244
Canter, M., 244
Carroll, J., 446–447
Carson, C., 88, 581
Cawelti, G., 49
Childs, V., 326–327
Clemetson, L., 25
Cobb, N., 6
Compton, M., 546, 578
Connors, N., 378
Connors, R., 310
Costa, A., 91
Cotton, N., 21
Cox, N., 260, 280, 288
Crow, G., 308
Cuban, L., 141
Cuff, W., 43

D

Daniels, H., 200
Davis, G., 4, 23, 48, 51, 57, 123, 254, 345, 352, 353, 501, 503, 515, 548, 549
DeFiore, D., 167
DeLauro, R., 273
Dengel, J., 190–191
Dental, K., 453, 455
Dickens, W., 12
Dickinson, T., 306, 345, 378, 576
Doda, N., 280, 286, 349, 352, 354, 535–537
Dodge, B., 203
Doherty, K., 78
Doreleijers, T., 8
Douglas, H., 112
Dow, J., 446, 448, 453
Dryfoos, J., 25
Dulik-Manes, A., 102
Dye, J., 450, 453, 454

E

Eccles, J., 25, 42, 289
Edwards, F., 549
Eggen, P., 202
Eichhorn, D., 3, 42, 390
Elkind, D., 131
Elliott, G., 4, 27
Epstein, J., 50, 549
Erb, T., 312, 345, 349, 354, 378
Erikson, E., 19–22
Eson, M., 10
Espin, O., 19
Evoy, K., 316

F

Farivar, S., 173
Feldman, S., 4, 27
Felner, R., 27, 29, 239, 289, 312, 353, 394, 514, 544, 546, 547, 582
Feuerstein, R., 13
Flowers, N., 308, 312
Fritz, S., 26–27
Frost, R., 309, 390
Furtwengler, W., 308

G

Galassi, J., 260, 280, 288
Gallagher, J., 446, 455
Gamoran, A., 414, 415, 416
Gardner, H., 13–15
Garrod, A., 20
Garvin, J., 253
Gately, F., 207
Gately, S., 207
George, E., 18, 193
George, P., 2, 18, 45, 49, 52, 55, 59, 78, 173, 193, 212, 213, 241, 242, 276, 302, 303, 305, 311, 312, 313, 328, 329, 349, 369, 383, 384, 396–397, 398–399, 415, 416, 417, 425, 446, 448, 453, 455, 468, 504, 514, 535–537, 549, 557, 563, 576
Gill, J., 378
Gilligan, C., 20
Glasser, W., 21
Glickman, C., 90
Goldberg, M., 27
Goleman, D., 15–16
Good, T., 160, 162, 163, 415
Goodenow, C., 19
Gonzalez, E., 27
Greeson, L., 22
Griffin, C., 402, 413, 556
Gruhn, W., 112
Gulledge, S., 260, 280, 288

H

Hackman, D., 448
Hall, G., 526
Hamdy, M., 454
Hanawald, S., 312
Hartman, C., 8

Hartzler, D., 547
Havighurst, R., 6–7
Hechinger, F., 24
Heistad, D., 160
Herman-Giddens, M., 1
Herrnstein, R., 12
Hertzog, J., 347
Hines, V., 546, 578
Hirsch, E., 90
Hodgkinson, H., 25–26
Holubec, E., 196–197
Honig, W., 46, 47
Hord, S., 526
Hoverstein, C., 280
Huelskamp, R., 88, 581
Hunter, M., 90
Husband, R., 353

I

Ianni, F., 22

J

Jackson, A., 4, 23, 48, 51, 57, 123, 254, 345, 352, 353, 501, 503, 515, 548, 549
Jacobsen, D., 202
Jenkins, D., 576
Jenkins, J., 55, 302
Jensen, A., 12
Johnson, D., 196–197, 384
Johnson, R., 196–197, 384
Johnston, H., 253, 254, 260
Jones, F., 244
Joyce, B., 193

K

Kagan, S., 184–189, 192
Kain, D., 312
Kane, T., 12
Kanter, R., 242
Kaplan, L., 562
Kauchak, D., 202
Kelsay, K., 232–233
Kilgore, K., 402, 413, 556
Kilkenny, L., 20
Kilpatrick, H., 141
King, T., 132
Klein, S., 8, 9, 11, 25, 29, 166
Knowles, T., 5, 154, 309
Kohlberg, L., 16–18

Kohn, A., 90, 125, 417
Kolstad, B., 414
Kozol, J., 24
Kozulin, A., 13

L

LaMorte, K., 198
Lane, M., 274–275
Lawrence, G., 328
Lee, V., 29, 289, 308, 309
Lessen, S., 8
Levine, A., 8
Levinson, D., 6
Lewis, A., 28, 414
Lewis, S., 198
Lindsay, D., 78
Lipsitz, J., 3, 416
Liu, J., 450, 454
Lord, S., 289
Lounsbury, J., 41, 212, 241, 242, 280, 349, 383, 384, 396–397, 468, 512–513
Lynch, J., 383

M

MacIver, D., 50
Madden, N., 423
Manzo, K., 538, 548, 562
Martin, H., 418–420
Marzano, R., 172, 194, 196, 197
Masci, D., 167
McEwin, C. K., 43, 55, 213, 254, 302, 303, 378, 549, 576
McLeland, B., 456
McTighe, J., 91
Medley, D., 160
Meier, D., 90
Mercer, A., 206, 404
Mercer, C., 206, 404
Merten, D., 23
Midgley, C., 42, 289
Miller, B., 9
Mills, G., 43
Mistretta, G., 454
Mizell, H., 27
Myhre, R., 478–479

N

Norton, J., 414

O

Oakes, J., 415
Oldaker, L., 45, 49
Olds, H., 304
Oliner, P., 22, 23
Olson, E., 309, 390
Osterman, K., 29, 289
Owings, W., 562

P

Peck, C., 141
Perkins, D., 155
Perkins, T., 291
Peshkin, A., 20
Peterson, J., 477–478
Piaget, J., 10, 16
Pickering, D., 172, 194, 196, 197
Pickler, G., 157, 261–262, 266, 271–272, 512
Plodzik, K., 305, 311
Polansky, H., 454
Pollock, J., 172, 194, 196, 197
Pounder, D., 308
Powers, S., 20
Prescott, D., 546, 578
Priddy, M., 576
Putbrese, L., 287

R

Reis, S., 173, 415
Renzulli, J., 173, 176, 415
Rettig, M., 448, 450, 454–455
Reynolds, M., 404
Rice, D., 208, 211
Richardson, V., 312
Roche, T., 133
Roesser, R., 5, 19, 21, 22, 23, 25, 27, 29
Romano, N., 126
Rosenshine, B., 161, 163
Roth, J., 7, 25, 30
Runkel, P., 533
Rutter, M., 239, 242

S

Sameroff, A., 25
Sanders, W., 158
Scheidlinger, S., 22
Schmoker, M., 76
Schmuck, R., 533
Schultze, C., 12
Schurr, S., 198
Schwartz, G., 23
Senge, P., 584
Sevick, M., 157
Shaplin, J., 304
Shave, B., 4
Shave, D., 4
Shewey, K., 198, 514, 549
Simmons, R., 5, 9
Sindelar, P., 402, 413, 556
Slavin, R., 27, 380, 415, 423
Smiel, R., 404
Smith, J., 29, 289, 308, 309
Smulyan, L., 20
Snider, C., 291
Snodgrass, D., 190–191
Soar, R., 160
Springer, M., 97, 99
Stahlman, T., 276
Steinberg, L., 8
Stevens, R., 161, 163
Stevenson, C., 305, 312, 313, 314–315, 317, 328, 345, 352
Strahan, D., 312

T

Tapscott, D., 132
Thomas, R., 157
Timmers, N., 126
Toepfer, C., 10
Tomlinson, C., 168, 180, 421

U

Urdan, T., 8, 9, 11, 25, 29, 166
Urich, T., 454

V

Valentine, J., 448
Valiquette, L., 309, 390
Van Dijk, M., 8
Van Til, W., 41
Vars, G., 41, 93–95, 100–102, 545

W

Walberg, H., 164
Walmsley, S., 10
Ward, M., 522–523
Weast, J., 576
Webb, N., 173
Webb, R., 402, 413, 556
Weilbacher, G., 545
Weinstein, M., 414, 415
Welch, R., 129
West, T., 404
Wheelock, A., 415
White, C., 20
Wilkinson, M., 414
Williams, E., 48, 546, 578
Williams, R., 22
Williamson, R., 510–511
Winebrenner, S., 177–178, 181–183
Winton, J., 125–126
Wittrock, M., 160
Wolff, H., 437
Wolfgang, C., 232–233
Woodall, T., 88, 581
Wormelli, R., 454

Y

Yair, G., 166–167
Young, M., 290
Ysseldyke, J., 164

Z

Zernicke, K., 467, 469
Ziegler, M., 95–97
Zigmond, N., 208, 211

Subject Index

A

Ability grouping, 414–428
  Alternatives to, 422–428
  De-tracking, 417–422, 517–519
  Research, 415–516
Academic achievement, 562–573
Adolescence, early, 2–22
  Characteristics of, 5
    Cognitive, 10–16
    Moral, 16–18
    Physical, sexual, 7–9
    Self-esteem, 21–23
  Developmental tasks, 6–7
  Identity formation, 19–21
  Management of, 226–252
    Middle school concept and, 238–243
    Relationships with, 226–227
    Student development and, 227–234
  Phases of, 3–5
Advisor, teacher as, 252–291
  Conducting a group, 278–281
  Activities for, 281–284
  Failure of, 578
  Planning, 506
  Research on, 284–289
Alternative grade configurations, 578–580
Arts, 82, 85
Association for Supervision and Curriculum Development, 41, 49
At-risk middle school students, 23–29

B

Batavia Middle School, 435, 436–437
Blue Valley Middle School, 484–486
Broomfield Heights Middle School, 268–270, 441–444, 505
  Schedule, 443
Brown Barge Middle School, 73, 105–109, 380
Buildings, 466–494
  Adapting older, 470–477
  Characteristics of exemplary, 477–494
  Middle school, 466–470
  Revitalizing existing buildings, 513–524
    Guilford County, 515–524
  Specifications, 493–494

C

Carnegie Council on Adolescent Development, 5, 24, 25, 49, 229, 501, 503
Chain of Lakes Middle School, 480–482
Cheerleading, 129–130
Cleveland Middle School, 482–484
Clubs and special interest activities, 118–121
Computers (*see* Technology)
Constructivism, 11

Consultation and co-teaching, 205–213
  Ability-grouping, 427
  Cooperative consultation, 206
  Co-teaching, 207–208
  Implementing, 209–210
  Precautions, 211
  Promises, 211–212
  Recommendations, 210–211
Cooperative learning, 192–198
Copernican schedules, 446–448
Corporate presence, 64–65
Counseling, 289–291
Crabapple Middle School schedule, 449
Creekland Middle School, 365
Curriculum of the middle school, 60–61, 73–150
  Alignment, 77, 566–567
  Compacting, 176–178
  Development, 95–97
  Exploratory, 112–121
  Interdisciplinary, integrated, 98–112
  Needs-based, 582–584
  Standards-based, 74–99
  Planning, 506
  Technology, 131–141

D

Definition of middle school, 45
Deland Junior High School, Deland Middle School, 471–473
Departmentalization, 372–374

Developmental-age grouping, 390–392
Developmental tasks, 6–7
Differentiating instruction, 166–205, 582
  Classroom workshop, 200–202
  Definition, 167
  Initial steps, 170–176
  Learning centers, 198–200
  Regular classroom, 168–169
  Technology in, 202–205
Discipline and classroom management, 225–252
Diversity, 580–582
Duke Middle School, 104–105

E
Educational zip code, 52–53
Emotional intelligence, 15–16
Erikson's theories of adolescence, 19–20
Evaluation of middle schools, 537–550
  Formative evaluation, 538–544
  Middle school movement, 548–549
  Summative evaluation, 544–548
Exploratory curriculum
  Band, 116–117
  Clubs and special interest activities, 118–121
  Courses, 113–115
  Wheel, 115–116
Exploratory teachers, 534–537
Extracurricular programs, 124–131

F
Facilities for middle schools (see Buildings)
Farnsworth Middle School, 138, 405–407, 488–489
Foreign language, 82, 85

G
Galaxy Middle School floor plan, 474
Generative middle school, 584–585
Goals of middle schools, 51–52
Grade levels in middle schools (see Grouping students in middle schools)

Grouping students in middle schools, 64, 365–434
Ability grouping, 414–428
  Advantages of alternatives, 395–400
  Alternatives to, 422–428
  De-tracking, 417–422
  Disadvantages of alternatives, 400
  Research, 415–416
Organization of middle schools, 235, 365–434, 505–506
  Elementary and high school, 366–368
  Student behavior management, 235–238
Student development and, 369–395
Guidance in the middle school, 289–291

H
Health curriculum, 83, 85, 121–123
Houses (see also School-within-school)
  Thematic, 389–390

I
Identity formation, 19–23
Inclusion, 401–414
  Continuum of placement, 405
  Model learning workshop, 406–408
  Regular teacher, 413–414
  Resource rooms, 404–408
  Schoolwide, 402–404
  With interdisciplinary teams, 408–412
Independent study (IS), 180–184
Instruction in middle schools, 63, 151–224
  Characteristics of, 152–158
  Consultation and co-teaching, 205–213
  Cooperative learning, 192–198
  Small group activities, 184–192
  Traditional whole class, 158–166
    Classroom management, 158–161

Differentiation, 166–205
  Modifications, 163–166,
  Steps, 161–166
  Supplementing, 176–184
    Grading contracts, 179–180
    Independent study, 180–184
    Learning contracts, 178–179
Integrated curriculum, 98–112
  Combined with standard, 98
  Criticism of, 109–111
  Rationale, 100–102
Intelligence, 11–16
  Emotional intelligence, 15
  Intelligence quotient (IQ), 11, 13
  Multiple intelligences, 13–14
Interdisciplinary team organization, 59, 301–364
  Alternative types, 313–323
    Four-teacher teams, 321–322
    Gradewide teams, 322–323
    Small teams, 313–320
    Three-teacher teams, 320–321
  Classroom discipline, 227–252
  Highly effective teams, 312–313
  Nature of, 304–305
  Phases of, 305–312
    Community, 308–310
    Governance in, 311–312
    Organization, 306–308
    Teamed instruction, 310–312, 327–331
  Precautions, 352–360
    Balanced teams, 352–353
    Team meetings, 357–359
  Purposes and possibilities, 344–352
    Advantages, 344–352
  Roles and responsibilities of members, 323–341
    Materials, 327
    Scheduling students, 325–327
    Team planning, 332–341

Sharing as the basis for, 302–304
Kid meetings, 249
Plans, 244–249
Team leaders, 341–344
Team spirit, sense of community, 250–252
Ten commandments of, 355–357
Interscholastic sports, 128–131
Intramurals, 124–128

J
Japanese schools, 52
Joplin-style plans, 423
Junior high schools, 40–41
Problems with, 235–238

K
Kanapaha Middle School, 451–453
King Middle School, 98
KWL charts, 189–191

L
Language arts curriculum, 80, 81, 83–84
Leadership in middle schools, 65–66, 555–589
Core components, 556
New challenges, 562–584
Shared decision-making, 557–562
Vision, 556–557
Learner-centered curriculum, 582–584
Learning centers, 198–200
Lincoln Middle School, 284–286, 343, 475–476, 555
Looping, 383–385

M
Mainstreaming, 402 (*see also* Inclusion)
Mandarin Middle School, 241
Mathematics, 80, 81, 84
Mebane Middle School, 301, 381–382
Mentoring (advising) middle school students, 252–291
Alternative designs for, 255–260
Daily large group, 255–258
One-on-one, 258–260

Goals of, 275–276
Purposes of, 272–275
Rationale for, 251–255
Requirements for success, 260–271
Teacher roles, 277–278
Middle schools
Accomplishments, 573–575
Buildings, 466–494
Concept, 54–58
Definition, 45–47
Exemplary, characteristics of, 48–51
Goals of, 51–52
Growth of, 41–44
History of, 39–45
Levels of community, 265
Schedules, 435–466
Size and complexity, 58–59
Trends, issues, 58–66
Moral development, 16–19
Mt. Slesse Middle School, 486–487
Multiage grouping (MAG), 106–108, 379–383
Multiple intelligences, 13–14

N
National Forum to Accelerate Middle-Grades Reform, 93
National Middle School Association (NMSA), 46, 92, 112
Nature versus nurture, 12–13
Ninth grade problems, 577
Numbered Heads Together, 184–185

O
Oak Hill Middle School, 490–492, 500
Organization of middle schools, 235, 365–434, 505–506
Compared with elementary and high school, 366–368
Student behavior management, 235–238
Student development and, 369–395

P
Parker Intensive Core Program, 392–393

Partner teams, 313–317
Pawtuxent Middle School, 411–412
Philosophy of middle school education, 502–505
Physical education curriculum, 80, 85, 123–131
Planning middle schools, 501–537
Exploratory teachers, 534–537
Six-step implementation plan, 501–502
Strategic planning, 502–513
Pod-style buildings, 479–494
Program Improvement Council (PIC), 558–562
Puberty, 1

R
Raising academic achievement, 562–573
Revitalizing existing middle schools, 513–524
Guilford County, 515–524
Staff development, 519, 524–534
Recommendations, 526–532
Skills, 532–534
Urban schools, 576–577

S
Scheduling, 61–62, 435–466
Designing, steps in, 459–465
Flexible block, 435–445
Long block, 445–466
Problems with, 457–459
Reasons supporting, 454–456
Varieties of, 446–454
Alternate Day Schedule (A/B), 448–450
Copernican, 446–448
4 × 4 Semester Plan, 450–452
Kanapaha model, 451–453
School-within-school, 385–389
Secretary's Commission on Achieving Necessary Skills (SCANS) report, 75
Self-study programs, 543–544
Shared decision-making, 557–562

Small group activities, 184–192
    Group Reporters, 187
    Inside-Outside Circles,
        186–187
    Jigsaw, 187–198
    KWL, 189–191
    Numbered Heads Together,
        184–185
    Solution Sort, 191
    Spontaneous Lectures, 185–186
    Stand and Share, 185
    Three-Step Interview, 192
Social studies, 80, 82, 84
Social support theory, 288–289
Spring Hill Middle School, 225
Staff development, 519–521,
    524–534, 566
Standards-based reform, 74–99
    Benchmarks, 83–85
    Criticism of, 87–92
    Example of, in Florida, 78–86
    Other states, 86–87
    Rapprochement with middle
        school education, 92–97
    Rationale for, 74–78
    Standards, 81–83
    Strands, 80–81

Student development and school
    organization, 369–395
    Core-style, 375–378
    Departmentalization, 372–374
    Grade level teams, 378–379
    Gradewide teams, 374–375
    Long-term teams, 379–390
        Developmental-age
            grouping, 390–392
        Looping, 383–385
        Multiage, 379–383
        School-within-school,
            385–389
    Model of, 370–372, 393–395
    Parker Intensive Core Program,
        392–393
Student Team Learning (STL),
    194–196
Summative evaluation of middle
    schools, 544–549
Sunshine State Standards, 78–86

T
Talent Middle School, 377
Teacher education, 577–578
Team leaders, 341–344
Team planning, 332–340

Teams–Games–Tournaments
    (TGT), 195–196
Technology, 62–63, 131–141
    Expectations for students,
        136–138
    Future, 140
    Magnet schools, 139
Three-teacher teams, 320–321
Time on task, 159–161
Tracking, 414–428
    Alternatives to, 422–428
    De-tracking, 417–422
    Research on, 415–416

W
Wakulla Middle School, 2, 237,
    239–240, 290, 316–317,
    385–386, 438–440
    Floor plan, 237
    Schedule, 438
Watershed project, 97, 99
Whole class instruction, 158–166
Winchester plan, 425–426

Z
Zip code of middle schools, 374